The Role of Media Pluralism in the Enforcement of EU Competition Law

Konstantina Bania

Foreword by Giorgio Monti

106 W 32nd St. New York, NY 10001, USA
www.concurrences.com
book@concurrences.com

Printed in the United States

First Printing, September 2019
978-1-939007-85-8 (paperback)
978-1-939007-86-5 (e-book)

Cover: Yves Buliard, www.yvesbuliard.fr
Book Design and Layout implementation: Darlene Swanson, www.van-garde.com

Concurrences Books

Antitrust Liber Amicorum

Eleanor Fox - Liber Amicorum, *Nicolas Charbit, Sonia Ahmad (ed.), 2021*

Richard Whish - Liber Amicorum, *Nicolas Charbit, Sonia Ahmad (ed.), 2020*

Herbert Hovenkamp - Liber Amicorum, *Nicolas Charbit, Sonia Ahmad (ed.), 2020*

Albert Foer - Liber Amicorum, *Nicolas Charbit, Sonia Ahmad (ed.), 2020*

Wang Xiaoye - The Pioneer of Competition Law in China, *Adrian Emch, Wendy Ng (ed.), 2019*

Frédéric Jenny - Standing Up for Convergence and Relevance in Antitrust, Vol. I
Nicolas Charbit, Sonia Ahmad (ed.), 2019

Douglas H. Ginsburg – An Antitrust Professor on the Bench, Vol. I
Nicolas Charbit, Sonia Ahmad (ed.),2018

Ian S. Forrester - A Scot Without Borders, Vol. I & II, *Assimakis Komninos et al. (ed.),2015*

William E. Kovacic: An Antitrust Tribute, Vol. I & II, *Nicolas Charbit et al. (ed.), 2013 & 2014*

Practical Law

Competition Women, Vol. I & II, *Kristina Nordlander & Evelina Kurgonaite (ed.), 2019*

Competition Law Inquiries in the EU - A Practitioner's Guide, *Nathalie Jalabert-Doury, 2019*

Gun-jumping in Merger Control: a Jurisdictional Guide, *Catriona Hatton, 2019*

Competition Digest – A Synthesis of EU and National Leading Cases, 3rd ed.
Frédéric Jenny (ed.), 2018

Choice - A New Standard for Competition Analysis?, *Paul Nihoul et al., 2016*

EU Law and Life Sciences, *Peter Bogaert, Damien Geradin (ed.), 2014*

PhD Theses

Buyer Power in EU Competition Law, *Ignacio Herrera Anchustegui, 2017*

The Role of Media Pluralism in the Enforcement of EU Competition Law, *Kostantina Bania, 2019*

Conference Proceedings

Antitrust in Emerging and Developing Countries – Vol II, *Eleanor Fox, Harry First (ed.), 2016*

Global Antitrust Law - Current Issues in Antitrust Law and Economics
Douglas Ginsburg, Joshua Wright (ed.), 2015

Antitrust in Emerging and Developing Countries – Vol. I, *Eleanor Fox, Harry First (ed.), 2015*

Competition Law on the Global Stage: David Gerber's Global Competition Law in Perspective, *David Gerber (ed.), 2014*

e-Book versions are available to Concurrences+ subscribers.

ACKNOWLEDGEMENTS

The present study is the result of five years of research that was mainly undertaken at the European University Institute (EUI). I am extremely grateful for the opportunities this institution has given me to grow as a scholar. Interactions with a range of brilliant minds and the innumerous conferences and seminars I attended have helped me find my personal academic identity. I am immensely grateful to the Greek Scholarships Foundation, the EUI, the Competition Law Scholars Forum and the European Broadcasting Union for granting the funds that allowed me to devote myself to writing the thesis on which this book is based.

Numerous people have contributed to this study one way or another. First and foremost, I am greatly indebted to my supervisor at the EUI, Giorgio Monti, for providing constant support and excellent guidance throughout. He taught me how to conduct thorough and relevant research and how to navigate the most complex questions facing competition enforcement in the digital economy. His inquisitive spirit, creativity and wisdom are inspirational. The impact of his mentorship on my work is far from limited to the writing of this book; it is manifested in every difficult assignment I carry out. In addition to my supervisor, other scholars have greatly contributed to my growth. Michal Gal, Peggy Valcke, Josef Drexl, Ioannis Lianos, Rachael Craufurd-Smith, Jonathan Faull and Youri Devuyst are among those whose interdisciplinary work, visionary approach to the interpretation of the law, and ethos are a continuing source of motivation.

My sincere thanks to the European Broadcasting Union for allowing me to put my knowledge into practice by being at the forefront of cutting-edge research in fascinating areas, including the implications of digitization for competition enforcement, platform responsibility, and the reform of telecoms regulation.

As with most products of hard work that involve a considerable amount of frustration, the writing and review of the present book would not have been possible without the support and encouragement of family and friends. He who deserves to be mentioned first is my husband, Michalis, who always pushes me to reach higher and do better. The contribution of his unconditional support to my professional and academic endeavors cannot be overstated. I am also grateful to my parents, Thomas and Litsa, and my sister Tania; they equipped me with the tools I needed to achieve even my most ambitious goals. Special thanks go to my Italian family, the Ambrogios. Lidia, Nino, Andrea e soprattutto Michele, grazie di tutto, vi voglio un bene dell'anima.

In the course of completing this project, I lost the single most important person in my life, my beloved grandmother. She raised me by giving me an immeasurable amount of affection and instilled in me all the morals and values I live by today. In the course of completing this project, I also gave birth to a beautiful boy, who taught me great strength and courage. This book is dedicated to my guardian angel, Soultana Pisiadou, and my living angel, Hermès T. Ditsas.

FOREWORD

Konstantina Bania's book makes the case for optimizing and sharpening the application of EU competition law to address the risk of reduced media pluralism. It offers a searching, multi-disciplinary reflection on a topic which has held the attention of policymakers for many years but which has gained increased prominence in spite of the emergence of the internet as a platform that, one might have thought, would create more open communication channels.

The book starts by exploring how far concerns about media pluralism remain in spite of the emergence of a wide variety of opportunities offered by the internet. Finding that risks to pluralism remain notwithstanding (and also because of) new technologies, she moves to explain that in the absence of either sufficiently powerful national rules or clear EU legislative competence, competition law may well offer options to protect EU media markets indirectly.

Her diagnosis is that the enforcement of competition law can do better by safeguarding both competition and pluralism more effectively. The analysis is retrospective (how well has the European Commission handled media markets?) and prospective (can we develop a pluralism friendly antitrust policy?). The assessment covers the range of anticompetitive conduct but at its heart is the notion of market foreclosure, and the risk of foreclosure that results when one entity controls an asset or factor of production. Whether control is over premium content, of retail prices, or a popular information gateway, the risk that control creates foreclosure up or downstream animates the analysis in this book. Unusually perhaps, the author does not just call for a recalibration of competition law to serve the interests of media pluralism. In other words, she does not advocate a weakened antitrust assessment to favour pluralism. Rather, the call here is for an integrated antitrust assessment of the impact of business practices on both competition and pluralism.

The scope of the project is ambitious: covering old and new media, from books to digital platforms. It considers the interdependence of various media and how regulatory responses in one media market might affect another. For example, one should study the impact that regulating an online platform's display of news may have on the market for newspapers: do platforms just steal content or do they enhance the visibility of newspapers and thus stimulate greater consumption of newspapers? The book digs into the economics of the relevant sectors, seeking to provide pathways for the adoption of more relevant economic models into the decision-making practice of the Commission.

The book contributes to scholarly discussions by the way it asks us to consider critically the contribution of EU competition law in media markets and by examining the synergies between competition and non-competition objectives. It asks enforcers to raise their game: exposing lessons to be learned about the past and considering how to shape enforcement in a fast-moving, uncertain future.

Giorgio Monti
Professor of Competition Law, LAW/RSCAS Joint Chair
European University Institute

TABLES OF LEGISLATION

TREATIES AND INTERNATIONAL CONVENTIONS

Treaty on European Union (consolidated version) [2008] OJ C 115/19.

Treaty on the Functioning of the European Union (consolidated version) [2012] OJ C 326/47.

Treaty on the Functioning of the European Union [2012] OJ C 326/1.

EU/EEA LEGISLATION

Commission (EEC) Regulation No. 67/67 on the application of Article 85(3) of the Treaty to certain categories of exclusive dealing agreements [1967] OJ 57/849.

Commission (EEC) Regulation No. 2349/84 on the application of Article 85(3) of the Treaty to certain categories of patent licensing agreements [1984] OJ L219/15, corrected by [1985] OJ L13/34.

Council Regulation (EEC) No. 2299/89 of 24 July 1989 on a code of conduct for computerized reservation systems [1989] OJ L220/1.

Council Directive 89/442/EEC of 3 October 1989 on the coordination of certain provisions laid down by law, regulation or administrative action in Member States concerning the pursuit of television broadcasting activities (Television Without Frontiers Directive) [1989] OJ L298/23.

Directive 95/46/EC of the European Parliament and of the Council of 24 October 1995 on the protection of individuals with regard to the processing of personal data and on the free movement of such data (Data Protection Directive) [1995] OJ L281/31.

Council Regulation (EC) No. 659/1999 of 22 March 1999 laying down detailed rules for the application of Article 93 of the EC Treaty [1999] L83/1.

Directive 2000/31/EC of the European Parliament and of the Council of 8 June 2000 on certain legal aspects of information society services, in particular electronic commerce, in the Internal Market (Directive on Electronic Commerce) [2000] OJ L178/1.

Directive 2001/29/EC of the European Parliament and of the Council of 22 May 2001 on the harmonization of certain aspects of copyright and related rights in the information society [2001] OJ L167/10.

Directive 2002/19/EC of the European Parliament and of the Council of 7 March 2002 on access to, and interconnection of, electronic communications networks and associated facilities (Access Directive) [2002] OJ L108/7.

Directive 2002/22/EC of the European Parliament and of the Council of 7 March 2002 on universal service and users' rights relating to electronic communications networks and services (Universal Service Directive) [2002] OJ L108/51.

Council Regulation (EC) No. 1/2003 of 16 December 2002 on the implementation of the rules on competition laid down in Articles 81 and 82 of the Treaty [2003] OJ L1/1.

Council Regulation (EC) No. 139/2004 of 20 January 2004 on the control of concentrations between undertakings (EC Merger Regulation) [2004] OJ L24/1.

Charter of Fundamental Rights of the EU [2006] OJ C 303/2.

Council Regulation (EC) No. 168/2007 of 15 February 2007 establishing a European Union Agency for Fundamental Rights OJ [2007] OJ L53/01.

Protocol No. 27 on the Internal Market and Competition [2008] OJ C 115/309.

Directive 2009/136/EC of the European Parliament and of the Council of 25 November 2009 amending Directive 2002/22/EC on universal service and users' rights relating to electronic communications networks and services, Directive 2002/58/EC concerning the processing of personal data and the protection of privacy in the electronic communications sector and Regulation (EC) No. 2006/2004 on cooperation between national authorities responsible for the enforcement of consumer protection laws (Text with EEA relevance) [2009] OJ L337/11.

Protocol No. 29 on the System of Public Broadcasting in the Member States [2010] OJ C 83/312.

Directive 2010/13/EU of the European Parliament and of the Council of 10 March 2010 on the coordination of certain provisions laid down by law, regulation or administrative action in Member States concerning the provision of audiovisual media services (Audiovisual Media Services Directive) [2010] OJ L332/27.

Commission Regulation (EU) No. 330/2010 of 20 April 2010 on the application of Article 101(3) of the Treaty on the Functioning of the European Union to categories of vertical agreements and concerted practices [2010] OJ L102/1.

Regulation (EU) 2016/679 of the European Parliament and of the Council of 27 April 2016 on the protection of natural persons with regard to the processing of personal data and on the free movement of such data, and repealing Directive 95/46/EC (General Data Protection Regulation) [2016] OJ L119/1.

EU/EEA LEGISLATIVE PROPOSALS

Commission. 'Proposal for a Council Regulation establishing a European Union Agency for Fundamental Rights' COM (2005) 280 final. <https://eur-lex.europa.eu/legal-content/EN/TXT/PDF/?uri=CELEX:52005PC0280(01)&from=EN>

Commission. 'Proposal for a Regulation of the European Parliament and of the Council on the protection of individuals with regard to the processing of personal data and on the free movement of such data (General Data Protection Regulation)' COM (2012) 11 final.

Commission. 'Proposal for a Regulation of the European Parliament and of the Council on promoting fairness and transparency for business users of online intermediation services' COM (2018) 238 final. <https://ec.europa.eu/digital-single-market/en/news/regulation-promoting-fairness-and-transparency-business-users-online-intermediation-services>

EU/EEA MEMBER STATES LEGISLATION

Act Against Restraints of Competition, version published on 15 July 2005 (Bundesgesetzblatt (Federal Law Gazette) I, p2114; 2009 I p3850), as last amended by Article 3 of the Act of 26 July 2011 (Federal Law Gazette I, p1554) <http://www.gesetze-im-internet.de/englisch_gwb/englisch_gwb.html> *Germany*

Bundesverfassungsgericht, 2270/05 from 11/09/2007, *Germany*.

Gesetz zur Umsetzung der Richtlinie 2000/52/EG der Kommission vom 26, Juli 2000 zur Änderung der Richtlinie 80/723/EWG über die Transparenz der finanziellen Beziehungen zwischen den Mitgliedstaaten und den öffentlichen Unternehmen (Transparenzrichtlinie-Gesetz – TranspRLG) <http://www.gesetze-im-internet.de/bundesrecht/transprlg/gesamt.pdf> *Germany.*

Greek Law No. 3592/2007 of 19/07/2007 on Media Concentration and Licensing Procedures [2007] Official Gazette 161/3371, *Greece.*

Interstate Treaty on Broadcasting and Telemedia (Interstate Broadcasting Treaty), version of the 12th Amendment to the Interstate Broadcasting Treaty dating from 18 December 2008, in force since 1 June 2009, *Germany.*

Ley 10/2007, de 22 de junio, de la lectura, del libro y de las bibliotecas Publicado en BOE núm. 150 de 23 de junio de 2007, Spain.

Ley 21/2014, de 4 de noviembre, por la que se modifica el texto refundido de la Ley de Propiedad Intelectual, aprobado por Real Decreto Legislativo 1/1996, de 12 de abril, y la Ley 1/2000, de 7 de enero, de Enjuiciamiento Civil. [2014] BOE Núm. 268 Sec. I. Pág. 90404 <http://www.boe.es/boe/dias/2014/11/05/pdfs/BOE-A-2014-11404.pdf> *Spain.*

Ley 7/2010, de 31 de marzo, General de la Comunicación Audiovisual, Official State Gazette 79, 1.4.2010, p. 30157, Spain.

Ley 8/2009, de 28 de agosto, de financiación de la Corporación de Radio y Televisión Española, Boletín Oficial del Estado, 210, 31.8.2009, p. 74003, Spain.

Loi n° 2011-590 du 26 mai 2011 relative au prix du livre numérique, Version consolidée au 15 janvier 2019 <http://www.legifrance.gouv.fr/affichTexte.do;?cidTexte=LEGITEXT000024082056> *France.*

LEGISLATION OF THE UNITED STATES OF AMERICA

Newspaper Preservation Act, U.S. Code, Title 15, Chapter 43.

Sherman Act 15 U.S.C. § 2 (2000).

TABLES OF CASES, OPINIONS AND DECISIONS

JUDGMENTS OF THE COURT OF JUSTICE OF THE EU

32/65 *Italian Republic v Council and Commission* [1966] ECR 234, 405.

56 and 58/64 *Consten SA and Grundig-Verkaufs GmbH v Commission of the European Economic Community* [1966] ECR 299, 340.

41 and 44/70 *NV International Fruit Company and others v Commission* [1971] ECR 411.

78/70 *Deutsche Grammophon Gesellschaft mbH v Metro-SB-Großmärkte GmbH & Co. KG* [1971] ECR 487.

8/72 *Vereeniging v Commission* [1972] ECR 977.

6/72 *Europemballage Corporation and Continental Can Company Inc v Commission* [1973] ECR 215.

155/73 Sacchi [1974] ECR 409 [1974] CMLR 177.

6/73 and 7/73 *Istituto Chemioterapico Italiano and Commercial Solvents v Commission* [1974] ECR 223.

26/75 *General Motors Continental NV v Commission of the European Communities* [1975] ECR 01367.

40-48, 50, 54-56, 111, 113 & 114/73 *Coöperatieve Vereniging 'Suiker Unie' UA and others v Commission of the European Communities* [1975] ECR I-1663.

26/76 *Metro-SB Großmärkte GmbH & Co. KG v Commission of the European Communities* [1977] ECR 1875.

27/76 *United Brands Company and United Brands Continentaal BV v Commission of the European Communities* [1978] ECR 207.

28/77 *Tepea BV v Commission* [1978] ECR 1391.

172/80 *Züchner* [1981] ECR 2021.

262/81 *Coditel SA and others v Ciné-Vog Films SA and others* [1982] ECR 3381.

322/81 *Nederlandsche Banden-Industrie-Michelin v Commission* [1983] ECR 3461.

319/82 *Kerpen & Kerpen* [1983] ECR 4173.

229/83 *Association des Centres distributeurs Édouard Leclerc and others v SARL 'Au blé vert' and others* [1985] ECR 1.

243/83 *SA Binon & Cie v SA Agence et messageries de la presse* [1985] ECR 2015.

42/84 *Remia and others v Commission* [1985] ECR 2545.

311/84 *Centre belge d'études de marché – Télémarketing (CBEM) v SA Compagnie luxembourgeoise de télédiffusion (CLT) and Information publicité Benelux (IPB)* [1985] ECR 3261.

311/85 *ASBL Vereniging van Vlaamse Reisbureaus v ASBL Sociale Dienst van de Plaatselijke en Gewestelijke Overheidsdiensten* [1985] ECR I-3801.

240/82 and others *Stichting Sigarettenindustrie and others v Commission of the European Communities* [1985] ECR 3831.

161/84 *Pronuptia de Paris GmbH v Pronuptia de Paris Irmgard Schillgallis* [1986] ECR 00353.

226/84 *British Leyland Public Limited Company v Commission* [1986] ECR 3263.

352/85 *Bond van Adverteerders v Netherlands* [1988] ECR 2085.

238/87 *Volvo v Veng* (UK) [1988] ECR 6211.

C-234/89 *Delimitis v Henninger Bräu AG* [1991] ECR I-935.

C-300/89 *Commission v Council* [1991] ECR I-2867.

C-62/86 *AKZO Chemie BV v Commission of the European Communities* [1991] ECR I-3359.

C-288/89 *Stichting Collectieve Antennevoorziening Gouda and others v Commissariaat voor de Media* [1991] ECR I-4007.

C-353/89 *Commission of the European Communities v Kingdom of the Netherlands* [1991] ECR I-4069.

C-295/90 *Parliament v Council* [1992] ECR I-4193.

C-211/91 *Commission v Belgium* [1992] ECR I-6757.

C-148/91 *Vereniging Veronica Omroep Organisatie v Commissariaat voor de Media* [1993] ECR I-487.

155/91 *Commission of the European Communities v Council of the European Communities* [1993] ECR I-00939.

C-320/91 *Corbeau* [1993] ECR I-2563.

C-393/92 *Municipality of Almelo and others v NV Energiebedrijf Ijsselmij* [1994] ECR I-01477.

C-18/93 *Corsica Ferries Italia Sri v Corpo dei Piloti del Porto di Genova* [1994] ECR I-1783.

C-360/92 *The Publishers Association v Commission* [1995] ECR I-23.

C-241/91 P and C-242/91 P *Radio Telefis Eireann (RTE) and Independent Television Publications Ltd v Commission* [1995] ECR I-743.

C-266/93 *Bundeskartellamt v Volkswagen AG and VAG Leasing GmbH* [1995] ECR I-3477.

C-7/97 *Oscar Bronner GmbH & Co. KG v Mediaprint Zeitungs- und Zeitschriftenverlag GmbH & Co. and others* [1998] ECR I-7791.

C-215/96 and C-216/96 *Carlo Bagnasco and others v Banca Popolare di Novara soc. coop. arl. (BNP) and Cassa di Risparmio di Genova e Imperia SpA (Carige)* [1999] ECR I-135.

C-75/97 *Maribel bis/ter* [1999] ECR I-3671.

C-395/96 P and C-396/96 P *Compagnie maritime belge transports and others v Commission* [2000] ECR I-1365.

C-9/99 *Echirolles Distribution SA v Association du Dauphiné and others* [2000] ECR I-8207.

C-163/99 *Portugal v Commission.* [2001] ECR I-2613.

C-377/98 *Netherlands v Parliament and Council* [2001] ECR I-07079.

C-310/99 *Italy v Commission* [2002] ECR I-2289.

C-314/03 *Commission v Grand Duchy of Luxembourg* [2004] ECR I-2257.

C-418/01 *IMS Health GmbH & Co. OHG v NDC Health GmbH & Co. KG* [2004] ECR I-5039.

C-217/05 *Confederación Española de Empresarios de Estaciones de Servicio v Compañía Española de Petróleos SA* [2006] ECR I-11987.

C-5/08 *Infopaq International A/S v Danske Dagblades Forening* [2009] ECR I-6569.

C-501/06 P, C-513/06 P, C-515/06 P and C-519/06 P *GlaxoSmithKline Services Unlimited v Commission* [2009] ECR I-9291.

C-52/09 *Konkurrensverket v TeliaSonera Sverige AB* [2011] ECR I-527.

C-403/08 and C-429/08 *Football Association Premier League Ltd and others v QC Leisure and others and Karen Murphy v Media Protection Services Ltd* [2011] ECR I-09083.

C-466/12 *Nils Svensson and others v Retriever Sverige AB* [2014] ECLI:EU:C:2014:76.

COURT OF FIRST INSTANCE

T-37/92 *Bureau Européen des Unions des Consommateurs (BEUC) v Commission of the European Communities* [1994] ECR II-285.

T-29/92 *Vereniging van Samenwerkende Prijsregelende Organisaties in de Bouwnijverheid (SPO)* [1995] ECR II-289.

T-141/89 *Tréfileurope* [1995] ECR II-791.

T-528/93, T-542/93, T-543/93 and T-546/93 *Metropole Television SA, Reti Televisive Italiane SpA, Gestevision Telecinco SA and Antena 3 de Television v Commission* [1996] ECR II-649, [1996] 5 CMLR 386.

T-229/94 *Deutsche Bahn AG v Commission* [1997] ECR II-1689.

T-374/94, T-375/94, T-384/94 and T-388/94 *European Night Services and others v Commission of the European Communities* [1998] ECR II-3141.

T-504/93 *Tiercé Ladbroke SA v Commission* [1997] ECR II-923.

T-25/95 and others *Cimenteries CBR and others v Commission of the European Communities* [2000] ECR II-491.

T-128/98 *Aéroports de Paris v Commission* [2000] ECR II-3929.

T-325/01 *DaimlerChrysler AG v Commission of the European Communities* [2005] ECR II-3319.

T-213 and 214/01 *Österreichische Postsparkasse AG and Bank für Arbeit und Wirtschaft AG v Commission of the European Communities* [2001] ECR II-03963.

T-168/01 *GlaxoSmithKline Services Unlimited v Commission* [2006] ECR II-2969.

T-201/04 *Microsoft Corp. v Commission of the European Communities* [2007] ECR II-03601.

T-289/03 *BUPA and others v Commission* [2008] ECR II-81.

T-442/03 *SIC v Commission* [2008] ECR II-1161.

T-568/08 and T-573/08 *Métropole télévision (M6) and Télévision française 1 SA* (TF1) [2010] ECR II-3397.

T-461/07 *Visa Europe and Visa International Service v Commission* [2011] ECR II-1729.

T-394/15 *KPN v European Commission* [2017] ECLI:EU:T:2017:756.

T-612/*17 Google and Alphabet v Commission* [2017] OJ C 369/37.

EUROPEAN COURT OF HUMAN RIGHTS

Case of *VGT Vereiniging gegen Tierfabriken v Switzerland.* Application no. 24699/94. Judgment of 28 June 2001.

EU/EEA NATIONAL CASE LAW

Court of First Instance of Brussels. *Copiepresse v Google*. No. 06/10.928/C.

Court of Appeal of Brussels. *Google Inc v Copiepresse*. R. No. 2011/2999, No. 817.

Cour de Cassation. Judgment of 12 February 2004, *NMPP v Conseil de la Concurrence*, BOCCRF n. 5 of 4 May 2004.

BGH. *Paperboy*. Judgment of 17 July 2003, I ZR 259/00. Available (in German) at: <http://juris.bundesgerichtshof.de/cgi-bin/rechtsprechung/document.py?Gericht=bgh&Art=en&Datum=2003&Sort=3&Seite=5&client=3&anz=1706&pos=171&nr=27035>.

Cour d'appel du Paris. *Société des Auteurs des Arts Visuels et de L'Image Fixe (SAIF) v Google France*, SARL, and Google Inc. Judgment of 26 January 2011, 08/13423.

US CASE LAW

Harper & Row, Publishers, Inc v Nation Enters 471 U.S. 539, 564–65 (1985).

International News Service v Associated Press 248 U.S. 215 (1918).

National Basketball Association v Motorola, Inc 105 F.3d 841, 41 U.S.P.Q.2d (BNA) 1585 (2d Cir. 1997).

West Virginia State Bd. Of Educ. v Barnette 319 U.S. 624 (1943).

United States v Apple Inc et al. 12 civ 02826 (DLC). (NY 2013) <http://www.justice.gov/atr/cases/f299200/299275.pdf>.

United States v Apple Inc. 2nd US Circuit Court of Appeals, No. 13-3741 <https://law.justia.com/cases/federal/appellate-courts/ca2/13-3741/13-3741-2015-06-30.html>.

Department of Justice (2012). Case 1:12-cv-02826-UA *United States of America v Apple Inc, Hachette Book Group Inc, HarperCollins Publishers LLC, The Penguin Group, A Division of Pearson PLC, Penguin Group (USA) Inc, Simon and Schuster Inc* (United States District Court, Southern District of New York) (Complaint) <http://www.justice.gov/atr/cases/f282100/282135.pdf>.

Department of Justice (2012). Civil Action No.1:12-CV-2826 *United States of America v Apple Inc, Hachette Book Group Inc, HarperCollins Publishers LLC, Verlagsgruppe Georg Von Holtzbrinck GmbH, Holtzbrinck Publishers, LLC d/b/a Macmillan, The Penguin Group, A Division of Pearson PLC, Penguin Group (USA) Inc, Simon and Schuster Inc.* Comments of Barnes & Noble on the proposed final judgment <http://www.justice.gov/atr/cases/apple/comments/atc-0097.pdf>.

Federal Trade Commission (2013a, January). *Google Agrees to Change Its Business Practices to Resolve FTC Competition Concerns In the Markets for Devices Like Smart Phones, Games and Tablets, and in Online Search.* Press Release <https://www.ftc.gov/news-events/press-releases/2013/01/google-agrees-change-its-business-practices-resolve-ftc>.

Federal Trade Commission (2013b, January). *Statement of the Federal Trade Commission Regarding Google's Search Practices In the Matter of Google Inc.* FTC File Number 111-0163 <https://www.ftc.gov/system/files/documents/public_statements/295971/130103googlesearchstmtofcomm.pdf>.

Federal Trade Commission (2013c, January). *Concurring and Dissenting Statement of Commissioner J. Thomas Rosch Regarding Google's Search Practices In the Matter of Google Inc. FTC File No. 111-0163* <https://www.ftc.gov/sites/default/files/documents/public_statements/concurring-and-dissenting-statement-commissioner-j.thomas-rosch-regarding-googles-search-practices/130103googlesearchstmt.pdf>.

Federal Trade Commission (2013d, January). *Statement of Commissioner Maureen K. Ohlhausen In the Matter of Google Inc. FTC File No. 111-0163* <https://www.ftc.gov/sites/default/files/documents/public_statements/statement-commissioner-maureen-ohlhausen/130103googlesearchohlhausenstmt.pdf>.

EUROPEAN COMMISSION DECISIONS

Decisions

1998 Football World Cup (Case IV/36.888) Commission Decision relating to a proceeding under Article 82 of the EC Treaty and Article 54 of the EEA Agreement [2000] OJ L5/55.

Ad hoc financing of Dutch public service broadcasters Commission Decision C 2/2004 [2006] OJ L49/1.

Ad hoc payments to RAI Commission Decision C 62/1999 [2004] OJ L119/1.

Ad hoc Payments to RTP Commission Decision ex NN133/B/01, NN85/B/2001 and NN94/B/99 [2002] OJ 85/5.

Amcor/Alcan (Case COMP/M.5599) [2010] OJ C 35/1.

Apple/Beats (Case COMP/M.7290) [2014] OJ C 260/8.

BBC Digital Curriculum (N37/2003) [2003] OJ C 271/47.

BBC License Fee [2003] OJ C 23/6.

BBC License Fee (N631/2001) [2002] OJ C 98/1.

BBC News 24 (NN88/98) [2000] OJ C78/6.

BBI v Boosey & Hawkes (IV/32.279) Commission Decision of 29 July 1987 [1987] OJ L286/36.

Bertelsmann/Kirch/Premiere (Case IV/M.993) [1999] OJ L053/1.

Bertelsmann/KKR (Case COMP/M.5533) [2009] OJ C 240/01.

Bertelsmann/Planeta/Circulo (Case COMP/M.5838) [2010] OJ C 228/3.

British Interactive Broadcasting/Open (Case IV/36.539) [1999] OJ 312/1.

BSkyB/Kirch Pay-TV (Case COMP/JV.37) [2000] OJ C 110/45.

Candover/Cinven/Bertelsmann-Springer (Case COMP/M.3197) [2003] C207/10.

CECED (Case IV.F.1/36.718) Commission Decision 2000/475/EC [2000] OJ L187/47.

Chaîne française d'information international (N54/2005) [2005] OJ C 256/25.

Comcast/NBC Universal (Case COMP/M.5779) [2010] OJ C228/2.

Decision of the Commission of the European Communities of 15 December 1975 relating to a procedure under Article 85 of the EEC treaty (IV/847 – SABA) [1976] OJ L28/19.

Deutsche Post AG – Interception of cross-border mail (COMP/C-1/36.915) [2002] OJ L331/40.

Deutsche Telekom/Beta Research (Case IV/M.1027) [1998] OJ C 37/4.

Decision of 4 May 2017 relating to a proceeding under Article 102 of the Treaty on the Functioning of the European Union (TFEU) and Article 54 of the EEA Agreement E-book MFNs and related matters (Amazon) (Case AT.40153). C(2017) 2876 final <http://ec.europa.eu/competition/antitrust/cases/dec_docs/40153/40153_4392_3.pdf>.

E-books (Case COMP/AT.39847) Commission Decision of 12 December 2012 addressed to Hachette Livre SA, HarperCollins Publishers Limited, HarperCollins Publishers LLC, Georg von Holtzbrinck GmbH & Co. KG, Verlagsgruppe Georg von Holtzbrinck GmbH, Simon & Schuster Inc, Simon & Schuster (UK) Ltd, Simon & Schuster Digital Sales Inc, Apple Inc relating to a proceeding under Article 101 TFEU and Article 53 of the EEA Agreement C(2012) 9288 (consolidated version).

E-books (Case COMP/39.847) Commission Decision of 25 July 2013 addressed to Penguin Random House Limited (formerly The Penguin Publishing Company Limited) and Penguin Group (USA) LLC (formerly Penguin Group (USA) Inc) relating to proceedings under Article 101 TFEU and Article 53 of the EEA Agreement C(2013) 4750.

EBU/Eurovision (Case IV/32.150) Commission Decision 93/403/EEC [1993] OJ L179/23.

EBU/Eurovision (Case IV/32.150) [2000] OJ L151/18.

European Sugar Industry Commission Decision 73/109/EC [1973] OJ L140/17

Facebook/WhatsApp (Case COMP/M.7217) [2014] OJ C 417/2.

Fox/Sky (Case COMP/M.8354) [2017] OJ 238/1.

Google/Doubleclick (Case COMP/M.4731) [2008] OJ C 184/6.

Google Search (Case AT.39740) Commission Decision of 27 June 2017 relating to proceedings under Article 102 TFEU and Article 54 of the EEA Agreement C (2017) 4444 final.

Greek Ferries (Case IV/D-2/34.466) Commission Decision of 9 December 1998 [1999] OJ L109/24.

Gruner + Jahr/Financial Times/JV (Case IV/M.1455) [1999] OJ C 80/5.

HBO Ziggo/HBO Nederland (Case COMP/M.6369) [2012] OJ C 72/2.

IBM personal computer (IV/30.849) Commission Decision 84/233/EEC of 18 April 1984 relating to a proceeding under Article 85 of the EEC Treaty [1984] OJ L118/24.

Intel (COMP/C-3/37.990) Commission Decision of 13 May 2009 relating to a proceeding under Article 82 of the EC Treaty and Article 54 of the EEA Agreement, D (2009) 3726 final.

Intel/McAfee (Case COMP/M.5984) [2011] OJ C 98/1.

JCB (Case COMP.F.1/35.918) Commission Decision of 21 December 2000 relating to a proceeding under Article 81 of the EC Treaty [2002] OJ L69/1.

Joint selling of the media rights of the FA Premier League on an exclusive basis (Notice published pursuant to Article 19(3) of Council Regulation No 17 concerning Case COMP/C.2/38.173 and 38.453) [2004] OJ C 115/02.

Joint Selling of the Media Rights of the FA Premier League (FAPL) (Case COMP/C.2/38.173) [2006] OJ L 176/104.

Joint Selling of the Media Rights to the German Bundesliga (Case COMP/C-2/37.214) [2005] OJ L134/46.

Kirch/Richemont/Multichoice/Telepiù (Case IV/M.584) [1995] OJ C 129/6.

KLM/Martinair (Case COMP/M.5141) [2009] C 51/4.

Lagardère/Natexis/VUP (Case COMP/M.2978) [2004] OJ L125/54.

Liberty Global Europe/Unitymedia (Case COMP/M.5734) [2010] OJ C36/1.

Liberty Global/Ziggo (Case COMP/M.7000) [2018] OJ C 125/4.

Lufthansa/SN Airholding (Case COMP/M.5335) OJ [2009] C 295/8.

Microsoft (Case COMP/C-3/37.792) Commission Decision of 24 March 2004 relating to a proceeding under Article 82 of the EC Treaty C [2004] 900 final.

Microsoft/Yahoo! Search Business (Case COMP/M.5727) C [2010] 1077.

MSG Media Service (Case IV/M.469) [1994] OJ L364/1.

Napier Brown – British Sugar (Case IV/30.178) Commission Decision of 18 July 1988 relating to a proceeding under Article 86 of the EEC Treaty [1988] OJ L284/41.

Nathan-Bricolux (Case COMP.F.1/36.516) Commission Decision of 5 July 2000 relating to a proceeding pursuant to Article 81 of the EC Treaty [2001] OJ L54/1.

Nestlé/Ralston Purina (Case COMP/M.2337) [2001] OJ C 239/7.

New Tax-Based Funding System for Public Broadcasting in Spain Commission Decision C 38/2009 [2011] OJ L1/9.

News Corp/BSkyB (Case COMP/M.5932) [2011] C 37/2.

News Corp/Premiere (Case COMP/M.5121) [2008] OJ C 219/4.

News Corp/Telepiù (Case COMP/M.2876) [2004] OJ L110/73.

News Corp/Telepiù (Case COMP/M.2876) C(2010) 4976 final.

Newspaper Publishing (Case IV/M.423) [1994] OJ C 85/5.

Nordic Satellite Distribution (Case IV/M.490) [1995] OJ L053/20.

Notice pursuant to Article 19(3) of Regulation No. 17 concerning Agence et Messageries de la Presse, Case IV/31.609 [1987] OJ C 164/02.

Notice pursuant to Article 19(3) of Council Regulation No. 17 concerning an application for negative clearance or exemption under Article 81(3) of the EC Treaty, Cases COMP/34.657, Sammelrevers and COMP/35.245 to 35.251, Einzelreverse [2000] OJ C 162/8.

Nutricia/de Rooij and Nutricia/Zuid-Hollandse Conservenfabriek Commission Decision of 12 December 1983 relating to a proceeding under Article 85 of the EEC Treaty [1983] OJ L376/22.

Pernod Ricard/V&S (Case COMP/M.5114) OJ [2008] C 219/5.

Philips/Osram (IV/34.252) [1994] OJ L378/37.

Public financing of public service broadcaster VRT Commission Decision E 8/2006 [2008] OJ C 143/1.

Publishers Association – Net Book Agreement (Cases IV/27.393 and IV/27.394) Commission Decision of 12 December 1988 relating to a proceeding under Article 85 of the EEC Treaty [1989] OJ L22/12.

Recoletos/Unedisa (Case IV/M.1401) [1999] OJ C 73/6.

Restrictions concerning ELT books (Case COMP/39771) C (2012)7141 final.

Rewe/Meinl (Case IV/M.1221) Commission Decision 1999/674/EC [1999] OJ L274/1

RTL/Veronica/Endemol (HMG) (Case IV/M.553) [1996] OJ L124/32.

RTVE (Case C 38/2009 (ex NN 58/2009)) Commission Decision on the State aid scheme which Spain is planning to implement for Corporación de Radio y Televisión Española C (2010) 4925 final.

Ryanair/Aer Lingus (Case COMP/M.4439) [2007] OJ C 10/6.

Scandlines Sverige AB v Port of Helsingborg (Case COMP/A.36.568/D3) [2006] CMLR 1298.

Sealink/B&I–Holyhead [1992] 5 CMLR 255.

SFR/Télé 2 France (Case COMP M.4504) [2007] OJ L316/57.

Star Alliance (Case AT.39595) Commission Decision of 23 May 2013 addressed to Air Canada, United Airlines Inc, and Deutsche Lufthansa AG relating to proceedings under Article 101 TFEU.

State aid financing of RTÉ and TNAG (TG4) (E4/2005) [2008] OJ C121/5.

Statoilhydro/Conocophilips (Case COMP/M.4919) [2009] OJ C 201/06.

Telenor/Canal+/Canal Digital (Case COMP/C.2/38.287) [2003] OJ C 149/10.

Tetra Pak II (IV/31043) Commission Decision of 24 July 1991 relating to a proceeding pursuant to Article 86 of the EEC Treaty [1992] OJ L72/1.

TPS Commission Decision 1999/242/EC [1999] OJ L90/6.

TPS (Case COMP/JV.57) [2002] OJ C 137/23.

Trans-Atlantic Conference Agreement (Case IV/35.134) [1999] OJ L95/1.

UEFA Broadcasting Regulations Commission Decision 2001/478/EC [2001] OJ L171/12.

UEFA Champions League (Case COMP/C.2-37.398) [2003] OJ L291/25.

Unilever/Sara Lee Body Care (Case COMP/M.5658) [2012] OJ C 23/10.

United International Pictures (UIP) [1989] OJ L226/25.

Universal Music Group/EMI Music (Case COMP/M.6458) [2012] OJ C 220/8.

VBBB/VBVB (Case IV/428) Commission Decision 82/123/EEC of 25 November 1981 relating to a proceeding under Article 85 of the EEC Treaty [1982] OJ L52/36.

VISA MIF (Case AT.39398) C (2014) 1199 final.

Vivendi/Canal+/Seagram (Case COMP/M.2050) [2000] OJ C 311/3.

Volkswagen (Case COMP/F-2/36.693) Commission Decision of 29 June 2001 relating to a proceeding under Article 81 of the EC Treaty [2001] OJ L262/14.

Wegener/PCM/JV (Case COMP/M.3817) [2005] C 191/3.

Yamaha (Case COMP/37.975) Commission Decision of 16 July 2003 relating to a proceeding under Article 81 of the EC Treaty and Article 53 of the EEA Agreement [not published].

PRESS RELEASES AND OTHER PUBLICATIONS REGARDING SPECIFIC DECISIONS

Brockhoff, J., Bertrand Jehanno, Vera Pozzato, Carl-Christian Buhr, Peter Eberl, and Penelope Papandropoulos (2008). *Google/DoubleClick: The first test for the Commission's non-horizontal merger guidelines,* Competition Policy Newsletter 2, 53–60.

Commission (2001, July). *Commission opens proceedings against UEFA's selling of TV rights to UEFA Champions League.* Press Release IP/01/1043. <http://europa.eu/rapid/press-release_IP-01-1043_en.htm?locale=it>.

Commission (2001, July). *Commission re-opens proceedings concerning the German system of fixed book prices because of its effects on cross-border Internet bookselling.* Press Release IP/01/1035. <http://europa.eu/rapid/press-release_IP-01-1035_en.htm?locale=it>.

Commission (2002, March). *Commission accepts undertaking in competition proceedings regarding German book price fixing.* Press Release IP/02/461. <http://europa.eu/rapid/press-release_IP-02-461_en.htm>.

Commission (2002, June). *Commission welcomes UEFA's new policy for selling the media rights to the Champions League.* Press Release IP/02/806. <http://europa.eu/rapid/press-release_IP-02-806_en.htm?locale=it>.

Commission (2002, June). *Commission clears B&W Loudspeakers distribution system after company deletes hard-core violations.* Press Release IP/02/916. <http://europa.eu/rapid/press-release_IP-02-916_en.htm?locale=en>.

Commission (2003, July). *New marketing system for Bundesliga broadcasting rights.* Press Release IP/03/1106. <http://europa.eu/rapid/press-release_IP-03-1106_en.htm?locale=it>.

Commission (2004, October). *Commission closes investigation into contracts of six Hollywood studios with European pay-TVs.* Press Release IP/04/1314. <http://europa.eu/rapid/press-release_IP-04-1314_en.htm>.

Commission (2010, November). *Antitrust: Commission probes allegations of antitrust violations by Google.* Press Release IP/10/1624. <http://europa.eu/rapid/press-release_IP-10-1624_en.htm?locale=en>.

Commission (2011, February). MEMO/11/89. *Media: Commission Vice-President Kroes welcomes amendments to Hungarian Media Law.* <http://europa.eu/rapid/press-release_MEMO-11-89_en.htm>.

Commission (2011, March). *Antitrust: Commission confirms unannounced inspections in the e-book publishing sector.* MEMO/11/126. <http://europa.eu/rapid/press-release_MEMO-11-126_en.htm?locale=en>.

Commission (2011, December). *Antitrust: Commission opens formal proceedings to investigate sales of e-books.* Press Release IP/11/1509. <http://europa.eu/rapid/press-release_IP-11-1509_en.htm>.

Commission (2013, January). *Mergers: Commission blocks proposed acquisition of TNT Express by UPS.* Press Release IP 13/68. <http://europa.eu/rapid/press-release_IP-13-68_en.htm>.

Commission (2013, April). *Commission seeks feedback on commitments offered by Google to address competition concerns – questions and answers.* <http://europa.eu/rapid/press-release_MEMO-13-383_en.htm>.

Commission (2012, May). Speech/12/372. *Statement of VP Almunia on the Google antitrust investigation.* <http://europa.eu/rapid/press-release_SPEECH-12-372_en.htm>.

Commission (2014a, February). *Antitrust: Commission obtains from Google comparable display of specialized search rivals – Frequently asked questions.* Memo 14/87. <http://europa.eu/rapid/press-release_MEMO-14-87_en.htm?locale=en>.

Commission (2014b, February). *Statement on the Google investigation.* <http://europa.eu/rapid/press-release_SPEECH-14-93_en.htm>.

Commission (2014, May). *Mergers: Commission clears acquisition of Telefónica Ireland by Hutchison 3G, subject to conditions.* Press Release IP 14/607. <http://europa.eu/rapid/press-release_IP-14-607_en.htm>.

Commission (2014, July). *Mergers: Commission clears acquisition of E-Plus by Telefónica Deutschland, subject to conditions.* Press Release IP 14/771. <http://europa.eu/rapid/press-release_IP-14-771_en.htm>.

Commission (2015, April), *Antitrust: Commission sends Statement of Objections to Google on comparison shopping service.* Fact Sheet. <http://europa.eu/rapid/press-release_MEMO-15-4781_en.htm>.

Commission (2015, June). *Antitrust: Commission opens formal investigation into Amazon's e-book distribution arrangements.* <http://europa.eu/rapid/press-release_IP-15-5166_en.htm>.

Commission (2016, July). *Antitrust: Commission takes further steps in investigations alleging Google's comparison shopping and advertising-related practices breach EU rules.* Press Release. <http://europa.eu/rapid/press-release_IP-16-2532_en.htm>.

Commission (2017, January). *Antitrust: Commission seeks feedback on commitments offered by Amazon in e-book investigation.* <http://europa.eu/rapid/press-release_IP-17-137_en.htm>.

Commission (2017, June). *Antitrust: Commission fines Google €2.42 billion for abusing dominance as search engine by giving illegal advantage to own comparison shopping service.* <http://europa.eu/rapid/press-release_IP-17-1784_en.htm>.

Commission (2017, July). *European Commission acts to preserve the rule of law in Poland.* <http://europa.eu/rapid/press-release_IP-17-2161_en.htm>.

Commission (2017, December). *Rule of Law: European Commission acts to defend judicial independence in Poland.* <http://europa.eu/rapid/press-release_IP-17-5367_en.htm>.

Commission (2018, July). *Antitrust: Commission fines Google €4.34 billion for illegal practices regarding Android mobile devices to strengthen dominance of Google's search engine.* <http://europa.eu/rapid/press-release_IP-18-4581_en.htm>.

Commission, D-G Competition (2002, June). *Commission ends competition proceedings regarding German book price fixing agreements following acceptance of an undertaking on cross-border sales.* Competition Policy Newsletter, 2, 35–37. <http://ec.europa.eu/competition/publications/cpn/2002_2_35.pdf>.

Google (2013, April). *Commitments in Case* COMP/C-3/39.740 – Foundem and others. <http://ec.europa.eu/competition/antitrust/cases/dec_docs/39740/39740_8608_5.pdf>.

Google (2013, October). *Commitments in Case* COMP/C-3/39.740 – Foundem and others. <http://www.consumerwatchdog.org/resources/googlesettlment102113.pdf>.

Google (2014, January). *Commitments in Case COMP/C-3/39.740 – Foundem and others.* <http://docs.dpaq.de/6448-google_commitments_full.pdf>.

ICOMP (2013, January). *Complaint of ICOMP against Google, Inc under Article 101 TFEU, pursuant to Article 7 of Regulation 9EC) No. 1/2003.* <http://www.i-comp.org/wp-content/uploads/2014/01/AnnexesICOMPMarketTestSubmission310513.pdf>.

ICOMP (2013, May). Response to the Remedies Proposed by Google Inc in Case COMP/C-3/39.740.

COUNCIL OF THE EUROPEAN UNION DECISIONS

Council Decision No. 252/2013/EU of 11 March 2013 establishing a Multiannual Framework for 2013–2017 for the European Union Agency for Fundamental Rights [2013] OJ L 79/1.

Council Decision (EU) 2017/2269 of 7 December 2017 establishing a Multiannual Framework for the European Union Agency for Fundamental Rights for 2018–2022 [2017] OJ L 326/1.

DECISIONS BY NATIONAL AUTHORITIES (INCLUDING PRESS RELEASES)

AGCom (2004). Delibera N. 360/04/CONS. <http://www.agcom.it/documents/10179/538769/Delibera+360-04-CONS/7b5b88af-14bc-4915-b264-dd1ca75e2ff9?version=1.0&targetExtension=pdf>.

AGCom (2010). A407- *Conto TV/Sky Italia, Provvedimento n. 21316.*

AGCom (2010). A420. *Federazione Italiana Editori Giornali/Google,* Provvedimento n. 21959.

AGCom (2013). *A429-RTI/SKY-Mondiali di Calcio, Provvedimento n. 24325.*

Bundeskartellamt (2013, November). *Amazon abandons price parity clauses for good.* <http://www.bundeskartellamt.de/SharedDocs/Meldung/EN/Pressemitteilungen/2013/26_11_2013_Amazon-Verfahrenseinstellung.html>.

Bundeskartellamt (2013). *HRS-Hotel Reservation Service Robert Ragge GmbH.* B.9-66/10. <http://www.bundeskartellamt.de/SharedDocs/Entscheidung/EN/Entscheidungen/Kartellverbot/B9-66-10.pdf?__blob=publicationFile&v=2>.

Bundeskartellamt (2013, March). *ARD/ZDF Online Platform 'Germany's Gold' raises competition concerns.* <http://www.bundeskartellamt.de/SharedDocs/Meldung/EN/Pressemitteilungen/2013/11_03_2013_Germanys-Gold.html>.

Conseil de la Concurrence (1998). *Décision n° 98-D-70 du 24 novembre 1998 relative à la saisine des sociétés Multivision et Télévision Par Satellite (TPS) dans le secteur des droits de diffusion audiovisuelle.* <http://www.autoritedelaconcurrence.fr/pdf/avis/98d70.pdf>.

Conseil de la Concurrence (2003). *Décision n° 03-MC-04 du 22 décembre 2003, Messageries Lyonnaises de Presse.* <http://www.autoritedelaconcurrence.fr/pdf/avis/03mc04.pdf>.

Danish Competition and Consumer Authority (2006, March). *Publishers right to fix book prices considerably reduced.* < https://www.en.kfst.dk/nyheder/kfst/english/decisions/20062903-publishers-right-to-fix-book-prices-considerably-reduced/ >.

Garante per la Protezione dei Dati Personali (2013, April). *Google: il Garante per la privacy avvia un'istruttoria sul rispetto della normativa italiana.* <http://www.garanteprivacy.it/web/guest/home/docweb/-/docweb-display/docweb/2348801>.

Hellenic Competition Commission (2008). Decision 422/V/2008, *RTL Central & Eastern Europe/Wakerock Limited.*

Information Commissioner's Office (2014). *Data Protection Act 1998 – Google Inc Undertaking. ICO Ref: ENF0492064.* https://www.pdpjournals.com/docs/88404.pdf.

Irish Competition Authority (2003, December). *Newspapers to amend business practices considered anti-competitive by The Competition Authority.*

Office of Fair Trading (2008). *Completed acquisition by Global Radio UK Limited of GCap Media plc.*

UK Department for Culture, Media and Sport (2011). *Notice on consultation on the proposed acquisition by News Corporation of up to 60.9% of British Broadcasting Group Plc – Undertakings given by News Corporation pursuant to paragraph 3 of Schedule 2 of the Enterprise Act 2002 (Protection of Legitimate Interests) Order 2003.*

TABLE OF SOFT LAW

EUROPEAN COMMISSION

Almunia, J. *Competition and personal data protection.* Speech given at the Privacy Platform event: Competition and Privacy in Markets of Data, 26 November 2012. <http://europa.eu/rapid/press-release_SPEECH-12-860_en.htm>.

Commission (1997, April). Press Release IP/97/313. *Electronic Commerce: Commission presents framework for future action.* <http://europa.eu/rapid/press-release_IP-97-313_en.htm?locale=it>.

Commission (2006). *The European Commission's Approach to Digital Interactive Television: Frequently Asked Questions.* Memo/06/60. <http://europa.eu/rapid/press-release_MEMO-06-60_en.htm>.

Commission (2007, January). Press Release IP/07/52. Media pluralism: *Commission stresses need for transparency, freedom and diversity in Europe's media landscape.*

Commission (2007). *Staff Working Document on Media Pluralism in the Member States of the EU* SEC (2007) 32.

Commission (2007). *White Paper on Sport* COM 391 final.

Commission. (2009). *Communication on the application of State aid rules to public service broadcasting (the Broadcasting Communication)* [2009] OJ C 257/1.

Commission (2013). *Public consultation on the Independent Report from the HLG on Media Freedom and Pluralism – Text of the consultation.* <https://ec.europa.eu/digital-agenda/en/news/public-consultation-independent-report-hlg-media-freedom-and-pluralism-—-read-contributions>.

Commission (2013). *Public consultation on the Independent Report from the HLG on Media Freedom and Pluralism – Contributions from Public Authorities.* <https://ec.europa.eu/digital-agenda/en/news/public-consultation-independent-report-hlg-media-freedom-and-pluralism-—-read-contributions>.

Commission, DG Competition (2004). *Best practices on the conduct of merger control proceedings.* <http://ec.europa.eu/competition/mergers/legislation/proceedings.pdf>.

Commission, DG Competition (2010). *Best Practices for the Submission of Economic Evidence and Data Collection in Cases Concerning the Application of Articles 101 and 102 TFEU and in Merger Cases. Staff Working Paper.* <http://ec.europa.eu/competition/antitrust/legislation/best_practices_submission_en.pdf>.

Commission, DG Enlargement (2014). *Guidelines for EU support to media freedom and media integrity in enlargement countries, 2014–2020.* <http://ec.europa.eu/enlargement/pdf/press_corner/elarg-guidelines-for-media-freedom-and-integrity_210214.pdf>.

Commission. *Communication from the Commission to the Council, the European Parliament, the European Economic and Social Committee and the Committee of the Regions on the future of European audiovisual regulatory policy* COM (2003) 784 final.

Commission. *Communication from the Commission to the Council and the European Parliament on Article 7 of the Treaty on European Union – Respect for and promotion of the values on which the Union is based* COM/2003/0606 final.

Commission. *Communication from the Commission to the European Parliament, the Council, the European Economic and Social Committee and the Committee of the Regions – A Quality Framework for Services of General Interest in Europe* COM(2011) 900 final. <http://ec.europa.eu/services_general_interest/docs/comm_quality_framework_en.pdf>.

Commission. *Communication from the Commission to the European Parliament and the Council on A New EU Framework to Strengthen the Rule of Law* COM(2014) 158 final, 2. <https://eur-lex.europa.eu/legal-content/EN/TXT/PDF/?uri=CELEX:52014DC0158&from=EN>.

Commission. *Communication on Services of General Interest* [2001] OJ C 17/04.

Commission. *Communication to the European Parliament, the Council, the European Economic and Social Committee and the Committee of the Regions on Tackling Online Disinformation: a European approach* COM(2018) 236 final.

Commission. *Declaration (No. 29) on Sport,* annexed to the final act of the Treaty of Amsterdam [1997] OJ C 340/136.

Commission. *Declaration on the specific characteristics of sport and its social function in Europe, of which account should be taken in implementing common policies,* Presidency conclusions, Nice European Council, Meeting, 7, 8, 9 December 2000.

Commission. *Guidance on the Commission's enforcement priorities in applying Article 82 of the EC Treaty to abusive exclusionary conduct by dominant undertakings* [2009] OJ C 45/2.

Commission. *Guidelines on the applicability of Article 101 of the Treaty on the Functioning of the European Union to horizontal cooperation agreements* [2011] OJ C 11/1.

Commission. *Guidelines on the Application of Article 101(3) TFEU* [2004] OJ C 101/08.

Commission. *Guidelines on the assessment of horizontal mergers under the Council Regulation on the control of concentrations between undertakings* [2004] OJ C 31/3.

Commission. *Guidelines on the assessment of non-horizontal mergers under the Council Regulation on the control of concentrations between undertakings* [2008] OJ C 265/7.

Commission. *Guidelines on Vertical Restraints* [2010] OJ C 130/1.

Commission. *Notice concerning agreements of minor importance which do not fall under Article 85(1) of the Treaty establishing the European Economic Community* [1997] OJ C 372/13.

Commission. *Notice of 18 December 1978 concerning its assessment of certain subcontracting agreements in relation to Article 85(1) of the EEC Treaty* [1979] OJ C 1/2.

Commission. *Notice on best practices for the conduct of proceedings concerning Articles 101 and 102 TFEU* [2011] OJ C308/6.

Commission. *Notice on Exclusive Dealing Contracts with Commercial Agents* [1962] OJ 139/2921.

Commission. *Notice on immunity from fines and reduction of fines in cartel cases* [2006] OJ C 298/11.

Commission. *Notice on remedies acceptable under Council Regulation (EC) No. 139/2004 and under Commission Regulation (EC) No. 802/2004.*

Commission. *Notice on the definition of relevant market for the purposes of Community competition law* [1997] OJ C 372/3.

Commission. *Notice on the handling of complaints by the Commission under Articles 81 and 82 of the EC Treaty* [2004] OJ C 101/05.

Commission. *Notice. Guidelines on the effect on trade concept contained in Articles 81 and 82 of the Treaty* OJ [2004] C 101/7.

Commission. *Pluralism and Media Concentration in the Internal Market – An Assessment of the Need for Community Action.* Green Paper COM (92) 480 final.

Commission. Staff Working Document (2008). *Accompanying document to the Communication from the Commission to the European Parliament, the Council, the European Economic and Social Committee and the Committee of the Regions – Eighth Communication on the application of Articles 4 and 5 of Directive 89/552/EEC 'Television without Frontiers', as amended by Directive 97/36/EC, for the period 2005–2006* SEC(2008) 2310._

Herbert, U. *Commercialising sport: Understanding the TV Rights debate.* Speech delivered in Barcelona, 2 October 2003. <http://ec.europa.eu/competition/speeches/text/sp2003_024_en.pdf >.

Lowe, P. *Consumer Welfare and Efficiency – New Guiding Principles of Competition Policy?* Speech given at the 13th International Conference on Competition and 14th European Competition Day, Munich, 27 March 2007.

Schaub, A. *Sports and Competition: Broadcasting rights for sports events. Speech delivered in Madrid,* 26 February 2002. <http://ec.europa.eu/competition/speeches/text/sp2002_008_en.pdf>.

Toft, T. (2003). *Football: joint selling of media rights.* Competition Policy Newsletter, 3, 47–52.

Wachtmeister, A. M. (1998), *Broadcasting of sports events and Competition law.* Competition Policy Newsletter, 2, 18–28.

EUROPEAN PARLIAMENT

European Parliament Resolution of 3 May 2018 on media pluralism and media freedom in the European Union (<2017/2209(INI)>).

European Parliament. Legislative resolution of 12 March 2014 on the proposal for a regulation of the European Parliament and of the Council on the protection of individuals with regard to the processing of personal data and on the free movement of such data (General Data Protection Regulation) (COM(2012)0011 – C7-0025/2012 – <2012/0011(COD)>).

European Parliament. Motion for a resolution on media law in Hungary, tabled by Daniel Cohn-Bendit, Rebecca Harms, Judith Sargentini, Helga Trüpel on behalf of the Greens/European Free Alliance Group, B7-0103/2011 of 9.2.2011. <http://www.europarl.europa.eu/sides/getDoc.do?type=MOTION&reference=B7-2011-103&language=EN>.

European Parliament. Motion for European Parliament Resolution on the situation as regards fundamental rights in the European Union (2002) (2002/2013(INI)).

European Parliament. Proposal for a Directive of the European Parliament and of the Council on copyright in the Digital Single Market COM/2016/0593 final. <https://eur-lex.europa.eu/legal-content/en/ALL/?uri=CELEX:52016PC0593>.

European Parliament. Resolution of 10 March 2011 on media law in Hungary P7_TA (2011) 0094. <http://www.europarl.europa.eu/sides/getDoc.do?pubRef=-//EP//TEXT+TA+P7-TA-2011-0094+0+DOC+XML+V0//EN>.

European Parliament Resolution of 25 November 2010 on public service broadcasting in the digital era: the future of the dual system [2010/2028 (INI)].

European Parliament. Resolution of 27 November 2014 on supporting consumer rights in the digital single market (2013/2973 (RSP)). <http://www.europarl.europa.eu/sides/getDoc.do?pubRef=-//EP//TEXT+TA+P8-TA-2014-0071+0+DOC+XML+V0//EN>.

European Parliament. Resolution of 22 April 2004 on the risks of violations, in the EU and especially in Italy, of freedom of expression and information (2003/2237(INI)).

European Parliament. Resolution of the Council and of the representatives of the Governments of the Member States meeting within the Council on public service broadcasting [1999] OJ C 30/1.

COUNCIL OF EUROPE

Council of Europe (2011, February). *Opinion of the Commissioner for Human Rights on Hungary's media legislation in light of Council of Europe standards on freedom of the media.* <https://wcd.coe.int/ViewDoc.jsp?id=1751289>.

Council of Europe. Recommendation No. R (2000) 23 on the independence and functions of regulatory authorities for the broadcasting sector and its Explanatory Memorandum, Pluralism in the multi-channel market: suggestions for regulatory scrutiny (MM-S-PL(1999) 012def).

Council of Europe. Recommendation No. R (94) 13 of the Committee of Ministers to Member States on measures to promote media transparency.

Council of Europe. Recommendation No. R (96) 10 on the guarantee of the independence of public service broadcasting and its Explanatory Memorandum.

Council of Europe. Recommendation No. R (99) 1 of the Committee of Ministers to Member States on Measures to Promote Media Pluralism and its Explanatory Memorandum.

OTHERS

AGCom (2010b). Libro bianco sui contenuti. <http://www.agcom.it/default.aspx?message=visualizzadocument&DocID=5558>.

Amnesty International (2007, March). Press Release. *EU Fundamental Rights: A long way to go.*

Article 29 Working Party (2013). *Opinion 03/2013 on purpose limitation.* <http://ec.europa.eu/justice/data-protection/article-29/documentation/opinion-recommendation/files/2013/wp203_en.pdf>.

BBC Response to Ofcom's Invitation to Comment on Measuring Media Plurality (2012). <http://stakeholders.ofcom.org.uk/binaries/consultations/measuring-plurality/responses/bbc.pdf>.

Bundeskartellamt (2017). *Background information on the Facebook proceeding.*

European Competition Network (2013, May). ECN *Brief.* <http://ec.europa.eu/competition/ecn/brief/05_2013/amaz_deuk.pdf>.

European Competition Network. *ECN Brief 02/2012.* <http://ec.europa.eu/competition/ecn/brief/02_2012/brief_02_2012.pdf>.

OSCE (2010, December). *Hungarian media law further endangers media freedom, says OSCE media freedom representative.* <http://www.osce.org/fom/74687>.

UK Department for Culture, Media, and Sport (2001). *Consultation on Media Ownership Rules.*

ABBREVIATIONS

CDMM	Council of Europe Steering Committee on the Mass Media
CFREU	Charter of Fundamental Rights of the European Union
CoE	Council of Europe
Commission	European Commission
EBU	European Broadcasting Union
ECJ	European Court of Justice
EUI	European University Institute
FCC	Federal Communications Commission
FRA	EU Fundamental Rights Agency
GDPR	General Data Protection Regulation
GCEU	General Court of the EU
NCA	National Competition Authority
OSCE	Organization for Security and Co-operation in Europe
RPM	Resale Price Maintenance
TEU	Treaty on European Union
TFEU	Treaty on the Functioning of the European Union

TABLE OF CONTENTS

CHAPTER 1
INTRODUCTION

1. Introduction

1. Digitization, the diffusion of broadband networks, and improvements in computing and wireless technologies are rapidly changing the media ecosystem as we know it. On the supply side, new distribution platforms have emerged, given that spectrum shortages and large upfront investments have been replaced by unlimited space and the ability to set up an outlet at almost no cost. As a result, there has been a proliferation of content and sources with the era of technical and economic scarcity gradually being succeeded by what is referred to as the 'era of communicative abundance'[1] or the 'age of plenty'.[2] On the user side, these developments have brought individuals to a whole other level. Consumers can now access content anytime, anywhere and on any digital device, from TV sets to tablets, from smartphones to laptops and desktops. Most importantly, Web 2.0 may lead to unprecedented levels of engagement because citizens can actively participate in public discourse, either by commenting on the content provided by mainstream media organizations or by creating their own outlets.

2. The digital revolution has undoubtedly brought significant benefits to media pluralism. As new sources may now instantly and effortlessly reach the public, audiences may access immeasurably more information than they could in the analogue environment. But the changes brought about by digital technologies have by no means rendered outdated the discussion over how media pluralism can be effectively protected. On the contrary, alongside concerns that policymakers have attempted to address in the past, such as concentration of ownership and interference with editorial freedom, which remain relevant,

---

1 Keane, J. (1999). *Public Life in the Era of Communicative Abundance*. Canadian Journal of Communication 24, 165–78

2 Ellis, J. (2002). *Seeing Things: Television in the Era of Uncertainty*. London and New York: I.B. Tauris

new concerns have arisen, posed by businesses that have emerged with the advent of the Internet.

3. More often than not, threats to media pluralism are not addressed in the domestic sphere. This is so for a number of reasons that may or may not be attributed to the Member States. For example, the legislator may have opted for a 'light' regulatory framework in order to advance national competitiveness vis-à-vis third countries. Where strict rules do apply, these cannot be enforced on media firms that are located outside the jurisdiction of the State whose citizens they reach. In many cases, the shape of national media markets depends on action taken by the EU. For instance, concentrations of an EU dimension are subject to the European Commission's approval.

4. What role, if any, should the EU play in safeguarding media pluralism in all the above cases? This issue has attracted wide attention in the scholarly literature, which offers several approaches to whether, and, if so, to what extent, the EU may act to protect this value. Avenues that have been explored thus far include human rights monitoring under Article 7 TEU, the enactment of a pan-European instrument setting minimum standards, and the development of soft-law initiatives that may lead to sound policymaking at a national level. Yet, action that could be taken under the branch of EU law that has played the most decisive role in shaping the European media markets, namely competition law, has received little attention to date. This is arguably because there has been a great deal of misunderstanding about its likely contribution to pluralism. The objective of this study is to resolve this misunderstanding by identifying the unexplored potential of strict competition enforcement for promoting a pluralistic offer.

2. Laying the groundwork: the Gordian knot of EU competence in the area of media pluralism

5. The relationship between EU law and media pluralism has been a thorny one, not least due to the complexities that arise in attempting to delineate competence boundaries. The Court of Justice of the EU has long held that media pluralism 'is connected with freedom of expression, as protected by Article 10 of the European Convention on Human Rights and Fundamental Freedoms, which is *one of the fundamental principles guaranteed by the [EU] legal order*' [emphasis added].[3] However, because the Member States have had a

3 See, for instance, ECJ, Case C-288/89 *Stichting Collectieve Antennevoorziening Gouda* [1991] ECR

general human rights competence since the inception of the European integration project, the endorsement by the Court of a principle that was construed as a manifestation of the exercise of a human right that received wide recognition among Member States was meant to ensure that *the EU institutions* would not develop policies that would force Member States to 'disapply constitutional rights or international human rights', and to bind Member States *only* when they applied EU law.[4] This division of competences has remained intact after the most recent amendments introduced by the Lisbon Treaty: the Charter of Fundamental Rights is now legally binding, however, it also explicitly provides that it does not afford new powers or tasks for the Union in the field of human rights.[5] Hence, even if Article 11(2) of the Charter establishes the obligation to 'respect' media pluralism, Member States are still primarily responsible for protecting this value in their jurisdiction.

6. Nevertheless, the EU does not lack competence altogether to act in support of media pluralism. Article 7 TEU introduces a mechanism that equips the EU institutions with the means of ensuring that all Member States respect the Union's founding principles: namely human rights, liberty, democracy, equality, and the rule of law.[6] More particularly, Article 7 establishes a procedure whereby the Council may determine whether there is a *clear risk of a serious breach* or whether there has been *a serious and persistent breach* by a Member State of one of the aforementioned principles.[7] Due to its deep-rooted relationship with freedom of expression, media pluralism is, *inter alia*, key to 'the democratic process in the Member States and in the European Union as a whole';[8] media has the capacity to mold public opinion and, by exposing citizens to diverse viewpoints, it enables them to make informed voting decisions. As a result, EU action against a Member State that engages in conduct harmful to media pluralism may rest on Article 7.

I-4007, paragraphs 23–29, and ECJ, Case C-353/89 *Commission of the European Communities v Kingdom of the Netherlands* [1991] ECR I-4069, paragraph 30. While the EU has not acceded to the European Convention on Human Rights yet, all Member States are signatories to the Convention and, on some occasions, they have been brought before the European Court of Human Rights for violations of media pluralism. For an overview of this case law and a criticism of the relevant judicial mechanism see, for instance, Komorek, E. (2013). *Media Pluralism and European Union*. Alphen aan den Rijn: Kluwer Law International, 61–81

4 Besson, S. (2011). *The Human Rights Competence in the EU – The State of the Question after Lisbon*, 39. In Kofler, G., Miguel Poiares Maduro and Pasquale Pistone (eds.). *Taxation and Human Rights in Europe and in the World*. Amsterdam: IBFD

5 See Treaty on European Union (consolidated version) [2008] OJ C 115/19, Article 6 (1) and (2), and Charter of the Fundamental Rights of the European Union [2010] OJ C 83/389, Article 51(1). Article 51(1) explicitly lays down that its provisions bind Member States only when they implement EU law and that the EU institutions must observe the principles enshrined therein 'respecting the limits of the powers of the Union as conferred on it in the Treaties'.

6 These principles are enshrined in the Treaty on European Union (consolidated version) [2008] OJ C 115/19, Article 2

7 For an overview of the actions that the Commission has undertaken in this field see: <http://europa.eu/legislation_summaries/human_rights/fundamental_rights_within_european_union/l33500_en.htm>

8 Commission (2007, January). Press Release IP/07/52. *Media pluralism: Commission stresses need for transparency, freedom and diversity in Europe's media landscape*

7. Moreover, media policies have traditionally been thought to form an integral part of Member States' cultural policies. This is so because one of the key roles that media is expected to play in a democracy is to advance social cohesion[9] by ensuring that the various linguistic, cultural, and ethnic minorities of a given society are fairly and diversely represented.[10] Pursuant to Articles 167(1) and 6(c) TFEU, the EU may carry out actions to support, coordinate or supplement action taken at the national level in order to contribute to the flowering of the cultures of the Member States.[11] Article 167(5) TFEU provides that, to fulfill the aforementioned objective, the EU may adopt incentive measures and recommendations,[12] but not instruments that would harmonize national media laws and regulations. The rationale that lies behind assigning the EU subordinate tasks in this domain is that Member States are better placed to develop the relevant legal tools in accordance with their traditions, community needs, and specificities of domestic markets.

8. Finally, the EU has extensive powers insofar as the economic aspects of this sector are concerned. More particularly, it has an exclusive competence to establish the competition rules that apply to undertakings that operate within the EU,[13] thereby including domestic and international media firms, and a shared competence to adopt legally binding acts for the completion of the single market.[14] Of course, regulating this industry in order to achieve the desired level of economic integration more often than not entails the adoption of measures that may somehow affect non-economic values. The TFEU itself acknowledges that tensions may arise as a result of the fact that media services are 'as much cultural services as they are economic services'[15] (the so-called culture/commodity conundrum), which explains why Article 167(4) TFEU establishes the duty of the EU institutions to take media pluralism into account under other provisions of the Treaties.[16]

---

9 On the link between social cohesion and democracy see, for instance, Henning, C. and Karin Renblad (eds.) (2009). *Perspectives on Empowerment, Social Cohesion and Democracy – An International Anthology*. Jönköping: School of Health Sciences, Jönköping University

10 Lefever, K., Ellen Wauters and Peggy Valcke (2013, July). *Media Pluralism in the EU – Comparative analysis of measurements systems in Europe and US*, 7. <http://www.steunpuntmedia.be/wp-content/uploads/2014/03/Steunpunt-Media_ICRI_Monitoring_D1D2.pdf>

11 Treaty on the Functioning of the European Union (consolidated version) [2012] OJ C 326/47 (TFEU)

12 The most widely known incentive measure adopted under Article 167(5) TFEU is the MEDIA program which ran from 1991 until 2013. On the strengths and weaknesses of measures adopted under this provision see, for instance, Hitchens, L. P. (1994). *Media Ownership and Control: A European Approach*. The Modern Law Review 57(4), 585–601; Craufurd-Smith, R. (2004). *Rethinking European Union competence in the field of media ownership: the internal market, fundamental rights and European citizenship*, European Law Review 29(5), 668; Komorek (2013), *supra* n. 3, 185–187

13 TFEU, Article 3(b)

14 ibid, Article 4(2)(a)

15 Directive 2010/13/EU of the European Parliament and of the Council of 10 March 2010 on the coordination of certain provisions laid down by law, regulation or administrative action in Member States concerning the provision of audiovisual media services (Audiovisual Media Services Directive) [2010] OJ L332/27, Recital (5)

16 This provision reads as follows: 'The Union shall take cultural aspects into account in its action under other provisions of the Treaties, in particular in order to respect and to promote the diversity of its cultures'.

9. As is clear from the above, the extent to which the EU may intervene in order to safeguard media pluralism is a labyrinthine, multi-layered competence matter involving several types of action that may be taken under different branches of EU law. On several occasions, this different set of competences has created considerable uncertainty over how far the EU can go to protect this value, for it is difficult, if not impossible, to isolate economic considerations from the social, cultural, and political functions that the media is expected to perform.

3. Background, state of the art, and research question

10. As already mentioned, media pluralism as an issue of concern to the EU is a topic that has been extensively discussed in the scholarly literature, which has explored the potential and weaknesses of the relevant EU legal toolkit from numerous perspectives. The purpose of this section is to summarize the major findings in this area, examine whether these findings remain relevant in light of recent market and legal/regulatory developments, and identify the gap in the knowledge in the current body of literature that the present study shall attempt to fill.

3.1 EU human rights law and media pluralism

11. In the field of human rights, Craufurd-Smith discussed the role of Article 7 TEU in ensuring that Member States provide an adequate level of protection of pluralism within their jurisdiction.[17] As noted above, this provision enables the EU institutions to act against a Member State that either clearly risks breaching[18] or has already committed a serious and persistent breach[19] of media pluralism. In the former case (e.g. where a Member State has enacted a law posing a threat to journalistic freedom[20]), the Council may (but is not required to) 'address recommendations' to the Member State concerned.[21] In the latter case (e.g. where a law posing threats to journalistic freedom has already been implemented[22]), the Council may (but is not bound to) suspend certain

17 Craufurd-Smith (2004), *supra n.* 12, 659–663

18 Treaty on European Union (consolidated version) [2008] OJ C 115/19, Article 7(1)

19 ibid, Article 7(2)

20 Communication from the Commission to the Council and the European Parliament on Article 7 of the Treaty on European Union – Respect for and promotion of the values on which the Union is based, COM/2003/0606 final, 7

21 Treaty on European Union (consolidated version) [2008] OJ C 115/19, Article 7(1)

22 *supra* n. 20, 8

of the rights deriving from the application of the Treaties to the Member State in question.[23] Craufurd-Smith maintains that, in theory, Article 7 is a powerful instrument in the hands of the EU on the grounds that it may produce a deterrent effect.[24] She acknowledges, however, that reliance on Article 7 to develop an EU policy that effectively protects media pluralism is problematic for many reasons: action under this provision is reactive in nature, suspension of Treaty rights may put in jeopardy the realization of the EU project by leading to anti-EU feeling within the Member State that is punished, and, perhaps more importantly, Article 7 has had limited-to-no practical significance in that the political sensitivities surrounding its implementation are difficult to overcome.[25] She illustrates this latter point by describing a process initiated by petitions made to the European Parliament in 2003 under Article 194 of the then EC Treaty (currently Article 227 TFEU[26]) regarding the level of concentration in the Italian broadcasting market.[27] The primary aim of the petitioners was for the Italian problem to be considered by the Council under Article 7.[28] Indeed, the European Parliament, having regard to Article 7, adopted a *Resolution on the risks of violations, in the EU and especially in Italy, of freedom of expression and information*.[29] After referring to, *inter alia*, the conflict of interest arising from the fact that (the then) Prime Minister Silvio Berlusconi owned the most powerful private media group in Italy, the Parliament instructed its President to forward the resolution to the Council.[30] Nevertheless, the Council did not take action under Article 7(1) in order to determine whether there was a clear risk of media pluralism violations in Italy.

12. The point that the role of Article 7 TEU was, is and will most likely remain purely symbolic, even in cases of outright violations by Member States,[31] has often been raised by human rights scholars.[32] A case involving the Hungarian

---

23 Treaty on European Union (consolidated version) [2008] OJ C 115/19, Article 7(3)

24 Craufurd-Smith (2004), *supra n.* 12, 661

25 ibid, 659–662

26 Article 227 TFEU reads as follows: 'Any citizen of the Union, and any natural or legal person residing or having its registered office in a Member State, shall have the right to address, individually or in association with other citizens or persons, a petition to the European Parliament on a matter which comes within the Community's fields of activity and which affects him, her or it directly'.

27 Petition 356/2003 by Federico Orlando and three co-signatories (Italian), on behalf of the 'Articolo 21 Liberi Di' association, on the implementation of Article 7 TEU regarding the protection of freedom of information in Italy, and Petition 1256/2003 by Ornella Erminio and Petition 35/2004 by Marco Canepari and 3,286 others on the breach committed by Italy of the freedom and pluralism of the media guaranteed by Article 6.

28 Craufurd-Smith (2004), *supra n.* 12, 660, referring to the text of the petition.

29 European Parliament Resolution of 22 April 2004, P5_ TA-PROV (2004) 0373

30 ibid, paragraph 88

31 Pinelli, C. (2012). *Protecting the Fundamentals. Article 7 of the Treaty on the European Union and beyond.* Foundation for European Progressive Studies Working Paper, 6. Note that, in addition to the tools provided by Article 7 TEU, Pinelli also explores the strengths and limitations of two further mechanisms that could contribute to the protection of human rights in the EU, namely 'purely judicial intervention' in cases of infringement of Article 20 TFEU and infringement proceedings under Articles 258–260 TFEU

32 See, for instance, de Búrca, G. and Paul Craig (2011). *EU Law: Text, Cases, and Materials* (5th edition), 390. Oxford: OUP, and Müller, J-W. (2013). *Safeguarding Democracy inside the EU: Brussels and the*

authorities lends further support to the argument that there is a 'sense of futility in looking to Art. 7 as a meaningful basis for policy'.[33] In 2010, Hungary adopted a controversial media law[34] that drew criticism from international organizations[35] and the governments of other Member States.[36] Media pluralism was found to be compromised, *inter alia*, because the law facilitated political interference with the appointment process of members of the national media regulator and because it did not define abstract terms, including especially the concept of 'public order', which could be misused to force journalists to disclose their sources.[37] In an attempt to convince Hungary to introduce substantial amendments to the law in question, the European Commission (hereinafter the Commission) embarked on a dialogue with the government,[38] while the European Parliament adopted a Resolution calling upon the State authorities 'to restore independence of media governance and halt state interference with freedom of expression ..., [for] over-regulation of the media is counterproductive, jeopardizing effective pluralism in the public sphere.'[39]

Future of Liberal Order. Transatlantic Academy Paper Series 2012–2013, No. 3, 17. For a general overview of the limitations of Article 7 TEU see, for instance, de Witte, B. and Gabriel N. Toggenburg (2004). *Human Rights and Membership of the European Union*. In Peers, S. and Angela Ward (eds.). *The EU Charter of Fundamental Rights*. Oxford: Hart Publishing, 59–82. Referring to Article 7 TEU, a report prepared for the European Parliament notes that '[i]n the history of the EU, neither of the Article 7 TEU procedures has ever been used. Their activation is in the hands of the various EU institutional actors, and is triggered only when high thresholds are exceeded. This leaves serious doubts as to the provision's operability'. See Bàrd, P. and Judit Bayer (2016). Study for the LIBE Committee. *A comparative analysis of media freedom and pluralism in the EU Member States*, 47. <http://www.europarl.europa.eu/RegData/etudes/STUD/2016/571376/IPOL_STU(2016)571376_EN.pdf>

33 Williams, A. (2006). *The indifferent gesture: Article 7 TEU, the Fundamental Rights Agency and the UK's invasion of Iraq*. European Law Review 31(1), 26

34 Commission (2011, February). MEMO/11/89. *Media: Commission Vice-President Kroes welcomes amendments to Hungarian Media Law*. <http://europa.eu/rapid/press-release_MEMO-11-89_en.htm>

35 See, for instance, Council of Europe (2011, February). *Opinion of the Commissioner for Human Rights on Hungary's media legislation in light of Council of Europe standards on freedom of the media*. <https://wcd.coe.int/ViewDoc.jsp?id=1751289>, and OSCE (2010). Analysis and assessment of a package Hungarian legislation and draft legislation *on media and telecommunications*. <http://www.osce.org/fom/71218?download=true>

36 See, for instance, *Chorus of Criticism: Germany Denounces New Hungarian Media Law*. 22 December 2010, Spiegel. <http://www.spiegel.de/international/europe/chorus-of-criticism-germany-denounces-new-hungarian-media-law-a-736206.html>

37 OSCE (2010, December). Press Release. *Hungarian media law further endangers media freedom, says OSCE media freedom representative*. <http://www.osce.org/fom/74687>

38 Commission (2011, January). Speech 11/6. *Hungary's new media law*. <http://europa.eu/rapid/press-release_SPEECH-11-6_en.htm>

39 European Parliament Resolution of 10 March 2011 on media law in Hungary P7_TA (2011) 0094, paragraph 7. <http://www.europarl.europa.eu/sides/getDoc.do?pubRef=-//EP//TEXT+TA+P7-TA-2011-0094+0+DOC+XML+V0//EN>. Note that, as opposed to the European Parliament's Resolution on the risks of violation, in the EU and especially in Italy, of freedom of expression and information (see *supra* n. 29, paragraph 83), the Resolution on the media law in Hungary does not make any reference to the right of the European Parliament to initiate the Article 7 TEU procedure. It is further worth noting that the motion for a resolution prepared by the political group of the Greens/European Free Alliance includes a paragraph recalling 'the possibility of the European Parliament to initiate the procedure under Article 7(1) TEU in view of determining whether there is a clear risk of a serious breach by Hungary of the values referred to in Article 2 TEU, such as respect for freedom, democracy and human rights', which was not incorporated into the final text of the resolution adopted by the European Parliament. See Motion for a Resolution on Media Law in Hungary, tabled by Daniel Cohn-Bendit, Rebecca Harms, Judith Sargentini, Helga Trüpel on behalf of the Greens/European Free Alliance Group, B7-0103/2011 of 9 February 2011, paragraph 9. <http://www.europarl.europa.eu/sides/getDoc.do?type=MOTION&reference=B7-2011-103&language=EN>

In spite of the fact that the above extra-legal initiatives[40] were not particularly fruitful, at the time of writing neither the Commission nor the European Parliament has initiated proceedings under Article 7 TEU.[41]

13. A more recent initiative that seeks to complement the mechanisms set out in Article 7 TEU also appears to have limited practical significance. Following events in certain Member States that demonstrated a lack of respect for the rule of law, former Commission President José Manuel Barroso made statements about the need to have a set of instruments ensuring that 'the "soft power" of political persuasion and the "nuclear option" of Article 7 TEU'[42] are not the only tools the EU has at its disposal.[43] Subsequently, the Commission adopted a Communication on a 'Framework for the Rule of Law' with a view to resolving threats to the rule of law *before* the conditions for activating the procedures under Article 7 TEU are met.[44] The Framework establishes a three-step process, comprising an objective and thorough *assessment* of the situation that is conducted by the Commission, a *recommendation* where the Commission calls upon the Member State concerned to resolve the problem within a given time limit, and *a follow-up* period during which the Commission monitors whether the Member State concerned implements the commitments it has made to resolve the issue at stake.[45] If there is no satisfactory follow-up to the recommendation, the Commission examines the possibility of triggering one of the procedures established under Article 7 TEU.[46] In 2016, the Commission activated the 'Framework for the Rule of Law' process with a view to addressing a number of concerns about a planned reform that would undermine the independence of the judiciary in Poland.[47] In December 2017, after almost two years of (unfruitful) attempts to find a solution in the context

40 Note that Article 7 TEU does not require the EU institutions that are competent to initiate proceedings under either Article 7(1) or 7(2) to invite the Member State to submit observations. This step is taken only after the Council has decided to engage in determining whether a clear risk exists or a breach has been committed.

41 Note that in this case the EU institutions were entitled to initiate proceedings under Article 7(2) because the government appears to have used the law to engage in practices that aimed at suppressing information. For instance, the media regulator, which is in charge of regulating media content and granting broadcast licenses, cancelled the license of the leading independent radio station Klub Radio that had been critical of the ruling party. More particularly, Klub Radio was refused the renewal of its license because the tender issued by the media regulator for its frequency called for a station that would broadcast 60% music, explicitly laying down that bids for this frequency would be evaluated based on that criterion. However, this condition would substantially change the news station's profile, which did not manage to get an approval decision. For more information about the implementation of the Hungarian media act see Human Rights Watch (2012, February). *Memorandum to the European Union on Media Freedom in Hungary*. <http://www.hrw.org/news/2012/02/16/memorandum-european-union-media-freedom-hungary>

42 Barroso, J.M. (2012). *State of the Union Address*. <http://europa.eu/rapid/press-release_SPEECH-12-596_en.htm>

43 Communication from the Commission to the European Parliament and the Council on A New EU Framework to Strengthen the Rule of Law COM(2014) 158 final, 2. <https://eur-lex.europa.eu/legal-content/EN/TXT/PDF/?uri=CELEX:52014DC0158&from=EN>

44 ibid, 3

45 ibid, 7–8

46 ibid.

47 Commission (2017, July). Press Release. *European Commission acts to preserve the rule of law in Poland*. <http://europa.eu/rapid/press-release_IP-17-2161_en.htm>

of the 'Framework for the Rule of Law' process, the Commission concluded that there is a clear risk of a serious breach of the rule of law and proposed to the Council to adopt a decision under Article 7(1) TEU.[48] However, the Council has not taken any steps towards evaluating the Polish situation (it is reminded that, under Article 7(1) TEU, the Council is not bound to determine whether the State under scrutiny indeed risks breaching the rule of law[49]). A possible explanation for the Council's inaction is that Member States are reluctant to 'discipline' others as they may fear a backlash.[50] It must be noted that, even if the Commission eventually triggered the procedure under Article 7(2), this latter provision establishes that the European Council may decide that there exists a serious and persistent breach only if it acts by *unanimity*;[51] Hungary has already vowed to veto any measures against Poland.[52] To conclude, '[t]he procedural requirements of and democratic implications for issuing sanctions pursuant to Article 7 TEU are such that the mechanism is not likely to be exercised'.[53]

14. Despite the fact that Article 7 has not been used to stigmatize or penalize a Member State that posed a threat to or has indeed harmed media pluralism, it has served as a basis on which the EU has attempted to build a system for regular monitoring of respect for human rights.[54] Perhaps the first notable example of this line of effort[55] is the Commission's decision to entrust a Network of Independent Experts with the task to prepare annual reports on the situation of fundamental rights in the EU. This Network was created in 2002

---

48 Commission (2017, December). Press Release. Rule of Law: European Commission acts to defend judicial independence in Poland. <http://europa.eu/rapid/press-release_IP-17-5367_en.htm>

49 Article 7(1) TEU reads as follows: 'On a reasoned proposal by one third of the Member States, by the European Parliament or by the European Commission, *the Council*, acting by a majority of four fifths of its members after obtaining the consent of the European Parliament, *may determine that there is a clear risk of a serious breach by a Member State of the values referred to in Article 2*. Before making such a determination, *the Council* shall hear the Member State in question and *may address recommendations to it*, acting in accordance with the same procedure. The Council shall regularly verify that the grounds on which such a determination was made continue to apply' [emphasis added]

50 Hotham, L. and Lucas Nacif. *Article 7 TEU and the Polish case – a recast.* 16 April 2018, KSLR EU Law Blog. <https://blogs.kcl.ac.uk/kslreuropeanlawblog/?p=1274#.W0SGeEiFO71>

51 Article 7(2) reads as follows: 'The European Council, *acting by unanimity* on a proposal by one third of the Member States or by the Commission and after obtaining the consent of the European Parliament, may determine the existence of a serious and persistent breach by a Member State of the values referred to in Article 2, after inviting the Member State in question to submit its observations' [emphasis added]

52 Hotham and Nacif (2018), *supra* n. 50, referring to Kelly, L. and Ralph Boulton. *Poland will not yield to EU over court reforms – Kaczynski.* 26 January 2018, Reuters. <https://uk.reuters.com/article/uk-poland-judiciary-kaczynski/poland-will-not-yield-to-eu-over-court-reforms-kaczynski-idUKKBN1FF13X?il=0>

53 ibid.

54 While no reference to 'regular monitoring' of human rights protection is made in Article 7 TEU, the Commission and the European Parliament are of the view that the provision opens the door to the establishment of such a mechanism. See, for instance, Communication from the Commission to the Council and the European Parliament *supra* n. 20, 9–310, and Motion for European Parliament Resolution on the situation as regards fundamental rights in the European Union (2002) (2002/2013(INI)), points 3 and 4. On this issue see, for instance, von Bogdandy, A. (2000). *The European Union as a Human Rights Organization? Human Rights and the Core of European Union.* Common Market Law Review 37(6), 1318, and de Búrca, G. (2004). *Beyond the Charter: How Enlargement has Enlarged the Human Rights Policy of the European Union.* Fordham International Law Journal 27(2), 713

55 See Communication from the Commission to the Council and the European Parliament, *supra* n. 20, 9

and produced a total of four reports.[56] It was subsequently incorporated into the EU Fundamental Rights Agency (hereinafter FRA) that was established in 2007[57] in order to provide the EU and the Member States (when implementing EU law) with assistance and expertise on fundamental rights. Regrettably, the FRA's mission is far more limited than originally envisaged. More particularly, while the Commission had initially suggested the creation of an agency that would systematically oversee the situation on the full spectrum of fundamental rights in the Member States of the EU,[58] it was ultimately decided that the FRA's remit would cover certain thematic areas[59] that would be defined in advance by a Multi-Annual Framework.[60] The FRA's duties mainly consist of collecting data, preparing studies, publishing reports, and networking with civil society.[61] This 'minimalist mandate',[62] attributed to Member States' unwillingness to allow the EU to expand its competence in the field of human rights,[63] was unsurprisingly considered a 'missed opportunity'.[64] Furthermore, the FRA does not have the power to decide on the topics that it studies, for it is the Council that adopts the Multi-Annual Framework.[65] This arguably undermines the FRA's independence[66] in that, as Williams puts it, it places the 'issue of human rights fully within the diplomatic realm allowing national government sensitivities to be protected'.[67]

15. For our purposes, it bears noting that media pluralism has not been included in the Multi-Annual Frameworks that have been adopted thus far (covering the periods 2007–2012, 2013–2017 and 2018–2022).[68] However, the EU has

56 The Reports of the Network are available at: <http://ec.europa.eu/justice/fundamental-rights/document/index_en.htm> along with the annual reports on the application of the CFREU

57 Council Regulation (EC) No. 168/2007 of 15 February 2007 establishing a European Union Agency for Fundamental Rights OJ [2007] OJ L53/01

58 European Policy Evaluation Consortium (EPEC) (2005). *Preparatory Study for Impact Assessment and Ex Ante Evaluation of Fundamental Rights Agency Final Report*, 42–43

59 See Commission proposal for a Council Regulation establishing a European Union Agency for Fundamental Rights, COM (2005) 280 final, 6. <https://eur-lex.europa.eu/legal-content/EN/TXT/PDF/?uri=CELEX:52005PC0280(01)&from=en>

60 *supra* n. 57, Recital (11)

61 ibid, Article 4(1)

62 Amnesty International (2007, March). Press Release. *EU Fundamental Rights: A long way to go*

63 Pinelli (2012), *supra* n. 31, 13

64 ibid. See also Amnesty International (2007, March) *supra* n. 62, and Alegre, S. (2008). *Human Rights and the Future of the European Union*. A Justice Futures Paper, 12. <http://www.antigone.gr/files/en/library/developments-in-human-rights-issues/080606.pdf >

65 *supra* n. 57, Recital (11)

66 Milanova, N. (2011). *EU Agency for fundamental rights (FRA): a reality check*. Report prepared for Human Rights Without Frontiers International, 34–35

67 Williams, A. (2010). *The Ethos of Europe. Values, Law and Justice in the EU*. Cambridge: CUP, 142

68 *supra* n. 57, Article 2; Council Decision No. 252/2013/EU of 11 March 2013 establishing a Multiannual Framework for 2013–2017 for the European Union Agency for Fundamental Rights [2013] OJ 79/1, Article 2; and Council Decision (EU) 2017/2269 of 7 December 2017 establishing a Multiannual Framework for the European Union Agency for Fundamental Rights for 2018–2022, Article 2. Note, however, that the fact that media pluralism has not been included in the Multi-Annual Frameworks that have been adopted to date does not imply that the FRA may not be involved in initiatives aimed at protecting media pluralism. For example, in 2016, the Colloquium on Fundamental Rights focused on media focused on media pluralism and democracy. In the context of this initiative, the FRA produced two

not deleted media pluralism from its human rights agenda. To the contrary, over the past years it has undertaken several initiatives that were based on its commitment to protect media pluralism 'as an essential pillar of the right to information and freedom of expression'.[69] For example, the Commission has published a number of texts that range from Working Papers on the status of media pluralism in the Member States[70] to Guidelines for EU support to media pluralism in enlargement countries.[71] The Commission has further financed studies in order to make available to the Member States instruments that would allow them to identify concerns over media pluralism. For instance, the Commission commissioned an independent study which delivered the Media Pluralism Monitor, a diagnostic tool for understanding risks to media pluralism.[72] This tool is based on indicators that cover a range of legal, economic and sociocultural dimensions in domains that are relevant to media pluralism, such as media ownership and control or safeguards for journalistic freedo.[73] Once this data is collected and processed by the software that was designed for its implementation, the Monitor may indicate a high risk, a moderate risk, or a low risk for media pluralism in the Member State concerned.[74] The Commission also assigned a group of experts, known as the High-Level Group on Media Freedom and Media Pluralism, to provide a set of recommendations for the protection of media pluralism and freedom in Europe.[75] The High-Level Group delivered a report that tackled several issues of concern to the competent policymakers, such as political and private interference with editorial independence, concentration of ownership, and the levels of funding received by public service broadcasters, and put forward a number of proposals to address these issues.[76] More recently, the Commission

studies that fed into the discussion. See Fundamental Rights Agency (2016). *Incitement in media content and political discourse in EU Member States*. <http://fra.europa.eu/en/publication/2016/incitement-media-content-and-political-discourse-member-states-european-union>; and Fundamental Rights Agency (2016). *Violence, threats and pressures against journalists and other media actors in the EU*. <http://fra.europa.eu/en/publication/2016/violence-threats-and-pressures-against-journalists-and-other-media-actors-european>

69 Commission. Staff Working Document on Media Pluralism in the Member States of the EU SEC (2007) 32. A (non-exhaustive) list of EU initiatives aimed at protecting and promoting media pluralism is available at: <https://ec.europa.eu/digital-single-market/en/policies/media-freedom-and-pluralism>

70 ibid. For additional documents the Commission has drafted in this area, as well as Resolutions adopted by the European Parliament, see fn. 3 and 2 of the Staff Working Document. See also Commission (2005). *Issues paper for the Liverpool Audiovisual Conference: Media pluralism – What should be the European Union's role?* Brussels: DG Information Society and Media

71 Commission, DG Enlargement (2014). *Guidelines for EU support to media freedom and media integrity in enlargement countries, 2014–2020*. <http://ec.europa.eu/enlargement/pdf/press_corner/elarg-guidelines-for-media-freedom-and-integrity_210214.pdf>

72 Commission (2009). *Independent Study on ndicators for Media Pluralism in the Member States: Towards a Risk-based Approach*, ix. <http://ec.europa.eu/information_society/media_taskforce/doc/pluralism/study/final_report_09.pdf>

73 ibid, ix

74 ibid, 109

75 High Level Group on Media Freedom and Pluralism (2013). *A free and pluralistic media to sustain European democracy*. <https://ec.europa.eu/digital-single-market/sites/digital-agenda/files/HLG%20Final%20Report.pdf >

76 ibid.

set up a High-Level Group of experts to advise on policy initiatives to counter fake news and disinformation spread online.[77] The Group delivered a report that makes several proposals to address this problem; these proposals are designed to enhance transparency of online news, promote media literacy, develop tools for empowering users and journalists, safeguard the diversity and sustainability of the European news media ecosystem, and promote research on the impact of disinformation in Europe.[78]

16. The above efforts (and any studies dealing with media pluralism that may be carried out by the FRA in the future) undoubtedly advance the debate on the challenges facing media pluralism. Furthermore, they involve independent reviewers, allow endemic violations of media pluralism to be identified, and, broadly speaking, they ensure that relevant suggestions are suited to the needs and traditions of the Member State concerned.[79] Yet, we cannot help but wonder whether the aforementioned initiatives will produce any meaningful effects on the design of national media policies. The remark made by Craufurd-Smith regarding the potential of the reports prepared by the Network of Independent Experts appears to be relevant in the post-Lisbon era: Member States have occasionally been willing to disregard Court rulings[80] and we should not expect that they will be eager to follow expert committee recommendations on how to safeguard media pluralism in their jurisdiction, no matter how well-formulated these recommendations are. An example illustrating this point is that no Member State has taken the initiative to implement the Media Pluralism Monitor to date.[81]

---

77 For a brief overview of this initiative and a summary of the report that was delivered see <https://ec.europa.eu/digital-single-market/en/news/final-report-high-level-expert-group-fake-news-and-online-disinformation>

78 High Level Group on Fake News and Online Disinformation (2018). *A multi-dimensional approach to disinformation*, 35. <https://ec.europa.eu/digital-single-market/en/news/final-report-high-level-expert-group-fake-news-and-online-disinformation> Following publication of this Report, the Commission adopted a Communication in which it puts forward an action plan to tackle the spread and impact of online disinformation in Europe. See Communication from the Commission to the European Parliament, the Council, the European Economic and Social Committee and the Committee of the Regions on Tackling Online Disinformation: a European approach COM(2018) 236 final. (NB: The Commission's action plan was announced at the time of going to press. As these initiatives are at a nascent stage, only time will tell whether they will manage to deliver the desired results). Another recent study in the area of fake news that was conducted by the Commission's Joint Research Centre is Martens, B., Luis Aguiar, Estrella Gomez-Herrera and Frank Mueller-Langer (2018). *The digital transformation of news media and the rise of disinformation and fake news*. <https://ec.europa.eu/jrc/en/news/digital-transformation-news-media-and-rise-fake-news>

79 Craufurd-Smith (2004), *supra* n. 12, 661. The same conclusion may be drawn in respect of any recommendations made by the Council under Article 7(1) TEU, if the latter provision is ever implemented.

80 ibid. 660–661

81 The EU assigned a research center, the Centre for Media Pluralism and Freedom, to conduct the implementation of the Media Pluralism Monitor, which, at the time of going to press, is an ongoing project.

3.2 Single market and media pluralism

17. Several studies discuss the impact of the completion of the single media market on media pluralism. This issue has been examined from two different perspectives: one, the desirability and legitimacy of adopting an instrument harmonizing national policies on media ownership that is based on one of the Treaty provisions related to the proper functioning of the internal market; and two, the effectiveness of existing instruments that primarily seek to facilitate the free movement of media services but also contain provisions that have as their objective the protection of media pluralism.

3.2.1 An instrument specifically aimed at addressing ownership concentration

18. The contribution that a pan-European legislative instrument addressing ownership concentration can make to the preservation of media pluralism is a long-standing debate that dates back to the early 1990s, when the European Parliament called upon the Commission to propose a measure so as to introduce restrictions on media consolidation.[82] Ownership of or control over media organizations has been subject to regulatory intervention both across and beyond the European Union[83] because it is generally believed that, due to the ability of the media to shape the political agenda and influence citizen behavior, accumulation of significant market power in the hands of a few 'may result in a skewed public discourse where certain opinions are excluded or under-represented'.[84] The means through which national laws aim at addressing concerns over media concentration vary from one country to another.[85] For example, certain Member States impose limitations on the number of licenses that may be acquired by the same person or organization, whereas others impose thresholds on the audience shares that may be held by an individual or firm.[86] These measures, however, have one thing in common: broadly speaking, they regulate economic aspects relating to the degree of market power any given media undertaking may exercise, but their primary objective is to ensure that the role of the media in maintaining a well-informed citizenry is not undermined.[87] As already seen, the Treaty does not provide the EU with

82 Commission. *Pluralism and Media Concentration in the Internal Market: An Assessment of the Need for Community Action*. COM (92) 480 final, 7

83 Valcke, P. (2011). *Looking For the User in Media Pluralism Regulation: Unraveling the Traditional Diversity Chain and Recent Trends of User Empowerment in European Media Regulation*. Journal of Information Policy 1, 291.

84 Commission. Staff Working Document on Media Pluralism in the Member States of the EU SEC (2007) 32, 5

85 For an overview of the different systems see Valcke, P. (2009). *From Ownership Regulation to Legal Indicators of Media Pluralism: Background, Typologies, and Methods*. Journal of Media Business Studies 6(3), 19–42

86 Valcke (2011), *supra* n. 83, 291

87 Note that certain Member States also impose qualitative requirements (e.g. requirements relating to man-

a strong legal basis to enact an instrument that is solely or mainly concerned with achieving this latter objective. Nevertheless, it has been argued that because the EU has the power to regulate media organizations as providers of 'services'[88] and because the European project has evolved in a way that encompasses, but is not limited to, economic integration, there would be scope for a supranational instrument *if* national measures and/or action on behalf of the Member States were inadequate or insufficient to address the cross-border concerns that arise from media concentration.[89]

19. Ariño puts forward two reasons why this may be the case. First, regulatory initiatives that sought to expedite the economic integration agenda allowed powerful media undertakings to expand into the markets of other Member States.[90] Perhaps the most prominent example of this type of initiative is the 'country of origin' principle, whereby only one Member State has jurisdiction over an audiovisual media service provider.[91] On the basis of this principle, the provider may operate across the EU provided that it complies with the rules of the Member State from which it emanates (the receiving State is not entitled to exercise secondary control.[92] The 'country of origin' rule enabled media service providers to engage in activities that transcend national frontiers, such as direct broadcasts and the sale of program rights.[93] The abolition of obstacles to intra-Union trade has also facilitated an intense process of cross-border mergers and acquisitions.[94] The reasons for this latter development are manifold: the option to merge with or acquire a company operating beyond national frontiers may be appealing to media firms that seek to attract critical mass to their content, or to share investment risks, or because the national competition authority of the jurisdiction under which they fall did not let them fulfill further consolidation plans.[95] As a result of the above, Ariño says, *it is becoming increasingly difficult for the Member States to apply their anti-concentration laws to media organizations with transnational ownership structures*, especially in cases where they deal with multinational corporations whose national affiliations are not strong enough to trigger the application of these laws.[96] There have been cases that lend support to this

agement board representation). For a brief overview see ibid, 291–294.

88 The term 'services' is defined in Article 57 TFEU.

89 Ariño, M. (2005). *Regulation and Competition in European Digital Broadcasting – A study of pluralism through access*. PhD thesis. Florence: European University Institute, 425–6

90 ibid, 426

91 Audiovisual Media Services Directive, *supra* n. 15, Recital (33)–(34)

92 ibid, Recital (36). There are some exceptions to this rule which are laid down in Article 3 of the Directive.

93 See, for instance, Commission. Staff Working Document on Media Pluralism in the Member States of the EU SEC (2007) 32, 9, and Commission. Communication on the application of State aid rules to public service broadcasting (the Broadcasting Communication) [2009] OJ C 257/1, paragraph 22

94 *supra* n.84, 9

95 Council of Europe (2004). *Report on Transnational Media Concentrations in Europe*. Report prepared by Advisory Panel to the CDMM on media concentrations, pluralism and diversity questions, 10

96 Ariño (2005), *supra* n. 89, 427. On this issue see also Picard, R. (2017). *The Sisyphean Pursuit of Media*

argument. For example, the Greek competition authority cleared the acquisition by the Luxembourg-based media conglomerate RTL of one of the most popular generalist TV channels in Greece, Alpha TV, on the grounds that RTL had no other interests in the Greek media market and that Alpha TV did not control more than 35% of the affected market, which is the threshold set by Law 3592/2007 on media concentration.[97]

20. Second, Ariño maintains that Member States may refrain from establishing strict ownership rules *or engage in a race-to-the bottom regulatory competition* in order to either attract profitable firms to their jurisdiction or provide them with the incentive not to move their operations to another State with less stringent regulation.[98] Indeed, over the past number of years, there has been 'a wave of deregulation in [media] ownership rules across Europe';[99] several Member States have either entirely abolished or significantly relaxed related restrictions.[100] The statement made by the UK authorities during the consultation on media ownership rules that preceded the adoption of the Communications Act 2003 is illustrative in that regard:

> [w]hilst the need for a plurality of media sources remains clear, we are committed to a deregulatory approach to media markets. From a commercial point of view, further liberalization would benefit existing and potential new investors, providing for further consolidation, greater efficiency, more scope for investment, and a more significant international presence.[101]

21. Another example that reveals Member States' unwillingness to address media pluralism concerns that arise from excessive concentration is that Article 21(4) of the Merger Regulation has had no practical significance;[102] this provision lays down that, if the Commission decides to clear a media concentration that does not raise concerns as to its compatibility with the common market, the Member States concerned may take appropriate measures to ensure that

Pluralism: European Efforts to Establish Policy and Measurable Evidence. Communication Law and Policy 22(3), 255–273; and Iosifidis, P. (2014). *Pluralism, Media Mergers and European Merger Control*. In Donders, K., Caroline Pauwels, and Jan Loisen. *The Palgrave Handbook of European Media Policy*. London: Palgrave Macmillan, 461–475

97 Hellenic Competition Commission (2008). Decision 422/V/2008, *RTL Central & Eastern Europe/ Wakerock Limited*, 13 and 19

98 Ariño (2005), *supra* n. 89, 427. On this issue see also Picard (2017). n. 96, 255–273

99 Commissariat voor de media (2011). *Media Monitor – The Dutch Media in 2010*, 6. <https://www.mediamonitor.nl/wp-content/uploads/2013/08/Mediamonitor-The-Dutch-media-in-20101.pdf >

100 See, for instance, Open Society Foundations (2012). *Mapping Digital Media in the European Union – A Report for the High-Level Group on Media Freedom and Pluralism*, 2. <http://www.opensocietyfoundations.org/sites/default/files/Mapping_Digital_Media_EU_20121217_0.pdf>; Ofcom (2009c). *Report on Media Ownership Rules*, 21 *et seq*.; and Freedom House (2013). *Report on Spain*. <https://www.freedomhouse.org/report/freedom-press/2013/spain#.VMJr_M016eY>

101 UK Department for Culture, Media, and Sport (2001). *Consultation on Media Ownership Rules*, paragraph 1.8.

102 Council Regulation (EC) No. 139/2004 of 20 January 2004 on the control of concentrations between undertakings (the EC Merger Regulation) OJ L24/1

the transaction in question does not damage media pluralism in the domestic sphere.[103]

22. Even if there is convincing evidence supporting the argument that, for a number of reasons, the Member States are not in the position or willing to deal with media concentration, the question remains as to what would be the appropriate legal basis for a supranational instrument that establishes restrictions on media ownership. Many claim that the instrument concerned may rest on Article 114 TFEU.[104] This provision stipulates that:

> The European Parliament and the Council shall, acting in accordance with the ordinary legislative procedure and after consulting the Economic and Social Committee, adopt the measures for the approximation of the provisions laid down by law, regulation or administrative action in Member States which have as their object the establishment and functioning of the internal market.

23. The Court has held that the EU may make use of Article 114 TFEU in situations where, in the absence of action at EU level, the laws and/or practices of Member States raise obstacles to the completion of the internal market.[105] In the case at hand, it has been contended that the disparities in the various anti-concentration measures that apply throughout the EU may lead to a drain of investment from countries with stringent ownership rules to countries where relaxed or no rules apply, ultimately fragmenting the internal market.[106] However,

---

103 For a detailed analysis of the role that Article 21(4) of the Merger Regulation has played thus far see, for instance, Whish, R. and David Bailey (2012). *Competition Law* (7th edition). Oxford: OUP, 852–4, and Ariño (2005), *supra* n. 89, 411. For our purposes here, suffice it to say that reference to media pluralism as a ground for application of Article 21(4) is made in three decisions, namely *Newspaper Publishing* (Case IV/M.423) [1994] OJ C 85/5; *News Corp/BSkyB* (Case COMP/M.5932) [2011] OJ C 37/2; and *Fox/Sky* (Case M.8354) [2017] OJ 238/1. It is worth mentioning that the UK authorities ultimately gave the green light to *Newspaper Publishing* and *News Corp/BSkyB* (the review of *Fox/Sky* is still ongoing). NB: in *News Corp/BSkyB*, the Secretary of State for Business, Innovation and Skills, who may intervene in mergers involving newspapers and/or broadcasting companies on public interest grounds, issued a 'European intervention notice', making the proposed operation subject to an additional review on media plurality issues by the competent UK authorities, namely OFT and Ofcom. After several undertakings proposed by the parties to the deal, the Secretary of State was willing to give the green light to the proposed transaction. However, due to a phone hacking scandal in which News Corp was found to be involved during the same period of time that the deal was being negotiated, News Corp ended up dropping its plans to take full ownership of BSkyB. In 2017, however, Fox (formerly known as News Corporation) re-notified to the Commission of its intention to purchase Sky. The Commission approved the deal, which, at the time of going to press, was still under review by the UK authorities. For recent developments in this case see, for instance, Waterson, J. *Sky takeover: Murdoch must offload Sky News to get green light*. 5 June 2018, The Guardian. <https://www.theguardian.com/business/2018/jun/05/sky-takeover-murdoch-sky-news-uk-fox-comcast>; Comcast likely to be new o*wner of Sky*. 19 July 2018, BBC. <https://www.bbc.com/news/business-44893625>

104 Craufurd-Smith (2004), *supra* n. 12, 663; Komorek (2013), *supra* n. 3, 254–257. Craufurd-Smith and Barzanti have also explored the potential of a handful of Treaty provisions outside the realm of the internal market that could be used by the EU to regulate media pluralism, namely Articles 352 and 25 TFEU and Article 11 TEU. They both acknowledge, however, that any action under these provisions faces significant competence limitations and is unlikely to be backed by Member States. See Craufurd-Smith (2004), *supra* n. 12, 664–666, and Barzanti, F. (2012). *Governing the European Audiovisual Space: What modes of governance can facilitate a European approach to media pluralism?* EUI Working Papers RSCAS 2012/49, 19–20

105 ECJ, Case C-377/98 *Netherlands v Parliament and Council* [2001] ECR I-07079

106 Note that this is one of the justifications the Commission put forward in its Green Paper on *Pluralism and*

Komorek identifies certain limitations that the use of Article 114 would entail which cannot be overlooked. More particularly, she notes that, when assessing whether an instrument rests on the correct legal basis, the Court takes account of the primary objective that the instrument pursues, the principles that underlie it and its ideological premises.[107] She refers to the case where the Court was called upon to determine whether the correct legal basis for the Framework Directive on Waste was Article 192 TFEU, which provides that the EU may adopt Directives that contribute to the preservation of the quality of the environment, or rather Article 114.[108] In this case, the Court held that, from the preambles of the Directive, it could be inferred that the instrument sought to achieve a high level of environmental protection and that, by virtue of the obligation it established (namely, the duty to take action in order to encourage the reduction of waste production) it had as its object the management of waste.[109] The Court acknowledged that waste is a 'good' and that as such its free movement should not be prevented,[110] as well as acknowledging that some of the provisions of the Directive, in particular the introduction of a common definition of waste, could affect the functioning of the internal market,[111] but it ruled that 'recourse to Article [114] is not justified where the measure to be adopted has only *the incidental effect of harmonizing market conditions* within the [EU]' [emphasis added].[112] Komorek claims that the Court is highly likely to follow a similar approach if it is called upon to examine whether an instrument harmonizing media ownership rules should rest on Article 114.[113] Indeed, as we have already seen, the anti-concentration laws of the Member States may regulate economic dimensions of the media, but the objective they seek to attain is a well-informed citizenry. It bears repeating that, contrary to environmental protection or any other area where the EU shares competence with the Member States, in the field of media the EU may solely take action to support national initiatives. In accordance with Article 167(5) TFEU, this action may not take the form of an instrument harmonizing national media laws and regulations. That is to say, as opposed to the Framework Directive on Waste referred to above, the EU institutions are not entitled to base an instrument on media ownership on Article 167 TFEU alone. Along the same line, Harcourt

---

Media Concentration in the Internal Market – An Assessment of the Need for Community Action. n. 82, 87 *et seq*.

107 Komorek (2013), *supra* n. 3, 256, referring to Chalmers, D. Gareth Davies and Giorgio Monti (2006). *European Union Law: Text and Materials*. Cambridge: CUP, 212. This is an approach that the Court has followed consistently throughout its case law. See, for instance, ECJ, Case C-295/90 *Parliament v Council* [1992] ECR I-4193, paragraph 13 and ECJ, Case C-300/89 *Commission v Council* [1991] ECR I-2867, paragraph 10

108 ECJ, Case 155/91 *Commission of the European Communities v Council of the European Communities* [1993] ECR I-00939

109 ibid, 8–10

110 ibid, 12

111 ibid, 18

112 ibid, 19

113 Komorek (2013), *supra* n. 3, 256–257

points to the weak terms in which Article 167 TFEU is drafted, remarking that the Court is highly unlikely to back media concentration legislation 'without an explicit Treaty statement from EU Member States'.[114]

24. Leaving the issue of legal basis aside, we must also consider the feasibility of any proposals to enact pan-European rules on media concentration. In the late 1990s, the Member States rejected the Commission's draft proposals for a 'Media Pluralism' Directive[115] that would set common rules on media ownership across the EU and there are no signs indicating that the tide may be turning. On the contrary, during the consultation conducted by the Commission in 2013 with the aim of collecting opinions on whether the EU should be considered competent to act in order to safeguard media pluralism at State level,[116] there was consensus among Member States that the EU lacks the power 'to develop a legislative framework to engage directly with media in an interventionist manner'.[117] In a similar vein, the draft proposal for the revised Audiovisual Media Services Directive (NB: at the time of going to press, the Directive was in the process of adoption) lays down that it is for each Member State to decide whether to adopt measures related to media ownership.[118]

3.2.2 Existing internal market instruments that include provisions specifically aimed at safeguarding media pluralism

25. As already mentioned, certain studies focus on the effectiveness of existing Directives that primarily facilitate the free movement of media services but which also contain provisions that seek to ensure that the single media market is not realized at the expense of media pluralism. While these provisions are an attempt to comply with Article 167(4) TFEU, there have been strong doubts raised over whether they make a meaningful contribution to that end. A good example illustrating that the duties the aforementioned instruments impose may not be appropriate or sufficient to safeguard media pluralism is the 'European works quota' rule laid down in the Audiovisual Media Services Directive. Article 16(1) of the Directive provides that 'Member States shall

114 Harcourt, A. (2005). *The European Union and the Regulation of Media Markets*. Manchester: Manchester University Press, 72

115 On this issue see, for instance, Doyle, G. (1997) *From 'Pluralism' to 'Ownership': Europe's emergent policy on Media Concentrations navigates the doldrums'*. Journal of Information Law and Technology 3. <http://www2.warwick.ac.uk/fac/soc/law/elj/jilt/1997_3>; Michalis, M. (1999). *European Union Broadcasting and Telecoms Towards a Convergent Regulatory Regime?* European Journal of Communication 14 (2), 147–171, and Iosifidis, P. (1997). *Pluralism and media concentration policy in the European Union*. Javnost – The Public 4(1), 85–104

116 Commission (2013). *Public consultation on the Independent Report from the HLG on Media Freedom and Pluralism-Text of the consultation*, 9. <https://ec.europa.eu/digital-agenda/en/news/public-consultation-independent-report-hlg-media-freedom-and-pluralism-—read-contributions>

117 ibid, 2

118 A draft proposal that leaked includes two recitals that refer to Member States' freedom to enact rules that seek to enhance transparency of media ownership

ensure, where practicable and by appropriate means, that broadcasters reserve for European works a majority proportion of their transmission time excluding the time allotted to news, sports events, games, advertising, teletext services and teleshopping'. In a similar vein, Article 17 provides that 'Member States shall ensure, where practicable and by appropriate means, that broadcasters reserve at least 10% of their transmission time, ... or alternately, at the discretion of the Member State, at least 10% of their programming budget, for European works created by producers who are independent of broadcasters'. The quota rule has traditionally been regarded as the main mechanism at EU level that is aimed at protecting pluralism,[119] on the grounds that it ensures that citizens will have access to content provided by firms that are not necessarily owned or controlled by the broadcasters bound by the rule, and that broadcasters established in the EU are not limited to the transmission of generic format programming produced by non-European, most notably US, media conglomerates.[120] Member States have undoubtedly made significant progress since the Television Without Frontiers Directive, which first introduced this rule, entered into force. For example, while in 1994 several broadcasters in eight out of (the then) thirteen Member States did not broadcast the requisite proportion of European works,[121] the most recent[122] report on the implementation of the Directive notes that the quotas are widely respected and that the average broadcasting time for European works in 2010 amounted to 64.3%.[123] However, this latter figure and any other related figure occasionally referred to by the Commission in its attempt to present the quota rules as a 'success story' have, arguably correctly, been treated with skepticism. Burri-Nenova, for instance, maintains that a high share of European productions is not a valid indication of a pluralistic offer for the reason that, for a work to be defined as 'European' for the purposes of the Directive, it is sufficient that the work originate in a Member State[124] and that no further conditions, including especially originality or quality requirements, need to be fulfilled.[125] This definition, Burri-Nenova says, is not adequate to address the challenges facing diversity in the current broadcasting landscape, such as the

119 Burri-Nenova, M. (2007). *The New Audiovisual Media Services Directive: Television Without Frontiers, Television Without Cultural Diversity*. Common Market Law Review 44(6), 1706

120 ibid, fn. 120

121 Commission. Report on application of Directive 89/552/EEC and proposal for a European Parliament and Council Directive amending Council Directive 89/552/EEC on the coordination of certain provisions laid down by law, regulation or administrative action in Member States concerning the pursuit of television broadcasting activities (presented by the Commission). COM (95) 86 final, 14

122 NB: While Article 33 imposes on the Commission the obligation to report on the implementation of the Directive on a regular (three-year) basis, it is not clear why no reports were produced in recent years. Related to this issue see Motion for a European Parliament Resolution on the Implementation of the Audiovisual Media Services Directive (2012/2132(INI))

123 Commission. First report on the application of Articles 13, 16 and 17 of Directive 2010/13/EU for the period 2009–2010. Promotion of European works in EU scheduled and on-demand audiovisual media services. COM (2012) 522 final, 9

124 Audiovisual Media Services Directive, *supra* n. 15, Article 1(1)(n)

125 Burri-Nenova (2007), *supra* n. 119, 1707

growing homogenization of content and the steady decline in quality TV.[126] As she so vividly puts it, 'a "Big Brother" type of show financed with European money qualifies perfectly as … a European work.'[127] The Directive provides that Member States are allowed to adopt a more detailed definition of the term 'European works'. Nevertheless, the vast majority of them transposed into national law the definition laid down in the Directive without establishing more stringent criteria.[128] Another criticism concerns the exclusion of news programming from the quota mechanism. Harrison and Woods note that the decision of the EU legislator to exclude from the quota calculation content with journalistic elements is an attempt to address industrial policy concerns; that is to say, an attempt to ensure that x amount of broadcast time is devoted to entertainment content created with 'European money',[129] rather than an effort to provide European citizens with more diverse programming, including especially factual programming.[130]

26. Another example is the Universal Services Directive, which forms part of the EU Telecoms Package[131] and which provides that, under certain circumstances, Member States may impose 'must-carry' obligations on undertakings providing electronic communications networks used for the distribution

---

126 ibid.

127 ibid, 1708. The same point is also raised by Harrison and Woods: the definition of European works 'does little or nothing to prevent the quotas being met by programmes that are of poor quality and which do not therefore meet informational, educational and cultural aims or goals'. See Harrison, J. and Lorna Woods (2007). *European Broadcasting Law and Policy*. Cambridge: CUP, 247

128 Graham, D. and Associates (2009). *Study on the application of measures concerning the promotion of the distribution and production of European works in audiovisual media services (i.e. including television programmes and non-linear services)*, 77. <http://ec.europa.eu/archives/information_society/avpolicy/docs/library/studies/art4_5/final_report.pdf>

129 This is also a point raised by Burri-Nenova. See *supra* n. 119, 1707

130 Harrison, J. and Lorna Woods (2007), *supra* n. 127, 248. For a critical overview of other aspects of the quota rules see Harrison and Woods, 249–265; de Witte, B. (1995). *The European Content Requirement – Five Years After* in Barendt, E. (ed.). *Yearbook of Media and Entertainment Law*. Oxford: OUP, 101–127; Harrison, J. and Lorna Woods (2001). *Television Quotas: Protecting European Culture?* Entertainment Law Review 12(1), 5–14; Lupinacci, T.M. (1991). *The Pursuit of Television Broadcasting Activities in the European Community: Cultural Preservation or Economic Protectionism?* Vanderbilt Journal of Transnational Law 24, 113–154; Katsirea, I. (2003). *Why The European Broadcasting Quota Should Be Abolished*. European Law Review 28 (2), 190–209; Drijber, B. J. (1999). *The Revised Television Without Frontiers Directive: Is It Fit For The Next Century?* Common Market Law Review 36(1), 87–122. For a more general discussion of the quota rules see Herold, A. (2009). *The New Audiovisual Media Services Directive* in Pauwels, C., Harri Kalimo, Karen Donders and Ben Van Rompuy (eds.), *Rethinking European Media and Communications Policy*. Brussels: VUB Press, 107–115. Two other provisions of the Audiovisual Media Services Directive that are related to the exercise of the right to information and hence, albeit indirectly, relate to media pluralism are Articles 14 ('listed events mechanism' for the broadcasting of events of major societal importance) and 15 (short news reporting on events of high interest to the public). For a critical overview of these provisions see Ariño, M. (2005), *supra* n. 89, 253–259; Lefever, K. (2012). *New Media and Sport: International Legal Aspects*. The Hague: T.M.C. Asser Press, 225–291; Helberger, N. (2006). *The 'right to information' and digital broadcasting – About monsters, invisible men, and the future of European broadcasting regulation*. Entertainment Law Review 17(2), 70–80

131 For a comprehensive overview of the rules established by the Telecoms Package see Helberger, N. (2005). *Regulating Conditional Access in Digital Broadcasting*. Alphen aan den Rijn: Kluwer Law International; Harrison, J. and Lorna Woods (2007), *supra* n. 127, 115–145. For a brief overview of rules adopted by Member States to regulate Electronic Program Guides see, for instance, van der Sloot, B. (2012). *Walking a Thin Line: The Regulation of EPGs*. JIPITEC 3, 138–147

of radio and television broadcasts to the public.[132] A must-carry obligation is the duty to carry certain channels that serve general interest objectives, which must be clearly defined by the Member State.[133] These channels are often (but not necessarily) channels offered by public service broadcasting organizations which are financed through state resources and entrusted by public authorities with safeguarding media pluralism by making available to the citizens balanced and varied programming. The Directive explicitly states that Member States may determine appropriate remuneration for offering these channels,[134] but in practice these are usually provided free of charge.[135] While 'must-carry' rules have sound theoretical foundations (e.g. a vertically integrated network provider has the ability and incentive to grant preferential treatment to its own channels, marginalizing competing content, including content that is created with the aim to advance important societal goals), their design and implementation have been far from perfect. A common criticism of the 'must-carry' rules is that they may bind the network providers *only*.[136] The Directive explicitly lays down that undertakings 'providing content such as the offer for sale of a package of sound or television broadcasting content', that is, undertakings that operate at the level of the supply chain that succeeds network provision (commonly referred to as service providers), are not subject to must-carry obligations.[137] The channel that benefits from the must-carry status must negotiate usage of the facilities controlled by the service providers (on which end-users' access to the content offered by the channel in question ultimately depends) on market terms. This, Varney and Feintuck say, is a 'weakness in the current provisions and perhaps prevents Member States from making effective use of [the must-carry rules] to promote pluralism'.[138] Indeed, if the objective of the must-carry duty is to establish a favorable regime for channels that bring an added value to the citizen, the exclusion of the service provider from the scope of the regime would appear to be a major

132 Directive 2002/22/EC of the European Parliament and of the Council of 7 March 2002 on universal service and users' rights relating to electronic communications networks and services (Universal Service Directive) [2002] OJ L108/51, Recital (43), (2002 USD), and Directive 2009/136/EC of the European Parliament and of the Council of 25 November 2009 amending Directive 2002/22/EC on universal service and users' rights relating to electronic communications networks and services, Directive 2002/58/EC concerning the processing of personal data and the protection of privacy in the electronic communications sector and Regulation (EC) No. 2006/2004 on cooperation between national authorities responsible for the enforcement of consumer protection laws (Text with EEA relevance) [2009] OJ L337/11, Recital (48) (2009 USD)

133 2009 Universal Services Directive, *supra* n. 132, Article 31(1)

134 2002 Universal Services Directive, *supra* n. 132, Article 31(2)

135 van Eijk, N. and Bart van der Sloot (2012). *Must-carry Regulation: a Must or a Burden?* foreword. In European Audiovisual Observatory (ed.). *Must-carry: Renaissance or Reformation?* IRIS plus, 2012–5

136 NB: At the time of going to press, the EU Telecoms Package, including the Universal Services Directive, was subject to review. The revision process is likely to address the problem by laying down that Member States may impose must-carry rules on both electronic communications network *and* service providers. For an overview of the revision process of the EU Telecoms Package see: <http://www.consilium.europa.eu/en/policies/electronic-communications-code/>

137 2002 Universal Services Directive, *supra* n. 132, Recital 45

138 Feintuck, M. and Mike Varney (2010). *Regulating Media Markets: The Need for Subsidiarity and Clarity of Principle.* In Birkinshaw, P. and Mike Varney (eds.). *The European Union Legal Order after Lisbon.* Alphen aan den Rijn: Kluwer Law International, 169

obstacle to achieving this objective. This is particularly so in cases where, even if the Member State has decided to establish must-carry rules, it may not enforce them on the network operator that carries the channels offered by the domestic service provider because the operator is established outside its jurisdiction.[139]

27. The European works quotas and must-carry obligations are two, perhaps the most notable, examples of the type of legislative action the EU has taken to ensure that the single media market is not realized in ways that undermine media pluralism. Scholarly literature has put forward a number of reasons why the mechanisms that the aforementioned rules establish have probably fallen foul of achieving that objective. Taking stock of the lessons learned, any legislative revisions would need to address the loopholes that have been left open (NB: while the Audiovisual Media Services Directive was recently revised, the definition of 'European works' remained intact[140]). However, the following two points must be borne in mind: first, any future provisions attempting to protect media pluralism will always need to respect the division of competences between the EU and the Member States in this area. Second, and related to the above, the fact that the overwhelming majority of Member States have decided not to attach quality or originality conditions to the term 'European works' illustrates that the national legislator may not be very keen to develop initiatives so as to ensure that relevant mechanisms will reach their full potential.

3.3 EU competition law and media pluralism

28. The question of whether, and if so to what extent, EU competition law can protect media pluralism has been a somewhat more complex topic, in that even those who argue in favor of an expansive approach to EU competence in the field of media adopt different and, in some cases, opposing perspectives. Broadly speaking, the studies that discuss the strengths and weaknesses of EU competition law can be divided into three categories.

29. First, certain authors contend that EU competition law in general, and merger control in particular, can play a major role in preventing the accumulation of significant power in the hands of a few media owners on the grounds that the compatibility of a concentration with the common market is assessed *ex ante* and an increasingly large number of mergers affecting the European media marketplace fall within the Commission's (exclusive) competence.[141]

---

139 On the issue of jurisdiction see Komorek (2013), *supra* n. 3, 168

140 See Directive (EU) 2018/1808 of the European Parliament and of the Council of 14 November 2018 amending Directive 2010/13/EU on the coordination of certain provisions laid down by law, regulation or administrative action in Member States concerning the provision of audiovisual media services (Audiovisual Media Services Directive) in view of changing market realities [2009] OJ L 303/69, Article 1

141 Craufurd-Smith (2004), *supra* n. 12, 669; Ariño (2005), *supra* n. 89, 405–412, and Komorek (2013), *supra* n. 3, 281–283

However, according to these authors, in order to ensure that it leads to an outcome that is pluralism-friendly, the EU merger control system needs an 'extra something'. This is because, so the argument goes, in certain cases the Commission is called upon to scrutinize concentrations that are not problematic from a competition perspective (e.g. where the merging firms are active in separate geographic markets), but which raise concerns over media pluralism (e.g. where the acquiring firm engages in practices that undermine journalistic freedom).[142] Proponents of this approach suggest that an obligation to conduct an assessment of the effects of the concentration on media pluralism be incorporated into the Merger Regulation.[143] They also recommend the establishment of a specialist body within the Commission, or even the creation of a European media concentration authority that would advise the Directorate-General for Competition on the pluralism-specific issues which the concentration in question would raise.[144] If this proposal materialized, EU merger control could indeed tackle problems that it cannot presently address. For example, currently, the Commission may check whether a merger will grant the involved firms the ability and incentive to foreclose competitors, thereby depriving consumers of a variety of choices.[145] Yet, a merger assessment that further seeks to determine the impact on media pluralism would also entail an analysis of whether the merged entity would acquire significant opinion-forming power, thereby being capable of marginalizing different viewpoints.[146] However, as advocates of this approach acknowledge, the above proposal raises at least three issues which might render it an unrealistic and possibly unattractive alternative to the *status quo*. First, given the (politically and culturally) sensitive nature of a pluralism review, it is questionable whether the Commission, that is, a supranational competition authority, is the most appropriate institution to decide relevant matters.[147] Second, the proposal to establish a European body entrusted with the duty to inform the Commission of the pluralism concerns that arise from media concentrations has, in the past, been turned down by the Commission.[148] Third, and perhaps

142 Ariño (2005), *supra* n. 89, 384–385; Komorek (2013), *supra* n. 3, 136–137, and Craufurd-Smith (2004), *supra* n. 12, 669

143 European Institute for the Media (2004). *The Information of the Citizen in the EU: Obligations for the Media and the Institutions concerning the Citizen's right to be Fully and Objectively Informed*, 251. <http://edz.bib.uni-mannheim.de/daten/edz-ma/ep/04/pe358896-en.pdf>; Craufurd-Smith (2004), *supra* n. 12, 669; Ariño (2005), *supra* n. 89, 405–410, and Komorek (2013), *supra* n. 3, 281–283

144 ibid.

145 See Commission Guidelines on the assessment of horizontal mergers under the Council Regulation on the control of concentrations between undertakings [2004] OJ C 31/3, paragraph 8, and Commission Guidelines on the assessment of non-horizontal mergers under the Council Regulation on the control of concentrations between undertakings [2008] OJ C 265/7, paragraph 10

146 See, for instance, Ofcom (2010b). *Report on public interest test on the proposed acquisition of British Sky Broadcasting Group plc by News Corporation*, paragraph 1.18. <http://www.culture.gov.uk/images/publications/OfcomPITReport_NewsCorp-BSkyB_31DEC2010.pdf>

147 Craufurd-Smith (2004), *supra* n. 12, 670; Komorek (2013), *supra* n. 3, 281, and Ariño (2005), *supra* n. 89, 405. Helberger takes the same position though she studies the application of EU competition law to media markets from a different perspective. See Helberger (2005), *supra* n. 131, 190

148 Craufurd-Smith (2004), *supra* n. 12, 670, referring to Palzer, C. and Caroline Hilger (2001). *Media Supervision on the Threshold of the 21st Century – Structure and Powers of Regulatory Authorities in the*

more importantly, Member States would most likely be unwilling to support this idea in that integrating a pluralism assessment into EU merger proceedings would probably be perceived 'as an illegitimate attempt to do indirectly what could not be agreed directly through the "appropriate" regulatory procedures'.[149]

30. The second avenue explored[150] is based on the same premise, namely that EU competition law can make an important contribution to the protection of media pluralism, but follows a more modest approach which does not involve legislative amendments. Proponents of this latter approach argue that the competition provisions of the Treaty cannot be applied in a vacuum: that is to say, detached from the non-economic values that the EU is bound to respect.[151] As Article 167(4) TFEU dictates, so the argument goes, concerns over media pluralism that may arise in the context of competition proceedings must be duly considered and balanced against considerations of a purely economic nature. These studies primarily seek to determine whether the Commission may either permit restrictions of competition or sacrifice efficiency in order to ensure that media pluralism or any other non-economic value that is at stake is taken into account. For example, Van Rompuy maintains that, in deciding whether to grant an exemption to an anti-competitive agreement under Article 101(3) TFEU, the Commission should assess the restrictions of competition introduced by the agreement concerned against the efficiencies it may generate, as well as against the contribution it may make to the enhancement of other public policy values.[152] In the case of mergers, Ariño argues that the Commission should opt for the 'second' or 'third best' alternative if the first, more efficient, solution is likely to endanger the democratic process.[153] In other words, according to Ariño, the Commission should be determined to forgo, to some extent, economies of scale and scope that could be achieved as a result of the merger in order to benefit media pluralism.[154] Advocates of this approach identify at least two weaknesses in attempting to apply competition law by reference to non-economic values. First, in cases where reconciliation between

Era of Convergence. European Audiovisual Observatory 8 IRIS plus. <https://rm.coe.int/1680783377>

149 Craufurd-Smith (2004), *supra* n. 12, 670; Scheuer, A. and Peter Strothmann (2002). *Media Supervision on the Threshold of the 21st Century What are the Requirements of Broadcasting, Telecommunications and Concentration Regulation?* Strasbourg: European Audiovisual Observatory, 7. <https://rm.coe.int/1680783385>

150 Note that certain authors explore both the first approach discussed above as well as the second approach discussed here. See, for instance, Ariño (2005), *supra* n. 89, 400–412

151 See, for instance, Van Rompuy, B. (2012). *Economic Efficiency: The Sole Concern of Modern Antitrust Policy?* Alphen aan den Rijn: Kluwer Law International, 283–404; Lefever (2012), *supra* n. 130, 118–128 (note that Van Rompuy and Lefever focus on broadcast rights to sports events); Ariño (2005), *supra* n. 89, 400–405, and Psychogiopoulou, E. (2006a). *The Cultural Mainstreaming Clause of Article 151(4) EC: Protection and Promotion of Cultural Diversity or Hidden Cultural Agenda?* European Law Journal 12, 585–591

152 Van Rompuy (2012), *supra* n. 151, 228–229

153 Ariño (2005), *supra* n. 89, 402–403

154 Ariño, M. (2004), *Competition Law and Pluralism in European Digital Broadcasting: Addressing the gaps*, Communications and Strategies 54, 118

competition considerations and considerations relating to the non-economic value concerned is impossible, the former must supersede the latter, for otherwise the Commission would act in violation of the Treaties.[155] Second, given that after the entry into force of Regulation 1/2003 national competition authorities are entitled to apply Articles 101 and 102 TFEU,[156] the integration of non-economic considerations in relevant analyses may jeopardize legal certainty by leading to an inconsistent application of the competition provisions across the EU, possibly subjecting the latter to opportunistic and arbitrary interpretation.[157]

31. Finally, there are studies that ascribe a negligible role to EU competition law as a tool for guaranteeing media pluralism.[158] Two arguments are typically put forward in the relevant literature. These arguments are intertwined and concern the trend that has emerged in EU competition enforcement over the past twenty years, namely the shift to a 'more economics-based' approach, which posits that economic efficiency and consumer welfare are the guiding principles of EU competition policy[159] and that, as a result, concerns over other public policy values, including media pluralism,[160] must be expelled from competition assessments. While critical of this paradigm shift, studies falling under the category examined here appear to have accepted that the Commission is unlikely to rearrange its priorities in order to make allowance for non-economic considerations.[161] On this basis, they identify the following two reasons why EU competition law is not adequate to safeguard media pluralism: first, *the application of EU competition law ensures market access* (e.g. by prohibiting a concentration that would grant the merging firms significant market power),[162] thereby potentially delivering an outcome that is of benefit to media pluralism, but this outcome is entirely dependent on the economic concerns the Commission attempts to address in each individual

155 Ariño (2005), *supra* n. 89, 402

156 Council Regulation (EC) No. 1/2003 of 16 December 2002 on the implementation of the rules on competition laid down in Articles 81 and 82 of the Treaty [2003] OJ L1/1

157 See Van Rompuy (2012), *supra* n. 151, 403, and Harrison and Woods (2007), *supra* n. 127, 166

158 Note that certain authors explore both the first approach discussed above as well as the third approach discussed here. See, for instance, Komorek (2013), *supra* n. 3, 135–142 and 281–283

159 See Lowe, P. *Consumer Welfare and Efficiency – New Guiding Principles of Competition Policy?* Speech given at the 13th International Conference on Competition and 14th European Competition Day, Munich, 27 March 2007

160 See, for instance, Ibáñez Colomo, P. (2006). *Saving the Monopsony: Exclusivity, Innovation and Market Power in the Media Sector*. Research Papers in Law, 07/2006, Global Competition Law Centre, 26

161 See, for instance, Barzanti (2012), *supra* n. 104, 14–15

162 Barzanti (2012), *supra* n. 104, 14–15; Komorek (2013), *supra* n. 3, 136–142; Ungerer, H. (2014). *The Reasons For Intervention Through Competition Policy*. In Donders, K., Caroline Pauwels and Jan Loisen (ed.). *The Palgrave Handbook of European Media Policy*. London: Palgrave Macmillan, 405–426. The Commission takes the same position. See, for instance, Commission (2005). *Issues paper for the Liverpool Audiovisual Conference: Media pluralism – What should be the European Union's role?* Brussels: DG Information Society and Media, 2; and Commission. Staff Working Document on Media Pluralism in the Member States of the EU, SEC (2007) 32, 7

case and hence is (at best) coincidental.[163] Second, it is claimed that, precisely because it is driven by efficiency considerations, EU competition law is incapable of grasping the '(coessential) qualitative (and not just quantitative) dimension' of pluralism. [164] That is to say, the narrowing of the objectives that competition law pursues makes it difficult, if not impossible, to embrace parameters other than cost reductions and lower prices.

32. While not entirely devoid of merit, the above two arguments raise strong doubts as to whether we should dismiss the idea that EU competition law can make a meaningful contribution to media pluralism, one that goes beyond the limits prescribed by the aforementioned studies. This is because, as opposed to all other suggestions that were examined above, the studies that belong to this category refer to the limitations without exploring the potential of strict competition enforcement. As a result, many questions remain unanswered. The loopholes left open by the above two arguments are examined in more detail below.

33. First, with respect to *access*, several authors refrain from testing the hypotheses on which the Commission has based its practice in order to ensure that media markets remain open to competition.[165] For example, to protect undistorted competition in broadcasting markets, the Commission has been mainly concerned with imposing behavioral remedies on undertakings that own or control access to premium content, i.e. content that has the capacity to attract large audiences.[166] The overwhelming majority of studies have been limited to discussing how these remedies were designed.[167] Of course, access to premium content is a significant bottleneck in broadcasting markets and thus a topic worthy of discussion, but the issue of whether there are other tools in the Commission's hands that are more effective than access remedies must also be examined. Moreover, even if one insists that access must be ensured through commitments relating to the acquisition of premium content, we would still need to evaluate the effectiveness of the remedies that have been imposed thus far against how the affected markets evolved. Impact assessment based on empirical data is key to sound economic policy-making. Another example

---

163 See Barzanti (2012), *supra* n. 104, 14–15, and Komorek (2013), *supra* n. 3, 136–142

164 Barzanti (2012), *supra* n. 104, 15. Harrison and Woods also appear to dismiss the idea that EU competition law may be applied by reference to qualitative considerations. See *supra* n. 127, 149–150

165 Nikolinakos, N. (2006). *EU Competition Law and Regulation in the Converging Telecommunications, Media and IT sectors*. Alphen aan den Rijn: Kluwer Law International, 138–161; Capito, R. and Moira Kettner (2008). *Excursus: EC Merger Regulation*. In Castendyk, O., Egbert J. Dommering and Alexander Scheurer. *European Media Law*. Alphen aan den Rijn: Kluwer Law International, 188–198; Psychogiopoulou, E. (2008). *The Integration of Cultural Considerations in EU Law and Policies*. Leiden, Boston: Martinus Nijhoff Publishers, 246–291; Ungerer (2014), *supra* n. 162, 409–416, and Komorek (2013), *supra* n. 3, 130–135. See also Lefever (2012), *supra* n. 130, 135–157. Note, however, that she discusses the issue from a different perspective, that of the exercise of the right to information.

166 See, for instance, *Vivendi/Canal+/Seagram* (Case COMP/M.2050) [2000] C 311/03; *News Corp/Telepiù* (Case COMP/M.2876) [2004] OJ L110/73; *BSkyB/Kirch Pay-TV* (Case COMP/JV.37) [2000] OJ C 110/45, and *SFR/Télé 2 France* (Case COMP M.4504) [2007] OJ L316/57

167 See *supra* n. 165

concerns resale price maintenance (hereinafter RPM) agreements in the print publishing sector. These arrangements usually fall foul of EU competition law,[168] however, they have traditionally been regarded as beneficial to media pluralism on the grounds that they facilitate the production and distribution of a wide variety of titles, including low-demand books.[169] The Commission has declared such agreements incompatible with the Treaty for the reason, *inter alia*, that they prevented booksellers from using low prices to penetrate the markets of other Member States.[170] Studies that discuss the relevant decision-making are restricted to condemning the Commission[171] for being unsympathetic to the non-economic pluralism-specific objectives they sought to achieve. Yet, these studies do not assess the decisions concerned against the backdrop of economics literature in this area that has provided convincing evidence that RPM can deliver a pluralistic outcome only under certain conditions.[172] The above examples illustrate why, when we draw conclusions on the weaknesses of ensuring market access as a proxy for media pluralism, we need to discuss whether the Commission's practice is well founded.

34. The second premise, namely that competition is mainly about cost efficiencies, tells only part of the story. A number of policy documents rightly point out that in a competition assessment several other factors come into play. For example, the (Horizontal and Non-Horizontal) Merger Guidelines lay down that the Commission's mission consists of preventing mergers that would be likely to significantly increase the market power of firms, and explains that an increase in market power refers to 'the ability of one or more undertakings *to profitably increase prices, reduce output, to cut choice or quality of goods and services or diminish innovation'* [emphasis added].[173] In other words, competition has several non-price dimensions. Whether, and if so to what extent,

---

168 In EU competition law, RPM has been treated as a 'hardcore restriction', that is, a restriction of competition 'by object' which, as such, results in the exclusion of the agreement from the scope of application of the Block Exemption Regulation. In cases where an RPM clause is contained in the agreement, that agreement is presumed to be caught by Article 101(1) TFEU, but it is established case law that parties to *any* agreement may plead an efficiency defense under Article 101(3) TFEU in an individual case. See Commission Guidelines on the Application of Article 101(3) TFEU [2004] OJ C 101/08, paragraph 47

169 For Member States where RPM laws for books apply as a means to protect media pluralism see Joint Research Centre (2012b). *Technical Report on Statistical, Ecosystems and Competitiveness Analysis of the Media and Content Industries: The Book Publishing Industry*, fn. 198. <http://ftp.jrc.es/EURdoc/JRC76642.pdf>

170 See *VBBB/VBVB* (Case IV/428) Commission decision 82/123/EEC of 25 November 1981 relating to a proceeding under Article 85 of the EEC Treaty [1982] OJ L52/36 and *Publishers Association – Net Book Agreement* (Cases IV/27.393 and IV/27.394) Commission decision of 12 December 1988 relating to a proceeding under Article 85 of the EEC Treaty [1989] OJ L22/12

171 See, for instance, Everling, U. (1997). *Book Price Fixing in the German Language Area and European Community Law*. Baden-Baden: Nomos, 112–118;, and Psychogiopoulou (2008), *supra* n. 165, 279–286

172 See, for instance, Appelman, M. and Marcel Canoy (2002). *Horses for Courses: Why Europe should not harmonize its book policies*. De Economist 150(5), 583–600, and Canoy, M., Jan C. van Ours and Frederick van der Ploeg (2005). *The Economics of Books*. CESifo Working Paper No. 1414, 12. <https://ideas.repec.org/p/ces/ceswps/_1414.html>

173 Commission Guidelines on the assessment of horizontal mergers under the Council Regulation on the control of concentrations between undertakings [2004] OJ C 31/3, paragraph 8 and Commission, Guidelines on the assessment of non-horizontal mergers under the Council Regulation on the control of concentrations between undertakings [2008] OJ C 265/7, paragraph 10

these dimensions influence the outcome of a competition analysis will depend on the particular characteristics of the market concerned and the importance that the consumers of the products or services offered by the undertakings under scrutiny attach to them. For example, in the market for recorded music, it is the quality of sound[174] whereas in server operating systems, it is the security features built into the system that aim to protect the user against unauthorized access, viruses, etc.[175] Similarly, in media markets, price is not necessarily the only or the most relevant parameter that drives competition. For example, demand for certain products, such as newspapers, is highly inelastic in price because it is spurred by the readers' political preferences.[176] In other cases, such as free-to-air television, it is the variety of content offered by the broadcasters or the availability of programming on catch-up TV.[177]

35. The above remarks indicate that the two assumptions on which the position that EU competition law can do little to nothing to protect media pluralism is based may be ill-founded. If so, EU competition law has potential that remains unexplored. The present study shall examine whether this is indeed the case by testing the accuracy of the above two assumptions. In doing so, it shall address two issues; the first is of a legal nature whereas the second is purely practical.

36. First, ascribing a very limited role to EU competition law is partly responsible for how scholarly literature in this area has evolved. More particularly, this approach has led the vast majority of authors who have dealt with the topic to focus on initiatives that could be developed under other branches of EU law, the main instruments of which were discussed above. Still, the question of whether EU competition law is applied to media markets properly, that is, by duly taking account of the parameters that drive competition in the media *and* by using the full toolkit the Commission has at its disposal, should precede any discussion over whether and, if so, what type of further action should be taken by the EU to preserve this value. This is because, as already discussed, the vast majority of proposals that have been put forward thus far raise competence issues that cannot be ignored and may not enjoy the necessary political will to materialize. It bears repeating that the EU has exclusive competence to establish the competition rules that apply to media undertakings operating within the EU. In light of the above, and even if opinions on

---

174 *Universal Music Group/EMI Music* (Case COMP/M.6458) [2012] OJ C 220/8, paragraph 127

175 CFI, Case T-201/04 *Microsoft Corp. v Commission of the European Communities* [2007] ECR II-03601, paragraph 652

176 Joint Research Centre (2012a). *Statistical, Ecosystems and Competitiveness Analysis of the Media and Content Industries: The Newspaper Publishing Industry*, 24. <http://publications.jrc.ec.europa.eu/repository/bitstream/JRC69881/jrc69881.pdf>

177 Csorgo, L. and Ian Munro (2011). *Market Definition Issues for Audio and Audio-Visual Distribution Products and Services in a Digital Environment, A Report Prepared for the Canadian Radio-television and Telecommunications Commission.* <http://www.crtc.gc.ca/eng/publications/reports/rp110215.htm#_ftn7>

what would be the best course of action to safeguard media pluralism at the EU level may pull in different directions, may we all agree that it is only after determining the point at which EU competition law exhausts its limits, we must ask what form of intervention, be it amendments to the Merger Regulation, soft law in the form of recommendations, or hard law in the form of instruments potentially stretching the Treaty boundaries, would address the issues that remain unresolved.

37. Second, from a practical perspective, a discussion over the contribution EU competition law enforcement can make to media pluralism may have more to offer than discussions over action under other branches of EU law. For example, as already seen, Article 7 TEU has never been applied, and only a handful of Member States have imposed stricter conditions to ensure that the term 'European works' corresponds to quality and innovative content. Moreover, in recent years, the Commission has explicitly stated that a harmonizing instrument in support of media pluralism is not in the EU legislative agenda.[178] Yet, at the time of going to press, the Commission has adopted 1,075 competition decisions affecting this sector.[179] It is not only the number of cases that has fallen under the Commission's scrutiny thus far that illustrates the impact of EU competition law on the structure of media markets. In implementing EU competition policy, the Commission has dealt with numerous undertakings such as broadcasters, newspaper publishers, digital retailers, and search engines whose practices may pose numerous threats to media pluralism. In light of the above, EU competition law has influenced media markets and, by extension, pluralism, significantly more than other branches of EU law and there are valid indications that this is not likely to change in the near future.

38. To sum up, the present study shall test the hypothesis that, if properly applied, EU competition law has the potential to protect media pluralism in a way which does not fit into the either excessively narrow or excessively broad frame molded by the relevant literature to date. It shall do so by focusing on the following three questions, which remain largely unanswered: has the Commission managed to prevent market foreclosure in the media sector? If not, what would be an alternative, proper application of the competition provisions of the Treaty to ensure that competition is not distorted? And would this alternative deliver an outcome that is more pluralism-friendly? This study is the first to adopt this novel approach to the application of EU competition rules to media markets and shall attempt to demonstrate that strict competition enforcement may go a long way towards protecting a non-economic value *without* stretching the Treaty limits.

---

178 See, for instance, Commission Staff Working Document on Media Pluralism in the Member States of the EU SEC (2007) 32, 4

179 Search by NACE code. <http://ec.europa.eu/competition/elojade/isef/index.cfm?fuseaction=dsp_result>

4. Research method

4.1 An interdisciplinary approach

39. A study exploring the contribution that strict competition enforcement can make to the protection of media pluralism cannot be approached from a legal standpoint only. In order to identify the challenges facing pluralism in the current media ecology and the lacunae in the Commission's decision-making, an in-depth understanding of relevant technological advancements and sector-specific economics is required. How has digitization affected the architecture of media markets? Has it altered content consumption patterns? Has scarcity of frequencies been replaced by other, possibly artificial, forms of scarcity? How does the two-sided nature of advertising-based media impact a competition assessment? These questions illustrate that the legal issues examined throughout this thesis cannot be considered in a vacuum. Moreover, new business models for the sale of media content have surfaced (e.g. online agency agreements for the sale of news subscriptions), the relationship between the consumer and the media content provider has undergone significant changes (e.g. atypical 'transactions' whereby the supplier offers content in exchange for personal data are becoming more and more common), and competition authorities are increasingly being called upon to assess practices the effects of which are not entirely clear (e.g. algorithm manipulation), finding themselves in uncharted territory. In view of the above, it is only through an interdisciplinary approach, whereby the legal analysis is informed and shaped by market and technological developments, economic theory, and empirical evidence, that any meaningful normative proposal on how EU competition law must be applied to media markets can be put forward.

4.2 The markets that will be examined: a dual (old/new) media perspective

40. The studies that discuss the role of EU competition law in protecting media pluralism have mainly focused on broadcasting markets.[180] The present study,

180 See, for instance, Komorek (2013), *supra* n. 3, 95–142; Ariño (2005), *supra* n. 89, and Harrison and Woods (2007), *supra* n. 127, 146–172. Note that more recent studies discussing the Commission's competition practice in media markets have also focused on the broadcasting sector. See, for instance, Van Rompuy (2012), *supra* n. 151, 319–390; Ungerer (2014), *supra* n. 162; Donders K. and Hallvard Moe (2014). *European State-Aid control and PSB: Competition Policy Clashing or Matching with Public Interest Objectives?* In Donders, K., Caroline Pauwels and Jan Loisen (eds.). *The Palgrave Handbook of European Media Policy*. London: Palgrave Macmillan, 426–441; Van Rompuy, B. (2014). *The Impact of EU Competition Policy on the Sale of Sports Media Rights: Trends and Developments at the National Level*. In Donders, K., Caroline Pauwels and Jan Loisen (eds.). *The Palgrave Handbook of European Media Policy*. London: Palgrave Macmillan, 442–460; and Iosifidis (2014), *supra* n. 96. 'Traditional' or 'old' media are media introduced prior to the advent of the Internet, such as television, newspapers, and magazines. New media is a broad concept 'used to describe the new generation of digital, computerized, or networked information and communication technologies'. This concept includes, for instance, social media such as Facebook and news aggregators such as Google News. See Electronic Frontiers

however, adopts a wider approach. More particularly, in addition to decisions concerning television, it will examine the Commission's practice in traditional print publishing as well as more recent cases dealing with new media markets, namely online search, news aggregation, and markets for the retail sale of e-content such as news apps and newspaper subscriptions. This dual (old/new media) perspective is driven by three considerations. First, in terms of use, traditional media still plays a major role in informing Europeans. For example, television is still their preferred source of news[181] on political matters.[182] However, alongside traditional media, entities that have emerged with the advent of the Internet, including digital intermediaries (that is, firms that deliver content produced by third-party suppliers to online users[183]) in particular, are now playing an important role in determining the amount and quality of information that citizens access and engage with. For example, based on the Reuters Institute *Digital News Report 2018*, the majority of users prefer to get to news through a side door, such as search engines and news aggregators, rather than going directly to a news website or application.[184] Second, and related to the above, in terms of policy, a discussion about the potential benefits to or dangers for media pluralism today cannot take place by focusing on one or the other type of media. For example, a key question is whether 'old' gatekeepers, which are more often than not (horizontally and/or vertically) integrated and which control traditional media markets, may still raise concerns over media pluralism. If this question is answered in the affirmative, does the new media environment, which makes available a vast amount of content, address the above concerns? Or do entities that operate in new media markets engage in practices that create additional risks for media pluralism? To put it simply, any meaningful policy proposal on how to safeguard pluralism in the current media landscape cannot be formulated without carefully considering how the perils posed by one type of media can be balanced against opportunities created by the other. Finally, from a competition law perspective, the Commission's decision-making in traditional media should not be studied in isolation from the practice it is currently developing in new media markets. For example, in cases dealing with free-to-air television, the Commission finds that the exercise of market definition should consist in identifying the

---

Foundation. *Definition of media*. IRM of 24/11/2009. This study uses the term 'traditional media providers' to refer to organizations that were established before the digital revolution commenced, such as broadcasters and newspaper publishers, and the term 'new media providers' to refer to firms that have emerged with the advent of the Internet such as blogs and wikis. The study, however, acknowledges that, as a result of technology convergence, this distinction is becoming increasingly blurred.

181 Commission (2017). *Media Use in the European Union*, 42

182 It bears noting that radio remains the medium that Europeans trust the most. See ibid, 24; also Commission (2016). *Special Eurobarometer 452. Media Pluralism and Democracy*, 10. <http://ec.europa.eu/information_society/newsroom/image/document/2016-47/sp452-summary_en_19666.pdf>

183 Foster, R. (2012). *News Plurality in a Digital World – Report prepared for the Reuters Institute for the Study of Journalism*, 25

184 Reuters Institute (2018). *Digital News Report 2018*, 13. <http://media.digitalnewsreport.org/wp-content/uploads/2018/06/digital-news-report-2018.pdf?x89475>

effective alternative sources of supply for the advertisers, not the viewers.[185] The Commission is of the opinion that a market for viewers need not be defined, on the grounds that the latter do not pay for the content they receive.[186] And yet, the opposite position would seem to find support in modern economic theory.[187] The attention that this issue deserves becomes clear if we think of the abundance of undertakings operating in the information economy that offer content for free. Another example concerns the publishing sector: as already mentioned, the Commission has declared RPM agreements between publishers and bricks-and-mortar retailers incompatible with the common market. Arrangements with RPM elements are making a comeback, but this time around they govern trade in digital content such as e-books and news apps. Was the approach to assessing RPM for traditional print titles based on a sound reasoning so that it can guide the Commission in digital content cases with a similar factual background? The above two examples illustrate that traditional and new media share certain characteristics (e.g. revenue model and pricing strategies) that are relevant for a competition analysis. Since the Commission's practice in traditional media markets is more mature than in new media markets, it is of utmost importance to assess the approach adopted in older cases in order to ensure that errors committed in the past are not incorporated into future decisions.

4.3 Book structure

41. In explaining the reasons why it is essential that the present study a) adopts an interdisciplinary approach and b) considers the Commission's decisional practice in both traditional and new media markets, I posed the key questions facing the topic that I shall examine, namely whether, and if so to what extent, a proper application of EU competition law can protect media pluralism. To answer the above questions, I structured the book as follows: one of the first issues that is raised in discussions concerning media pluralism is whether, in light of the advancements that have taken place over the past few years, policy intervention in support of this value is still needed. Many argue that in today's media landscape the citizen is given access to a wide range of information and given countless opportunities to participate in public discourse. Through an analysis of how market, regulatory and technological developments have

---

185 Commission notice on the definition of relevant market for the purposes of Community competition law [1997] OJ C 372/3, paragraph 13. See, for instance, *News Corp/Telepiù* (Case COMP/M.2876) [2004] OJ L110/73 paragraph 24; *News Corp/BSkyB* (Case COMP/M.5932) [2011] OJ C 37/2 paragraph 97; *SFR/Télé 2* (Case COMP/M.4504) [2007] OJ L316/57, paragraph 45; *News Corp/Premiere* (Case COMP/M.5121) [2008] OJ C 219/4, paragraph 19; *Telenor/Canal+/Canal Digital* (Case COMP/C.2/38.287) [2003] OJ C 149/10 paragraph 28; *BSkyB/Kirch Pay-TV* (Case COMP/JV.37) [2000] OJ C 110/45, paragraph 24; *Bertelsmann/Kirch/Premiere* (Case IV/M.993) [1999] OJ L053/1, paragraph 18; *Kirch/Richemont/Multichoice/Telepiù* (Case IV/M.584) [1995] OJ C 129/6, paragraph 15

186 ibid.

187 See, for instance, Filistrucchi, L., Damien Geradin, Eric van Damme, E. and Pauline Affeldt (2012). *Market Definition in Two-Sided Markets: Theory and Practice*. TILEC Discussion Paper No. 2013-009. Available through SSRN at: <http://papers.ssrn.com/sol3/papers.cfm?abstract_id=2240850>

affected supply and consumption of media content, Chapter 2 dismantles the argument that digital technologies have remedied concerns over media pluralism. In doing so, Chapter 2 exposes the reader to the main challenges confronting the realization of a pluralistic offer, such as a natural tendency of (traditional and new) media markets to concentration, content homogenization, and practices impairing the free flow of media content in the online universe.

42. As already mentioned, at EU level, cases that have raised pluralism issues have been mainly examined by the Directorate-General for Competition. After establishing in Chapter 2 that media pluralism is (still) worthy of protection, Chapter 3 will inquire whether, and if so to what extent, EU competition law has been/can be applied in a pluralism-friendly manner. By pinpointing the loopholes the Commission has left open in a number of (antitrust and merger) cases that touched upon issues that arise in relevant competition investigations, such as access to valuable inputs (e.g. premium content) and the role of the non-price dimensions of competition in market definitions and competitive assessments, the Chapter puts forward two claims: first, the practice that the Commission has developed in media markets has fallen short of protecting *either competition or media pluralism*. And second, EU competition law can be applied in a way which goes beyond the Commission's predispositions and which may lead to *competition decisions that are more accurate and pluralism-friendly* without giving rise to controversies over competence.

43. Chapters 4 to 6 are concerned with testing the above two claims. They do so by attempting to encapsulate the main issues the Commission has encountered in older and more recent cases that raise both competition and pluralism concerns. The decisional practice the Commission has developed under Article 101, Article 102, and merger control will be examined by reference to a specific sector in a way that reflects a business strategy (e.g. consolidation), practice (e.g. algorithm manipulation), or pricing model (e.g. RPM), that has been a major (competition and media) policy matter in the market concerned.

44. More particularly, Chapter 4 will explore the parameters against which the Commission exercises merger control in cases concerning broadcasting markets. In this sector, mergers and acquisitions have had a broad appeal due to the significant economies of scale and scope that broadcasters can achieve by integrating with other firms that operate at the same (horizontal integration) or different (vertical integration) levels of the supply chain. For our purposes, it bears noting that, from a competition perspective, a concentration may increase the ability and incentive of the merging firms to crowd out competing suppliers whereas, from a pluralism perspective, a concentration may allow the individuals controlling the merged entity to marginalize opposing viewpoints.

45. Consolidation has not been as popular in the publishing sector as it has been in television.[188] In the publishing industry, as indicated above, a popular strategy has been RPM, whereby the publisher sets the retail prices of the titles it produces and the retailer is not permitted to offer discounts or any other form of promotion unless the publisher explicitly grants its authorization. For this reason, Chapter 5 examines how the Commission has applied/may apply Article 101 TFEU to agreements with RPM elements governing the sale of (e-)newspapers and (e-)books. Depending on market conditions, RPM may promote competition for titles and/or encourage small publishers to penetrate the market. The analysis seeks to identify these conditions.

46. With respect to online intermediation activities, such as online search and news aggregation, *Google Search*, a case that deals with a number of practices in which an entity leading such activities engages, is particularly relevant for the purposes of this study. More particularly, the Commission recently adopted a decision that Google has abused its dominant position in online search (the investigation into practices related to content aggregation is still open[189]).[190] As mentioned above, by acting as intermediaries between content providers and audiences, search engines and news aggregators are gradually playing an important role in determining the amount and quality of information that consumers access and engage with. It will be seen in greater detail in Chapter 2 that there are several areas in which the activities they develop may impact undistorted competition and pluralism, including the control they exercise over what may be regarded as *distribution bottlenecks* through which users access content, the *editorial-like judgments* they perform in selecting the content they link to or carry, and their role in shaping *future economic models for news provision.*[191] *Google Search* is a vivid illustration of the above issues. For example, insofar as news economics is concerned, one of the complaints has to do with the practice of copying and displaying parts of news articles (also referred to as 'scraping') in Google's news aggregation platform, Google News.[192] Does scraping affect the ability of news providers to generate (advertising and subscription) revenues? If so, are the effects positive or negative? If the effects are negative, can news providers rely on Article 102 TFEU to prevent Google from using their content? A complaint

---

188 For recent developments regarding M&A activity in television see, for instance, Evens, T. and Karen Donders (2016). *Mergers and acquisitions in TV broadcasting and distribution: Challenges for competition, industrial and media policy.* Telematics and Informatics 33(2), 674–682

189 Commission (June, 2017). Press Release. *Antitrust: Commission fines Google €2.42 billion for abusing dominance as search engine by giving illegal advantage to own comparison shopping service.* <http://europa.eu/rapid/press-release_IP-17-1784_en.htm>

190 *Google Search* (Case AT.39740) Commission decision of 27 June 2017 relating to proceedings under Article 102 TFEU and Article 54 of the EEA Agreement C (2017) 4444 final

191 Foster (2012), *supra* n. 183, 6–7

192 For an overview of the complaints against Google see, for instance, Commission (2014a, February). Memo 24/87. *Antitrust: Commission obtains from Google comparable display of specialized search rivals – Frequently asked questions.* <http://europa.eu/rapid/press-release_MEMO-14-87_en.htm?locale=en>

that exemplifies the role of an intermediary as a distribution bottleneck concerns Google's retaliation practices, whereby news providers that object to the use of their stories on the Google News website are excluded from Google's services altogether, including general search results.[193] To what extent does this practice deprive users of discovering news online? Could this conduct be regarded as abusive tying for the purposes of Article 102 TFEU? Finally, with respect to editorial-like judgments, Google was found to deliberately demote competing websites whilst ensuring prominent display for its own content.[194] Does this practice affect the range of content to which users are exposed? And under what conditions is preferential treatment of one's own products a violation of EU competition law? The above issues will be discussed in detail in Chapter 6, which, building around the issues that have arisen throughout the *Google Search* investigation (including issues on which a decision has not yet been adopted), will examine how Article 102 TFEU may be applied to digital intermediaries that engage in conduct introducing artificial forms of information scarcity.

47. The main theme that cuts across Chapters 4 to 6 is control over an asset or factor that may somehow affect competition and pluralism in the affected markets. For example, in broadcasting, it is control over premium content or infrastructure; in publishing, it is control over price; and in online search and news aggregation, it is control over a vastly popular online platform through which users access information.

48. A few final remarks on the topics that will be covered: naturally, in addition to the business strategies/practices, pricing models, and revenue mechanisms described above, traditional and new media entities may affect competition and media pluralism in an abundance of ways which, given the complexity of the relevant markets (and the structures of the companies operating therein), are difficult – if not impossible – to study in an exhaustive manner. However, this study aspires to expose the reader to the main issues that have arisen thus far in competition cases concerning the most widely used media and to explore a variety of 'traditional' and 'new' concerns over pluralism that can be addressed under EU competition law. Moreover, the term 'EU competition law' that is used throughout this book refers to EU antitrust and merger control. In other words, the present study does not deal with State aids granted to the media sector. This approach is not meant to underestimate the contribution of public funding to promoting media pluralism nor to minimize the Commission's efforts to ensure that relevant schemes observe certain basic principles, including, especially, independent supervision of the undertaking

193 ibid.

194 *Google Search* (Case AT.39740) Commission decision of 27 June 2017 relating to proceedings under Article 102 TFEU and Article 54 of the EEA Agreement C (2017) 4444 final

in receipt of public money and proportionality of funding.[195] There are two reasons why State aid control does not serve the purposes of this study. First, contrary to antitrust and merger control,[196] the Commission's competence in the field of State aids is limited. This is because, on the basis of the principle of subsidiarity, EU Member States get to decide whether public funding is necessary to promote media pluralism and how the relevant scheme must be designed in order to deliver a pluralistic outcome. As opposed to in antitrust and merger control, where the Commission exercises full control over the shape of the obligations imposed on the undertakings concerned, in State aid control[197] it is restricted to ensuring that the measure under scrutiny does not allow the beneficiary of aid to misuse the public funds it receives. Put differently, given Member States' discretion to define the obligations that an undertaking in receipt of public money must fulfil in order to enhance media pluralism,[198] an evaluation of whether the aid measures concerned indeed achieve that objective must primarily be based on how the *national* laws establishing these measures are formulated and implemented. The focus of this study is on *Union* law. Moreover, and related to the competence restrictions discussed above, the standards that are used in conducting the relevant assessments vary. Consider the example of an assessment involving a broadcaster. On the one hand, if that broadcaster concluded an anti-competitive agreement with another entity, the restrictions to competition that the agreement in question would introduce would primarily be assessed against efficiencies and consumer welfare. On the other hand, in State aid control, the harm to competition is balanced against social welfare,[199] including equity,

195 See Communication on the application of State aid rules to public service broadcasting (the Broadcasting Communication) [2009] OJ C 257/1, paragraphs 50 *et seq.* and 70 *et seq.*

196 Compare, for instance, Article 3(1)(b) TFEU with Article 106(2) TFEU

197 For example, Lefever examines the effects of State aid decisions on the exercise of the right to information on sports competitions. See *supra n.* 133, 172–177. Donders looks into whether and, if so, to what extent State aid control obstructs the realization of the public broadcasting project and is driven by a one-size-fits-all approach towards national policies that are heterogeneous. See Donders, K. (2011). *Public Service Media and Policy in Europe*. London: Palgrave Macmillan. Other studies with a different focus include: Donders, K. and Hallvard Moe (eds.) (2011). *Exporting the Public Value Test. The regulation of public broadcasters' new media services across Europe*. Göteborg: Nordicom; Donders, K. (2009). *State Aid and Public Service Broadcasting. How Future Proof is the Remit of Public Broadcasting Organizations?* In Pauwels, C., Harri Kalimo, Karen Donders and Ben Van Rompuy (eds.), *Rethinking European Media and Communications Policy*. Brussels: VUB Press, 206; Schulz, W. (2009). *The Legal Framework for Public Service Broadcasting in Germany: Procrustean Bed or Hammock?* Journal of Media Law 1(2), 219–241, and Donders, K. (2011). *Superficial Harmonization Versus One-Size-Fits-All: The Implementation of European State Aid Principles in Flanders and the Netherlands*. Journal of Media Law 3(2), 237–261

198 See, for instance, Protocol No. 29 on the System of Public Broadcasting in the Member States [2010] OJ C 83/312, which reads as follows: 'The High Contracting Parties, considering that the system of public broadcasting in the Member States is directly related to the democratic, social and cultural needs of each society and to the need to preserve media pluralism, have agreed upon the following interpretive provisions, which shall be annexed to the Treaty on European Union and to the Treaty on the Functioning of the European Union: *The provisions of the Treaties shall be without prejudice to the competence of Member States to provide for the funding of public service broadcasting* and in so far as such funding is granted to broadcasting organizations for the fulfillment of the *public service remit as conferred, defined and organized by each Member State*, and in so far as such funding does not affect trading conditions and competition in the Union to an extent which would be contrary to the common interest, while the realization of the remit of that public service shall be taken into account' [emphasis added]

199 See Commission (not dated). *Common Principles for an Economic Assessment of the Compatibility of*

considerations[200] and it is established case law that the Commission may not carry out efficiency assessments when deciding whether aid schemes in support of public service broadcasters, which have traditionally been regarded as a vehicle for media pluralism, are compatible with the common market.[201] That is to say, in the case of State aid control, the Treaty leaves considerable room for non-economic concerns to be considered; to the extent that public funding is not 'disproportionate', some harm to competitors is tolerated to advance media pluralism. The key question that the present study seeks to answer, however, is whether media pluralism can be protected when the Treaty leaves no room for non-economic goals to supersede competition considerations.

State Aid Under Article 87(3). <http://ec.europa.eu/competition/state_aid/reform/economic_assessment_en.pdf>

200 For example, in the case of public service media, those equity objectives consist of, e.g. offering society (including disadvantaged groups such as low-income citizens who may not be able to afford TV subscriptions) access to information, providing content that addresses the needs of cultural and linguistic minorities, etc. These objectives are determined by each Member State individually. For more information regarding how a selected set of Member States defined the equity objectives public broadcasters are required to attain see, for instance, Katsirea, I. (2008). *Public Broadcasting and European Law: A Comparative Examination of Public Service Obligations in Six Member* States. Alphen aan den Rijn: Kluwer Law International

201 See GCEU, Joined Cases T-568/08 and T-573/08 *Métropole télévision (M6) and Télévision française 1 SA (TF1)* [2010] ECR II-3397, paragraph 141 and Case T-275/11 *Télévision française 1 (TF1) v European Commission* (not yet reported), paragraphs 130, 133–4 and 138

CHAPTER 2

MEDIA PLURALISM AND THE MYTH OF COMMUNICATION ABUNDANCE

1. Introduction

49. In the midst of the changes brought about by digital technologies, policymakers from across Europe have started rethinking the status of media pluralism as a fundamental communications policy principle. More particularly, as already mentioned in Chapter 1, the argument that media pluralism is to a large extent a natural outcome of the digital revolution is gaining ground. This argument is based on the following two assumptions that are increasingly being reflected in media policies. First, digital technologies are believed to have remedied concerns relating to concentration of ownership. The fear that significant opinion-forming power may end up in the hands of a few is said to have diminished on the grounds that currently, alongside well-established media organizations, there are many other sources providing information, as well as several platforms through which marginalized viewpoints, which would not have found their way to audiences in an analogue environment, may reach the public. Second, citizens are believed to use the media in ways that strengthen citizenship. The abundance of information they can now access, the control they can exercise over content, and the ability to create and distribute content on matters of common concern are considered to create ideal conditions for exposure to diverse ideas and active participation in public discourse.

50. The objective of this Chapter is three-fold. First, to explain the approach of the present study to media pluralism as a normative concept in the light of the aforementioned developments (Part 2). The aim is not to propose a new legal definition, but to illustrate that the evolution of communication

technologies and markets has had implications for media pluralism as a policy goal. Second, to discuss whether policy intervention to protect and promote media pluralism is still needed by examining whether the above two assumptions, on which modern media policymaking is being built, are well-grounded. For that purpose, I shall analyze the conditions that reflect the current state of European media markets and inquire whether these assumptions are supported by empirical evidence. More particularly, Part 3 examines whether concerns regarding concentration of ownership have indeed subsided, whereas Part 4 focuses on the demand side, discussing habits that have emerged with the advent of new media. Third, through the study of (old and new) supply and consumption patterns and sector-specific economics, to lay the groundwork for subsequent Chapters, which will discuss the characteristics of traditional and new media markets that the Commission must take into consideration when it is called upon to assess unilateral conduct, mergers, or anti-competitive agreements.

2. The legal definition of media pluralism: is it still about what the market has to offer?

51. Media pluralism is widely perceived as a prerequisite for democracy, *inter alia*, on the grounds that access to a broad range of information strengthens citizenship and advances social cohesion. Yet, in spite of the broad respect it generates for these merits, a definition of media pluralism does not exist in international statutory law.[202] The lack of a definition of media pluralism in international legal texts is largely attributed to the fact that this value has been thought to be better conceptualized by reference to the specific political, social, cultural and economic conditions of a given State on the basis of a number of criteria, such as the presence of linguistic and/or ethnic minorities[203] and policy approaches to the media industry. As any description of media pluralism involves choices about the types of content that should be provided to audiences, as well as choices about the parameters that are appropriate for assessing whether a media landscape is pluralistic or not, achieving 'a meeting of minds' when drafting an international legal document that touches upon this issue has proven to be an insurmountable goal.[204] With regard to the European Union, several legal texts,

202 Valcke, P. (2011). *Looking For the User in Media Pluralism Regulation: Unraveling the Traditional Diversity Chain and Recent Trends of User Empowerment in European Media Regulation*. Journal of Information Policy 1, 288. <http://jip.vmhost.psu.edu/ojs/index.php/jip/article/view/31>

203 For instance, the preservation of linguistic diversity would not play a major role in the Netherlands, a linguistically homogeneous country, as opposed to Belgium, which has three official languages.

204 Karpinnen, K. (2007). *Making a difference to media pluralism. A critique of the pluralistic consensus in European media policy*. In Cammaerts, B. and Nico Carpentier (eds.). *Reclaiming the Media*. Bristol: Intellect Books, 21

including primary EU law such as the Charter of Fundamental Rights[205] and the Amsterdam Protocol on Public Service Broadcasting,[206] refer to media pluralism. These texts, however, do not go so far as to describe its nature, scope or meaning.[207] In addition to the heterogeneity characterizing the media landscapes of the various Member States,[208] this definitional lacuna relates to the EU's competence limitations in the field of media, which were extensively discussed in Chapter 1. Therefore, Member States have been free to give form to this value in accordance with national traditions and the peculiarities of domestic media markets. However, a description of media pluralism is not to be found in national law either. For example, while throughout their case law national constitutional courts have established that media pluralism is a value inherently related to the exercise of freedom of expression and, as such, a necessary condition for a well-functioning democratic society, they have refrained from providing a precise definition of the term.[209] National legislators from across Europe have adopted the same approach.[210]

52. Nonetheless, descriptions of media pluralism can be found in numerous policy texts.[211] Most comprehensively, the concept of media pluralism has been elaborated by the Council of Europe (CoE) and its advisory committees.[212] Among other documents of a non-legally binding character, the Explanatory

205 Charter of Fundamental Rights of the European Union [2000] C 364/1, Article 11. The provision reads as follows: '1. Everyone has the right to freedom of expression. This right shall include freedom to hold opinions and to receive and impart information and ideas without interference by public authority and regardless of frontiers. 2. The freedom and *pluralism of the media shall be respected*' [emphasis added]

206 Protocol No. 29 on the System of Public Broadcasting in the Member States [2010] OJ C 83/312, which reads as follows: 'The High Contracting Parties, considering that *the system of public broadcasting in the Member States is directly related to the democratic, social and cultural needs of each society and to the need to preserve media pluralism*, have agreed upon the following interpretive provisions, which shall be annexed to the Treaty on European Union and to the Treaty on the Functioning of the European Union: The provisions of the Treaties shall be without prejudice to the competence of Member States to provide for the funding of public service broadcasting and in so far as such funding is granted to broadcasting organizations for the fulfillment of the public service remit as conferred, defined and organized by each Member State, and in so far as such funding does not affect trading conditions and competition in the Union to an extent which would be contrary to the common interest, while the realization of the remit of that public service shall be taken into account' [emphasis added]

207 Valcke (2011), *supra* n. 1. On secondary EU law which refers to media pluralism see, for instance, Audiovisual Media Services Directive [2010] OJ L332/27, Recitals 8, 12, 34, 48 and 94; Communication on the application of State aid rules to public service broadcasting (the Broadcasting Communication) [2009] OJ C 257/1, paragraphs 2, 11, 14–16 and 47; and Council Regulation (EC) No. 139/2004 of 20 January 2004 on the control of concentrations between undertakings (the EC Merger Regulation) [2004] OJ L24/1, Article 21(4)

208 Commission (2009). *Independent Study on Indicators for Media Pluralism in the Member States – Towards a Risk-based Approach*, 1. <http://ec.europa.eu/information_society/media_taskforce/doc/pluralism/pfr_report.pdf>

209 Valcke (2011), *supra* n. 1, 288. For more information about the relevant case law of national courts and the Council of Europe see references in ibid, fn. 2.

210 All Member States of the EU have adopted regulatory instruments that aim to safeguard media pluralism. In some cases, the constitution explicitly refers to media pluralism. Yet, to my knowledge, neither regulation nor the constitutions in question define media pluralism.

211 For an EU perspective see, for instance, Commission. *Pluralism and Media Concentration in the Internal Market – An Assessment of the Need for Community Action*. Green Paper COM (92) 480 final; and Commission. Staff Working Document on Media Pluralism in the Member States of the EU SEC (2007) 32

212 Valcke (2011), *supra* n. 1, 288 referring to Klimkiewicz, B. (2009). *Is the Clash of Rationalities Leading Nowhere? Media Pluralism in European Regulatory Policies*. In Czepek, A., Melanie Hellwig, and Eva Nowak, *Press Freedom and Pluralism in Europe: Concepts and Conditions*. Bristol: Intellect Books, 46

Memorandum of Recommendation No. R (99)1 on Measures to Promote Media Pluralism, which was adopted by the CoE's Committee of Ministers in 1999, refers to media pluralism as:

> a *diversity of media supply*, reflected, for example, in the existence of a plurality of independent and autonomous media (generally called structural pluralism) as well as a *diversity of media types and contents (views and opinions)* made available to the public. [emphasis added][213]

53. The Memorandum correctly makes a distinction between diversity of media supply and diversity of media types and contents. This is because in media markets the former does not automatically guarantee the latter.[214] In other words, even if there are many structurally separated media organizations operating in a given market, this does not necessarily mean that these organizations will ensure that audience members will have access to diverse ideas and/or that the needs of niche audiences will be catered to. One example that illustrates why diversity of supply should not be relied upon to achieve diversity of contents and types is commercial free-to-air TV, which is mainly funded by advertisers. As free-to-air broadcasters depend on ad revenues, they usually opt for distributing programs that appeal to the masses with a view to attracting advertisers.[215] This means that they tend to provide programming similar to that which has already proven successful for a competitor and/or to recycle programming which has received high audience ratings in the past. In other words, commercial free-to-air broadcasters are usually reluctant to offer original programming with highly uncertain demand or programming which serves the needs of cultural or linguistic minorities and which attracts too small an audience to generate cost recovery revenues. As a result, companies in a competitive broadcasting market may be inclined to fill the same middle ground,[216] in which case an anomaly may arise whereby a considerable number of broadcasters does not lead to a varied offer but rather to program duplication.[217] Diversity of supply is therefore distinguished from diversity of type and content because the relationship between the number of media organizations active in a given market and the range of content that is made available to consumers is not necessarily causal.[218]

213 Explanatory Memorandum to Recommendation No. R (99) 1 on Measures to Promote Media Pluralism. <https://wcd.coe.int/ViewDoc.jsp?Ref=ExpRec(99)1&Language=lanEnglish&Ver=original&Site=CM&BackColorInternet=C3C3C3&BackColorIntranet=EDB021&BackColorLogged=F5D383>

214 Empirical research has not provided definitive evidence on the relationship between supply and content diversity. However, traditional media regulation in support of media pluralism has used supply diversity-related measures as a proxy for content diversity. For more information about this issue see, for instance, Valcke (2011), *supra* n. 1, 294–5 and Napoli, P. M. (1999). *Deconstructing the Diversity Principle*, Journal of Communication 49(4), 7–34

215 Ariño, M. (2005). *Regulation and Competition in European Digital Broadcasting – A study of pluralism through access*. PhD thesis. Florence: European University Institute, 58

216 Prosser, T. (2005). *The Limits of Competition Law: Markets and Public Services*. Oxford: OUP, 209

217 Craufurd-Smith, R. (2004). *Rethinking European Union competence in the field of media ownership: The internal market, fundamental rights and European citizenship*. European Law Review 29(5), 653

218 On the relationship between supply and content diversity see Part 3.1.

54. The dichotomy between supply and content diversity has not only been the epicenter of the relevant standard-setting work of the CoE:[219] policymakers,[220] media regulators,[221] competition authorities[222] and constitutional courts[223] from across Europe have adopted the same distinction.

55. However, this definition of pluralism, albeit accommodating certain particularities of the media markets (see above example of how advertising affects the diversity of content broadcast), is incomplete because it only takes account of the supply side.[224] In other words, it is concerned with what media organizations provide, but not with what individuals really read and watch. Yet, if one accepts that the ultimate goal of any policy intervention to support media pluralism is at least[225] 'this exposure to diverse ideas, sources, and perspectives that facilitates the well-informed decision-making that is central to the democratic notion of effective self-governance',[226] media pluralism cannot be properly conceptualized without regard to the amount and type of content that audiences access and engage with. This is simply because the diversity of sources and content actually consumed, also referred to as *exposure* or *use diversity*, may be different from the diversity of sources and

219 See, for instance, CoE. Recommendation No. R (99) 1 of the Committee of Ministers to Member States on Measures to Promote Media Pluralism; Recommendation No. R (2000) 23 on the independence and functions of regulatory authorities for the broadcasting sector and its Explanatory Memorandum, Pluralism in the multi-channel market: suggestions for regulatory scrutiny (MM-S-PL(1999) 012def); and Recommendation No. R (96) 10 on the guarantee of the independence of public service broadcasting and its Explanatory Memorandum; and Recommendation No. R (94) 13 of the Committee of Ministers to Member States on measures to promote media transparency

220 This distinction has influenced media policy and law-making in, for instance, Germany, Greece, Denmark, and Belgium. See German Interstate Broadcasting Treaty (Rundfunkstaatsvertrag), Articles 25(1) and 26(2); ELIAMEP (2010). *MEDIADEM background information report on media policies and regulatory practices in a selected set of European countries, the European Union and the Council of Europe: the case of Greece*, 23; Greek Law 3592/2007 on media concentrations and licensing rules applicable to media organizations, Article 3(3); ELIAMEP (2010). *MEDIADEM background information report on media policies and regulatory practices in a selected set of European countries, the European Union and the Council of Europe: the case of Denmark*, 18 and 20; ELIAMEP (2011). *MEDIADEM Case study report: Does media policy promote media freedom and independence? The case of Belgium*, 22 *et seq*. On a supranational level, see, for instance, Commission. Staff Working Document on Media Pluralism in the Member States of the EU SEC (2007) 32, 5

221 See, for instance, Ofcom (2010b). *Report on public interest test on the proposed acquisition of British Sky Broadcasting Group plc by News Corporation*, paragraph 1.18. <http://www.culture.gov.uk/images/publications/OfcomPITReport_NewsCorp-BSkyB_31DEC2010.pdf>

222 See, for instance, UK Competition Commission (2007). *Report on the Acquisition by BSkyB plc of 17.9% of the shares in ITV Plc sent to Secretary of State (BERR) of 14 December 2007*, paragraph 30

223 For a discussion of the relevant case law in a selected set of EU countries (France, Italy, Germany) see, for instance, Valcke, P. (2004), *Digitale Diversiteit: Convergentie van Media-, Telecommunicatie- en Mededingingsrecht (Digital Diversity – Convergence of Media, Telecommunications and Competition Law)*. Brussels: Larcier, 127–148

224 Klimkiewicz (2009), *supra* n. 11, 46

225 Helberger notes that policy intervention in support of media pluralism may go 'beyond facilitating autonomous choices', in which case an additional role for media regulation 'would be to guide users in their choices'. On the different conceptions of exposure diversity as a policy goal see Helberger, N. (2011). *Diversity Label: Exploring the Potential and Limits of a Transparency Approach to Media Diversity*. Journal of Information Policy 1, 345 *et seq*.

226 Napoli, P. (2001, October). *Diversity and Localism: A Policy Analysis Perspective*. Paper presented at an FCC Roundtable on Media Ownership, 4 <http://transition.fcc.gov/ownership/roundtable_docs/napoli-stmt.pdf>

content that is made available in the market.[227] In fact, empirical studies show that the diversity provided does not coincide with the diversity consumed.[228]

56. The integration of exposure diversity considerations in media policies has always been important. As an economic policymaker needs to know how consumers react to price changes, a communications policymaker needs to know how audiences react to changes in their media system.[229] If not, there is the risk that a given regulatory instrument that seeks to safeguard (or otherwise affects) media pluralism is based upon false assumptions. In spite of the above, exposure diversity has largely been ignored thus far. This is so mainly for two reasons. First, traditional media policymaking has been based on the passive consumption theory, according to which audiences are powerless to resist the persuasive messages that the media carries.[230] Second, in the past, due to high entry barriers relating to, *inter alia*, spectrum shortages and large upfront investments, the sources and content that found their way to the audiences were scarce.[231] Hence, individuals were expected to consume most of what was offered.[232]

57. However, exposure diversity can no longer be marginalized. As a result of technological developments, there exist plenty of sources and content which individuals may now access, including pay-per-view services, blogs, wikis and online newspapers that operate alongside well-established media organizations. It is therefore becoming increasingly important to determine how audience members behave in an environment where content and sources are abundant. For example, do consumers continue to concentrate around a few familiar brands or do they actively look for diverse content? Has consumption of news content increased? If so, do new information sources play an important role in the process of public opinion formation? In addition, digital technologies allow citizens to comment on the content provided by mainstream media and/or establish their own outlets. Do audience members use the media in order to actively engage in public discourse? If citizens indeed search for diverse information, consult with several sources and produce and distribute content on matters of common concern, then regulating the media to guarantee source and content diversity would not seem to be as important as it once was.

---

227 ibid, 3–4

228 See, for instance, Cooper, C. and Tang Tang (2009). *Predicting Audience Exposure to Television in Today's Media Environment: An Empirical Integration of Active-Audience and Structural Theories*. Journal of Broadcasting & Electronic Media 53(3), 400–418; Webster, J. G. (2005). *Beneath the Veneer of Fragmentation: Television Audience Polarization in a Multi-Channel World*. Journal of Communication 55(2), 366–382, and Prior, M. (2005). *News vs. Entertainment: How Increasing Media Choice Widens the Gap in Political Knowledge and Turnout*. American Journal of Political Science 49(3), 577–592

229 Napoli (2001), *supra* n. 25, 4

230 Valcke (2011), *supra* n. 1, 304

231 Helberger, N. (2011). *Media Diversity from the User's Perspective: An Introduction*. Journal of Information Policy 1, 242

232 Goodman, E. (2004). *Media Policy Out of the Box: Content Abundance, Attention Scarcity, and the Failures of Digital Markets*. Berkeley Technology Law Journal 19, 1457

58. There is evidence that policymakers are increasingly starting to consider exposure diversity. For example, in its Green Paper on Pluralism and Media Concentration of 1992, the European Commission (the Commission), clearly focusing on the supply side, noted that diversity of information can be assessed 'according to the *editorial content* of the broadcasts or the press, according to the *number of channels* or titles, and according to the *number of* media controllers or *owners*' [emphasis added].[233] However, in its Staff Working Document on Media Pluralism in the Member States of the EU, published in 2007, the Commission adopted a broader approach that arguably encompasses demand-side considerations. The document lays down that 'although pluralism of ownership is important, it is a necessary but not sufficient condition for ensuring media pluralism. ... *Ensuring media pluralism*, in our understanding, implies *all measures that ensure citizens' access* to a variety of information sources, opinion, voices, etc. in order to form their opinion' [emphasis added].[234] In a similar vein, in its Communication on Tackling Online Disinformation that was published in 2018, the Commission notes that one of the overarching principles that must guide initiatives seeking to address the spread of fake news online is the promotion of diversity of information through, *inter alia*, support for high quality journalism 'in order to enable citizens to make informed decisions based on critical thinking'.[235]

59. Similar remarks can be made with respect to the approach followed by national policymakers. For example, in its 2010 report on the status of the Dutch media, media regulator Commissariaat voor de media underlined that:

233 Commission. Staff Working Document on Media Pluralism in the Member States of the EU SEC (2007) 32, 19

234 ibid, 5. Similar to the Staff Working Document, the Independent Study that followed its publication noted that pluralism is a multi-layered concept encompassing 'the *diversity of media supply, use and distribution*, in relation to 1) ownership and control, 2) media types and genres, 3) political viewpoints, 4) cultural expressions and 5) local and regional interests' [emphasis added]. Examples of exposure diversity-related indicators that the Independent Study identified include the range of citizens and citizens' groups using online media for posting content relevant for political debate, and the level of influence on political and public debate by bloggers. See Commission (2009). *supra* n. 7, 5 and 106

235 Communication from the Commission to the European Parliament, the Council, the European Economic and Social Committee and the Committee of the Regions on Tackling Online Disinformation: a European approach COM(2018) 236 final, 6. <https://ec.europa.eu/digital-single-market/en/news/communication-tackling-online-disinformation-european-approach> In addition to the aforementioned Communications, a number of EU policy texts illustrate the shift to an increasing consideration of exposure diversity. For example, one of the recommendations made in a study which was commissioned by the European Parliament in order to strengthen media pluralism is the use of preventive policy instruments in the form of educational projects on the grounds that '*conscious decisions concerning content selection need to be made by the users in order to achieve exposure to plural media content*'. Bàrd, P. and Judit Bayer (2016). Study for the LIBE Committee. *A comparative analysis of media freedom and pluralism in the EU Member States*, 15. <http://www.europarl.europa.eu/RegData/etudes/STUD/2016/571376/IPOL_STU(2016)571376_EN.pdf> See also European Parliament Resolution of 3 May 2018 on media pluralism and media freedom in the European Union (2017/2209(INI)), paragraphs 32 and 36. <http://www.europarl.europa.eu/sides/getDoc.do?pubRef=-//EP//TEXT+TA+P8-TA-2018-0204+0+DOC+XML+V0//EN>

> [a]lthough the news market share per independent supplier is considered one of the most important indicators of opinion power ... another indicator is the number of news sources consumers consult. Even though there is an incredible amount of information available, *actual exposure to a wide range of sources is not guaranteed*' [emphasis added].

60. The report concludes that 'media are in transition ... and *exposure diversity should also be measured for the news market*' [emphasis added].[236]

61. This change of direction is welcomed because it (at least) seeks to ensure that media pluralism as a normative concept is adapted to the conditions that characterize the modern media ecosystem (whether the mere ability to get exposed to various sources and content has been used to justify (de-)regulatory reforms that were not well-grounded will be discussed in more detail below). Similarly, the present study, conducted in the midst of changes brought about by digitization, acknowledges the importance of taking account of all three components, that is, diversity of suppliers, diversity of content and type, and diversity of exposure.[237]

62. These three components have been defined and further broken down into subcomponents by Napoli and Valcke. More particularly, drawing on the goals that have been (or should be) pursued by the competent policymaker in the US, Napoli distinguishes between source, content and exposure diversity, and sub-categorizes each of these three dimensions as follows:

236 Commissariaat voor de Media (2011). *MEDIAMONITOR – The Dutch Media in 2010*, 90–91. <https://www.mediamonitor.nl/wp-content/uploads/2013/08/Mediamonitor-The-Dutch-media-in-20101.pdf>. See also Ofcom (2012). *Measuring Media Plurality*, paragraph 1.3, where Ofcom defines pluralism as 'a) ensuring there is a *diversity of viewpoints available and consumed* across and within media enterprises and b) preventing any one media owner or voice having too much influence over public opinion and the political agenda' [emphasis added]. Ofcom then referred to several parameters that would characterize an ideal plural outcome, including a variety of independent news media voices across all platforms *and* active multisourcing, that is, the consumption of a range of different news sources (see paragraph 3.22)

237 Recent studies that explore the concept of media pluralism or how to measure it include Raeijmaekers, D. and Pieter Maeseele (2015). *Media pluralism and democracy: what's in a name?* Media, Culture and Society 37(7), 1042–1059; Karpinnen, K. (2015). *The Limits of Empirical Indicators: Media Pluralism as an Essentially Contested Concept*. In Valcke, P., Miklós Sükösd and Robert G. Picard. *Media Pluralism and Diversity. Concepts, Risks and Global Trends*. London: Palgrave Macmillan, 287–296; Jakubowicz, K. (2015). *New Media Ecology: Reconceptualizing Media Pluralism*. In Valcke, Sükösd and Picard. *Media Pluralism and Diversity. Concepts, Risks and Global Trends*, 23–53; Napoli, P. (2015). *Assessing Media Diversity in the U.S.: A Comparative Analysis of the FCC's Diversity Index and the EU's Media Pluralism Monitor*. In Valcke, Sükösd and Picard. *Media Pluralism and Diversity. Concepts, Risks and Global Trends*, 141–151; Helberger, N. (2015). *Media Pluralism Policies from the User Perspective*. In Valcke, Sükösd and Picard. *Media Pluralism and Diversity. Concepts, Risks and Global Trends*, 325–340; and Ceron, A. and Sergio Splendore (2016). *From contents to comments: Social TV and perceived pluralism in political talk shows*. New Media and Society 20(2), 659–675

Source Diversity	Content Diversity	Exposure Diversity
1. Ownership a. Programming b. Outlet	1. Format/Program Type	1. Horizontal
2. Workforce	2. Demographic	2. Vertical
	3. Idea/Viewpoint	

Source: Napoli (2001:2), Figure 1

63. Napoli's model builds upon and extends the diversity framework that has traditionally been employed by the US media regulator, the Federal Communications Commission.[238] The concept of source diversity is defined in terms of both outlet *and* content ownership.[239] Indeed, outlet and content ownership do not necessarily coincide. For example, a TV channel may choose to distribute content the broadcast rights to which it purchased from a film studio. Workforce diversity is defined in terms of the gender and ethnic composition of a media outlet's workforce.[240] The second component, content diversity, is defined in terms of diversity of ideas/viewpoints, which refers to the diversity of political, social and cultural perspectives represented within the media, diversity of programs/types (e.g. drama, comedies, news programs, talk shows, etc.),[241] and demographic diversity, which refers to the gender and ethnic composition of those represented in media content.[242] Finally, horizontal exposure diversity refers to the distribution of viewers/readers/users across all available content options, whereas vertical exposure diversity refers to the diversity of content consumption within individual audience members.[243]

64. Valcke identifies the same components, but makes a further distinction between a quantitative and qualitative sub-component in each of these three elements.[244] According to Valcke, quantitative refers to a simply numerical assessment of diversity whereas qualitative diversity of suppliers, product and use is determined by parameters such as religion, ethnicity or program type.[245] Listed below are some examples of how Valcke sub-categorizes each component:

---

238 Napoli (2001), *supra* n. 25, 3

239 ibid.

240 ibid, 4. See also Napoli, P. (2011). *Exposure Diversity Reconsidered*. Journal of Information Policy 1, 247

241 Napoli (1999), *supra* n. 13, 18 and 22

242 ibid.

243 ibid, 5

244 Valcke (2011), *supra* n. 1, 291. Note that Valcke refers to *source diversity*, *supplier diversity*, and *provider diversity* interchangeably. She does the same with the notions of *content diversity* and *product diversity* on the one hand, and *exposure diversity* and *use diversity* on the other.

245 ibid.

Source/Supplier/ Provider Diversity	Product/Content Diversity	Exposure/Use Diversity
Quantitative: How many independent owners are active in a given market?	Quantitative: How many book titles are available in the market?	Quantitative: How many news sources do online users consult on a daily basis?
Qualitative: Are politicians prevented from owning media organizations?	Qualitative: Does TV programming serve the needs of linguistic minorities?	Qualitative: Can online users critically evaluate media content?

65. The analysis conducted throughout this book will be guided by Valcke's model for two reasons. First, Valcke's distinction is particularly useful for the purposes of this study because one of the main arguments put forward herein is that EU competition law, as applied to media markets, must be concerned with quantitative *and* qualitative considerations. As a result, Valcke's model may capture parameters which are arguably relevant to a competition analysis. Take a merger between two competing free-to-air generalist TV channels, by way of example. We assume that, post-merger, both channels continue to operate *and* that their programming remains the same. However, the merging firms decide to increase the advertising/content ratio in their news programs. For the avoidance of confusion, we assume that, following this change, the amount of time devoted to different viewpoints post-merger is redistributed proportionately.[246] Based on Napoli's categorization and given that program/ format types and viewpoint representation remain essentially unchanged, the merger does not appear to adversely affect content diversity. However, if the amount of time devoted to the transmission of advertisements is a quality indicator that determines demand-side substitutability, the increase in the advertising/content ratio could, based on Valcke's distinction, be regarded as a decrease in qualitative content diversity. Second, Valcke's categorization is based on policies that were developed by the Member States of the EU. As a result, it takes account of policies, such as fixed book pricing mechanisms, which have not played an important normative role in the US system. Given the focus of this study on EU competition law, the reader will be able to better understand where the Commission positions itself in respect of such policies.

66. Prior to delving into the opportunities for and challenges facing media pluralism in the current media landscape, a note to the reader regarding the types of media content that will be covered throughout this book. Broadly speaking, there are two approaches to measuring media pluralism. The first takes

246 For example, before the merger, left wing politicians would get a 5-minute coverage whereas right-wing politicians would get a 10-minute coverage. Post-merger, leftwing politicians get a 2.5-minute coverage whereas right-wing politicians a 5-minute coverage.

account of all media content, that is, it does not attempt to measure whether the outcome is pluralistic by reference to a specific genre.[247] The second focuses on news mainly on the grounds that '[t]he unrestricted dissemination of a diverse range of information, opinions and arguments about the day's news and events provides the greatest potential to inform citizens and ensure an effective democratic process.'[248] The present study acknowledges that, when we refer to media pluralism as a prerequisite for a socially cohesive, democratic society, news content is perhaps more relevant than other content, e.g. a US comedy series. For this reason, it intends to study a number of issues that are relevant to news markets, including resale price maintenance for the sale of print newspapers, and online agency agreements for the sale of news subscriptions. However, the analysis will not be restricted to news markets for the following two reasons. First, as already discussed in Chapter 1, the purpose of this study is to explore how far a proper application of the EU competition rules can go to safeguard media pluralism. Were we to limit our analysis to cases that deal exclusively with news provision, we would fall short of grasping in its full extent the impact that EU competition enforcement has had on media markets, including news markets. For example, while the Commission may not have scrutinized mergers between thematic news channels, it examined a vast number of mergers involving generalist free-to-air channels that provide news as well as pay-TV operators that provide a bouquet of channels devoted to the analysis of current affairs. Second, while undoubtedly justifiable from a practical perspective (basing a media pluralism measurement on news content *only* is more manageable than putting all media content into the mix),[249] focusing on news may run the risk of ignoring content that fulfills the democratic functions the media is expected to perform. For example, is 'infotainment' more relevant to the democratic process in a given State than a documentary about indigenous peoples residing in the territory of the State in question?[250]

67. Having explained what my approach to media pluralism as a normative concept is, I will now examine whether policy intervention to support this value is still needed.

247 Ofcom (2012), *supra* n. 35, 9

248 ibid, 9–10

249 ibid. See also Centre for Media Pluralism and Media Freedom (2013). *European Union Competencies in Respect of Media Pluralism and Media Freedom*, 13. <http://cadmus.eui.eu/bitstream/handle/1814/26056/RSCAS_PP_2013_01.pdf?sequence=1&isAllowed=y>

250 See Craufurd-Smith, R. and Damian Tambini (2012). *Measuring Media Plurality in the United Kingdom: Policy Choices and Regulatory Challenges*. Journal of Media Law 4(1), 54: 'although news is centrally important for the democratic process and plays a key role in opinion formation, other genres also provide information and can be socially and culturally influential'

3. Assumption no. 1: Media concentration is no longer a problem – the market will provide

68. Media policymakers and commentators alike are increasingly putting forward the argument that the proliferation of sources and content that citizens can now access and engage with resolves the problems originating from the concentration of ownership that was pervasive in the traditional media landscape. With the amount of information that citizens now have at their fingertips, they say, rules aimed at addressing concentration of ownership are becoming obsolete. This view is progressively being integrated in media regulation, the most blatant example being the trend towards relaxation (or abolition) of ownership restrictions that has emerged over the past few years. This section discusses whether digital technologies have indeed rendered concerns about media concentration superfluous. I first explain the economic and political reasons why traditional media markets in Europe are concentrated, as well as the implications of concentration for pluralism. After introducing the reader to the main issues related to concentration of ownership, I inquire whether a decline of 'old gatekeepers', such as TV broadcasters and newspapers, has indeed taken place and if not, whether communicative abundance in the digital environment ensures a balance of opinion-forming power.

3.1 Why are traditional media markets in Europe concentrated?

69. Traditional media markets have a natural tendency to concentration. This has been confirmed by empirical studies that have examined the structure of the media industry in Europe and beyond.[251]

---

251 See, for instance, Brogi E., Konstantina Bania, Iva Nenadic, Alina Ostling and Pier Luigi Parcu (2017). *Monitoring Media Pluralism in Europe: Application of the Media Pluralism Monitor 2016 in the European Union, Montenegro and Turkey*, 27. <http://cadmus.eui.eu/bitstream/handle/1814/46786/CMPF-MPM_PolicyReport2017.pdf?sequence=1&isAllowed=y>; Autorità per le Garanzie nelle Comunicazioni (2012). *Indagine conoscitiva sul settore della raccolta pubblicitaria* (Allegato A alla Delibera 551/12/CONS). <http://www.agcom.it/documents/10179/1/document/bd184d98-cdcd-41e1-b141-9864dcfba8d6>; and Ward, D., Oliver Carsten Fueg and Alessandro D'Armo (2004). *Mapping Study of Media Concentration and Ownership in Ten European Countries*. <http://citeseerx.ist.psu.edu/viewdoc/download?doi=10.1.1.691.2674&rep=rep1&type=pdf>. In addition to the above, other studies that examine the phenomenon of media concentration include the following: Open Society Institute (2005). *Television across Europe – Monitoring Report*; Council of Europe (2002). *Media Diversity in Europe. Report prepared by the Advisory Panel to the CDMM on media concentrations, pluralism and diversity questions*. <https://rm.coe.int/CoERMPublicCommonSearchServices/DisplayDCTMContent?documentId=0900001680483b2c>; European Federation of Journalists (2005). *Media power in Europe: The big picture of ownership*. For the study of the phenomenon of media concentration in non-European markets see, for instance, Mastrini, G. and Martin Becerra (2011). *Estructura, concentración y transformaciones en los medios del Cono Sur latinoamericano*. Scientific Journal of Media Literacy 36, 51–59, and Noam, E. M. (2009). *Media ownership and concentration in America*. Oxford: OUP.

High Entry Barriers

70. The reasons why traditional media markets have high concentration ratios are manifold and strongly linked to an array of obstacles that make it difficult for new businesses to break through and compete effectively with well-established media organizations. Let's take television broadcasting by way of example: launching a TV channel requires compliance with sector-specific rules that determine the number of competitors in a given market. More particularly, television broadcasting has traditionally been subject to a licensing regime; due to spectrum shortages, governments across the EU have adopted laws regulating how much of the usable frequency shall be used for broadcasting as well as the broadcast power and locations of broadcast licenses.[252] Moreover, the new entrant needs to make an exceptionally large investment to set up operations and pay start-up losses.[253] This initial investment includes investment in premium content, that is, content that has the capacity to attract mass audiences (e.g. Hollywood blockbusters and major sporting competitions). Purchasing premium content is a daunting task and may amount to an entry barrier not only because the rights holders usually charge the licensees excessive prices, but also because the content in question is often controlled by already existing broadcasters through long-term exclusive agreements.[254] Competition authorities have attempted to address foreclosure concerns relating to exclusivity by imposing remedies, most notably by requiring the broadcasters involved in the transaction under scrutiny to reduce the duration and/or scope of exclusivity.[255] However, these attempts have largely failed to ensure that the market for the acquisition of premium content remains open to competition.[256] Consumers' unwillingness to bear high switching costs, that is, costs incurred as a result of changing suppliers, is another obstacle difficult to overcome. For example, in the case of satellite TV, if existing operators do not provide interoperability, consumers may refrain from changing to a new channel aggregator in order to avoid buying a new set-top box (the satellite receiver).[257] Switching costs can also be psychological; audience members

252 Communication on the application of State aid rules to public service broadcasting (the Broadcasting Communication) [2009] OJ C 257/1, paragraph 1; Picard, R. and Bum Soo Chon (2004). *Managing Competition Through Barriers to Entry and Channel Availability in the Changing Regulatory Environment*. The International Journal on Media Management 6(3), 168–170

253 See, for instance, Commission. Guidelines on the Application of Article 101(3) TFEU [2004] OJ C 101/08, paragraph 115 and Guidance on the Commission's enforcement priorities in applying Article 82 of the EC Treaty to abusive exclusionary conduct by dominant undertakings [2009] OJ C 45/2, paragraph 17

254 These agreements usually include holdback and pre-emption rights. For a detailed analysis of the entry barriers in the markets for acquisition of premium content rights see Geradin, D. (2005). *Access to content by new media platforms: A review of the competition law problems*. European Law Review 30(1), 68–94

255 See, for instance, *Joint Selling of the Media Rights of the FA Premier League* (*FAPL*) (Case COMP/C.2/38.173) [2006] OJ L176/104, paragraph 16 and *News Corp/Telepiù* (Case COMP/M.2876) [2004] OJ L110/73, paragraph 225

256 For a detailed analysis of access to premium content-related remedies see Chapter 3, Part 2.1. and Chapter 4, Parts 3.2. and 4.3.

257 OECD (2003a). *Policy Roundtable on Media Mergers*, 22

have long-established content consumption habits that are strongly associated with existing providers. For example, in the case of a broadcaster, this may be a popular soap opera or a trusted anchorman. In the case of newspapers, one of the main factors determining customer loyalty is family heritage.[258] This makes the creation of new viewing and reading patterns a slow process that may demand years of unprofitable wait.[259]

High production costs + low distribution costs = Economies of scale = Integration

71. In addition to the above, media content has high first-copy costs (e.g. labor costs, purchase of equipment, promotion and brand-development costs, etc.).[260] But, once the provider has produced the content, the incremental cost to an additional consumer is low.[261] For example, in the case of newspapers, costs incurred in news-gathering and the acquisition of a printing mechanism are necessary to create even one copy. However, the next copies may be produced at negligible marginal costs (the paper and ink to print an additional newspaper).[262] The fact that media content is very expensive to create but fairly cheap to deliver incentivizes media companies to expand into every possible distribution platform and succeeding and/or preceding levels of the supply chain[263] because it gives them the opportunity to exploit large economies of scale and scope. By enabling established firms to rationalize resources, reduce transaction costs and spread the related risks, large economies of scale and scope stimulate horizontal (expansion at the same level of the supply chain, e.g. television broadcaster merges with television broadcaster), vertical (expansion at different levels of the supply chain, e.g. television broadcaster acquires film studio) and/or diagonal (diversification into new business areas, e.g. newspaper diversifies into magazine publishing)[264] integration.

Two-sidedness

72. Another element that reinforces the tendency of traditional media markets to concentration is their two-sided nature. A two-sided market is generally

258 *News Corp/BSkyB* (Case COMP/M.5932) [2011] C 37/2, paragraph 231

259 Picard and Chon (2004), *supra* n. 51, 171

260 OECD (2003a), *supra* n. 56, 21. See also Goodman (2004), *supra* n. 31, 1433–4. For example, in 2009, the New York Times reportedly spent $63 million per quarter on raw materials and $148 million on wages and benefits. See Carlson, N. *Printing The NYT Costs Twice As Much As Sending Every Subscriber A Free Kindle*. 30 January 2009, Business Insider. <http://www.businessinsider.com/2009/1/printing-the-nyt-costs-twice-as-much-as-sending-every-subscriber-a-free-kindle?IR=T#ixzz3PXgJfaiY>

261 Goodman (2004), *supra* n. 31, 1432–1434

262 Norton, S. W. and Will Norton Jr. (1986). *Economies of Scale and the New Technology of Daily Newspapers: A Survivor Analysis*. University of Nebraska – Lincoln College of Journalism & Mass Communications, Working Paper 6

263 Doyle, G. (2002). *Media Ownership: The Economics and Politics of Convergence and Concentration in the UK and European Media*. London: Sage Publications, 4

264 ibid, 4–5

defined as a market in which '1) two sets of agents interact through an intermediary or platform, and 2) the decisions of each set of agents affect the outcomes of the other set of agents.'[265] Two-sided platforms arise in cases in which there are externalities and in which transaction costs do not allow the two sets of agents to address the externality directly.[266] The platform is the intermediary that solves the externality by minimizing the costs that a transaction between entities belonging to these groups of agents would entail.[267] The type of two-sided markets in which several types of traditional media are active is advertising-based media. Advertising-based media use the content they provide to attract audiences and then sell access to these audiences to advertisers.[268] Therefore, in order to generate profit, they must engage both the audience members (through the provision of attractive content) and the advertisers (through the provision of a large pool of audience members to whom advertisers can address their ads). The relationship between these two sets of agents is characterized by indirect network effects[269] that create what Caillaud and Jullien call 'a chicken and egg dynamic'.[270] This means in practice that the broadcaster with the largest audience base or the newspaper with the highest circulation will tend to attract more advertisers. The more appealing that broadcaster or newspaper becomes to advertisers, the more the other providers' ad revenues decline. The fewer advertisers the latter attract, the fewer resources they have at their disposal to produce or acquire attractive content. This leads to a decline in audience which causes a further drop in advertisers. Charging less for ad space is not the solution to the problem because advertisers are not so interested in paying lower prices as in reaching as many viewers/readers as possible. As a result of the above, smaller firms find themselves in a downward spiral, which, if it does not eventually crowd them out, at least results in one or very few providers enjoying significant market power.[271]

73. It bears noting that the relationship between each of the above characteristics and concentration varies from medium to medium. For example, compared with newspapers and television, magazines and radio have low first-copy

---

265 Rysman, M. (2009). *The Economics of Two-sided Markets*. Journal of Economic Perspectives,23(3), 125

266 Evans, D.S. and Richard Schmalensee (2007). *Industrial Organization of Markets with Two-Sided Platforms*. Competition Policy International 3, 154

267 OECD (2009). *Policy Roundtable Report on Two-Sided Markets*, 11–12. <http://www.oecd.org/daf/competition/44445730.pdf>

268 Evans and Schmalensee (2007), *supra* n. 65, 155

269 OECD (2003a), *supra* n. 56, 21 and 26. Network effects arise in situations where the size of one group of agents has an impact on another group of agents. See OECD (2012), *Policy Roundtable on Market Definition*, 54. <http://www.oecd.org/daf/competition/Marketdefinition2012.pdf>. For instance, the number of audience members that watch a given channel has a positive impact on the advertisers, in that more audience members increase the possibility that their ads will be watched, thereby possibly leading to a profitable transaction.

270 Caillaud, B. and Bruno Jullien (2003). *Chicken & egg: competition among intermediation service providers*. RAND Journal of Economics 34(2), 309–328

271 OECD (2003a), *supra* n. 56, 21

costs.[272] Moreover, producing a TV series is more expensive than producing a newspaper, but distributing a newspaper is more expensive than distributing a TV series.[273] However, these differences cannot be relied upon to draw definitive conclusions regarding which sector is more concentrated than others. For example, radio has lower first-copy *and* lower distribution costs than newspapers, but in certain Member States newspaper publishing markets are less concentrated than radio markets.[274] This means that a policymaker that seeks to address concerns relating to (mono- *and* cross-media) concentration of ownership, including market foreclosure and threats to pluralism, needs to understand the role that each of the above parameters plays in the market under scrutiny in order to be able to select the best course of action (e.g. what are the most appropriate remedies in a merger transaction, how to design a regulatory instrument in order to lower entry barriers where necessary, etc).

Liberalization/Deregulation

74. Besides the economic rationales behind the industry's movement for consolidation, a series of national and supranational policies have facilitated, if not encouraged, media concentration across the EU. First, in 1989, the Television Without Frontiers (now Audiovisual Media Services or AVMS[275]) Directive[276] was adopted with the aim to liberalize the broadcasting (and, after the AVMS Directive entered into force, audiovisual media) markets. As already mentioned in Chapter 1, pursuant to the Directive, for an audiovisual media provider to operate across the whole of the EU, it suffices that it complies with the rules of the Member State from which it emanates (country of origin principle).[277] This rule has played a major role in the expansion of media undertakings into other countries. While fewer than eighty-five cross-border television channels existed in 1989, twenty years later at least 650 channels targeted the market of a Member State other than the country of establishment.[278] Combined with the increasing acceptance of generic formats such as reality TV programs and comedy series, which has reduced cultural barriers, liberalization allowed

272 Bardoel, J. and Jan van Cuilenburg (2008). *Strategic Media Management*. In Fourier, P. J. (ed.). *Media Studies – Policy, Management and Media Representation* (2nd edition). Cape Town: Juta & Co, 176

273 ibid.

274 For example, this was the case in the Netherlands and Italy as documented in Ward, Fueg and D'Armo (2004), *supra* n. 50, 8 and 13

275 Directive 2010/13/EU of the European Parliament and of the Council of 10 March 2010 on the coordination of certain provisions laid down by law, regulation or administrative action in Member States concerning the provision of audiovisual media services (Audiovisual Media Services Directive) [2010] OJ L332/27

276 Council Directive 89/442/EEC of 3 October 1989 on the coordination of certain provisions laid down by law, regulation or administrative action in Member States concerning the pursuit of television broadcasting activities (Television Without Frontiers Directive) [1989] OJ L298/23

277 See Audiovisual Media Services Directive, Articles 2 and 3

278 Commission, *Seventh report from the Commission to the European Parliament, the Council, the European Economic and Social Committee and the Committee of the Regions on the application of Directive 89/552/EEC 'Television without Frontiers'*, 3 COM (2009) 309 final

(formerly purely national) media groups to grow significant business outside their primary markets.[279] The expansion of media undertakings into the markets of other Member States has also been facilitated by a wave of deregulation. National governments have gradually been abolishing or relaxing ownership rules in order to attract new investors and ultimately become more competitive vis-à-vis third countries.[280] Deregulation is also the outcome of initiatives which supranational policymakers undertook throughout the 1990s with a view to creating a 'Global Information Society';[281] the denationalization of the processes of media production and distribution was largely pushed by the International Monetary Fund and other international regulatory bodies.[282] Finally, the Commission, which has exclusive competence to decide whether a concentration of a Union dimension is compatible or not with the common market,[283] has adopted a very tolerant approach to the expansion plans of undertakings, including US firms that provide media services across the EU. Since the Merger Regulation entered into force, only six concentrations affecting the traditional media sector were prohibited,[284] out of a total of 184 operations that have sought regulatory approval thus far.[285] In some cases, the Commission has gone so far as to clear transactions in spite of the fact that clearance would lead to a near-monopoly in the affected markets.[286]

3.2 What is the impact of media concentration on pluralism?

75. Diversity of ownership or control over media organizations is the dimension that has received the most attention[287] in regulation supporting media

279 Council of Europe (2004). *Transnational media concentrations in Europe*. Report prepared by the Advisory Panel to the CDMM on media concentrations, pluralism and diversity questions, 7. On this issue see also Commission. Staff Working Document on Media Pluralism in the Member States of the EU SEC (2007) 32, 9; Communication on the application of State aid rules to public service broadcasting (the Broadcasting Communication) [2009] OJ C 257/1, paragraph 22; and Harcourt, A. (2004). *Institution-driven competition: The regulation of cross-border broadcasting in the EU*. European University Institute Working Papers, RSCAS No. 2004/44, 1. Also published in Journal of Public Policy, 27(3), 293-317.

280 Since the early 1980s, the governments of several European countries such as the UK, Finland, Greece, Italy and Bulgaria have been promoting deregulation in the media industry. For more information on the process of liberalization and deregulation see, for instance, ELIAMEP (2010). *MEDIADEM background information report on media policies and regulatory practices in a selected set of European countries, the EU and the Council of Europe*. The Commission has been supportive of this approach on the grounds that 'too restrictive ownership rules might hinder European companies from competing globally'. See Commission. Staff Working Document on Media Pluralism in the Member States of the EU SEC (2007) 32, 9

281 Doyle (2002), *supra* n. 62, 2

282 See Arsenault, A.H. and Manuel Castells (2008). *The Structure and Dynamic of Global Multi-Media Business Networks*, International Journal of Communication 2, 708–711

283 Council Regulation (EC) No. 139/2004 of 20 January 2004 on the control of concentrations between undertakings (the EC Merger Regulation) OJ L24/1, Article 4(1)

284 Search by NACE Code. <http://ec.europa.eu/competition/elojade/isef/index.cfm?fuseaction=dsp_result> Note that this list has omitted *MSG Media Service* (Case IV/M.469) [1994] OJ L364/1

285 Search by NACE Code and based on a calculation of transactions that have sought clearance up to August 2018. <http://ec.europa.eu/competition/elojade/isef/index.cfm?fuseaction=dsp_result>

286 *News Corp/Telepiù* (Case COMP/M.2876) [2004] OJ L110/73, paragraph 140

287 Valcke (2011), *supra* n. 1, 291

pluralism, both across[288] and beyond[289] the European Union. Ensuring that significant opinion-forming power is not concentrated in the hands of a few has been (or, at least until recently, was) a priority because of the presumed negative effects of concentration on media pluralism.[290] To quote Lord McIntosh of Haringey, former UK Minister for Media and Heritage at the Department for Culture, Media and Sport, the principle underlying media ownership restrictions 'is that it would be dangerous for any person to control too much of the media because of his or her ability to influence opinions and set the political agenda'.[291]

76. Saying that *every* media concentration is *always only* harmful to pluralism is not accurate. Depending on the circumstances, a concentration may have some positive effects on media pluralism.[292] For example, if a mainstream publisher acquires a niche publisher that is on the verge of bankruptcy, or headed for some serious financial difficulties, an outlet that offers alternative content survives. Similarly, a merger between two local newspapers that keep their editorial departments separate post-merger may enhance pluralism if the advertising market is so small that it cannot sustain both newspapers.[293] A merger between two local broadcasters may lead to the creation of a strong national player with a program offer that is different from the generic programming of competing multinational broadcasters.

77. However, experience shows that a concentration is highly likely to have negative consequences for pluralism.[294] From a purely economic perspective, a

288 The relevant measures that the EU Member States have adopted vary. For instance, as already mentioned in Chapter 1, some Member States impose limitations on the number of licenses that may be held by the same person, whereas others impose limitations on the total amount of audience, capital, or market shares that a single person, natural or legal, can control. For an overview of the different systems see Valcke, P. (2009). *From Ownership Regulation to Legal Indicators of Media Pluralism: Background, Typologies, and Methods*. Journal of Media Business Studies 6(3), 19–42

289 For instance, media ownership is regulated in the US and Australia. For an overview of the US rules see the website of the FCC, available at: <http://www.fcc.gov/guides/review-broadcast-ownership-rules>; for an overview of the Australian framework see the website of the Parliament of Australia, available at: <http://www.aph.gov.au/About_Parliament/Parliamentary_Departments/Parliamentary_Library/Publications_Archive/archive/mediaregulation>

290 Valcke (2011), *supra* n. 1, 291

291 Ofcom (2010b), *supra* n. 20, 17

292 Recent studies that explore the relationship between concentration and media pluralism include Garcia Pires, A. (2017). *Media pluralism and competition*. European Journal of Law and Economics 43(2), 255–283; and Allen, H. and Sara Connolly (2017). *Media pluralism: What matters for governance and regulation?* Journal of Media Economics 30(2), 47–64

293 Commission. Staff Working Document on Media Pluralism in the Member States of the EU, SEC (2007) 32, 8. Note that in the US this is encouraged under the Newspaper Preservation Act, U.S. Code, Title 15, Chapter 43

294 The examples here concern the impact of an individual operation on media pluralism. As regards the impact of a concentrated market structure, there are studies that found that the more concentrated the sector, the less pluralistic the media landscape. See, for instance, Humphreys, P. (1996). *Mass media and media policy in Western Europe*. Manchester: Manchester University Press; Einstein, M. (2002). *Media Diversity: Economics, Ownership, and the FCC*. New York: Routledge; and La Porte Alfaro, M. T. and Teresa Sabada (2001). *Globalization of the Media Industry and Possible Threats to Cultural Diversity – A Study prepared for the European Parliament*. Final Study. Working document for the STOA Panel. There are also studies that did not manage to identify a relationship between ownership concentration and media pluralism, especially content diversity, in *quantitative* terms. See, for instance, Berry, S. and Joel

concentration increases the incentive to crowd out competing content suppliers. Consider vertical mergers affecting broadcasting markets, for example – in several cases where competition authorities found that the merged entity would enjoy significant power in the upstream market for the purchase of premium content, they imposed upon the involved firms the obligation to sub-license the acquired content to competitors post-merger.[295] However, in the vast majority of cases, the merged entities deprived other broadcasters of the ability to effectively compete in the downstream market for TV audiences.[296] Equally ineffective were sublicensing mechanisms establishing the duty to grant access to infrastructure that is essential to competition but cannot feasibly be duplicated (e.g. a cable network).[297] These examples illustrate that a vertically integrated firm with access to a valuable input will do everything within its power to foreclose the market to other content providers, potentially harming supply diversity. An integrated media organization may also negatively impact content diversity, most notably through decisions relating to the use of the outlets' resources. For example, horizontally integrated newspapers tend to use the same content across all titles held in common ownership in order to reduce the costs incurred in the news-gathering process.[298]

78. From a non-economic perspective, concentration may have adverse effects on pluralism when individuals controlling several (and/or popular) media seek to promote a certain political agenda; history is full of examples of media moguls, often linked to political parties, that have used the opinion-forming power of their outlets in order to protect their own interests, rather than to expose the audiences to opposing viewpoints or inconvenient truths.[299] These

---

Waldfogel (2001). *Do mergers increase product variety? Evidence from radio broadcasting*. Quarterly Journal of Economics 116, 1009–1025 and Ward, D. (2006). *Final Report on the Study Commissioned by the MC-S-MD – The Assessment of Content Diversity in Newspapers and Television in the Context of Increasing Trends Towards Concentration of Media Markets*, MC-S-MD (2006) 001, 4. Strasbourg: Council of Europe. However, even in the latter case, there are *qualitative* parameters and, in particular, parameters that determine whether the power that goes with ownership is used to direct editorial decisions, which are key to understanding whether concentration harms pluralism (e.g. are politicians prevented from owning a media outlet? Does the owner promote a self-censorship culture?). These parameters have been the subject of other studies (see, for instance, *infra n.* 103)

295 For an analysis of sublicensing mechanisms imposed by the Commission see Chapter 3, Part 2.1. and Chapter 4, Part 3.1. For an analysis of sublicensing mechanisms imposed by national competition authorities see Ofcom (2009a). *Wholesale must-offer remedies: International examples*

296 ibid.

297 On this issue see Chapter 4, Part 4.3.

298 Doyle (2002), *supra* n. 62, 23. Drawing on empirical research on media companies' behavior to multi-use their products, Murray notes that 'once hit content has been identified it can be milked for revenue almost ad infinitum'. See Murray, S. (2005). *Brand loyalties: rethinking content within global corporate media*, *Media, Culture & Society*, 27(3), 431

299 A good example is former Prime Minister of Italy, Silvio Berlusconi who, in the March 1994 elections, 'used his three TV stations reaching 40% of the Italian audience to give unremitting support to his own political party'. Subsequent research proved 'not only that there was a bigger swing to the right (3.5% more) among Berlusconi viewers than in the electorate in general, but also that this swing could not be explained by the fact that viewers of Berlusconi channels were already more right wing. Viewers of these channels were found to be middle of the road and only shifted their voting *after* watching the Berlusconi channels. See Owen, B. (2006). *The tragedy of broadcast regulation*. In Hassan, R. and Julian Thomas (eds.), *The New Media Theory Reader*. Berkshire UK: Open University Press, 82. Berlusconi won these and subsequent elections with numerous supranational initiatives stressing that Italy was (and

individuals have interfered with journalistic autonomy either directly (by literally making day-to-day editorial decisions) or indirectly (e.g. by appointing only like-minded people or by creating a spirit of obedience that leads to self-censorship).[300] Practices undermining the editorial independence of the media are facilitated by a number of lacunae in the applicable legal framework of several Member States, including the absence of transparency rules requiring media firms to publish their ownership structure,[301] the lack of regulatory safeguards against commercial influence over editorial content,[302] and/or the absence of rules preventing political parties from holding broadcast licenses or running newspapers.[303]

3.3 Is concentration in traditional media markets still a concern?

79. The concern that traditional media organizations may impair the fair and free flow of information is still pervasive in the EU. This is so for the following three reasons.

80. First, as discussed above, because the economics of media markets encourages, if not dictates, concentration, and because policymakers have become more permissive vis-à-vis ownership restrictions, traditional media markets in Europe are already concentrated. Evidence suggests that a shift to disintegration is unlikely to occur: in 2017, the Commission alone received eleven merger notifications in the traditional media sector involving giants such as Fox, Sky, Vivendi and Discovery.[304] On a national level, over the past years,

---

still is) in desperate need of effective regulation addressing the conflict of interest that arises in cases where a politician may own shareholdings in media organizations. See, for instance, EU Network of Independent Experts on Human Rights (2003). *Report on the Situation of Fundamental Rights in the European Union and its Member States in 2002*, 110; European Parliament Resolution of 22 April 2004 on the risks of violations, in the EU and especially in Italy, of freedom of expression and information (2003/2237(INI)). Similar remarks can be made when an owner uses the outlet to promote a certain corporate agenda. A good example is the following: UK newspapers the Times and the Sun, which belong to media tycoon Rupert Murdoch, had a favorable attitude towards UK's former Prime Minister David Cameron because Murdoch was hoping to get, in return, approval to acquire the 61% of the BSkyB stock that he did not already own. Both newspapers changed attitude though, after Cameron announced his decision to appoint a judge to investigate a phone-hacking scandal involving another Murdoch newspaper, News of the World. See, for instance, Burns, J. F. and Alan Cowell. *Cameron Defends Handling of Murdoch Bid to Take Over Sky Broadcasting*. 25 May 2012, New York Times. <http://www.nytimes.com/2012/05/26/world/europe/e-mail-shows-murdoch-bid-maneuvering.html?_r=0>; Holton, K. *UK's Cameron defends role in Murdoch takeover deal*. 25 May 2012, Reuters. <http://www.reuters.com/article/2012/05/25/britain-hacking-cameron-idUSL5E8GP7PN20120525>; and Simons, N. *Rupert Murdoch Uses Twitter To Attack David Cameron Over Donor Row*. 26 March 2012, The Huffington Post. <http://www.huffingtonpost.co.uk/2012/03/26/rupert-murdoch-turns-on-david-cameron-over-cash-for-access-allegations_n_1379057.html>.

300 Doyle (2002), *supra* n. 62, 19–20

301 See, for instance, Brogi et al. (2017), *supra* n. 50, 25–26; Commission (2016). *Media pluralism and democracy: outcomes of the 2016 Annual Colloquium on Fundamental Rights*, 3; and OSCE (2003). *The Impact of Media Concentration on Professional Journalism*, 56

302 Brogi et al. (2017), *supra* n. 50, 31–34

303 ibid, 38–40; Commission. Staff Working Document on Media Pluralism in the Member States of the EU SEC (2007) 32, 6–7

304 Search by NACE Code. <http://ec.europa.eu/competition/elojade/isef/index.cfm?fuseaction=dsp_result>

several Member States (e.g. the UK, Spain, and the Netherlands) have further relaxed their mono- and cross-media ownership rules.[305] These developments cannot be expected to reduce the ability and incentive of powerful media organizations to engage in practices undermining journalistic autonomy. To the contrary, as a result of a tolerant approach towards concentration, there has reportedly been 'a rise in political ownership – in some cases clandestine – as well as a resurgence of "press baronism"'.[306]

81. Second, traditional media are a big part of Europeans' media diet. For example, television is still the most popular medium in the EU.[307] In 2017, the Internet may have overtaken radio,[308] but radio remains the medium that Europeans trust the most.[309] In terms of use, written press comes fourth, but a considerable percentage of Europeans (28%) continue to read newspapers every day, or almost every day.[310] For the purposes of this study, it bears noting that television is still the main medium for molding the citizen's view on matters of common concern: television remains Europeans' preferred source of news on both national and European political affairs.[311] Moreover, qualitative research showed that television continues to have the most impact on public opinion due to 'its immersive audiovisual qualities that bring stories to life'.[312]

82. Third, as the analysis below will demonstrate, the new media environment has not created a 'diverse'-enough offer that can be balanced against the content supplied by traditional media outlets. Put simply, new media have not yet fully addressed the concerns relating to the excessive opinion-forming power the 'old gatekeepers' enjoy.

---

305 See Open Society Foundations (2012). *Mapping Digital Media in the European Union – A Report for the High-Level Group on Media Freedom and Pluralism*, 2. <http://www.opensocietyfoundations.org/sites/default/files/Mapping_Digital_Media_EU_20121217_0.pdf>; Ofcom (2009c). *Report on Media Ownership Rules*, 21 *et seq*.; and Freedom House (2013). *Report on Spain*. <https://www.freedomhouse.org/report/freedom-press/2013/spain#.VMJr_M016eY>

306 Open Society Foundations (2012), *supra* n. 104, 2. Similarly, the 2012 MEDIADEM Report found that, in their effort to be loyal to the outlet's private interests, editors more often than not 'promote unprofessional and unethical practices in the newsrooms'. See ELIAMEP (2012), *MEDIADEM Comparative Report on Media freedom and Independence in 14 European* countries, 146–147. <https://www.eliamep.gr/wp-content/uploads/2012/09/media-freedom.pdf> On the state of editorial autonomy across Europe see also Brogi et al. (2017), *supra* n. 50, 40–43

307 Commission (2017). *Media Use in the European Union*, 4

308 ibid.

309 ibid, 20. See also Commission (2016). Special Eurobarometer 452. *Media Pluralism and Democracy*, 10. <http://ec.europa.eu/information_society/newsroom/image/document/2016-47/sp452-summary_en_19666.pdf>

310 Commission (2017), *supra* n. 106, 11

311 ibid, 37 and 42

312 See, for instance, Ofcom (2012), *supra* n. 35, 14. The popularity of this medium combined with the great influence it may exert on viewers has underpinned the methodologies that media regulators have designed and employed in recent years to measure media pluralism; TV is assigned greater weight than other media. See, for instance, Ofcom (2010b), *supra* n. 20, 58. The FCC's Diversity Index also assigns greater weight to television than to other media. For an overview and criticism of the methodology see, for instance, Hill, B. C. (2006). *Measuring media market diversity: concentration, importance, and pluralism*. Federal Communications Law Journal 58, 169–194

3.4 The advent of digital media: is concentration no longer a problem?

83. Among the many developments that have occurred over the past few years, two technologies have had a particularly significant impact on the media marketplace, namely the introduction of Digital Terrestrial Television (DTT) and the Internet.[313] Digital television is a new broadcasting technology that is gradually replacing the traditional analogue model. In analogue broadcasting, the signal takes the form of a continuous wave whereas digital technology converts analogue signals into binary code of zeros and ones.[314] One of the main advantages of digital broadcasting is that it releases spectrum, the so-called digital dividend; due to advanced compression, the technology may transmit eight digital TV channels using the same amount of spectrum needed to transmit one analogue TV channel. As for the Internet, not only does it provide unlimited space, but it also allows the production and distribution of content at (almost) no cost.[315]

84. These technologies have marked the beginning of the end of the spectrum scarcity era and significantly lowered the barriers that new providers need to overcome in order to penetrate the market.[316] As a result, new information sources have proliferated. Despite the fact that both technologies are relatively new (the Internet started an expansion to Europe less than fifteen years ago and most Member States have only recently completed the digital switchover, that is, the transition from analogue to digital broadcasting[317]), relevant figures are impressive: in the period 2003–2004, when the first major steps for the transition from analogue to digital broadcasting were made, 860 channels with potential national coverage were broadcast across Europe,[318] whereas in 2010, according to the Commission, there were 7,500 broadcasters available across the EU.[319] As regards the Internet, raw data merely gives us an idea of the amount of information that may be found online. For example, based on data collected in June 2018, 473,400 tweets are sent by Twitter users per minute.[320]

313 See Centre for Media Pluralism and Media Freedom (2013), *supra* n. 48, and Council of Europe (2002), *supra* n. 50, 26, para 101

314 Commission (2006). *The European Commission's Approach to Digital Interactive Television: Frequently Asked Questions*, Memo/06/60. <http://europa.eu/rapid/press-release_MEMO-06-60_en.htm>

315 Communication on the application of State aid rules to public service broadcasting (the Broadcasting Communication) [2009] OJ C 257/1, paragraph 5

316 Centre for Media Pluralism and Media Freedom (2013), *supra* n. 48, 27

317 More information about the digital switchover process is available at: http://europa.eu/legislation_summaries/audiovisual_and_media/l24223a_en.htm>

318 Commission. *Fifth Report from the Commission to the Council, the European Parliament, the European Economic and Social Committee and the Committee of the Regions on the application of Directive 89/552/EEC 'Television without Frontiers'*, SEC (2006) 160, 4. <http://eur-lex.europa.eu/legal-content/EN/TXT/PDF/?uri=CELEX:52006DC0049&from=EN>

319 Commission. *First Report from the Commission to the European Parliament, the Council, the European Economic and Social Committee and the Committee of the Regions on the application of Directive 2010/13/EU 'Audiovisual Media Service Directive'* COM (2012) 203 final, 3

320 Statista (2018). *Media usage in an internet minute as of June 2018*. <https://www.statista.com/statis-

85. This revolution has sparked a polarized debate about whether the long-standing concern over concentration of ownership has subsided.[321] On the one hand, the 'media optimists', that is, those who are enthusiastic about the effects of new technologies on media pluralism, argue that since the fear that certain players will take advantage of technical or economic scarcity to dominate the marketplace has diminished, the circumstances for the creation of a pluralistic media environment are more favorable now than ever before. Digital media, the media optimists say, have made access to the audiences easy and cheap[322] whereas new horizontal networks, the development of which was prompted by the Internet, facilitate the multimodal exchange of interactive messages from many to many.[323] According to the optimists, due to accessibility, affordability and interactivity, cultural and social boundaries are increasingly dissolving,[324] and insurgent politics can now intervene more decisively in the new communication space.[325] These changes, they believe, will ultimately dismantle the power held by the traditional media system where news production is defined by the interaction between political elites and journalists, and create a 'multiaxility' structure where non-mainstream political actors can set the political agenda.[326] On the other hand, the 'media pessimists' argue that digital media have fallen short of resolving issues relating to concentration of power in the hands of a few gatekeepers. New technologies, they say, are stuck in old hierarchies that still determine the amount and type of content ultimately reaching the citizens.[327] These hierarchies use new technologies either to protect and promote certain political interests[328] or, taking advantage of the increasing acceptance of generic format content, to maximize profit.[329] The pessimists also distrust new media businesses which are increasingly playing a major role in finding and selecting content that is (or should be)

---

tics/195140/new-user-generated-content-uploaded-by-users-per-minute/> Based on an older report, over 160 billion videos were produced and shared by Internet users in 2012 alone. See Helberger, N., Guibault, L. and Janssen E. H. (2012). *User-Created-Content: Supporting a Participative Information Society. Understanding the Digital World.* Amsterdam Law School Research Paper No. 2012-32, 80–81

321 For a comprehensive overview of the arguments put forward by media optimists and those supported by media pessimists, see Karppinen, K. (2009). *Rethinking media pluralism and communicative abundance.* Observatorio Journal 3(4), 151–169

322 Compaine, B.M. and Douglas Gomery (2000). *Who owns the media? Competition and concentration in the mass media industry.* Mahwah, NJ: L. Erlbaum Associates, 575

323 Castells, M. (2007). *Communication, power and counter-power in the network society.* International Journal of Communication 1, 247

324 McNair, B. (2006). *Cultural Chaos – Journalism, News and Power in a Globalized World.* London: Routledge, 6

325 Castells (2007), *supra* n. 122, 248

326 Williams, B. A. and Michael X. Delli Carpini (2004). *Monica and Bill all the time and everywhere: The collapse of gatekeeping and agenda setting in the new media environment.* American Behavioral Scientist 47(9), 1213

327 Hindman, M. (2008). *The Myth of Digital Democracy.* Princeton, NJ: Princeton University Press, 18

328 Braman S. (2004). *Where Has Media Policy Gone? Defining the Field in the Twenty-First Century.* Communication Law and Policy 9(2), 153–182

329 Council of Europe (2004), *supra* n. 78, 25–26; Fenton, N. (2010). *Drowning or Waving? New Media, Journalism and Democracy.* In Fenton, N. (ed.), *New Media, Old News. Journalism and Democracy in the Digital Age.* London: Sage, 3–16

of interest to the user; they believe that these businesses create new silos of information instead of breaking down the old ones.[330]

86. Regulatory reforms that took place over the past decade suggest that the optimists have greatly influenced modern media policymaking. For example, in 2003, the Federal Communications Commission (FCC) approved new media ownership rules that allowed TV broadcasters to reach 45% of the national audience, an increase of 10% from the previous restrictions.[331] The document outlining the amendments to the then applicable media ownership thresholds lays down that citizens

> have more choices, more sources of news and information, and more varied entertainment programming available to them than ever before … and via the Internet, Americans can access virtually any information, anywhere, on any topic. … [O]wnership rules, like a distant echo from the past, continue to restrict who may hold radio and television licenses as if broadcasters were America's gatekeepers.[332]

87. More recently, in 2017, the FCC voted in favor of a further relaxation of the media ownership restrictions that apply in the US. Commenting on the rationale for this reform, FCC Chairman Ajit Pai said that '*[t]he media ownership regulations of 2017 should match the media marketplace of 2017*', adding that the changes concerned are needed 'given current consumer habits, as people get their news not just from local stations, but from websites, podcasts, and social media'.[333] In a similar vein, in its report on the status of Dutch media in 2010, the Commissariaat voor de Media notes that 'a wave of deregulation in ownership rules seems to go through Europe. This also applies to the Netherlands where the Temporary Act Media Concentration was repealed as of the first of January 2011. *The increasing amount of news sources is one of the reasons why concerns about media diversity gradually seem to move away from measures which aim to secure a minimal number of players in a market*' [emphasis added]. [334]

---

330 Verhulst, S. (2007). *Mediation, Mediators and New Intermediaries. Implications for the Design of New Communications Policies*. In Napoli, P. (ed.). *Media Diversity and Localism: Meaning and Metrics*. Mahwah, NJ: Lawrence Erlbaum, 113–137

331 For an overview and critical analysis of these changes see, for instance, Miller, D. S. (2004). *Limits on Media Ownership: Should the FCC Curb Its Reliance on Deregulation?* U. ILL. J.L. Tech. & Pol'y 2, 345–367

332 FCC (2003). *Report and Order and Notice of Proposed Rulemaking*, FCC 03-127, points 3 and 4

333 Johnson, T. *The FCC just passed the most significant changes to media ownership regulations in a generation*. 16 November 2017, Business Insider UK. <http://uk.businessinsider.com/fcc-passes-media-ownership-regulations-rules-2017-11?r=US&IR=T>

334 Commissariaat voor de Media (2011), *supra* n. 35, 6. See also Commission. Staff Working Document on Media Pluralism in the Member States of the EU SEC (2007) 32, 4 and 15–16: The Commission has taken the stance that the adoption of pan-European media ownership rules would not be appropriate, *inter alia*, because '*the Internet [allows] licensed media and unlicensed media to compete on the web using a mixture of text, graphics, photographs and video … without the high entry costs and entry barriers inher-*

88. The assumption on which the aforementioned regulatory reforms are based is arguably not well-grounded, for a numerical increase in sources and content has not made concerns relating to media concentration disappear with a magic wand. I am certainly not saying that the media ownership rules that were repealed or relaxed were well-designed and implemented in an effective manner. Nevertheless, and without undermining the role that they may play (or have already played) in reducing the power held by old gatekeepers, I am skeptical about whether, in the absence of ownership restrictions, media can indeed reach their full potential. Evidence on supply and demand patterns in digital television and Internet markets suggests that new technologies have not remedied the communicative inequalities that result from media concentration. This is so mainly for two reasons: first, traditional media organizations still hold significant opinion-forming power because they have managed to reposition and establish a very strong presence in digital content markets. Second, new media businesses that have emerged with the advent of the Internet, most notably digital intermediaries, may engage in practices that hinder the fair and free flow of information, introducing artificial forms of scarcity. Each of these two issues is examined separately below.

3.4.1 Traditional media organizations repositioning in digital broadcasting markets: the wolf changes its coat, but not its nature

89. The introduction of digital television has not made market-entry easy for new content suppliers, or at least not as easy as originally anticipated. This may be inferred from recent research that shows that the European audiovisual marketplace remains highly concentrated[335] *and* that the most profitable companies are businesses that were already well established before the digital revolution commenced.[336] There are several reasons that can explain why new entrants have been unable to challenge older competitors.

90. First, the positive impact that lower production and distribution costs may have on diversity has arguably been exaggerated. As Owen correctly notes, 'access' is different from 'success';[337] while establishing a media outlet is not as expensive as it once was, costs incurred in the creation of *attractive* content

ent in broadcast or traditional print media'.

335 Brogi et al. (2017), *supra* n. 50. See in particular p. 27–29

336 Information retrieved from the Yearbook Online Service of the European Audiovisual Observatory, available at: <http://yearbook.obs.coe.int/>

337 Owen, B. M. (2004). *Confusing Success with Access: 'Correctly' Measuring Concentration of Ownership and Control in Mass Media and Online Services*. Paper prepared for the 'Media Concentration and the Internet – Empirical, Business and Policy Research', a Symposium at the Columbia Institute for Teleinformation (CITI), Columbia Business School

that manages to generate the advertising[338] or subscription revenues[339] that will ensure the longevity of the outlet remain high.[340] For example, in the US, the most-watched TV shows of the 2016–2017 season were produced and/or distributed by established providers, such as AMC, NBC and Fox.[341] Big ratings require, as a rule, big budgets. For example, the actors that star in CBS' *The Big Bang Theory* (fifth in the list)[342] are each paid $1 million per episode.[343] AMC's *The Walking Dead* (first in the list) reportedly costs $3 million per episode.[344] TV series produced by companies established in the EU may not be as 'lavish' as US shows, but they are not cheap either. For example, the BBC reportedly spent £800,000 for the pilot of its mini-series *Sherlock Holmes*.[345] The 'megabucks' spent to create a first copy combined with the high audience ratings that content distributed by established providers achieves may be the digital media outcome to which Baker refers as 'the Hollywood effect'.[346] Baker expects that the ability to create and deliver content at less or almost no cost will have two implications for diversity.[347] First, it will lead to a numerical increase in commercial and non-commercial product offerings, which he calls the 'diversity effect'.[348] Second, it will incentivize existing providers to invest more in first copies.[349] This latter effect, which corresponds to how Hollywood's capacity to spend significant amounts of money on the first copy allowed it to dominate the world's film industry, will result in the concentration of the audiences around the products of established firms, ultimately leading to a decrease in the diversity of sources and contents that are actually consumed.[350]

---

338 See, for instance, the TV series of which suppliers secured the highest advertising revenues in 2013: De Moraes, L. *NBC's 'The Blacklist' Tops Annual New-Series Ad Price Survey*. 14 October 2013, Deadline Hollywood. <http://deadline.com/2013/10/nbcs-the-blacklist-tops-annual-new-series-ad-price-survey-610874/>

339 Note that consumers are more willing to bear the extra cost of new hardware or subscriptions if the new product is provided by recognizable brands. This is so because consumers seek to avoid psychological discomfort, which they experience when switching to providers with whom they are not familiar. See Murray (2005), *supra* n. 97, 431 and Picard and Chon (2004), *supra* n. 51, 170

340 Karppinen (2009), *supra* n. 120, 158

341 Schneider, M. *These Are the 100 Most-Watched TV Shows of the 2015-16 Season: Winners and Losers*. 31 May 2016, IndieWire. <https://www.indiewire.com/2016/05/most-watched-tv-show-2015-2016-season-game-of-thrones-the-walking-dead-football-1201682396/>

342 ibid.

343 Berg, M. The World's Highest-Paid TV Actors: Jim Parsons Leads With $27.5 Million. 28 September 2017, Forbes. <https://www.forbes.com/sites/maddieberg/2017/09/28/the-worlds-highest-paid-tv-actors-jim-parsons-leads-with-27-5-million/#949d9e851a30>

344 Surrey, M. Here's how much it costs to make an episode of 'The Walking Dead'. 11 December 2016, Mic. <https://mic.com/articles/161740/here-s-how-much-it-costs-to-make-an-episode-of-the-walking-dead#.fjP53F4FP>

345 Heritage, S. Sherlock Holmes's smarter brothers: the best pilots that never made it to air. 28 May 2010, The Guardian. <http://www.theguardian.com/tv-and-radio/tvandradioblog/2010/may/28/sherlock-holmes-best-pilots-never>

346 Baker, C. E. (2007). Media concentration and democracy: why ownership matters, 105. Cambridge/New York: CUP

347 ibid.

348 ibid.

349 ibid.

350 ibid, 102

91. Second, there are indications that lower technical barriers to entry have not enhanced supply diversity; the possibility of increased efficiency from economies of scale makes it fairly easy for traditional media companies to expand and solidify their presence in neighboring media markets. More particularly, while the switch-off of analogue television releases spectrum, instead of creating opportunities for new entrants, it may well favor existing media conglomerates that have both the financial resources to invest in new and multiple channels and enough content to 'feed' them.[351] The UK market is a good example to illustrate how (communicative and market) power is distributed in digital television: In the UK, which completed the digital switchover in 2012, 567 international, national and local channels are currently available.[352] All of these channels are delivered by a handful of well-known groups such as CBS, Viacom, Sky and Discovery.[353] It is therefore important to make a clear distinction between entry barriers and economies of scale; it may be less complicated to enter the market now than it was in the past, but this does not make efficiencies irrelevant. Noam, who studied the evolution of information markets, found that when entry barriers drop and economies of scale rise, a U-shaped effect is created whereby there will initially be more operators but ultimately fewer survivors, those that benefit from large economies of scale.[354] In view of the above, and given that the digital switchover has only recently been completed in most Member States, it remains to be seen how many of the thousands of channels which are now available in the European audiovisual space and which do not belong to powerful media organizations will continue to exist in the next few years.

92. Third, and related to the above, previously different communication infrastructures now use the same transport protocols. This means that television broadcasts can currently be delivered on multiple platforms with significantly less cost.[355] For example, besides terrestrial, direct-to-home satellite and cable networks, TV programming is also available on Internet Protocol television, offered by telecommunication providers over managed network with high quality of service, and Over-The-Top (OTT) television, provided by the content owners themselves (e.g. BBC iPlayer, Hulu, YouTube,[356] etc.) without the ISP or network operator controlling viewer access.[357] As a result,

---

351 European Federation of Journalists (2005), supra n. 50, 5–6

352 See <http://mavise.obs.coe.int/country?id=14>

353 ibid.

354 Noam (2009), *supra* n. 50, 37

355 Pavlik, J. (2005). Understanding Convergence and Digital Broadcasting Technologies for the Twenty-First Century. NHK Broadcasting Studies. <https://www.nhk.or.jp/bunken/english/reports/pdf/05_no4_08.pdf>

356 YouTube, which started as a peer video upload website, now provides access to programming posted by mainstream broadcasters. See OECD (2013a). *Competition Issues in Television and Broadcasting*, 2

357 ibid, 9–10. For more information on technology convergence and how it affects broadcasting see, for instance, EBU (2013). Reply to the European Commission Green Paper – Preparing for a Fully Converged Audiovisual World: Growth, Creation and Values. <https://www.ebu.ch/files/live/sites/ebu/files/Publications/Position%20papers/EBU-Position-EN%20reply%20Green%20Paper%20convergence%2010.9.2013.pdf>

the same content can be delivered on multiple devices (e.g. traditional TV set, tablets and smartphones) and in several formats (e.g. linear transmission, catch-up and on-demand). This feature, one of the many facets of convergence, incentivizes media companies to distribute the same content across all new platforms.[358] Doyle studied the impact of this practice on the new media offer. More particularly, Doyle studied the strategy that UK television suppliers are increasingly employing to produce and deliver content, known as '360-degree commissioning', whereby, from their earliest stages, decisions on what type of content to invest in are determined by the content's ability to generate revenue through multiple platforms.[359] Doyle concludes that this practice undoubtedly improves the use of resources,[360] but that it also results in established media outlets recycling those themes and genres that appeal to the masses.[361] One of the messages that this empirical research conveys is that, to the extent that and as long as existing media firms rely on tried recipes to reposition in neighboring content markets, the emergence of distribution platforms may have a chilling effect on content diversity.

3.4.2 Concentration online and digital intermediaries (aka the new information gatekeepers)

93. Alongside traditional media organizations, businesses that have emerged with the advent of the Internet, most notably digital intermediaries, are increasingly determining the amount and quality of information that citizens can access and engage with. For the purposes of this study, digital intermediaries may be defined as undertakings which bring content from third-party suppliers to users 'using a variety of digital software, channels, and devices'.[362] Broadly speaking, digital intermediaries can be classified into four groups: search engines like Google and Bing, news aggregators like Yahoo, social media like Facebook, and digital stores like Apple.[363]

---

358 For example, BBC news program Question Time is available on linear TV via BBC One, and on-demand via the BBC's iPlayer (through which it can be streamed, watched on catch-up TV and downloaded). Video highlights of the program are made available on BBC iPlayer, the BBC News and the BBC One websites. Finally, a text summarizing the content broadcast accompanies the video highlights. See <http://www.bbc.co.uk/programmes/b006t1q9>; <http://www.bbc.co.uk/iplayer/episode/b04v85qt/question-time-11122014> and <http://www.bbc.co.uk/iplayer/categories/news/highlights>.

359 Doyle, G. (2010). From Television to Multi-platform: Less from more or more for less? Convergence: The International Journal of Research into New Media Technologies 16(4), 432

360 ibid, 444

361 ibid, 446

362 Foster, R. (2012). News Plurality in a Digital World – Report prepared for the Reuters Institute for the Study of Journalism, 25

363 ibid, 6

94. The markets in which digital intermediaries operate are highly concentrated[364] for largely the same reasons traditional media markets have high concentration ratios. For example, the market for online search has high entry barriers, relating to, *inter alia*, hardware acquisition, web-indexing costs, IP patents and costs incurred in the development of algorithms.[365] Moreover, several, if not most, intermediaries operate as advertising-based media; the indirect network effects that are created as a result of their acting as two-sided platforms usually results in the market 'tipping' in favor of existing operators.[366] Entry barriers are higher in cases where a popular intermediary imposes long-term exclusivity agreements on its advertising partners.[367] Switching costs vary depending on the intermediary, but these also can prevent market entry in that they may create lock-in effects.[368] Finally, the products that intermediaries offer such as search results and 'news feeds' are characterized by high fixed costs (mainly associated with the development of innovative technologies) and low distribution costs. As already seen, this characteristic encourages concentration because it allows the merged entity to reap economies of scale. The opportunity to achieve scale economies largely explains Google's decision to acquire control of online ad services provider Doubleclick,[369] Apple's decision to acquire audio product designer Beats[370] and, more recently, Facebook's decision to acquire popular communications app WhatsApp.[371]

95. Broadly speaking, digital intermediaries do not create content as traditional media organizations do.[372] Nor do they seem to generate significant revenues for news providers, which means that we (still) cannot establish a direct and

---

364 For example, Google controls well above 90% of the general online search and general search advertising markets in most Member States. See *Google Search* (Case AT.39740) Commission decision of 27 June 2017 relating to proceedings under Article 102 TFEU and Article 54 of the EEA Agreement C (2017) 4444 final, Table 2, p. 58

365 Reference to these factors is made in Microsoft/Yahoo! (Case COMP/M.5727) Commission Decision C (2010) 1077, paragraph 111. As for the total cost, Microsoft submitted in its comments that the capital expenditure required to enter the market is approximately USD1,000 million in hardware, USD1,000 million in human capital and several billions of dollars to develop and update the algorithm.

366 See Google/Doubleclick (Case COMP/M.4731) [2008] OJ C 184/6, paragraph 290: 'Given that online advertising is a two-sided market characterized by network effects, scale and access to user data are important ingredients of success. ... As the network of the merged entity would become larger and "information-richer", it would attract more publishers and more advertisers up to the point where the market would "tip" in favour of the network of the merged entity, enabling it to raise the price of its offering.'

367 Google has entered into exclusive agreements with its ad partners; these arrangements are currently being scrutinized by the European Commission. See, for instance, Commission (June, 2017). Press Release. Antitrust: Commission fines Google €2.42 billion for abusing dominance as search engine by giving illegal advantage to own comparison shopping service. <http://europa.eu/rapid/press-release_IP-17-1784_en.htm>

368 Foster (2012), supra n. 161, 32

369 Google/Doubleclick (Case COMP/M.4731) [2008] OJ C 184/6

370 Apple/Beats (Case COMP/M.7290) [2014] OJ C 260/8

371 Facebook/WhatsApp (Case COMP/M. 7217) [2014] OJ C 417/2

372 Foster (arguably correctly) draws a distinction between news aggregators and the other three types of digital intermediaries. He explains that: 'While the former present a carefully curated package of news and are similar in many ways to print newspapers of old, the latter position themselves as gateways to an almost unlimited amount of content from many different suppliers. While the former present plurality challenges which are similar to those associated with established media, the latter are rather different animals with potentially different implications for plurality'. See Foster (2012), supra n. 161, 28

causal relationship between intermediaries and high-quality investigative journalism.[373] However, in an environment where content is abundant and attention scarce, the process of discovering content is becoming increasingly challenging. Digital intermediaries play a major role in facilitating this process. For example, news aggregators and search engines provide access to a wide range of news material from an abundance of different sources that could not have easily been consulted in the analogue landscape.[374] Social media may be used as a source of news traffic.[375] Digital stores create new opportunities for news providers which may develop and make available on these platforms applications that offer access to their packages of branded news and commentary.[376] However, these benefits can be realized *if* intermediaries are indeed used as a tool to search for alternative sources *and if* they indeed facilitate wide and open access to content, two assumptions that can be questioned.

96. In respect of the role of digital intermediaries in facilitating exposure to diverse sources and ideas, Hindman asks: are digital intermediaries 'strong gatekeepers, with a great deal of autonomous influence in directing web traffic?' Or are they 'simply mediators, mirroring existing institutions?'[377] The answer is 'both' and performance of each of these two functions has different implications for media pluralism.

97. Starting from their role as 'simple mediators', I already mentioned that digital intermediaries undoubtedly make a significant contribution to the creation of a media environment where diverse information can be easily identified and accessed. However, this does not necessarily mean that citizens have taken advantage of the (theoretically) endless opportunities these platforms offer: data shows that online users are inclined to consume content produced by established media organizations instead of actively looking for online content that may complement their traditional media experience.[378] Based on the

373 Foster (2012), supra n. 161, 24. In fact, there is considerable tension between digital intermediaries and traditional media organizations, for the latter argue that the former 'steal' their audiences and ad revenues. See, for instance, the practice of 'scraping' in which news aggregators engage (this practice will be discussed in detail in Chapter 5, Part 3). Similar concerns have also been raised in the context of the debate on 'fake news'. See, for instance, Hubbard, S. Fake News is a Real Antitrust Problem. December 2017. Competition Policy International Antitrust Chronicle, 2–3 <https://www.competitionpolicyinternational.com/wp-content/uploads/2017/12/CPI-Hubbard.pdf> Hubbard notes that '[w]hile on the one hand acting as gatekeepers for the flow of information worldwide, Facebook and Google on the other hand compete against legitimate news companies for user attention, user data and ad dollars. Google and Facebook both have incentives to keep users within their digital walls, engaging with content on the Facebook platform or on Google search pages, web properties and apps, rather than on news publishers' properties' [emphasis added].

374 Foster (2012), supra n. 161, 18 and 26

375 ibid, 20. However, Foster correctly notes that the news stories shared on these outlets mainly originate from mainstream sources. For example, according to Ofcom, the three most popular news sites whose stories were shared on Facebook and Twitter were the online versions of The Daily Mail, The Guardian and BBC News. See Ofcom (2012a). Communications Market Report, 275–6

376 Foster (2012), supra n. 161, 27

377 Hindman (2008), supra n. 126, 80

378 See, for instance, Ofcom (2018). News Consumption in the UK: 2018, 11 <https://www.ofcom.org.uk/__data/assets/pdf_file/0024/116529/news-consumption-2018.pdf>

results of the Reuters Institute Digital News Report 2018, this would seem to apply to online news consumption in several EU Member States.[379] The above must be considered against the fact that content delivered by non-mainstream media, including especially websites for political advocacy and political blogs, may 'get only a tiny fraction of the attention that traditional news outlets receive'.[380] The conclusion to draw here is that, as long as established providers control the market for news provision,[381] alternative content may drown in the ocean of content abundance.[382] Therefore, to the extent that audiences are prone to concentrate around the online content provided by traditional media, intermediaries may end up 'mirroring existing institutions', rather than serving as platforms used to discover new sources.

98. As regards their role as 'gatekeepers with autonomous influence in directing web traffic', Foster identifies four broad areas in which their activities may have negative consequences for pluralism: a) their control of what may be considered as distribution bottlenecks through which users, especially younger generations, access content; b) the editorial-like judgments they make about the content they link to or carry (e.g. they select and display content 'relevant' to the user's query, decide which sources of news to feature prominently); c) their role in shaping future economic models for news provision (e.g. they enable disaggregation of news content, which makes it increasingly difficult for news providers to generate ad revenues), and d) their inclination and ability to set the political agenda (e.g. when they invest in media in their own right).[383] This classification grasps the main areas where pluralism concerns relating to intermediaries' behavior have arisen thus far. Let's take search engines and news content by way of example. Search engines in general, and Google in particular, play a key role in channeling news to Europeans: general search engines seem to be the intermediaries that citizens use the most to find news stories[384] and Google controls over 90% of the general online search market in most Member States.[385] Starting from its role as a distribution bottleneck, several news providers maintain that Google exercises excessive control over the

379 Reuters Institute (2018). *Digital News Report 2018*, 58 *et seq.* <http://media.digitalnewsreport.org/wp-content/uploads/2018/06/digital-news-report-2018.pdf?x89475>

380 Hindman (2008), supra n. 126, 80–81

381 Arsenault and Castells (2008), supra n. 81, 719

382 Hindman (2008), supra n. 126, 18. Baker discusses the influence that blogs may exercise and notes that 'as long as traditional news and cultural media continue to dominate, as they do now, in performing (even if inadequately) their traditional roles, the mere possibility of this development has no obvious bearing on existing issues of concentration'. See Baker (2007), supra n. 145, 100

383 Foster (2012), supra n. 161, 6–7. On how search engines impact media pluralism see also van Hoboken, J. (2015). Search Engines, Pluralism and Diversity: What Is at Stake and How to Move Policy Forward? In Valcke, P., Miklós Sükösd, and Robert G. Picard. Media Pluralism and Diversity. Concepts, Risks and Global Trends. London: Palgrave Macmillan, 341–357

384 Reuters Institute (2017). Digital News Report, 14. <https://reutersinstitute.politics.ox.ac.uk/sites/default/files/Digital%20News%20Report%202017%20web_0.pdf?utm_source=digitalnewsreport.org&utm_medium=referral>

385 *Google Search* (Case AT.39740) Commission decision of 27 June 2017 relating to proceedings under Article 102 TFEU and Article 54 of the EEA Agreement C (2017) 4444 final, Table 2, p. 58

way in which they reach online users. More particularly, news providers that operate paywalls claim that, unless they agree to some of their content being made available for free via Google Search, they automatically lose visibility in Google's search results.[386] If this is indeed the case, then Google artificially limits the number of sources that are available in the market. This practice could also be a concern if paywalls become essential for the economic viability of news provision.[387] An issue related to the above is how integration between intermediaries can affect diversity. For example, Italian newspaper and magazine publishers alleged that Google's news aggregator, Google News, was free-riding on their content and that, if they extracted their publications from the aggregator, they would be excluded from Google Search altogether.[388] To the extent that they prevent news providers from directing traffic to their websites or deprive them of the ability to generate ad revenues, such 'retaliatory' practices may harm pluralism in the long run. Elements of editorial-like judgments made by search engines are present in, for instance, the presentation of their search results or the construction of their algorithms.[389] For example, a search engine may sell high positions on the list of search results or priority-index the pages of partners so that the latter rank higher than non-partner sites.[390] As a result, visibility is ensured for the news providers that paid, but not necessarily for those that may be providing more accurate or higher quality content. Another example concerns editorial-like judgments that have contributed to the widespread dissemination of 'fake news', a problem that has grown more acute in recent years with the increasing use of digital intermediaries; algorithms that have been designed in a way that ensures that content that gets more clicks, 'shares', 'likes' or comments receives a high ranking.[391] As Pasquale puts it, '[intermediaries] make the metric of success online 'virality', promoting material that has received a good deal of attention or seems to match a sub-public's personalization profile, regardless of whether it is true or even minimally decent. That reduces pluralism by elevating profit considerations over the democratizing functions of public discourse.'[392] Digital intermediaries also make editorial-like judgments when

386 Foster (2012), supra n. 161, 31

387 ibid, 39

388 In 2010, the Italian competition authority adopted a commitments decision with respect to Google's alleged tying between Google Search and Google News. See Agcm (2010). *A420 Federazione Italiana Editori Giornali/Google,* Provvedimento n. 21959. <http://www.agcm.it/dotcmsDOC/allegati-news/p21959.pdf>

389 Foster (2012), *supra* n. 161, 34

390 van Eijk, N. (2009). *Search Engines, the New Bottleneck for Content Access*. In Preissel, B., Justus Haucap and Peter Curwen (eds.), *Telecommunication Markets: Drivers and Impediments*. Berlin: Springer-Verlag, 141–156

391 See, for instance, Roberts, H. Google made changes to its search algorithm that unintentionally made it vulnerable to the spread of fake news, sources say. 10 December 2016, Business Insider. <http://uk.businessinsider.com/google-algorithm-change-fake-news-rankbrain-2016-12>; and Krishna, S. Facebook's News Feed change may amplify fake news. 16 January 2018, Engadget. <https://www.engadget.com/2018/01/16/facebook-news-feed-tweak-could-make-fake-news-worse/>

392 Pasquale, F. (2018). The Automated Public Sphere. In Seatnan, A. R., Ingrid Schneider, and Nicola Green (eds.). The Politics of Big Data. Big Data, Big Brother? Oxon: Routledge. For an overview of the causes

they decide how to profile their own services vis-à-vis the services offered by their competitors.[393] For example, search engines may decide to downgrade search results of competing services and grant preferential treatment to their own services. This issue was examined by the Commission in the context of an antitrust investigation into how Google would display search results of websites competing with it in a neighboring market.[394] This case concerns the possible exclusion of competing price comparison websites from general online search, in other words, websites providing content that is not essential to consume in order to make informed voting decisions. However, Google, among other intermediaries, has been expanding into (news) content markets,[395] thereby having the incentive to downgrade competing services. Moreover, given that there exist substantial information asymmetries between search engines and online users, Google may also have the ability to reduce visibility of competing news services. The impact of downgrading on competition is still not clear. However, were this practice to produce exclusionary effects, it could harm pluralism. Finally, and related to the above, an experiment that was conducted by Epstein and Robertson shows that were search engines to promote a certain political agenda, downgrading could prove as harmful as interfering with the editorial policies of a newspaper; the experiment in question shows that downgrading search results influences voters' preferences and may ultimately affect election results.[396]

99. The above analysis makes clear that the proliferation of sources and content does not automatically ensure pluralism. It is against the background of off- and online concentration, which may weaken democracy in many ways (some of which are already known and studied, whereas others are new and still shady), that arguments on the decreasing importance of powerful media organizations in the process of public opinion formation must be carefully

---

of 'fake news' dissemination, the effects it may have on the process of public opinion formation, and possible (regulatory) responses to its proliferation see, for instance, High Level Group on fake news and online disinformation (2018). A multi-dimensional approach to disinformation. <https://ec.europa.eu/digital-single-market/en/news/final-report-high-level-expert-group-fake-news-and-online-disinformation>; and Communication from the Commission to the European Parliament, the Council, the European Economic and Social Committee and the Committee of the Regions on Tackling Online Disinformation: a European approach COM(2018) 236 final. <https://ec.europa.eu/digital-single-market/en/news/communication-tackling-online-disinformation-european-approach>

393 Foster (2012), supra n. 161, 34

394 *Google Search* (Case AT.39740) Commission decision of 27 June 2017 relating to proceedings under Article 102 TFEU and Article 54 of the EEA Agreement C (2017) 4444 final

395 For example, Yahoo has its own news service, Google owns one of the most popular news aggregation services on the web, and AOL, a US search portal, acquired control of The Huffington Post, a popular news blog. See, for instance, AOL/Huffington Post. AOL Agrees To Acquire The Huffington Post. 7 February 2011, The Huffington Post. <http://www.huffingtonpost.com/2011/02/07/aol-huffington-post_n_819375.html>, and Peters, J. Y. and Verne G. Kopytoff. Betting on News, AOL Is Buying The Huffington Post. 7 February 2011, The New York Times. <http://www.nytimes.com/2011/02/07/business/media/07aol.html?_r=0>

396 Epstein, R. and Ronald E. Robertson (2013). Democracy at Risk: Manipulating Search Rankings Can Shift Voting Preferences Substantially Without Voter Awareness. American Institute for Behavioral Research and Technology Working Paper Series. Paper presented at the 25th annual meeting of the Association for Psychological Science, Washington, D.C. A summary of the paper is available at: <http://aibrt.org/downloads/EPSTEIN_and_Robertson_2013-Democracy_at_Risk-APS-summary-5-13.pdf>

considered. Accordingly, policymakers should realize that 'communicative abundance alone does not render questions about the distribution of communicative power and political voice obsolete, but only reconfigures them in a more complex form'.[397]

4. Assumption no. 2: The citizens will act (consume diverse content) and interact (create and distribute content that strengthens democracy)

100. As previously mentioned, traditional media policymaking is rooted in the passive consumption theory according to which audiences are powerless to resist the persuasive messages that media carry. In the linear age, the consumer was thought of as an impotent receiver whose ability to choose was limited to 'switching between different predefined program packages'.[398] However, related regulation is currently undergoing significant changes. For example, as discussed above, the relaxation of ownership restrictions that took place in several Member States has largely been based on the wide array of content that consumers may now access.[399] This is probably the most blatant example, but certainly not the only sign suggesting that the tide has turned. For example, in its 2011–2013 Strategy Statement, the Broadcasting Authority of Ireland notes that new technologies herald a new era in which '[r]ather than being passive consumers', audiences can '*critique broadcasting content*'.[400] Similarly, the Commission's 2009 Broadcasting Communication lays down that '[t]he traditional passive consumption model has been gradually turning into ... *control over content by consumers*' [emphasis added].[401] In the same vein, in its 2010 Annual Report, the Dutch media regulator states that citizens now 'have a certain responsibility in *finding their way* in the media landscape and *consulting different voices*' [emphasis added].[402]

101. These statements are indicia that there is a gradual shift to a regulatory model that is assigning more duties to the individuals. However, without suggesting that traditional media regulation is (always or still) appropriate to address pluralism concerns relating to exposure diversity, the conditions for this shift to

397 Karppinen (2009), *supra* n. 120, 160

398 Valcke (2011), *supra* n. 1, 304

399 Open Society Foundations (2012), supra n. 104, 2

400 Broadcasting Authority of Ireland (2010). Strategy Statement 2011–2013, 22. <http://www.bai.ie/wordpress/wp-content/uploads/BAI_Strategy_2011-13_v2ENG.pdf>

401 Communication on the application of State aid rules to public service broadcasting (the Broadcasting Communication) [2009] OJ C 257/1, paragraph 5

402 Commissariaat voor de media (2011), *supra* n. 35, 91

take place have arguably not matured yet. This is so mainly for three reasons: first, content may be abundant, but attention is scarce. This reality distorts the communication process and deeply affects the quality of content that media organizations produce. Second, the ability to control what type of content they are exposed to allows individuals to create a private information universe. This may impair the free flow of information and eventually weaken social cohesion. Third, Europeans do not create content that contributes to better public governance, at least not as much as was originally anticipated.

102. Before I discuss the above three issues, it is important to point out that, for Europeans to consume content that is made available online and to engage actively in public discourse that takes place in the online arena (e.g. create a blog, post comments on a newspaper's site, etc.), a fundamental requirement has not been met yet. Achieving exposure diversity naturally presupposes access to the content that media outlets have to offer. While in the traditional media environment access *per se* is easy in that, broadly speaking, it only requires buying a newspaper or switching on the TV or radio, access to online information is far more complicated because it depends on various parameters, including the motivation to use a computer, access to the Internet and skills to look for and choose content of interest. Entering the communicative abundance era does not mean that citizens are ready to benefit from the variety of output that may be found online. To the contrary, recent data published by Eurostat shows that new technologies may have caught many off-guard: 13% of Europeans have never used the Internet, while in seven Member States this amount exceeds 20% of the population.[403] Moreover, and perhaps more importantly, until recently, 88% of Europeans using the Internet did not have 'a high level of basic Internet skills'.[404] It must be noted that a 'high level of basic Internet skills' was measured by reference to – what may seem to many – low standards.[405] It is clear from the above considerations that to achieve other, more challenging conditions, including the ability to work with the necessary hardware and software, identify and process information, and ultimately engage in online political activity, there is still a long way to go. But, for the sake of the issues I raise below, let us assume that all Europeans have access to and use the Internet. Does this mean that they automatically choose to be exposed to diverse content or produce content to interact with others in ways that strengthen citizenship?

403 See <http://epp.eurostat.ec.europa.eu/tgm/table.do?tab=table&init=1&language=en&pcode=tin00093&plugin=1>

404 See <http://epp.eurostat.ec.europa.eu/tgm/refreshTableAction.do?tab=table&plugin=1&pcode=tsdsc470&language=en>

405 A 'high level of basic Internet skills' was measured by reference to whether users had carried out five or six of the following Internet-related activities: use a search engine to find information; send an email with attached files; post messages to chat rooms, newsgroups or any online discussion forum; use the Internet to make telephone calls; use peer-to-peer file sharing for exchanging movies, music etc.; and create a web. See supra n. 203

4.1 The citizens will act responsively by consuming diverse content

4.1.1 Content abundance = attention scarcity

103. Levels of exposure diversity were higher in the analogue landscape than in the digital media environment. As discussed above, in traditional media markets, output was scarce and hence consumers could be expected to 'bump into' information they did not initially demand.[406] This is no longer the case, for in the digital media ecosystem content is abundant and attention scarce. This reality has created two effects. The first relates to how much attention audiences pay to the content they are (voluntarily or involuntarily) exposed to and the second has to do with how the market responds to the audiences' behavior.

104. On the demand-side, starting from how much attention we pay to the content we are exposed to, one of the most striking examples about media consumption today is that the use of one medium is not inversely proportional to the use of others. More particularly, while regular Internet usage has been increasing across Europe,[407] TV usage has not decreased.[408] In fact, 2017 marked an increase in both Internet and TV usage.[409] How is that possible? Audiences are engaging in media multitasking.[410] Simultaneous media use must be considered alongside the fact that online activity is not necessarily related to the TV program that is being watched.[411] This online activity includes texting, general web surfing, social networking, and gaming.[412] This means that multitaskers do not necessarily complement their viewing experience by gathering more information about the content being broadcast but rather engage in a different media experience. It goes without saying that media multitasking distorts the communication process, the effectiveness of which depends not only on whether the message that is being transmitted is received, but also on whether the receiver has actually made sense of the message in question and reflected on its content. In other words, simultaneous media use leads to an information

406 Goodman (2004), *supra* n. 31, 1457

407 Based on data collected by Eurostat between 2006 and 2017. See: <http://epp.eurostat.ec.europa.eu/tgm/table.do?tab=table&init=1&language=en&pcode=tin00091&plugin=1>

408 Commission (2017), *supra* n. 106, 4

409 See <http://epp.eurostat.ec.europa.eu/tgm/table.do?tab=table&init=1&language=en&pcode=tin00091&plugin=1> and Commission (2017), supra n. 106, 4

410 Based on a study published in 2017, about 73% of the adult population in the US will use their mobile phone, laptop, or tablet while watching television. See eMarketer (2017). US Simultaneous Media Users. <https://www.emarketer.com/Report/US-Simultaneous-Media-Users-eMarketers-Estimates-2017/2002163> In some European countries, such as France and the UK, the figures on simultaneous media use may exceed 60%. For more information see Simultaneous media use rises in Europe. 1 June 2012, Warc.com. <http://www.warc.com/Content/News/Simultaneous_media_use_rises_in_Europe.content?ID=fed4dca7-bca7-44b6-b42a-dbf941b155c2>

411 See, for instance, IAB (2013). Mediascope Europe 2012 Pan-European Launch Presentation Summary, 16 et seq. <http://www.iabeurope.eu/files/6713/8720/0955/MEDIASCOPE_2012_PAN-EUROPEAN_SUMMARY_LAUNCH_PRESENTATION_public.pdf>

412 eMarketer (2017), *supra* n. 209. See also Microsoft (2009). *Meet Europe's media multi-taskers*, 6

overload that 'exceeds the interpretative capacity of the subject'.[413]

105. However, even when consumers use only one medium, this does not ensure exposure to diverse content. In an environment where content is scarce and attention abundant, more content increases the diversity of items individuals are aware of.[414] Once information becomes abundant though, attention is essentially drawn to a smaller set of sources. But, as information is an experiential good and may therefore be evaluated only after it has passed the perceptual filter, the items that are chosen to form part of this smaller set of sources are not selected on the basis of the content they contain, but on the basis of the content users *think* they contain.[415] This explains why 'in an information-rich economy there is no guarantee that the perceived items are the best possible items'.[416]

106. On the supply-side, how does attention scarcity affect the content offer? First, it creates entry barriers. As long as content is scarce and attention abundant, a content creator who has an original idea has good chances to reach the user she addresses because there are still entries on the user's mind.[417] These chances are significantly reduced in a content abundant–attention scarcity market because the entries on the user's mind are exhausted.[418] Second, content abundance results in price reductions (simple economics of supply and demand where prices fall when the supply curve shifts outward).[419] Attention, however, is becoming scarce and hence more and more valuable.[420] In other words, competition focuses less on price (evidence of this is the amount of content that is now made available for free) and more on the audience's perception filter. To pass the perception filter, media suppliers seek to capture the audience's attention either by privileging the sexy, violent and vulgar[421] or by forcing the audience to relate to their brands (read: excessive investments in brand promotion and star power).[422] News providers in particular, no longer

---

413 Stevenson, N. (1995). Understanding Media Cultures. Social Theory and Mass Communication. Thousand Oaks, CA: Sage Publications, 157

414 Falkinger, J. (2005). Attention Economies. CESifo Working Paper No. 1079, 26. <https://ideas.repec.org/p/ces/ceswps/_1079.html>

415 ibid, 26

416 ibid, 27

417 ibid, 26

418 ibid.

419 Bardoel and van Cuilenberg (2008), *supra* n. 71, 130–131

420 For more on the attention economy see, for instance, Simon, H. A. (1971). Designing Organizations for an Information-rich World. In Greenberger, M. (ed.), Computers, Communications, and the Public Interest,. Baltimore: Johns Hopkins Press, 38–52 (Cited after reprint in: Simon, H.A. (1982). Models of bounded rationality. Volume 2: Behavioural Economics and Business Organization, Cambridge/Massachussets: MIT Press). For more on the attention economy see, for instance, Hargittai, E. (2004). The Changing Online Landscape: From Free-for-All to Commercial Gatekeeping. In Day, P. and D. Schuler (eds.), Community Practice in the Network Society: Local Actions/Global Interaction. New York: Routledge, 66–76.

421 Goodman (2004), *supra n.* 31, 1460

422 See Haque, U. The Attention Economy. 8 November 2005, Bubblegeneration.com. <http://www.bubble-

having the luxury of spending time applying themselves to additional fact-gathering or explaining the facts more critically, may favor fast exposure over refined analysis.[423] This makes it difficult for audiences to absorb and reflect on the news content they consume.[424]

4.1.2 The 'Daily Me' culture

107. What about the content which consumers choose to be exposed to when they engage in a more meaningful media experience? I mentioned above that one of the main changes brought about by digital technologies, and to which policy and regulatory texts are increasingly referring, is the ability to exercise control over content. The freedom to determine what type and how much content to consume is one of the two reasons (the other reason being content abundance) why the Audiovisual Media Services Directive establishes a lighter regulatory regime for on-demand services than for traditional broadcasting.[425] This approach seems to imply that the individual is in a position to create a 'healthy varied diet'.

108. Instead of a 'healthy varied diet', however, the ability to exercise control over content may have created what Nicholas Negroponte called in the early days of the digital revolution 'the Daily Me', that is, a communications package that is individually designed, with each item selected in advance.[426] The increasing use of services that deliver tailored information are indicative of the users' eagerness to personalize as much as possible the content they consume on a daily basis.[427] This habit creates a culture of content customization that may disincentivize citizens from discovering content which they did not originally seek and which does not necessarily fit their existing dispositions. Critical of this trend, democratic theorist Habermas notes that 'the rise of millions of fragmented chat rooms across the world ... leads to the fragmentation of *large but politically focused mass audiences into a huge number of isolated issue publics*' [emphasis added].[428] Following the same line of reasoning, political philosopher Mouffe takes the view that new media 'are making it possible to *only read and listen to things that completely reinforce what you*

generation.com/2005/11/attention-economy-across-consumer.cfm> As Haque puts it, 'each marketing dollar [is now] chasing a smaller and smaller return on attention, just to keep margins constant'.

423 Goodman (2004), supra n. 31, 1460

424 ibid.

425 Audiovisual Media Services Directive, Recital (58)

426 Sunstein, C. (2007). Republic.com 2.0. Princeton, NJ: Princeton University Press, 4, referring to Negroponte, N. (1995). Being Digital. New York: Knopf, 153

427 For more examples on personalized consumption of media products see Sunstein (2007), *supra* n. 225, 1–18

428 Habermas, J. (2006). Political Communication in Media Society: Does Democracy Still Enjoy an Epistemic Dimension? The Impact of Normative Theory on Empirical Research. Communication Theory 16(4), 423

believe in' [emphasis added].[429] In other words, new technologies create the conditions for a private information universe that may facilitate exposure to 'more', except in this case 'more' may mean 'more of the same'.

109. '*What's the harm in it?*' one might ask. If the individual wishes to learn more about what interests her the most and share her opinions with others that have similar viewpoints, she should go ahead and do it. The answer to this question, however, is not as straightforward as it may seem. 'The Daily Me' culture may have far-reaching effects on pluralism and ultimately democracy. These effects become clear if we think of how social cohesion, a prerequisite for democracy,[430] relates to exposure to different opinions: It has long been acknowledged that a society that aspires to be cohesive must not seek to transform heterogeneity into homogeneity but to embrace diversity in all its facets (e.g. religious, ethnic, cultural or political).[431] Rather than a meeting of the minds, social cohesion refers to the creation of a *de facto* solidarity that is built among the various members of a community. As Dahrendorf *et al.* put it, '[s]ocial cohesion should not be thought of as harmony, but as a condition of lively civil societies held together by a framework of citizenship.'[432] In this sense, social cohesion has been proven to be strongly linked to better public service delivery, financial accountability, political stability, educational attainment and economic prosperity.[433] Therefore, in order to ensure the well-being of its members, a society must work towards creating a framework which reduces disparities, avoids social fractures,[434] and establishes strong social ties among the groups that form it.[435]

---

429 Carpentier, N. and B. Cammaerts (2006). Hegemony, Democracy, Agonism, and Journalism. An Interview with Chantal Mouffe. Journalism Studies 7(6), 968. For a different view on the impact of new media on democracy see, for instance, Rogers, R. (2004). Information Politics on the Web. Cambridge, MA: MIT Press, and McNair (2006), supra n. 123.

430 On the link between social cohesion and democracy see, for instance, Henning, C. and Karin Renblad (2009). Perspectives on Empowerment, Social Cohesion and Democracy – An International Anthology. Jönköping: School of Health Sciences, Jönköping University

431 In West Virginia State Bd. Of Educ. v Barnette, 319 U.S. 624 (1943), the US Supreme Court stroke down a state law demanding children to salute the American flag on the grounds that '[c]ompulsory unification of opinion achieves only the unanimity of the graveyard'. In *VGT Vereiniginggegen Tierfabriken v Switzerland* (2), which dealt with the question whether the refusal to broadcast a provocative commercial on industrial animal production and animal experiments violates freedom of expression as enshrined in Article 10 of the ECHR, the Court found that the principle is 'applicable not only to information or ideas that are favorably received or regarded as inoffensive or as a matter of indifference, but also to those that offend, shock or disturb. Such are the demands of pluralism, tolerance and broadmindedness without which there is no democratic society'. See ECtHR 28 June 2001, *VGT Vereiniging gegen Tierfabriken v Switzerland*, paragraph 66.

432 Dahrendorf, R., F. Field and C. Hayman (1995). Report on Wealth Creation and Social Cohesion in a Free Society (the Dahrendorf Report). London: Commission on Wealth Creation and Social Cohesion, 34

433 Foa, R. The Economic Rationale for Social Cohesion: Cross-Country Evidence, 1. Paper presented at the International Conference on Social Cohesion and Development, 20 and 21 January 2011. <http://www.oecd.org/dev/pgd/46908575.pdf> See also Sarikakis, K. (2007). Mediating Social Cohesion: Media and cultural policy in the European Union and Canada. European Studies, 24, 68

434 Council of Europe (2008). *Report of high-level task force on social cohesion in the 21st century – Towards an active, fair and socially cohesive Europe*. TFSC (2007) 31E

435 For a comprehensive overview of the notion of social cohesion see Noll, H.H. (2009). The Impact of Cultural and Citizenship Education on Social Cohesion. Input Statement The Impact of Cultural and Citizenship Education on Social Cohesion: Chances – Challenges – Changes, Vilnius, Lithuania

110. The relationship between media and social cohesion can be seen from two different angles: media can be either 'centripetal', promoting integration, or 'centrifugal', encouraging division.[436] If the effect of new technologies is indeed the creation of an information micro-mundus at the expense of the free flow of information, then media inevitably becomes 'centrifugal'. This poisons one of the main functions that media are expected to perform in and for a democracy, namely to expose the views of and the problems facing each and every group of the society they are meant to serve and to advance a culture of common understanding.[437] Failure to perform this function could result in what Sunstein calls group polarization,[438] which occurs when citizens choose to cage themselves in 'echo chambers' or 'information cocoons' in order to avoid listening to dissenting voices.[439] Customized media consumption may then become an instrument used by radical groups to breed hostility towards those with conflicting opinions.[440]

111. By pointing out that content personalization may have a negative impact on democracy in order to illustrate that the ability to control our own media universe does not necessarily lead to exposure diversity, I do not seek to undermine the contribution digital media can make to the advancement of social cohesion. For example, digital media facilitate multisourcing, thereby enabling citizens to access multiple information sources.[441] Moreover, to the extent that they bring together people who share the same beliefs, digital media may also serve as a platform through which views that would otherwise not have found their way to the audiences manage to reach the public. To quote the EU High Level Group on Media Freedom and Pluralism, '[t]he media are part and parcel of the overall social fabric of society and may either help or hinder communication and mutual understanding between different parts of it, fostering or suppressing democratic debate, as the case may be.'[442] Opinions about whether 'the Daily Me' culture enhances diversity or not are

436 McQuail, D. (2010). McQuail's Mass Communication Theory (6th edition). London: Sage, 90 (summary of academic debates on the relationship between media and social order)

437 Drawing on this role, in its report 'A free and pluralistic media to sustain European democracy', the High Level Group on Media Freedom and Pluralism called upon Member States to have independent media councils with a politically and culturally balanced and socially diverse membership. See High Level Group on Media Freedom and Pluralism (2013). A free and pluralistic media to sustain European democracy, 7. <https://ec.europa.eu/digital-single-market/sites/digital-agenda/files/HLG%20Final%20Report.pdf>

438 Sunstein, C. (2003). Why Societies Need Dissent. Cambridge MA: Harvard University Press, 111–144

439 Sunstein (2007), supra n. 225, 46–96

440 See Hamelink, C. (1997). Media, Ethnic Conflict and Culpability. In Servaes, J. & Lie, R. (eds.). Media in Transition. Leuven/Amersfoort: Acco

441 See Reuters Institute (2017), supra n. 183, 11. The report notes that '[t]he reality is that, for most of us, social media are not something different but increasingly just part of the everyday media mix. Two-thirds of social media news users in the United States also … visit mainstream websites or apps (66%) – a bit more than the the general population. Just 2% ONLY use social media for news in an average week. This evidence acts as counter to the often-cited theories that we live in our echo chambers much of the time. Most people combine a number of different sources and platforms for news'

442 High Level Group on Media Freedom and Pluralism (2013), *supra* n. 236, 11

polarized[443] whereas the findings of relevant empirical research are either inconclusive[444] or interpreted in opposing ways.[445] Therefore, we cannot draw safe conclusions as to the extent to which personalized communication has created marginalization.[446] It is true, however, that we have already witnessed cases that show how audience polarization may be used to cultivate fanaticism and anarchy as well as the potential it has to destroy the social tissue. In Europe, for instance, extremist groups have been using new media to recruit members or advance their propaganda[447] with their 'groups of friends' calling for violence, discrimination against communities of different ethnicities and religions, and segregation.[448] Populist politicians also use social media to spread their fragmented ideology.[449] These examples illustrate why concerns relating to the personalized content consumption paradigm may not have been exaggerated.

443 See, for instance, Pariser, E. (2011). The Filter Bubble: What the Internet is Hiding from You. New York: Penguin Press, and Berners-Lee, T. Long Live the Web: A call for continued open standards and neutrality. 22 November 2010, Scientific American. <http://www.scientificamerican.com/article/long-live-the-web/> Both Pariser and Berners-Lee believe that personalized search has an adverse effect on exposure to conflicting ideas. Compare their views with Foster (supra n. 161, 22) who argues that personalization does not prevent users from seeking a diversity of voices.

444 See, for instance, Boukes, M., Hajo G. Boomgaarden, Marjolein Moorman and Claes H. De Vreese (2014). News With an Attitude: Assessing the Mechanisms Underlying the Effects of Opinionated News. Journal of Mass Communication and Society 17(3), 354–378

445 See, for instance, how the results of the 2012 On the State of the News Media Report that was prepared by the Pew Research Center Project for Excellence in Journalism concerning, *inter alia*, the role of social media in facilitating exposure to diverse sources/ideas have been interpreted by the European Commission: 'Much has been said about the use of social networks as a major driver of news, but recent research in the US has shown that this is not the case as only 9% of adults get news very often through social networks and the large majority of them still go to news websites, use keyword search or get news through a news organizing web site or application'. Compare the Commission's view with Foster's interpretation of whether social media create a 'filter bubble' or not: 'Recent research carried out in the US by the Pew Research Center concludes, for example, that social media are currently more used as an additional source of news rather than as a replacement source, hence widening not narrowing the 'filter'. For example, 71% of those who ever follow news on Facebook (and 76% on Twitter) also get news somewhat or very often from a news organization's website or app. Twitter scored relatively well in providing news which users felt they would never have found elsewhere'. See Commission (2012). *Digital Agenda for Europe – Scoreboard 2012*, 28 and Foster (2012), *supra* n. 161, 22

446 Karppinen (2009), supra n. 120, 163

447 For an overview of examples of online extremist narratives see, for instance, Radicalization Awareness Network (2012). Proposed Policy Recommendations for the High Level Conference. <http://ec.europa.eu/dgs/home-affairs/what-we-do/networks/radicalisation_awareness_network/ran-high-level-conference/docs/proposed_policy_recommendations_ran_at_en.pdf>

448 See, for instance, Sikorski, R. In Europe, a new wave of terrorism driven by social media. 17 October 2017, Euractiv. <https://www.euractiv.com/section/freedom-of-thought/opinion/in-europe-a-new-wave-of-terrorism-driven-by-social-media/>

449 See, for instance, Engesser, S., Nicole Ernst, Frank Esser and Florin Büchel (2016). Populism and social media: how politicians spread a fragmented ideology. Journal of Information, Communication and Society 20(8), 1109–1126. It must further be noted that research conducted by the Fundamental Rights Agency showed that, in the period between 1 January 2014 and 1 September 2016, courts, national equality bodies, independent press councils and independent regulatory or supervisory bodies for broadcasting organizations found incitement to hatred, discrimination or violence in media content in a number of instances. See Fundamental Rights Agency (2016). Incitement in media content and political discourse in EU Member States, 7 et seq. <http://ec.europa.eu/information_society/newsroom/image/document/2016-47/fra_media_and_incitement_paper_19752.pdf>

4.2 The citizens will interact (create and distribute content that strengthens democracy)

112. As previously noted, digitization and improvements in computing and wireless technologies have heralded a new era in which the role of the individual in the communication process is undergoing significant changes. The citizens may now set up outlets such as blogs and wikis, and influence and/or comment on the content provided by well-established media organizations by giving feedback to editors via, for instance, emails, test screenings and focus groups. Individuals are no longer powerless eyeballs, but may actively participate in the dissemination of information on issues of public concern, a function that was, until recently, reserved to professional journalists. Indeed, user-generated or user-created content (UGC and UCC respectively), that is, content produced and made available over the Internet 'outside of professional routines and practices',[450] may promote a more diverse and transparent media system; users may, for instance, create content that complements or even questions the accuracy of the content provided by mainstream media.[451]

113. In certain cases, UGC has had extreme democratic significance. One of the most prominent examples is the Arab Spring movement: Facebook and Twitter allowed citizen-journalists to communicate the atrocities of suppressive regimes in the Arab World, and spread awareness about and publicize protests aiming to bring down longtime political systems, even when leading media organizations were blocked.[452] The Arab Social Media Report, prepared by the Dubai School of Government, shows that the primary purpose of social media use during the uprisings for 55% of the population of the Arab world was to spread information around the globe about the uprisings, whereas for 66% the main goal of social media use was to raise awareness inside the country on the causes of the revolutions.[453] Another striking example of citizen journalism is WikiLeaks. Started by Australian activist Julian Assange, WikiLeaks operates as an online, not-for-profit organization that publishes leaks of confidential information of interest to the public, among which are included classified documents relating to wars, detention and torture, spying and (counter-) intelligence and government and corporate conspiracies.[454]

---

450 OECD (2007). Participative Web: User-Created Content, 4. <http://www.oecd.org/internet/interneteconomy/38393115.pdf>

451 Newman, N. (2009). The rise of social media and its impact on mainstream journalism: A study of how newspapers and broadcasters in the UK and US are responding to a wave of participatory social media, and a historic shift in control towards individual consumers. Oxford Reuters Institute for the Study of Journalism Working Paper, 5 (summarizing the literature regarding the impact of UGC on mainstream media). <https://reutersinstitute.politics.ox.ac.uk/sites/default/files/2017-11/The%20rise%20of%20social%20media%20and%20its%20impact%20on%20mainstream%20journalism.pdf>

452 For the role of social media in the organization of the Arab Spring protests see, for instance, Huang, C. Facebook and Twitter key to Arab Spring uprisings: report. 6 June 2011, The National. <http://www.thenational.ae/news/uae-news/facebook-and-twitter-key-to-arab-spring-uprisings-report>

453 Dubai School of Government (2011). Arab Social Media Report, Vol. 1 No. 2, 8

454 See <http://wikileaks.org/About.html> WikiLeaks became internationally famous for detailing corre-

Engaging in discovering and reporting on corporate and political mishandlings transforms individuals into community-serving citizens, a transformation which, in the absence of new media, could not easily occur.[455] However, in the EU, UGC has not reached its democratic potential yet. In a report which was published in 2012 and which deals with, *inter alia*, Internet usage in the EU, the Commission laments that in the year of the 'Indignados' and the Arab Spring, only 10% of Europeans participated in online consultations and voting to define civic or political matters.[456] Engagement in such activities does not seem to have increased since 2011; to the contrary, according to Eurostat, in 2017, only 9% of Europeans used the Internet to take part in online consultations and voting.[457] Based on recent survey data, in the UK, a Member State with one of the highest percentages of frequency of Internet use,[458] only 12% of the respondents reported that they had commented on news using social media in 2017.[459]

114. The above must be considered against the nature of UGC, whose impact on culture and democracy has been discussed by many contemporary social thinkers.[460] Keen, for instance, is of the view that:

---

spondence between the US State department and its diplomatic missions around the world, numbering around 250,000 cables. For more information see, for instance, Stein, S. Gibbs On Legal Action Against WikiLeaks: 'I Wouldn't Rule Anything Out'. 29 November 2010, The Huffington Post. <http://www.huffingtonpost.com/2010/11/29/gibbs-on-legal-action-aga_n_789311.html> and Fantz, A. See yourself as the next Assange? Good luck. 30 June 2012, CNN. <http://edition.cnn.com/2012/06/29/world/future-leaking-online/index.html> WikiLeaks is placed among many other similar initiatives, for instance, <www.opensecrets.org>, the website of the Center for Responsive Politics, a nonprofit research group that tracks money in politics and its effects on elections and public policy and the POGO project (Project on Government Oversight <www.pogo.org>), a non-partisan non-profit organization which investigates and exposes systemic abuses of power, mismanagement and subservience by the US government to powerful special interests

455 For more examples on the impact of UGC on politics see OECD (2007), supra n. 249, 36–37

456 Commission (2012). A vibrant digital single market, 28. <https://ec.europa.eu/digital-agenda/sites/digital-agenda/files/KKAH12001ENN-chap2-PDFWEB-2.pdf>

457 <http://ec.europa.eu/eurostat/tgm/table.do?tab=table&init=1&language=en&pcode=tin00129&plugin=1>

458 <https://ec.europa.eu/eurostat/statistics-explained/index.php/Digital_economy_and_society_statistics_-_households_and_individuals#Internet_usage> (one needs to click on 'Internet usage' to access the information

459 Ofcom (2017). International Communications Market Report, 144. <https://www.ofcom.org.uk/__data/assets/pdf_file/0032/108896/icmr-2017.pdf> Equally disappointing were the findings of older empirical research on user involvement with media production in national markets. For instance, a study prepared by the Cardiff School of Journalism, Media and Cultural Studies showed that, in the period 2007–2008, only 4% of the British public contributed content to a news media website. Wardle, C. and Andrew Williams (2008). ugc@thebbc. Understanding its impact upon contributors, non-contributors, and BBC News. Cardiff School of Journalism, Media and Cultural Studies. The final report is available at: <http://orca.cf.ac.uk/48158/> Another study focusing on the Greek media landscape concluded that in 2011 only 3% of users' comments enriched content by providing original, unreported information to mainstream media, and that on very few occasions users broadened the media agenda through their comments. See Milioni, D., Konstantinos Vadratsikas and Venetia Papa (2012). Their two cents' worth: Exploring user agency in readers' comments in online news media. Observatorio (OBS) Journal 6(3), 35

460 See, for instance, Baker (2007), supra n. 145; Sunstein (2007), supra n. 225, and Carr, N.G. (2010). The Shallows: What the Internet Is Doing to Our Brains. New York City: W. W. Norton & Company

> YouTube eclipses even the blogs in the inanity and absurdity of its content. ... The site is an infinite gallery of amateur movies showing poor fools dancing, singing, eating, washing, shopping, driving, cleaning, sleeping, or just staring into their computers. ... In a flattened, editor-free world where independent videographers, podcasters, and bloggers can post their amateurish creations at will, and no one is being paid to check their credentials or evaluate their material, media is vulnerable to untrustworthy content of every stripe.[461]

115. Keen's observations point to the main issues that must be taken into account when arguing (or, even worse, basing a regulatory instrument on the assumption) that the ability to create and distribute content has transformed the passive consumer into a perfectly conscious citizen. First, UGC may take different forms, including forms that awaken the audience's lowest instincts. In such cases, UGC cannot be expected to contribute to the mission of the media to provide content that advances self-development, an essential ingredient for effective citizenship and in general for behaviors that strengthen democracy.[462] Second, where UGC indeed feeds established media organizations with important unreported information, it may only complement rather than replace the latter which would verify the accuracy of the content concerned.[463]

116. Finally, when discussing the role of online users in promoting media pluralism through content that strengthens democracy, we must also consider their contribution to the dissemination of 'fake news'. Though misleading information is not produced by the users themselves, the flow of 'fake news' is largely attributed to the fact that users are more likely to share, like or comment on sensational stories; a recent empirical study found that, contrary to conventional wisdom, 'fake news' appears to spread more than the truth because humans, *not robots*, are more likely to spread it.[464]

117. The extent to which audience empowerment advances pluralism is still difficult to define. More research is undoubtedly needed to examine this phenomenon in order to define relevant policy priorities.[465] What the above analysis

461 Keen, A. (2007). The cult of the amateur. London: Nicholas Brealey Publishing, 5, 16 and 19

462 Chickering, A. R. (2008). Strengthening democracy and personal development through community engagement. New Directions for Adult and Continuing Education, 118, 87–95

463 Newman (2009), supra n. 250, 2. Newman conducted empirical research discussing the impact of UGC on British media and reports that in many cases traditional media organizations received a significant amount of false information which was deliberately posted to influence coverage of the events or the debate they generated.

464 Vosoughi, S., Deb Roy, and Sinan Aral (2018). The spread of true and false news online. Science 359(6380), 1146–1151. Available at: <http://science.sciencemag.org/content/359/6380/1146>

465 As was pointed out by the Council of Europe, '[i]t would ... be useful to explore the use and creation of media by the audience, which is changing with the new technologies, and examine if it is nowadays enough to offer what has traditionally been considered important information for a democracy' [emphasis added]. See Council of Europe (2009). Methodology for monitoring media concentration and media con-

makes clear, however, is that it is not reasonable to believe that the individual has been mutated from a set of powerless eyeballs in a fully enlightened and vigilant citizen. As Helberger puts it, 'ill-advised is the idea that governments can simply shift the responsibility for qualitative and diverse information away from the suppliers onto the ... consumers'.[466]

5. Conclusions

118. While the discussion concerning the extent to which the effects of digital technologies on media pluralism have been positive is still unsettled, the above analysis makes clear that concerns over its protection have by no means been rendered obsolete. 'Old gatekeepers' dominate the European marketplace, because traditional media still occupy a central position in media consumption and because existing firms have managed to reposition and solidify their presence in digital content markets. Technological developments may have lowered entry barriers, but money, reputation and the large customer base that goes with them are still important to attract eyeballs. Moreover, new businesses that have emerged with the advent of the Internet, including especially digital intermediaries, operate in ways that may disrupt the fair and free flow of information by introducing artificial forms of scarcity. In view of the above, a numerical increase in diversity has not remedied communicative inequalities resulting from concentration of ownership. To the contrary, the ways in which off- and online concentration are now mingled, affecting the amount and type of content to which citizens are exposed, are more difficult to define which in turn makes the pluralism concerns that arise more challenging to address.

119. Furthermore, it was seen that the wide array of information citizens now have at their fingertips or the ability to exercise control over content does not guarantee that they will choose to be exposed to diverse ideas. Individuals are increasingly engaging in simultaneous media use, a consumption pattern that prevents them from meaningfully engaging with the messages they receive. They may also be creating a private information microcosm where they speak only with others that think alike. To the extent that it isolates other viewpoints, control over content cannot be expected to advance pluralism. As to whether European audiences use digital media in ways that strengthen citizenship, this is hardly supported by empirical evidence.

---

tent diversity. Report prepared by the Group of Specialists on Media Diversity (MC-S-MD), 13

466 Helberger, N. (2008), From Eyeball to Creator – Toying with Audience Empowerment in the Audiovisual Media Service Directive. Entertainment Law Review 6, 134–5

120. To sum up, it is not safe to assume that media pluralism is an almost natural outcome of the digital media environment. Instead of gradually adopting a hands-off approach, policymakers, within each field of competence, should carefully reflect on the threats that both old and new gatekeepers pose to pluralism and create a framework within which marginalized viewpoints reach the audiences and audiences become more responsive to diversity.

CHAPTER 3

EU COMPETITION LAW AND MEDIA PLURALISM: IS PLURALISM A MARKET ACCESS EQUIVALENT, A RESTRICTION OF COMPETITION, OR MAYBE SOMETHING ELSE?

1. Introduction

121. The previous Chapter examined whether digital technologies have rendered concerns over media pluralism obsolete. Having analyzed the conditions that reflect the current state of European media markets, the Chapter concluded that, alongside issues that policymakers attempted to remedy in the past such as concentration of ownership, which remain pervasive, new perils posed by undertakings that operate in the online universe have emerged. At the EU level, cases that have given rise to pluralism concerns have fallen under *competition law*. This is so for the following three reasons, which have been discussed in Chapter 1. First, Article 7 TEU, which entitles the EU to take action in cases where there is a clear risk of a serious breach or a serious and persistent breach of media pluralism has had no practical significance. Equally negligible has been the role of Article 21(4) of the Merger Regulation, which allows Member States to take appropriate measures to protect media pluralism in cases where a concentration that has been cleared by the Commission raises the concern that the involved undertakings may hold significant opinion-forming power post-merger. Finally, due to competence limitations in the media domain, no pan-European sector-specific regulation applies to concentrations which do not pose threats to competition but which are likely to harm media pluralism.

122. What can or must the Directorate-General for Competition of the Commission do if it is called upon to examine a case that raises concerns over media pluralism? Primary EU law neither explicitly excludes the possibility that pluralism may impact the application of the EU competition rules nor remains silent on the issue; Article 167(4) TFEU provides that the Commission must take media pluralism into account in the definition and implementation of the EU competition policy and Article 11(2) CFREU imposes on the Commission the duty to 'respect' media pluralism. However, these provisions do not explain how competition may be balanced against pluralism considerations in cases of conflict.

123. As a result of the above, the relationship between EU competition law and media pluralism has been rather uneasy. The Commission itself has supported contradictory ideas about whether and, if so, how the application of the former may safeguard the latter. Over the past twenty years, it has moved from boldly stating that competition law prevents 'a degree of cumulative control or participation in media companies which might endanger the existence of a wide spectrum of views and opinions in the media markets'[467] to openly rejecting a conception of competition law that is concerned with pluralism considerations.[468] The Commission's decisional practice reflects this contradiction, thereby lacking consistency. Moreover, whether the Commission has indeed disregarded pluralism in recent cases is debatable, for some of the decisions it has adopted suggest otherwise.

124. This Chapter will explore whether and, if so, to what extent EU competition law, as interpreted and applied by the Commission, has contributed to maintaining media pluralism. To this end, I shall examine how the Commission's perceptions have filtered into its decisional practice. The Commission seems to have adopted two different approaches: it has regarded media pluralism either as an almost spontaneous result of unhindered market access, or as a value the protection of which would require restrictions of competition that it believes is not entitled to allow. The Chapter argues that these two approaches, which will be discussed in Parts 2 and 3 respectively, are not solid and have fallen short of protecting both competition and pluralism. But, applying EU competition law in a way that delivers pluralism-friendly results may go beyond the Commission's predispositions. Part 4 identifies a third approach to the relationship between competition and pluralism which appears to have more potential than the other two, for it may lead to competition decisions that are more accurate *and* pluralism-friendly without giving rise to controversies over competence.

---

467 Commission Communication from the Commission to the Council, the European Parliament, the European Economic and Social Committee and the Committee of the Regions on the future of European audiovisual regulatory policy, COM (2003) 784 final, 8

468 News Corp/BSkyB (Case COMP/M.5932) [2011] OJ C37/2, paragraphs 306–309

2. Media pluralism as a result of unhindered market access

125. On several occasions, the Commission has taken the stance that media pluralism is an almost spontaneous result of the undistorted functioning of the markets. For example, in the Issues Paper for the Liverpool Audiovisual Conference, the Commission states that '[t]he application of European competition law plays an important role in ... *ensuring market access* for new entrants. *Thus, ... competition policy can make an important contribution to maintaining and to developing media pluralism*, both in traditional television markets and in new upcoming markets' [emphasis added].[469] This is repeated verbatim in the Commission's Staff Working Document on Media Pluralism in the Member States of the EU[470] and, as a policy priority, it is reflected in several merger and antitrust decisions. These decisions can be divided into two categories. First, there have been decisions where the Commission was limited to noting that, since the transaction under scrutiny did not raise any foreclosure concerns, diversity could not be harmed.[471] Second, there have been cases where the Commission found that the involved undertakings would have the ability and incentive to foreclose the affected markets, but instead of adopting a prohibition decision, it attempted to address related concerns through 'access' remedies. In these decisions, which concerned traditional and emerging broadcasting markets, 'access' has come to mean almost exclusively 'access to the market for the acquisition of *premium content*', which is content that has the ability to attract mass audiences (e.g. box-office blockbusters and major sports events).[472] The implications of the first category of decisions for pluralism have already been examined in Chapter 2, where I discussed why it is not correct to assume that keeping the markets open to competition will produce a pluralism-friendly outcome; traditional and new media markets have high entry barriers and, even if diverse suppliers do enter the market, this cannot be expected to automatically guarantee content and exposure diversity. The analysis below will focus on the reasoning adopted in decisions falling under the second category. More particularly, I shall study whether the commitments that were made legally binding on undertakings selling rights to premium content have indeed facilitated market access as well as the relationship between these remedies and media pluralism.

469 Commission (2005). Issues paper for the Liverpool Audiovisual Conference: Media pluralism – What should be the European Union's role? Brussels: DG Information Society and Media, 2

470 Commission. Staff Working Document on Media Pluralism in the Member States of the EU SEC (2007) 32, 7

471 See, for instance, Bertelsmann/Planeta/Circulo (Case COMP/M.5838) [2010] OJ C 228/3, paragraphs 16, 39, 49, 57 and 59; HBO/Ziggo/HBO Nederland (Case COMP/M.6369) [2012] OJ C 72/2, paragraph 53, and Bertelsmann/KKR (Case COMP/M.5533) [2009] OJ C 240/01, paragraph 79

472 See the 'Media' Section of the website of DG Competition: 'Access to content is crucial to enable competition in media markets. This applies to infrastructure, platforms and devices (satellite, cable and terrestrial networks, TV sets, PCs, mobile devices)'. <http://ec.europa.eu/competition/sectors/media/overview_en.html>

2.1 Ensuring access to premium content as a means to protect undistorted competition

126. Premium content is undoubtedly a valuable input, for its transmission may generate significant advertising revenues on which the survival of media firms largely depends. For example, sports programming is of high value to advertisers and hence to content distributors because it is particularly appealing to men who are in the age groups 16 to 20 and 35 to 40; compared with other consumer groups, young men have a less-fixed spending pattern and are therefore more likely to try new products and services.[473] More particularly, football, a mass-attractive sport with high viewing figures, seems to be the most effective tool to address this group of the population which does not, as a rule, watch much television.[474] There are several examples illustrating how the possession (or lack thereof) of this type of content may affect market structures. For example, in the early 1990s, after acquiring the exclusive rights to the English Premier League, Sky was transformed from a loss-making company to a very profitable one.[475] Sky, which 'has built its business … on the back of live top football',[476] has dominated the UK pay-TV market ever since. In December 2005, Premiere, the German media group, lost 42% of its market value and a large part of its subscriber base after it released a statement that it had not managed to purchase the rights to the Bundesliga, whereas the new Bundesliga licensee Unity/Arena attracted over 900,000 subscribers within a few months.[477] Likewise, seven years of growth turned to a substantial decrease in subscriber numbers for TPS in France upon losing its broadcast rights to Ligue 1 matches.[478]

127. It bears noting that premium content is a crucially valuable input in digital markets despite the abundance of services currently available online. As the Commission noted in the Preliminary Report on the E-Commerce Sector Inquiry,[479] '[w]hile online transmission offers the possibility to innovate the

473 See UEFA Champions League (Case COMP/C.2-37.398) [2003] OJ L291/25, paragraph 73. See also EBU/Eurovision (Case IV/32.150) [2000] OJ L151/18, paragraph 50: 'pay-TV broadcasters, particularly in France, the United Kingdom and Spain have discovered that having attractive sporting events is an enormously motivating factor in recruiting subscribers, in particular young males with disposable income'

474 UEFA Champions League (Case COMP/C.2-37.398) [2003] OJ L291/25, paragraph 74

475 Ariño, M. (2005). Regulation and Competition in European Broadcasting – A study of pluralism through access. PhD thesis. Florence: European University Institute, 222

476 Gibson, O. Premier League lands £3bn TV rights bonanza from Sky and BT. 13 June 2012, The Guardian. <http://www.theguardian.com/media/2012/jun/13/premier-league-tv-rights-3-billion-sky-bt>

477 Hatton, C., Christoph Wagner and Hector Armengod (2007). Fair Play: How Competition Authorities have Regulated the Sale of Football Media Rights in Europe. European Competition Law Review 28(6), 346

478 Ofcom (2009b). Pay TV Phase Three Document: Proposed Remedies, paragraph 3.31. <http://stakeholders.ofcom.org.uk/binaries/consultations/third_paytv/summary/paytv_condoc.pdf>

479 The E-Commerce Sector Inquiry is an industry investigation into the main e-commerce market trends and competition concerns, which the Commission launched in 2015. It led to the publication of a Preliminary Report and a Final Report setting out the main findings of the audit. For more information see: <http://ec.europa.eu/competition/antitrust/sector_inquiries_e_commerce.html>

provision of access to products and services, *demand for digital content services is ultimately driven by demand for the content offered.* From this perspective, the main driver of competition remains the same: attractive content' [emphasis added].[480] This is illustrated by how premium content is valued by providers such as digital platforms and electronic communications service providers. For example, in 2016, Twitter purchased the worldwide rights to broadcast ten games of the US National Football League.[481] In 2018, Facebook hired Eurosport's CEO to lead the social network's efforts to broker worldwide deals for live-streaming sports.[482] Based on the results of a recent survey conducted by the Body of European Regulators for Electronic Communications, electronic communications service providers are increasingly acquiring (or producing) premium content in order to attract subscribers to their fixed and/ or mobile offers.[483] These examples illustrate that 'Content is (still) King'.[484]

128. While in theory ensuring access to premium content seems appropriate to address some of the issues undercutting competition in media markets, such as the indirect network effects created by exclusive transmission and the resulting downward spirals that lead to quasi-monopolistic or oligopolistic market structures, the analysis that follows will show that the Commission's interventions have done little to nothing to protect undistorted competition.[485] I shall attempt to demonstrate the above by examining the Commission's decisional practice in the area of joint selling of broadcast rights to sports events, in particular, football.[486]

480 Commission (2016). Preliminary Report on the E-Commerce Sector Inquiry, paragraph 924

481 European Audiovisual Observatory (2016). Audiovisual sports rights between exclusivity and right to information, 10. <https://rm.coe.int/1680788a5d>

482 See, for instance, Spangler, T. Facebook Recruits Eurosport Chief Peter Hutton to Lead Global Sports-Rights Deals. 21 January 2018, Variety. <http://variety.com/2018/digital/global/facebook-hires-eurosport-peter-hutton-global-sports-deals-1202671505/>

483 BEREC (2018). Report on the impact of premium content on ECS markets and the effect of devices on the open use of the Internet, 10–11. <https://berec.europa.eu/eng/document_register/subject_matter/berec/reports/8013-berec-report-on-the-impact-of-premium-content-on-ecs-markets-and-the-effect-of-devices-on-the-open-use-of-the-internet>

484 For more information about this quote see Heath, E. 'Content is King'–Essay by Bill Gates 1996. 29 January 2017, Medium <https://medium.com/@HeathEvans/content-is-king-essay-by-bill-gates-1996-df74552f80d9>

485 On the practice the Commission developed in the area of joint acquisition of rights to premium content see, for instance, Van Rompuy, B. and Karen Donders (2013). The EBU's Eurovision System Governing the Joint Buying of Sports Broadcasting Rights: Unfinished Competition Business. Competition Law Review 9(1), 7–28; Van Rompuy, B. and Karen Donders (2012). Competition Law, Sports, and Public Service Broadcasting: The Legal Complexity and Political Sensitivity of Measuring Market Distortion and Public Value. Journal of Media Law 4(2), 213–228, and Herold, A. (2002). Rules Governing the Acquisition by Third Parties of Television Rights for Sporting Events under Eurovision in Breach of the European Competition Law. International Journal of Communications Law and Policy 7, 1–9

486 It should be noted that access to a valuable input in general and access to premium content in particular is a cross-cutting theme in this book. The access to premium content remedies the Commission has imposed on media undertakings that acquire exclusive rights from football associations and then sell them to competing content providers will also be discussed in Chapter 4, which discusses the relevant decisional practice in the area of merger control and which reaches similar conclusions regarding the ineffectiveness of access remedies. In this Chapter we focus on joint selling by football associations, that is, concentration at the rights holder (not the licensees) level. As will be seen in greater detail below and in Chapter 4, the Commission's tolerance towards concentration at the upstream level adversely affected competition in downstream broadcasting and neighboring content markets. On the practice the Commission developed in the area of access to premium films see, for instance, Ariño (2005), supra n. 9, 261–271

129. In the Netherlands,[487] Spain[488] and Portugal,[489] broadcast rights to football matches are sold by the football clubs individually. But the general trend across Europe has been the implementation of a joint selling model, whereby a national association/federation is assigned by the various clubs the task of selling the rights to the matches of the competition for the national championship concerned.[490] International competitions such as the UEFA Champions League[491] and the World Cup[492] are also controlled by single entities that trade the rights on behalf of the participants.

130. The first case in this area that was examined by the Commission concerned the central marketing of broadcast rights to the UEFA Champions League.[493] Initially, the Commission refused to grant a negative clearance as well as an exemption under Article 101(3) TFEU because UEFA would sell all the free and pay-TV rights on an exclusive basis to a single broadcaster per territory for a period lasting several years.[494] This commercial policy was found to reduce output and eliminate price competition.[495] Following negotiations with the Commission, UEFA introduced changes to its collective selling scheme that were considered appropriate to address the concerns the Commission had identified throughout its investigation. These changes can be summarized as follows:

» The media rights were split into fourteen smaller packages;

» Contrary to the previous arrangement, individual clubs would have the right to exploit deferred rights as well as certain rights that were previously sold exclusively by UEFA;

487 In the Netherlands, broadcast rights are sold on the basis of the 'home rights game' model whereby each football club is allowed to sell the rights to the matches played at its stadium. Dutch football clubs have been employing this model since the national competition authority considered that joint selling should be regarded as a price-fixing arrangement which does not qualify for an exemption. See Comisión Nacional de la Competencia (CNC) (2008). Informe sobre la competencia en los mercados de adquisición y explotación de derechos audiovisuales de fútbol en España, fn. 58

488 ibid, see in particular p. 22 et seq. In Spain, the visiting club must grant an authorization to the home team for the rights to the game to be sold to a media provider

489 See Peeters, T. Competitive balance in European football leagues. 14 August 2012, Football Perspectives. <http://footballperspectives.org/competitive-balance-european-football-leagues>

490 Ariño (2005), supra n. 9, 233. For example, the Football Association Premier League (FAPL) sells the rights to the UK Premier League, the Deutsche Fußball Liga GmbH is the federation charged with selling the rights to the German Bundesliga, and rights to the French Ligue are sold by Ligue de Football Professionnel (LFP).

491 See, for instance, UEFA Champions League (2014). Media content rights sales: UEFA Champions League/UEFA Super Cup. <http://www.uefa.org/MultimediaFiles/Download/Publications/competitions/Marketing/01/96/76/90/1967690_DOWNLOAD.pdf>

492 <http://www.fifa.com/aboutfifa/organisation/tv/salesdistribution.html>

493 UEFA Champions League (Case COMP/C.2-37.398) [2003] OJ L291/25

494 Commission (2001, July). Commission opens proceedings against UEFA's selling of TV rights to UEFA Champions League. Press Release IP/01/1043. <http://europa.eu/rapid/press-release_IP-01-1043_en.htm?locale=it>

495 Commission (2002, June). Commission welcomes UEFA's new policy for selling the media rights to the Champions League, Press Release IP/02/806. <http://europa.eu/rapid/press-release_IP-02-806_en.htm?locale=it>

» All media rights would be made available, including those rights UEFA was reluctant to sell such as Internet and UMTS rights; and

» The media rights contracts would be awarded for a period not exceeding three years through a public bidding procedure.[496]

131. The same approach was adopted in *German Bundesliga* (Deutschen Fußball Liga, DFL)[497] and in *English Football Association Premier League* (FAPL);[498] the Commission exempted the agreements upon the condition that rights would be broken down into several packages that could only be acquired on the basis of a transparent and non-discriminatory bidding procedure, previously unexploited rights would be made available on the market, contracts with media operators would not exceed three seasons, and individual clubs would retain the right to sell certain rights.[499]

132. The above remedies proved to be ineffective. For example, FAPL segmented the rights for the 2004–2007 seasons into four packages; all packages, however, were ultimately acquired by Sky.[500] A similar scenario emerged in Germany. In January 2012, the Bundeskartellamt accepted DFL's commitment to divide the rights into more than one package.[501] Yet, this did not prevent Sky Deutschland from purchasing the exclusive rights to the Bundesliga for pay-TV, IPTV *and* mobile for the 2013–2017 seasons.[502] Therefore, despite what the Commission expected, these arrangements did not 'enhance the possibility for more broadcasters, including small and medium-sized companies, to obtain [premium sports] content'.[503]

133. Stricter remedies have also failed to achieve this goal. For example, because Sky acquired all of the Premier League packages for the 2004–2007 seasons

496 ibid.

497 Joint Selling of the Media Rights to the German Bundesliga (Case COMP/C-2/37.214) [2005] OJ L134/46

498 Joint Selling of the Media Rights of the FA Premier League (Case COMP/C.2/38.173) [2006] OJ L176/104

499 Commission (2003, July). New marketing system for Bundesliga broadcasting rights. Press Release IP/03/1106. <http://europa.eu/rapid/press-release_IP-03-1106_en.htm?locale=it>; Joint Selling of the Media Rights to the German Bundesliga (Case COMP/C-2/37.214) [2005] OJ L134/46, Annex, paragraphs 2.1 et seq.; Notice published pursuant to Article 19(3) of Council Regulation No. 17 concerning Case COMP/C.2/38.173 and 38.453, Joint selling of the media rights of the FA Premier League on an exclusive basis [2004] OJ C 115/02, paragraphs 16 et seq. On the practice the Commission developed in the area of joint selling rights and in particular on whether the relevant decision-making has benefited the consumer see Lefever, K. and Ben Van Rompuy (2009). Ensuring Access to Sports Content: 10 Years of Intervention. Time to Celebrate? Journal of Media Law, 1(2), 243-268

500 Notice published pursuant to Article 19(3) of Council Regulation No. 17 concerning Case COMP/C.2/38.173 and 38.453, Joint selling of the media rights of the FA Premier League on an exclusive basis [2004] OJ C 115/02, paragraphs 10 and 11

501 European Competition Network. Brief 02/2012, 6. <http://ec.europa.eu/competition/ecn/brief/02_2012/brief_02_2012.pdf>

502 See Briel, R. Sky Deutschland wins all live Bundesliga rights. 18 April 2012, Broadband TV News. <http://www.broadbandtvnews.com/2012/04/18/sky-deutschland-wins-live-bundesliga-rights/>

503 UEFA Champions League (Case COMP/C.2-37.398) [2003] OJ L291/25, paragraph 171

during the Commission's investigation, FAPL further undertook to specify in the invitations to future tenders that no single operator would be entitled to acquire all of the live audiovisual packages (no single buyer obligation).[504] The no single buyer obligation may have resulted in Setanta entering the market, but this was of little value. Sky won the rights to five of the six packages (the maximum available to a single bidder) whereas Setanta purchased the rights to the remaining package, 'generally recognized to be the least attractive'.[505] Moreover, Setanta did not manage to exert effective competitive constraints on Sky; in June 2009, it went into administration and its rights were awarded to ESPN, which concluded a wholesale deal with Sky for distribution of the package on Sky's DSat platform.[506] As a result, Setanta customers were ultimately forced to buy a Sky subscription.[507]

134. The above examples illustrate why concerns over distortion of competition in media markets that arise from joint selling agreements are not likely to be addressed through unbundling obligations.[508] Given that antitrust intervention to split up rights into different packages has been far from a success story, it is striking that the Commission is *still* of the view that 'unbundling' is an effective means to boost competition in (digital) media markets.[509]

2.2 Ensuring access to premium content as a means to protect media pluralism

135. The contribution of the Commission's efforts to ensuring access to premium content is questionable, not only from a competition but also from a pluralism perspective. First, premium content, be it an UEFA Champions League match, the World Cup finals or a Hollywood film, is the same irrespective of whether it is provided by a well-established media organization or a new entrant. Second, ensuring that more than one company acquires this content does not necessarily incentivize the provision of more original or marginalized content that has the capacity to advance democracy. For example, it was a *sports* broadcaster (Setanta) that managed to purchase the license to exploit certain

504 Joint Selling of the Media Rights of the FA Premier League (Case COMP/C.2/38.173) [2006] OJ L176/104, paragraph 3.2.

505 Ofcom (2009b), supra n. 12, paragraph 2.53

506 ibid, paragraph 1.17, fn. 42

507 ibid, paragraph 12.40

508 Ariño (2005), supra n. 9, 242

509 See Commission (2016), supra n. 14, paragraph 642. The Commission notes that 'splitting up rights in order to allow a variety of digital content providers to offer their services by using different technologies may increase competition in digital content markets'. For a detailed analysis of the issues that arise from how the Commission defines 'bundling' in the E-Commerce Sector Inquiry Reports as well as from the potential implications of 'unbundling' for competition and consumer welfare see Bania, K. The Effects of Broadcasting Digitization on EU Competition Law: A Tale of National and EU Politics. Paper presented at the 13th Conference of the Academic Society for Competition Law, 21–23 June 2018, New York University

football rights as a result of the no single buyer remedy imposed on FAPL.[510] Third, and related to the above, the argument that the acquisition of premium content allows providers to promote their overall program, thereby leading to the exposure of the audiences to content that strengthens citizenship, is weak. As Ladeur observes, somewhat cynically, 'the likelihood that a spectator may acquire an interest in political background information by watching top sporting events is perhaps not particularly high'.[511] Finally, as already mentioned, even if the Commission intervenes to limit the scope and duration of an exclusive contract between the rights holder and a media provider, this does not mean that a new entrant will have the financial resources to successfully bid for the rights after the contract in question expires. Hence, ensuring access to premium content does not necessarily guarantee media pluralism. Where it indeed allows new entrants or established firms to build or maintain a customer base respectively, it *may* cater to supply diversity. However, the connection with content and exposure diversity is far more uncertain.

136. In light of the above, the practice the Commission has developed in the media sector to ensure market access seems to be, from a competition perspective, ineffective and, from a pluralism angle, theoretically unfounded.

3. Media pluralism as a restriction of competition

137. As previously noted, the Commission has occasionally stated that, in applying EU competition law, its greatest contribution to addressing pluralism concerns consists in its interventions to ensure that market access is not hindered. But, what position has the Commission taken in cases where it found that keeping the affected markets open to competition would not necessarily remedy these concerns? This section will explore whether the Commission has attempted to reconcile competition and media pluralism in cases of conflict, and whether, and if so to what extent, pluralism can justify restrictions of competition. Where appropriate, I will refer to cases that do not involve pluralism-specific concerns.

138. Recent decisional practice shows that the Commission has been keen to distance itself from values which, in its view, are irreconcilable with the value of undistorted competition and which could be harmed as a result of a transaction it examined. For example, in *News Corp/BSkyB*, the Commission scrutinized a concentration by which News Corporation[512] would acquire sole

510 Ofcom (2009b), supra n. 12, paragraph 2.53

511 Ladeur, K. H. (2004). Guaranteeing the Programming Mandate of Public Broadcasters and Restraints on Private Broadcasters' Programmes in Multimedia Conditions, German Law Journal 5(8), 915

512 News Corp/BSkyB (Case COMP/M.5932) [2011] C 37/2, paragraph 3

control of BSkyB.[513] In addition to the possible anti-competitive effects it was likely to create,[514] the proposed concentration also raised major pluralism concerns.[515] The Commission was limited to noting that relevant issues are for the UK authorities to address under Article 21(4)[516] of the Merger Regulation[517] and decided to approve the concentration on the grounds that it did not raise serious doubts as to its compatibility with the common market.[518] The Commission followed a similar approach in *Google/Doubleclick*, which dealt with the acquisition by Google of rival online advertising services provider Doubleclick.[519] In this case, several market participants and civil society groups voiced concerns about the combination of the databases held by Google and Doubleclick.[520] It was argued that, as a result of the merger, user privacy could be undermined because the combination of the databases in question would increase the power of the merging firms to track customer online behavior and use it for advertising purposes.[521] The Commission cleared the concentration for the reason that it was not likely to significantly impede effective competition in the common market and that, irrespective of the approval of the merger, the merging parties were obliged to respect EU and national privacy regulation in their day-to-day business.[522]

139. The Commission has not always disassociated competition from other public policies. To the contrary, in the past, non-competition policy considerations have significantly influenced the outcome of competition decisions.[523] For example, agreements were granted an exemption under Article 101(3) TFEU[524] on the grounds that the anti-competitive concerns they raised could be outweighed

---

513 ibid, paragraphs 1 and 4

514 ibid, paragraph 28

515 See, Ofcom (2010b). Report on public interest test on the proposed acquisition of British Sky Broadcasting Group plc by News Corporation

516 See Chapter 1, n. 103

517 News Corp/BSkyB (Case COMP/M.5932) [2011] C 37/2, paragraph 309

518 ibid, paragraph 310. The Commission made the same remarks in the decision dealing with Murdoch's second attempt to acquire control of Sky. See Fox/Sky (Case COMP/M.8354) [2017] OJ C238/1, paragraphs 469 et seq.

519 Google/Doubleclick (Case COMP/M.4731) [2008] OJ C 184/6, paragraph 1

520 Brockhoff, J., Bertrand Jehanno, Vera Pozzato, Carl-Christian Buhr, Peter Eberl, and Penelope Papandropoulos (2008). Google/DoubleClick: The first test for the Commission's non- horizontal merger guidelines. Competition Policy Newsletter 2, 59

521 ibid.

522 *Google/Doubleclick* (Case COMP/M.4731) [2008] OJ C 184/6, paragraph 368. For a critical analysis of how the Commission has dealt with recent cases raising data protection concerns see Bania, K. (2018). *The Role of Consumer Data in the Enforcement of EU Competition Law*. European Competition Journal 14(1), 38–80

523 For instance, Townley estimates that between 1993 and 1 May 2004, when Regulation 1/2003 on the modernization of the rules implementing Articles 101 and 102 TFEU started to apply, non-economic considerations were decisive in over 32% of formal Commission decisions that were adopted under Article 101(3) TFEU. See Townley, C. (2009). *Article 81 EC and Public Policy*. Oxford: Hart Publishing, 5–6

524 For a comprehensive overview of how public policy concerns were taken into account by the Commission in the application of Article 101(3) TFEU see Monti, G. (2002). *Article 81 EC and Public Policy*. Common Market Law Review 39(5), 1057–1099

by their contribution to employment stabilization[525] or pollution reduction.[526] A similar reasoning can be traced to old decisions in the media sector.[527] For instance, in *EBU/Eurovision*, the Commission decided that the agreement entitling the members of the European Broadcasting Union, a professional association of broadcasting organizations, to participate in a system of joint acquisition of television rights, justified an exemption under Article 101(3) TFEU on the basis that it enabled EBU members 'to provide a broader range of sports programs, including minority sports and sports programs with education, cultural or humanitarian content'.[528] Another notable example is a series of concentrations in the broadcasting sector that were blocked throughout the 1990s.[529] Embedded in the relevant prohibition decisions is the belief that the strict application of competition rules may not only protect competitive market structures in the media but may 'also contribute to maintaining plurality in this sensitive sector'.[530]

140. *News Corp/BSkyB* and *Google/Doublick* are illustrative of the process of modernization of EU competition law. This modernization process, which started in the late 1990s and which was largely influenced by changes in US antitrust policy that were prompted by a general acceptance of the law and economics analysis of the 'Chicago School',[531] includes two components.[532] The first involves a narrowing of the objectives of competition law: the new conception of competition law posits that economic efficiency and consumer welfare, as understood by neoclassical economics, are the guiding principles of EU competition policy.[533] The second, which follows from the first, posits that formal economic methodology is the central organizing structure for applying competition law.[534] Together, these two components are commonly

525 See, for instance, *Decision of the Commission of the European Communities of 15 December 1975 relating to a procedure under Article 85 of the EEC treaty* (IV/847 – SABA) [1976] OJ L28/19. The Commission's decision was later upheld by the Court. See ECJ, Case 26/76 *Metro-SB Großmärkte GmbH & Co. KG v Commission of the European Communities* [1977] ECR 1875, paragraph 43. The same approach was followed in Commission decision of 12 December 1983, relating to a proceeding under Article 85 of the EEC Treaty [1983] OJ L376/22. The Court upheld the Commission's decision. See ECJ, Case 42/84 *Remia and others v Commission* [1985] ECR 2545, paragraph 42

526 See, for example, *Philips/Osram* (Case IV/34.252) [1994] OJ L378/37, paragraph 27 and *CECED*, Commission Decision 2000/475/EC [2000] OJ L187/47, paragraphs 47–51 and 55–57

527 For a comprehensive overview of the Commission decisions in the media sector where non-economic concerns were decisive see Arino (2005), *supra* n. 9, 139–144

528 *EBU/Eurovision* (Case IV/32.150) Commission decision 93/403/EEC [1993] OJ L179/23, paragraph 62. This decision was subsequently annulled by the Court. See CFI, Joined Cases T-528, 542, 543 & 546/93 *Métropole télévision SA and others v Commission* [1996] ECR II-649

529 These decisions will be analyzed in Chapter 4

530 Harcourt, A. (2005). *The European Union and the Regulation of the Media Markets*. Manchester: Manchester University Press, 51

531 Anderman, S. (2007). *The Interface between Intellectual Property Rights and Competition Policy*. Cambridge: CUP, 7

532 Gerber, D. J. (2008). *Two Forms of Modernization in European Competition Law*. Fordham International Law Journal 31(5), 1247

533 See Lowe, P. Consumer Welfare and Efficiency – New Guiding Principles of Competition Policy? Speech given at the 13th International Conference on Competition and 14th European Competition Day, 27 March 2007, Munich

534 Gerber (2007), *supra* n. 66

referred to as the 'more economic approach'.[535]

141. There is already a large body of literature discussing the objectives of EU competition law in general and the shift to a more economic approach in particular.[536] While conflicting views pull in many different directions, broadly speaking, at one end of the spectrum are those that argue that interference from other policies that have thus far influenced competition law should be eliminated altogether.[537] EU competition law, they say, should be allowed to become 'as in the USA, antitrust law pure and simple'.[538] As regards media pluralism specifically, it is not clear, so the argument goes, why competition law 'should suffer from such concerns, in particular at a time where the Commission seems to have reached a clear stance on the aims of competition policy'.[539] At the other end of the spectrum are those that maintain that competition law should be enforced by reference to media pluralism. Advocates of this latter view suggest that an obligation to assess the effects of media concentrations on pluralism be incorporated into the Merger Regulation.[540] They recommend the establishment of a specialist body that would advise the Directorate-General for Competition on pluralism-specific concerns raised by concentrations affecting media markets.[541]

142. These opposite views are arguably equally problematic. On the one hand, competition law cannot be solely concerned with efficiency and welfare considerations. From a teleological perspective, competition has never been referred to in the EU Treaties as an objective in its own right. To the contrary, competition was embedded in primary EU law right from the start as one of the key *instruments* towards the objective of European integration in general and the completion of the single market in particular.[542] That competition is a

---

535 ibid.

536 See, for instance, Akman, P. (2009a). Consumer Welfare and Article 102 EC: Practice and Rhetoric. World Competition, 32, 71–90; Akman, P. (2009b). Searching for the Long-Lost Soul of Article 82 EC. Oxford Journal of Legal Studies, 29 (2), 267–303; Andriychuk, O. (2010). Rediscovering the Spirit of Competition: On the Normative Value of the Competitive Process. European Competition Journal, 6(3), 575–610; Drexl, J., Kerber, W. Podszun, R. (eds.) (2010). Competition Policy and the Economic Approach – Foundations and Limitations. Cheltenham: Edward Elgar; Lovdahl-Gormsen, L. (2007). The Conflict Between Economic Freedom and Consumer Welfare in the Modernization of Article 82 EC. European Competition Journal 3(2), 329–344; Odudu, O. (2010). The Wider Concerns of Competition Law. Oxford Journal of Legal Studies 30(3), 599–613; and Zimmer, D. (ed.) (2012). The Goals of Competition Law. Cheltenham: Edward Elgar

537 See, for instance, Motta, M. (2004). Competition Policy: Theory and Practice. Cambridge: CUP, Section 1.3; and Bishop, S. and Mike Walker (2002). The Economics of EC Competition Law (2nd edition). London: Sweet and Maxwell, 23–27

538 Amato, G. (1997). Antitrust and The Bounds of Power – The Dilemma of Liberal Democracy in the History of the Market. Oxford: Hart Publishing, 116

539 Ibáñez Colomo, P. (2006). Saving the Monopsony: Exclusivity, Innovation and Market Power in the Media Sector. Research Papers in Law, 7/2006, Global Competition Law Centre, 26

540 See, for instance, Craufurd-Smith (2004). Rethinking European Union competence in the field of media ownership: the internal market, fundamental rights and European citizenship. European Law Review 29(5), 669; Ariño (2005), supra n. 9, 405–410, and Komorek, E. (2013). Media Pluralism and European Union, 281–283. Alphen aan den Rijn: Kluwer Law International

541 ibid.

542 Jones, A. and Brenda Sufrin (2014). EU Competition Law – Texts, Cases and Materials (5th edition). Oxford: OUP, 35–40

means to an end, rather than an end in itself, continues to hold true in the post-Lisbon era.[543] The Court of Justice has repeatedly favored this teleological interpretation, holding that Articles 101 and 102 TFEU should be implemented in light of the overall objectives of the Union.[544] A literal interpretation of the Treaties leads to the same conclusion. More particularly, the Treaty on the Functioning of the European Union includes several 'cross-sectional'[545] provisions that establish that non-economic considerations relating to environmental[546] and consumer protection,[547] employment,[548] human health, education, adequate social protection, social exclusion, training,[549] development cooperation,[550] welfare of animals,[551] economic, social and territorial social cohesion[552] and, of particular relevance for this study, cultural diversity,[553] must be 'integrated', 'ensured' or 'taken into consideration' in the definition

543 It bears noting that neither the TEU nor the TFEU replicates Article 3(f) of the Treaty of Rome, which established that one of the main activities through which the Community should fulfill the objectives laid down in Article 2 EEC consisted in 'the institution of a system ensuring that competition in the common market is not distorted'. In the context of the amendments introduced by the Lisbon Treaty, the principle of undistorted competition was transferred to a Protocol (Protocol No. 27 on the Internal market and Competition [2008] OJ C 115/309) and Article 3 TEU now lays down in broad terms that one of the Union's tasks is the establishment of an internal market. This does not mean that the EU attaches less importance to competition now than before; Article 51 TEU explicitly states that the Protocol forms 'an integral part' of the Treaties. The ECJ has also ruled that moving the principle of undistorted competition to a Protocol has no legal consequence (see Case C-52/09, Konkurrensverket v TeliaSonera Sverige AB [2011] ECR I-527. However, the fact that the Protocol repeats Article 3(f) of the Treaty of Rome almost verbatim corroborates the view that competition continues to be a means to serve the internal market

544 Van Rompuy, B. (2012). Economic Efficiency: The Sole Concern of Modern Antitrust Policy? Alphen aan den Rijn: Kluwer Law International, 219, referring to ECJ, Joined Cases 56 and 58/64 Consten SA and Grundig-Verkaufs GmbH v Commission of the European Economic Community [1966] ECR 299, 340; ECJ, Case 32/65 Italian Republic v Council and Commission [1966] ECR 234, 405; ECJ, Joined Cases 41 and 44/70 NV International Fruit Company and others v Commission [1971] ECR 411, paragraphs 86–89; ECJ, Case 6/72 Europemballage Corporation and Continental Can Company Inc v Commission [1973] ECR 215, paragraphs 23–24; ECJ, Case 229/83 Leclerc/Au blé vert [1985] ECR 1, paragraph 8, and ECJ, Case 26/76 Metro-SB Großmärkte GmbH & Co. KG v Commission of the European Communities [1977] ECR 1875, paragraph 20

545 Monti (2002), supra n. 58, 1069, noting that this term is used mostly by German scholars (see fn. 48)

546 Article 11 TFEU: 'Environmental protection requirements must be integrated into the definition and implementation of the Union's policies and activities, in particular with a view to promoting sustainable development'

547 Article 12 TFEU: 'Consumer protection requirements shall be taken into account in defining and implementing other Union policies and activities'

548 Article 147(2) TFEU: 'The objective of a high level of employment shall be taken into consideration in the formulation and implementation of Union policies and activities'

549 Article 9 TFEU: 'In defining and implementing its policies and activities, the Union shall take into account requirements linked to the promotion of a high level of employment, the guarantee of adequate social protection, the fight against social exclusion, and a high level of education, training and protection of human health'; Article 168(1) TFEU: 'A high level of human health protection shall be ensured in the definition and implementation of all Union policies and activities'

550 Article 208(1) TFEU: 'Union policy in the field of development cooperation shall be conducted within the framework of the principles and objectives of the Union's external action'

551 Article 13 TFEU: 'In formulating and implementing the Union's agriculture, fisheries, transport, internal market, research and technological development and space policies, the Union and the Member States shall, since animals are sentient beings, pay full regard to the welfare requirements of animals, while respecting the legislative or administrative provisions and customs of the Member States relating in particular to religious rites, cultural traditions and regional heritage'

552 Article 175 TFEU: 'The formulation and implementation of the Union's policies and actions and the implementation of the internal market shall take into account the objectives set out in Article 174 and shall contribute to their achievement'

553 Article 167(4) TFEU: 'The Union shall take cultural aspects into account in its action under other provisions of the Treaties, in particular in order to respect and to promote the diversity of its cultures'

of other Union policies and activities, including competition enforcement. Article 7 TFEU, introduced by the Lisbon Treaty, solidifies this need for coherence by establishing a general obligation of the EU to 'ensure consistency between its policies and activities, taking all of its objectives into account and in accordance with the principle of conferral of powers'. As a matter of law, the extent to which these cross-sectional clauses impact the application of the EU competition rules is not clear.[554] It can be noted that the wording of some cross-sectional provisions is stronger than others.[555] For example, under Article 168(1) TFEU, in its action under other provisions of the Treaties, the Union is obliged to 'ensure' a 'high level' of human health whereas pursuant to Article 167(4) TFEU the Union is bound to 'take cultural aspects into account'. The wording of the latter suggests a weaker level of integration than the one required by the former.[556] However, Article 167(4) TFEU, albeit loosely drafted, cannot be rendered devoid of any mandatory effect. In other words, the duty it enshrines cannot be disregarded altogether when applying the EU competition provisions of the Treaty; Article 167(4) TFEU and similar cross-sectional clauses require compromise.[557] The Court of Justice has traditionally supported this approach, corroborating the position that the EU competition policy cannot be implemented in a vacuum, that is to say, completely detached from other EU values.[558] On the other hand, rendering undistorted competition dependent on the protection of media pluralism is not appropriate either. Article 167 TFEU lacks both a strong wording to support the counter-argument *and* direct effect.[559] Competition rules, however, are directly applicable and in a higher position in the hierarchy of the priorities of the Union 'in view of the generality of their reach, the strength of their wording, and their close link with essential objectives of the EU'.[560] Even under

554 Van Rompuy (2012), *supra* n. 78, 220

555 Ariño (2005), supra n. 9, 141. For a detailed comparison of these clauses, including the different ways in which they were implemented, see Psychogiopoulou, E. (2008). The Integration of Cultural Considerations in EU Law and Policies. Leiden: Martinus Nijhoff Publishers, 6–84

556 Van Rompuy (2012), supra n. 78, 225

557 ibid. referring to Kingston, S. (2010). *Integrating Environmental Protection and EU Competition Law: Why Competition Isn't Special*. European Law Journal 16(6), 789; Casey, D. (2009). *Disintegration: Environmental Protection and Article 81 EC*. European Law Journal 15(3), 367; Townley (2009), *supra* n. 57, 55, 62–63; Schweitzer, H. (2007). *Competition Law and Public Policy: Reconsidering an Uneasy Relationship. The Example of Article 81*, 5. EUI Working Paper, No. 2007/32; Psychogiopoulou, E. (2006a). *The Cultural Mainstreaming Clause of Article 151(4) EC: Protection and Promotion of Cultural Diversity or Hidden Cultural Agenda?* European Law Journal 12(5), 585; Lafferty W. M. and Eivind Hovden (2003). *Environmental Policy Integration: Towards an Analytical Framework*. Environmental Politics 12(1), 16; and Sevenster, H.G. and Hans Vedder (2000). *Integreren or concurrenen? De rol van niet-mededingingsbelangen, in het bijzonder milieubescherming, in het kartelbeleid*, Tijdschrift voor Europees en Economisch Rect 2(1), 4–5. For a different view see, for instance, Komninos, A. P. (2005). *Non-competition concerns: Resolution of Conflicts in the Integrated Article 81 EC*. The University of Oxford Centre for Competition Law and Policy Working Paper No. 08/05, and Odudu, O. (2006). *The Boundaries of EC Competition Law: The Scope of Article 81*, 158–174. Oxford: OUP

558 For a detailed analysis of the relevant case law see Townley, (2009), supra n. 57, 55–86. Note that the Commission has been severely criticized for supporting in its Guidelines on Article 101(3) TFEU an interpretation that seeks to marginalize non-competition policy considerations, which clearly goes against this case law

559 Van Rompuy (2012), *supra* n. 78, 225

560 ibid. referring to Cruz, J. B. (2002). Between Competition and Free Movement: The Economic

the broadest reasonable interpretation, concerns over media pluralism cannot override competition considerations in cases of conflict. Hence, the proposal to build into the Merger Regulation a requirement to conduct a full-fledged analysis of the effects of a transaction on media pluralism (with a view to prohibiting concentrations which pose pluralism concerns but which are not likely to distort competition) seems to go beyond what EU law sanctions.

143. An interpretation that would seem sound in terms of law and policy is in between the two extremes outlined above, a position which many have already supported.[561] As regards the question of whether and, if so, to what extent the Commission should take into account non-economic considerations when deciding whether an anti-competitive agreement qualifies for an exemption under Article 101(3) TFEU, Monti, for example, maintains that 'an agreement which contributes to a Community policy but is inefficient, or partitions the common market, should not be exempted … but an agreement which results in increased efficiency *and* which contributes to other Community goals is exempted because the combination of these two benefits outweighs the restriction of competition.'[562] Monti and other commentators[563] convincingly contend that under this interpretation unnecessary restrictions of competition are not accepted, whereas the cross-sectional clauses are not rendered devoid of any legal effect.[564] But, many, including those same commentators that argue in favor of a moderate approach,[565] have expressed skepticism about whether the above proposed interpretation applies to the cross-sectional clause on culture. More particularly, it has been asserted that the Commission's task to take cultural aspects into account under Article 167(4) TFEU should be read as a *renvoi* to the laws of the Member States.[566] Due to the Union's quasi non-existent competence to regulate culture, so the argument goes, the only plausible interpretation of Article 167(4) TFEU is 'respect for the national legislator's political discretion'.[567] While competence limitations cannot be overlooked,[568] this argument is not ultimately conclusive. Even if the stronger wording of other cross-sectional clauses allows for the non-economic goals they pursue to be weighed more heavily against undistorted competition,

---

Constitutional Law of the European Community. Oxford: Hart Publishing, 63–66

561 See, supra n. 91

562 Monti (2002), supra n. 58, 1070

563 See, for instance, Wesseling, R. (2000). The Modernization of Antitrust Law. Oxford: Hart Publishing, and Van Rompuy (2012), supra n. 78, 403

564 Monti (2002), supra n. 58, 1070–1

565 ibid, 1084

566 Schmid, C. U. (2000). Diagonal Competence Conflicts between European Competition Law and National Regulation – A Conflict of Laws, Reconstruction of the Dispute on Book Price Fixing. European Review of Private Law, 8, 164

567 ibid.

568 As already discussed in detail in Chapter 1, Article 167(5) TFEU explicitly excludes the adoption of a harmonizing instrument protecting media pluralism and Article 6 TFEU limits the Union's relevant legislative competence to actions that solely support, supplement and coordinate the actions taken by Member States.

there is arguably some room for cultural, including media, policy considerations to be taken into account in the application of the EU competition rules. In several instances, the Court has been asked to rule on the compatibility with the internal market of national measures that aimed at safeguarding media pluralism. In these cases, the Court refused to read media pluralism within one of the narrowly interpreted grounds for justification laid down in Article 52 TFEU.[569] It has, however, acknowledged that a media policy may constitute an overriding requirement relating to the general interest, thereby justifying restrictions on the freedom to provide services.[570] In other words, in interpreting the provisions on free movement, the Court has attempted to resolve the conflict by compromise. It should also be noted that the Note from the Praesidium that drafted the Charter of Fundamental Rights of the EU (CFREU) explains that Article 11(2), which establishes the EU's duty to abstain from taking action that would undermine media pluralism, is to be interpreted in light of the aforementioned case law.[571] The question then arises as to whether we should adopt a different approach to the interpretation of restrictions on competition introduced by arrangements that could potentially enhance media pluralism. The Treaties would not seem to support this approach, for free movement and competition are equally important for the achievement of the internal market.

144. The main conclusion to draw from the above analysis is that both a teleological and a literal interpretation of the Treaties may support the argument that media pluralism concerns can justify restrictions of competition. However, it should be borne in mind that the extent to which pluralism concerns can affect the outcome of a competition decision is fairly limited. Article 167(4) TFEU has no direct effect and, post-Lisbon, the EU continues to have limited competence to regulate this area.[572] As a result, the legal basis for resolving any conflict by compromise, albeit existent, remains rather thin.

569 See, for instance, ECJ, Case 352/85 Bond van Adverteerders v Netherlands [1988] ECR 2085, paragraphs 31 et seq.; and ECJ, Case C-211/91 Commission v Belgium [1992] ECR I-6757, paragraphs 7 et seq.

570 See, for instance, ECJ, Case C-288/89 Stichting Collectieve Antennevoorziening Gouda and others v Commissariaat voor de Media [1991] ECR I-4007, paragraphs 23–29; ECJ, Case C-353/89 Commission of the European Communities v Kingdom of the Netherlands [1991] ECR I-4069, paragraphs 29–31, and ECJ, Case C-148/91 Vereniging Veronica Omroep Organisatie v Commissariaat voor de Media [1993] ECR I-487, paragraphs 9–13

571 Praesidium of the Convention which drafted the Charter of Fundamental Rights of the EU (2000). Text of the explanations relating to the complete text of the Charter as set out in CHARTE 4487/00 CONVENT 50, 14. <http://www.europarl.europa.eu/charter/pdf/04473_en.pdf>

572 As already mentioned in Chapter 1, even if post-Lisbon the Charter of Fundamental Rights has been made legally binding on the EU institutions, Article 51(2) explicitly states that the CFREU 'does not establish any new power' for the Union.

4. Media pluralism considerations as an integral part of competition assessments: rethinking 'competition' in the media

145. It was seen above that in recent years the Commission has taken the stance that, in cases where preventing market foreclosure is not sufficient to remedy concerns over media pluralism, it lacks the competence to examine these concerns further.[573] Competence limitations, however, were not the only reason put forward in justification of this approach. This is illustrated by *News Corp/ BSkyB* where the Commission stated that the scope and purpose of competition and pluralism assessments '*are very different*',[574] clearly implying that a pluralism review would have led to findings different from those in its decision.[575] However, contrary to the Commission's opinion, these two types of analyses are not irreconcilable. In this section, I shall attempt to demonstrate a) that the objectives of and legal frameworks for competition and pluralism assessments may, but do not always, produce different outcomes, and b) that, if the EU competition rules are properly adapted to the particularities of media markets, competition assessments may deliver pluralism-friendly results.

4.1 Why can competition and media pluralism assessments lead to different outcomes?

146. The goals of and rules underpinning competition and media pluralism reviews may produce different, even opposing, outcomes. This is so for at least three reasons. First, concentration as prohibited by media regulation, and concentration as a competition concern, do not necessarily coincide as normative concepts.[576] The accumulation of significant market power is not a breach of EU competition law; Article 102 TFEU does not prevent an undertaking from acquiring and holding, on its own merits, a dominant position, but only the abuse thereof.[577] Yet, from a pluralism perspective, centralization of market power, which is the presumed equivalent of opinion-forming power, would be sufficient to trigger the application of media ownership restrictions.[578]

573 News Corp/BSkyB (Case COMP/M.5932) [2011] C 37/2, paragraph 306

574 ibid, paragraph 307

575 The same remark is made by the Commission in the decision dealing with Murdoch's second attempt to acquire control of Sky. See Fox/Sky (Case COMP/M.8354) [2017] OJ C238/1, see in particular paragraph 471. For more information about this case see Chapter 1, n. 103

576 Ariño (2005), supra n. 9, 384

577 See, for instance, ECJ, Case C-52/09 Konkurrensverket v TeliaSonera Sverige AB [2011] ECR I-527, paragraph 24; ECJ, Case 322/81 Nederlandsche Banden-Industrie-Michelin v Commission [1983] ECR 3461, paragraph 57, and ECJ, Joined Cases C-395/96 P and C-396/96 P Compagnie maritime belge transports and others v Commission [2000] ECR I-1365, paragraph 37

578 Ariño (2005), *supra* n. 9, 385

Nevertheless, there are examples illustrating that in some cases concentration is not understood very differently under the two regimes. For example, in cases where ownership rules apply,[579] the market-share thresholds, above which it is inferred that media firms hold appreciable opinion-forming power, do not always differ from market-share thresholds that could suggest that the firms concerned have the ability and incentive to significantly impede effective competition. For instance, on the one hand, the Greek law on media concentration lays down that a media undertaking may not hold more than 35% of the market in which it operates.[580] In Germany, this threshold is set at 30%.[581] On the other hand, in exercising merger control, which resembles media ownership control in that the decision to oppose a merger is based on the *likelihood* that the concentration under scrutiny will grant the merging parties the power to engage in undesirable practices, the Commission has occasionally found that market shares between 25% and 35%, which would be held by the involved undertakings post-merger, were an indication that the transaction could significantly impede effective competition.[582] These examples illustrate that, unless an undertaking becomes dominant as a result of internal growth, which for competition purposes would not in itself trigger intervention against the undertaking concerned but which for pluralism purposes would be forbidden, there may be cases where action to address concentration under the two frameworks would not necessarily go in different directions.

147. Second, it has been contended that competition and pluralism assessments are likely to produce different outcomes for the reason that competition law protects competition whereas regulation in support of media pluralism protects competitors.[583] However, what or whom EU competition law protects is not entirely clear, for the case law and the Commission's decisional practice are ambiguous on this matter. More particularly, and especially in the past, the Commission seems to have used competition policy to safeguard competitors. This policy, which is also referred to as the policy of 'economic

579 And this is the case with the vast majority of Member States. However, in most cases, the rules require the media company concerned to control at least 25% of the market. For an overview of the restrictions that apply in each Member State see Commission (2009). Independent Study on Indicators for Media Pluralism in the Member States – Towards a Risk-based Approach. Annex III – Country Reports

580 Law No. 3592/2007 of 19/07/2007 on Media Concentration and Licensing Procedures [2007] Official Gazette 161/3371, Article 3(3). It should be noted that this restriction applies to mono-media concentration.

581 This is expressed in terms of the audience share of all viewers. Interstate Broadcasting Treaty (2009), Article 26(2).

582 See, for instance, Rewe/Meinl (Case IV/M.1221) Commission decision 1999/674/EC [1999] OJ L274/1, paragraphs 98–114; Nestlé/Ralston Purina (Case COMP/M.2337) [2001] OJ C 239/7, paragraphs 44–47. The Block Exemption Regulation on the application of Article 101(3) TFEU to certain categories of vertical agreements is based on a similar presumption. More particularly, the Regulation provides that the exemption from the rules on competition applies on condition that the market shares held by the parties to the agreement do not exceed 30% of the relevant market in which each party operates. See Commission Regulation (EU) No. 330/2010 of 20 April 2010 on the application of Article 101(3) TFEU to categories of vertical agreements and concerted practices [2010] OJ L102/1, Article 3(1)

583 Ariño (2005), *supra* n. 9, 385

freedom',[584] supports the idea that individuals should be allowed to participate in the market unobstructed from the economic power held by other market participants.[585] The influence it has exercised on the Commission is exemplified by documents where explicit references to individual economic freedom as a goal of EU competition law are made,[586] as well as by policy and legislative action that was driven by the aim to protect competitors rather than rivalry as a value in itself. For example, the Commission has exempted certain types of agreements from general prohibitions on restrictive practices with a view to offering SMEs the opportunity to compete with larger firms.[587] More recently, however, the EU institutions appear to advocate the position that a restriction of competition is not equivalent to a restriction of the parties' individual freedom. In addition to statements made by the Commission,[588] this is illustrated by the shift underpinning the refusal to supply case law: in the late 1980s and early 1990s, the Commission adopted a broad interpretation of the term 'abusive refusal to supply', whereby companies which held a dominant position and which refused to grant their competitors access to a valuable input were deemed to act in violation of Article 102 TFEU.[589] In recent times, however, stricter tests have been introduced that limited the scope of Article 102 TFEU in cases of refusal to deal.[590] Yet, at least in the media domain, the issue remains unsettled; the imposition of remedies that seek to ensure access to premium content does not protect the process of competition but competing content providers, for otherwise the Commission would allow the company that made the highest bid to transmit the acquired content on an exclusive

584 Jones and Sufrin (2014), *supra* n. 76, 17

585 ibid.

586 See, for instance, Commission (1986). Annual Report on Competition Policy 1985, 11: Effective competition 'preserves the freedom and right of initiative of the individual economic operators and it fosters the spirit of enterprise. … Competition policy should ensure that the abusive use of market power by a few does not undermine the rights of the many.'

587 See, for instance, Commission Notice of 18 December 1978 concerning its assessment of certain subcontracting agreements in relation to Article 85(1) of the EEC Treaty [1979] OJ C 1/2, paragraph 1; Commission Notice concerning agreements of minor importance which do not fall under Article 85(1) of the Treaty establishing the European Economic Community [1997] OJ C 372/13, paragraph 19; Commission (EEC) Regulation No. 67/67 on the application of Article 85(3) of the Treaty to certain categories of exclusive dealing agreements [1967] OJ 57/849; Commission (EEC) Regulation No. 2349/84 on the application of Article 85(3) of the Treaty to certain categories of patent licensing agreements [1984] OJ L219/15, corrected by [1985] OJ L13/34

588 See, for instance, Commission (2013, April). Commission seeks feedback on commitments offered by Google to address competition concerns – questions and answers: 'The Commission does not act to protect competitors as such, but to preserve the competitive process for the benefit of consumers. It acts only when there is harm to competition with negative effects on consumers, in particular in terms of reduced choice and less innovation' [emphasis added]. <http://europa.eu/rapid/press-release_MEMO-13-383_en.htm>

589 See, for instance, Sealink/B&I–Holyhead [1992] 5 CMLR 255

590 See, for instance, CFI, Case T-504/93 Tiercé Ladbroke SA v Commission [1997] ECR II-923; ECJ, Case C-7/97 Oscar Bronner GmbH & Co. KG v Mediaprint Zeitungs- und Zeitschriftenverlag GmbH & Co. and others [1998] ECR I-7791; ECJ, Joined cases T- 374/1994, T-375/1994, T-384/1994 and T-388/1994 European Night Services and others v Commission of the European Communities [1998] ECR II-3141. For more information on this paradigm shift and the conditions introduced by the more restrictive case law see, for instance, van den Bergh, R. and Peter Camesasca (2006). European Competition Law and Economics – A Comparative Perspective, 274–276. Antwerpen, Groningen, Oxford: Intersentia-Hart Publishing

basis without requiring it to share the content in question with its rivals.[591]

148. Finally, and arguably more fundamentally, competition and pluralism reviews may lead to different outcomes because the 'public interest' they seek to protect is not the same.[592] On the one hand, for the purposes of competition, the public interest is primarily understood as the 'satisfaction of consumer preferences'.[593] The audience member as consumer has traditionally been perceived as 'someone who measures quality in terms of quantity, maximum pleasure and price'.[594] Audiences as consumers are solely concerned with serving their individual needs and preferences,[595] and hence tend to focus on a limited amount of content that reflects those needs and preferences.[596] Along this line, the consumer can get the content she wants at a low price through open and competitive markets[597] and effective competition enforcement. On the other hand, for the purposes of pluralism, the public interest is understood as the collective benefit that results from an informed and cohesive citizenry.[598] The audience member as citizen has an interest in having the media perform functions that are vital for a well-functioning democracy (e.g. provide accurate and unbiased information about matters of common concern, control the power holders[599]).[600] This interest is protected through the effective exercise of freedom of expression,[601] which is enshrined in Article 10 ECHR, the Constitutions of Member States, Article 11 CFREU, and sector-specific regulation.[602]

149. Yet, the nature of this distinction is not absolute, and not only because we are both consumers and citizens.[603] The EU competition rules have occasionally been interpreted and applied in order to serve a 'public interest' that went

591 See, for instance, UEFA Champions League (Case COMP/C.2-37.398) [2003] OJ L291/25, paragraph 171: These arrangements should 'enhance the possibility for more broadcasters, including small and medium-sized companies, to obtain UEFA Champions League content'

592 Ariño (2005), *supra* n. 9, 384

593 ibid.

594 Helberger, N. (2008). From Eyeball to Creator – toying with audience empowerment in the Audiovisual Media Service Directive. University of Amsterdam, Institute for Information Law, Working Paper, 5 <http://www.ivir.nl/publicaties/download/239>, also published in Entertainment Law Review 6, 128–137

595 Hasebrink, U. (2011). Giving the audience a voice: The role of research in making media regulation more responsive to the needs of the audience. Journal of Information Policy 1, 324

596 Harrison, J. and Lorna Woods (2007). European Broadcasting Law and Policy. Cambridge: CUP, 9

597 Lefever, K. (2012). New Media and Sport: International Legal Aspects. The Hague: T.M.C. Asser Press, 78

598 Ariño (2005), *supra* n. 9, 384

599 Nieminen, H. and Josef Trappel (2011). *Media serving democracy*. In Trappel□, J., Werner A. Meier, Leen D'Haenens□, Jeanette Steemer and Barbara Thomass (eds.). *Media in Europe Today*. Bristol: Intellect, 141–143

600 Hasebrink (2011), supra n. 129, 324

601 Lefever (2012), supra n. 131, 79

602 Related to this issue see also Karppinen, K. and Halvard Moe (2014). What we talk about when we talk about 'the market': Conceptual contestation in contemporary media policy research. Journal of Information Policy 4, 327–341

603 Harrison and Woods (2007), supra n. 130, 8

beyond the accommodation of 'consumer interests', as defined above. For example, in *CECED*, an agreement bound the parties to refrain from producing washing machines that did not meet the energy efficiency standards they had agreed upon;[604] the Commission decided that the consumer benefit condition set by Article 101(3) TFEU was fulfilled on the grounds that:

> the benefits to society brought about by the CECED agreement appear to be more than seven times greater than the increased purchase costs of more energy-efficient washing machines. *Such environmental benefits for society would adequately allow consumers a fair share of the benefits even if no benefits accrued to individual purchasers of machines* [emphasis added].[605]

150. The 2006 Leniency Notice, which sets out the framework for rewarding cooperation by undertakings which are or have been party to cartels, states that '[t]he interests of consumers *and* citizens in ensuring that secret cartels are detected and punished outweigh the interest in fining those undertakings that enable the Commission to detect and prohibit such practices' [emphasis added].[606] In *Konkurrensverket v TeliaSonera*, the Court ruled that the function of the competition rules is 'to prevent competition from being distorted *to the detriment of the public interest, individual undertakings and consumers, thereby ensuring the well-being of the European Union*' [emphasis added].[607] By referring to these examples, I do not attempt to argue that the concept of consumer interest can be stretched to an extent that encompasses all that is of concern to the audience member as a citizen. For example, a citizen may benefit from rules preventing journalists from holding a political mandate, but this is not necessarily a conflict of interest that can be addressed by EU competition law. However, in all the above cases, the Commission and the Court understand that competition law is in a public interest that embraces but is not confined to consumer satisfaction, that is to say, they endorse the idea that competition law may deliver a collective outcome that is not necessarily the sum of individual gains.

151. It is made clear from the above considerations that the purpose of, and legal frameworks for, competition and pluralism reviews may be at odds from the outset, but, depending on how EU competition law is interpreted, convergent outcomes cannot be excluded.

---

604 Commission decision 2000/475/EC relating to a proceeding under Article 81 of the EC Treaty and Article 53 of the EEA Agreement, CECED (Case IV.F.1/36.718) [2000] OJ L187/47, paragraph 30

605 ibid, paragraph 56

606 Commission Notice on immunity from fines and reduction of fines in cartel cases [2006] OJ C 298/11, paragraph 3

607 ECJ, Case C-52/09 Konkurrensverket v TeliaSonera Sverige AB [2011] ECR I-527, paragraph 22

4.2 Can EU competition assessments deliver pluralism-friendly results? The Commission's narrow understanding of 'competition' in the media

152. The focus of competition assessments and the scope of pluralism reviews are different for the reason that an authority entrusted with deciding on the impact of a conduct or transaction on pluralism has the power to examine whether the firms or individuals under scrutiny may misrepresent facts, marginalize opposing viewpoints, and control the political agenda, in violation of the applicable media laws and principles. For example, in assessing the likely effects of the *News Corp/BSkyB* deal on media pluralism, Ofcom examined, *inter alia*, whether News Corp would interfere with Sky News' editorial policies and whether existing regulatory safeguards, such as impartiality requirements on TV broadcast news, were sufficient to ensure no undue influence on Sky News' independence.[608] The EU competition watchdog is not entitled to carry out these tasks. Does this, however, exclude a pluralism-friendly interpretation of the competition rules? The answer is no, especially if this interpretation allows the Commission to reach more accurate competition decisions. As will be seen in greater detail below, the Commission has ignored the possibilities of a pluralism-friendly competition analysis that is based on neither controversial and ineffective access remedies nor disproportionate restrictions of competition. This is because it has adopted a narrow understanding of the concept of 'competition' in media markets.

153. In applying EU competition rules to media markets, the Commission has disregarded altogether parameters of competition that drive demand for content. For example, the Commission has maintained that assessments of mergers affecting the media sector focus on checking 'whether there is ... *the ability of the merged entity to profitably increase prices* on defined antitrust markets post-merger' [emphasis added].[609] Yet, competition is not only about prices, as a number of policy documents binding on the Commission rightly point out. For example, as already mentioned in Chapter 1, the (Horizontal and Non-Horizontal) Merger Guidelines lay down that the Commission's mission consists in preventing mergers that would be likely to significantly increase the market power of firms, and explain that an increase in market power refers to 'the ability of one or more undertakings to profitably increase prices, *reduce output, choice or quality of goods and services or diminish innovation*' [emphasis added].[610] This is repeated verbatim in several other documents in

608 Ofcom (2010b), *supra* n. 49, 70 *et seq*.

609 News Corp/BSkyB (Case COMP/M.5932) [2011] C 37/2, paragraph 307

610 Commission Guidelines on the assessment of horizontal mergers under the Council Regulation on the control of concentrations between undertakings [2004] OJ C 31/3, paragraph 8 and Commission Guidelines on the assessment of non-horizontal mergers under the Council Regulation on the control of concentrations between undertakings [2008] OJ C 265/7, paragraph 10

which the Commission provides guidance on how it applies EU competition law,[611] including the Guidelines on Vertical Restraints[612] and the Guidance on the Commission's enforcement priorities in applying Article 102 TFEU to abusive exclusionary conduct by dominant undertakings.[613]

154. The non-price dimensions of competition seem to have played a major role in the Commission's decisional practice in several sectors on various occasions. For example, the Commission's decisions have occasionally been based on quality as a feature of product differentiation in order to delineate the boundaries of the relevant product market(s).[614] In *UPS/TNT*, the Commission distinguished express services from slower services on the grounds that customers that need to be sure that the items they ship will reach their destination within one day are not willing to switch to slower services as a result of a price increase.[615] Based on this distinction, the Commission found that the merging firms were close competitors and decided to block the notified transaction because it would have reduced the number of significant players in the market for express services to only three or two.[616] In *Unilever/Sara Lee*, the Commission concluded that the merging parties' deodorant brands *Dove* and *Sanex* were substitutable because they shared the same skin-caring attributes.[617] This concentration was approved subject to, *inter alia*, the condition that Unilever would not enter the affected markets with the *Sanex* brand.[618] In *Universal/EMI*, the Commission found that recorded music in physical format and recorded music in digital format belong to separate markets because they

611 For example, the Guidelines on Horizontal Cooperation Agreements illustrate how various forms of cooperation agreement between actual or potential competitors can positively or adversely affect product quality or variety. Communication from the Commission – Guidelines on the applicability of Article 101 of the Treaty on the Functioning of the European Union to horizontal cooperation agreements [2011] OJ C 11/1. See, for instance, paragraphs 183, 185 and 190. The Notice on Market Definition provides instructions on how quality characteristics can inform the relevant market definition analysis. See Commission Notice on the definition of relevant market for the purposes of Community competition law [1997] OJ C 372/3, paragraph 22

612 Commission Guidelines on Vertical Restraints [2010] OJ C 130/1. See, for instance, paragraph 91

613 The Commission states in its Guidance on the Commission's enforcement priorities in applying Article 82 of the EC Treaty to abusive exclusionary conduct by dominant undertakings [2009] OJ C 45/2 (paragraph 11) that it 'considers that an undertaking which is capable of profitably increasing prices above the competitive level for a significant period of time does not face sufficiently effective competitive constraints and can thus generally be regarded as dominant. In this Communication, the expression 'increase prices' includes the power to maintain prices above the competitive level and is used as short-hand for the various ways in which the parameters of competition – such as prices, output, innovation, the variety or quality of goods or services – can be influenced to the advantage of the dominant undertaking and to the detriment of consumers' [emphasis added]. Similarly, the Guidelines on the Application of Article 101(3) TFEU (paragraph 16) [2004] OJ C 101/08 lay down that '[a]greements between undertakings are caught by the prohibition rule of Article 101(1) when they are likely to have an appreciable adverse impact on the parameters of competition on the market, such as price, output, product quality, product variety and innovation' [emphasis added].

614 OECD (2013c). The Role and Measurement of Quality in Competition Analysis, 79. <http://www.oecd.org/competition/Quality-in-competition-analysis-2013.pdf>

615 Commission (2013, January). Mergers: Commission blocks proposed acquisition of TNT Express by UPS. Press Release IP 13/68. <http://europa.eu/rapid/press-release_IP-13-68_en.htm>

616 ibid.

617 Unilever/Sara Lee Body Care (Case COMP/M.5658) [2012] OJ C 23/10, paragraphs 579 et seq.

618 ibid, paragraph 1388

have different sound quality.[619] Having defined the relevant markets in this way, the Commission concluded that the transaction would grant the merged entity the ability to extract onerous licensing terms from digital retailers[620] and adopted a clearance decision after the entity undertook to divest a significant part of its digital repertoire.[621] The Commission has also used quality standards as a parameter against which it assessed supply-side substitutability. For example, in *Amcor/Alcan*, the Commission found that, within the flexible packaging market, pharmaceutical flexible packaging should be regarded as a separate market for the reason that it is characterized by high hygiene requirements and highly risk-aversive customers.[622] The concentration was approved subject to the condition that Amcor would divest its pharmaceutical flexible packaging arm.[623]

155. Originality, variety and quality considerations have influenced decisions not only because they led to narrower market definitions, but also because they were taken into account in the assessment of the effects of a merger transaction or unilateral conduct on competition. For example, in *Intel/McAfee*, one of the main concerns was that Intel could foreclose competing providers of anti-virus software by degrading interoperability of its hardware with security solutions other than the acquired McAfee products.[624] The Commission found that lack of interoperability would negatively impact the affected markets, 'in particular with regard to innovation and choice'.[625] The same conclusion was reached in *Microsoft* concerning the impact of tying Windows Media Player and Windows PCs on the delivery of content over the Internet and on multimedia software.[626] Similarly, in *Intel*, the Commission concluded that, absent the exclusionary pricing practices in which Intel had engaged, customers would have had 'a wider quality choice'.[627]

156. However, the non-price dimensions of competition seem to have played little or no role in the Commission's decisional practice in the media sector. For our purposes, relevant decisions can be divided into two categories. First, there have been decisions where the Commission shows a clear preference for price competition. For example, in assessing mergers affecting free-to-air TV (i.e. advertising-financed television) markets, the Commission has

619 Universal Music Group/EMI Music (Case COMP/M.6458) [2012] OJ C 220/8, paragraph 127

620 ibid, paragraph 636

621 ibid, paragraphs 826 *et seq.* and 880 *et seq.*

622 Amcor/Alcan (Case COMP/M.5599) [2010] OJ C 35/1, paragraphs 23 and 137 et seq.

623 ibid, paragraphs128 et seq.

624 Intel/McAfee (Case COMP/M.5984) [2011] OJ C 98/1, paragraphs 154 et seq.

625 ibid, paragraph 172. Note that in this case the Commission imposed upon Intel a wide range of commitments to ensure that no technical tying of Intel hardware and McAfee security solutions would occur (see paragraphs 301 et seq. and 341 et seq.)

626 Microsoft (Case COMP/C-3/37.792) Commission Decision C (2004) 900 final, paragraphs 782 and 1067

627 Intel (COMP/C-3/37.990) Commission Decision D (2009) 3726 final, paragraph 1603

repeatedly taken the stance that, even though the audience's preferences are 'an important indicator of the attractiveness and acceptance of the broadcasting channels',[628] the exercise of market definition should consist in identifying the effective alternative sources of supply for the advertisers on the grounds that viewers do not pay for the content broadcast.[629] As a result, merger decisions in the broadcasting sector have been limited to discussing the effect of the concentration under scrutiny on advertising markets. Similar remarks can be made with respect to decisions in the book publishing sector. Parties to fixed book pricing agreements, which establish that booksellers shall sell books at the price that is set by the publisher that produced them, occasionally put forward the argument that the agreement under consideration qualified for an exemption under Article 101(3) TFEU because it enabled publishers to cross-subsidize less popular titles through the profits they made on fast-selling books.[630] As a result, the parties claimed, the agreement led to a wider range of books made available on the market, thereby allowing consumers to receive a fair share of the benefits resulting from the agreement.[631] The Commission rejected this argument on the basis that, even if a variety of titles is to be regarded as benefiting the consumers, the price of the product is the key element in their decision to purchase a book.[632]

157. Second, there have been decisions where the Commission has made incidental references to quality, variety or originality as features of product differentiation, but these features have not influenced the outcome of the decisions concerned. For example, in merger decisions in the newspaper sector, the Commission has repeatedly noted that the market for national daily newspapers might be divided into smaller markets according to the editorial line of newspapers or the quality of the publications (e.g. quality press as opposed to tabloids).[633] Nevertheless, in these cases, the Commission meticulously avoided delineating the boundaries of the markets affected by the transaction,[634] whereas, to my knowledge, in none of these decisions was

628 See, for instance, *RTL/Veronica/Endemol (HMG)* (Case IV/M.553) [1996] OJ L124/32, paragraph 20

629 See, for instance, News Corp/Telepiù (Case COMP/M.2876) [2004] OJ L110/73 paragraph 24; News Corp/BSkyB (Case COMP/M.5932) [2011] OJ C37/2 paragraph 97; SFR/Télé 2 (Case COMP/M.4504) [2007] OJ L316/57, paragraph 45; News Corp/Premiere (Case COMP/M.5121) [2008] OJ C 219/4, paragraph 19; Telenor/Canal+/Canal Digital (Case COMP/C.2/38.287) [2003] OJ C 149/10, paragraph 28; BSkyB/Kirch Pay-TV (Case COMP/JV.37) [2000] OJ C 110/45, paragraph 24; Bertelsmann/Kirch/Premiere (Case IV/M.993) [1999] OJ L053/1, paragraph 18, and Kirch/Richemont/Multichoice/Telepiù (Case IV/M.584) [1995] OJ C 129/6, paragraph 15

630 *VBBB/VBVB* (Case IV/428) Commission decision 82/123/EEC of 25 November 1981 relating to a proceeding under Article 85 of the EEC Treaty [1982] OJ L52/36, paragraph 50

631 ibid, paragraph 54

632 ibid, paragraph 55

633 Gruner + Jahr/Financial Times/JV (Case IV/ M. 1455) [1999] OJ C 80/5, paragraph 17; Wegener/PCM/JV (Case COMP/M.3817) [2005] C 191/3, paragraph 10; Newspaper Publishing (Case IV/M.423) [1994] OJ C 85/5, paragraph 18, and Recoletos/Unedisa (Case IV/M.1401) [1999] OJ C 73/6, paragraph 18

634 Recoletos/Unedisa (Case IV/M.1401) [1999] OJ C 73/6, paragraph 28; Newspaper Publishing (Case IV/M.423) [1994] OJ C 85/5, paragraphs 13–16; Wegener/PCM/JV (Case COMP/M.3817) [2005] C 191/3, paragraph 20, and Gruner + Jahr/Financial Times/JV (Case IV/M.1455) [1999] OJ C 80/5, paragraph 20

quality degradation or reduction in 'editorial' competition post-merger taken into account. Likewise, non-price dimensions of competition in news provision relating to consumption habits that have emerged over the past few years have occasionally been mentioned but they had no impact whatsoever on the final decision.[635]

158. Placing an excessive focus on prices or, even worse, ignoring the non-price dimensions of competition in the media altogether translates into a decision that fails to adapt 'to the particular facts and circumstances of each case'.[636] In a case of the media sector, these particular facts and circumstances are at least the following: an abundance of undertakings operating in today's information economy such as free-to-air broadcasters, social networking sites, online search engines, and news aggregators offer content for free. Furthermore, content consumers are not 'strongly homogeneous', i.e. they have neither the same single interest nor the same array of interests and identical preferences through that array.[637] Even in cases where the provider charges for the content it distributes, consumer interests are more relevant than price. For example, if a pay-per-view subscriber wants to be entertained but does not like football, it is highly unlikely that she will purchase access to a football match because the match is cheaper than a movie. Finally, there are media markets, most notably in the publishing sector, where demand is highly price-inelastic.[638] As the Commission has occasionally noted, 'out of the factors motivating readers to purchase a particular newspaper, *price is not the first factor*, and only one out of several important factors influencing purchasing decisions and determining customer loyalty. *The perceived political stance of a newspaper, family heritage, social-economic factors and the type of content are more important factors*' [emphasis added].[639] The above characteristics provide sufficient proof that, from a viewer/end-user/reader perspective, price is not the main demand-driver. As a result, a competition analysis that is mainly or solely concerned with price disregards key elements that determine substitutability, ultimately jeopardizing the accuracy of the decision.

159. A similar conclusion can be reached with respect to the other drawback I identified above, that is, the Commission's insistence on adopting decisions that are based on inconclusive market definitions or remain stuck to consumption patterns that do not reflect the current state of play in media supply and usage. A good example is *News Corp/BSkyB*, already discussed above in

635 See, for instance, News Corp/BSkyB (Case COMP/M.5932) [2011] OJ C 37/2, paragraphs 207–216

636 Commission Guidelines on the assessment of horizontal mergers under the Council Regulation on the control of concentrations between undertakings [2004] OJ C 31/3, paragraph 5

637 OECD (2003a). Policy Roundtable on Media Mergers, 43

638 See, for instance, Joint Research Centre (2012a). Statistical, Ecosystems and Competitiveness Analysis of the Media and Content Industries: The Newspaper Publishing Industry, 24. < http://publications.jrc.ec.europa.eu/repository/bitstream/JRC69881/jrc69881.pdf>

639 News Corp/BSkyB (Case COMP/M.5932) [2011] C 37/2, paragraph 231

different contexts. In this case, the Commission noted that one of the broad markets affected by the transaction was newspaper publishing[640] (where News Corp was particularly active) without, however, discussing whether consumers regard news delivered by print publications as substitutable with news delivered by other content providers. Instead, the Commission preferred to refer to the conclusions of market definitions that had determined merger decisions it had adopted throughout the 1990s.[641] News consumption, however, has undergone significant change since then. For example, newspapers and broadcasters, including Sky, have moved online, competing for the same audiences and advertisers.[642] Moreover, the question of whether and, if so, to what extent the provision of news content online exerted competitive constraints on print newspapers was left open on the grounds that the transaction would not raise any competitive concerns under any of the alternative product market definitions considered.[643] This, however, is highly questionable for at least two reasons. First, the data on which the Commission based this conclusion could support the opposite conclusion. More particularly, according to the Commission's findings, even under the broadest possible definition, which would include print newspapers and online news websites, the entity would hold between 35% and 55% of the UK market post-merger.[644] The Commission's Merger Guidelines lay down that these market shares could be an indication that the concentration may impede effective competition.[645] Second, measurements of the impact of the merger on the UK news market, which took account of the audience share and reach of the involved undertakings within individual platforms (e.g. papers, TV, radio, online) *and* cross-platform usage,[646] led Ofcom to conclude that the merged entity would hold a strong position with respect to the consumption of news content across all media.[647] Attached to arguably outdated market definitions and having abstained

640 ibid, paragraph 28

641 ibid, paragraph 214

642 For a comprehensive overview of the changes that the market for news provision has undergone over the past years see, for instance, Foster, R. (2012). News Plurality in a Digital World – Report prepared for the Reuters Institute for the Study of Journalism

643 News Corp/BSkyB (Case COMP/M.5932) [2011] C 37/2, paragraph 216. The alternative product market definitions considered were the following: the market for news content as a broad market, which could be further divided into a market for print newspapers and a market for online news services; a market for print newspapers v a market for paid-for online news services; a market for news delivery through new digital devices v print v online newspapers. It must be noted that the Commission adopted the same approach to the assessment of the more recent attempt of News Corp (now Fox) to acquire control of Sky. See Fox/Sky (Case COMP/M.8354) [2017] OJ C238/1, paragraphs 119 et seq.

644 News Corp/BSkyB (Case COMP/M.5932) [2011] C 37/2, see Tables 2 and 4

645 Commission Guidelines on the assessment of horizontal mergers under the Council Regulation on the control of concentrations between undertakings [2004] OJ C 31/3, paragraph 17. Note that, with respect to the other markets possibly affected by the transaction, no clear data was provided. For example, the Commission does not distinguish between paid-for online news services and free news services. See News Corp/BSkyB, Case COMP/M.5932 [2011] C 37/2, Table 5

646 Ofcom (2010b), supra n. 49, paragraph 5.17

647 ibid, paragraph 5.32. It should be noted that Ofcom's analysis discussed the pluralism issues the transaction raised. However, it was heavily based on methodologies employed in competition law (e.g. degree of substitutability between different platforms, media, and providers). Moreover, the metrics on which Ofcom based its analysis, including audience share and reach, are measures that can (and arguably

from delving into the substitutability issues related to news consumption, the Commission ignored altogether any horizontal effects the merger was likely to create.

160. Narrow-minded or incomplete assessments of the parameters that determine demand and supply in media markets have a negative impact on both competition and pluralism. As regards supply-side considerations, from a competition perspective, it can be clearly inferred from the above analysis that the approach the Commission has followed thus far inherently entails the risk that the adopted decisions are based on erroneous findings that range from flawed market definitions to underestimating the market power[648] of the undertakings under scrutiny. This has been exemplified by the factors that should play a role in the definition of the news markets affected by *News Corp/BSkyB* compared with those factors on which the Commission based its decision. The same decision offers another similar example that illustrates the implications for pluralism. In this case, the Commission divided the upstream broadcasting market for the acquisition of content into the market for sports events, the market for premium films, and the market for *other TV* content, without, however, specifying what it meant by 'other TV content'.[649] This term may include different types of content such as news, documentaries and TV series, which, from the viewers' perspective, serve different purposes and could therefore imply the existence of narrower market segments.[650] If the Commission had conducted the market definition exercise properly, and if the analysis had concluded that the market for the acquisition of news content was a separate market, it would have been able to examine concerns over distortions of

---

should) be used in competition cases involving free content markets, e.g. free-to-air television. These issues will be examined in more detail in Chapter 4

648 In a recent judgment, the General Court of the EU annulled a decision where the Commission failed to explain why a merger would not significantly impede effective competition in the market for premium pay-TV sports channels. The Court ruled that 'the Commission decided to leave open the definition of the relevant product market because, in its view, there would be no competition concerns in any event. Consequently, the Commission could not, subsequently, avoid its obligation to explain, at least briefly, why there would be no vertical competition concerns regarding the possible market for premium pay TV sports channels'. See GCEU, Case T394/15 KPN v European Commission ECLI:EU:T:2017:756. Following the annulment, the Commission adopted a new decision. See Liberty Global/Ziggo (Case COMP/M.7000) [2018] OJ C 125/4. This rare example of annulment of an approval decision illustrates the implications that incomplete assessments may have for the merging parties and competitors alike. For a brief anaylsis of such implications see, for instance, Powell, M., Jérémie Jourdan, and Strati Sakellariou-Witt. EU Court annuls a 2014 European Commission merger clearance for insufficient reasoning. 27 October 2017, White & Case. <https://www.whitecase.com/publications/alert/eu-court-annuls-2014-european-commission-merger-clearance-insufficient-reasoning>

649 News Corp/BSkyB (Case COMP/M.5932) [2011] C 37/2, paragraph 30. See also Fox/Sky (Case COMP/M.8354) [2017] OJ C238/1, paragraph 63 where the Commission identifies the market for other TV content as a separate product market without engaging in an analysis of whether this market should be further divided into smaller markets.

650 This is a possibility the Commission considered but did not discuss in detail in other cases. See, for instance, TPS (Case COMP/JV.57) [2002] OJ C 137/23, paragraph 16, where it considered whether the market for pay-TV channels should be further segmented by thematic content (such as premium, sports, movies, news, youth channels). For a US perspective of how markets have been (or should be) defined on the basis of genre/type see, for instance, Nesvold, P. (1996). Communication Breakdown: Developing an Antitrust Model for Multimedia Mergers and Acquisitions. Fordham Intellectual Property, Media and Entertainment Law Journal, 6(2), 781–869

competition in the affected news markets. For example, it is not excluded that under a more meticulous approach the Commission could have found that the merger could afford the parties a greater ability to bid for and win wholesale news deals.[651] The acquisition of significant market power to consistently outbid competitors in upstream markets is a valid competition concern and has influenced the outcome of merger decisions in several instances.[652] The finding that the merging firms could foreclose upstream news markets could lead to the imposition of remedies, such as the divestment of news assets,[653] to ensure that competition for news content is not eliminated. This would clearly have positive spillover effects on media pluralism, as the sale of such assets to a provider that is structurally independent from the merged entity would reduce the parties' opinion-forming power.

161. As regards the demand side, from a competition perspective, the Commission's decisional practice arguably falls short of serving the audience member as consumer for the reason that it equates consumer welfare with consumer surplus. Consumer welfare, defined as 'the individual benefit derived from the consumption of goods and services',[654] is a normative concept broader than consumer surplus, which represents the difference between the buyers' reservation price (the maximum price a consumer is willing to pay for a product) and the market price.[655] Irrespective of whether consumer welfare is the ultimate objective that EU competition enforcement pursues or one of the results it is intended to deliver,[656] it was demonstrated above that consumer surplus is one, and perhaps not the most relevant, benchmark against which to measure consumer satisfaction. Moreover, as already mentioned, in

651 This was an issue that Ofcom considered in the assessment of the same transaction. See Ofcom (2010b), supra n. 49, 14

652 For examples in the media sector see Chapter 4, Part 3.

653 Ofcom (2010b), supra n. 49, 90. This was a solution that was proposed by stakeholders that responded to Ofcom's consultation regarding the News Corp/BSkyB deal. Structural remedies are fairly common in EU merger practice. For recent merger decisions where structural remedies were imposed see, for instance, Commission (2014, July). Mergers: Commission clears acquisition of E-Plus by Telefónica Deutschland, subject to conditions. Press Release IP 14/771. <http://europa.eu/rapid/press-release_IP-14-771_en.htm>, and Commission (2014, May). Mergers: Commission clears acquisition of Telefónica Ireland by Hutchison 3G, subject to conditions. Press Release IP 14/607. <http://europa.eu/rapid/press-release_IP-14-607_en.htm> On the issue of structural remedies in EU merger control see, for instance, Wand, W. (2011). Structural Remedies in EU Antitrust and Merger Control. World Competition 34(4), 571–596, and Papandropoulos, P. and Alessandro Tajana (2006). The Merger Remedies Study – In Divestiture We Trust? European Competition Law Review, 27(8), 443–454

654 OECD (1993). Glossary of Industrial Organization Economics and Competition Law, compiled by R. S. Khemani and D. M. Shapiro, commissioned by the OECD Directorate for Financial, Fiscal and Enterprise Affairs. <http://stats.oecd.org/glossary/detail.asp?ID=3177>

655 Jones and Sufrin (2014), *supra* n. 76, 4–5

656 See, for instance, CFI, Joined Cases T-213/01 and T-214/01 Österreichische Postsparkasse AG and Bank für Arbeit und Wirtschaft AG v Commission [2006] ECR II-1601, paragraph 115; CFI, Case T-168/01 GlaxoSmithKline Services Unlimited v Commission [2006] ECR II-2969, paragraph 118, and compare ECJ, Joined Cases C-501/06 P, C-513/06 P, C-515/06 P and C-519/06 P GlaxoSmithKline Services Unlimited v Commission [2009] ECR I-9291, paragraphs 59–60; GCEU, Case T-461/07 Visa Europe and Visa International Service v Commission, paragraph 126 ECR II-1729; and ECJ, Case C-52/09 Konkurrensverket v TeliaSonera Sverige AB [2011] ECR I-527, paragraph 22. The last three cases suggest that the ultimate objective of EU competition law is the protection of competition, not consumer welfare.

cases of markets offering content for free (online search, free-to-air TV, online news…), the Commission focuses on the anti-competitive effects that may arise in the advertising markets concerned on the grounds that the viewers/ users do not pay for the content they receive. This inevitably leads to an assessment that ignores the impact on the non-price dimensions of competition. If one accepts that demand-side considerations relating to content quality and variety are features of product differentiation that determine competition in the media, then non-price effects should also be measured for the purposes of a competition analysis.[657] This is far from uncommon; the above overview of Commission decisions involving a wide range of products, from deodorants to software to postal services, clearly shows that the EU competition rules are sufficiently flexible to allow for an interpretation that seeks to protect non-price competition. It is submitted that, were the Commission willing to take these factors into account as it did in cases in other sectors, and to be guided by a definition of consumer welfare that takes account of the specificities of demand in media markets, the outcome of competition decisions would not only be more accurate, but also more friendly to pluralism. This is because the analysis would manage to grasp certain quantitative and qualitative dimensions of diversity, as defined in Chapter 2.

162. The potential of EU competition law for a pluralism-friendly interpretation that is based on sound economic principles is illustrated by an old decision,[658] *United International Pictures (UIP)*, which concerned the creation of a joint venture, UIP, by three Hollywood studios. The object of UIP would be the distribution and licensing on an exclusive basis of feature motion pictures produced by the involved studios.[659] Based on the finding that UIP's parent companies accounted for almost a quarter of the gross box-office receipts from feature films and because the parties were among the largest film distributors within the EU,[660] the Commission feared that the agreement could foreclose the market to competing content. The Commission exempted the agreement subject to conditions that aimed at preventing the above from happening. For example, UIP and the parent companies agreed to make themselves available to produce, finance, acquire distribution rights to, and distribute feature

657 For the weaknesses that a price-oriented definition of 'consumer welfare' entails in the case of competition enforcement in digital markets see Coyle, D. (2018). Practical competition policy implications of digital platforms. Bennett Institute for Public Policy Working Paper 1/2018. See in particular p. 4: 'Clearly when the consumer-side price is zero, as on many platforms, all the direct competitive pressure is exerted through service quality and innovative features. Although competition guidelines often pay lip service to quality and other characteristics as features of competition, in practice there is a focus on price as it is definitionally crisp and easier to measure.' On this issue see also Burnside, A. Bob Dylan and Consumer Welfare. Paper presented at the Centre for Competition Law and Policy Conference, 27 May 2017, Oxford University. See Online Markets and Offline Welfare Effects, 4–8. <https://www.law.ox.ac.uk/sites/files/oxlaw/online_markets_and_offline_welfare_effects.pdf>

658 A more recent example is Lagardère/Natexis/VUP (Case COMP/M.2978) [2004] OJ L125/54 where the Commission discussed the effects of vertical integration on the diversity of books produced and distributed by the merged entity. For an overview of this case see Psychogiopoulou (2008), supra n. 89, 277–279

659 United International Pictures (UIP) [1989] OJ L226/25, paragraph 7

660 ibid, paragraph 43

films of third parties in the EU.[661] To allow the Commission to check compliance with related obligations, the parties committed to maintain records that showed the titles of local products of third parties produced, financed or distributed by UIP, and the identity of local products for which a formal written offer was made by third parties to UIP for production, financing or distribution.[662] Remedies intended to ensure that competition for content is not eliminated may rest upon an entirely economic foundation. It was discussed in detail that vertically integrated media undertakings like UIP may decrease diversity either by granting their own products preferential treatment (in order to eliminate competition) or by distributing popular content in as many markets and across as many platforms as possible (in order to maximize profit). These remedies, however, also embrace pluralism, for they allow content produced by suppliers independent from the parties to the agreement to find its way to the audiences. Given the positive implications for non-price competition and pluralism, it is unfortunate that this approach has been abandoned in recent cases.

5. Conclusions

163. This Chapter sought to assess whether EU competition law, as interpreted and applied by the Commission, has contributed to the protection of media pluralism. It was seen that the Commission has adopted two different approaches to this issue. Under the first, media pluralism has been regarded as an almost spontaneous result delivered by unhindered market access. Under the second, pluralism has been treated as a value, the protection of which would require restrictions of competition that, due to competence limitations, the Commission believes is not entitled to allow. The Chapter extensively discussed the practice the Commission has developed under both approaches and, having identified several shortcomings that involve the implementation of ineffective access policies and an inconsistent (and, to some extent, unjustifiably restrictive) interpretation of the Treaties, concluded that the Commission's interventions have not been particularly beneficial to pluralism.

164. The analysis, however, was not limited to the discussion of the Commission's existing predisposition towards the relationship between competition and pluralism; a third approach whereby pluralism-related considerations form an integral part of a competition assessment was also identified. By studying the factors that influenced the Commission's decisions on several occasions,

661 ibid, paragraph 27

662 ibid, paragraph 32

I attempted to demonstrate that the Commission's understanding of how competition law applies to media markets has certain lacunae that may first and foremost imperil the accuracy of competition decisions. I maintained that, were the Commission willing to fill these lacunae by developing a framework which grasps the particularities of media markets and which makes full use of the toolbox it has at its disposal, the decisions would also deliver a more pluralism-friendly outcome. The Chapters that follow are devoted to identifying the drawbacks of the Commission's decisional practice in the media sector and to exploring the potential of this third approach in the role of competition enforcement in safeguarding pluralism.

CHAPTER 4

EU MERGER CONTROL IN THE BROADCASTING SECTOR

1. Introduction

165. One of the first steps in answering the question of how EU competition law can be applied so as to take account of media pluralism was to showcase that digital technologies have not remedied concerns relating to concentration of ownership across the European Union. This, I said, is largely due to the fact that horizontally and/or vertically integrated traditional media organizations occupy a central position within the European media market. More particularly, traditional media still play a major role in content consumption. For example, television is still the most popular medium in the EU.[663] In addition, consumers are attached to traditional providers; empirical research on demand-side concentration in the news market has shown that citizens are still inclined to consume content distributed by 'old' media outlets.[664] Finally, the fact that the same content can be easily distributed in the new media ecosystem makes it fairly easy for traditional media firms to expand into and dominate emerging markets.

166. Having argued in the previous Chapter that EU competition law is flexible enough to prevent concentration-related risks for pluralism, this Chapter will examine the role that EU merger control can play in ensuring that significant power does not end up in the hands of a few entities that would 'control' broadcasting markets. In the case at hand, 'control' is understood as control of the acquired entity and, by extension, control of an asset, such as premium content, that shapes market structures.

---

663 Commission (2017). Media Use in the European Union, 4

664 See, for instance, Reuters Institute (2018). *Digital News Report 2018*, 58 *et seq*. <http://media.digitalnewsreport.org/wp-content/uploads/2018/06/digital-news-report-2018.pdf?x89475>

167. The Chapter focuses on mergers in the broadcasting industry because, as I have already explained in Chapter 1, the decisional practice the Commission has developed will be examined by reference to a specific sector in order to reflect a business strategy, practice, and pricing model that has been a major (competition and media) policy matter in the sector concerned. In broadcasting, mergers and acquisitions have had a broad appeal due to the significant economies of scale and scope that broadcasters can achieve by integrating with other firms that operate at the same or at different levels of the supply chain. Cross-border integration has undoubtedly been more attractive to TV providers than it has been to providers of other traditional media. A vivid illustration of this latter point is that, at the time of going to press, 107 transactions in the broadcasting sector have sought EU regulatory approval[665] whereas in the newspapers/journals/periodicals sector only fifteen transactions have been notified to the Commission.[666] For our purposes, it further bears noting that, by virtue of the fact that mergers and acquisitions have been very popular in broadcasting markets and because TV remains Europeans' preferred source of news on political affairs,[667] the likelihood that ownership concentration may lead to a distorted public discourse, where certain opinions are silenced or improperly represented, seems to be greater in mergers of a EU dimension affecting TV markets than in mergers affecting other traditional media.

168. This Chapter shall attempt to assess merger decisions and the applicable legal framework against the main claims that were put forward in Chapter 3, namely that, by ignoring the particular characteristics of media markets, the practice the Commission has developed has fallen short of protecting both competition and media pluralism, and that EU competition law can be applied in a way which may lead to competition decisions that are more accurate *and* pluralism-friendly without stretching the Treaty boundaries.

169. The Chapter is structured as follows: I will begin by examining how the Commission has defined the relevant product markets in cases involving free-to-air broadcasters, arguing that failing to take account of the viewers' market falls short of grasping the demand-side substitution dynamics of markets where content is provided for free (Part 2). I then make a critical analysis of how the Commission has occasionally assessed the effects of the merger on the broadcasting markets concerned. I argue that, as opposed to its current, more permissive, stance towards integration, the restrictive approach it had adopted in earlier cases was far more appropriate to protect both competition and pluralism. I demonstrate this by examining the impact of prohibition decisions on the development of broadcasting markets and compare it with that

665 Search by NACE Code. <http://ec.europa.eu/competition/elojade/isef/index.cfm?fuseaction=dsp_result>

666 ibid.

667 Commission (2017), supra n. 1, 37 and 42

of the remedies subject to which more recent mergers were cleared (Part 3). Part 4 inquires into how pluralism-specific considerations can be injected into each step of a merger analysis by means of examples.

2. Relevant product market for free-to-air television: is advertising the only content broadcast?

170. In decisions dealing with mergers affecting the retail distribution of broadcasting services, the Commission finds that the key parameter to define the relevant markets is the revenue model used by program suppliers.[668] Thus, according to the Commission, in the case of free-to-air (FTA) TV (i.e. advertising-financed television), even if the audiences' preferences are 'an important indicator of the attractiveness and acceptance of the broadcasting channels', the exercise of market definition should consist in identifying the effective alternative sources of supply for the advertisers, not the viewers.[669]

171. Focusing on advertising markets is justified, the Commission says, on the ground that there is no trade relationship between the broadcaster and the viewer.[670] However, the Commission's perception of trade is mistaken because there are transactions that have an economic value without necessarily entailing the exchange of products or services for money.[671] In FTA TV, there appears to be a transaction whereby, on the one hand, the broadcaster offers content to the consumer (which the consumer values because, by accessing the content, she gets informed, educated or entertained), and on the other hand, the consumer provides access to herself, i.e. her attention, to the broadcaster (which the broadcaster values because eyeballs are necessary to generate advertising revenues).[672] Hence, if trade is defined in a broad manner as the

---

668 See, for instance, News Corp/Telepiù (Case COMP/M.2876) [2004] OJ L110/73, paragraph 24; News Corp/BSkyB (Case COMP/M.5932) [2011] OJ C37/2, paragraph 97; SFR/Télé 2 (Case COMP/M.4504) [2007] OJ L316/57, paragraph 45; News Corp/Premiere (Case COMP/M.5121) [2008] OJ C 219/4, paragraph 19; Telenor/Canal+/Canal Digital (Case COMP/C.2/38.287) [2003] OJ C 149/10, paragraph 28; BSkyB/Kirch Pay-TV (Case COMP/JV.37) [2000] OJ C 110/45, paragraph 24; Bertelsmann/Kirch/Premiere (Case IV/M.993) [1999] OJ L053/1, paragraph 18; and Kirch/Richemont/Multichoice/Telepiù (Case IV/M.584) [1995] OJ C 129/6, paragraph 15

669 See, for instance, RTL/Veronica/Endemol (HMG) (Case IV/M.553) [1996] OJ L124/32, paragraph 20

670 See supra n. 6

671 Polverino, F. (2012). Hunting the Wild Geese: Competition Analysis in a World of 'Free'. In Ghidini, G., Piergaetano Marchetti, Marcello Clarich and Fabiana di Porto (eds.). Concorrenza e Mercato. Roma: Giuffrè Editore, 547. For a comprehensive overview of how 'free product markets' impact competition enforcement see Gal, M. and D. L. Rubinfeld (2015). The Hidden Costs of Free Goods: Implications for Antitrust Enforcement. NYU Center for Law, Economics and Organization Working Paper Series, Working Paper No. 14–44. Available at SSRN: <http://papers.ssrn.com/sol3/papers.cfm?abstract_id=2529425#%23>

672 Europe Economics (2002). Market Definition in the Media Sector: Economic Issues. Report for the

act of exchanging one's goods or services for goods or services that someone else offers to cover a – what seems to be rather common and increasingly popular – type of transaction in today's information economy, an exchange of content for attention 'can properly be termed trade'.[673] Accordingly, there is a market for audiences to define. In this market, basic economic principles apply: a) audiences incur some cost in watching TV, that is, the opportunity cost of the time spent in front of the TV or the opportunity cost of the time spent watching the programs of a particular broadcaster and b) attention is a scarce resource because the interpretative capacity of the individual is not infinite.[674] It follows logically from the above that broadcasters compete for eyeballs by seeking to offer attractive content.[675]

172. The market for viewers' attention must be defined for the purposes of competition law for mainly two reasons. First, the relevant advertising market does not indicate which is the viewers' market affected by the merger. Broadcast programming and advertising space are different products serving different purposes. On the one hand, viewers will seek to use their 'time budget' efficiently by accessing content that fulfills their need to be informed about current affairs, desire to be entertained, etc. Advertisers, on the other hand, will seek to use their marketing budget efficiently by purchasing the attention of the largest possible audience. In other words, advertisers will show little to no interest in minority-taste programming.[676] Audience size is not the only parameter responsible for the divergence between advertiser and viewer preferences. In addition to mass audiences, advertisers will seek to buy 'viewer attention adjusted for the likelihood that the viewer will buy the goods and services being advertised'.[677] Baker convincingly demonstrates that advertisers opt for 'light' programming, whilst avoiding 'content that offends or takes a

European Commission, DG Competition, 42. See also Stucke, M. and Allen Grunes (2001). Antitrust and the Marketplace of Ideas. Antitrust Law Journal, 69(1), 297

673 Europe Economics (2002), supra n. 10, 44. The importance of attention as a rivalrous good may have increased now with the advent of digital media, but the emergence of an attention economy was pointed out as early as 1971 by Herbert A. Simon who noted that in a content-abundant economy, a new problem of scarcity arises: '[w]hat information consumes is rather obvious: it consumes the attention of its recipients. Hence a wealth of information creates a poverty of attention, and a need to allocate that attention efficiently among the overabundance of information sources that might consume it'. Simon, H. A. (1971). Designing Organizations for an Information-rich World. In Greenberger, M. (ed.). Computers, Communications, and the Public Interest. Baltimore: Johns Hopkins Press, 38–52 (Cited after reprint in: H.A. Simon (1982). Models of bounded rationality. Volume 2: Behavioural Economics and Business Organization. Cambridge, MA: MIT Press). For more on the attention economy see, for instance, Hargittai, E. (2004). The Changing Online Landscape: From Free-for-All to Commercial Gatekeeping. In Day, P. and Doug Schuler (eds.). Community Practice in the Network Society: Local Actions/Global Interaction. New York: Routledge, 66–76, and Falkinger, J. (2005). Attention Economies, CESifo Working Paper, No. 1079. Available at: <https://ideas.repec.org/p/ces/ceswps/_1079.html>

674 Goldhaber, M. H. (1997). The Attention Economy and the Net. 7 March 1997, First Monday 2(4). <http://firstmonday.org/article/view/519/440>, and Davenport, T. H. and John C. Beck (2001). The Attention Economy: Understanding the New Currency of Business. Boston: Harvard Business School Press, 11

675 Europe Economics (2002), supra n. 10, 44

676 Owen, B.M. and Steven Wildman (1992). Video Economics. Cambridge, MA: Harvard University Press, 91–92

677 Goodman, E. (2004). Media Policy Out of the Box: Content Abundance, Attention Scarcity, and the Failures of Digital Markets. Berkeley Technology Law Journal, 19, 1425

position on a controversial issue' because they 'want the surrounding content to promote a frame of mind that leaves ... viewers most open to advertising messages'.[678] As is clear from the above, programs that are regarded as substitutes by the advertisers are not necessarily representative of viewers' interests.

173. Second, the market for free-to-air TV is a two-sided market.[679] It was explained in Chapter 2 that a two-sided market is a market in which '1) two sets of agents interact through an intermediary or platform, and 2) the decisions of each set of agents affect the outcomes of the other set of agents.'[680] Two-sided platforms arise in cases in which there are externalities and in which transaction costs do not allow the two sets of agents to address the externality directly.[681] The platform is the intermediary that solves the externality by minimizing the costs that a transaction between entities belonging to these groups of agents would entail.[682] The type of two-sided markets in which FTA broadcasters are active is advertising-based media. As mentioned above, advertising-based media use the content they provide to attract audiences and then sell access to these audiences to advertisers.[683] Where a viewer ended up buying the advertised product, the broadcaster facilitated the completion of a transaction that would not have taken place otherwise.

174. The profit-maximizing logic of a two-sided intermediary is different from that of one-sided businesses[684] because, in addition to the costs that it must bear to operate the platform and the demand for the two different types of products it offers, the intermediary must also take into account the interdependence between the two different types of consumers it targets.[685] In our case, advertising prices depend on whether there are other broadcasters attracting viewers with the same demographic profile *and* on how viewers react to advertising. But, while identifying which broadcasters appeal to the audiences that advertisers aim to reach is a rather straightforward exercise, the way in which advertisers and viewers interact with each other is not self-evident. On the one

678 Baker, C. E. (1992). Advertising and a Democratic Press. U. PA. L. REV. 140, 2153, 2156. For more on the commodification of the audiences see, for instance, Streeter, T. (1996). Selling the Air: A Critique of the Policy of Commercial Broadcasting in the United States. Chicago, IL: University of Chicago Press

679 See, for instance, Rochet, J.C. and J. Tirole (2003). Platform Competition in Two-sided Markets. Journal of the European Economic Association 1, 990–1029; Argentesi, E. and Lapo Filistrucchi (2007). Estimating market power in a two-sided market: The case of newspapers. Journal of Applied Econometrics 22(7), 1247–1266; Kaiser, U. and Julian Wright (2006). Price Structure in two-sided markets: Evidence from the magazine industry. International Journal of Industrial Organization 24, 1–28

680 Rysman, M. (2009). The Economics of Two-sided Markets. Journal of Economic Perspectives, 23(3), 125

681 Evans, D.S. and Richard Schmalensee (2007). Industrial Organization of Markets with Two-Sided Platforms. Competition Policy International 3, 154

682 OECD (2009). Policy Roundtable Report on Two-Sided Markets, 11–12. <http://www.oecd.org/daf/competition/44445730.pdf>

683 Evans and Schmalensee (2007), supra n. 19, 155

684 For the problems that arise from the application of a traditional one-sided logic to two-sided markets see Wright, J. (2003). One-Sided Logic in Two-Sided Markets. Review of Network Economics 3(1), 44–64

685 Evans, D.S. (2009). Two-Sided Market Definition. In ABA Section of Antitrust Law. Market Definition in Antitrust: Theory and Case Studies, 7

hand, it is quite clear that the more viewers watch the content broadcast, the more attractive the platform becomes to advertisers because a large user base increases the possibilities for value-creating exchanges. On the other hand, it is not clear whether audiences appreciate ads. If they wish to purchase a given product, the more ads they watch, the more likely it is that they will find the product that fits their preferences.[686] If, however, they are not interested in buying anything, transmitting too many ads may cause their dissatisfaction and force them to switch to another broadcaster or even discourage them from watching TV. Alternatively, they may simply choose to ignore ads.[687] In this case, putting up with the advertisements may be perceived as the 'price' that viewers pay to access the broadcaster's programming.

175. The above remarks indicate the existence of indirect network effects between the advertisers and the viewers. Determining whether these effects are positive or negative is necessary[688] to understand whether or not the broadcaster faces effective constraints. For instance, based on the above, on the advertisers' side there is a positive network effect. Yet, it is hard to tell whether on the viewers' side the net effect is positive or negative. How would the answer to this question affect the competition assessment in the case of a merger involving FTA broadcasters? If the users dislike ads and the merged entity decides to increase the advertising/content ratio, the viewers may switch to an alternative broadcaster. That other broadcaster should be regarded as a competitor that is capable of constraining the merging parties' behavior.[689] Network effects between the two sides should also be measured. In the above example, network effects may be large enough to create a downward spiral (the more ads, the fewer viewers, the fewer viewers, the fewer advertisers…), ultimately weakening the broadcaster's market position. In view of the above, a competition analysis that focuses on the level of advertising rates fails to take account of the demand-side substitution dynamics of FTA TV markets; as opposed to what the Commission implies, demand in FTA markets is not driven solely by low advertising prices, for advertisers also care about reaching sizeable audiences that are likely to buy their products. Similarly, from the viewers' perspective, attention, i.e. the 'price' audiences are willing to pay, depends on

686 See Evans, D. S. (2008). Competition and Regulatory Policy for Multi-sided Platforms with Applications to the Web Economy. Concurrences 2, 57–62

687 In other words, in this case, the broadcaster internalizes the cost of viewing ads by providing free content. See Evans, D. S. and Richard Schmalensee (2007). The Industrial Organization of Markets with Two-Sided Platforms. In Collins, W.D. (ed.). Issues in Competition Law and Policy. Chicago: American Bar Association, 670–1

688 Filistrucchi, L., Damien Geradin, Eric van Damme, E. and Pauline Affeldt (2012). Market Definition in Two-Sided Markets: Theory and Practice. TILEC Discussion Paper No. 2013-009, 9. Available through SSRN at: <http://papers.ssrn.com/sol3/papers.cfm?abstract_id=2240850> Filistrucchi et al. explain that 'positive indirect network effects occur when the value obtained by one group of customers increases with the number of customers (or, more generally, the demand) of the other group' whereas 'negative indirect network effects occur … when the value obtained by one group of customers decreases with the number of customers (or, more generally, the demand) of the other group'

689 Commission Notice on the definition of relevant market for the purposes of Community competition law [1997] OJ C 372/03, paragraph 2

both the content provided by the broadcaster *and* the amount of time devoted to the transmission of ads.

176. This approach, whereby the relevant product market for free-access TV is defined by reference to the contractual arrangements between the broadcaster and the advertisers, essentially aims to protect price competition without regard for content competition. From a pluralism perspective, this has an impact on the variety and quality of the programs broadcast. More particularly, as previously seen, in a merger between FTA broadcasters, the SSNIP test would be based on a price charged to an advertiser that prefers content capable of both reaching a large audience and boosting its buying mood. As a result, the demand-side substitutability analysis would lead to an assessment that ignores the effects of the merger on niche programming or programming that generates disputes, is 'too depressing' or 'too serious'.[690] Moreover, post-merger, the firms may decide to increase the advertising/content ratio.[691] The resulting increase in ad space may lead to price reductions (simple economics of supply and demand where prices fall when the supply curve shifts outward). Under the approach currently followed, the merged entity's behavior would not raise anti-competitive concerns; on the contrary, it would be found to promote price competition. Similarly, no competition problems would be identified if the merging parties started to use the same programming across different channels in order to reduce production costs.[692] Hence, this type of analysis fully neglects content quality and variety reductions (this issue will be discussed in more detail in Parts 3 and 4).

3. Competitive assessment

3.1 Shift from platform competition at any cost to regulated consolidation of the market

177. Since the Merger Regulation entered into force, the Commission has refused to clear five concentrations in the broadcasting sector.[693] What these five cases have in common is that the notified operations involved broadcasters, content

690 Sunstein, C. (2000). Television and the Public Interest. California Law Review 88(2), 515 referring to Baker (1992), supra n. 16, 2153–4

691 Note that the advertising limits under the Audiovisual Media Services Directive [2010] OJ L332/27 are fairly relaxed: broadcasters are entitled to interrupt their programming every thirty minutes provided that the proportion of the spots within a given clock hour does not exceed 20%. This means that broadcasters may devote up to twelve mins/hour to advertising (see Articles 20(2) and 23(1)).

692 OECD (2003a). Policy Roundtable on Media Mergers, 25

693 Reference is made to Bertelsmann/Kirch/Premiere (Case IV/M.993) [1999] OJ L053/1; Deutsche Telekom/Beta Research (Case IV/M.1027) [1998] OJ C 37/4; MSG Media Service (Case IV/M.469) [1994] OJ L364/1; Nordic Satellite Distribution (Case IV/M.490) [1995] OJ L053/20; RTL/Veronica/Endemol (HMG) (Case IV/M.553) [1996] OJ L124/32

providers, and infrastructure operators, thereby raising vertical integration concerns.[694] In these decisions, the Commission found that the undertakings concerned were already holding or would hold as a result of the transaction significant market power, which in turn would result in the merged entity sealing off the affected markets. For instance, the first prohibited concentration, *MSG Media Service*, concerned the creation of a joint venture by Bertelsmann, a German media group with holdings in commercial television, Kirch, the leading German supplier of feature films and television programming, also active in commercial television, and Deutsche Telekom, the German telecommunications incumbent.[695] The object of the joint venture was the technical and administrative handling of mainly pay-TV services and the provision of the necessary technical infrastructure for the supply of such services.[696] The relevant markets identified by the Commission were the market for technical and administrative services for pay-TV suppliers, the market for pay-TV and the market for cable television networks.[697] In its competitive assessment, the Commission was mainly concerned with MSG's first-mover advantage, which was likely to create a long-term monopoly in the market for technical and administrative services for pay-TV in Germany and further strengthen the position of Bertelsmann and Kirch in the market for the retail distribution of pay-TV services.[698] With respect to the above, the Commission noted that suppliers wishing to enter the pay-TV market following digitization would be forced to receive the relevant technical and administrative services from a company controlled by competitors that were already in a leading position.[699] Additionally, it feared that the concentration would have adverse effects on the market for cable networks. The Commission found that the administrative practice regarding the granting of authorizations to establish the required reception equipment largely protected Telekom from competition.[700] In its view, even if this practice were abandoned, cable network operators would find it difficult to compete with Telekom.[701] There was, in particular, the risk that private operators could not access the program licensed by Bertelsmann and Kirch, which the Commission considered necessary for the creation of attractive program packages, or could purchase it only on unfavorable conditions.[702] Based on the above, the Commission concluded that the concentration would

694 For an overview of these and other mergers that fell under the Commission's scrutiny see, for instance, Nikolinakos, N. (2006). EU Competition Law and Regulation in the Converging Telecommunications, Media and IT sectors. Alphen aan den Rijn: Kluwer Law International, 138–161; and Nitsche, I. (2001). Broadcasting in the European Union. The Role of Public Interest in Competition Analysis. Alphen aan den Rijn: Kluwer Law International, 111–124

695 MSG Media Service (Case IV/M.469) [1994] OJ L364/1, paragraphs 1 and 5–7

696 ibid, paragraph 8

697 ibid, paragraph 19

698 ibid, paragraph 55 et seq.

699 ibid, paragraph 82

700 ibid, paragraph 93

701 ibid, paragraph 92

702 ibid, paragraph 93

probably wall off all three markets and decided to ban the transaction.[703]

178. An approach similar to the one followed in *MSG Media Service* was adopted in the assessment of the other four prohibited operations. The Commission's reasoning in all these decisions is underpinned by its willingness to ensure inter-platform competition.[704] In spite of not being entirely certain about how the markets concerned were likely to evolve, the Commission took a strict stance against vertical integration and did not hesitate to sacrifice the provision of new services in the short term so as to guarantee that a variety of suppliers could operate in these markets in the long run.[705] Indeed, vertical integration in the media markets may have several anti-competitive effects, for '[i]f the content provider is dominant, a competing carrier might be unable to obtain enough valuable content in the appropriate language to offer a satisfactory selection of channels and programs. If the carrier is dominant, a competing provider might be unable to find satisfactory alternative broadcasters.'[706] The Commission's determination to prevent market foreclosure resulting from vertical integration is also demonstrated by the fact that in all the above cases the parties to the transactions proposed undertakings that were rejected on the grounds that they were 'mere pledges of conduct',[707] 'meaningless',[708] 'insufficient',[709] or 'inadequate'[710] to address the competition problems that had arisen.

179. This set of negative decisions represents almost 20% of all transactions the Commission has blocked thus far.[711] Yet, this does not mean that the Commission has treated concentration in the broadcasting sector more restrictively than in other industries. These transactions were notified to the Commission when the Commissioner responsible for the EU Competition Policy was Karel Van Miert. Instilled in these decisions is Van Miert's belief that the strict application of competition rules may not only protect competitive market structures in the media but also contributes to maintaining media pluralism.[712] But the Commission's eagerness to ensure inter-platform competition has undergone significant changes over the past twenty years: since

703 ibid, paragraph 102

704 Ariño, M. (2005). Regulation and Competition in European Broadcasting – A study of pluralism through access. PhD thesis. Florence: European University Institute, 111

705 Harrison, J. and Lorna Woods (2007). European Broadcasting Law and Policy. Cambridge: CUP, 164

706 Temple Lang, J. (1997). Media, multimedia, and European Community antitrust law. Fordham International Law Journal 21(4), 1359. <http://ir.lawnet.fordham.edu/cgi/viewcontent.cgi?article=1569&context=ilj>

707 MSG Media Service (Case IV/M.469) [1994] OJ L364/1, paragraph 99

708 Deutsche Telekom/Beta Research (Case IV/M.1027) [1998] OJ C 37/4, paragraph 65

709 See *Nordic Satellite Distribution* (Case IV/M.490) [1995] OJ L053/20 paragraph 154 and *RTL/Veronica/Endemol (HMG)* (Case IV/M.553) [1996] OJ L124/32, paragraph 112

710 Bertelsmann/Kirch/Premiere (Case IV/M.993) [1999] OJ L053/1, paragraph 155

711 According to the Merger Statistics Table published by the Commission, a total of twenty-four operations have been rejected between 21 September 1990 and 30 June 2018. The table is available at: <http://ec.europa.eu/competition/mergers/statistics.pdf>

712 Harcourt, A. (2005). The European Union and the Regulation of the Media Markets. Manchester: Manchester University Press, 51

May 1998,[713] the Commission has given the green light to all notified transactions in the broadcasting sector, several of which subject to (structural and/or behavioral) conditions.[714]

180. A good example of the Commission's apparently more permissive approach towards consolidation is *Vivendi/Canal+/Seagram* in which the Commission was asked to assess the acquisition of Seagram (active in different segments of the entertainment business and owner of Universal, one of the six Hollywood majors), by Vivendi (active in, *inter alia*, cinema and television through equity interests in Canal+ and BSkyB, two leading pay-TV operators, and a majority stake in CDCA, which holds film catalogues and licenses broadcasting rights to French channels).[715] In its analysis, the Commission found that the concentration would result in a company with the world's largest film library, the second largest library of TV programming in the EEA and the first acquirer of output deals signed with US studios.[716] The Commission also noted that, as a result of structural and other[717] links between Vivendi or Universal and other Hollywood majors, Canal+ was likely to have preferential access to movie rights.[718] In spite of the above, the Commission approved the operation. An amalgamation of behavioral and structural commitments proposed by the parties was found to eliminate the anti-competitive concerns that the concentration raised. For instance, Vivendi undertook to divest its entire stake in BSkyB and not to grant Canal+ the first-window rights covering more than 50% of Universal's production, thereby leaving the remaining 50% to other operators.[719]

181. Another example is the high-profile (horizontal) merger *News Corp/Telepiù* dealing with a concentration by which media conglomerate News Corporation (now 21st Century Fox), operating at all tiers in the broadcast supply chain (e.g. production and distribution of motion pictures and TV programming, production and distribution of advertising products and services, the development of digital broadcasting, the development of conditional access and subscriber management systems, the creation and distribution of online programming) would acquire control, via a special purpose vehicle company, of the Italian pay-TV companies Telepiù and Stream.[720] Under the proposed transaction,

713 Last in the series of prohibited operations previously discussed were Deutsche Telekom/Beta Research (Case IV/M.1027) [1998] OJ C 37/4 and Bertelsmann/Kirch/Premiere (Case IV/M.993) [1999] OJ L053/1 (both of them adopted on 27 May 1998)

714 Search by NACA Code. NB: Commission decision BSkyB/Kirch Pay-TV, which was adopted in 2000 and which declared the concentration compatible with the common market under Article 6(1)(b), does not appear in the Commission's list

715 Vivendi/Canal+/Seagram (Case COMP/M.2050) Commission Decision (2000) C 311/03, paragraphs 1 and 4–8

716 ibid, paragraph 15

717 ibid, paragraph 49

718 ibid, paragraph 49

719 ibid, p. 20 and 22

720 News Corp/Telepiù (Case COMP/M.2876) [2004] OJ L110/73, paragraphs 1 and 7–9

Telepiù and Stream would merge their activities in a combined Direct-to-Home (DTH) satellite platform in which Telecom Italia, the Italian telecom incumbent, would hold a minority stake.[721] While the Commission found that the merged entity would have a monopoly as regards the DTH means of transmission and would also have the incentive to foreclose actual and potential competitors wishing to enter the market through the same or other means of transmission,[722] it declared the concentration compatible with the common market subject to a number of behavioral and structural remedies. For instance, News Corporation committed to waive exclusive rights for pay-per-view, video on demand and near video on demand on all platforms and not to conclude contracts exceeding a duration of two years with football clubs and of three years with film studios. The decision also established the obligation of News Corporation to offer third parties, on an unbundled and non-exclusive basis, the right to distribute on platforms other than DTH any premium content if (and for as long as) the combined platform would offer such premium contents to its retail customers. Telepiù undertook to divest its digital and analogue terrestrial broadcasting assets and not to enter into any further digital terrestrial television activities, neither as network nor as retail operator.[723]

182. Similarly, the Commission decided to clear the acquisition by BSkyB of a stake in Kirch, despite its concerns that the concentration would result in Kirch acquiring significant power in the German pay-TV market resulting from the influx of financial resources from BSkyB.[724] The transaction was approved upon the condition that the parties would respect a bundle of (behavioral) commitments proposed to the Commission. More particularly, Kirch committed to offer to all interested third parties access to its technical platform on a fair, reasonable and non-discriminatory basis.[725] BSkyB and Kirch also undertook that, in the event they acquired rights for the exploitation of a major live international sports event on a multinational basis, they would not give to one another the status of preferred bidder for such rights by granting, for instance, a right of first negotiation, first refusal or first offer.[726] This condition was imposed so as to address the possible adverse effects on the market for the acquisition of TV rights to pan-European sports events.[727]

183. A package of behavioral commitments was also accepted in the more recent *SFR/Télé 2* decision dealing with the plans of SFR, jointly controlled by

721 ibid, paragraph 1

722 ibid, paragraph 140

723 ibid, paragraph 225(c), (d), (i), (g) and (k)

724 BSkyB/Kirch Pay-TV (Case COMP/JV.37) [2000] OJ C 110/45. See in particular paragraphs 1, 5–7, 9, 51 and 80

725 ibid, p. 20

726 ibid, p. 25

727 ibid, see paragraphs 90 *et seq.*

Vivendi and Vodafone, to acquire sole control of the Internet access and fixed telephone business of Télé 2.[728] The Commission feared that, as a result of the proposed project, Vivendi would have the ability and incentive to grant its SFR/Télé2 subsidiary preferential access to the television content it had in its possession.[729] Such conduct could lead to a severe weakening of other DSL operators in the downstream distribution market as well as in the upstream market for the acquisition of television content.[730] In order to eliminate these concerns, Vivendi committed to offer its channels to all DSL operators on normal market terms, which could not be less favorable than those provided to SFR. With a view to ensuring an adequate monitoring of this undertaking, Vivendi was asked to keep separate accounts for each channel distributed wholesale in this way.[731]

184. This move from inter-platform competition to regulated consolidation suggests that the Commission has gradually succumbed to the tendency of the industry towards concentration. The Commission, commentators say, has become increasingly 'aware of the reasons that lead companies to seek further integration'[732] and has therefore decided to adopt an approach that heralds 'a new era of realistic appraisal of the underlying financial conditions in which the sector operates'.[733] This logic is arguably ill-advised. The analysis that follows will demonstrate that the Commission's leniency combined with remedies that fell short of capturing the dynamics of media markets have harmed consumer welfare and that, in retrospect, despite its lacunae, the reasoning it applied to the prohibited operations discussed above was far more adequate to protect competition and pluralism.

3.2 Ensuring market access = pluralistic and/or competitive broadcasting markets?

185. While the shift from inter-platform competition to regulated consolidation marks a significant policy change, the objective under both approaches is the same: market access should not be prevented as a result of the notified transaction. In the first case, the Commission pursues this objective by prohibiting concentrations that would confer an unparalleled first-mover advantage on the merged entity. In the second case, the Commission seeks to guarantee that

728 SFR/Télé 2 France (Case COMP M.4504) [2007] OJ L316/57, paragraphs 1, 6 and 7

729 ibid, see paras 92 et seq.

730 ibid, paragraph 101

731 ibid, paragraph 117

732 Mendes-Perreira, M. (2003). Vertical and horizontal integration in the media sector and EU competition law. Paper presented at the Workshop 'The ICT and Media Sectors within the EU Policy Framework', Brussels, 7 April 2003, 10 <http://ec.europa.eu/competition/speeches/text/sp2003_009_en.pdf>

733 Alexiadis, P. and Miranda Cole (2004). Revisiting Competition Law and Regulatory Analyses of Consolidations in the Communications Sector. Financier Worldwide, Industry Sector Review: Technology, Media & Telecommunications 2004, 14. See also Nikolinakos (2006), supra n. 32, 170

the merger does not deter access to key elements, namely premium content and infrastructure, which allow broadcasters to effectively compete.[734] In both cases, the underlying assumption is that broadcasters that do not fall within the sphere of influence of one of the merging firms will be able to undertake activities in the affected markets. For example, the Commission refused to clear *Bertelsmann/Kirch/Premiere*, which concerned the plans of CLT-UFA and Kirch to merge their digital television activities in Germany into the Premiere venture,[735] on the grounds that other 'providers of digital pay-TV and multimedia services [would] be unable to develop freely and without restriction'.[736] Similarly, in the approved *News Corp/Telepiù*, it explained that, if the merged undertakings restricted access to premium content, 'competitors [would] not be in a position to create an alternative successful pay-TV platform'.[737] The Commission seems to imply that market access, guaranteed either through a negative decision or through a conditional clearance, caters to supply diversity.[738]

186. Under both approaches, the effects of a concentration on content diversity have largely been marginalized. For instance, in *NSD*, the Commission was limited to noting that the operation would lead to 'less variety in the offer to Nordic TV households'.[739] In *Bertelsmann/Kirch/Premiere*, it mentioned that a horizontally integrated undertaking active in both the pay- and free-to-air TV markets could negatively influence the range of programs in each of the two segments.[740] However, these and other similar remarks are incidental rather than parts of a full-fledged analysis of whether the transaction would adversely affect minority-taste, assorted and/or high value programming. The reasoning behind these decisions seems to be based on the premise that such programming is a natural outcome of supply diversity. For instance, in *News Corp/Telepiù*, in its assessment of the impact of the merger on the market for the acquisition of TV channels, the Commission observed that, 'should the merged entity decide to ... exert its monopsonist power to such an extent that some TV channel providers exit the market ..., *consumers would*

734 This is the Commission's main concern when assessing mergers in the media sector. See, for instance, <http://ec.europa.eu/competition/sectors/media/overview_en.html> See also Mendes-Perreira. (2003), supra n. 70, 12

735 Bertelsmann/Kirch/Premiere (Case IV/M.993) [1999] OJ L053/1, paragraph 1

736 ibid, paragraph 122

737 News Corp/Telepiù (Case COMP/M.2876) [2004] OJ L110/73, paragraph 184

738 The Commission supported this position in several policy documents. See, for instance, Commission (2005). Issues Paper for the Liverpool Audiovisual Conference Media Pluralism – What should be the European Union's role?, 2, and Staff Working Document on Media Pluralism in the Member States of the EU SEC (2007) 32, 7

739 Nordic Satellite Distribution (Case IV/M.490) [1995] OJ L053/20, paragraph 151

740 Bertelsmann/Kirch/Premiere (Case IV/M.993) [1999] OJ L053/1. See in particular paragraphs 87–88: 'the more varied and attractive the programs offered by the free broadcasters, the less incentive there is for viewers to subscribe to pay-TV as well. ... The attractiveness of a channel is largely dependent on the program rights available to it. When a television operator has a leading position in pay-TV and free-TV, and also holds the main program rights for free-TV and pay-TV, he is in a position to control the interaction between free- and pay-TV'

enjoy a greatly reduced variety of products and freedom of choice' [emphasis added].[741]

187. Two problems arise from the Commission's merger practice in the broadcasting sector as described above. The first is related to the assumption that content diversity derives from supply diversity, whereas the second concerns the remedies imposed in the post-Van Miert era, which did not manage to ensure market access.

188. The assumption that supply diversity will lead to content diversity is weak. The main reasons explaining why in media markets the former does not necessarily guarantee the latter have already been discussed in Chapter 2.[742] With respect to the broadcasting sector, the following features are particularly counterproductive to a varied programming, even in markets where several channel distributors are active: first, as I explained above, the use of advertising results in programming which seeks to attract mass audiences and promote materialism.

189. Second, TV content produced in-house has, as a rule, high first-copy costs. For example, the sixth season of HBO's *Game of Thrones* cost an average of $10 million per episode.[743] Acquired content is also very expensive. For instance, for a premium drama series, the BBC pays the independent producer an average of GB £650k – £1,000k per hour.[744] In Germany, Sky currently pays the Bundesliga a license fee of €876 million per season[745] and, in the UK, Premier League rights cost Sky £3.579 billion.[746]

190. Third, as opposed to producing (or purchasing) attractive content, distributing TV programming is fairly cheap, and even more so with technology convergence. It was explained in Chapter 2 that previously different communication infrastructures now use the same transport protocols. This means that television broadcasts can currently be delivered on multiple platforms with

741 News Corp/Telepiù (Case COMP/M.2876) [2004] OJ L110/73, paragraph 173

742 As discussed in detail in Chapter 1, this is also an assumption that seems to have underpinned regulation in support of media pluralism. For an overview see, for instance, Napoli, P. M. (2011). Exposure diversity reconsidered. Journal of Information Policy 1, 246–259, and Valcke, P. (2011). Looking For the User in Media Pluralism Regulation: Unraveling the Traditional Diversity Chain and Recent Trends of User Empowerment in European Media Regulation. Journal of Information Policy 1, 294–5. Note that content diversity may be further undermined by factors that were examined in detail in Chapter 2, Parts 3.4.1. and 3.4.2.

743 Martin, E. Here's how much it costs HBO to produce one episode of 'Game of Thrones'. 6 August 2017, CNBC. <https://www.cnbc.com/2017/08/04/it-costs-millions-to-produce-one-episode-of-hbos-game-of-thrones.html>

744 BBC Tariff Prices for Independents. <http://www.bbc.co.uk/commissioning/tv/how-we-work/business-requirements/tariff-ranges.shtml>

745 These fees cover the period from 2017–2018 until 2020–2021. See, for instance, Barraclough, L. Pay-TV Operator Sky Pays Almost $4 Billion for German Soccer Rights. 9 June 2016, Variety. <https://variety.com/2016/tv/global/pay-tv-sky-german-soccer-rights-1201792143/>

746 These fees cover the period from 2019 until 2022. See Conn, D. Sky and BT Sport retain grip on Premier League rights but TV frenzy cools. 13 February 2018, The Guardian. <https://www.theguardian.com/football/2018/feb/13/sky-bt-sport-premier-league-tv-rights>

significantly less cost.[747] Besides terrestrial, direct-to-home satellite and cable networks, TV programming is also available on Internet Protocol television, offered by telecommunication providers over managed networks, and Over-The-Top (OTT) television, provided by the content owners themselves (e.g. BBC iPlayer, Hulu, YouTube,[748] etc.) without the ISP or network operator controlling viewer access.[749] As a result, the same content can be delivered on multiple devices (e.g. traditional TV set, tablets, and smartphones) and in several formats (e.g. linear transmission, on-demand).

191. Finally, content is a product with highly uncertain consumer demand. There is little doubt that the success of a film, series or anchorman depends on viewer preferences that are not easy to predict. This is not just common sense, but an empirically verified hypothesis. For example, De Vany and Walls tested the assumption that the variance of the probability distribution of movie outcomes is infinite by developing a model that makes distribution conditional on a list of choice variables that may alter the location of the probability mass of distribution.[750] After applying their model to a sample of 2,015 movies, De Vany and Walls concluded that it is impossible to determine the parameters that make a movie successful. Factors such as release strategies, budget and aggressive marketing made no difference, since no pattern could be identified. This finding illustrates why content production (or acquisition) is a very risky undertaking.[751]

192. High production and low distribution costs and uncertain consumer demand create 'biases in favor of programming that mimics existing programming successes and/or that holds out the promise of a long and extended life ... In either case, the programming produced may systematically shortchange niche audiences.'[752]

193. In view of all the above parameters, market access should not be regarded as a vehicle for content diversity.

194. As regards access remedies imposed on broadcasters in the post-Van Miert era, these were poorly conceived and therefore proved inadequate in keeping

---

747 Pavlik, J. (2005). Understanding Convergence and Digital Broadcasting Technologies for the Twenty-First Century. NHK Broadcasting Studies, 142 <https://www.nhk.or.jp/bunken/english/reports/pdf/05_no4_08.pdf>

748 YouTube, which started as a peer video upload website, now provides access to programming posted by mainstream broadcasters. See OECD (2013a). Competition Issues in Television and Broadcasting, 2

749 ibid, 9–10. For more information on technology convergence and how it affects broadcasting see, for instance, EBU (2013). Reply to the European Commission Green Paper – Preparing for a Fully Converged Audiovisual World: Growth, Creation and Values. <https://www.ebu.ch/files/live/sites/ebu/files/Publications/Position%20papers/EBU-Position-EN%20reply%20Green%20Paper%20convergence%2010.9.2013.pdf>

750 De Vany, A. and W. David Walls (1999). Uncertainty in the Movie Industry: Does Star Power Reduce the Terror of the Box Office? Paper presented at the annual meeting of the American Economic Association, New York, January 1999. <http://pages.stern.nyu.edu/~wgreene/entertainmentandmedia/Devany&Walls.pdf>

751 Goodman (2004), supra n. 15, 1435

752 ibid.

the markets affected by the transaction open to competition. Take, as an example, the commitments that were made legally binding on a number of merging firms with a view to ensuring access to premium content. As already seen, the merging parties occasionally undertook to reduce the duration of exclusivity contracts with rights holders. The rationale behind this solution is that rivals will not be forced to exit the market permanently whilst the acquiring entity is granted a certain amount of time to recoup the investment. However, an obligation whereby auctions for the content rights must be organized every *x* years is not sufficient to guarantee that the rights will be purchased by a different provider. Premium content is very expensive and antitrust intervention to limit the contract length does not necessarily mean that a smaller competitor will have the financial resources to successfully bid for the rights after the contract expires. For example, as already seen in Chapter 3, the Commission decision dealing with the TV rights to the English FA Premier League (FAPL) provides that related agreements shall be concluded for a period not exceeding three seasons.[753] This, however, did not prevent Sky from successfully bidding for the rights in every single auction that was organized after the decision was adopted.[754] Interestingly, the prohibition decisions discussed above were partly based on the concern that, even after termination of their output deals for pay-TV rights with film studios, the merging parties, given their financial strength, were most likely to acquire those rights for another term.[755]

195. Another remedy imposed on the merging parties in order to guarantee access to premium content is the duty to sublicense rights acquired on an exclusive basis. However, these sublicensing schemes have been far from a success story. The difficulties that competitors have encountered in their attempt to acquire premium content will be illustrated through an analysis of the wholesale must-offer mechanism subject to which the *News Corp/Telepiù* merger was cleared.

196. ***How is premium content sublicensed?*** In *News Corp/Telepiù*, the merged entity undertook to offer third parties the right to distribute premium content on the basis of the *retail-minus principle*.[756] This is a principle whereby the wholesale price is calculated as the retail price charged by the sub-licensor

753 Joint Selling of the Media Rights of the FA Premier League (FAPL) (Case COMP/C.2/38.173) [2006] OJ L176/104, paragraph 16

754 In fact, Sky Sports has been broadcasting the Premier League to UK TV-viewing audiences since the launch of the league in 1992. See Harris, C. BSkyB Retains Majority of TV Rights to Premier League On UK TV For 2013–16. 13 June 2012, World Soccer Talk. <http://worldsoccertalk.com/2012/06/13/bskyb-retains-majority-of-tv-rights-to-premier-league-on-uk-tv-for-2013-16/> For recent developments see Williams, C. Virgin Media urges Ofcom crackdown on Premier League TV prices. 30 September 2014, The Telegraph. <http://www.telegraph.co.uk/finance/newsbysector/mediatechnologyandtelecoms/media/11131139/Virgin-Media-urges-Ofcom-crackdown-on-Premier-League-TV-prices.html>

755 See, for instance, Bertelsmann/Kirch/Premiere (Case IV/M.993) [1999] OJ L053/1, paragraphs 49–50, and Deutsche Telekom/Beta Research (Case IV/M.1027) [1998] OJ C 37/4, paragraphs 31–32

756 News Corp/Telepiù (Case COMP/M.2876) [2004] OJ L110/73, see Section 10 of the Commitments, p. 8–11

minus the cost of an efficient undertaking.[757] For retail-minus pricing to protect competition, it is necessary that the sub-licensor faces competitive pressure. If not, a retail-minus mechanism does not prevent it from charging excessive retail prices (which automatically translate into excessive wholesale prices).[758] In *News Corp/Telepiù*, the competitive analysis had concluded that the merged entity would acquire a near-monopoly position in the pay-TV market, thereby having both the ability and incentive to foreclose competitors by raising rivals' costs.[759] It is therefore odd that the Commission found that, in the case of Sky, a sublicensing scheme based on the retail-minus pricing principle would allow other pay-TV operators 'to access premium contents which would otherwise be too costly for them to purchase directly'.[760] If the Commission carefully weighed the position Sky would hold in the market post-merger against the condition under which retail-minus pricing can be an effective means to safeguard competition, it could have predicted what happened one year after the decision was adopted: following complaints by competitors, the Italian media regulator, AGCom, intervened to change Sky's method of calculating the 'minus' because its wholesale offers were unsustainable.[761]

197. ***What is sublicensed?*** Problems arise if content that is indeed 'premium' is excluded from the scope of the wholesale must-offer regime, thereby allowing the incumbent to empty content markets, including emerging content markets. In the case of *News Corp/Telepiù*, the Commission left out the 'basic packages' carrying several popular channels (e.g. MTV and Discovery) and US series (e.g. Desperate Housewives and Lost).[762] Following the decision, Sky went on to sign a series of exclusive agreements with these basic package channels.[763] As a result, this content, which, according to former IPTV provider Fastweb, was the main reason for becoming a pay-TV subscriber for 70% of the viewers,[764] was not available to other pay-TV operators. This may go part-way towards

757 For more details on the method applied in News Corp/Telepiù see Section 10 of the Commitments, paragraphs 10.5. and 10.6.

758 ERG (2009). Report on price consistency in upstream broadband markets, 15.

See also Geradin, D. (2005). Access to content by new media platforms: A review of the competition law problems. European Law Review, 30(1), 84. On the inadequacy of retail–minus mechanisms to protect competition see also Geradin, D. and Michel Kerf (2003). Controlling Market Power in Telecommunications: Antitrust vs Sector-specific Regulation. Oxford: OUP

759 News Corp/Telepiù (Case COMP/M.2876) [2004] OJ L110/73, paragraph 140

760 ibid, paragraph 246

761 See AGCom (2004). Delibera N. 360/04/CONS. <http://www.agcom.it/documents/10179/538769/Delibera+360-04-CONS/7b5b88af-14bc-4915-b264-dd1ca75e2ff9?version=1.0&targetExtension=pdf> In this case, e.Biscom argued that the price charged by Sky Italia was too high and asked for a 50% discount on the retail price. AGCom agreed with e.Biscom and imposed on Sky the obligation to modify its wholesale offer as follows: the minus value of the six packages subject to the must-offer regime should be between 51.6% (the most expensive package) and 62.6% (the cheapest packages) of the retail price of the premium package. See paragraph 3, p. 20 of the decision

762 Ofcom (2009a). Wholesale must-offer remedies: International examples, 9

763 ibid, 14

764 ibid.

explaining how things evolved in the Italian IPTV market.[765] In the second half of 2012, Wind and Fastweb, finding themselves unable to create a sustainable customer base, closed their IPTV services.[766] This shows that, in addition to distortions of competition, an ill-designed sublicensing mechanism may also have a chilling effect on innovation (IPTV delivers better picture and sound quality and has richer functionality[767] than DTH).

198. ***When is premium content sublicensed?*** In *News Corp/Telepiù*, the Commission does not set a deadline by which Sky must grant access to the rights. The decision lays down that the wholesale offer 'shall be made on reasonable terms and conditions (including, without limitation, reasonable provision as to notice periods)',[768] but without explaining what is meant by 'reasonable'. Again, this is not enough to prevent the incumbent from engaging in anti-competitive practices. Furthermore, introducing a binding arbitration system does not fully address the concerns that may arise from failure to comply with the obligation to sublicense content within a 'reasonable' time frame; an alternative dispute resolution mechanism is undoubtedly faster than regular court proceedings, however, recourse to arbitration does not mean that the dispute will be resolved overnight. For example, it took the International Court of Arbitration two years to decide whether the FIFA World Cup was must-offer content[769] and AGCom another two to conclude whether Sky implemented its cost-allocation strategies on a discriminatory basis.[770]

199. But, what best illustrates the limitations of this mechanism is that, long before the commitments expired, IPTV operators and Sky Italia abandoned the wholesale must-offer and signed unregulated commercial agreements whereby IPTV players would act as Sky's distributors and be remunerated on the basis of a

---

765 In 2008, the aggregate market share of all telecoms operators providing pay-TV services was 3.7% whereas Sky Italia controlled 88.8% of the market. See News Corp/Telepiù (Case COMP/M.2876) C(2010) 4976 final, paragraph 31. In 2009, Fastweb had 200,000 subscribers, a figure which was nowhere near Sky's 4.4 million. See Ofcom (2009a), supra n. 100, 7

766 See, for instance, Malachiti, A. *Fastweb chiude con Sky e con la Iptv*. 7 September 2012. InfoOggi < https://www.infooggi.it/articolo/fastweb-chiude-con-sky-e-con-la-iptv/31058>; and Chiusura definitive offerta 'Infostrada TV' dal 22 giugno 2012. 30 maggio 2012. CellularItalia <http://www.cellularitalia.com/news/wind1104chiusura-infostrada-tv22-06.php>

767 For example, IPTV has the ability to provide on-demand content channels and interactive content applications

768 News Corp/Telepiù (Case COMP/M.2876) [2004] OJ L110/73, section 10.4 of the Commitments

769 In News Corp/Telepiù, the combined platform undertook not to make any exclusivity arrangements for means of transmission other than DTH in future agreements concerning worldwide sports rights (see News Corp/Telepiù Case (COMP/M.2876) [2004] OJ L110/73, section 8.1 of the Commitments). In November 2008, Sky purchased from RAI the transmission rights for pay-TV on all platforms, including DTT, of the FIFA World Cup. In February 2010, RTI, the broadcast media subsidiary of the Mediaset group, brought a complaint before the International Court of Arbitration (ICC) arguing that Sky had violated the above obligation. The ICC held that the FIFA media rights were not covered by the commitments on the grounds that the event did not have the capacity to generate a 'regular' customer base (and hence constant revenues) and did not therefore qualify as 'premium content'. See AGCom (2013). A429-RTI/SKY-Mondiali di Calcio, Provvedimento n. 24325, paragraphs 17 and 19

770 See AGCom (2010). A407-Conto TV/Sky Italia, Provvedimento n. 21316, para 6. This decision is discussed in more detail in Part 4.

revenue-sharing model.[771] Sky Italia would bill the viewer directly and own the customer relationship.[772] Apparently, these arrangements also fell short of boosting competition because, as already seen, two of the three IPTV providers (Fastweb, Wind and Telecom Italia) were forced to exit the market in 2012.

200. With respect to pluralism, I explained in Chapter 3 why the contribution of a competition policy facilitating access to premium content to the protection of media pluralism should not be overestimated. *News Corp/Telepiù* is a vivid illustration of this point in that the competitor that seems to have been favored by the remedies the most is Mediaset. This is because the merged entity, Sky Italia, committed not to develop activities on DTT,[773] which Mediaset penetrated after the decision was adopted[774] and has been controlling ever since.[775] Being the leading commercial FTA broadcaster, Mediaset has the deep pockets to acquire premium content and provide an offering alternative to that of Sky. Mediaset is, however, owned by Silvio Berlusconi, known for controlling the group's editorial policies in order to advance his own political and commercial interests.[776]

3.3 Public policy considerations in the Commission's merger practice: how decisive have they been?

201. The Commission may have regard to public policy considerations when it is called upon to assess whether a concentration between media undertakings is compatible or not with the common market. As far as the media sector is concerned, the legal basis for integrating such considerations into a competition analysis is Article 167(4) TFEU, which envisages the Commission's duty to take cultural aspects into account when action is taken in the framework of other Union policies, as well as Article 11(2) CFREU, which establishes the obligation to respect freedom and pluralism of the media. In addition to these provisions of primary EU law, Article 2(1)(b) of the Merger Regulation

771 This was based on the number of subscribers and the value of the acquired package. See Ofcom (2009a), supra n. 100, 15

772 ibid.

773 News Corp/Telepiù (Case COMP/M.2876) [2004] OJ L110/73, section 10.4 of the Commitments. Note that, following Sky's request to revise this commitment, the Commission lifted the obligation in 2010 and allowed Sky Italia to apply for an authorization with the competent Italian authorities for the award of one DTT multiplex. See News Corp/Telepiù (Case COMP/M.2876) C(2010) 4976 final

774 Ofcom (2009a), supra n. 100, 7

775 News Corp/Telepiù (Case COMP/M.2876) C(2010) 4976 final, paragraphs 31–32

776 See, for instance, EU Network of Independent Experts on Fundamental Rights (2004). Synthesis Report: Conclusions and Recommendations on the situation of fundamental rights in the European Union and its Member States in 2003, 40 <https://www.ab.gov.tr/files/ardb/evt/1_avrupa_birligi/1_6_raporlar/1_3_diger/human_rights/report_on_fundamental_rights_2003.pdf>; EU Network of Independent Experts on Fundamental Rights (2005). Synthesis Report: Conclusions and Recommendations on the situation of fundamental rights in the European Union and its Member States in 2004, 62.; and EU Network of Independent Experts on Fundamental Rights (2006). Report on the Situation of Fundamental Rights in the European Union and its Member States in 2005, 109<http://www.statewatch.org/news/2006/jun/EU-funrights-report05.pdf>

lays down that the Commission must consider the development of technical progress and the interests of intermediate and ultimate consumers when scrutinizing a merger. The question which therefore arises and seeks an answer in this section is whether, and if so how and to what extent, the Commission has made use of the above provisions so as to protect Union values other than (price) competition. The cases discussed below mainly concern merger transactions affecting the broadcasting markets. However, where appropriate, reference is also made to decisions dealing with concentrations in other sectors of the media industry to complement the analysis.

3.3.1 Public policy considerations under Article 2(1)(b) of the Merger Regulation: development of technical progress and consumer interests

202. In *Bertelsmann/Kirch/Premiere*, the parties to the merger argued that the proposed project, the creation of a digital pay-TV program and marketing platform using d-box technology,[777] required a significant investment. According to the parties, it was only by joining forces that the infrastructure necessary for the breakthrough of digital television in Germany could be established.[778] If the operation were approved, the parties said, it would promote technical progress. In the Commission's view, however, it was extremely doubtful whether the merger would indeed have a positive impact on technical progress because the transaction was likely to seal off the (then emerging) pay-TV market.[779] The Commission further noted that even if the project could contribute to technical progress, this was irrelevant under Article 2(1)(b) because the criterion of technical progress contained therein 'is subject to the proviso that it does not form an obstacle to competition'.[780] Based on the above, it decided to reject the parties' argument. The Commission had reached the same conclusion in *MSG Media Service*, the earlier unsuccessful attempt of Bertelsmann and Kirch to solidify their presence in the German pay-TV market.[781]

203. The first problem with the above reasoning is that it renders Article 2(1)(b) devoid of substance. It is built on 'a contradiction in terms, for it would impose the interpretation that ... the presence of economic and technical progress would be unnecessary to authorize a transaction in the absence of anticompetitive

777 *Bertelsmann/Kirch/Premiere* (Case IV/M.993) [1999] OJ L053/1, paragraph 8

778 ibid, paragraph 119

779 ibid, paragraph 122

780 ibid.

781 *MSG Media Service* (Case IV/M.469) [1994] OJ L364/1, paragraph 100: while '[i]t is true that the successful spread of digital television presupposes a digital infrastructure and hence that an enterprise with the business object of MSG can contribute to technical and economic progress ... the reference to this criterion in Article 2(1)(b) of the Merger Regulation is subject to the reservation that no obstacle is formed to competition'.

effects'.[782] This interpretation has justifiably been criticized by commentators and practitioners alike because it deprives the merging parties of the ability to put forward any dynamic efficiency claims.[783] The second problem arising from the above decisions is that no reliable economic data was relied upon to assess whether or not the notified operation could enhance technical progress. For example, in *MSG Media Service*, the Commission based its conclusion on a series of opinions of competing enterprises surveyed; unsurprisingly, competitors stated that if the concentration were cleared, 'they would have to review and possibly abandon existing plans or thoughts on future pay-TV supply in the digital television area'.[784] Instead of deriving this conclusion from competitors' views, which have 'limited, if any, evidentiary value', the Commission should have attempted to establish the causality link between the impact of the new entity on the ability and incentive of other companies to penetrate the affected market.[785]

204. It is not excluded that a rational interpretation of Article 2(1)(b) or a detailed economic analysis could have led to the same conclusion, that is, that the merger would likely harm both technical progress and competition. It bears noting that the decision to ban these mergers was not wrong, if for other reasons. We have already seen that the prohibitions were largely based on the assumption that vertical integration combined with an unparalleled first-mover advantage would grant the merged entity the ability and incentive to foreclose the market for pay-TV. It was on the basis of these foreclosure concerns that the Commission rejected the parties' argument that it was only by pooling their resources that the infrastructure necessary for the breakthrough of digital pay-TV television in Germany could be established.[786] The way the market developed proved the Commission right. Bertelsmann (now part of RTL Group)[787] is still alive and kicking in both free-to-air and pay-TV.[788] Deutsche Telekom has been very successful in the IPTV segment.[789] In 2010, an SES Astra subsidiary launched the HD+ program package which is becoming increasingly popular,[790] thereby potentially having the capacity to exercise

782 Lascowska, M. (2013). Dynamic Efficiencies and Technological Progress in EC Merger Control. The University of Oxford, Centre for Competition Law and Policy Working Paper CCLP (L) 29, 5. <http://papers.ssrn.com/sol3/papers.cfm?abstract_id=2336956>

783 Butorac Malnar, V. (2008). The Role of Efficiencies in Merger Control: Comparative EU–USA Perspective. Zb. Prav.fak. Sveuc. Rij 29(2), 864–5

784 *MSG Media Service* (Case IV/M.469) [1994] OJ L364/1, paragraph 101

785 Lascowska (2013), supra n. 120, 6. Lascowska convincingly argues that the assessment of whether the merging parties in Bertelsmann/Kirch/Premiere can contribute to technical progress also lacks a sound economic reasoning, see in particular p. 9–11

786 See Bertelsmann/Kirch/Premiere (Case IV/M.993) [1999] OJ L053/1, paragraph 119

787 Note that in 2000 Bertelsmann CLT-UFA merged with Pearson TV and became RTL Group. See <http://www.rtlgroup.com/www/htm/AboutUs_History.aspx>

788 <http://mavise.obs.coe.int/company?id=2093>

789 <http://mavise.obs.coe.int/country?id=2>

790 According to SES, within three years after its launch, HD+ had been activated in 1.1 million households. In 2016, it exceeded the two million subscriber mark. See Lilie, F. Number of HD+ Subscribers in

constraints on Sky Deutschland (former Kirch)[791] and RTL. Finally, it is worth mentioning that, in the period following the prohibition decisions, the average prices for pay-TV in Germany were significantly lower than in several other European countries.[792]

205. Compared with *MSG Media Service* and *Bertelsmann/Kirch/Premiere*, the Commission follows an apparently more permissive approach in *News Corp/ Telepiù*. This latter case did not concern the development of technical progress, but the interests of end consumers. As already mentioned, the Commission found that the concentration would lead to the creation of a near-monopoly in the pay-TV market in Italy[793] and that the conditions for the transaction to qualify as 'rescue merger' due to the financial difficulties faced by Stream were not fulfilled.[794] Nevertheless, the Commission concluded that a conditional clearance of the merger would be more beneficial to consumers than a disruption caused by a potential closure of Stream.[795] A factor influencing the Commission's decision seems to have been that neither Stream nor Telepiù had been profitable. It was therefore likely that one of them would exit the market anyway, resulting in the market being controlled by an unregulated monopolist. Put simply, the Commission felt that 'regulated' consolidation was less detrimental to (actual or potential) pay-TV subscribers.[796] However, it reached this conclusion without making any reference to Article 2(1)(b) and, most importantly, without substantiating in which way the consumers would be worse off if Stream went bankrupt. It is therefore difficult to determine to what extent consumer protection factored into its decision to clear the merger.

206. Considering how the market evolved post-merger, the outcome of the decision appears to have harmed rather than improved consumer welfare. As already seen, consumers have been deprived of choice. Moreover, in the period following the decision, pay-TV prices in Italy were the second highest in Europe.[797]

Germany Passes Two Million Mark. Press Release. 13 February 2017, SES website. <https://www.ses.com/press-release/number-hd-subscribers-germany-passes-two-million-mark>

791 Note that in 2008, Premiere AG (former Kirch) was acquired by News Corporation.

792 Padilla, J., Matthew Bennett and Wim Koevoets (2007). Pay-TV prices in Europe – An Econometric Analysis, 6.

793 News Corp/Telepiù (Case COMP/M.2876) [2004] OJ L110/73, paragraph 114

794 ibid, paragraph 205 et seq.

795 ibid, paragraph 221

796 Nikolinakos (2006), supra n. 32, 168

797 Padilla, Bennett and Koevoets (2007), supra n. 130

3.3.2 Media pluralism and cultural diversity considerations

207. In *MSG Media Service*, the Commission seems to have taken account of the concerns related to the concentration of significant (opinion-forming) power in the hands of one media owner. In assessing the competitive constraints that potential competitors could exert on the merged entity, the Commission noted that

> [t]he only currently known company wishing to offer in Germany similar services to those to be provided by MSG is Selco ... Selco is a joint venture between the private television broadcaster PRO 7 (50.1%) and News Corporation Ltd (49.9%), which belongs to the Murdoch group. ... It should ... be noted that *47.7 % of the shares in PRO 7 are held by Mr. Thomas Kirch, the son of the owner of the Kirch group. ... PRO 7 therefore should probably be included at least in the sphere of influence of the Kirch group*. Against this background it is hardly to be expected that Selco will enter into active competition against MSG [emphasis added].[798]

208. National regulatory instruments in support of media pluralism adopt the same approach. For example, Article 5(3) of Greek Law 3592/2007 on media concentration provides that the rules established therein apply to both the person in 'control' of a media undertaking and her family members.[799] But, achieving the same objective as a regulatory tool aiming to protect media pluralism does not imply that the Commission's reasoning in *MSG* cannot be grounded on economic principles. In other words, this approach should not necessarily be regarded as an exception to competition law. For example, it is a commonly accepted principle that a vertically integrated company enjoying significant market power will have the ability and incentive to favor its own upstream or downstream services.[800] The same logic may apply by analogy to the situation in which two undertakings are controlled by two persons that are connected by blood or marriage. Moreover, including Pro 7 in the sphere of influence of the Kirch group is supported by the Merger Regulation, which defines the concept of 'control' in a flexible and broad manner. More particularly, Article 3(2) lays down that 'control shall be constituted by rights, contracts *or any other means which*, either separately or in combination and *having regard to*

---

798 MSG Media Service (Case IV/M.469) [1994] OJ L364/1, paragraph 65

799 Law No. 3592/2007 of 19 July 2007 on Media Concentration and Licensing Procedures, Official Gazette, No. 161, 3371. See in particular Article 5(3)(a) and (b): 'Έλεγχος υφίσταται όταν φυσικό ή νομικό πρσωπο, που συμμετέχει και σε άλλο ηλεκτρονικό μέσο ενημέρωσης της αυτής μορφής, επηρεάζει με οποιονδήποτε τρόπο ουσιωδώς τη λήψη αποφάσεων της επιχείρησης σχετικά με τον τρόπο διοίκησης και την εν γένει λειτουργία της. ... Οι ανωτέρω προϋποθέσεις ελέγχου ισχύουν και για τους συζύγους και τους συγγενείς σε ευθεία γραμμή απεριορίστως και εκ πλαγίου μέχρι και τρίτου βαθμού εξ αίματος ή εξ αγχιστείας'

800 See Guidelines on the assessment of non-horizontal mergers under the Council Regulation on the control of concentrations between undertakings [2008] OJ C 265/7, paragraphs 31 et seq.

the considerations of fact or law *involved, confer the possibility of exercising decisive influence on an undertaking*' [emphasis added].[801] Even if the son of the owner of the Kirch group was not a majority stakeholder in Pro 7, the 47.7% of shares he held in the company was, based on existing case law, enough to consider that he (and, by extension, his father) was in control of Pro 7.[802] The Commission would have reached the same conclusion by examining the coordinated effects to which the concentration could give rise. Pursuant to the Horizontal Merger Guidelines, coordination may take various forms, including market division, for instance by customer characteristics.[803] In this case, market division arrangements seem to have taken place. As opposed to the merged entity, Pro 7 would only market *foreign-language* programs in Germany and, according to the information available to the Commission at the time of the decision, it was not planning to engage in the provision of TV content in the German language, but rather to keep operating 'in a niche market with a limited subscriber base'.[804] The above analysis clearly illustrates that if the Commission is willing to apply competition law in a pluralism-friendly manner, it can do so without necessarily deviating from an economics-based analysis.

209. In recent years, the Commission has disassociated merger control from pluralism and cultural diversity considerations. Two examples of this arguably rigid application of competition law are *News Corp/BSkyB* and *NBC/Comcast*.[805] The former has already been extensively discussed in Chapter 3 (Part 3). For our purposes here, it bears repeating that, in addition to the possible anti-competitive effects it was likely to create,[806] the proposed concentration also raised major pluralism concerns. More particularly, it was feared that, if the transaction were approved, it would give media entrepreneur, Rupert Murdoch, a dangerous level of control of the UK media.[807] The Commission was limited to noting that relevant issues are for the UK authorities to address under Article

801 In an equally flexible and broad manner, Article 3(3)(b) provides that 'control is acquired by persons or undertakings which: (a) are holders of the rights or entitled to rights under the contracts concerned; or (b) while not being holders of such rights or entitled to rights under such contracts, have the power to exercise the rights deriving therefrom' [emphasis added]

802 There are Commission decisions finding that minority shareholdings of between 25.96% and 36.9% can confer de facto sole control on an undertaking (I refer to percentages because the decision does not give any details on Kirch's son's voting and other rights in Pro 7). For an overview of the relevant decisional practive see, for instance, Frazer, T. and Susan Hinchliffe. Proposed changes to the EU merger control regime. EU & Competition briefing from Arnold & Porter LLP published in the December 2012/January 2013 issue of The In-House Lawyer. <https://www.arnoldporter.com/~/media/files/perspectives/publications/2012/12/proposed-changes-to-the-eu-merger-control-regime/files/publication/fileattachment/ihl206-arnold.pdf>

803 Guidelines on the assessment of horizontal mergers under the Council Regulation on the control of concentrations between undertakings [2004] OJ C 31/3, paragraph 40

804 MSG Media Service (Case IV/M.469) [1994] OJ L364/1, paragraph 65

805 Comcast/NBC Universal (Case COMP/M.5779) [2010] OJ C228/2

806 News Corp/BSkyB (Case COMP/M.5932) [2011] C 37/2, paragraph 28

807 See, Ofcom (2010b). Report on public interest test on the proposed acquisition of British Sky Broadcasting Group plc by News Corporation

21(4) of the Merger Regulation[808] and decided to approve the concentration on the grounds that it did not raise serious doubts as to its compatibility with the common market.[809] In *NBC/Comcast*, the Commission was called upon to decide whether the creation of a joint venture by Comcast (a cable network operator which is also involved in the licensing of TV programming and TV channels to pay-TV operators and in the production of motion pictures and TV programs) and NBCU (a global media and entertainment company, active in the development, production, marketing and distribution of entertainment, news and information) is compatible with the common market.[810] After a brief analysis of the structure of the affected markets, the Commission concluded that the notified operation would not have any significant impact on the availability of TV content and was therefore unlikely to harm cultural diversity.[811] The reasoning that led to this conclusion is problematic for three reasons: first, the Commission seems to have accepted the parties' argument that the transaction should be approved because, as a result of the significant growth in the number of new TV channels across Europe, there has been an increase in the demand for new content.[812] However, as was already seen above and in Chapter 2, an increase in the number of TV channels is neither an indication that the market is competitive (e.g. the channels may be owned by the same group) nor an incentive to provide original content. Second, the Commission appears to have accepted the parties' claim that European TV program producers are strong competitors *inter alia* because, under the Audiovisual Media Services Directive, broadcasters are required to reserve the majority of their broadcasting time for European works.[813] The assumption that European TV program producers exert competitive constraints on their US counterparts due to the European works quota rule is unfounded. As explained in Chapter 1 (Part 2), from a cultural diversity perspective, this rule is ill-designed because it imposes no quality requirements. Third, the Commission refrains from considering the effects of the concentration on cultural diversity. The conclusion that cultural diversity is not threatened as a result of the creation of the joint venture is derived from the finding that the transaction will not significantly impede effective competition.[814] The Commission followed this approach in several other cases, including *HBO/Ziggo*,[815] *Bertelsmann/Planeta/Circulo*,[816]

808 News Corp/BSkyB (Case COMP/M.5932) [2011] C 37/2, paragraph 309

809 ibid, paragraph 310. Identical remarks were made by the Commission in the decision dealing with Murdoch's second attempt to acquire control of Sky. See Fox/Sky (Case COMP/M.8354) [2017] OJ C238/1, paragraphs 469 et seq. For more information about this case see Chapter 1, n. 103.

810 ibid, paragraphs 2–6

811 ibid, paragraph 44

812 ibid, paragraph 41

813 ibid, paragraph 42

814 ibid, paragraphs 36 et seq.

815 HBO/Ziggo/HBO Nederland (Case COMP/M.6369) [2012] OJ C 72/2, paragraph 53

816 Bertelsmann/Planeta/Circulo (Case COMP/M.5838) [2010] OJ C 228/3, see in particular, paragraphs 39, 49, 57 and 59

and *Bertelsmann/KKR*.[817] There have also been cases such as *SFR/Télé 2*,[818] and *Liberty Global Europe/Unitymedia*,[819] where no mention of cultural diversity is made. Mere or no references to this value in the assessment of a merger affecting cultural industries renders Article 167(4) TFEU devoid of any mandatory effect (the problems that arise from this approach have been examined in Chapter 3, Part 3).

210. The above analysis sufficiently proves that public policy considerations have, at best, played a limited to no role in determining the outcome of a merger decision. The approach followed in *NBC/Comcast* suggests that the Commission perceives cultural diversity as a spontaneous result delivered by the undistorted functioning of the markets, objectives whose realization depends on the outcome of market forces. In *News Corp/Telepiù*, the interests of the consumers seem to have been taken into account as an exception to competition law but the Commission abstained from conducting a detailed assessment to substantiate this finding and therefore the extent to which such interests determined the outcome of the decision is not quantifiable. Lately, the Commission seems eager to distance itself from the protection of objectives that it does not consider relevant to EU merger control, including media pluralism, the *Newcorp/BSkyB* decision being the most prominent example of this approach.

4. Rethinking the Commission's merger practice in the broadcasting sector: exercising merger control in a pluralism-friendly manner

211. Moving from theory to practice, this section will examine how pluralism-specific considerations can be integrated into each step of the assessment of a merger affecting the broadcasting sector. I will use the example of a concentration involving two free-to-air broadcasters. However, as I will explain in more detail below, the suggestions made throughout this section are also appropriate for the assessment of mergers involving other players that provide content for free as well as for the assessment of mergers affecting markets that entail the exchange of content for money.

817 Bertelsmann/KKR (Case COMP/M.5533) [2009] OJ C 240/01. See in particular paragraph 79

818 SFR/Télé 2 (Case COMP M.4504) [2007] OJ L316/57

819 Liberty Global Europe/Unitymedia (Case COMP/M.5734) [2010] OJ C36/1

4.1 Market definition in the assessment of mergers affecting FTA TV markets: what is the relevant viewers' market?

212. As discussed above, in the case of a merger affecting free-to-air TV markets, the Commission is willing to identify the advertising markets affected by the transaction but not the relevant audience markets. The argument it puts forward to explain this approach is that, in the absence of a trade relationship between the broadcaster and the viewer, there is no market to define. This argument, I say, is unconvincing on the grounds that viewers' attention is a valuable input and a scarce resource allocated between broadcasters through competition. Hence there is a market for audiences, which must be defined for the purposes of competition law for at least two reasons. First, content that advertisers regard as substitutable is not a proxy for content that viewers regard as substitutable. Second, FTA TV is a two-sided platform exhibiting indirect network effects that need to be defined and measured because the interdependence between the two demands exercises competitive constraints on the broadcaster that affect the outcome of the decision. In view of the above, the exercise of market definition should consist in identifying the effective alternative sources of supply for both the advertisers *and* the viewers.

213. The fact that in the case of FTA TV there is no exchange of money, i.e. no benchmark price against which to apply the hypothetical price increase to run a traditional SSNIP test, is not a valid reason for refusing to define the viewers' markets affected by the notified transaction. The instruments used to exercise merger control must be flexible enough to be able to grasp dimensions of competition that are relevant to the market under scrutiny. In its notice on the definition of the relevant market for the purposes of Community competition law, the Commission itself notes that '[t]here is a range of evidence permitting an assessment of the extent to which substitution would take place ..., *depending very much on the characteristics and specificity of the industry and products or services that are being examined.* The same type of evidence may be of no importance in other cases' [emphasis added].[820] As the example that follows will illustrate, if adjusted to the particularities of free content markets, a SSNIP test has the capacity to identify what are the viewers' switching rates and how they affect competition.

214. In the case of a traditional application of the SSNIP test, the first step would consist in examining how consumers would react to price increases. In our case, however, content is provided for free. We may overcome this barrier by asking what viewers would do if there was a change in quality rather than price.[821] A widely accepted quality indicator in FTA TV that could be used to

820 Commission Notice on the definition of relevant market for the purposes of Community competition law [1997] OJ C 372/3, paragraph 25.

821 Europe Economics (2002), supra n. 10, 88

conduct the substitutability assessment is the amount of time devoted to the transmission of advertisements. The assumption that viewers dislike advertising has been verified by empirical studies.[822] On this basis, it is possible to run a hypothetical monopolist test by considering the likely effects of a small but significant increase in the number of advertising minutes per hour, keeping other broadcasters' content constant.[823] If this change leads viewers to watch more of the other available channels, this would imply that the broadcaster competes in a wider viewer market which includes these other channels. If this change, however, leads viewers to spend less time watching television, this would indicate that the hypothetical monopolist holds significant power in attracting viewers to its content.[824]

215. This type of analysis need not be limited to one quality parameter. The 'stated preferences' method, and more particularly conjoint analysis, may lead to a more nearly complete assessment of the viewer-side constraints exerted on the broadcasters concerned. Conjoint analysis 'confronts respondents with hypothetical choices among different products, which are carefully made different on different aspects while keeping constant the others'.[825] It is in essence a SSNIP test that takes account of more than one dimension of competition. For example, in the case of advertising markets, a conjoint analysis may ask advertisers which broadcaster they would prefer if they had to choose between two broadcasters that charge the same price but appeal to viewers with different demographic profiles and vice versa.[826] In the case of the viewers' market, in addition to the amount of time devoted to the transmission of advertisements, variables that may be used to conduct a conjoint analysis include content variety, availability of programming, i.e. whether the broadcaster makes its programming available when the consumer wants to see it (e.g. through catch-up TV or archive),[827] and even the introduction of a subscription fee.[828]

216. This market definition analysis would largely depend on data collected with consumer surveys. The Commission itself acknowledges that surveys on

822 See, for instance, Wilbur, K. C. (2008). A Two-Sided, Empirical Model of Television Advertising and Viewing Markets. Marketing Science, 27(3), 356–378, and Jeziorski, P. (2010). Merger enforcement in two-sided markets. Economics Working Paper Archive 570, Johns Hopkins University. <https://ideas.repec.org/p/jhu/papers/570.html>

823 Europe Economics (2002), supra n. 10, 89

824 ibid.

825 Filistrucchi, L., Damien Geradin and Eric van Damme (2012). Identifying two-sided markets. Discussion Paper, TILEC DP 2012-008, 15

826 ibid.

827 Csorgo, L. and Ian Munro (2011). Market Definition Issues for Audio and Audio-Visual Distribution Products and Services in a Digital Environment, A Report Prepared for the Canadian Radio-television and Telecommunications Commission. <http://www.crtc.gc.ca/eng/publications/reports/rp110215.htm#_ftn7> Comparable parameters were used in Universal/EMI where the Commission based the assessment of whether recorded music in physical format is a substitute for recorded music in digital format on characteristics such as sound quality, usage restrictions and the art work (covers, booklets and lyrics). See Universal Music Group/EMI Music (Case COMP/M.6458) [2012] OJ C 220/8, paragraph 127

828 YouTube introduced subscription fees for content without ads. See: <https://www.youtube.com/premium>

usage patterns and attitudes are an appropriate instrument to establish whether an economically significant proportion of consumers considers two products as substitutable[829] and has relied on their results in merger investigations, but unfortunately, only on a few occasions.[830]

217. The proposed method has several advantages. First, as opposed to qualitative techniques,[831] a conjoint analysis would not simply define the nature of the indirect network effects between the viewers and the advertisers, but would further allow the Commission to measure their size, thereby leading to a more accurate assessment of the competitive constraints exerted on the merging parties.[832] Moreover, consumer surveys may play a major role in informing the substitutability assessment in cases where econometric data such as diversion ratio estimates are not available.[833] Even in cases where econometric analyses were available,[834] consumer surveys have proved useful for complementing or testing the validity of their results.[835]

218. These consumer surveys can be conducted by the parties to the transaction or by the Commission itself. If the survey is conducted by the parties, the report should include detailed information about how the research was carried out.[836] This would allow the Commission to check whether the parties committed errors or made choices that may have produced biased results. For example, in the case concerning the joint venture between the BBC, Channel Four and ITV relating to the video on demand sector (Project Kangaroo), the results of the survey conducted by the parties were not relied upon by the Competition Commission because, contrary to the 'small price increases' logic underpinning the SSNIP test, consumers were asked what they would do if content

829 See, for instance, Commission Notice on the definition of relevant market for the purposes of Community competition law [1997] OJ C 372/3, paragraph, 41; Commission (EU) Guidelines on the assessment of horizontal mergers under the Council Regulation on the control of concentrations between undertakings [2004] OJ C 31/3, paragraph 29; DG Competition (2010). Best Practices for the Submission of Economic Evidence and Data Collection in Cases Concerning the Application of Article 101 and 102 TFEU and in Merger Cases. Staff Working Paper. <http://ec.europa.eu/competition/antitrust/legislation/best_practices_submission_en.pdf>

830 See, for instance, Ryanair/Aer Lingus (Case COMP/M.4439) [2007] OJ C 10/6; KLM/Martinair (Case COMP/M.5141) [2009] C 51/4; Pernod Ricard/V&S (Case COMP/M.5114) OJ [2008] C 219/5; Lufthansa/SN Airholding (Case COMP/M.5335) OJ [2009] C 295/8; Ryanair/Aer Lingus (Case COMP/M.4439) [2007] OJ C 10/6; Statoilhydro/Conocophilips (Case COMP/M.4919) OJ [2009] C 201/6

831 Take the example of deductive reasoning which is premised on a logical assumption. In the case of advertising-financed TV, we would take for granted that viewers dislike advertising. This would be correct but we would be unable to draw any conclusions on the size of the network effects. For an overview of the qualitative methods that may be employed when defining two-sided markets see Filistrucchi, Geradin and van Damme (2012), supra n. 163, 12–15

832 ibid, 13–15

833 See OECD (2011). Economic Evidence in Merger Analysis, 255. In our case, it would be an increase in advertising minutes per hour or any other negative change in quality.

834 This was, for instance, the case in Ryanair/Aer Lingus (Case COMP/M.4439) [2007] OJ C 10/6. While the Commission found the econometric analysis useful, it also found it incomplete because it did 'not address the loss in potential competition between the merging parties, nor competition on factors other than price, such as frequencies, advertising or ancillary services'. See OECD (2011), supra n. 171, 258

835 DG Competition (2010), supra n. 167, paragraph 30

836 ibid, paragraph 39

prices increased by as much as 200%.[837] If the Commission takes the initiative to commission its own consumer survey, it would need to grasp the most relevant demand parameters prior to conducting the interviews. To this end, interested third parties, i.e. the consumers, should have a say in the questionnaire design and instruments of data collection.[838] In the case of the viewer market, an interested third party which could help the Commission choose relevant variables or more generally provide useful information on consumption habits in the media markets affected by the merger is Euralva, an alliance of national associations representing the interest of listeners and viewers of broadcasting.[839]

219. This approach has certain drawbacks, most notably the possibility for a divergence between stated and real preferences;[840] if what consumers say they prefer is different from what they actually prefer, the surveys, no matter how well designed, will produce inaccurate findings. This obstacle, however, can be overcome by running a 'revealed preferences' study. The revealed preferences method is based on 'data on the actual behavior of market participants as well as the estimation of demand for the two sides of the market'.[841] For example, to measure demand on the advertisers' side, it would be necessary to collect data on advertising rates, the quantity of advertising slots, and the demographic profile of the viewers to which a broadcaster appeals.[842] On the viewers' side, we could measure the volume of consumption (minutes of watching TV), reach (the percentage of people who are exposed to a broadcaster in a given period of time), the amount of time the broadcaster in question devotes

837 Competition Commission (2009). A report on the anticipated joint venture between BBC Worldwide Limited, Channel Four Television Corporation and ITV plc relating to the video on demand sector, paragraph 4.10: 'The survey carried out by the parties was intended to inform our understanding of the substitutability of UK and non-UK content. However, in our view, the results might overestimate actual switching ... [C]onsumers were asked about their likely responses to relatively large increases in the price of UK TV archive content relative to other options. They were asked how they would respond if UK TV archive content, instead of being free, cost £0.50, and how they would respond if prices increased from £0.50 to £1.50, while the price of other options (such as non-UK TV content) was variously free or cost £0.50. This makes it difficult to interpret the results of the survey within the context of the SSNIP test, which is based on proportionately small price increases.' See also Office of Fair Trading (2008). Completed acquisition by Global Radio UK Limited of GCap Media plc, paragraph 201

838 The Commission itself notes in its Staff Working Document (SWD) on Best Practices for the submission of economic evidence in competition cases that, if it decides to run a survey, it is appropriate to consult interested third parties. See DG Competition (2010), supra n. 167, fn. 30. While this SWD does not define the term 'interested third parties', the document outlining DG Competition's best practices on the conduct of merger control proceedings explicitly refers to consumer associations as third persons whose views the Commission welcomes throughout a merger investigation. See DG Competition (2004). Best practices on the conduct of merger control proceedings, paragraph 34. <http://ec.europa.eu/competition/mergers/legislation/proceedings.pdf> The legal basis is Article 16(3) of Commission Regulation (EC) No. 802/2004 the implementing Council Regulation (EC) No. 139/2004 on the control of concentrations between undertakings [2004] OJ L133/1

839 For more information about Euralva see: http://www.euralva.wordpress.com/>

840 Camesasca, P.D., Maarten Meulenbelt, Thomas Chellingsworth, Ief Daems and Julie Vandenbuccche (2009). The Dutch Yellow Pages Merger Case – 2-1 Will Go! European Competition Law Review 30(1), 7 referring to Louviere, J.J., D.A. Hensher and J.D. Swait (2000). Stated choice methods: Analysis and applications. Cambridge: CUP

841 Filistrucchi, Geradin and van Damme (2012), supra n. 163, 17

842 ibid.

to advertising, and multisourcing (the average number of broadcasters that viewers used in a given period of time).[843] In each Member State there is at least one company (e.g. Nielsen, GfK, TNS, etc.) providing audience measurement services and, in most cases, broadcasters have access to (their own *and* their competitors') audience behavior-related data. Under Article 11(1) of the Merger Regulation, the Commission may, by simple request or decision, obtain the above data from the merging broadcasters, the broadcasters' competitors and other relevant parties as it sees fit.[844]

220. While one may argue that the Commission has only ninety working days to decide whether or not to approve a merger,[845] the methodology applied to the prohibition decision concerning the proposed acquisition of sole control by Ryanair of Aer Lingus clearly shows that the proposed analysis is not only defensible in theory but also workable in practice. To assess demand-side substitutability, the Commission conducted consumer surveys at Dublin airport. Where data regarding distances and travelling times derived from the responses to the questionnaire were incomplete or manifestly questionable, the Commission obtained the information it needed from websites providing mapping and route planning services.[846] The Commission also took into account the views of airports and of Member States' civil aviation authorities that were expressed during the course of the investigation, *after* comparing them with the results of reports such authorities made independently of the proposed transaction.[847] The Commission complemented its analysis with other data, including the estimated proportion of leisure passengers on a route, the impact of the regulatory framework on substitutability, the merging parties' marketing practices and the results of a price correlation analysis it conducted during the investigation.[848]

221. One might ask whether the proposed method can really make a difference. The answer is yes, a big one. The approach the Commission followed in *News Corp/BSkyB* illustrates why its lack of interest in examining substitutability from a viewer's perspective is likely to lead to erroneous or incomplete market definitions that may ultimately affect the outcome of the decision. For example, in this case, the Commission avoided defining the market for audiences, implicitly assuming that viewers are indifferent to advertising.[849] Adopting the Commission's reasoning would mean accepting that a broadcaster may raise

843 Ofcom (2012b). Measuring media plurality, 19–20. <https://www.ofcom.org.uk/consultations-and-statements/category-1/measuring-plurality>

844 See also DG Competition (2004), supra n. 176, paragraphs 26–28

845 Council Regulation (EC) No. 139/2004 of 20 January 2004 on the control of concentrations between undertakings (the EC Merger Regulation) OJ L24/1, Article 10(3)

846 Ryanair/Aer Lingus (Case COMP/M.4439) [2007] OJ C 10/6, paragraph 99(1)

847 ibid, at (3)

848 ibid, at (4)–(8)

849 Filistrucchi, Geradin and van Damme (2012), supra n. 163, fn. 54

ad prices and/or increase the advertising/content ratio without worrying about viewers switching to another provider. However, as previously mentioned, empirical studies have found that demand for advertising affects demand for content because audiences dislike advertising.[850]

222. In *News Corp/BSkyB*, the Commission also found that the market for the provision of broadcasting services to end-users in the UK and Ireland encompasses all technical means of distribution, including satellite, DTT and IPTV.[851] It based this finding on the replies given by content distributors, not viewers.[852] However, in its report on the same transaction, Ofcom found that IPTV was not (and is unlikely to become in the near future), a traditional TV substitute. Ofcom's conclusion was based on TV content viewing habits.[853]

223. Failure to take account of what type of content audiences regard as interchangeable may also lead to the definition of the relevant product market in a broad manner, thereby making it less likely to find that the merger will adversely affect competition. For example, in *News Corp/BSkyB*, the Commission made a distinction between the market for sports events, the market for premium films and the market for *other TV content* without, however, specifying what it meant by 'other TV content'.[854] It simply referred to documentaries and TV series as examples of the types of content covered by that category.[855] Unsurprisingly, the Commission found that neither News Corporation nor BSkyB were holding significant market power in the markets for sale and acquisition of other TV content respectively.[856] However, in its report on Project Kangaroo, the Competition Commission, which was largely based on consumer survey results, concluded that the market for TV content was further subdivided into different markets on the basis of form, availability, origin and genre as follows:

> (a) Short form vs long form. Short-form video includes clips from longer videos or short video clips uploaded by users (user-generated content). Long-form content refers to full-length material.

---

850 Wilbur (2008), supra n. 160

851 News Corp/BSkyB (Case COMP/M.5932) [2011] C 37/2, see paragraphs 100 et seq.

852 ibid, paragraph 104

853 Ofcom (2010b). Report on public interest test on the proposed acquisition of British Sky Broadcasting Group plc by News Corporation, paragraph A2.267. See also Ofcom (2012c). Securing long term benefits from scarce low frequency spectrum, paragraph 1.26, p. 6. <http://stakeholders.ofcom.org.uk/binaries/consultations/uhf-strategy/statement/UHF_statement.pdf>

854 News Corp/BSkyB (Case COMP/M.5932) [2011] C 37/2, paragraph 30

855 ibid.

856 For a detailed discussion of the approach to market definition the Commission followed in this case and its implications for competition and media pluralism see Chapter 3, Part 4

(b) Catch-up vs archive. Catch-up content is made available soon after it is first broadcast on linear TV (generally within hours and for up to 30 days). Archive content is content that is no longer available within the catch-up window.

(c) Content of UK origin vs content of non-UK, primarily US, origin

(d) Genre (including drama, entertainment, comedy, sport, news, etc.).[857]

224. It bears noting that, while in several decisions the Commission has considered subdividing the market[858] in a way similar to the above, it has meticulously left open the question of whether the market for *other TV content* should be further segmented.[859]

225. The above analysis convincingly demonstrates that the Commission can and must define the relevant viewers' market in cases involving FTA broadcasters. This is becoming more pressing and imperative because, with the advent of digital media, public broadcasters are increasingly getting involved in projects aiming to deliver free content on new distribution platforms. For example, in the UK, BBC Worldwide partnered with, *inter alia* ITV, Channel 4 and Channel 5 and created a digital terrestrial TV/on-demand platform called YouView.[860] YouView provides access to free-to-air TV channels and its Electronic Program Guide does *not* carry advertising.[861] A similar platform involving public broadcasters ARD and ZDF was also envisaged by German operators.[862] As hybrid distribution platforms constantly emerge, the

857 Competition Commission (2009), supra n. 175, paragraph 2.6. For more details see paragraphs 4.15 et seq. Similar remarks can be made about the different approaches followed by the European Commission and the Conseil de la Concurrence concerning the French broadcasting market. See Commission decision of 3 March 1999 relating to a proceeding pursuant to Article 85 of the EC Treaty, (Case IV/36.237) [1999] OJ L90/6, paragraphs 34–36 (the Commission refrained from delineating the boundaries of the market for the acquisition of sports and film rights) and compare Décision n° 98-D-70 du 24 novembre 1998 relative à la saisine des sociétés Multivision et Télévision Par Satellite (TPS) dans le secteur des droits de diffusion audiovisuelle (p. 17) where the Conseil de la Concurrence, based on a study submitted by the Conseil supérieur del'audiovisuel (CSA) on film consumption that concluded that the offer of American films does not fulfill the needs of French audiences, divided the market into two segments, namely the market for French films and the market for American films.

858 See, for instance, News Corp/BSkyB (Case COMP/M.5932) [2011] C 37/2, paragraph 63, where it was considered dividing the market for films in a market for US-produced films and a market for European films, and TPS (Case COMP/JV.57) [2002] OJ C 137/23, paragraph 16, where it was considered whether the market for pay-TV channels should be further segmented by thematic content (such as premium, sports, movies, news, youth channels).

859 See News Corp/BSkyB (Case COMP/M.5932) [2011] C 37/2, paragraph 66; News Corp/Premiere (Case COMP/M.5121) [2008] OJ C 219/4, paragraph 35; and TPS (Case COMP/JV.57) [2002] OJ C 137/23, paragraph 16

860 <http://www.youview.com/>

861 McCabe, M. YouView will encourage competition, says chief. 16 September 2010, MediaWeek. <http://www.mediaweek.co.uk/article/1028931/youview-will-encourage-competition-says-chief>

862 However, the transaction failed to get regulatory approval by the Bundeskartellamt. For more information on this project see, for instance, Krieger, J. ARD and ZDF establish German VOD portal. 25 April 2012, RapidTVNews. <http://www.rapidtvnews.com/index.php/2012042521488/ard-and-zdf-establish-german-vod-portal.html>; and Bundeskartellamt ARD/ZDF Online Platform 'Germany's Gold' raises

Commission may soon be called upon to clear a transaction in which broadcasters, entirely or partly financed through license fees, participate. In such a case, an examination of whether the new platform will have the ability and incentive to raise advertising prices post-merger can hardly produce accurate conclusions on the effects of the platform on competition.[863] But the suggestions made above are by no means limited to the broadcasting sector. Most companies in today's digital media economy are advertising-based. Hence, if properly adapted to the particularities of each case, the proposed approach to market definition may be used in competition cases involving undertakings that provide free content in exchange for an intangible asset (e.g. attention, data,[864] etc.), including online search engines such as Google and Bing,[865] news aggregators such as Feedly and Google News, social networking sites like Facebook and LinkedIn.

226. The proposed methods may (and, arguably, should) also be used in cases of two-sided markets where audiences are required to pay to access the platform. For example, in mergers affecting the pay-TV markets, the Commission has referred to the level of subscriptions that viewers are willing to pay as a key parameter to define the markets affected by the merger.[866] However, pay-TV programming is sold in bundles of several channels and, as a result, audiences are not able to indicate their preferences for a particular channel or for a specific program provided by that channel.[867] This criterion leads to a substitutability analysis that has the main drawback of market definition in FTA TV markets, that is, a focus on ad prices casts a shadow on the audience's voice. Taking viewers' interests into account as suggested above would address this problem.[868]

---

competition concerns. Press Release, 11 March 2013. <http://www.bundeskartellamt.de/SharedDocs/Meldung/EN/Pressemitteilungen/2013/11_03_2013_Germanys-Gold.html>

863 On this issue see, for instance, Bania, K. and Richard Burnley (2014). Co-operation between broadcasters in the new media age: Rethinking national competition policy. European Competition Law Review 35(5), 220

864 On how my proposed approach would apply to data-driven markets see Bania, K. (2018). The Role of Consumer Data in the Enforcement of EU Competition Law. European Competition Journal 14(1), 38–80

865 In the recent case dealing with Google's discriminatory practices affecting price comparison websites, the Commission found that one of the relevant product markets affected by Google's conduct was the market for general search services, noting that 'even though users do not pay a monetary consideration for the use of general search services, they contribute to the monetization of the service of providing data with each query'. The Commission's finding was based on the lack of substitutability between general search and other online services, such as specialized search services and social networking sites. See *Google Search* (Case AT.39740) Commission decision of 27 June 2017 relating to proceedings under Article 102 TFEU and Article 54 of the EEA Agreement C (2017) 4444 final, paragraphs 158 et seq.

866 See supra n. 6

867 Goodman (2004), supra n. 15, 1426

868 Note that the Commission has acknowledged that viewer interests should be taken into account when defining the relevant pay-TV markets. However, it largely refrained from conducting a detailed analysis of the factors that shape the provision of pay-TV services from the audience's perspective. For example, in News Corp/BSkyB and SFR/Tele2, it based the assessment on replies given by distributors (the platforms carrying the content) and TV channel suppliers, not the subscribers themselves. See News Corp/BSkyB (Case COMP/5932) [2011] OJ C 37/02, paragraph 46, fn. 35 and SFR/Télé 2 France (Case COMP/M.4504) [2007] OJ L316/57, paragraphs 98–104

4.2 Competitive assessment: how can the effects on content diversity and quality be measured?

227. In Part 3, I mentioned that the Commission refrained from discussing the likely adverse effects of a concentration on content diversity and quality. I also demonstrated why its assumption that supply diversity will deliver varied and high-value content is ill-founded. In this section, I attempt to show how theory and practice can guide the Commission in incorporating related considerations into its merger decisions in the broadcasting industry.

228. The argument that the impact of a concentration on content diversity should not be marginalized is not democracy rhetoric. In Chapter 3 (Part 4) it was extensively discussed that competition in media markets has several non-price dimensions, including variety and quality. Naturally, assessing whether a merger will have adverse effects on non-price competition is a question of fact that cannot be determined in the abstract. However, developing a framework within which this assessment can be conducted is far from an impossible task. For example, the question of whether a merger is likely to reduce content diversity can be answered by reference to the importance of fixed costs. The higher these costs are, the more the new entity will be incentivized to provide the same content over all its constituent parts.[869] For instance, provided that both of them continue to exist post-merger, two broadcasters attracting viewers with the same demographic profiles can be expected to depend on the same content (e.g. a successful TV series) or the same content provider (e.g. a news agency) to generate audiences. This assumption is based on sector-specific economics; we have already seen in media markets in general and in broadcasting markets in particular that content creation (or acquisition) is very expensive but distribution fairly cheap. In their attempt to rationalize resources, broadcasters are highly likely to seize the opportunity to exploit large economies of scale. Content diversity reductions may also be linked to the incentive to preempt entry into the market.[870] This incentive is particularly strong in the case of new media markets because they involve significant network effects, thereby being vulnerable to tipping in favor of the first-mover.[871] Pre-emption becomes easier in cases where the merging parties control access to a valuable input. As seen above, the Commission partly based its early prohibition decisions dealing with mergers affecting the then nascent pay-TV market on this concern,[872] and rightly so. Market data needed to conduct an

869 OECD (2003a), supra n. 30, 44

870 ibid.

871 ibid, 40

872 See, for instance, MSG Media Service, paragraphs 56 and 62: '[E]xperience in other countries shows that pay-TV suppliers or cable network operators are the most likely suppliers of technical and administrative services for pay-TV … As the only supplier of pay-TV so far, Bertelsmann/Kirch already have, through Premiere, a subscriber base which they can also use in future digital pay-TV. The parties object in this respect that Premiere's subscriber base would not be sufficient to ensure a pay-back on the investment in MSG. This may be true. However, the risk of investment in a digital infrastructure is significantly reduced

analysis, as suggested above, are not difficult to collect from the merging parties, their competitors, other interested third parties (e.g. companies operating upstream such as news wholesalers), and publicly available sources.

229. As regards quality, one may argue that this depends on the idiosyncrasy of each viewer and that, as a result, no meaningful analysis of the quality of the content offered or the provider itself can take place in a merger decision. Indeed, quality is a subjective variable. However, subjective does not mean immeasurable. The approach followed in the prohibition decision concerning the proposed acquisition by Ryanair of sole control of Aer Lingus is a good example, illustrating how related considerations can inform a competition analysis. Based on the results of the consumer survey conducted at Dublin airport, the Commission decided to ban the transaction *inter alia* because the elimination of competition between the two air carriers would 'result in a reduction of service quality' and 'of choice between service models'.[873] Similar to *Ryanair/Aer Lingus*, the Commission can integrate degradation of quality into the theory of harm with reference to parameters to which viewers, not the merging parties or their competitors, attach particular importance.

230. Another example exemplifying an economics-based approach that seeks to understand the impact of a concentration on non-price competition is *Universal/EMI*, where the Commission found that the notified transaction would adversely affect the development of emerging online platforms and their ability to geographically expand into various digital markets, ultimately depriving EU consumers of innovative services.[874] This was likely to materialize, the Commission said, because the concentration would grant the merged entity the ability and incentive to extract more onerous licensing terms from these platforms. The link between an entity that may leverage its combined size in relation to its customers/platforms that bring new ways to consume music and the potential harm to innovation is rather straightforward. What deserves a closer look is the approach the Commission followed to determine whether the entity would, as a result of the merger, acquire the power to engage in exploitative practices that could produce this negative effect. In the event, the Commission conducted an econometric analysis which used the retail revenue share as the measure of each company's size in a given country/platform/period triplet. This retail revenue share was a measure adjusted to the

---

if the service provider can build on a subscriber base of analogue pay-TV customers. Each competitor of MSG would have to build on a subscriber base which the pay-TV suppliers handled by them would have to first acquire. Competitors of Bertelsmann/Kirch on the market for pay-TV would, in contrast to the parent companies of Premiere, have to start from scratch. The same applies to potential competitors of MSG in the area of technical and administrative services.'

873 Ryanair/Aer Lingus (Case COMP/M.4439) [2007] OJ C 10/6, paragraph 497. For the role that quality aspects played in the Commission's decision see paragraphs 492 et seq.

874 Universal Music Group/EMI Music (Case COMP/M.6458) [2012] OJ C 220/8, paragraph 636

quality of the record company's repertoire.[875] To control for repertoire quality, the Commission took account of variables such as the chart position of each track, age (months since first scale) and the proportion of hits (top fifty songs) in each company's repertoire.[876] Using the above method, the Commission found that the proposed transaction would increase by 10–20% the merged entity's share and that, due to the resulting increase in its product line, the entity would likely be able to impose on its digital customers disadvantageous commercial conditions.[877]

231. The Commission may conduct an analysis similar to the one in *Universal/EMI* in order to check whether a merger between two broadcasters would grant the merged entity the ability and incentive to extract better terms and conditions from independent TV content producers. Qualitative criteria that may be used with a view to measuring the broadcaster's program quality have been suggested by the Copé Commission, a committee of experts appointed by the French government to examine the role that public television should play in the digital era. These criteria comprise measurement of the program's audience on all platforms/networks for a long time period, and measurement of the usage rate (percentage of persons having accessed at least once a program offered by the broadcaster on a given period).[878] Depending on the resulting increase in the size of the broadcasters' repertoire, the Commission may be led to the conclusion that, as a result of the merger, the entity may exert significant bargaining power vis-à-vis production companies to which it is not structurally linked, thereby potentially depriving viewers of original content.

232. The above analysis inevitably gives rise to the following question: if the Commission found that the merger could have a negative impact on diversity or quality, would that be a good enough reason to prohibit (or attach conditions to) the merger concerned? The answer to this question depends on several parameters. But, if the need to conduct a balancing exercise indeed arises, there is no *a priori* reason why price reductions should prevail over diversity reductions. Consider again a merger between two FTA broadcasters. Post-merger, the broadcasters will be less restrained than before in increasing the advertising/content ratio (bad for quality). An increase in that ratio would lead to an increased supply of advertising space and a possible ad price reduction (good for price competition).[879] The likely positive effects on price competition should be carefully considered against the overall market structure (i.e.

875 ibid, Summary of the Economic Analysis, paragraph 20

876 ibid, paragraph 46, p. 328

877 ibid, paragraph 614

878 Commission pour la nouvelle télévision publique (2008). Rapport Présenté au Président de la République par Jean-François Copé le 25 juin 2008, 15. <http://www.culture.gouv.fr/culture/actualites/dossiers/Rapport_Cope/rapport_commission.pdf>

879 OECD (2003a), supra n. 30, 25

concentration levels) and the popularity of the merged entity. Moreover, the possible ad price reduction is subject to the condition that both broadcasters will continue to operate post-merger. For example, if the acquiring entity plans to shut down the acquired outlet to eliminate competition or if the parties intend to merge their broadcasting operations (as was, for instance, the case with Stream and Telepiù in *News Corp/Telepiù*) no ad space increase and hence no ad price reduction can be expected. If both broadcasters remain active post-merger, and assuming that ad prices may decrease, the final effect would, *inter alia*, depend on whether the merger could result in an increase in the prices of advertised products.[880]

4.3 Structural and behavioral commitments: designing remedies that protect supply and content diversity

233. As already seen in Part 3, one of the most common remedies imposed on undertakings involved in transactions affecting the broadcasting sector has been the obligation to sublicense premium content. Following the analysis of how these mechanisms were designed and implemented, I reached the conclusion that they did not manage to ensure that competition (and pluralism) would not be adversely affected post-merger. I shall now demonstrate that this conclusion is equally valid for other commitments the Commission has occasionally accepted and make some proposals to address their lacunae.

234. Structural remedies alone may not address foreclosure or ownership concentration concerns in the case of a merger involving a vertically integrated undertaking.[881] Put simply, the parties' commitment to divest assets does little to nothing if it fails to take account of the purchaser's (or any other competitor's) dependence on the seller in an upstream or downstream market.[882] Even if it does, an ill-designed obligation to behave in a certain way in that other market is unlikely to resolve the issue in a satisfactory manner. For example, as already seen, in *News Corp/Telepiù*, Telepiù undertook to divest its digital terrestrial broadcasting assets and not to enter into any further digital terrestrial television (DTT) activities, whether as network or as retail operator.[883] However, the merged entity was not prevented from controlling the market for the acquisition of premium content in *all* distribution platforms, including DTT, as a wholesaler.[884] As we have already seen, the wholesale offer mechanism has created several hurdles.

880 ibid.

881 Note that the vast majority of concentrations notified to the Commission that affect the broadcasting markets involve companies that are active on several levels of the supply chain.

882 Commission (2005). Merger Remedies Study, 23. <http://ec.europa.eu/competition/mergers/legislation/remedies_study.pdf>

883 News Corp/Telepiù (Case COMP/M.2876) [2004] OJ L110/73, paragraph 225(k)

884 ibid, at (g)

235. Related to the above, a duty to divest assets in a market where there is no overlap between the merging parties is only partly appropriate to eliminate concerns over market foreclosure. In *News Corp/Telepiù*, both Stream and Telepiù operated as pay-TV broadcasters via DTH, but only Telepiù broadcast on DTT.[885] There may have been a good reason why Telepiù was asked to sell its DTT assets, that otherwise the merger would bring both platforms under Sky's control on a lasting basis, but there was no structural remedy concerning the satellite platform, which the merged entity would clearly control post-merger. Instead of divestiture, the Commission accepted the parties' proposal to grant access to new DTH entrants through a 'cost-oriented non-discriminatory formula based on directly attributable costs of the services, a share of relevant technical costs (fixed and common costs) and a reasonable return over an appropriate period'.[886] This loosely defined obligation led to Sky Italia imposing onerous access conditions. More particularly, absent any specifications on behalf of the Commission as to how the 'common costs' related to the use of the platform should be calculated, Sky opted for a method that was based on the 'expected benefit' third parties would accrue from using the platform.[887] This 'expected benefit' was a percentage of the revenue generated from the sale of subscriptions or, in the case of pay-per-view, events.[888] This method raised two concerns: first, it established a causal link between the wholesale price charged by Sky and the retail price charged by competitors. In other words, it made the wholesale price dependent on the type of content transmitted, not on the use of the platform.[889] Second, it required third parties to provide Sky with sales volumes data, i.e. commercially sensitive information.[890] Following a lengthy investigation, AGCom decided to modify Sky's method so that the wholesale price would reflect the cost Sky would bear in the daily management of the platform.

236. Furthermore, even when certain aspects of an access mechanism are sufficiently precise or unambiguous, this does not mean that the merged entity will not breach the commitments it made to the Commission with a view to granting its own subsidiaries preferential treatment. In the above example, in violation of the obligation established in the decision,[891] Sky refrained from implementing and maintaining accounting separation between its broadcasting, retail distribution and platform operations,[892] thereby making it

885 ibid, paragraphs 8 and 9

886 ibid, paragraph 225(h)

887 AGCom (2010). A407-Conto TV/Sky Italia, Provvedimento n. 21316, paragraph 8. See also Delibera n. 233/09/CONS, paragraphs 24 et seq.

888 AGCom (2010). A407-Conto TV/Sky Italia, Provvedimento n. 21316, paragraph 8

889 ibid, paragraph 21

890 ibid, paragraph 22

891 News Corp/Telepiù (Case COMP/M.2876) [2004] OJ L110/73, section 10.6 of the Commitments

892 AGCom (2010). A407-Conto Vv/Sky Italia, Provvedimento n. 21316, paragraph 58

impossible to examine whether it respected the arm's length principle. AGCom had to intervene again to ensure that Sky complied with its accounting separation/transparency obligations.[893]

237. The above findings are consistent with the Commission's Merger Remedies Study, which concludes that remedies aiming to grant access to IPRs or know-how have deterred rather than encouraged market entry, the prices charged by the wholesaler being 'the single most essential element affecting the effectiveness of licensing remedies'.[894] In its report concerning the wholesale premium content packages supplied by Sky in the UK, Ofcom made similar remarks.[895]

238. In light of the above, we may draw the following conclusions: with respect to behavioral commitments, theory says and experience shows that they do not reduce the incentive to act anti-competitively. This means that access remedies must be described in as much detail as possible to reduce the firms' ability to engage in exclusionary practices post-merger. For example, in the case of wholesale must-offer regimes, the pricing method applied by the incumbent should be clearly defined and assessed prior to merger clearance.[896] As for the scope of the sublicensing mechanism, this should be determined by reference to the type of content (e.g. major sports competitions, Hollywood first-run movies) rather than channels. We have already seen in *News Corp/Telepiù* that the exclusion of 'basic' package channels carrying premium content from the sublicensing scheme resulted in Sky concluding a series of exclusive agreements with these channels,[897] thereby making them unavailable to other pay-TV operators, including operators active on platforms into which Sky was not planning to expand. In France and Spain, inclusion of channels in the sublicensing scheme led to the merged entity reducing the investment in those channels, making them less attractive to competitors.[898] Finally, it bears noting that the EU merger control toolbox provides the Commission with two apparatuses that could be used to improve the effectiveness of access remedies. First, if the parties fail to act in accordance with the commitments they made to get the merger cleared, the Commission may impose fines.[899] Second, in the case of access remedies, 'which may be on-going for a number of years and for which not all contingencies can be predicted at the time of the adoption of the ... decision', the Commission has the power to modify

893 ibid.

894 Commission (2005), supra n. 220, 118

895 Ofcom (2010a). Competition issues in premium pay TV movies, paragraph 6.26, p. 61. <http://stakeholders.ofcom.org.uk/binaries/consultations/movies_reference/summary/moviescondoc.pdf>

896 Commission (2005), supra n. 220, 120

897 Ofcom (2009a), supra n. 100, 14

898 ibid, 4

899 Council Regulation (EC) No. 139/2004 of 20 January 2004 on the control of concentrations between undertakings (the EC Merger Regulation) OJ L24/1, Article 14(2)(d)

or substitute the commitments that have failed to achieve their objective.[900] These two possibilities have largely been ignored to date.

239. As already seen, access to premium content remedies does not guarantee that content diversity will not be adversely affected post-merger. Hence, if, following the approach proposed above, the Commission finds that a concentration is likely to have a negative impact on non-price competition, other undertakings should be preferred in order to alleviate concerns arising from diversity reductions. Establishing behavioral obligations with a view to preserving competition in the content market is not as inconceivable as one might think. For example, in *Canal+/TPS*, in order to ensure that the quality of certain channels carried by the merging parties would not be reduced post-merger, the Conseil de la Concurrence imposed on the merging firms the obligation to broadcast for 50% of these channels' total transmission time films that were not available on another channel.[901] In the case of vertical mergers or mergers involving firms that are already vertically integrated, the entity should be required to acquire content from producers that have no structural links to the merging parties. The flipside of the remedy proposed in *Vivendi/Canal+/Seagram* could be an option here. As mentioned above, to get the merger approved, Vivendi undertook not to grant Canal+ the first-window rights covering more than 50% of the production of Universal Studios,[902] implying that Universal would need to conclude acquisition agreements with other content providers for the remaining 50%. I have already demonstrated that such remedies may be ineffective because the obligation to sell does not guarantee acquisition by other firms. In fact, the parties to the transaction were not bound by this obligation in cases where there was 'no competing offer at fair market value for all or part of the balance of Universal's film production'.[903] A duty to acquire content from independent producers would address the concerns identified above; it would limit the ability to foreclose competitors in the downstream market and result in the distribution of content that would not necessarily carry the editorial stamp of the merging parties.

240. With respect to the design of structural remedies, the most important issue consists in what should be divested. Structural remedies must first and foremost concern assets that the parties own in the market where there is substantial overlap.[904] Moreover, the divested activities must consist of *viable*

900 Commission Notice on remedies acceptable under Council Regulation (EC) No. 139/2004 and under Commission Regulation (EC) No. 802/2004, paragraph 74

901 Ofcom (2009a), supra n. 100, 21

902 Vivendi/Canal+/Seagram (Case COMP/M.2050) [2000] C 311/03, 20

903 ibid.

904 In its Merger Remedies Study the Commission found that 'less than overlap' divestiture commitments have been 'ineffective or risky'. See Commission (2005), supra n. 220, paragraph 34, p. 38, noting that '[r]esults from "less than the overlap" divestiture remedies suggest that such remedies were often ineffective or risky'.

businesses, including businesses, which, if run by a suitable purchaser, can compete effectively with the merged entity on a lasting basis. This should be borne in mind if the merger is likely to affect the market for news provision. Even if they attract audiences, from a revenue perspective, news outlets are more often than not 'loss-making entities owned by broader, profitable media companies, so there is no guarantee that the loss-making news outlet that might be ordered to be sold out would find a buyer'.[905] If substantial overlap is found in the market for news provision and the entity is not likely to find a credible purchaser, the proposal that was made in the assessment of the *News Corp/BSkyB* merger investigation by the UK authorities can be considered here. In brief, the proposal was that Sky News would start to operate as an *independent* public limited company. Its shares would be distributed among the existing shareholders of Sky in line with their existing shareholdings. As a result, post-merger, Sky News' structure would remain as if the concentration had not happened.[906] While this remedy would not result in the acquisition of the outlet by a provider that is not linked to the merged entity, it would at least not lead to a more concentrated market for news provision post-merger.

5. Conclusions

241. The objective of this Chapter was to examine the role that EU merger control has played/may play in ensuring that significant (market and opinion-forming) power is not concentrated in only a handful of traditional media owners. For that purpose, I examined the reasoning the Commission developed in merger decisions in the broadcasting sector. Some decisions were adopted several years ago and this has allowed me to assess the impact of a number of decisions on the affected markets. After identifying the drawbacks of the relevant decisional practice, I inquired whether the applicable legal framework may be interpreted and applied in a way that leads to a more complete assessment of the effects of a concentration on competition post-merger and explored to what extent my proposed approach might also benefit pluralism. In light of the results of the study of these cases and, based on the theoretical framework developed throughout this Chapter and Chapters 2 and 3, the following conclusions can be drawn.

905 BBC (2012). Response to Ofcom's Invitation to Comment on Measuring Media Plurality, 12. <http://stakeholders.ofcom.org.uk/binaries/consultations/measuring-plurality/responses/bbc.pdf>

906 Department for Culture, Media and Sport (2011). Notice on consultation on the proposed acquisition by News Corporation of up to 60.9% of British Broadcasting Group Plc – Undertakings given by News Corporation pursuant to paragraph 3 of Schedule 2 of the Enterprise Act 2002 (Protection of Legitimate Interests) Order 2003, 2

242. As regards market definition, identifying the relevant viewers' market and examining how viewers and advertisers interact with each other will allow the Commission to accurately measure the competitive constraints exerted on the merged entity. However, the proposed approach to market definition, which is largely based on consumer surveys, will also allow viewers to explain what their preferences are. From a pluralism perspective, this is a step forward because content appealing to advertisers, i.e. content that can attract large audiences and promote materialism, is not representative of viewers' interests. As a result, exposure diversity, the dimension of pluralism which concerns the amount and type of content audiences access and/or would like to engage with, is taken into account. Moreover, because there is a direct link between market definition and the theory of harm that is formulated in assessing possible anti-competitive behavior post-merger, defining the markets by reference to the content viewers regard as substitutable leaves room for considering the impact of the merger on more niche programming, thereby potentially leading to a more content diversity-friendly outcome. Content diversity may also be enhanced if the Commission abandons the assumption that supply diversity will guarantee a broad range of programming to choose from and accepts that the parameters of non-price competition in media markets are equally, if not more, important than price competition. Finally, with respect to remedies, the problems that have arisen in the implementation of must-offer mechanisms, such as loosely constructed pricing methods or inadequate definitions of the term 'premium content', may provide guidance in the design of similar schemes in the future with a view to avoiding opportunistic interpretations on the part of the merged entity that will attempt to game the commitments to its advantage. However, I have expressed strong doubts about the effectiveness of behavioral remedies that seek to ensure access to infrastructure or attractive content. If properly designed, structural remedies are far more appropriate to address both competition and pluralism concerns. From a competition perspective, compared with access remedies, structural solutions have been far more successful: the Commission's Merger Remedies Study, which analyzed forty decisions adopted in the five year period 1996–2000,[907] found that in the cases where structural remedies were imposed on the merging parties, '94% of the divested businesses were still operating and therefore exercising some degree of competitive constraint on the merged entity.'[908] Structural commitments are also more appropriate to protect pluralism because the sale of the divested business to a provider that is not structurally linked to the merged entity reduces the merging parties' opinion-forming power, thereby safeguarding supply diversity.

907 Commission (2005), *supra* n. 220, 11

908 ibid, 128

CHAPTER 5

ANTITRUST CONTROL IN PRINT AND DIGITAL PUBLISHING

1. Introduction

243. The previous Chapter dealt with mergers and acquisitions in the broadcasting sector. It was seen that, due to the significant economies of scale and scope broadcasters can achieve by integrating with other firms that operate at the same or at different levels of the supply chain, mergers and acquisitions have been a rather common business strategy in television. Consolidation has not had the same appeal to newspaper and book publishers; in the publishing industry, two popular business strategies have been Resale Price Maintenance (hereinafter RPM) governing trade in print titles and, more recently, (RPM-based) agencies governing trade in digital publications. The connecting thread remains the application of EU competition law to media undertakings that are in control of an asset or parameter that may somehow affect competition in the markets concerned. But, while in television this is control of the acquired entity, in the case of books and newspapers it is control over price.

244. RPM in publishing refers to an arrangement whereby the publisher sets the retail prices of the titles it produces and the retailer is not permitted to offer discounts or any other forms of promotion unless the publisher explicitly grants its authorization. RPM is a very controversial issue from both a competition and a media pluralism perspective. Conflicting views on the pros and cons of this pricing model pull in many different directions. For example, as regards competition, opponents maintain that the ban on price competition eliminates the incentive for dynamic efficiencies whereas proponents argue that the protected profit margin encourages market entry. With respect to media pluralism, opponents say that the ban on price competition deprives readers of the ability to buy publications at lower prices and proponents claim that

the protected profit margin promotes supply and content diversity. Empirical research dealing with the impact of RPM on either competition or media pluralism is scarce, which is why we are still in limbo over the effects fixed prices may generate.

245. The picture is equally complex when we discuss the legal aspects of RPM as a business model employed to sell content. In some Member States, laws establishing an exemption from the general competition rules apply on the grounds that fixed prices help advance pluralism in print publishing.[909] At EU level and in Member States where no RPM laws apply, agreements establishing fixed prices are presumed to be caught by Article 101(1) TFEU (or the national equivalent), but it is generally accepted that the parties may put forward efficiencies under Article 101(3) TFEU (or the national equivalent). Naturally, this has created a legal patchwork. For example, in Germany, news publishers fixing the retail prices of their titles benefit from a derogation under the *Act Against Restraints of Competition*[910] whereas in the Netherlands they enjoy no such privilege.[911] National Competition Authorities (NCAs) and the EU institutions have approached this issue in different ways. For example, the Dutch[912] and Irish[913] NCAs have dismantled the respective RPM systems governing trade in newspapers whereas in the UK the scheme has been treated favorably.[914] At EU level, the Commission has been permissive towards RPM for newspapers[915] whereas it appears to have taken a strict stance on RPM for books.[916] The Court has been sympathetic to RPM arrangements by reason of

909 See, for instance, the Spanish Ley 10/2007, de 22 de junio, de la lectura, del libro y de las bibliotecas Publicado en BOE núm. 150 de 23 de Junio de 2007, Preàmbulo: 'La regulación sobre la comercialización del libro y publicaciones afines parte de la convicción de que se ofrece un producto que es más que una mera mercancía: se trata de un soporte físico que contiene la plasmación del pensamiento humano, la ciencia y la creación literaria, posibilitando ese acto trascendental y único para la especie humana, que es la lectura. La difusión de esas creaciones, su valor cultural y su pluralidad requieren una cierta garantía tanto en el control de calidad del texto como en su comercialización para que puedan ser accesibles al mayor número de potenciales lectores' [emphasis added]. For Member States where RPM laws for books still apply see Joint Research Centre (2012b). Technical Report on Statistical, Ecosystems and Competitiveness Analysis of the Media and Content Industries: The Book Publishing Industry, fn. 198. <http://ftp.jrc.es/EURdoc/JRC76642.pdf> (NB: in Greece, this law was recently abolished). On the generalized adoption of fixed prices for newspapers see, for instance, Kjolby, H. (2008). Denmark. In Yamey, B. S. (ed.) Resale Price Maintenance. A Comparative American–European Perspective (3rd Edition), 145–178, 157. New Brunswick: Aldine Transaction, and OECD (1997). Policy Roundtable on Resale Price Maintenance. <http://www.oecd.org/competition/abuse/1920261.pdf>

910 Act Against Restraints of Competition. Published on 26 June 2013 (Bundesgesetzblatt I, 2013, p. 1750, 3245), as last amended by Article 1 of the law of 1 June 2017 (Bundesgesetzblatt I, p. 1416), paragraph 30. <http://www.gesetze-im-internet.de/englisch_gwb/englisch_gwb.html#p0145>

911 Netherlands Competition Authority (1999). NMa and DTe Annual Report, 59

912 ibid.

913 Irish Competition Authority (2003, December). Newspapers to amend business practices considered anticompetitive by The Competition Authority

914 Office of Fair Trading (2008a). Newspaper and magazine distribution. Opinion of the Office of Fair Trading. Guidance to facilitate self-assessment under the Competition Act 1998

915 Commission Notice pursuant to Article 19(3) of Regulation No. 17 concerning Agence et Messageries de la Presse, Case IV/31.609 [1987] OJ C 164/02

916 See VBBB/VBVB (Case IV/428) Commission decision 82/123/EEC of 25 November 1981 relating to a proceeding under Article 85 of the EEC Treaty [1982] OJ L52/36, and Publishers Association – Net Book Agreement (Cases IV/27.393 and IV/27.394) Commission decision of 12 December 1988 relating to a proceeding under Article 85 of the EEC Treaty [1989] OJ L22/12

both the contribution newspaper publishing can make to media pluralism[917] and the role of books in protecting cultural unity between linguistically homogeneous areas.[918] This legal patchwork is not a problem because it leads to opposing outcomes across the EU. It is a problem because, as already mentioned, there is not enough evidence (including especially studies dealing with the particularities of each national market) suggesting whether RPM leads to higher prices and, if this is indeed the case, whether it stimulates non-price competition, thereby outweighing the harm that results from higher prices.

246. The RPM-based agency model was introduced by Apple and major book publishers in 2010. It has since become an attractive strategy for the sale of digital content services that range from e-books to apps (including news apps), to newspaper subscriptions. It bears noting that, while often finding themselves in a weaker bargaining position, this model has been embraced by book and newspaper publishers alike. As far as the legal status of agencies is concerned, the issues that arise go far beyond the controversies of fixed prices. Under certain conditions, an agency contract falls outside Article 101(1) TFEU.[919] In such cases, agencies are different from 'traditional' RPM agreements in terms of competition enforcement. However, the case law is far from consistent with respect to the conditions under which an agency relationship may indeed benefit from antitrust immunity.

247. It is clear from the above considerations that, while the focus of the analysis will be on EU competition law, the issues that will be examined throughout this Chapter go beyond a) the application of Article 101 TFEU to print and digital publishing, and b) the Commission's approach to RPM as a pricing strategy in the media. The issue of fixed prices for publications is currently in a state of flux across Europe. In Greece, the RPM law for books was recently abolished[920] whereas the French legislator has extended its applicability to digital books.[921] What such legislative initiatives appear to lack is a sound economic foundation. Hence, in discussing whether and, if so, under what

917 ECJ, Case 243/83 SA Binon & Cie v SA Agence et messageries de la presse [1985] ECR 2015

918 ECJ, Case C-360/92 The Publishers Association v Commission [1995] ECR I-23, paragraph 44. In this judgment, the Court condemned the Commission for not having carefully considered whether the agreement concerned was essential to promote cultural unity between the UK and Ireland, in which case it could be eligible for exemption under Article 101(3) TFEU. Sadly, we cannot assess the impact of this judgment on the reasoning that the Commission would have adopted in the examination of the RPM agreements the second time around: one month before the ruling, publishing house Hodder Headline withdrew from the agreement, a move that heralded the collapse of the RPM mechanism. After most of the major publishers pulled out of the NBA, the system was dismantled and the Commission did not bother to adopt a new decision. For more information see MacDonald, M. Collapse of Net Book Agreement 'within months'. 26 December 1994, The Independent. <http://www.independent.co.uk/news/uk/collapse-of-net-book-agreement-within-months-collapse-1388530.html>

919 Commission Guidelines on Vertical Restraints [2010] OJ C 130/01, paragraph 18

920 Venizelos, T. Greece to liberalize fixed system of book pricing. 18 March 2014, Press TV News. <https://www.youtube.com/watch?v=cTeRM3Kj-x0>

921 Loi n° 2011-590 du 26 mai 2011 relative au prix du livre numérique. Version consolidée au 15 janvier 2019. <http://www.legifrance.gouv.fr/affichTexte.do;?cidTexte=LEGITEXT000024082056>

conditions RPM may benefit from an exemption under Article 101(3) TFEU, I shall attempt to develop a framework within which national legislators may assess whether an RPM scheme may indeed lead to the pluralism-friendly outcome it is intended to deliver. Moreover, although the Commission now rarely dedicates its resources to enforcement in this field, a number of NCAs, which – post-modernization of EU competition law – may pursue infringements of Article 101 TFEU,[922] have often taken cases involving RPM arrangements for the sale of publications.[923]

248. Following the same approach as Chapter 4, this Chapter seeks to test the main claims that were put forward in Chapter 3, namely that by failing to take due account of the particular characteristics of the markets concerned, the Commission's practice imperils the accuracy of competition decisions and that, if properly applied, EU competition law may lead to a pluralism-friendly outcome without giving rise to controversies over competence.

249. The Chapter is structured as follows: Part 2 discusses how Article 101(3) TFEU may be interpreted to ensure that RPM agreements fostering non-price competition benefit from the exemption. To this end, I examine the approach followed in *VBBB/VBVB* because this is the only decision in which the Commission conducted a complete assessment of the arguments that are commonly put forward in support of RPM. Building around the reasoning the Commission adopted in *VBBB/VBVB*, I shall attempt to clarify the conditions under which RPM may deliver the efficiencies that are relevant for our purposes. Part 3 discusses antitrust control in digital publishing. The analysis will revolve around the *E-books* case,[924] which concerns the agency agreements signed between Apple and major publishers for the sale of e-books. This case is important to discuss for mainly three reasons. First, from a competition perspective, these agreements were the first[925] of their kind that fell under the

922 Council Regulation (EC) No. 1/2003 of 16 December 2002 on the implementation of the rules on competition laid down in Articles 81 and 82 of the Treaty [2003] OJ L1/1

923 For action taken by the Swedish competition authority see, for instance, Joint Research Centre (2012a), supra n. 1, 81. See also Danish Competition and Consumer Authority (2006, March). Publishers right to fix book prices considerably reduced. < https://www.en.kfst.dk/nyheder/kfst/english/decisions/20062903-publishers-right-to-fix-book-prices-considerably-reduced/ > and supra n. 3 – n. 6 for action taken by other competition authorities

924 E-books (Case COMP/AT.39847) Commission decision of 12 December 2012 addressed to Hachette Livre SA, HarperCollins Publishers Limited, HarperCollins Publishers LLC, Georg von Holtzbrinck GmbH & Co. KG, Verlagsgruppe Georg von Holtzbrinck GmbH, Simon & Schuster Inc, Simon & Schuster (UK) Ltd, Simon & Schuster Digital Sales Inc, Apple Inc relating to a proceeding under Article 101 TFEU and Article 53 of the EEA Agreement C(2012) 9288 (consolidated version)

925 More recently, the Commission opened an investigation into certain clauses included in Amazon's contracts with publishers. The clauses concerned required publishers to inform Amazon about more favorable terms offered to Amazon's competitors and/or offer Amazon similar terms and conditions. For an overview of the case see Commission (2015, June). Antitrust: Commission opens formal investigation into Amazon's e-book distribution arrangements. <http://europa.eu/rapid/press-release_IP-15-5166_en.htm>; and Commission (2017, January). Antitrust: Commission seeks feedback on commitments offered by Amazon in e-book investigation. <http://europa.eu/rapid/press-release_IP-17-137_en.htm> The Commission closed the investigation by adopting a commitments decision. See Commission decision of 28 July 2017, E-book MFNs and related matters (Amazon) (Case AT.40153). <http://ec.europa.eu/competition/antitrust/cases/dec_docs/40153/40153_4392_3.pdf>

Commission's antitrust microscope. Second, and related to the above, the arrangements between Apple and the involved publishers that were scrutinized by the Commission, such as the 70/30 revenue-sharing rule,[926] have apparently had an industry-wide appeal. Therefore, the decision raises issues that are not limited to the facts of that particular case. Third, as already discussed in Chapter 2, Apple, as a digital intermediary, may affect media pluralism by shaping economic models for news publishing.[927] Since agency was introduced by Apple and later on adopted by news publishers, it is essential that we discuss the potential impact of this business strategy on news provision. Part 4 discusses the Commission's approach in *Sammelrevers*,[928] which dealt with an RPM agreement governing trade in German-language books and other print products and in which the Commission attempted to resolve a conflict between (price) competition and (what it thought would be beneficial to) book diversity in a rather unconventional manner.

> ***Note to the Reader***:
>
> *– Prior to delving into the issues outlined above, it bears clarifying for methodological purposes why this Chapter deals with both books and newspapers. It was mentioned in Chapter 2 that, when we refer to media pluralism as a prerequisite for democracy, news is perhaps more relevant than other types of content. However, it was also explained that if we restricted our analysis to cases that deal exclusively with news provision, we would fall short of grasping in its full extent the impact that the application of the EU competition rules has had on media pluralism, including news provision. In the case at hand, the Commission's decisional practice concerns almost exclusively book publishing, but the arguments in support of and against RPM as a means to protect pluralism in newspaper publishing are essentially the same. Moreover, unlike RPM for the sale of newspapers, there is a wealth of literature examining RPM for books. The Chapter will attempt to properly adjust the relevant economic arguments to the particularities of news markets and shed some light on a largely neglected topic, that is, why RPM has been regarded as beneficial to news provision.*
>
> *-Some background information on the use of books and newspapers and changes in the value chain will allow the reader to*

926 See, for instance, Foros, Ø., Hans Jarle Kind, and Greg Shaffer (2013). Turning the Page on Business Formats for Digital Platforms: Does Apple's Agency Model Soften Competition? CESIFO Working Paper No. 4362, 1–2 <http://papers.ssrn.com/sol3/papers.cfm?abstract_id=2317715>

927 See Foster, R. (2012). News Plurality in a Digital World – Report prepared for the Reuters Institute for the Study of Journalism, 6–7

928 Commission Notice pursuant to Article 19(3) of Council Regulation No. 17 concerning an application for negative clearance or exemption under Article 81(3) of the EC Treaty, Cases COMP/34.657 Sammelrevers, and COMP/35.245 to 35.251 Einzelreverse, [2000] OJ C 162/8

better understand the issues that will be discussed throughout the Chapter:

Books *Book reading occupies a central position in content consumption; it is currently the second most popular cultural activity among EU citizens.*[929] *It should be noted that when we discuss book reading in Europe, we mainly refer to the traditional print book; in 2017, print books accounted for almost 80% of total sales.*[930] *The traditional value chain remains to a large extent unchallenged. Upstream, self-publishing is in its nascent stages but publishing houses, which have traditionally been responsible for, inter alia, the editing, presentation, pricing and promotion of the book, are still 'at the core of the business'.*[931] *Downstream, the main disruption concerns the growth of large chains such as Fnac and online distributors, most notably Amazon. This has shifted market power away from the publishers to retailers; the latter are not only in a position to extract more onerous conditions from the former, but they also have access to reader data which they may not share.*[932] *This raises issues in cases where the retailer is integrated with a publisher because the former is in the position to provide the latter with valuable insight into consumption preferences, allowing the firm to establish a profitable relationship with the readership.*

Newspapers *Newspapers make a significant contribution to news dissemination; 'they provide space for opinion, in-depth analysis and a reflection on recent events ... helping citizens understand issues.'*[933] *In terms of media use, 28% of Europeans continue to read the paper every day or almost every day.*[934] *Contrary to the book market, the traditional value chain has been significantly disrupted. With the advent of the Internet, newspaper publishers have suffered significant revenue losses. This is largely attributed to advertisers preferring behavioral targeting, which means that newspapers now have to compete with a much wider*

929 European Parliamentary Research Service (2017). Access to Culture in the European Union, 15. <http://www.europarl.europa.eu/RegData/etudes/IDAN/2017/608631/EPRS_IDA(2017)608631_EN.pdf>; Ernst and Young (2014). Creating Growth. Measuring cultural and creative markets in the EU, 31. <http://www.ey.com/Publication/vwLUAssets/Measuring_cultural_and_creative_markets_in_the_EU/$FILE/Creating-Growth.pdf>

930 Statista (2018). E-book market share in Europe in 2013 and 2017. <https://www.statista.com/statistics/292092/ebook-market-share-europe/>. For more information see Joint Research Centre (2012a) supra n. 1, 16. <http://ftp.jrc.es/EURdoc/JRC76642.pdf>

931 Joint Research Centre (2012a), supra n. 1, 14

932 ibid, 71; for the importance the publishing trade attaches to consumer data see Rimm, A. M. (2014). Conditions and Survival: Views on the Concentration of Ownership and Vertical Integration in German and Swedish Publishing. Publishing Research Quarterly 30(1), 77–92

933 ibid, 12

934 Commission (2017). Media Use in the European Union, 11

range of firms, including real estate, dating and job recruitment portals.[935] *Moreover, due to the vast amount of information currently available on the Internet for free, consumers are not willing to pay for online news content.*[936] *That users are increasingly consuming news within distributed environments, such as social media and news aggregators, is also worth mentioning.*[937] *As a result of the above realities, over the past few years newspapers have been actively searching for a successful business model in the online news segment.*

2. Resale Price Maintenance: a conduit for non-price competition in print product markets?

250. As already discussed in the Introduction, RPM has been a popular business model in the print product industry. By 'Resale Price Maintenance' we refer to agreements or practices that have 'as their direct or indirect object the establishment of a fixed or minimum resale price or a fixed or minimum resale price level to be observed by the buyer'.[938] In EU competition law, RPM has been treated as a 'hardcore restriction', that is, a restriction of competition 'by object'[939] which, as such, results in the exclusion of the agreement from the scope of application of the Block Exemption Regulation.[940] In cases where an RPM clause is contained in the agreement, that agreement is presumed to be caught by Article 101(1) TFEU, but it is established case law that parties to *any* agreement may plead an efficiency defence under Article 101(3) TFEU in an individual case.[941]

251. The discussion over the effects of RPM on competition is far from settled. Proponents mainly contend that, while it eliminates intra-brand *price*

935 Joint Research Centre (2012a). Technical Report on Statistical, Ecosystems and Competitiveness Analysis of the Media and Content Industries: The Newspaper Publishing Industry, 6. <http://publications.jrc.ec.europa.eu/repository/bitstream/JRC69881/jrc69881.pdf>

936 ibid.

937 For more information about online news consumption see Reuters Institute (2017). Digital News Report. <https://reutersinstitute.politics.ox.ac.uk/sites/default/files/Digital%20News%20Report%202017%20web_0.pdf?utm_source=digitalnewsreport.org&utm_medium=referral>

938 Commission Guidelines on Vertical Restraints [2010] OJ C 130/01, paragraph 48.

939 See, for instance, Commission Regulation (EU) No. 330/2010 of 20 April 2010 on the application of Article 101(3) TFEU to categories of vertical agreements and concerted practices [2010] OJ L102/1, Article 4(a) of the BER; ECJ, Case 243/83 SA Binon & Cie v SA Agence et messageries de la presse [1985] ECR 2015; ECJ, Case 161/84 Pronuptia de Paris GmbH v Pronuptia de Paris Irmgard Schillgallis [1986] ECR 00353; Commission Guidelines on the Application of Article 101(3) TFEU [2004] OJ C 101/08, paragraph 23.

940 Commission Guidelines on the Application of Article 101(3) TFEU [2004] OJ C 101/08, paragraph 47.

941 ibid, paragraph 60; CFI, Case T-168/2001 GlaxoSmithKline Services Unlimited v Commission [2006] ECR II-2969, paragraphs 247–252.

competition, RPM promotes intra-brand *service* competition, eliminates the risk of free-riding on another distributor's investments to improve quality of service, and addresses the problem of double marginalization.[942] Opponents argue that RPM facilitates horizontal collusion both upstream and downstream and, because it prevents any form of price competition (discounts, promotional offers, etc.), it does not allow distributors to engage in price discrimination which may result in output increases and cost savings that may be passed on to the consumer in the form of lower prices.[943] But, empirical research discussing the positive or negative effects of RPM on competition is scarce.

252. The discourse surrounding the impact of RPM on media pluralism is equally unsettled. Advocates claim that fixed prices mitigate the risks associated with newspaper and book publishing and, in doing so, they allow publishers to produce a broad range of print products, including slow-moving esoteric books and new newspaper titles, thereby contributing to content diversity. It is also argued that the protected profit margin resulting from RPM encourages small publishers and independent non-integrated retailers to penetrate the market, thereby increasing supply diversity. Opponents mainly argue that RPM does not benefit media pluralism because it deprives customers of the ability to buy content at lower prices. Again, however, robust empirical research testing the above claims is scarce and, where it exists, incomplete. For example, in the late 1990s, the UK book market switched from fixed to free pricing. Empirical findings demonstrate that following the dismantlement of the RPM system the number of books published increased.[944] Yet, no systematic content analysis was carried out that addressed the question of whether the number of titles represented more diversity. Cross-country comparative studies, that is, studies comparing markets with RPM against markets with free prices, have also failed to reach definitive conclusions.[945]

253. The consumer of print products is another big mystery. For example, to date, there are no studies on the price elasticity of demand for books, but only some studies on the price elasticity of the *total* demand for books.[946] While these latter provide some insight into whether books are interchangeable with other media products,[947] they say nothing about substitutability *within* the book market.

942 Petit, N. and David Henry (2010). Vertical Restraints under EU Competition Law: Conceptual Foundations and Practical Framework, SSRN Working Paper, 9–10. <http://papers.ssrn.com/sol3/papers.cfm?abstract_id=1724891>.

943 ibid, 8–9.

944 Bennett, M., Amelia Fletcher, Emanuele Giovannetti and David Stallibrass (2010). Resale Price Maintenance: Explaining the controversy, and small steps towards a more nuanced policy. Fordham International Law Journal 33, 1295.

945 Appelman, M. and Marcel Canoy (2002). Horses for Courses: Why Europe should not harmonize its book policies. De Economist 150(5), 592

946 Canoy, M., Jan C. van Ours and Frederick van der Ploeg (2005). The Economics of Books. CESifo Working Paper No. 1414, 12. <https://ideas.repec.org/p/ces/ceswps/_1414.html>

947 ibid.

Moreover, the lack of rigorous empirical research results in fragmentary knowledge about consumption habits such as brand loyalty, genre preferences, etc. Bookstores, especially large book chains, engage in gathering data about their customers, but this information is, naturally, not publicly available.

254. In this section, I shall examine whether and, if so, under what conditions an RPM agreement governing trade in books or newspapers may indeed deliver non-price efficiencies which can lead to an exemption under Article 101(3) TFEU and which can be beneficial for media pluralism. This analysis shall be conducted in the light of *VBBB/VBVB*.[948] This case concerned an RPM agreement which provided that Dutch and Belgian publishers would fix the retail price of the titles they produced and that booksellers would not offer any discounts except in cases where this was explicitly allowed by the publishers.[949] The focus of my analysis is on *VBBB/VBVB* because this is the only decision in the print publishing sector where the Commission conducted a full-fledged assessment of whether all four conditions laid down in Article 101(3) TFEU were met. *Sammelrevers*,[950] which dealt with an RPM agreement governing trade in books and magazines between Germany and Austria (this decision raised other issues which will be discussed in more detail in Part 4 of this Chapter), and *Agence et Messageries de la Presse*,[951] which concerned an RPM system for the sale of Belgian and foreign newspapers in Belgium, are clearance notices, lacking a detailed analysis of the factors that led to granting the exemption. In *Net Book Agreement*,[952] a decision on the RPM mechanism governing trade in books between the UK and Ireland, the Commission assessed only whether the agreements concerned were indispensable to alleviate administrative burdens on publishers (e.g. whether, absent price fixing, it would not be practicable for publishers to give notice to every bookstore of the publishers' individual conditions of sale) and therefore the decision does not reflect the Commission's position on the role of RPM as a conduit for non-price competition.

255. From the outset it bears noting that, in *VBBB/VBVB*, the parties did not provide sufficient evidence to substantiate that the first condition under Article 101(3) TFEU, namely that the agreement improves production and/or distribution, was met. Therefore, the Commission correctly found that the arrangements could

948 VBBB/VBVB (Case IV/428) Commission decision 82/123/EEC of 25 November 1981 relating to a proceeding under Article 85 of the EEC Treaty [1982] OJ L52/36

949 ibid, paragraph 9

950 Commission Notice pursuant to Article 19(3) of Council Regulation No. 17 concerning an application for negative clearance or exemption under Article 81(3) of the EC Treaty, Cases COMP/34.657 Sammelrevers, and COMP/35.245 to 35.251 Einzelreverse, [2000] OJ C 162/8

951 Commission Notice pursuant to Article 19(3) of Regulation No. 17 concerning Case IV/31.609, Agence et Messageries de la Presse [1987] OJ C 164/02

952 *VBBB/VBVB* (Case IV/428) Commission decision 82/123/EEC of 25 November 1981 relating to a proceeding under Article 85 of the EEC Treaty [1982] OJ L52/36 and *Publishers Association – Net Book Agreement* (Cases IV/27.393 and IV/27.394) Commission decision of 12 December 1988 relating to a proceeding under Article 85 of the EEC Treaty [1989] OJ L22/12

not benefit from the exemption. Despite the fact that it was not required to examine whether the other three conditions set by Article 101(3) TFEU were fulfilled (the four conditions laid down in Article 101(3) TFEU must be met cumulatively), the Commission went on to conduct a complete assessment because it considered it useful to discuss '*certain aspects of collective resale price maintenance in general*'.[953] Hence, it would seem that the positions the Commission takes in *VBBB/VBVB* are not limited to the facts of that particular case.

2.1 Can RPM contribute to improvements in the production and distribution of print products?

256. As already mentioned, the first condition of Article 101(3) TFEU requires that the agreement contribute to 'improving the production or distribution of goods'. Pursuant to the Guidelines on the Application of Article 101(3) TFEU, the aim of the analysis is to determine what are the objective efficiencies[954] created by the agreement and their economic importance.[955] The Guidelines explicitly state that, in addition to cost efficiencies, parties may put forward efficiencies of a qualitative nature.[956] It bears noting that the wording of the Guidelines does not suggest a preference for cost efficiencies. To the contrary, the Commission acknowledges that in several instances, 'the main efficiency enhancing potential of the agreement is not cost reduction, it is quality improvements and other efficiencies of a qualitative nature. Depending on the individual case, such efficiencies may therefore be of equal or greater importance than cost efficiencies.'[957] This nicely fits media markets because, as already explained in Chapter 3, price is not the main parameter driving demand for content. In our case, the publishing trade has traditionally contended that RPM arrangements protect and promote non-price competition in the form of a broad range of titles *and* a variety of publishers and retailers serving the consumer. It is noted that, for the purposes of this thesis, a broad range of titles would be a reflection of content diversity, whereas a variety of publishers and retailers would be a reflection of supply diversity. The term 'non-price competition' that is used throughout this Chapter refers to both these pluralism-friendly outcomes unless otherwise stated.

257. The following analysis will examine whether RPM may indeed stimulate non-price competition in print publishing and how open the Commission has been to related arguments.

---

953 *VBBB/VBVB* (Case IV/428) Commission decision 82/123/EEC of 25 November 1981 relating to a proceeding under Article 85 of the EEC Treaty [1982] OJ L52/36, paragraph 48

954 Commission Guidelines on the Application of Article 101(3) TFEU [2004] OJ C 101/08, paragraph 49. According to established case law 'only objective benefits can be taken into account. This means that efficiencies are not assessed from the subjective point of view of the parties.'

955 ibid, paragraph 50

956 ibid, paragraph 59

957 ibid, paragraph 69

258. In *VBBB/VBVB*, the parties argued that the agreement allowed publishers to offer a wide variety of titles, including less popular books.[958] With fixed prices, the parties said, the publishers, especially smaller houses that sought to fill market niches, were certain that retailers would be willing to stock and promote low-demand books that entailed high inventory costs.[959] In the publishing trade, this is usually referred to as the *inventory hypothesis*.[960] The Commission rejected the parties' claim by simply noting that book pricing is '*in general, an individual, independent decision by each publisher* when he sets his selling prices to the trade' [emphasis added].[961] The general wording of the Commission's answer suggests that it altogether dismisses the idea that RPM, as a pricing strategy, could somehow result in a broader range of books. However, this reply is arguably oversimplified: literary success is highly unpredictable,[962] which may discourage market players from investing in original projects. Fixed prices may offset the associated risks. This is based on economic theory on the efficiencies on RPM and in particular on the demand uncertainty theory whereby, in cases of uncertain consumer demand, manufacturers are willing to take risks more easily if they are permitted to set a minimum price for their products.[963] Since the profit margin is protected, so the argument goes, manufacturers are sure that distributors will order inventories before the uncertainty is resolved.[964] In the book context, this means that publishers may use the protected margin to promote esoteric titles, literary experiments and unknown authors.[965]

259. It bears noting, however, that the Commission's decision to reject the parties' claim, albeit lacking solid economic foundations, was not, in and of itself, erroneous. The efficiencies to be generated by the agreement under scrutiny 'must be derived from empirical data and facts not just economic theory'.[966] Or, as noted in the Guidelines, the information submitted by the parties must be 'verifiable' because otherwise there is not 'sufficient certainty that the

958 VBBB/VBVB (Case IV/428) Commission decision 82/123/EEC of 25 November 1981 relating to a proceeding under Article 85 of the EEC Treaty [1982] OJ L52/36, paragraph 50

959 ibid.

960 Appelman and Canoy (2002), supra n. 37, 591

961 VBBB/VBVB (Case IV/428) Commission decision 82/123/EEC of 25 November 1981 relating to a proceeding under Article 85 of the EEC Treaty [1982] OJ L52/36, paragraph 51

962 For an interesting analysis of why the success of a book cannot be predicted see Vanderbilt, T. Why is literary fame so unpredictable? 21 May 2012, The New Yorker. <http://www.newyorker.com/books/page-turner/why-is-literary-fame-so-unpredictable>

963 For an overview of the efficiencies brought about by RPM see, for instance, Peepercorn, L. (2008). Resale price maintenance and its alleged efficiencies. European Competition Journal 4(1), 201–212; Elzinga, K. G. and David E. Mills (2010). Leegin and Procompetitive Resale Price Maintenance. The Antitrust Bulletin 55(2), 349–379, and Petit and Henry (2010), supra n. 34

964 Deneckere, R., H.P. Marvel, and J. Peck (1997). Demand Uncertainty and Price Maintenance: Markdowns as Destructive Competition. American Economic Review 87(4), 634

965 International Publishers Association (2014). Global Fixed Book Price Report, 3. <http://www.snel.org.br/wp-content/themes/snel/docs/Material/global.pdf>

966 Jones, A. and Brenda Sufrin (2014). EU Competition Law – Texts, Cases and Materials (5th Edition). Oxford: OUP, 253

efficiencies have materialized or are likely to materialize'.[967] In the case at hand, fixed prices *per se* do not reduce the incentive to fund or carry titles that fill a safe middle ground[968] and hence, absent any relevant data (e.g. a clause in the agreement which binds the retailers to display an *x* amount of slow-moving books for a certain period of time and proof that the clause is effectively enforced), it is not possible to establish a direct and causal relationship[969] between the RPM agreement and the array of books placed on the market.[970] In *VBBB/VBVB*, it appears that the parties did not provide any evidence to substantiate how the collective fixed pricing system they had set up advanced the production and distribution of Dutch-language titles. Consequently, even if the Commission had been open to the argument that RPM may generate this efficiency, it would not have been able to determine whether the arrangements under scrutiny had indeed delivered the claimed result.[971]

260. The inventory hypothesis may hold not only in cases of products with uncertain consumer demand, but also in cases of products with little to no scrap value.[972] In situations where it is known in advance that the value of the traded asset will be insignificant or nil at the end of its useful life, RPM enables the manufacturer to take the revenue risk of supplying it. This is particularly relevant for the newspaper sector.[973] Publishers print newspapers as late as possible (between 22:30 and 03:00) in order to make sure that they have not left out the latest news, especially late breaking news.[974] Newspapers are delivered to wholesalers between 03:00 and 04:00 and subsequently to retailers between 05:00 and 07:00.[975] The vast majority of newspapers are bought before 10:00, which demands that distribution take place within tight time limits, for 'those copies left unsold at the end of the day are effectively worthless'.[976] In this case, fixed prices may be regarded as a means to mitigate the financial risks

967 Commission Guidelines on the Application of Article 101(3) TFEU [2004] OJ C 101/08, paragraph 56

968 Appelman and Canoy (2002), supra n. 37, 590; Gippini-Fournier, E. (2010). Resale Price Maintenance in the EU: in statu quo ante bellum? SSRN Working Paper, 15. <http://papers.ssrn.com/sol3/papers.cfm?abstract_id=1476443> Also available in Hawk, B. (ed.). Annual Proceedings of the 36th Annual Conference on International Antitrust Law and Policy – Fordham Corporate Law Institute. Huntington, NY: Juris Publishing

969 Commission Guidelines on the Application of Article 101(3) TFEU [2004] OJ C 101/08, paragraph 53

970 The same conclusion can be drawn with respect to the cross-subsidization claim that the parties put forward, that is, the argument that the agreement enabled publishers and distributors alike to subsidize works of literary merit that were unlikely to cover their production and storage costs out of the profits they made from bestsellers. See paragraph 50 of the decision. For a critical analysis of whether RPM in the book industry achieves the cultural objectives it is meant to deliver see van der Ploeg, F. (2004). Beyond the Dogma of the Fixed Book Price Agreement. Journal of Cultural Economics 28(1), 16

971 Failure to submit empirical data in support of the argument that RPM improved production by contributing to better editorial content appears to have been one of the main reasons why, in the late 1990s, the Dutch competition authority dismantled the fixed pricing mechanism established by the Netherlands Daily Newspaper Association. See Netherlands Competition Authority (1999), supra n. 3, 59

972 Deneckere, Marvel and Peck (1997), supra n. 56, 634

973 Office of Fair Trading (2008a), supra n. 6, paragraph 3.4.

974 ibid.

975 ibid.

976 ibid.

that arise from unsold copies.[977] In an opinion concerning the compatibility of the UK newspaper distribution system with the Competition Act, the Office of Fair Trading (OFT) embraced the inventory hypothesis, noting that with a distribution system based on RPM newspaper publishers are certain that retailers will be willing to sell new titles or, in cases where publishers want to use availability as a promotional instrument to boost circulation, to take additional copies of an already existing title.[978]

261. In *VBBB/VBVB*, the parties further argued that their RPM arrangements improved distribution by contributing to the preservation of an extensive network of retailers.[979] This claim has validity in economic terms because the protected profit margin ensured through RPM shields small bookshops from large retailers that can afford to engage in a race to the bottom on price.[980] The Commission, however, rejected this claim on the grounds that, even if an RPM agreement somehow contributes to the widespread supply of books at the retail level, overall it has a negative impact on distribution because it bans price competition. According to the Commission, '[t]his is particularly damaging since … competition on the price of individual titles within the distributive trade is an important means of rationalizing and improving the distribution system.'[981] This reply embodies one of the main criticisms of RPM, that is, fixed prices eliminate the retailers' incentive for efficiencies in the form of innovation.[982] This is illustrated by the following example: a bookseller wishes to promote the sales of audio books that her store offers. She decides to create a space with the necessary equipment where readers can sit and listen to the book of their choice. However, to generate the resources necessary in order to undertake this investment, the bookseller needs to increase sales. One way to increase sales is to reduce book prices. Under an RPM system, the bookseller, deprived of the right to offer discounts, does not manage to boost sales of either traditional or new products. But, this is only one side to the story; improvements in distribution in the form of increased sales may originate from price reductions *as much as* from an extensive network of retailers. This is because demand for a product does not depend solely

977 ECJ, Case 243/83 *SA Binon & Cie v SA Agence et messageries de la presse* [1985] ECR 2015, paragraph 46

978 Office of Fair Trading (2008a), supra n. 6, 3.10

979 VBBB/VBVB (Case IV/428) Commission decision 82/123/EEC of 25 November 1981 relating to a proceeding under Article 85 of the EEC Treaty [1982] OJ L52/36, inferred from paragraph 51

980 Appelman and Canoy (2002), supra n. 37, 591

981 *supra* n. 71, paragraph 53

982 Orbach, B. Y. (2008). Antitrust Vertical Myopia: The Allure of High Prices. Arizona Law Review 50, 270; Lao, M. (2009). Resale price maintenance: A reassessment of its competitive harms and benefits. SSRN Working Paper, 16. <http://papers.ssrn.com/sol3/papers.cfm?abstract_id=1434984> Also in Drexl, J., Warren S. Grimes, Clifford A. Jones, Rudolph J. R. Peritz and Edward T. Swaine (eds.) (2011). More common ground for International Competition Law? Cheltenham Glos, UK: Edward Elgar; Appelman and Canoy (2002), supra n. 37, 593; Ringstad, V (2004). On the cultural blessings of fixed book prices. International Journal of Cultural Policy 10(3), 356

on price, but also on the number of outlets offering the product.[983] That is, 'the price-demand schedule for a product shifts outward if the number of retailers carrying the product increases [because] … the inconvenience of shopping is reduced when retail density is higher.'[984] The same logic would apply to newsstands. Again, however, moving from theory to practice, the parties to *VBBB/VBVB* do not appear to have provided the Commission with any factual data in order to substantiate their claim.

262. The final argument raised by the parties in *VBBB/VBVB* was that RPM allowed retailers to provide ancillary services to the public, including placing orders for individual customers.[985] In RPM literature this is also referred to as *the service hypothesis* or *elimination of free-riding*: Proponents of RPM maintain that, in cases where a distributor provides some sort of service on behalf of the producer that entails certain costs for the distributor, there is a risk that, in the absence of fixed prices, distributors which do not provide the service will offer discounts and win over customers that benefited from the extra efforts of that other distributor.[986] In our case, a concern would be that a retailer employed and trained staff to inform the reader about the books it carries, but the reader ended up buying the book from the cheapest bookstore. If this materializes, the distributor no longer has the incentive to provide the service, adversely affecting both producers and consumers.[987] This argument, however, is not particularly relevant for book or newspaper publishing because 'service' does not appear to influence the consumers' purchase decisions. Empirical research suggests that, in-store, most books are discovered on the shelves or on a promotional stand[988] whereas newspapers have, as a rule, a very loyal and dedicated readership which depends on factors such as political preferences and the type of content (e.g. tabloid v quality) they offer and not on the newsstand retailers' suggestions. In view of the above, the Commission rightly set this allegation aside.[989]

---

983 Appelman and Canoy (2002), supra n. 37, 590–591

984 ibid, 591, referring to Verouden, V. (2001). Essays in Antitrust Economics. PhD thesis. Tilburg: Center for Economic Research

985 *supra* n. 71, paragraph 50

986 Bennett et al. (2010), supra n. 36, 1289

987 ibid. For an overview of the free-riding theories in support of RPM see Orbach (2008), supra n. 74, 271–274. For a critical view on free riding as a justification for RPM see Lao, M. (2008). Free Riding: An Overstated, and Unconvincing, Explanation for Resale Price Maintenance, 196–231. In Pitofsky, R. (ed.). How the Chicago School Overshot the Mark: Effect of Conservative Economic Analysis on U.S. Antitrust. Oxford: OUP

988 For recent research on book consumption patterns see, for instance, BNC Research (2013). The Canadian Book Consumer, 6

989 supra n. 71, paragraph 54

2.2 Is RPM indispensable to produce and distribute a wide range of books and/or to ensure an extensive network of retailers?

263. Assuming that an RPM agreement may indeed improve the production and distribution of books (and the above section demonstrated that this argument may be supported by economic theory), the parties would still need to demonstrate that the ban on price competition is, according to Article 101(3) TFEU, 'indispensable' to the attainment of the claimed efficiencies. The Guidelines on the Application of Article 101(3) TFEU lay down that, in examining whether this condition is met, the main determinant is whether or not the agreement '[makes] it possible to perform the activity in question more efficiently than would likely have been the case *in the absence of the agreement or the restriction concerned*' [emphasis added].[990] The Guidelines further note that, in making this assessment, due regard must be had to the context in which the agreement operates and in particular 'the market conditions and business realities facing the parties to the agreement'.[991] Applying the above to fixed book pricing arrangements, the factual data submitted by the parties should be examined in light of a) whether the qualitative efficiencies which fixed prices may generate, namely a broad range of books and an extensive network of suppliers, may also be realized under a free pricing system, and b) the market circumstances under which the parties operate.

264. As regards the first element, it bears noting that the Commission has forcefully denied that a wide variety of books, including more literary creations, cannot be attained under a free pricing system. More particularly, in *VBBB/VBVB*, it stated that, for publishers to be able to pursue more risky ventures, 'there is no need for a system under which the resale price of every book is set by the publisher right down to the final stage of distribution'.[992] Aside from the fact that it provided no further explanations supporting this finding, the Commission also fell short of considering book-specific economics: books have high fixed but low marginal costs.[993] Fixed costs include authors' advances, costs incurred in the editorial, production and distribution processes (e.g. proofreading, cover design, typesetting, copy-editing, order processing, warehouse management, physical transportation, storage expenses), and marketing/advertising costs.[994] In recent years, developments such as new prepress technologies have lowered some of these costs,[995] but creating a print

990 Commission Guidelines on the Application of Article 101(3) TFEU [2004] OJ C 101/08, paragraph 74

991 ibid, paragraph 75

992 *supra* n. 71, paragraph 51

993 Canoy, van Ours and van der Ploeg (2005), supra n. 38, 11

994 Joint Research Centre (2012a), supra n. 1, 14, 61 and 74

995 Turku School of Economics and Business Administration (2005). Publishing Market Watch Final Report. Prepared for DG Enterprise, European Commission, 70. <http://ec.europa.eu/information_society/me-

book remains a rather expensive undertaking. In view of the above, a logic similar to that governing broadcast content applies to the book market: demand uncertainty combined with high fixed and low marginal costs incentivize publishers and booksellers to focus on titles that have the capacity to attract a mass readership. In a free pricing system, it is safer to opt for easily digestible content within one of the most widely preferred genres, such as romance, crime, or science fiction,[996] than invest in controversial books written by unknown authors. This may go partway towards explaining the conclusion reached by a study of the European book market that one of the main weaknesses of the sector is that 'a large number of new products are created that are very similar to previous products. Major product innovations happen more rarely and this has conditioned the culture of the publishing industry.'[997] Empirical evidence suggests that free prices may not be able to deliver an extensive network of retailers either. For example, in the UK, following the switch from fixed to free prices, the market shares of supermarkets and other large discount stores rose dramatically at the expense of independent bookstores, a large number of which were forced to exit the market.[998] The theoretical explanation for this is pretty straightforward: large multiple retailers have the incentive to engage in aggressive price competition in order to either attract new clientele or promote the other products they offer. These entities may even decide to sell books below cost; they can afford to engage in this pricing strategy because they can cross-subsidize related losses out of the profits they make from those other products. A race to the bottom on price is not, however, a strategy that will necessary pay off for the small independents. Surely, one may contend (and this is one of the oft-repeated arguments against RPM) that a free pricing system does nothing more than obligate non-efficient retailers to exit the market. However, it should be borne in mind that exit comes at a 'price'; large multiple retailers have traditionally focused on a very limited array of books, mostly, if not exclusively, on bestsellers,[999] because they want to sell volume, not variety.[1000]

265. As regards the second element of the indispensability assessment identified above, that is, the market conditions facing the parties, Appelman and Canoy, who conducted empirical research on the effects of both free and fixed prices on the book markets of several Member States, identify the following three

dia_taskforce/doc/pmw_20050127.pdf>

996 On which genres are currently most popular see, for instance, Turner-Francis, M. Book Genres That Make the Most Money. 6 January 2017, Bookstr. <https://www.bookstr.com/book-genres-that-make-the-most-money>

997 Turku School of Economics and Business Administration (2005), supra n. 87, 70

998 Office of Fair Trading (2008b). An evaluation of the impact upon productivity of ending resale price maintenance on books. Report prepared for the OFT by the Centre for Competition Policy at University of East Anglia, 43–44. <https://research.aston.ac.uk/portal/files/3507622/Evaluation_of_the_impact_upon_productivity_of_ending_resale_price_maintenance_on_books.pdf>

999 ibid, fn. 52

1000 ibid. See also Canoy, van Ours and van der Ploeg (2005), supra n. 38, 11

characteristics that, for our purposes, may determine whether RPM is indispensable. The first is 'language size', which refers to the number of people speaking the language in which the book is written.[1001] Language size determines the size of the risk associated with the decision to publish and market a book; a widely spoken language mitigates this risk because if the book turns out a success, publishers and booksellers may achieve significant economies of scale.[1002] The second is population density.[1003] In States such as Finland, Ireland or Greece, which are sparsely populated, it is unlikely to have a large retail network catering to demand, including especially demand in remote areas, unless the profit margin of booksellers is protected.[1004] Finally, and related to the above, population density may not matter if readers buy books online.[1005] Broadly speaking, population density would still be relevant across the EU, for at least two reasons. While Internet penetration and online consumption vary from country to country, in several Member States more than 50% of the population has never purchased goods or services over the Internet.[1006] Moreover, bricks-and-mortar stores are Europeans' preferred purchase channel.[1007]

266. The picture is slightly different and apparently less complex in the case of newspapers where it seems that 'the economic risks'[1008] as a 'business reality facing the parties' would play the most important role in the indispensability assessment. The perishability of newspapers is a peculiarity that the production and distribution system of other media products does not have and the argument commonly raised is that RPM is necessary to ensure that an extensive network of retailers will be able to serve readers, especially those readers residing in remote areas in the territory covered by the agreement. This claim is particularly likely to hold in cases where RPM imposed on retailers is combined with the wholesalers' obligation to supply low-demand outlets.[1009] It bears noting that it may be inferred from *Binon* (a preliminary ruling concerning, *inter alia*, a series of RPM agreements governing trade in newspapers in Belgium) that both the Court and the Commission were largely sympathetic to the perishable nature of newspapers as a factor that would determine the indispensability assessment in relevant cases.[1010]

1001 Appelman and Canoy (2002), *supra* n. 37, 595

1002 ibid.

1003 ibid.

1004 On population density in the Member States see http://appsso.eurostat.ec.europa.eu/nui/show.do?dataset=demo_r_d3dens&lang=en>

1005 Appelman and Canoy (2002), supra n. 37, 595

1006 <http://ec.europa.eu/eurostat/statistics-explained/index.php/Digital_economy_and_society_statistics_-_households_and_individuals#Ordering_or_buying_goods_and_services>

1007 BNP Paribas (2017, May). E-Commerce. Online Sales in Europe, 2

1008 Commission Guidelines on the Application of Article 101(3) TFEU [2004] OJ C 101/08, paragraph 80

1009 This is, for instance, the case in the UK. See Office of Fair Trading (2008a), supra n. 6, paragraphs 4.54 et seq.

1010 ECJ, Case 243/83 *SA Binon & Cie v SA Agence et messageries de la presse* [1985] ECR 2015, paragraphs 43 and 46

2.3 Can RPM benefit the readership?

267. For an agreement restrictive of competition to be eligible for an exemption under Article 101(3) TFEU, consumers must receive a fair share of the resulting benefits. Based on the relevant case law, the Guidelines explain that 'the pass-on of benefits must at least compensate consumers for any actual or likely negative impact caused to them by the restriction of competition'.[1011] The Guidelines explicitly refer to quality improvements and product variety as forms of consumer pass-on that must be considered in the analysis.[1012] As already mentioned, cost efficiencies are not given preference over qualitative efficiencies in the assessment of the first condition of Article 101(3) TFEU, and reading the Guidelines' paragraphs that describe how the Commission would conduct an analysis of whether the 'consumer benefit' criterion is fulfilled suggests the same thing. However, whether the Commission has been willing to accept that an RPM agreement (or any other agreement for that matter[1013]) may generate consumer gains other than lower prices is questionable. More particularly, in *VBBB/VBVB*, the Commission gives the following reply to the argument that RPM passes a variety of books on to the consumer:

> [E]ven if a wide range of titles … [is] to be regarded as benefiting the consumer, the consumer generally cannot benefit from the advantages of any rationalization that takes place in the book trade. … *Since the price of the product is, for many consumers, an important element in their decision to purchase – and this applies to books as much as to other products – … the consumer is not receiving a fair share* [emphasis added].[1014]

268. This finding is based on two assumptions: first, that fixed prices are higher than those that retailers would charge if they were allowed to offer discounts. And second, that price is the main demand driver in book markets. Both assumptions are arguably equally problematic.

1011 Commission Guidelines on the Application of Article 101(3) TFEU [2004] OJ C 101/08, paragraph 85

1012 ibid, paragraph 102 et seq.

1013 The Commission has been reluctant to accept qualitative efficiencies. See, for instance, Trans-Atlantic Conference Agreement (Case IV/35.134) [1999] OJ L95/1, paragraph 410. Even in cases where it did acknowledge that the agreement could improve quality, it found that the resulting benefit could not outweigh the overall harm to competition. See, for instance, Star Alliance (Case AT.39595) Commission decision of 23 May 2013 addressed to Air Canada, United Airlines Inc, and Deutsche Lufthansa AG relating to proceedings under Article 101 TFEU, paragraphs 78–79. Also note that the Commission has not been willing to accept arguments that RPM agreements qualify for an exemption under Article 101(3) TFEU. See JCB (Case COMP.F.1/35.918) Commission decision of 21 December 2000 relating to a proceeding under Article 81 of the EC Treaty [2002] OJ L69/1; Nathan-Bricolux (Case COMP.F.1/36.516) Commission decision of 5 July 2000 relating to a proceeding pursuant to Article 81 of the EC Treaty [2001] OJ L54/1; Volkswagen (Case COMP/F-2/36.693) Commission decision of 29 June 2001 relating to a proceeding under Article 81 of the EC Treaty [2001] OJ L262/14; Yamaha (Case COMP/37.975) Commission decision of 16 July 2003 relating to a proceeding under Article 81 of the EC Treaty and Article 53 of the EEA Agreement [not published]; and Commission (2002). Press Release IP/02/916. Commission clears B&W Loudspeakers distribution system after company deletes hard-core violations. <http://europa.eu/rapid/press-release_IP-02-916_en.htm?locale=en>

1014 *supra* n. 71, paragraphs 54–55

269. As regards the assumption that RPM forces consumers to pay more than they would have under a free pricing system, intuitively, one might say that this makes sense; once demand uncertainty is resolved and the product turns out a success, customers are charged the 'high' fixed price.[1015] If the product turns out to be a failure, customers are still charged the 'high' fixed prices because retailers are prevented from lowering prices.[1016] Following this line of reasoning, the argument that RPM may enhance consumer welfare in the form of surplus would not hold under any circumstances. However, the impact of RPM on consumer surplus is not so straightforward. While studies have shown that RPM results in higher prices,[1017] we may still not draw any definitive conclusions because these studies have tested the price effects of RPM in a very limited number of industries.[1018] The most compelling piece of evidence that their findings should not be generalized and/or that they do not necessarily apply to our case is the conclusion reached by Fishwick in his *ex ante/ex post* study of the UK book market: Fishwick showed that after the collapse of the RPM system, prices increased.[1019] It is submitted that, in cases involving RPM, instead of directly assuming that an RPM agreement reduces consumer surplus, it would be more appropriate to examine whether the publishers' incentives to pass on benefits in the form of lower prices are stronger than the incentives of distributors. For example, in the opinion mentioned above concerning the compatibility of the UK newspaper distribution system with the Competition Act, the OFT noted that there are at least two elements supporting the position that publishers' control over price may translate into lower prices for the consumer.[1020] First, the newspaper market is two-sided. This means that, in deciding whether or not to charge higher prices, distributors will only consider the profit margin they will forego as a result of a subsequent fall in sales.[1021] But, a fall in sales would make the paper less attractive to advertisers, thereby negatively affecting ad revenues.[1022] Hence, compared with distributors, publishers are more likely to lower prices because, to maximize profit, they need to take account of both circulation *and* ad revenues.[1023] This hypothesis was

1015 Lao (2009), *supra* n. 74, 27

1016 ibid.

1017 For studies suggesting or finding that RPM results in lower prices see, for instance, Areeda, P. E. and Herbert Hovenkamp (2004). Antitrust Law (2nd Edition New York: Aspen Publishers, 1604b, 40; Steiner, R. L. (1991). Sylvania Economics – A Critique. Antitrust Law Journal 60(1), 56; Overstreet, T. R. (1983). Resale Price Maintenance: Economic Theories and Empirical Evidenc. FTC Bureau of Economics Staff Report, 160; Mueller, W. F. (1989). The Sealy Restraints: Restrictions on Free Riding or Output? Wisconsin Law Review 1255;and Scherer, F.M. (2005). Comment on Cooper et al.'s 'Vertical Restrictions and Antitrust Policy'. Competition Policy International, 1(2), 71–74. <http://www2.owen.vanderbilt.edu/lukefroeb/froeb.papers/Vertical/2005.CPI.scherer.pdf>

1018 Lao (2009), supra n. 74, 34

1019 Fishwick, F. (2008). *Book Prices in the UK Since the End of Resale Price Maintenance.* International Journal of the Economics of Business 15(3), 359–377

1020 Office of Fair Trading (2008a), supra n. 6, 4.77

1021 ibid, paragraph 4.78

1022 ibid.

1023 ibid.

supported by empirical evidence gathered by the OFT, which suggested that the main concern of retailers in regard to fixed prices was that they were prevented from *increasing* prices.[1024] In the case of books, while the market is not two-sided, it cannot be excluded that publisher and retailer incentives are not aligned. If publishers have an interest in charging less (e.g. because the more books they sell, the more reputable the house becomes, the more reputable the house becomes, the more authors or literary agents the house attracts…) than booksellers, then RPM may lead to lower prices for the consumer. Second, the OFT said, retailers may not be incentivized to cut prices in cases where consumers are not willing to switch from one outlet to another.[1025] This is so in cases where consumers do not wish to travel all the way to another outlet (e.g. a small newsstand may be closer to their home than a hypermarket offering discounts) or simply because they do not wish to change consumption habits.[1026] This latter element could apply to books in cases of sparsely populated areas and/or in cases where consumers do not regard purchase through the online distribution channel as substitutable with purchase at bricks-and-mortar stores. Again, if the publisher is interested in boosting an increase in sales and the bookseller is able to extract monopoly profits from the readers, RPM may lead to lower prices.[1027] It should also be borne in mind that the studies that have concluded that RPM results in higher prices have not demonstrated that RPM indeed harms consumer welfare. This is because they have not dealt with whether consumers received benefits that compensated for the higher prices.[1028] In our case, widespread availability could, for instance, lead to an increase in sales (i.e. more profits for the publishers), which in turn could result in higher quality[1029] whereas retailers carrying a variety of titles would give the consumers more choice. Even if the RPM agreement under scrutiny were likely to lead to higher prices, we would still need to check whether this harm might be outweighed by the aforementioned benefits.[1030]

270. With respect to the second assumption underpinning the Commission's assessment of whether the 'consumer benefit' criterion was met in *VBBB/VBVB*, that is, that price is the key element in the reader's decision to purchase a book, it is far from obvious whether this is indeed the case, for several other factors seem relevant for determining demand-side substitutability. For example, in book economics literature, it is an oft-repeated saying that the opportunity cost of consuming a book is usually greater than the price of the

1024 ibid.

1025 ibid, paragraph 4.79

1026 ibid.

1027 ibid, paragraph 4.80

1028 Lao (2009), supra n. 74, 13

1029 For example, Gabszewicz et al. found that, in the case of newspapers, sales and quality are positively correlated. See Gabszewicz, J. J., Paolo, G. Garella, and Nathalie Sonnac (2007). Newspapers' Market Shares and the Theory of the Circulation Spiral. Information Economics and Policy 19(3–4), 405–413

1030 Commission Guidelines on the Application of Article 101(3) TFEU [2004] OJ C 101/08, paragraph 85

book.[1031] Other parameters include publisher/author loyalty,[1032] and format (e.g. large v pocket format).[1033] But, most importantly, prices do not appear to be the decisive factor in regard to purchase because books, as goods, are not homogeneous. Nor are consumer interests. As the Commission itself noted in the *Candover/Cinven/Bertelsmann* merger decision, '[f]rom a demand-side point of view it is rare that two different publications be viewed as perfect substitutes. There usually are differences in the coverage, comprehensiveness and content provided by two different publications. … Therefore, *consumers will rarely substitute one publication for another in reaction to their relative prices*' [emphasis added].[1034] Related to the above, it is generally assumed that popular books are price elastic[1035] because they appeal to a broad audience, including low-income groups, whereas slow-moving titles are price inelastic because consumers either belong to high-income groups or need to buy these titles for professional or academic purposes.[1036] While this makes sense at first, even this assumption is open to debate. For example, if a *Lord of the Rings* book is out, the consumer wants to buy *that* book and it is highly unlikely that in such cases she will be price sensitive. Finally, it bears repeating that there are no studies dealing with the price elasticity of demand for either popular or more esoteric titles,[1037] that is, empirical research has not verified the above assumption yet.

271. Similar remarks can be made in respect of newspapers. In the case of newspapers, the purchase decision may depend on the 'political stance of a newspaper, family heritage, social-economic factors and the type of content' rather than on price.[1038] While price elasticity varies from newspaper to newspaper,[1039] there is evidence suggesting that in many cases demand is highly inelastic.[1040]

272. Since robust empirical research regarding demand-side substitutability is lacking, and given the heterogeneity of the book and newspaper markets across the EU, issues regarding reading habits, the importance consumers attach to price, and how they prioritize the factors that determine their decision to purchase

1031 Canoy, van Ours and van der Ploeg (2005), supra n. 38, 11

1032 Lee, E. and Byungtae Lee (2013, June). Dynamics of Price Elasticity Over Time: Evidence from the E-Book Industry. PACIS Proceedings. Paper 124, 3–4. <https://pdfs.semanticscholar.org/19b2/d5211a-8fae5f18ec6b865b0a7ada43c4ba3d.pdf>

1033 For a distinction between large and pocket format titles see, for instance, Lagardère/Natexis/VUP (Case COMP/M.2978) [2004] OJ L125/54, paragraphs 95 et seq.

1034 Candover/Cinven/Bertelsmann-Springer (Case COMP/M.3197) [2003] C207/10, paragraph 13

1035 Note that the Guidelines explicitly refer to elasticity of demand as one of the factors to take into account when assessing whether the consumer benefit criterion is met. See Commission Guidelines on the Application of Article 101(3) TFEU [2004] OJ C 101/08, para 96

1036 Canoy, van Ours and van der Ploeg (2005), supra n. 38, 12

1037 ibid.

1038 News Corp/BSkyB (Case COMP/M.5932) [2011] C 37/2, paragraph 231

1039 Doyle, G. (2002). Understanding Media Economics. London: Sage Publications, 129

1040 ibid. See also Joint Research Centre (2012b), supra n. 27, 24 should be considered on a case-by-case basis and related questions should be answered by the readership itself through qualitative research, including consumer surveys. The contribution of qualitative research to improving the accuracy of substitutability and competitive assessments has been illustrated in Chapter 4.

2.4 Does RPM eliminate competition?

273. The final condition of Article 101(3) TFEU requires that the agreement does not afford the undertakings concerned the possibility of eliminating competition in respect of a substantial part of the products concerned. In *VBBB/VBVB*, in assessing whether this condition is met, the Commission first noted that dimensions of competition such as stocking, specialization, service offered and ordering facilities should be regarded as secondary to price competition and that, since the agreement between the two associations prevented retailers from offering discounts to their customers, competition was eliminated in the affected market.[1041] Second, with a view to rebutting the parties' argument that publishers participating in the RPM system compete with one another within individual categories of books, the Commission took the stance that competition of this type is restricted to a small number of titles or series.[1042] More particularly, it noted that:

> As a rule most *books are completely original works*, written by an author following his inspiration at the time of writing. *They cannot be compared with one another*. In a number of cases, certainly, it is not the author's subjective creativity which is the principal feature, but rather the objective information which the book is intended to convey. *Books covering the same ground can therefore to some extent be regarded as substitutes, and may thus constitute a single market. But these works account for only a limited share of the total number of books in the market* [emphasis added].[1043]

274. The contradiction that arises here is obvious: on the one hand, the Commission finds that parameters of competition related to the quality of book or the service offered by bookstores are not as important as price. On the other hand, it notes that books with a high elasticity of demand represent a small percentage of the books sold. However (and this applies to *VBBB/VBVB* as much as it does to books in general), since competition on the upstream level is driven by the originality of the content produced by the author and price competition is relevant for a limited number of books that have close substitutes (e.g. dictionaries, travel guides, etc.),[1044] then an RPM agreement would not seem

1041 *supra* n. 71, paragraphs 61–62

1042 ibid.

1043 ibid.

1044 van der Ploeg (2004), *supra* n. 62, 13

to result in an elimination of competition in a substantial part of the products under consideration. Adjusted accordingly, a similar argument may be raised in the case of newspapers: where demand depends on factors such as the editorial position of the title, the agreement would fulfill the fourth condition laid down in Article 101(3) TFEU. The clearance notice the Commission adopted in *Agence et Messageries de la Presse*[1045] suggests that, despite a ban on price competition, related arrangements may qualify for an exemption.

275. The above analysis shows that Article 101(3) TFEU is flexible enough to allow for the non-price dimensions of competition to be taken into account in cases concerning RPM agreements for the sale of print products. Moreover, and relevant for the purposes of this study, economic theory supports the argument that, depending on the specific conditions of the market examined (e.g. the perishable nature of newspapers, language size, population density, etc.), RPM may be both appropriate and essential to deliver qualitative efficiencies in the form of a wide variety of titles or an extensive network of retailers, thereby remedying certain challenges facing media pluralism in the publishing sector, including especially marginalization of low-demand content.

3. Antitrust control in digital publishing: the agency model

276. The Commission decisions that concern RPM agreements governing print products were adopted between 1981 and 2002. Following *Sammelrevers*,[1046] the most recent of these decisions, competition issues relating to agreements that establish fixed prices for books and newspapers went dormant for about eight years when, in early 2010, arrangements made between book publishers and tech giant Apple revivified the debate. These arrangements, which were the first of their kind that fell under the Commission's antitrust microscope, were similar to those discussed above in that the publishers concerned set the prices for the e-books sold on Apple's iBookstore and Apple was not allowed to offer any discounts.[1047] However, the agreements between Apple and the involved publishers were substantially different from 'traditional' RPM agreements in the business model that was employed by the parties, namely the agency model, under which the retailer does not buy the content but rather

1045 Commission Notice pursuant to Article 19(3) of Regulation No. 17 concerning Case IV/31.609, Agence et Messageries de la Presse [1987] OJ C 164/02

1046 Commission Notice pursuant to Article 19(3) of Council Regulation No. 17 concerning an application for negative clearance or exemption under Article 81(3) of the EC Treaty, Cases COMP/34.657, Sammelrevers and COMP/35.245 to 35.251, Einzelreverse [2000] OJ C 162/8

1047 E-books (Case COMP/AT.39847) Commission Decision C(2012) 9288 (consolidated version), fn. 4 and paragraphs 31 and 36

acts as an intermediary between the provider and the end-consumer. For our purposes, agency agreements in general and the *E-books* case in particular are important for three main reasons.

277. First, as regards competition issues, agency agreements such as those in the case at hand raise questions that go far beyond the controversies of fixed prices. More particularly, under certain conditions, an agency contract, including any restrictions 'by object' it may contain, falls outside Article 101(1) TFEU.[1048] By contrast, as seen above, 'traditional' RPM agreements between a bricks-and-mortar bookstore and a publisher are presumed to be caught by Article 101(1) TFEU; to comply with EU competition law, they must fulfill all four requirements set by Article 101(3) TFEU. Hence, agencies with an RPM element are distinct from 'traditional' RPM agreements as far as competition enforcement is concerned. Furthermore, and related to the above, the case law is far from clear as to the conditions under which an agency relationship may indeed benefit from antitrust immunity. The particularities of digital markets add to the already existing ambivalence.

278. Second, with respect to media pluralism and as already mentioned in Chapter 2, digital stores such as Apple's iBooks Store act as intermediaries between the publisher and the readership.[1049] In Chapter 2, we also saw that one of the main areas in which the activities of intermediaries may affect media pluralism is the shaping of economic models for news publishing.[1050] Given that over the past few years newspaper publishers have engaged in a quest for a successful business model that is key to the survival of high quality journalism, we cannot refrain from discussing the possible implications of the agency model (first used by Apple and major book publishers and subsequently adopted by other powerful online retailers[1051] and newspaper publishers[1052]) for the future of news provision.

1048 Commission Guidelines on Vertical Restraints [2010] OJ C 130/01, paragraph 18

1049 Foster (2012), supra n. 19, 25

1050 ibid, 6–7

1051 For example, in the e-book sector, Apple may have been the first but it certainly is not the only firm to use agency agreements; major digital retailers such as Amazon, Barnes & Noble, Kobo and Sony also entered into agency agreements with publishers. See, for instance, Campbell, L. HC and Hachette UK Refine Agency Model. 3 April 2013, The Bookseller. <http://www.thebookseller.com/news/hc-and-hachette-uk-refine-agency-model>; Department of Justice (2012). Civil Action No.1:12-CV-2826, United States of America v Apple Inc, Hachette Book Group Inc, HarperCollins Publishers LLC, Verlagsgruppe Georg Von Holtzbrinck GmbH, Holtzbrinck Publishers LLC d/b/a Macmillan, The Penguin Group, A Division of Pearson PLC, Penguin Group (USA) Inc and Simon & Schuster Inc, Comments of Barnes & Noble on the proposed final judgment, 3. <http://www.justice.gov/atr/cases/apple/comments/atc-0097.pdf>; Whithall, Z. Kobo switches to agency terms with major U.S. publishers. 1 April 2010, Quill & Quire. <http://www.quillandquire.com/omni/kobo-switches-to-agency-terms-with-major-us-publishers/>; and Jones, P. Amazon, Sony agree to agency deals over e-books in US. 1 April 2010, The Bookseller. <http://www.thebookseller.com/news/amazon-sony-agree-agency-deals-over-e-books-us.html>

1052 See, for instance, Kahn, J. Cue on agency model: 'I don't think you understand. We can't treat newspapers or magazines any differently than we treat FarmVille.' 23 April 2012, 9to5Mac. <http://9to5mac.com/2012/04/23/cue-on-agency-model-i-dont-think-you-understand-we-cant-treat-newspapers-or-magazines-any-differently-than-we-treat-farmville/>

279. Finally, while in the commitments decision it adopted the Commission focused on the collusion aspects of the case, that is, the allegedly unlawful coordination between the undertakings concerned, the arrangements between Apple and the involved publishers have apparently influenced agreements concluded between other entities marketing content online.[1053] Since the commitments that were made legally binding concern the above arrangements, the decision hints at how the Commission may treat related issues in the future and provides the basis for an analysis of the framework within which antitrust control of online agencies should be conducted.

3.1 The *E-Books* case: the facts and the outcome

280. The *E-books* case concerns the allegedly[1054] anti-competitive conduct of Apple and publishers[1055] Hachette, HarperCollins, Penguin,[1056] Macmillan and Simon & Schuster (hereafter collectively referred to as the 'Publishers') in respect of the sale of e-books to consumers. The facts of this case may be summarized as follows: in January 2010, the Publishers signed agency agreements with Apple that would govern the sales of their e-books in the US. Under these agreements, the Publishers would set the prices for e-books made available on Apple's iBooks Store, while Apple would be remunerated by payment of a commission equal to 30% of the retail price paid by consumers.[1057] This contractual relationship was substantially different from the one the Publishers had established with Amazon in 2007 when, after Amazon launched its e-reader 'Kindle', demand for e-books significantly increased.[1058] More particularly, prior to signing the agreements with Apple, the Publishers sold e-books to retailers, including Amazon, under

1053 See, for instance, Foros, Jarle Kind, and Shaffer (2013), supra n. 18, 1–2

1054 'Allegedly' anti-competitive conduct because, as opposed to a prohibition decision, a commitments decision makes the commitments binding without concluding 'whether there was or still is an infringement'. See Commission Notice on best practices for the conduct of proceedings concerning Articles 101 and 102 TFEU [2011] OJ C308/6, paragraph 117

1055 E-books (Case COMP/AT.39847) Commission Decision C(2012) 9288 (consolidated version), paragraph 1

1056 It is noted that the commitments decision, which will be discussed in more detail below, is not addressed to Penguin because the latter had not proposed any commitments that could address the Commission's concerns. Commitments Decision, p. 7, fn. 2 clarifies as follows: 'The Commission also opened proceedings against Pearson plc ("Pearson"). Pearson is the parent company of the Penguin group ("Penguin"), one of the largest English-language trade book publishers in the world. Pearson was, however, not an addressee of the Preliminary Assessment. The Commission is still examining Pearson's conduct and its compatibility with Article 101 of the Treaty. Pearson remains, therefore, a party to the proceedings in case COMP/39.847/E-Books.' However, in practice, since Apple undertook to terminate agency agreements it had concluded with the Publishers prior to the decision, its contractual relationship with Pearson came to an end (see paragraph 105). A few months after the adoption of this decision, Pearson proposed commitments which were essentially the same as those offered by the other Publishers involved in the case. After they were market tested, these commitments were accepted by the Commission. See Commission decision of 25/07/2013 addressed to Penguin Random House Limited (formerly The Penguin Publishing Company Limited) and Penguin Group (USA) LLC (formerly Penguin Group (USA) Inc) relating to proceedings under Article 101 TFEU and Article 53 of the EEA Agreement in E-books (Case COMP/39.847) C(2013) 4750

1057 E-books (Case COMP/AT.39847) Commission Decision C(2012) 9288 (consolidated version), fn. 4 and paragraphs 31 and 36

1058 ibid, paragraph 18

the wholesale model.[1059] Under this model, e-books are sold to the retailers at a wholesale price below the suggested retail price set by publishers.[1060] In the case at hand, wholesale prices were up to 50% of the e-book list price.[1061] The key element of wholesale agreements is that retailers are free to determine the retail prices charged to consumers.[1062] Between March and December 2010, the Publishers initiated negotiations with Apple regarding sales of e-books under the agency model in the UK, France and Germany.[1063] The agreements, which were signed shortly thereafter, were very similar to the US contracts.[1064] In addition to the 70/30 revenue sharing rule explained above, all agreements included maximum retail price grids for newly released e-books[1065] and a retail parity MFN clause.[1066] This MFN clause provided that, if another retailer sold a particular e-book at a lower price, including in cases where that retailer was party to a wholesale agreement, the Publisher was bound to lower the retail price of the e-book in the iBooks Store to match that other lower price.[1067] The retail parity MFN arrangements between Apple and the Publishers eventually forced Amazon to switch to agency arrangements.[1068]

281. In March 2011,[1069] the Commission confirmed that it had initiated inspections at the premises of firms active in the e-book market.[1070] Based on the results of these inspections, the Commission decided to open formal antitrust proceedings to investigate whether the Publishers had engaged in practices violating EU competition law.[1071] Throughout its inquiry, the Commission concentrated on the collusion aspects of the case. The Commission placed particular emphasis on the exchange of contacts between the Publishers who, concerned about Amazon's heavy discounts policy, reportedly came together to coordinate the pricing terms of the agreements signed with Apple. [1072] According to the Commission, Apple played a major role in this attempt by ensuring that each of

1059 ibid, paragraph19

1060 ibid, paragraph 20

1061 ibid.

1062 ibid, paragraph 21

1063 ibid, paragraph 40

1064 ibid, paragraph 41 et seq.

1065 ibid, paragraph 32

1066 ibid, paragraph 31

1067 ibid.

1068 ibid, paragraphs 38–9

1069 Note that an investigation into whether the agreements between the Publishers and Apple had breached competition rules had been initiated by the UK Office of Fair Trading two months earlier. However, with a view to avoiding duplication of the investigation, the OFT closed the case and the Commission took over. The documents relating to the OFT's investigation are available at: http://webarchive.nationalarchives.gov.uk/20140402142426/http://www.oft.gov.uk/OFTwork/competition-act-and-cartels/ca98/closure/e-books>

1070 Commission (2011, March). Antitrust: Commission confirms unannounced inspections in the e-book publishing sector. MEMO/11/126. <http://europa.eu/rapid/press-release_MEMO-11-126_en.htm?locale=en>

1071 Commission (2011, December). Antitrust: Commission opens formal proceedings to investigate sales of e-books. Press Release IP/11/1509. <http://europa.eu/rapid/press-release_IP-11-1509_en.htm>

1072 E-books (Case COMP/AT.39847) Commission Decision C(2012) 9288 (consolidated version), paragraphs 22–23

the Publishers knew that the others were negotiating with it on the same pricing conditions.[1073] This coordination gave strong indications that the Publishers and Apple 'engaged in a concerted practice with the object of raising retail prices of e-books in the EEA or preventing the emergence of lower prices in the EEA for e-books, in breach of Article 101(1) TFEU'.[1074] In subsequent discussions with the Commission, the parties proposed undertakings which, following a market test, were considered appropriate to address the Commission's concerns and, as such, led to the adoption of a commitments decision.[1075]

282. The undertakings that were made legally binding on the Publishers and Apple were the following:

» Publishers and Apple committed to terminate the agency agreements that were concluded as a result of the concerted practice;[1076]

» For a period of five years, each of the Publishers and Apple undertook not to enter into any agreement for the sale of e-books that contains an MFN clause.[1077] Apple further committed to inform all publishers with which it had an agency agreement that it would not enforce the MFN clause included therein; and[1078]

» For a two-year ('cooling-off') period, each of the Publishers undertook not to restrict a retailer's ability to set retail prices of e-books.[1079] However, it was clarified in the decision that both the Publishers and Apple remained free to enter into agency agreements.[1080] If they indeed opted for agency, the Publishers would not restrict the retailer's freedom to reduce retail prices 'by an aggregate amount equal to the total commission the publisher pays to the e-book retailer, over a period of at least one year … and/or to use that amount to offer any other forms of promotions'.[1081] In fact, shortly after the commitments decision was adopted, HarperCollins, Hachette, Simon & Schuster[1082] and Macmillan[1083] reportedly concluded agency agreements with Amazon.[1084]

1073 ibid, paragraphs 33–34

1074 Commission. Final Report of the Hearing Officer COMP/39.847 – E-Books [2013] OJ C 73/06, paragraph 4. <http://eur-lex.europa.eu/legal-content/EN/TXT/PDF/?uri=CELEX:52013XX0313(02)&from=EN>

1075 E-books (Case COMP/AT.39847) Commission Decision C(2012) 9288 (consolidated version), paragraph 5

1076 ibid, paragraphs 97 and 130

1077 ibid, paragraphs 101, 102 and 106

1078 ibid, paragraph 107

1079 ibid, paragraph 99

1080 ibid, paragraph 153

1081 ibid, paragraph 100

1082 Pilkington, M. Simon & Schuster Adopts Refined Agency Pricing with Amazon UK. 29 April 2013, The Good E-reader. <http://goodereader.com/blog/electronic-readers/simonschuster-adopts-refined-agency-pricing-with-amazon-uk>

1083 Shaffi, S. Macmillan US does agency deal with Amazon. 19 December 2014, The Bookseller. <http://www.thebookseller.com/news/macmillan-us-does-agency-deal-amazon>

1084 Campbell, L. HC and Hachette UK Refine Agency Model. 3 April 2013, The Bookseller. <http://www.

3.2 The *E-Books* decision: the question left unanswered and an assessment of the accepted undertakings

283. In the commitments decision, the Commission carefully avoided taking a stance on the agency agreements concluded between Apple and the Publishers *absent the concerted practice*. While this issue was raised by interested stakeholders in the context of the market test that took place prior to the final assessment of the undertakings proposed by the Publishers, the Commission was limited to noting that its concerns 'do not relate to the legitimate use of the agency model for the sale of e-books'.[1085] In strict procedural terms, the Commission was not bound to assess whether these agreements (or the agency model as a business strategy in general) were aligned with EU competition law. The Commission enjoys a large margin of discretion in defining the scope of an antitrust inquiry[1086] and, since it decided to investigate the *way* in which the Publishers had switched to agency rather than the *content* of the agreements, the commitments procedure essentially sought to identify the most adequate solution to restore the conditions of competition that existed prior to the possible concerted practice. However, in effect, the Commission has more often than not given its opinion on issues it was not required to address in its decisions, formulating competition policy through the back door. For example, as already mentioned, in *VBBB/VBVB*, after finding that the agreement did not contribute to improvements in the production or distribution of books, it considered it '*useful to look more closely at the parties' arguments in relation to all the conditions* of Article [101(3) TFEU], *although it is ... unnecessary* to consider whether an agreement satisfies all the conditions of Article [101(3) TFEU] when it has already been found to fail one of those conditions' [emphasis added].[1087] Since the agency model is gaining popularity in the digital economy, it is much to be lamented that the Commission did not grasp the opportunity to clarify the rather blurred lines of the legal framework that applies to businesses entering into an agency contract. In our case, it is far from clear whether, and if so under what conditions, *individual* agency agreements, that is, *agreements without elements of cartel conduct*,[1088] may

---

thebookseller.com/news/hc-and-hachette-uk-refine-agency-model>

1085 E-books (Case COMP/AT.39847) Commission Decision C(2012) 9288 (consolidated version), paragraph 153

1086 Commission Notice on best practices for the conduct of proceedings concerning Articles 101 and 102 TFEU [2011] OJ C308/6, paragraphs 17 et seq.

1087 *VBBB/VBVB* (Case IV/428) Commission decision 82/123/EEC of 25 November 1981 relating to a proceeding under Article 85 of the EEC Treaty [1982] OJ L52/36, paragraph 48

1088 It should be noted that, even in cases of 'genuine' agency, Article 101(1) TFEU may apply if the agency facilitates (hub-and-spoke) collusion. See Commission Guidelines on Vertical Restraints [2010] OJ C 130/01, paragraph 20, which notes that this is the case 'when a number of principals use the same agents ... to collude on marketing strategy or to exchange sensitive market information between the principals'. Similarly, the Commission Guidelines on Horizontal Cooperation Agreements note that competition law may be violated in cases of information exchange 'indirectly through ... a third party such as a market research organization or through the companies' suppliers or retailers'. See Guidelines on the applicability of Article 101 TFEU to horizontal cooperation agreements [2011] OJ C 11/1, paragraph 55. On the issue of hub-and-spoke collusion see, for instance, Odudu, O. (2011). Indirect Information Exchange: The Constituent Elements of Hub-And-Spoke Collusion. European Competition Law Journal 7(2), 205–242

be regarded as 'genuine' agency structures, thereby rendering Article 101(1) TFEU inapplicable. In this section, I shall attempt to answer this question and explore, in light of the prevailing market conditions, the implications for media pluralism were individual agency arrangements to be granted antitrust immunity.

3.2.1 Could agency agreements between online retailers and content providers be regarded as 'genuine' agency agreements?

284. Pursuant to the Guidelines on Vertical Restraints, 'an agent is a legal or physical person vested with the power to negotiate and/or conclude contracts on behalf of another person (the principal), either in the agent's own name or in the name of the principal, for the purchase of goods or services, or sale of goods or services by the principal.'[1089] From a commercial perspective, agency is a very attractive structure. Principals, especially those who are considering entering new markets, do not need to establish a distribution network using their own resources, whereas agents, who do not buy the principals' products but are solely bound to conclude contracts on their behalf, face significantly lower barriers to entry than other types of distributors.[1090] Agency agreements are not caught by Article 101(1) TFEU;[1091] it is established case law that since the agent follows the principal's instructions and thus acts 'like a commercial employee, [it] forms an economic unit with this undertaking'.[1092] The underlying rationale for the exception is rather straightforward. Article 101 TFEU applies to agreements 'between' undertakings, not entities that operate 'within' the same undertaking (this is commonly referred to as the 'single economic entity' doctrine).[1093] To make this assessment, 'formal separation of two companies resulting from their having distinct legal identity, is not decisive. The test is whether or not there is *unity in their conduct on the market*' [emphasis added].[1094] If the incentives of principal and agent are indeed aligned, then the agency structure is akin to a vertically integrated firm.[1095] As a result, clauses restrictive of competition, including 'hardcore' restrictions such as the assignment of exclusive territories and resale price maintenance, escape Article

1089 Commission Guidelines on Vertical Restraints [2010] OJ C 130/01, paragraph 12

1090 See Geradin, D., Anne Layne-Farrar, and Nicolas Petit (2012). EU Competition Law and Economics. Oxford: OUP, paragraph 3.13

1091 ibid, paragraph 18

1092 ECJ, Joined Cases 40-48, 50, 54-56, 111, 113 & 114/73 Coöperatieve Vereniging 'Suiker Unie' UA and others v Commission of the European Communities [1975] ECR-1663, paragraph 480

1093 For an overview of the relevant case see Odudu, O. and David Bailey (2014). The Single Economic Entity Doctrine in EU Competition Law. Common Market Law Review 51, 1721–1758

1094 CFI, Case T-325/01 DaimlerChrysler AG v Commission of the European Communities [2005] ECR II-3319, paragraph 85

1095 Bennett, M. (2013, June). Online Platforms: Retailers, Genuine Agents or None of the Above? Competition Policy International, 4 <https://www.competitionpolicyinternational.com/assets/Uploads/EuropeJune.pdf>

101(1) TFEU[1096] provided they form part of a 'genuine' agency arrangement. But, while the legal *implications* of establishing an agency relationship have long been clear,[1097] the *conditions* under which agency agreements may benefit from antitrust immunity have been rather ambiguous.

285. The first (and – what seems to be in current practice – decisive) condition relates to the allocation of commercial and financial risks; where the agent assumes no such risks, it is deemed to be a genuine agent.[1098] Two criteria appear to be the key factors to determine this. First, ownership of the contract goods should not be vested in the agent and second, the agent should not bear any direct or indirect risks in respect of the contracts concluded by itself on behalf of the principal, including transport costs, advertising costs, liability vis-à-vis third parties and liability vis-à-vis the principal for customers' non-performance.[1099] Determining whether the 'risk' criterion is met is not a straightforward exercise, for the relevant case law has produced rather contradictory outcomes. For example, one issue that is still unsettled concerns the risks the principal requires the agent to undertake in closely related markets. In *DaimlerChrysler*, the Court held that qualifying as a genuine agent for the sale of the principal's goods or services (sale of new cars) does not depend on whether the principal commands the agent to bear risks in other, neighboring markets (provision of after-sales servicing and performance of guarantee work on vehicles).[1100] This approach is contrasted with the one the Court followed in *VAG Leasing* where, in assessing the applicability of Article 101(1) to the arrangements between Volkswagen and its dealers which acted as agents leasing Volkswagen vehicles, it took account of the fact that the latter were obliged by the former to provide after-sales services.[1101] Another question that still seeks an answer is whether some risks may be borne by the agent without related obligations jeopardizing the qualification of the relationship as a genuine agency. For instance, in its 1962 Notice on Exclusive Dealing Contracts with Commercial Agents, the Commission noted that agents could assume the *del credere* guarantee[1102] whereby 'the agent acts not only as a salesperson

1096 Commission Guidelines on Vertical Restraints [2010] OJ C 130/01, paragraph 18

1097 The Commission affirmed the special regime that agency agreements enjoy as early as 1962. See Commission Notice on Exclusive Dealing Contracts with Commercial Agents [1962] OJ 139/2921

1098 See, for instance, Commission Notice on Exclusive Dealing Contracts with Commercial Agents [1962] OJ 139/2921, paragraph 1; ECJ, Joined Cases 40-48, 50, 54-56, 111, 113 & 114/73 Coöperatieve Vereniging 'Suiker Unie' UA and others v Commission of the European Communities [1975] ECR-1663, paragraphs 482 and 541; ECJ, Case C-266/93 Bundeskartellamt v Volkswagen AG and VAG Leasing GmbH [1995] ECR I-3477, paragraph 19; Commission Guidelines on Vertical Restraints [2000] OJ C 291/01, paragraphs 13–15; Commission Guidelines on Vertical Restraints [2010] OJ C 130/01, paragraphs 13–15

1099 Commission Guidelines on Vertical Restraints [2010] OJ C 130/01, paragraph 16. The Guidelines distinguish between contract-specific, market-specific and other risks. For the relevant definitions see paragraph 14.

1100 CFI, Case T-325/01 DaimlerChrysler AG v Commission of the European Communities [2005] ECR II-3319, paras 66 and 81–120

1101 ECJ, Case C-266/93 Bundeskartellamt v Volkswagen AG and VAG Leasing GmbH [1995] ECR I-3477, paras 19–21

1102 Commission Notice on Exclusive Dealing Contracts with Commercial Agents [1962] OJ 139/2921, paragraph 1

or broker for the principal, but also as a guarantor of the credit extended to the buyer'.[1103] Yet, in *VAG Leasing* the Court adopted a more stringent approach, holding that the agents should not 'bear *any* of the risks resulting from the contracts negotiated on behalf of the principal' [emphasis added].[1104] The Guidelines on Vertical Restraints, which state that Article 101(1) TFEU does not apply if the agent 'bears *only insignificant* risks' [emphasis added][1105] are thereby not particularly helpful in resolving this controversy.

286. The second criterion is 'integration' of the agent with the principal's business. More particularly, for an agency agreement to render Article 101(1) TFEU inapplicable, the agent should 'neither undertake nor engage in activities proper to an independent trader'.[1106] This criterion, which is also referred to as criterion of economic dependence, excludes from the favorable regime cases where the agent enjoys significant commercial autonomy, acting in the name of various principals or developing simultaneously other commercial activities.[1107] However, there is uncertainty over the extent to which this condition has been embraced by either the Court or the Commission. In the past, Court rulings and Commission decisions have largely been based on whether the agent acted as an 'integral part' of the principal.[1108] In recent years, the main focus has been on how risks are allocated,[1109] but the relevant case law still makes reference to the role of the agent as an 'auxiliary organ'[1110] and

1103 Definition <http://www.investopedia.com/terms/d/del-credere-agency.asp>

1104 ECJ, Case C-266/93 *Bundeskartellamt v Volkswagen AG and VAG Leasing GmbH* [1995] ECR I-3477, paragraph 19. In a more recent case, the Court ruled that 'the fact that the intermediary bears *only a negligible share of the risks* does not render Article 85 [now Article 101] of the Treaty applicable' [emphasis added]. See ECJ, Case C-217/05 *Confederación Española de Empresarios de Estaciones de Servicio v Compañía Española de Petróleos SA* [2006] ECR I-11987, paragraph 61

1105 Commission Guidelines on Vertical Restraints [2010] OJ C 130/01, paragraph 15

1106 Commission Notice on Exclusive Dealing Contracts with Commercial Agents, OJ 1962 139/2921, paragraph 1

1107 Lianos, I. (2007). Commercial Agency Agreements, Vertical Restraints, and the Limits of Article 81(1) EC: Between Hierarchies and Networks. Journal of Competition Law and Economics 3(4), 632

1108 See, for instance, ECJ, Joined Cases 40-48, 50, 54-56, 111, 113 & 114/73 Coöperatieve Vereniging 'Suiker Unie' UA and others v Commission of the European Communities [1975] ECR-1663, paragraphs 545–546: The Court based its ruling on the fact that 'the agents in question are large business houses, which at the same time as they distribute sugar for the account of the applicant ..., undertake a very considerable amount of business for their own account ..., in particular in the field of exports to third countries ... Thus, these representatives are authorized to act as independent dealers in those transactions'. See also ECJ, Case C-311/85 ASBL Vereniging van Vlaamse Reisbureaus v ASBL Sociale Dienst van de Plaatselijke en Gewestelijke Overheidsdiensten [1985] ECR I-3801 which was a case of multiple agency (travel agent acting on behalf of several tour operators): 'A travel agent ... must be regarded as an independent agent who provides services on an entirely independent basis. He sells travels organized by a large number of different tour operators and a tour operator sells travel through a very large number of agents ... A travel agent cannot be treated as an auxiliary organ forming an integral part of a tour operator's undertaking' (paragraph 20). A similar reasoning has also been adopted by the Commission. See, for instance, European Sugar Industry, Commission decision 73/109/EC [1973] OJ L140/17

1109 For a comprehensive overview of the evolution of the relevant case law see Zhang, A. H. (2013). Toward an Economic Approach to Agency Agreements. Journal of Competition Law and Economics, 9(3), 565–570, and Lianos (2007), supra n. 199, 631–648

1110 See, for instance, ECJ, Case C-266/93 Bundeskartellamt v Volkswagen AG and VAG Leasing GmbH [1995] ECR I-3477, paragraph 19; ECJ, Case C-217/05 Confederación Española de Empresarios de Estaciones de Servicio v Compañía Española de Petróleos SA [2006] ECR I-11987, paragraphs 42–44. It should be noted that these judgments are somewhat misleading in that they make reference to the 'integration' criterion without, however, addressing the question of whether the criterion is actually met. The

has occasionally focused on the fact that the agent did not have the power to alter retail prices as a valid indication that the agent had 'no authority to act independently of the principal'.[1111] These considerations suggest that the 'integration' criterion has not been abandoned altogether.

287. Putting the above analysis into context, the following question seeks an answer: could agency agreements between online platforms and content providers, such as those concluded between Apple and the Publishers, fall outside Article 101(1) TFEU? Starting from the condition that the agent should be integrated with the principal's business, we cannot predict with certainty how the Commission would deal with the fact that Apple (or any other multi-sided retailer) sells the books of more than one publisher or that Apple develops in parallel a considerable amount of other activities for its own account (sale of e-readers, sale of apps, etc.). The Commission may state in its Guidelines that an entity may qualify as an agent irrespective of whether it acts in the name of one or more principals,[1112] but, as previously mentioned, its decisional practice is not entirely immune to 'economic dependence' considerations. With respect to risk, and without access to the agreements concerned, we cannot assess whether Apple assumed any responsibilities that would render Article 101(1) TFEU inapplicable[1113] (note that the commitments decision is not helpful in that regard, because it is limited to the description of certain pricing terms of the agreements). For now, we may only conjecture whether or not Apple could be perceived as a 'genuine agent' for the purposes of EU competition law: in principle, a narrow interpretation of the above two criteria would lead to the conclusion that Article 101(1) TFEU applies. In addition to the fact that this is a case involving a retailer that operates to a large extent independently of one single publisher, Apple also seems to have incurred some costs in promoting the Publishers' e-books. For example, it has created an instrument, the Widget Builder, which allows publishers to increase sales of their books on the iBooks Store by adding interactive widgets to their websites and blogs.[1114] If the creation of this and other similar instruments were an obligation under the agency agreement signed with the Publishers, this could be regarded as an 'investment in sales promotion',[1115] which, according to the Guidelines, is a type of risk that should not be borne by the agent for the agreement to escape Article 101(1) TFEU.

---

focus in both cases is on risk allocation.

1111 See CFI, Case T-325/01 DaimlerChrysler AG v Commission of the European Communities [2005] ECR II-3319, paragraphs 92–93. For an overview of this judgment see Jones, A. and Brenda Sufrin (2008). EC Competition Law (3rd Edition), 687–688. Oxford: OUP

1112 Commission Guidelines on Vertical Restraints [2010] OJ C 130/01, paragraph 13

1113 E-books (Case COMP/AT.39847) Commission Decision C(2012) 9288 (consolidated version), see in particular paragraphs 31 et seq.

1114 See <https://widgets.itunes.apple.com/> For further investments Apple has made to promote e-authors and publishers see: <http://www.apple.com/support/mac-apps/ibooksauthor/>

1115 Commission Guidelines on Vertical Restraints [2010] OJ C 130/01, paragraph 16(e)

288. Nevertheless, it is highly questionable whether such a narrow interpretation serves the purposes for which the special regime for agencies has been established in the first place. Excluding from said regime multiple agencies[1116] or cases where the agent develops a strategy to market the principal's products[1117] would likely result in preventing most agency arrangements from qualifying for immunity. In the case of online agency agreements, such as those signed between Apple and the Publishers, it should be borne in mind that the content provider holds control over both ownership of the content (the agent/digital store does not purchase the IPRs to the content concerned)[1118] *and* price. Moreover, given the digital nature of e-books, the agent does not need to incur any transport or storage costs. Finally, customers' non-performance is irrelevant as a financial risk in online markets because consumers' debit or credit cards are, broadly speaking, charged at the moment of purchase. In view of the above, it is submitted that there are legitimate grounds for granting immunity to RPM-based agencies.

3.2.2 Granting antitrust immunity to agencies: then what?

289. The above section concludes that there are valid reasons to grant immunity to RPM-based agencies. The question that inevitably arises is the following: if we were to treat these arrangements favorably, what would be the impact on the market and what would be the implications for media pluralism given the current business realities? I shall answer this question by looking into possible price and non-price effects. From the outset, it bears noting that it is too soon to draw any definitive conclusions. Only time and empirical research will tell whether the arguments that are raised below indeed hold.

290. ***Genuine agency and price effects*** The impact of the agency model on prices is a hotly contested and largely unsettled issue. In the *E-books* case, the Commission took the preliminary view that the Publishers concluded the agency agreements with Apple in order to increase prices but, since this was a commitments decision, proof substantiating this view was not provided.[1119] On the other side of the Atlantic, the Court of the Southern District of New York found that within a few weeks of switching to agency (voluntarily or otherwise), the prices of e-books produced by the Publishers increased.[1120]

1116 Lianos (2007), supra n. 199, 634

1117 Bennett, M. (2013, June), supra n. 187, 8–9

1118 ibid.

1119 E-books (Case COMP/AT.39847) Commission Decision C(2012) 9288 (consolidated version), paragraph 32

1120 'The increases at Amazon within roughly two weeks of moving to agency amounted to an average per unit e-book retail price increase of 14.2% for their New Releases, 42.7% for their NYT Bestsellers, and 18.6% across all of the Publisher Defendants' e-books'. United States Southern District of New York (2013). United States v Apple Inc et al. Case 1:12-cv-02826-DLC Document 326, 94. <http://www.justice.gov/atr/cases/f299200/299275.pdf> This judgment was upheld by the Appeals Court. See U.S. v Apple Inc, 2nd US Circuit Court of Appeals, No. 13-3741. <https://law.justia.com/cases/federal/appellate-courts/ca2/13-3741/13-3741-2015-06-30.html> Apple challenged the appellate court's decision but the Supreme

However, this finding concerns the defendants' books only[1121] and it may well be attributed to the cartel, not the agency model *per se*. It further bears noting that looking at price effects immediately after the industry adopts agency may lead to erroneous conclusions. Johnson, for example, examined the effects of the agency model on pricing when there is consumer lock-in, which is likely to occur in the e-book market because a consumer is tied to a particular book-reading device, and found that switching to agency may lead to higher prices for e-books initially but eventually prices decrease, similar to the wholesale model.[1122] Foros *et al.* reach a similar conclusion, albeit from a different perspective, that of the current market structure; their model shows that, under the prevailing e-book market conditions where the degree of competition is higher upstream than downstream, prices would be lower *with* rather than without an industry-wide adoption of the agency mechanism.[1123]

291. The premise that agency may lead to lower prices may hold if we also take into account the interplay with the market for print books, which is something Johnson and Foros *et al.* intentionally refrained from considering[1124] but which Abhishek *et al.* examined. More particularly, Abhishek *et al.* convincingly argue that when e-sales have a negative impact on sales through traditional channels,[1125] the publisher has the incentive to limit e-sales.[1126] Therefore, if a wholesale arrangement is made, the publisher will set a high wholesale price for the agent which will ultimately result in higher retail prices.[1127] This will reduce negative spillover effects in the offline channel but will

---

Court refused to hear the case. See, for instance, Hurley, L. Supreme Court rejects Apple e-books price-fixing appeal. 7 March 2016, Reuters. <https://www.reuters.com/article/us-usa-court-ebooks-idUSKCN0W91LQ>

1121 Associations of authors that were not in a contractual relationship with the Publishers maintained that, following the adoption of agency by Apple, prices of their books fell. See, for instance, Coker, M. Does Agency Pricing Lead to Higher Book Prices? 28 March 2012, Smashwords. <http://blog.smashwords.com/2012/03/does-agency-pricing-lead-to-higher-book.html>

1122 Johnson, J. P. (2013). The Agency and Wholesale Models in Electronic Content Markets. SSRN Working Paper, 1–2 <http://papers.ssrn.com/sol3/papers.cfm?abstract_id=2126808>

1123 Foros, Jarle Kind, and Shaffer (2013), supra n. 18, 10–14. Note that Foros et al. assume that the principal fixes the retail price at which the agent sells the contract goods and that the agreement establishes a 70/30 revenue sharing rule, which are provisions identical to the agreements made between Apple and the Publishers

1124 ibid, 3

1125 Note that the issue of how e-book sales affect sales at the bricks-and-mortar stores is far from settled. There are numerous studies suggesting that sales in the e-channel have a negative impact on sales through traditional distribution networks. See, for instance, Brynjolfsson, E., Yu J. Hu, and Mohammad S. Rahman (2009). Battle of the Retail Channels: How Product Selection and Geography Drive Cross-Channel Competition. Management Science 55(11), 1755–1765, and Goolsbee, A. (2001). Competition in the Computer Industry: Online versus Retail. The Journal of Industrial Economics, 49(4), 487–499. Other studies reach the opposite conclusion. See, for instance Smith, M. D. and Rahul Telang (2010). Piracy or Promotion? The Impact of Broadband Internet Penetration on DVD Sales. Information Economics and Policy 22(4), 289–298. Special Issue: Digital Piracy. And certain studies suggest that the effect of online sales on sales through traditional networks may be positive but insignificant. See, for instance, Hilton, J. and David Wiley (2010). The Short-Term Influence of Free Digital Versions of Books on Print Sales. BYU Faculty Publications. Paper 1358. <http://scholarsarchive.byu.edu/cgi/viewcontent.cgi?article=2357&context=facpub>

1126 Abhishek, V., Kinshuk Jerath and Z. John Zhang (2016). Agency Selling or Reselling? Channel Structures in Electronic Retailing. Management Science 62(8), 2259–2280

1127 ibid.

aggravate double marginalization[1128] in the online channel.[1129] By contrast, under agency, the principal has the incentive to charge lower prices because with agency the higher the retail price, the higher the commission it has to pay the agent.[1130] This leads to the agency structure being more efficient[1131] and ultimately lower prices for the end consumer.[1132]

292. ***Genuine agency and non-price effects in the book market*** Starting from the upstream markets, authors appear to earn more with agency rather than with a wholesale model. The usual revenue sharing under agency is 40/30/30 (40% for the author, 30% for the publisher and the remaining 30% for the retailer) whereas under Amazon's wholesale arrangements the revenue split used to be 8/32/60.[1133] Higher royalties may encourage new authors, including indie authors, to enter the market, stimulate creativity and eventually lead to an increase in the range of titles that is available to consumers.[1134]

293. Moreover, because the publisher controls price, agency may address concerns relating to heavy discount strategies, which powerful retailers are not prevented from following under a wholesale deal. This is also referred to as 'the 9.99 problem' raised by Amazon's pricing before it switched to agency. More particularly, as soon as it launched its e-reader, 'Kindle', in an attempt to boost sales of the device,[1135] Amazon began offering e-books, including newly released English-language bestsellers, for US$9.99.[1136] This price was not only substantially below the retail price proposed by the Publishers, but also below the wholesale price at which Amazon was buying the e-books.[1137] The effects of this practice on book consumption are not clear but the argument may be made that, with Amazon charging such low prices, consumers may refrain from buying content that costs more because this is what they expect *any* title to cost. Put simply, this practice may devalue the book as a literary creation

1128 For an analysis of the effects of double marginalization on innovative products see Shen, W. (2012). Examining Double Marginalization Effect for Innovative Product Supply Chain. International Journal of Operations Research and Information Systems, 3(1), 37–52

1129 Abhishek, Jerath and Zhang (2016), supra n. 218

1130 ibid.

1131 ibid.

1132 Note that Condorelli et al. reach the same conclusion. See Condorelli, D. Andrea Galeotti and Vasiliki Skreta (2013). Selling Through Referrals. NYU Working Paper No. 2451/31774. <http://papers.ssrn.com/sol3/papers.cfm?abstract_id=2260874> For a comprehensive overview of the economic studies conducted in this area see Wirl, F. (2017). Agency Model and Wholesale Pricing: Apple versus Amazon in the E-Book Market. International Journal of the Economics of Business 25(2), 243–245

1133 OECD (2012). E-books: Developments and Policy Considerations. OECD Digital Economy Papers, No. 208, 27–29

1134 Epstein. R. Not Proven: The DoJ Suit Against Apple for E-book Pricing. 10 April 2014, Ricochet. <https://ricochet.com/archives/not-proven-the-doj-suit-against-apple-for-ebook-pricing/>

1135 Joint Research Centre (2012a), supra n. 1, 73

1136 In 2011, Amazon's Kindle store offered 950,000 e-book titles, of which 800,000 cost $9.99 or less. See Wischenbart, R. The Global eBook Market. Current Conditions and Future Projections, 5. <http://www.publishersweekly.com/binary-data/ARTICLE_ATTACHMENT/file/000/000/522-1.pdf>

1137 E-books (Case COMP/AT.39847) Commission Decision C(2012) 9288 (consolidated version), paragraph 22

and marginalize well-researched works or more esoteric titles. Furthermore, if e-books cost substantially less than hardcover versions, publishers face pressure to reduce prices of print books.[1138] This may result in lower prices for the consumers, but as I have already explained, a race to the bottom on price has a negative impact on content diversity.

294. As regards downstream markets, in cases where online sales have adverse effects on sales through traditional channels, an RPM-based agency may stimulate competition between retailers; as already seen, RPM may encourage market entry, for it protects the distributor's profit margin. Moreover, to the extent that it contributes to the survival of bricks-and-mortar bookstores or the survival of the traditional product in and of itself, control over prices would be to the benefit of the majority of consumers, including younger generations, that seem to prefer print to e-books.[1139]

295. ***Genuine agency and non-price effects in the news market*** As already mentioned, one of the main areas in which the activities of digital stores may impact media pluralism is the shaping of news economics, that is to say, the ways in which they may affect the ability of newspaper publishers to earn (advertising and subscription) revenues. Hence, when we discuss the non-price pluralism-specific effects of granting immunity to 'genuine' agency arrangements the question that arises is whether these arrangements may somehow interfere negatively with the publishers' ability to generate the financial resources necessary to invest in high quality journalism. The answer is likely no, for mainly three reasons. First, previous revenue models have been far from successful. For example, certain publishers have attempted to introduce paywalls, however, this model was quickly abandoned because the earnings from subscriptions could not make up for the drop in advertising revenues that followed the massive loss of audiences.[1140] Other publishers, in their effort to reduce the high fixed costs that the production and distribution of newspapers entails, decided to go online-only.[1141] Yet, this also proved a risky undertaking. For instance, Thurman and Myllylahti examined the switch to online-only of Finnish financial newspaper Taloussanomat and found that, while the title managed to reduce costs by 50%, revenues decreased by 75%.[1142] The adoption of the agency model, combined with the introduction of tablets and new generations of e-readers, which make digital newspapers more appealing to

1138 Department of Justice (2012), supra n. 143, 9

1139 See, for instance, Hom, M. Why Humans Prefer Print Books. 4 January 2016, Elsevier SciTech Connect. <http://scitechconnect.elsevier.com/why-humans-prefer-print-books/>; Robb, A. 92 Percent of College Students Prefer Reading Print Books to E-Readers. 14 January 2015, New Republic. <http://www.newrepublic.com/article/120765/naomi-barons-words-onscreen-fate-reading-digital-world>; and Bury, L. Young adult readers 'prefer printed to ebooks'. 25 November 2013, The Guardian. <http://www.theguardian.com/books/2013/nov/25/young-adult-readers-prefer-printed-ebooks>

1140 Joint Research Centre (2012b), supra n. 27, 8

1141 ibid, 24

1142 ibid.

the readership,[1143] has opened up a new market for publishers, and evidence suggests that agency is the first ever viable income-generating strategy for online news provision.[1144]

296. Second, compared with an emerging and – what appears to be – efficient charging mechanism set up by the *Financial Times*, agency has a distinctive advantage. More particularly, instead of entering into a contractual relationship with Apple under the 'standard' (70/30) agency terms, the *Financial Times* created a web-based product using HTML5, which is accessible via any smartphone web browser.[1145] While this allows the publishers to establish a direct relationship with the readership, it is an expensive alternative (it entails significant software development and subscriber management costs) which not all news providers can afford.[1146] It bears repeating that not having to incur the costs that the establishment of a full-grown distribution network would require is what makes agency so attractive. Third, in the case of a 'genuine' RPM-based agency, publishers maintain control over price.

297. In summary, in the current market conditions, granting immunity to agency agreements,[1147] which allow the provider to fix the retail price of the content and which introduce a revenue-sharing arrangement that contributes to the viability of both principal and agent, is more likely to enhance rather than negatively affect media pluralism.

298. *Would non-pure agencies be different?* The above conclusion would not necessarily hold in the case of non-pure agency agreements[1148] under which 'the agent cannot be validly prevented from passing on part or all of its

1143 ibid, 8

1144 ibid, 65. See also Foster (2012), supra n. 19, 39

1145 Foster (2012), supra n. 19, 31 referring to Smith, P. Fts Mobile Web App Shows Apples Are Not the Only Fruit. 8 June 2011, Themediabriefing.com, and Prodhan, G. Financial Times pulls its apps from Apple store. 31 August 2011, Reuters. <http://www.reuters.com/article/2011/08/31/us-apple-ft-idUSTRE77U1O020110831>

1146 ibid.

1147 Note that, even if for one reason or another an RPM-based agency does not qualify as a 'genuine' agency relationship, the agreement may still qualify for an exemption under Article 101(3) TFEU. The economic studies cited in this Part of the Chapter pinpoint the factors that must be considered in an assessment under Article 101(3) to ensure that the non-price dimensions of competition that are relevant for our purposes are sufficiently taken into account.

1148 Note that the case law and the Commission's decisional practice are not entirely clear as to whether an agreement which allows the agent to forego its commission qualifies as a genuine agency or not. For example, in DaimlerChrysler the Court held that, provided that the agent is not required to forego its commission, the agreement concerned falls outside Article 101(1) TFEU. See CFI, Case T-325/01 DaimlerChrysler AG v Commission of the European Communities [2005] ECR II-3319, paragraph 99. In ASBL, the Court ruled that agreements prohibiting agents from sharing their commission are incompatible with Article 101(1) TFEU but where the agent acts on behalf of many principals it is not a genuine agent. See ECJ, Case C-311/85 ASBL Vereniging van Vlaamse Reisbureaus v ASBL Sociale Dienst van de Plaatselijke en Gewestelijke Overheidsdiensten [1985] ECR I-3801, paragraphs 20 and 24. In E-books, the Commission imposed on the Publishers the obligation not to restrict the agent's freedom to reduce retail prices 'by an aggregate amount equal to the total commission the publisher pays to the e-book retailer … for a period of two years' [emphasis added]. It may be inferred from this time restriction that, upon expiry of the commitments, the Publishers may prevent the retailer from foregoing its commission. See E-books (Case COMP/AT.39847) Commission Decision C(2012) 9288 (consolidated version), paragraph 100

commission payment to the customer in order to reduce the effective sale price paid by the customer for the product'.[1149] As already indicated above, the establishment of a non-pure agency for a period of two years was the third and final commitment that was made legally binding on the undertakings involved in the E-books cartel.[1150] This is arguably not an optimal solution because powerful digital stores with significant resources at their disposal have the ability and incentive to forego their commission altogether. To the extent that it reinforces downstream concentration, this measure may generate exclusionary effects. This should be considered alongside the fact that, unlike powerful US retailers, domestic firms operating in Member States where RPM laws apply are not allowed to offer discounts.[1151] Given these regulatory conditions and the relevant markets' tendency to concentration, a non-pure agency would not seem appropriate to protect competition or pluralism.

4. Sammelrevers: media pluralism as a restriction of competition

299. As already discussed in Chapter 3, the Commission has occasionally (especially in the past) attempted to reconcile competition and non-economic values by accepting restrictions of competition to the benefit of those other values.[1152] In the publishing sector, the case where the Commission appears to have made a considerable allowance for restrictions of competition as a

1149 Van Bael, I. and Jean-François Bellis (2005). *Competition Law of the European Community* (4th Edition). Aphen aan den Rijn: Kluwer Law International, 229

1150 E-books (Case COMP/AT.39847) Commission Decision C(2012) 9288 (consolidated version), paragraphs 99–100

1151 ibid, paragraph 120

1152 In Chapter 2, it was demonstrated that this is one of the Commission's two approaches to dealing with the relationship between competition and media pluralism. It is worth mentioning briefly that, in the book publishing sector, the other approach (pluralism as a result of unhindered market access) was followed in *Bertelsmann/Planeta/Circulo* where the Commission was limited to noting that, since the transaction under scrutiny did not raise any foreclosure concerns, diversity could not be harmed. See Case COMP/M.5838 [2010] OJ C 228/3, paragraphs 16, 39, 49. A criticism of this approach and its implications for non-price competition and media pluralism took place in Chapter 2, Part 2. The *E-books* commitments decision makes reference to cultural diversity, but it is clear that the value had no impact whatsoever on the Commission's assessment of the commitments. See *E-books* (Case COMP/AT.39847) C(2012) 9288 (consolidated version), paragraphs 127 and 152. In the other two antitrust decisions in the sector, namely *VBBB/VBVB* and *Net Book Agreement*, the parties claimed that the agreements were eligible for exemption under Article 101(3) TFEU on the grounds that they protected the cultural and linguistic unity between the Netherlands and Flanders and between the UK and Ireland respectively, but the Commission rejected the argument in both cases (See *VBBB/VBVB* (Case IV/428) Commission decision 82/123/EEC of 25 November 1981 relating to a proceeding under Article 85 of the EEC Treaty [1982] OJ L52/36, paragraph 60, and *Publishers Association – Net Book Agreement* (Cases IV/27.393 and IV/27.394) Commission decision of 12 December 1988 relating to a proceeding under Article 85 of the EEC Treaty [1989] OJ L22/12, paragraph 43). It further bears noting that in merger decisions in the book publishing sector and in antitrust and merger decisions in newspaper and magazine publishing, there is generally no mention of cultural diversity or media pluralism. In newspaper publishing, the only exceptions are *News Corp/BSkyB* (Case COMP/M.5932) [2011] OJ C37/2, and *Newspaper Publishing* (Case IV/M.423) [1994] OJ C 85/5. Both these decisions have already been discussed in Chapter 3, Parts 3 and 4.

means to protect pluralism is *Sammelrevers*,[1153] which dealt with an RPM agreement governing trade in German-language books and other print products. The main issue was whether an RPM system confined to the territory of a Member State had no effect on trade, thereby rendering Article 101(1) TFEU inapplicable. *Sammelrevers* deserves a closer look because the approach the Commission followed in this case is a rather unorthodox and arguably illegitimate way to address conflicts between competition and pluralism. For the avoidance of confusion, it should be noted from the outset that a case with facts similar to those of *Sammelrevers* should be distinguished from cases of genuine agency discussed above in that in situations of genuine agency the contractual relationship is granted immunity *because* it does not harm competition, not *despite* the harm to competition.

4.1 Could Sammelrevers indeed escape antitrust scrutiny?

300. In 1993, Austrian and German publishers filed an application to the Commission for negative clearance or, alternatively, for exemption under Article 101(3) TFEU apropos their RPM agreements covering books and other print products in Austria and Germany, also known as *Sammelrevers* system.[1154] In 2000, the notifying parties sent the Commission a modified version of *Sammelrevers*,[1155] lifting the cross-border element of the mechanism.[1156] As a result of this amendment, the RPM agreements between German publishers and Austrian booksellers on the one hand and Austrian publishers and German booksellers on the other were annulled.[1157] Subsequently, the Commission issued a notice clearing the new Sammelrevers system on the grounds that, while the agreements embodied therein restricted price competition,[1158] they would not have any appreciable effect on trade between Member States in the sense of Article 101(1) TFEU.[1159] This was so, the Commission said, because the system would only apply to the sale of books from German publishing houses by German booksellers to final consumers in Germany and because it would not restrict price competition for books re-imported into Germany.[1160] However, a few months later, after receiving complaints by Internet booksellers established outside Germany that German publishers and book wholesalers

1153 Commission notice pursuant to Article 19(3) of Council Regulation No. 17 concerning an application for negative clearance or exemption under Article 81(3) of the EC Treaty, Cases COMP/34.657 Sammelrevers and COMP/35.245 to 35.251 Einzelreverse OJ [2000] OJ C 162/8

1154 ibid, paragraph 1. Note that publishers of non-Member States (Switzerland, China, the Czech Republic and the United States of America) were also parties to the agreement (see paragraph 2)

1155 ibid, paragraph 2

1156 ibid.

1157 ibid.

1158 ibid, paragraphs 11 and 12

1159 ibid, paragraph 13

1160 ibid. This was subject to the condition that the exportation and re-importation of these books was not solely aimed at evading the system

refused to supply them in order to prevent direct cross-border sales at a price lower than the fixed price set by Sammelrevers members, the Commission reopened antitrust proceedings.[1161] Based on the preliminary results of its investigation, the Commission noted that the agreement '[had] been applied in a way that [continued] to have an effect on trade'.[1162] In subsequent discussions with the Commission, German publishers and booksellers made the commitment to refrain from raising obstacles to direct cross-border selling, which resulted in a negative clearance comfort letter in March 2002.[1163]

301. The preliminary conclusion that Sammelrevers had produced an effect on trade could have led to a decision finding that a violation of Article 101(1) had taken place. Under such circumstances, the Commission has the power to impose on the entities concerned fines that may amount to 10% of the total turnover of each firm involved in the infringement.[1164] Considering that the second clearance was subject to the same condition as the first (i.e. that the German RPM arrangements would not affect direct cross-border sales),[1165] the following questions inevitably arise: since in its second attempt to restore competition in the market for German-language books the Commission accepted a behavioral undertaking that did not manage to address the problem the first time around, and since in both decisions the Commission refused to subject the agreement to antitrust scrutiny, does *Sammelrevers* indicate a high degree of tolerance towards 'purely national' fixed book pricing (FBP) agreements? If so, is the approach followed in *Sammelrevers* a good path to follow in cases of conflict between competition and media pluralism?

302. In order to answer the first question, we need to examine how the 'appreciable effect on trade' criterion, the fulfillment of which would trigger Article 101(1) TFEU in this case, has been applied, and then assess the Commission's approach in *Sammelrevers* in light of the political and economic context in which this decision was adopted. As already mentioned, for an agreement restrictive of competition to be caught by Article 101(1) TFEU, it must be capable of appreciably affecting trade between Member States. This is a jurisdictional condition that defines the scope of application of EU competition law.[1166] In examining whether

1161 Commission (2001, July). Commission re-opens proceedings concerning the German system of fixed book prices because of its effects on cross-border Internet bookselling. Press Release IP/01/1035. <http://europa.eu/rapid/press-release_IP-01-1035_en.htm?locale=it>

1162 ibid.

1163 DG Competition (2002, June). Commission ends competition proceedings regarding German book price fixing agreements following acceptance of an undertaking on cross-border sales. Competition Policy Newsletter 2, 35–37. <http://ec.europa.eu/competition/publications/cpn/2002_2_35.pdf>

1164 Council Regulation (EC) No. 1/2003 of 16 December 2002 on the implementation of the rules on competition laid down in Articles 81 (now 101) and 82 (now 102) of the Treaty [2003] OJ L1/1, Articles 7 and 23(2)

1165 Commission notice pursuant to Article 19(3) of Council Regulation No. 17 concerning an application for negative clearance or exemption under Article 81(3) of the EC Treaty, Cases COMP/34.657 Sammelrevers and COMP/35.245 to 35.251 Einzelreverse OJ [2000] OJ C 162/8, paragraph 10

1166 Commission Notice. Guidelines on the effect on trade concept contained in Articles 81 and 82 of the

this condition applies, three elements need to be addressed, namely the notion 'may affect', the notion of 'appreciability', and the notion of 'trade between Member States'.[1167] The Commission lays down in its Guidelines on the Effect on Trade Concept the principles developed by EU Courts in respect of the interpretation of these terms.[1168] Under a standard test applied by the Court of Justice, the notion 'may affect' suggests that 'it must be possible to foresee with a sufficient degree of probability on the basis of a set of objective factors of law or fact that the agreement may have an influence, direct or indirect, actual or potential, on the pattern of trade between Member States'.[1169] For the 'pattern of trade' to be influenced, trade need not be negatively affected, that is, the Union may establish jurisdiction also when the arrangements are likely to lead to an increase in trade.[1170] The notion of 'appreciability' is the quantitative dimension of the effect on trade condition, in that it restricts EU jurisdiction to agreements that may produce effects 'of a certain magnitude'.[1171] Each case is assessed on an individual basis by reference to parameters such as the *nature* of the agreement and the *position* that the involved undertakings hold in the relevant product market.[1172] For example, agreements that are by nature capable of appreciably affecting trade are those that may affect imports or exports or that cover several Member States.[1173] As regards the position of the parties in the affected market(s), there exist no pre-established rules, but the Commission usually applies presumptions based on market shares and aggregate annual turnovers.[1174] Finally, the notion of 'trade between Member States' does not imply that the agreement under examination must be implemented in several Member States. Trade between Member States may be affected also in cases where the relevant market is national in scope,[1175] provided that there is 'an impact on cross-border economic activity involving at least two Member States'.[1176]

Treaty OJ [2004] C 101/7, paragraph 12, referring to ECJ, Joined Cases 56 and 58/64 Consten SA and Grundig-Verkaufs GmbH v Commission of the European Economic Community [1966] ECR 299, 340, and to ECJ, Joined Cases 6/73 and 7/73 Istituto Chemioterapico Italiano and Commercial Solvents v Commission [1974] ECR 223

1167 ibid, paragraph 18

1168 ibid, paragraph 3

1169 ibid, paragraph 23, referring to ECJ, Case 172/80 Züchner [1981] ECR 2021, fn. 11; ECJ, Case 319/82 Kerpen & Kerpen [1983] ECR 4173; ECJ, Joined Cases 240/82 and others Stichting Sigarettenindustrie and others v Commission of the European Communities [1985] ECR 3831, paragraph 48; CFI, Joined Cases T-25/95 and others Cimenteries CBR and others v Commission of the European Communities [2000] ECR II-491, paragraph 3930. The 'pattern of trade' test is further explained in paragraphs 24–43 of the Guidelines.

1170 ibid, paragraph 34, referring to CFI, Case T-141/89 Tréfileurope [1995] ECR II-791; CFI, Case T-29/92 Vereniging van Samenwerkende Prijsregelende Organisaties in de Bouwnijverheid (SPO) [1995] ECR II-289, and Commission decision of 29 June 2001 relating to a proceeding under Article 81 of the EC Treaty (Case COMP/F-2/36.693) Volkswagen [2001] OJ L262/14

1171 ibid, paragraph 44

1172 ibid, paragraphs 44, 45 and 50

1173 ibid, paragraph 48

1174 ibid, paragraphs 50–57

1175 ibid, paragraph 22

1176 ibid, paragraph 21

303. Two remarks can be made with respect to the above. First, it is clear that the effect on trade concept has been interpreted in a rather broad manner; EU competition law will apply even if the agreement binds undertakings that operate in the territory of one Member State and irrespective of whether the effect is actual or potential, positive or negative. It is therefore not surprising that in very few cases this condition was not fulfilled.[1177] Second, had the Commission applied the principles set out in the aforementioned Guidelines, *Sammelrevers* would not have escaped Article 101(1) TFEU. More particularly, according to the relevant case law, cartels and vertical agreements covering a single Member State are 'by nature' capable of affecting intra-Union trade in that they may partition the common market by raising obstacles to the economic penetration which the Treaty aspires to achieve.[1178] In *Sammelrevers*, it was clear that the parties could prevent retailers from other Member States from selling books to German consumers at low prices, for they had the incentive to ensure the sustainability of the price level introduced by the (national) RPM mechanism.[1179] It is accepted that, in cases of arrangements that may by their very nature impact trade between Member States, it is not necessary to define the relevant product market and the market shares held by the involved undertakings in order to assess whether the appreciability requirement is met.[1180] It may, however, be necessary to take account of the possible aggregate effects of parallel networks of similar or identical agreements.[1181] The Guidelines lay down that '[e]ven if a single agreement or network of agreements is not capable of appreciably affecting trade between Member States, the effect of parallel networks of agreements, taken as a whole, may be capable of doing so'.[1182] In our case, while in theory the system did not hinder price competition, in that neither publishers nor booksellers were obliged to enter into an RPM contractual relationship, in practice almost all market players participated in the system.[1183] Moreover, since most German-language books were published in Germany, the mechanism also governed a substantial proportion of the trade of such titles. Were the above realities to be taken into account, the Commission would have inevitably been led to the conclusion that, as a result of *Sammelrevers*, the parties could appreciably affect trade in the market for German-language books.

1177 See, for instance, ECJ, Joined Cases C-215/96 and C-216/96 *Carlo Bagnasco and others v Banca Popolare di Novara soc. coop. arl. (BNP) and Cassa di Risparmio di Genova e Imperia SpA (Carige)* [1999] ECR I-135. In this case, the Court ruled that the pattern of trade would not be affected, see paragraphs 47 *et seq*. See also ECJ, Case 28/77 *Tepea BV v Commission* [1978] ECR 1391. In this case, the Court ruled that the 'appreciability' requirement was not met, see paragraphs 46–48.

1178 Commission Notice. Guidelines on the effect on trade concept contained in Articles 81 and 82 of the Treaty OJ [2004] C 101/7, paragraphs 78 and 86.

1179 ibid, paragraph 88.

1180 ibid.

1181 ibid.

1182 ibid, paragraph 49.

1183 Appelman and Canoy (2002), supra n. 37, 588.

304. That the Commission has been overly permissive in this case is further illustrated by comparing the analysis in *Sammelrevers* with the assessment of whether the effect on trade is met in other cases.[1184] A good example is *British interactive Broadcasting (BiB)*, a decision concerning the creation of a Joint Venture (JV), the purpose of which would be the provision of digital interactive television services.[1185] While the JV agreement provided that BiB's activities would be confined to the UK territory, the Commission found that the agreement could have an effect on trade.[1186] This was so, the Commission said, for at least three reasons. First, due to continuous developments in the market for digital interactive services, it was highly likely that the technical difficulties associated with offering these services to consumers in other Member States would be overcome in the near future.[1187] Second, Sky, one of the parent companies,[1188] was already present in the Irish market; since there were no linguistic barriers between the UK and Ireland, it could not be excluded that BiB's services would soon be made available to Irish consumers.[1189] Finally, even if Sky did not expand into other markets, the agreement could still affect trade between Member States for the reason that non-UK competitors would not be able to rely on the investments of BiB's parent companies.[1190] This latter conclusion was reached after the Commission examined the clauses of the JV agreement,[1191] which established, *inter alia*, the parent companies' obligation to refrain from holding more than 20% in a competing company.[1192] It is submitted that the Commission could have approached *Sammelrevers* with a similar insight; the first clearance notice was issued one month *after* the E-Commerce Directive (on which the Commission had been working since 1997[1193]) was adopted with a view to enabling 'European citizens and operators to take full advantage, without consideration of borders, of the opportunities afforded by electronic commerce.'[1194] It was therefore far

1184 See, for instance, ECJ, Case 8/72 Vereeniging v Commission [1972] ECR 977, paragraphs 28–29. This case concerns a different sector but greatly resembles the facts of Sammelrevers: a Dutch trade association (in which most Dutch cement dealers participated) recommended the prices at which its members would sell in the Netherlands. The parties claimed that, as the arrangement did not apply to exports, it did not affect trade between Member States. The Court, however, rejected this argument on the grounds that '[a]n agreement extending over the whole of the territory of a Member State by its very nature has the effect of reinforcing the compartmentalization of markets on a national basis.'

1185 British Interactive Broadcasting/Open (Case IV/36.539) [1999] OJ L312/1, paragraph 2.

1186 ibid, 153 et seq.

1187 ibid.

1188 ibid, paragraph 1

1189 ibid, paragraph 155

1190 ibid, paragraph 156

1191 The approach whereby the specific economic and legal context of the agreement under scrutiny is examined was followed by the Court in ECJ, Case C-234/89 Delimitis v Henninger Bräu AG [1991] ECR I-935. See in particular paragraphs 19 et seq.

1192 ibid.

1193 See, for instance, Commission (1997, April). Press Release IP/97/313. Electronic Commerce: Commission presents framework for future action. <http://europa.eu/rapid/press-release_IP-97-313_en.htm?locale=it>

1194 Directive 2000/31/EC of the European Parliament and of the Council of 8 June 2000 on certain legal aspects of information society services, in particular electronic commerce, in the Internal Market (Directive on Electronic Commerce) [2000] OJ L178/1, Recital (3)

from difficult to predict how a national cartel could inhibit the development of the then emerging market for online book sales.

305. Yet, the Commission's persistence to grant immunity to this particular arrangement should not be regarded as a turning point in its decisional practice. In other words, this decision does not suggest that the Commission has thereby established a favorable antitrust regime for 'purely national' RPM agreements in order to enable them to achieve non-economic pluralism-specific objectives in spite of the anti-competitive effects they are likely to create. The approach followed in *Sammelrevers* is largely explained by the fact that the German legislator was planning to adopt a national law on fixed book prices, a parameter that the Commission took into account when it adopted its commitments decision.[1195] It is established case law that Member States may enact RPM laws provided that they do not raise obstacles to the free movement of goods.[1196] With that said, the decision to clear *Sammelrevers* on the grounds that the system was incapable of affecting trade between Member States should be regarded as a temporary solution (aimed at ensuring a smooth transition from the RPM system that private actors had set up to an RPM system that would be established by the State) rather than a case of lenient competition enforcement. In subsequent cases, the Commission applied the principles enunciated in the Guidelines, as discussed above.[1197]

1195 DG Competition (2002). Commission ends competition proceedings regarding German book price fixing agreements following acceptance of an undertaking on cross-border sales. Competition Policy Newsletter, Issue 2. <http://ec.europa.eu/competition/publications/cpn/2002_2_35.pdf> See in particular paragraph 7 of the Undertaking (attached to the Newsletter) which reads as follows: 'This Undertaking is only valid during the maintenance in force of the Sammelrevers 2000 governing the retail price maintenance of books and other printed products in Germany. As soon as the Sammelrevers is repealed by State measures governing the retail price maintenance this Undertaking ceases its validity.'

1196 See, for instance, ECJ, Case 229/83 Association des Centres distributeurs Édouard Leclerc and others v SARL 'Au blé vert' and others [1985] ECR 1; ECJ, Case C-9/99 Echirolles Distribution SA v Association du Dauphiné and others [2000] ECR I-8207

1197 For example, in a case regarding funding arrangements for RTVE, the Commission rejected the argument put forward by the party to the proceedings that there could be no effect on trade on the grounds that RTVE would not broadcast outside Spain and that it was not planning to export programming to other Member States. Commission decision on the State aid scheme No. C 38/2009 (ex NN 58/2009) which Spain is planning to implement for Corporación de Radio y Televisión Española (RTVE) C (2010) 4925 final, paragraph 42. For the avoidance of confusion, the effect on trade criterion in State aid cases has been interpreted in a way similar to the one in used in antitrust cases. See, for instance, ECJ, Case C-75/97 Maribel bis/ter [1999] ECR I-3671, paragraph 47 and ECJ, Case C-310/99 Italy v Commission [2002] ECR I-2289. I did, however, trace an inconsistency in recent practice. See Restrictions concerning ELT books (Case COMP/39771) paragraph 17: '[Y]our complaint is limited to conduct directed towards your business operations, all of which are located in Greece. In particular, you allege that you are unable to purchase books for your company in Greece from the publishers' distributors situated outside Greece. The main effects of the alleged infringement therefore relate to Greece, i.e. one single Member State, whereas the Commission is generally well placed to deal with infringements that relate to three or more Member States.'

4.2 Is Sammelrevers a good path to follow in order to resolve conflicts between competition and pluralism?

306. For the purposes of this study, we need to answer the question of whether, in cases of conflict between competition and media pluralism, we should advocate for an approach similar to that adopted by the Commission in *Sammelrevers*. The answer is no, for at least three reasons. The first has to do with how non-economic pluralism-specific concerns should be taken into account in the application of EU competition rules. The Commission's second decision clearing Sammelrevers was accompanied by the following statement made by the then Commissioner responsible for Competition Policy, Mario Monti: 'By clearing the German price fixing system the Commission, in a perspective of subsidiarity, also takes account of the national interest in maintaining these systems which are aimed at preserving cultural and linguistic diversity in Europe.'[1198] This statement implies that the application of Article 101(1) TFEU is contingent on the protection of the non-economic values enshrined in Article 167(4) TFEU. However, as was already discussed in detail in Chapter 3, neither an interpretation of the Treaties nor the Court's case law support the argument that, in cases of tension between competition considerations and considerations relating to cultural/media policies, the former may supersede the latter.

307. Second, finding that a condition set by Article 101(1) TFEU is not met when it is actually met in order to 'protect' agreements restrictive of competition that are intended to enhance other public policy objectives would undermine legal certainty; in such cases, there would be considerable ambivalence about the reasons why and the extent to which those other public policies factored into the Commission's decision to render EU competition law inapplicable. For example, in *Sammelrevers*, Monti's statement was the only indication that cultural and linguistic diversity took precedence over competition. In view of the above, the reasoning in *Sammelrevers* is arguably an opaque and unlawful method to address non-economic concerns in the implementation of the EU competition rules. It is submitted that the possible benefits of an RPM arrangement for pluralism should rather be considered under Article 101(3) TFEU, for otherwise it would be fairly easy for the parties to bypass antitrust law (as in *Sammelrevers*, they could simply commit not to engage in anti-competitive practices against undertakings providing the same print products from other Member States). The approach proposed here was followed by the Court in *Binon*[1199] where it was held that if an agreement between publishers of newspapers and periodicals and distributors includes arrangements which

1198 Commission (2002, March). Commission accepts undertaking in competition proceedings regarding German book price fixing. Press Release IP/02/461. <http://europa.eu/rapid/press-release_IP-02-461_en.htm>

1199 ECJ, Case 243/83 SA Binon & Cie v SA Agence et messageries de la presse [1985] ECR 2015

'by definition' restrict competition,[1200] Article 101(1) TFEU applies, and that if 'the fixing of the retail price by publishers constitutes … the sole method by which a wide selection of newspapers and periodicals can be made available to readers, the Commission *must take account of those factors when examining an agreement for the purposes of Article [101](3)*' [emphasis added].[1201] Balancing restrictions of competition against non-economic concerns under the umbrella of Article 101(3) TFEU[1202] is a more transparent method than the adoption of a notice stating that the agreement is not subject to antitrust scrutiny. Moreover, the proposed method would not result in granting immunity in cases where competition concerns exist or are likely to arise.[1203]

308. Third, related to the above and as extensively discussed throughout this Chapter, RPM is not necessarily beneficial for media pluralism. In fact, absent a series of conditions, RPM may be to the detriment of diversity. Conducting an analysis under Article 101(3) TFEU within the framework that was proposed in Part 2 of this Chapter would allow the Commission to check whether RPM may indeed produce positive effects on media pluralism in the form of qualitative efficiencies.

309. The three reasons that are put forward as to why in cases of conflict between competition and pluralism we should not defend an approach similar to that adopted by the Commission in *Sammelrevers* lend further support to one of the claims put forward in Chapter 3, namely that strict competition enforcement that takes due account of the particularities of the media markets under scrutiny has more potential than the approaches to the relationship between the two values the Commission has followed to date, including the acceptance of arbitrary restrictions of competition.[1204]

1200 Note that, although the case concerned mainly the 'selective distribution' aspects of the case, it is relevant for our case because the selective distribution system introduced quantitative restrictions which are subject to Article 101(1) TFEU. See ibid, paragraph 29.

1201 ibid, paragraph 46. Note that the same approach was followed by the Commission in VBBB/VBVB. In this case, the parties claimed that the effect on trade criterion was not fulfilled because the agreement applied to a linguistically homogeneous area and was intended to protect cultural unity, however, the Commission – arguably rightly – rejected the claim on the grounds that it would otherwise 'diminish the applicability' of Article 101(1) TFEU. See VBBB/VBVB (Case IV/428) Commission decision 82/123/EEC of 25 November 1981 relating to a proceeding under Article 85 of the EEC Treaty [1982] OJ L52/36, paragraph 44

1202 For more information on the issue of resolution of conflict through exclusion and resolution of conflict through compromise, and an analysis of the very few cases where exclusion was preferred over compromise see Van Rompuy, B. (2012). Economic Efficiency: The Sole Concern of Modern Antitrust Policy? Alphen aan den Rijn: Kluwer Law International, 219–229

1203 Monti, G. (2007). EC Competition Law. Cambridge: CUP, 105

1204 See Chapter 3, Part 3

5. Conclusions

310. This Chapter examined two popular business models that have been employed to sell books and newspapers, that is, RPM for print titles and RPM-based agency for digital publications. It assessed the Commission's practice in publishing markets against the claims that were put forward in Chapter 3, namely that by failing to adapt competition enforcement to the particular characteristics of the media market under scrutiny, competition decisions lack a sound reasoning and that, if properly applied, EU competition law may lead to an outcome that is of benefit to pluralism. These claims were tested against the three issues which the application of Article 101 to publishing markets has raised to date, that is, whether RPM agreements qualify for an exemption under Article 101(3) TFEU (*VBBB/VBVB*), whether RPM agreements benefit from immunity from Article 101 in spite of their harming competition (*Sammelrevers*), and whether RPM-based agency agreements qualify for immunity from Article 101 on the grounds that they do not harm competition (*E-books*).

311. As regards the first issue, an exhaustive analysis of *VBBB/VBVB* provides sufficient proof that the Commission has paid little to no attention to sector-specific economics. Ignoring altogether features such as demand uncertainty and the tendency to content homogenization, the Commission based its decision on the contestable assumptions that RPM leads to higher prices and that readers prefer lower prices to variety. Following a detailed overview of book and newspaper economics, the analysis showed that RPM may confer several non-price benefits upon the readership; provided that certain market conditions are fulfilled, an RPM agreement may deliver qualitative efficiencies in the form of, *inter alia*, a broad range of titles and an extensive network of retailers, thereby contributing to the preservation of content and supply diversity.[1205] These efficiencies may be realized *without* necessarily involving higher retail prices.

312. The approach followed in *Sammelrevers*, where the Commission declared Article 101 inapplicable to a 'purely national' RPM agreement, is problematic for a number of reasons. Clearing an RPM agreement on the grounds that granting antitrust immunity protects media pluralism goes beyond what is allowed by the Treaties. As extensively discussed in Chapter 3, in cases of conflict between competition considerations and considerations relating to

1205 Note that, naturally, as technology advances, some of the efficiency justifications that are put forward in support of RPM will become irrelevant. For example, print-on-demand equipment, which currently delivers an inferior product, will gradually replace traditional printing processes and significantly reduce storage costs. When this happens, the retailers' cross-subsidization argument is unlikely to hold. On print-on-demand technology see, for instance, Snow, D. O. Print-on-Demand: the best bridge between new technologies and established markets. Booktech – The Magazine for Publishers (January–February 2001). <http://www.u-publish.com/pod2.htm> On a recent dispute between Amazon and small publishers regarding the use of print-on-demand equipment see Miller, J. Amazon accused of 'bullying' smaller UK publishers. 26 June 2014, BBC News. <http://www.bbc.com/news/technology-27994314>

media pluralism, the former may not supersede the latter. This approach further undermines legal certainty and transparency, two principles that should guide the implementation of EU competition law, including especially in cases where the Commission attempts to conduct a competition assessment in a way that resolves tensions between competition and another public policy value. But, most importantly, given that RPM is not a *condicio sine qua non* for the preservation of media pluralism, refraining from examining whether the agreement concerned may indeed generate the (qualitative) efficiencies it is meant to deliver may run counter to pluralism.

313. Finally, as far as online agencies are concerned, in *E-books*, the Commission avoided taking a position on whether the arrangements between Apple and major book publishers, which have had an industry-wide appeal, come within the scope of Article 101. Nonetheless, this Chapter examined in detail the characteristics of RPM-based agencies and concluded that there are plausible arguments supporting why they should benefit from antitrust immunity. Contrary to traditional RPM agreements, agents do not need to buy the product and, to the extent that the incentives of digital stores and publishers remain aligned after the contract is concluded, the retailer may well be regarded as the extension of the will of the publisher. Interestingly, in the prevailing market conditions, granting the immunity is *not* likely to harm media pluralism, thereby lending further support to the point raised in Chapter 3 that competition and media pluralism are to a great extent reconcilable; the analysis illustrated that digital stores have opened up a market for authors, who apparently receive more favorable conditions now than they did in the past. With respect to the role of digital stores in shaping the economics of news provision, the agency model that was introduced by Apple appears to have been the first successful charging mechanism for newspaper subscriptions and is far cheaper than other alternatives that are currently available. Hence, the adoption of the agency model by digital retailers appears to have produced a positive impact on pluralism. Would the same conclusion apply to business practices affecting the economics of news provision in which other digital intermediaries such as search engines and news aggregators engage? Or, does the fact that digital retailers have enabled news publishers to generate revenues in online markets preclude that they may behave in ways that adversely affect media pluralism? Maybe not. But the issues raised by the above two questions are not directly related to pricing strategies and will be examined in detail in the next Chapter.

CHAPTER 6

DIGITAL INTERMEDIARIES AND ARTICLE 102 TFEU: THE CASE OF GOOGLE

1. Introduction

314. The previous Chapter studied, *inter alia*, the role of a category of digital intermediaries, namely digital stores, in shaping media markets. It did so by examining the effects of the RPM-based agency model on the economics of news provision. As already seen in Chapter 2, molding the future of news provision is one of the main areas illustrating the role that digital intermediaries may play in harming or promoting media pluralism.

315. Moving away from Article 101 TFEU but remaining within the confines of antitrust, this Chapter will discuss issues that relate to the application of Article 102 TFEU to digital intermediaries. In addition to practices affecting *news economics*, this Chapter will examine other types of conduct potentially beneficial or damaging to media pluralism that were mentioned in Chapter 2,[1206] namely the *editorial-like judgments* digital intermediaries perform in selecting, ranking and displaying information and practices in which they engage in their role as *distribution bottlenecks*. To this end, the Chapter will use as a case study the Commission's investigation into Google's abuse of dominance in general online search,[1207] part of which is still ongoing. The Google antitrust case has been chosen mainly for two reasons. First, this is the first case where the Commission has dealt with anti-competitive unilateral conduct in markets

1206 See Part 3.4.2.

1207 Commission (2010, November). Antitrust: Commission probes allegations of antitrust violations by Google. Press Release IP/10/1624. <http://europa.eu/rapid/press-release_IP-10-1624_en.htm?locale=en>

where digital intermediaries operate.[1208] As a result, it sheds light on the intricacies of the markets in question and illustrates the challenges with which the Commission has to cope in reaching a decision. Second, the complaints against Google are numerous, ranging from the anti-competitive use of third-party content to algorithm manipulation to restrictions on data portability. The issues that arise from these practices cover the full spectrum of the aforementioned types of conduct. For example, insofar as the impact on *news economics* is concerned, one of the issues we shall examine concerns the copying of parts of news articles in Google's news aggregation platform, Google News. A matter that exemplifies the role of an intermediary as a *distribution bottleneck* concerns Google's retaliation practices whereby news providers that object to the use of their stories on the Google News website may be excluded from Google's services altogether, including general search results. Finally, with respect to *editorial-like judgments*, Google was found to have demoted competing websites whilst granting preferential treatment to its own content.[1209]

316. As in Chapters 4 and 5, this Chapter discusses the application of EU competition law to undertakings that control an asset or parameter that affects competition. In Chapter 4 it was control of the acquired entity, whereas in Chapter 5 it was control over the retail price of newspaper and book titles. In the case at hand, it is control of a popular information gateway, namely Google's search engine, which Google is said to use to expand into and dominate adjacent markets such as news aggregation and vertical search markets.

317. Consistent with the direction followed in assessing the Commission's practice in broadcasting and publishing markets, this Chapter seeks to establish whether the Commission has made proper use of the EU competition law toolbox to address the issues it has identified and, if not, to explore whether, if properly applied, Article 102 may address concerns over media pluralism in the affected markets. The Chapter is structured as follows: Part 2 is an overview of the facts of the case and exposes the reader to the main aspects of Google's business model. Part 3 examines the allegations that concern the possible impact of Google's conduct on the economics of news provision.

1208 At the time of going to press, the Commission adopted the Google Android decision, fining Google €4.34 billion. The case concerns illegal practices regarding Android mobile devices in which Google was found to engage with a view to strengthening its position in general internet search. For example, Google has required manufacturers to pre-install the Google Search app and browser app (Chrome) as a condition for licensing Google's app store. While the text of the decision is not yet publicly available, the Commission outlines the reasoning of its decision in Commission (2018, July). Antitrust: Commission fines Google €4.34 billion for illegal practices regarding Android mobile devices to strengthen dominance of Google's search engine. <http://europa.eu/rapid/press-release_IP-18-4581_en.htm> For an analysis of this case see, for instance, Ibáñez Colomo, P. The Android decision is out: the exciting legal stuff beneath the noise. 18 July 2018, Chillin' Competition. <https://chillingcompetition.com/2018/07/18/the-android-decision-is-out-the-exciting-legal-stuff-beneath-the-noise-by-pablo/>

1209 See Commission (2010, November), supra n. 2; Commission (2017, June). Antitrust: Commission fines Google €2.42 billion for abusing dominance as search engine by giving illegal advantage to own comparison shopping service. Press Release IP/17/1784. <http://europa.eu/rapid/press-release_IP-17-1784_en.htm>

Part 4 explores issues related to Google's role as a distribution bottleneck, namely retaliatory practices that affect news markets, restrictions of data portability, and the exploitative gathering and processing of user data. Part 5 focuses on the editorial-like judgments which Google performs, that is, the discriminatory practices which were found to divert traffic from competing websites to Google's content.

2. Google under the European antitrust microscope: the scope of the Commission's investigation in *Google Search*

318. On 30 November 2010, the European Commission announced that it decided to initiate an investigation into allegations that Google has abused its dominant position in the online search market, in violation of Article 102 TFEU.[1210] The decision to open a formal investigation was based on complaints launched by Foundem, a UK price comparison website, Ciao, a German price comparison website and Microsoft subsidiary, and eJustice, a French legal portal.[1211] All three complainants are vertical search engines. These are distinct from general search engines in that, instead of indexing large portions of the Internet through a web crawler,[1212] they index content by reference to a specific topic, location, and/or industry. Google is a general search engine, but over the past few years it has expanded into neighboring vertical search markets such as product and flight price comparison. The complainants put forward that Google has been abusing its dominant position in general online search with the aim of pushing competing services out of vertical search markets.[1213] Before discussing in more detail what the case is about, it is essential to explain some key aspects of Google's business model.

319. Google Search is an advertising-based medium, which means that it supplies search results for free and that its revenues come from advertising. Google delivers two types of results, namely unpaid results and paid results/sponsored links. The unpaid results, which are also known as 'natural', 'organic' or 'algorithmic' results, are the results that are returned based on 'the natural indexing of the Web site'.[1214] The paid results or sponsored links are third party

1210 Commission (2010, November), supra n. 2

1211 Google Search (Case AT.39740) Commission decision of 27 June 2017 relating to proceedings under Article 102 TFEU and Article 54 of the EEA Agreement C (2017) 4444 final

1212 Microsoft/Yahoo! (Case COMP/M.5727) C(2010) 1077, paragraph 31

1213 Commission (2010, November), supra n. 2

1214 Definition <http://www.webopedia.com/TERM/N/natural_search.html>

advertisements displayed at the top and at the right hand side of Google's search results page.[1215] Google sells this ad space through its auction-based advertising platform, Google Ads.[1216] After creating a Google account, the advertiser chooses keywords that are words or phrases relevant to its business. The position that an advertiser is allocated in the list of paid search results depends on the bid the advertiser makes for a given keyword and its 'Quality Score'.[1217] The Quality Score is an approximate calculation of how relevant the advertiser's ads, keywords and website are to a person seeing the ad.[1218] It is determined by several factors such as the keyword's past click-through rate (i.e. how often that keyword led to clicks on the ad), the quality of the landing page (i.e. how relevant, transparent, and easy-to-navigate the advertiser's website is) and geographic performance (i.e. how successful the advertiser's account has been in the regions it is targeting).[1219] The price an advertiser must pay Google is the bid that it made for a keyword multiplied by its Quality Score.[1220]

320. Going back to the antitrust proceedings, the complainants put forward that Google has been lowering the ranking of their websites in the list of organic results, whilst ensuring prominent display for its own services.[1221] In June 2017, the Commission adopted a decision finding that Google abused its dominant position in general online search by giving illegal advantage to its own comparison shopping service.[1222] Google appealed the decision before the General Court of the EU.[1223]

321. The investigation remains open with respect to the other practices in which Google has allegedly engaged. More particularly, the Commission is concerned about the exclusivity obligations that Google imposes on its advertising partners. As regards advertising with Google Ads, Google appears to restrict advertisers to exporting ad campaign data into competing platforms, including general search engines.[1224] The other concern relates to how Google does business

1215 Commission (2010, November), supra n. 2

1216 See <http://support.google.com/adwords/bin/answer.py?hl=en&answer=1704410>

1217 Information retrieved through: http://support.google.com/adwords/bin/answer.py?hl=en&answer=2454010>

1218 ibid.

1219 ibid.

1220 Varian, H. (2010, March). *Search Advertising With Google: Quality Score Explanation by Google Chief Economist*. <http://www.youtube.com/watch?v=qwuUe5kq_O8>

1221 Commission (2010, November), *supra n.* 2

1222 *Google Search* (Case AT.39740) Commission decision of 27 June 2017 relating to proceedings under Article 102 TFEU and Article 54 of the EEA Agreement C (2017) 4444 final

1223 GCEU, Case T-612/17 *Google and Alphabet v Commission*, Action brought on 11 September 2017 [2017] OJ C 369/37

1224 Commission (2012, May). *Statement of VP Almunia on the Google antitrust investigation*. Speech/12/372. <http://europa.eu/rapid/press-release_SPEECH-12-372_en.htm>; Commission (2016, July). *Antitrust: Commission takes further steps in investigations alleging Google's comparison shopping and advertising-related practices breach EU rules*. Press Release. <http://europa.eu/rapid/press-release_IP-16-2532_en.htm>

as an intermediary in the online advertising market. In *Google/Doubleclick*, the Commission explains that 'intermediaries pool advertising space made available for sale by publishers [i.e. website owners] and advertisers wishing to buy advertising space and facilitate the matching between the supply of ad space and the demand for ad space to place ads'.[1225] Google provides intermediation services through its AdSense platform: website owners make ad spaces available by pasting ad codes on their sites, and advertisers bid for their ads to be displayed in these spaces.[1226] According to the information that is currently publicly available, Google imposes upon the website owners a series of obligations, including the obligation not to source ads from Google's competitors, which may have produced exclusionary effects in the affected markets.[1227]

322. The final concern has to do with 'scraping' third-party content. More particularly, Google copies material offered by other websites and uses it in its own offerings without seeking permission from the websites concerned.[1228]

323. To sum up, Google's conduct has been found to raise concerns regarding the following practices:[1229]

» Manipulation of general search results, which was found to give an illegal advantage to its comparison shopping service;

» Exclusivity restrictions imposed on advertisers and web publishers, possibly foreclosing advertising markets; and

» Scraping third-party content, potentially reducing competitors' incentive to innovate.

324. The Commission initially stated that it would follow a commitments procedure on the grounds that, compared with 'a more adversarial path',[1230] this process was more appropriate 'to swiftly restore competitive conditions on a [fast-moving] market'.[1231] Google proposed commitments three times:[1232] the

1225 *Google/Doubleclick* (Case COMP/M.4731) [2008] OJ C 184/6, paragraph 18

1226 Information <http://www.google.com/adsense/start/>

1227 Commission (2010, November), *supra n.* 2; Commission (2016, July), *supra* n. 19

1228 Commission (2014a, February). *Antitrust: Commission obtains from Google comparable display of specialized search rivals – Frequently asked questions*. Memo 14/87. <http://europa.eu/rapid/press-release_MEMO-14-87_en.htm?locale=en>; Commission (2016, July), *supra* n. 19

1229 Note that since 2010, other companies have filed complaints similar to those initially raised by Foundem. See, for instance, Microsoft (March, 2011). *Adding our Voice to Concerns about Search in Europe*. <http://blogs.microsoft.com/on-the-issues/2011/03/30/adding-our-voice-to-concerns-about-search-in-europe/>

1230 Commission (2014b, February). *Statement on the Google investigation*. <http://europa.eu/rapid/press-release_SPEECH-14-93_en.htm>

1231 Commission (2013, April). *Commission seeks feedback on commitments offered by Google to address competition concerns – questions and answers*. <http://europa.eu/rapid/press-release_MEMO-13-383_en.htm>

1232 See Google (2013, April). *Commitments in Case COMP/C-3/39.740 – Foundem and others*. <http://ec.europa.eu/competition/antitrust/cases/dec_docs/39740/39740_8608_5.pdf>; Google (2013, October). *Commitments in Case COMP/C-3/39.740 – Foundem and others*. <http://www.consumerwatch-

first two proposals were expressly rejected. In February 2014, the Commission announced that the third set of undertakings submitted by Google was 'capable of addressing' its concerns.[1233] But, in April 2015, that is, more than one year later, the Commission stated that it decided to send Google a Statement of Objections relating to the allegations of preferential treatment *only* and that this '[would] not in any way prejudge the outcome of the Commission's investigation' into Google's conduct as regards the other issues'.[1234] As already mentioned, in June 2017, the Commission adopted a decision finding that, by engaging in preferential treatment of its own services, Google violated Article 102 TFEU.[1235] With respect to the allegations of scraping and exclusivity, the Commission may still be considering the adoption of a commitments decision on the basis of the final set of undertakings proposed by Google.[1236]

325. Having explained the conduct that is being investigated and how the Commission may proceed in the future, two remarks should be made regarding the scope of my analysis. First, the Chapter will not examine the concerns that arise from the restrictions imposed on web publishers. Currently, there is insufficient factual information that would allow me to engage in an assessment of the agreements concerned. Suffice it to say that, from the statements the Commission has made on certain occasions, the scope of these restrictions appears to be wide. For example, the Commission noted that publishers have been required 'not to source search ads from Google's competitors'.[1237] It may be inferred from such statements that the restrictions in question may amount to 'exclusive purchasing' deals, which may breach Article 102 TFEU if they 'have the effect of preventing the entry or expansion of competing undertakings'.[1238] Second, given that the Commission appears to have left the door

---

dog.org/resources/googlesettlment102113.pdf>; and Google (2014, January). *Commitments in Case COMP/C-3/39.740 – Foundem and others*. <http://docs.dpaq.de/6448-google_commitments_full.pdf>

1233 Commission (2014a, February), *supra* n. 23

1234 Commission (2015, April). *Antitrust: Commission sends Statement of Objections to Google on comparison shopping service*. <http://europa.eu/rapid/press-release_MEMO-15-4781_en.htm>

1235 *Google Search* (Case AT.39740) Commission decision of 27 June 2017 relating to proceedings under Article 102 TFEU and Article 54 of the EEA Agreement C (2017) 4444 final

1236 The most recent statement regarding scraping and restrictions on data portability is rather vague. The Commission notes that 'it will continue to investigate … concerns with regard to copying of rivals' web content (known as 'scraping'), and undue restrictions on advertisers.' See Commission (2016, July), *supra* n. 19

1237 Commission (2016, July), *supra* n. 19; Commission (2013, April), *supra* n. 26

1238 Guidance on the Commission's enforcement priorities in applying Article 82 of the EC Treaty to abusive exclusionary conduct by dominant undertakings [2009] OJ C 45/2, paragraph 34. On the parameters the Commission would take into account to conduct an assessment of exclusive purchasing deals, see paragraphs 33 *et seq*. of the Guidance. It is worth mentioning that, in addition to preventing web publishers from doing business with competing search engines, Google appears to have concluded a series of exclusivity agreements with a number of key players in markets adjacent to online search that may have had far-reaching effects on competition. For example, Google has signed exclusivity agreements with a number of popular web-browsers such as Safari, Firefox, and Opera, in order to become the default search engine. While competitors brought this issue to the attention of the Commission, the latter apparently decided not to include related deals in its investigation. For more information on the competitors' allegations see ICOMP (2013, January). *Complaint of ICOMP against Google, Inc under Article 101 TFEU, pursuant to Article 7 of Regulation 9EC) No. 1/2003*. <http://www.i-comp.org/wp-content/uploads/2014/01/AnnexesICOMPMarketTestSubmission310513.pdf>

open for a commitments decision to be adopted with respect to scraping and data portability restrictions on the basis of the most recent proposals submitted by Google, I shall examine whether the suggested undertakings are indeed appropriate to alleviate the concerns which they raise.

3. Scraping third-party content: feed aggregators and Article 102 TFEU

326. As already discussed in Chapter 2, digital intermediaries may impact media pluralism by, *inter alia*, affecting the ability of news providers to generate (advertising and/or subscription) revenues. Chapter 5 examined the effects that the agency model has had on newspaper publishing and concluded that in light of current business realities, these effects appear to be positive; evidence suggests that the agency model has been the first viable income-generating strategy for online news provision.[1239] Moreover, even if publishers usually find themselves in a weaker bargaining position vis-à-vis the digital retailers that provide access to the audiences that are locked into the hardware devices they manufacture, they maintain control over price *and* ownership of the content that is made available to the readership whilst getting 70% of the retail proceeds. This section will discuss how another category of intermediaries, namely news aggregators, may affect publishers' ability to generate the financial resources that are necessary to gather and report news. I will focus on the practice on which the very existence of news feed aggregators depends, that is, the 'scraping' of third party content, which, as already mentioned, the Commission is currently investigating in the context of the Google antitrust case.[1240] For our purposes, 'scraping' refers to the act of copying the headline and (usually) small excerpts of a news story (commonly referred to as 'snippets') without remunerating the news outlet that wrote the story.

327. The term news aggregator refers to 'a website that takes information from multiple sources and displays it in a single space'.[1241] News aggregators resemble traditional news providers more than other digital intermediaries; they choose the information that reaches the readership[1242] and some of them run their own

1239 Joint Research Centre (2012a). *Technical Report on Statistical, Ecosystems and Competitiveness Analysis of the Media and Content Industries: The Newspaper Publishing Industry*, 65. < http://publications.jrc.ec.europa.eu/repository/bitstream/JRC69881/jrc69881.pdf>

1240 Commission (2013, April), *supra* n. 26

1241 Isbell, K. (2010). *The Rise of the News Aggregator: Legal Implications and Best Practices*. Berkman Center Research Publication No. 2010-10, 2. Available at SSRN through: <https://papers.ssrn.com/sol3/papers.cfm?abstract_id=1670339>

1242 On how news aggregation works in practice see, for instance, Anderson, C. W. (2010). *What Aggregators Do: Rhetoric, Practice, and Cultures of Digital and Analog Evidence in Web-Era Journalism*. Paper Submitted to the 12th International Symposium for Online Journalism Austin, Texas, 2–3 April

news production operations.[1243] While they may take various forms,[1244] 'feed' aggregators such as Google News and Yahoo! News are the most common type. A feed aggregator 'contains material from a number of websites organized into various "feeds", typically arranged by source, topic, or story'.[1245] Feed aggregators usually 'display the headline of a story and, sometimes, the first few lines of the story's lede, with a link to where the rest of the story appears on the original website'.[1246] The business models of feed aggregators vary. For example, Google News is ad-free, whereas Yahoo! News is ad-based. In terms of use, while the majority of users still go directly to branded sites to read news,[1247] news aggregators are becoming a popular means of finding news online.[1248]

328. The emergence and increasing use of news aggregators has sparked a hot debate over how 'scraping' may affect news supply and consumption. Proponents claim that aggregators are beneficial to content providers in that they divert traffic to the original websites, thereby allowing them to reach new audiences and increase ad revenues.[1249] It is also said that even in cases where news aggregators do not divert traffic to the source, they may increase brand awareness, which 'may be more valuable to the producer than any resulting decrease in revenue'.[1250] Opponents, including especially news providers, claim that news aggregators do nothing but steal from media organizations that spend significant amounts of money to gather facts and report them. As Rupert Murdoch famously put it, 'producing journalism is expensive. We invest tremendous resources in our project from technology to our salaries. To aggregate stories is not fair use.[1251] To be impolite, it is theft' [footnote added].[1252] Since the audiences get all the information they need by reading the first few lines of the story, so the argument goes, they have no interest whatsoever in accessing the full text.[1253] However, the results of empirical research on the impact of aggregation

1243 Foster, R. (2012). *News Plurality in a Digital World – Report prepared for the Reuters Institute for the Study of Journalism*, 25

1244 Other categories are specialty aggregators, blog aggregators, and user-curated aggregators. For their definitions and the ways in which they operate see Isbell (2010,) *supra* n. 36, 2–5

1245 ibid, 2

1246 ibid.

1247 Reuters Institute (2017). *Digital News Report*, 14 <https://reutersinstitute.politics.ox.ac.uk/sites/default/files/Digital%20News%20Report%202017%20web_0.pdf?utm_source=digitalnewsreport.org&utm_medium=referral>

1248 See, for instance, Reuters Institute (2018). *Digital News Report 2018*, 13; and Ofcom (2013). *International Communications Market Report*, Figure 1.57.

1249 Lee, A. M. and Hsiang Iris Chyi (2015). *The Rise of Online News Aggregators: Consumption and Competition*. International Journal on Media Management, 17(1), 4

1250 McDonnell, J. C. (2012). *The Continuing Viability of the Hot News Misappropriation Doctrine in the Age of Internet News Aggregation*. Northwestern Journal of Technology and Intellectual Property, 10(3), 256

1251 Fair use is a term used in copyright law: if usage of third party content fulfills the conditions of fair use, the usage does not amount to a copyright infringement

1252 Bunz, M. *Rupert Murdoch: 'There's no such thing as a free news story'*. 1 December 2009, The Guardian. <http://www.theguardian.com/media/2009/dec/01/rupert-murdoch-no-free-news>

1253 See, for instance, European Press Publishers (2014). *Press Publishers' Response to Google's Third Commitments Proposal. European Commission's Competition Investigation of Google – AT.39740*, 10

on news providers are mixed. Some found that a significant proportion of online news consumers scan the headlines without clicking through to the original websites,[1254] whereas others found that news aggregators and traditional news media outlets are in a symbiotic, non-competitive relationship.[1255] Hence, the issue of whether news aggregation substitutes or complements news outlets is, at the time of writing, far from settled.

329. Prior to delving into the intricacies of competition law, I must underline that, while determining whether news aggregators are substitutes for or complements to news outlets is key to understanding how they may influence the future of news provision, the ways in which they may affect the demand side of the market, namely the readership, and media pluralism is a far more complex issue. On the one hand, those aggregators that license content from news agencies and produce their own news reports contribute to supply and content diversity. Moreover, to the extent that they facilitate and (one may say encourage) active multisourcing,[1256] they enhance exposure diversity. On the other hand, one may question whether news aggregators indeed engage the readership in a meaningful media experience. To put it bluntly, what makes the reader more knowledgeable? Scanning the ledes of the stories of ten different news outlets or reading the full story distributed by one single provider? And how do news aggregators, which facilitate news customization, affect one's vision of the world? Attention scarcity and content personalization and, more particularly, their possible effects on news consumption and media pluralism have been explored in Chapter 2[1257] and are undoubtedly worthy of further empirical research.

1254 See, for instance, Commission (2016). *Commission Staff Working Document – Impact Assessment on the modernisation of EU copyright rules*, Part 1, 157. <https://ec.europa.eu/digital-single-market/en/news/impact-assessment-modernisation-eu-copyright-rules>; and Wauters, R. *44% Of Google News Visitors Scan Headlines, Don't Click Through*. 19 January 2010, Techcrunch. <http://techcrunch.com/2010/01/19/outsell-google-news/> Two studies examined the effects of incorporating local news links to Google News on visits to local news outlets. The first study, conducted by Athey and Mobius, concluded that, while visits to local news outlets initially increase, they reduce over time and ultimately users rely on Google News exclusively to consume local news. See Athey, S. and Markus Mobius (2012). *The Impact of News Aggregators on Internet News Consumption: The Case of Localization*. Working Paper. <https://www.law.northwestern.edu/research-faculty/searlecenter/workingpapers/documents/Athey_Impact_News_Aggregators_on_Internet_News_Consumption.pdf> The second study, conducted by George, finds that total visits increase by less than 1% and that, as a result, adding local news links to Google News is unlikely to 'have an economically meaningful impact on local news outlets'. See George, L. (2013). *Local News Online: Aggregators, Geo-Targeting and the Market for Local News*, 27. Time Warner Cable Research Program on Digital Communications. Report Series Winter 2013. <http://www.twcresearchprogram.com/pdf/TWC_George_Report.pdf> Another study found that, while aggregators may expand the readership for some articles, they also reduce traffic to newspapers' home pages. See Jeon, Doh-Shin and Nikrooz Nasr (2016). *News Aggregators and Competition among Newspapers on the Internet*. American Economic Journal: Microeconomics 8(4), 91–114

1255 See, for instance, Lee and Hsiang (2015), *supra* n. 44; Yang, M. J., and Hsiang Iris Chyi (2011). *Competing with whom? Where? And why (not)? An empirical study of U.S. online newspapers' competition dynamics*. Journal of Media Business Studies 8(4), 59–74; Huang, J. S., Yang, M. J., and Hsiang Iris Chyi (2013). *Friend or foe? Examining the relationship between news portals and newspaper sites in Taiwan*. Chinese Journal of Communication 6(1), 103–119. For a different perspective of how the existence of a news aggregator may affect competition among newspapers see Esfahani, N. N. and Don-Shin Jeon (2013). *News Aggregators and Competition Among Newspapers in the Internet*. IDEI Working Paper, no. 770

1256 Foster (2012), *supra* n. 38, 25

1257 See Part 4.1.

3.1 News aggregation and EU competition law

330. From the outset, it bears noting that the practice of scraping raises both competition and copyright issues. Given the focus of this study on EU competition law, this section will explore the former (but without altogether ignoring the latter). Two remarks must be made here. First, at *EU* level, there are no statutory provisions for the copyright protection of headlines and small excerpts of news stories. The EU Copyright Directive imposes on Member States the obligation to harmonize their national laws for three types of works, namely computer programs, databases and photographs.[1258] As a result, the question of whether headlines and small excerpts are copyrightable is answered by the national legislator or judge, depending on the criteria that each Member State has set to determine whether a work is 'original' and thus deserving of protection. However, this is expected to change with the Directive on Copyright in the Digital Single Market, currently in the process of adoption: the Directive may establish Member States' obligation to grant press publishers (ancillary) copyright protection for the digital use of the articles they produce.[1259] Second, copyright law does not pre-empt EU competition law.[1260] It further goes without saying that EU competition rules prevail over national copyright laws.[1261]

331. This section will build around the above two issues from two different perspectives. First, irrespective of whether news outlets benefit from copyright protection in the Member State(s) where they operate (*irrespective* because action taken to cease a copyright infringement does not preclude action under EU competition law), and bearing in mind that the ability of news outlets to generate revenues is key to the production of high-quality investigative journalism, does EU competition law equip them with any tools to prevent aggregators from using their content? Second, bearing in mind that news aggregators may bring added value to the readership and assuming that headlines and small excerpts are protected by copyright, does EU competition law equip aggregators with any tools[1262] to force publishers to grant access to their content?

1258 Directive 2001/29/EC of the European Parliament and of the Council of 22 May 2001 on the harmonization of certain aspects of copyright and related rights in the information society [2001] OJ L167/10, Articles 1.3, 3.1. and 6

1259 See Proposal for a Directive of the European Parliament and of the Council on copyright in the Digital Single Market COM/2016/0593 final, Article 11. The proposal is available at: <https://eur-lex.europa.eu/legal-content/en/ALL/?uri=CELEX:52016PC0593>

1260 Our approach would not be different even if one accepted that the Infopaq judgment has such far-reaching effects that it extends the copyright protection afforded under the EU Copyright Directive to newspaper articles. See ECJ, Case C-5/08 *Infopaq International A/S v Danske Dagblades Forening* [2009] ECR I-6569

1261 See, for instance, ECJ, Joined Cases C-241/91 P and C-242/91 P *Radio Telefis Eireann e Independent Televisión Publications Ltd. v Commission* [1995] ECR I-743, paragraph 28

1262 Note that, from a copyright law perspective, Article 5 of the Copyright Directive allows Member States to provide for exceptions or limitations to the rights enshrined in Articles 2 and 3 the Directive. The derogation laid down in Article 5(3)(c) seems at first sight relevant here. This provision reads as follows: '[the Member State may exempt] reproduction by the press, communication to the public or making available of published articles on current economic, political or religious topics or of broadcast works or other subject-matter of the same character, in cases where such use is not expressly reserved, and as long as

3.1.1 Can EU competition law help publishers prevent news aggregators from scraping their content?

332. The question that seeks an answer here is whether a news aggregator which uses the headlines and the first few lines of a news story without remunerating the undertaking that produced the story in question violates EU competition law. To my knowledge, no case with comparable facts has fallen under the EU antitrust microscope thus far. In certain States in the US, cases brought by news publishers that allege that a firm has engaged in anti-competitive behavior by copying their content without their permission have been dealt with under the Hot News Misappropriation doctrine. The Hot News Misappropriation doctrine emerged as early as 1918 in *International News Service v Associated Press*, a judgment rendered by the US Supreme Court.[1263] International News Service (INS) and the Associated Press (AP), two organizations consisting of newspapers published throughout the United States, were competing 'in the gathering and distribution of news and its publication for profit'.[1264] INS bribed employees of AP members to furnish news prior to publication and copy news from early editions of AP newspapers which it would subsequently sell, either bodily or after rewriting it.[1265] Interestingly, the Court noted that it would 'spend no time' upon the question of application of the Copyright Act on the grounds that the case turned upon 'the question of what is unfair competition business'.[1266] This latter question, the Court said, should be answered with due regard to the nature and conditions of the business concerned.[1267] The Court held that AP gathered news at the cost of 'organization, skill, labor, and money'[1268] and that, unless it benefited from a 'quasi-property right in the results of its enterprise as against a rival in the same business',[1269] it would no longer have the incentive to offer this 'extremely useful' service to the readers.[1270] Based on the above, the Court ruled that INS's practices harmed AP's business 'precisely at the point where the profit [was] to be reaped, in order to divert a material portion of the profit from those who have earned it to those

---

the source, including the author's name, is indicated, or use of works or other subject-matter in connection with the reporting of current events, to the extent justified by the informatory purpose and as long as the source, including the author's name, is indicated, unless this turns out to be impossible'. However, this is not a powerful tool in the hands of news aggregators, not least because in several Member States, reproduction under the provisions implementing Article 5(3)(c) is allowed only by 'the press', that is, newspapers or other 'similar' media organizations. For more on this issue see Xalabarder, R. (2011). *Google News and Copyright*. In Lopez-Tarruella, A. (ed.). *Google and the Law: Empirical Approaches to Legal Aspects of Knowledge-Economy Business Models*. The Hague: T.M.C. Asser Press, 145

1263 *International News Service v Associated Press*, 248 U.S. 215 (1918)

1264 ibid, 229

1265 ibid, 234–236

1266 ibid, 236

1267 ibid, 248

1268 ibid.

1269 ibid, 234

1270 ibid, 235

who have not'.[1271] The Hot News Misappropriation has been endorsed by five States thus far, where it forms part of unfair competition law.[1272] Courts in these States have expanded the doctrine and further elaborated upon the conditions for its application.[1273] In the leading judgment, *National Basketball Association v Motorola*,[1274] which concerned a complaint brought by the National Basketball Association (NBA) against Motorola for selling a paging device that supplied 'real-time' NBA scores,[1275] the Second Circuit laid down the following five conditions under which the doctrine may apply:

> i) a plaintiff *generates or gathers information at a cost*;
>
> (ii) the information is *time-sensitive*;
>
> (iii) a defendant's use of the information constitutes *free-riding* on the plaintiff's efforts;
>
> (iv) the defendant is *in direct competition* with a product or service offered by the plaintiffs; and
>
> (v) the ability of other parties to free-ride on the efforts of the plaintiff or others would so *reduce the incentive* to produce the product or service that its existence or quality would be substantially threatened [emphasis added].[1276]

333. In the US, the rise and increasing popularity of news aggregators have prompted a feverish debate over whether the Hot News Misappropriation tort, as exemplified by *NBA*, should also cover their activities.[1277] At the time of writing, views are polarized and, while proposals have been put forward to federalize the tort,[1278] Congress has not taken any relevant initiative so far.

334. Given the lack of any relevant case law in the EU, could the elements set out in *NBA* draw from EU competition law principles, thereby providing news

1271 ibid, 240

1272 These States are: New York, Pennsylvania, Missouri, California, and Illinois. See McDonnell (2012), *supra* n. 45, 256 and 262. On the hot news misappropriation doctrine and the relevant US case law see also Rosenfeld, S. (2014). *How Far Will News Organizations Go to Take the 'Lede?' Hot News Misappropriation in the Digital Age*. Berkeley Journal of Entertainment and Sports Law, 3(1), 86–92; Montgomery, S. W. (2012). *Extra!! Extra!!: The Viability of the Hot News Misappropriation Claim Is in Jeopardy*. Loyola L.A. Entertainment Law Review 32, 365-398; Schmidt, E. P. (2011). *Hot News Misappropriation in the Internet Age*. Journal on Telecommunications and High Technology Law, 9, 313–343; Beaton, G. D. (2012). *The Cold Reality of the Ineffective Hot News Remedy, and the Case for Contract*. Columbia Law Review, 112, 2068–2109

1273 McDonnell (2012), *supra* n. 45, 260

1274 *National Basketball Association v Motorola, Inc*, 105 F.3d 841, 41 U.S.P.Q.2d (BNA) 1585 (2d Cir. 1997)

1275 ibid, paragraphs 2 and 5

1276 ibid, paragraph 16

1277 On developments in recent case law and relevant literature see *supra* n. 67

1278 See, for instance, McDonnell (2012), *supra* n. 45, 273 referring to Deutsch, A. L. (2010). *Protecting News in the Digital Era: The Case for a Federalized Hot News Misappropriation Tort*. In Advanced Seminar on Copyright Law, PLI Patents, Copyrights, Trademarks, & Literary Prop., Course Handbook Series No. 1003, 2010, 511

outlets active in the EU with a means to impede aggregators from scraping their content? For the avoidance of confusion, I am not suggesting importing the *NBA* test into EU competition law as such. Because the facts in *NBA* and the Google case are very similar, the criteria the Second Circuit established in this judgment may serve as useful indicators; the test would still need to be adapted to the standards set by EU competition law.

335. We should start our analysis by noting that in the US a news provider may invoke violations under Hot News Misappropriation without the defendant enjoying 'monopoly power'.[1279] In EU competition law, however, the only provision that may apply to a case with comparable facts is Article 102 TFEU. Hence, in addition to any evidence supporting their complaint that an abuse has taken place, news providers would need to demonstrate that a news aggregator such as Google News is in a dominant position in the affected market. At EU level, decisional practice does not shed light on this or closely related issues because, as already discussed in Chapter 3, the Commission has more often than not refrained from completing the market definition exercise in decisions concerning news provision.[1280] National courts have not been particularly helpful either. For example, in *Copiepresse*, which dealt with, *inter alia*, the legitimacy of the use by Google News of snippets of articles produced by French and German-speaking Belgian publishers, the Brussels Appeal Court refused to '[dwell] on the twists and turns on competition law, notably … market definition'.[1281] As explained in detail in Chapter 3, this approach may jeopardize the accuracy of the decision, adversely affecting both competition and media pluralism. In the case at hand, from a statement the Commission made on, *inter alia*, the scraping allegations, it may be inferred that it is inclined to think that Google News and online news websites are competitors.[1282] However, as will be seen below, this is not so straightforward. Hence, were a commitments decision to be adopted (i.e. a decision where the Commission would not need to conduct a full-fledged market definition analysis), remedies may penalize Google News without good reason, possibly to the detriment of innovation and consumer choice. It further bears noting that in this particular area, an additional problem arises, that of establishing that a copyright infringement has taken place. For example, in *Copiepresse*, the Court held that reading the headlines and the first few lines of a news story removed readers' incentive to click through to the original websites,[1283] without, however, basing this finding on any evidence.[1284] Having assumed

1279 This would be the equivalent of 'dominance' under Article 102 TFEU. See Sherman Act 15 U.S.C. § 2 (2000)

1280 Chapter 3, Part 4.2.

1281 Court of Appeal of Brussels, *Google Inc v Copiepresse*. R. No. 2011/2999, No. 817, paragraph 62

1282 Commission (2013, April), *supra* n. 26: 'Google uses on its own specialized search services original material taken from the websites of its competitors.'

1283 Court of Appeal of Brussels, *Google Inc v Copiepresse*. R. No. 2011/2999, No. 817, paragraph 28

1284 Docquir, P. F. and Bart Van Besien (2014). *Changing Conditions of Competition for Public Service and*

that Google News was a substitute for rather than a complement to the websites of news providers, the Court concluded that the use by Google News of headlines and excerpts could not be regarded as 'reproduction for legitimate purposes', thereby falling foul of copyright law.[1285] Refraining from defining the market(s) affected by Google News' practices may have led to an erroneous finding.[1286] The Court was, arguably correctly, criticized on this point.[1287]

336. A recent Commission decision where the substitution dynamics in today's news markets were considered (but not discussed in detail) is *News Corp/BSkyB*.[1288] While not dealing with news aggregation, the brief analysis the Commission conducted raises some issues that are relevant here. For example, News Corp submitted that the relevant product market is the market for the supply of print newspapers *and* online news services.[1289] More particularly, News Corp argued that print titles face significant competitive constraints from branded websites, including websites of established broadcasters such as the BBC, Internet portals such as Yahoo!, search engines and blogs.[1290] In *News Corp/BSkyB*, it was further mentioned that whether or not the provider charges for news might play a pivotal role in assessing demand-side substitutability. If so, print newspapers may be interchangeable with online paid-for services,[1291] but not with online news content offered for free. The issue of whether online news provision is an alternative to print titles is still unresolved. While regulatory authorities have occasionally treated off- and online news as complements rather than substitutes,[1292] empirical research has produced mixed outcomes.[1293] As regards the distinction between paid-for and

---

Commercial Media in Belgium: Implications for Media Independence. In Psychogiopoulou, E. *Media Policies Revisited. The Challenge for Media Freedom and Independence*. London: Palgrave Macmillan, 154

1285 Court of Appeal of Brussels, *Google Inc. v Copiepresse*. R. No. 2011/2999, No. 817, paragraphs 27–29 and 44

1286 This example illustrates another function that EU competition law may perform: tools used to assess demand-side substitutability may also inform an analysis under IP law.

1287 See, for instance, Xalabarder (2011), *supra* n. 57, 160

1288 *News Corp/BSkyB* (Case COMP/M.5932) [2011] C 37/2. See also *Fox/Sky* (Case M.8354) [2017] OJ 238/1, paragraphs 129–133

1289 *News Corp/BSkyB* (Case COMP/M.5932) [2011] C 37/2, paragraph 207

1290 ibid, paragraph 209

1291 ibid, paragraph 211

1292 See, for instance, Ofcom (2012b). *Measuring Media Plurality*, paragraph 4.3.: 'TV, Radio, Newspapers, Online should not be seen as direct substitutes; rather, they complement each other in many ways', and FCC – Waldman, S. and the Working Group on Information Needs of Communities (2011). *The Information Needs of Communities. The changing media landscape in a broadband age*: '[i]t may be premature to give a full-throated endorsement to new media platforms as a substitute for traditional media'. <http://www.fcc.gov/info-needs-communities>

1293 See, for instance, Gentzkow, M. (2007). *Valuing New Goods in a Model with Complementarity: Online Newspapers*. The American Economic Review 97(3), 713–744; De Waal, E., Klaus Schönbach and Edmund Lauf (2005). *Online newspapers: A substitute or complement for print newspapers and other information channels?* Communications: The European Journal of Communication Research 30, 55–72; Filistrucchi, L. (2005). *The Impact of Internet on the Market for Daily Newspapers in Italy*. EUI Working Paper ECO No. 2005/12. <http://cadmus.eui.eu/bitstream/handle/1814/3353/ECO2005-12.pdf>; Kaiser, U. and Hans Christian Kongsted (2005). *Do Magazine's 'Companion Websites' Cannibalize the Demand for the Print Version?* Centre for Applied Microeconometrics – Institute of Economics University of Copenhagen Working Paper 2005–07. <http://ftp.zew.de/pub/zew-docs/dp/dp0549.pdf>

free news content, in the past, the Commission found that national dailies and free newspapers belong to separate markets.[1294] This distinction may be relevant in the online world. As already seen in Chapter 5, given the amount of information that is currently available online for free, users are not willing to pay for content.[1295] Of course, reaching conclusions on the above issues depends on a number of factors (Internet penetration and use, demographics, news consumption habits in the relevant market, etc.). Any decision would therefore require a fact-intensive analysis that takes account of the particularities of the market(s) under scrutiny. However, if we indeed define the market as broadly as suggested in *News Corp/BSkyB* (market for the supply of news or market for paid-for v market for free news content), Google News is unlikely to be found dominant.

337. But, one might also ask whether there is a distinct market for news consumers' attention, that is, a market for the supply of content (headlines and small excerpts) that attracts users to one website or another.[1296] This should not be excluded. In Chapter 4, I illustrated why in cases where the consumer pays with her attention in order to access a content platform, a market for audiences may need to be defined for antitrust purposes. This is where the third condition set in *NBA*, namely that the firm misappropriating the content is in direct competition with news outlets, comes in. If we indeed identify a market for news consumers' attention, then Google News and news providers could be competing. If so, Google News could be found to possess the market power required to trigger the application of Article 102 TFEU.

338. The first and second conditions imposed in *NBA* (information is gathered at a cost and news is time-sensitive) are both fairly easy to fulfill and reflect factors that have long been taken into account in EU competition law assessments. As regards the first, the Commission's Guidance Paper on the application of Article 102 TFEU lays down that the existence of high barriers to entry is a parameter for assessing the foreclosure effects that the conduct of the dominant firm may generate.[1297] As discussed in detail in Chapter 2, the production of news content, which involves exceptionally high news-gathering costs, labor costs, etc.,[1298] is a rather expensive undertaking. With respect to the second condition, the Guidance Paper also lays down that, in examining foreclosure effects, the Commission will take into account the conditions of

1294 See, for instance *Newspaper Publishing* (Case IV/M.423) [1994] OJ C 85/5, paragraph 17; and *Recoletos/Unedisa* (Case IV/M.1401) [1999] OJ C 73/6, paragraph 29

1295 Joint Research Centre (2012), *supra* n. 34, 6

1296 Note that this has been logic has been applied to cases concerning copyright infringements. See, for instance, *Harper & Row, Publishers, Inc v Nation Enters* 471 U.S. 539, 564–65 (1985)

1297 Guidance on the Commission's enforcement priorities in applying Article 82 of the EC Treaty to abusive exclusionary conduct by dominant undertakings [2009] OJ C 45/2, paragraphs 16–17 and 20

1298 Norton, S. W. and Will Norton Jr. (1986). *Economies of Scale and the New Technology of Daily Newspapers: A Survivor Analysis*. University of Nebraska – Lincoln College of Journalism & Mass Communications, Working Paper 6

the market affected by the conduct concerned. Applied to the newspaper industry, an argument echoing the US Supreme Court's approach in *INS* could be raised here; news has a short life cycle and a dominant news aggregator may harm competition to the extent that it negatively impacts a news provider's 'legitimate business precisely at the point where the profit is to be reaped'.[1299] In Chapter 5, where I discussed the highly perishable nature of newspapers, I referred to cases indicating that the Commission and the Court were largely sympathetic to this particularity of news markets.[1300]

339. Fulfillment of the final two criteria, namely free-riding on the competitors' efforts and reduction or elimination of the incentive to compete as a result of the unlawful conduct, could, under certain conditions, support the claim that Google News has abused its position. In the EU, free-riding as behavior that raises anti-competitive concerns has mostly been dealt with in the literature regarding vertical restraints. For example, advocates of Resale Price Maintenance (RPM) contend that the obligation to sell at a retail price set by the manufacturer eliminates the risk of free-riding on a distributor's investments to improve quality of service.[1301] In a similar vein, proponents of Most-Favored-Nation clauses (MFNs) maintain that MFNs encourage a distributor to make the contract-specific investment required to penetrate a risky (downstream) market because it provides it with some certainty that the manufacturer will not free-ride on its efforts by offering subsequent entrants better deals in order to expand its distribution network.[1302] In explaining under what conditions a restraint may fulfill the 'indispensability' condition under Article 101(3) TFEU, the Commission Guidelines give an example of an exclusive distribution agreement between a manufacturer and a distributor that undertakes, *inter alia*, to advertise the product, survey consumers and ensure quick delivery.[1303] The Commission notes that a ban on active sales preventing other firms from selling into the territory of the distributor could be regarded as indispensable on the grounds that the latter would lack the motivation to

1299 *International News Service v Associated Press*, 240 U.S. 215 (1918)

1300 See Commission Notice pursuant to Article 19(3) of Regulation No. 17 concerning Case IV/31.609 *Agence et Messageries de la Presse* [1987] OJ C 164/02; and ECJ, Case 243/83 *SA Binon & Cie v SA Agence et messageries de la presse* [1985] ECR 2015

1301 See, for instance, Petit, N. and David Henry (2010). *Vertical Restraints under EU Competition Law: Conceptual Foundations and Practical Framework*. SSRN Working Paper, 9–10. <http://papers.ssrn.com/sol3/papers.cfm?abstract_id=1724891>; Peepercorn, L. (2008). *Resale price maintenance and its alleged efficiencies*. European Competition Journal 4(1), 201–212; Elzinga, K. G. and David E. Mills (2010). *Leegin and Procompetitive Resale Price Maintenance*. The Antitrust Bulletin 55(2), 349–379. SSRN Working paper. <https://papers.ssrn.com/sol3/papers.cfm?abstract_id=1885001>; Gippini-Fournier, E. (2010). *Resale Price Maintenance in the EU: in statu quo ante bellum?* SSRN Working Paper, 15. <http://papers.ssrn.com/sol3/papers.cfm?abstract_id=1476443> Also available in Hawk, B. (ed.). *Annual Proceedings of the 36th Annual Conference on International Antitrust Law and Policy – Fordham Corporate Law Institute*. Huntington, NY: Juris Publishing

1302 See Vanderborre, I. and Michael J. Frese (2014). *Most Favored Nation Clauses Revisited*. European Competition Law Review 12, 589, and Baker, J. B. and Judith A. Chevalier (2013). *The Competitive Consequences of Most-Favored-Nation Provisions*. Antitrust Magazine 27(2), 20–21

1303 Commission Guidelines on the Application of Article 101(3) TFEU [2004] OJ C 101/08, paragraph 82

sell the product if other firms could free-ride on its investments.[1304] As regards the relationship between unilateral conduct and free-riding, Article 102 TFEU has occasionally been applied in a way that favored the *competitors* of the dominant firm rather than *competition* as a value in itself. I mentioned in Chapter 3 that in the late 1980s and early 1990s the Commission adopted a broad definition of the term 'abusive refusal to supply' whereby companies which held significant market power and which refused to grant access to an input they controlled were almost axiomatically deemed to act in violation of Article 102 TFEU.[1305] This approach, which mainly aimed to liberalize former State monopolies,[1306] was subsequently modified and stricter tests introduced that limit the scope of Article 102 TFEU.[1307] Yet, while the approach to complaints alleging abuses of dominance has undoubtedly gradually become more stringent, Petit and Neyrinck make a convincing case that, even in more recent case law such as *Microsoft*, Article 102 TFEU was instrumentalized in order to put competitors on a par with a dominant firm that possessed a valuable input, allowing competitors to free-ride to some extent on the dominant firm's efforts.[1308] Indeed, the Court has interpreted Microsoft's refusal to supply rather flexibly, enabling competitors to be granted access to the input to which they sought access, namely interoperability information.[1309]

340. Adapting the above to the case at hand, we should first say that the thread joining the theories in favor of introducing restraints that seek to address this type of conduct is the concern that, absent the restraint, the incentive to penetrate a market, invest in risky projects, etc. would be significantly reduced or altogether eliminated.[1310] Similar remarks can be made with respect to the logic underpinning the decisional practice in cases of abuse of dominance. For example, as will be seen in greater detail below (Part 5), in *Microsoft*, the Commission has sought to ensure that the dominant firm's incentive to innovate would be preserved (Microsoft was not required to disclose source code

---

1304 ibid.

1305 See, for instance, *Sealink/B&I-Holyhead* [1992] 5 CMLR 255

1306 For more information on this issue see, for instance, van den Bergh, R. and Peter Camesasca (2006). *European Competition Law and Economics – A Comparative Perspective*, 274–6. Antwerpen, Groningen, Oxford: Intersentia-Hart Publishing

1307 See, for instance, Case T-504/93 *Tiercé Ladbroke SA v Commission* [1997] ECR II-923; Case C-7/97 *Oscar Bronner GmbH & Co. KG v Mediaprint Zeitungs- und Zeitschriftenverlag GmbH & Co. and others* [1998] ECR I-7791; Joined cases T- 374/1994, T-375/1994, T-384/1994 and T-388/1994 *European Night Services and others v Commission of the European Communities* [1998] ECR II-3141

1308 Petit, N. and Norman Neyrinck (2011). *Droit de la Concurrence et Instrumentalisation Parasitaire*. Working Paper. Institut d'Etudes Juridiques Européennes, Université de Liège, 10–16 <http://orbi.ulg.ac.be/handle/2268/98911>

1309 CFI, Case T-201/04 *Microsoft Corp. v Commission of the European Communities* [2007] ECR II-03601, paragraphs 630 *et seq*. For a critical view on the Commission's approach in the Microsoft case see Jones, A. and Brenda Sufrin (2008). *EU Competition Law – Texts, Cases and Materials* (3rd Edition). Oxford: OUP, 571–574

1310 See, for instance, Commission Guidelines on the Application of Article 101(3) TFEU [2004] OJ C 101/08, paragraph 82; Vanderborre and Frese (2014), *supra* n. 97, 589; Baker and Chevalier (2013), *supra* n. 97, 20; and Orbach, B. Y. (2008). *Antitrust Vertical Myopia: The Allure of High Prices*. Arizona Law Review 50, 276

but interoperability information, which is a less invasive alternative).[1311] To ensure consistency with economic theory and the relevant case law, Google's free-riding could be regarded as abusive *if* it reduced or eliminated the incentive of newspapers to gather and report news. Here, one would need to check whether readers indeed replace news outlets with Google News, thereby potentially depriving the former of the ability to generate revenues. It bears noting that in the FTC proceedings, this issue created considerable tension between the Commissioners because, from the evidence submitted, it could be inferred that scraping *favored* rather than harmed websites competing with Google. For example, in his (dissenting) statement, Commissioner Rosch noted that 'the investigation revealed that the alleged "victims" of Google's scraping were *not* injured: overall traffic to the alleged victims increased substantially while the alleged scraping was occurring and traffic to these websites from Google grew at an even faster rate.'[1312] Google ultimately committed to refrain from scraping third-party content,[1313] but, if the relevant data indeed lent support to Google's argument that no harm was done to competitors, it is questioned whether the FTC followed the right approach to this issue.

341. The above analysis shows that, provided that Google News holds a dominant position in the affected market, news providers could bring a complaint under Article 102 TFEU. However, a decision dealing with whether scraping amounts to an abuse should be based on proof demonstrating that copying and displaying snippets has indeed diverted traffic away from the publishers' websites on to the aggregating platform. In the absence of relevant evidence, the Commission would commit an error to punish a firm which a) has not harmed the complainants, and b) possibly brings added value to the readership.

3.1.2 Can publishers be forced to grant access to their content under EU competition law?

342. Assuming that news aggregators bring added value to the readership and that the headlines and small excerpts of a news story enjoy copyright protection, I shall also attempt to answer the flipside to the question posed above, that is, whether EU competition law equips news aggregators with any tools to force

---

1311 See *infra*, Part 5. On this issue see also Massadeh, A. A. (2011). *The Essential Facilities Doctrine Under Scrutiny: EU and US Perspective*. UEA Working Paper Series 2011-AM-1 (see in particular p. 20 *et seq.*)

1312 See Federal Trade Commission (2013c, January). *Concurring and Dissenting Statement of Commissioner J. Thomas Rosch Regarding Google's Search Practices In the Matter of Google Inc.* FTC File No. 111-0163. <https://www.ftc.gov/sites/default/files/documents/public_statements/concurring-and-dissenting-statement-commissioner-j.thomas-rosch-regarding-googles-search-practices/130103googlesearchstmt.pdf>; and Federal Trade Commission (2013d, January). *Statement of Commissioner Maureen K. Ohlhausen In the Matter of Google Inc.* FTC File No. 111-0163. <https://www.ftc.gov/sites/default/files/documents/public_statements/statement-commissioner-maureen-ohlhausen/130103googlesearchohlhausenstmt.pdf>.

1313 See Federal Trade Commission (2013b, January). *Statement of the Federal Trade Commission Regarding Google's Search Practices In the Matter of Google Inc. FTC File Number 111-0163*, fn. 2. <https://www.ftc.gov/system/files/documents/public_statements/295971/130103googlesearchstmtofcomm.pdf>.

news outlets to license their content. As already indicated above, the issue of whether snippets of news articles are indeed copyrightable is still unsettled across the EU. Court rulings and recent legislative action in a handful of Member States suggest a tendency toward granting news publishers benefits of copyright protection[1314] whereas the Directive on copyright in the Digital Single Market is highly likely to establish the Member States' obligation to grant press publishers ancillary copyright protection for the digital use of their articles.[1315] Whether news scraping should qualify as a copyright infringement falls outside the scope of this study. Suffice it to say that granting news outlets exclusivity over snippets of articles which they produced and which are publicly available on the Internet has generated much controversy. Many have argued that snippets are not worthy of copyright protection and that the public authorities' move to regulate this area was an ill-founded attempt to milk profitable US companies[1316] that stretched the boundaries of IP law in an excessive manner.[1317] Hence, the below analysis is based on a premise that represents a recent trend that has emerged in copyright law across the EU, but this should not be understood to mean that the headline and the first few lines of the lede of a news story should enjoy copyright protection.

343. For our purposes, we assume that all or the vast majority of news outlets that produce the content to which access is sought jointly decide to refuse to supply Google News. In other words, we assume that news outlets enjoy a collective dominant position which is, *inter alia*, determined by whether a group of undertakings 'adopt the same conduct on the market' concerned.[1318] Albeit outside the boundaries of the EU, this has happened. In Brazil, newspapers collectively decided to opt out of Google News.[1319]

1314 See, for instance, Court of Appeal of Brussels, *Google Inc v Copiepresse* R. No. 2011/2999, No. 817, 52–55; *supra* n. 54; and *infra* ns. 124 and 127.

1315 See Proposal for a Directive of the European Parliament and of the Council on copyright in the Digital Single Market COM/2016/0593 final, Article 11.

1316 See, for instance, Ibáñez Colomo, P. *The Spanish Google tax, or (twice) the perfect cartel*. 19 March 2014, Chillin' Competition. <http://chillingcompetition.com/2014/03/19/the-spanish-google-tax-or-twice-the-perfect-cartel/>.

1317 See, for instance, Rosati, E. *Fordham Focus 9: News Aggregators and Fair Use*. 5 April 2013, The IPKat. <http://ipkitten.blogspot.it/2013/04/fordham-focus-9-news-aggregators-and.html> Another case with a similar factual background is *NMPP v Conseil de la Concurrence*, which concerned the refusal of NMPP, the largest press distributor in France, to grant access to its software system and database. The Cour de Cassation annulled a judgment of the Paris Court of Appeals that had upheld the decision of the Conseil de la Concurrence which ordered NMPP (in the context of interim proceedings) to offer access to its system. NMPP's competitor had successfully argued before the Conseil de la Concurrence that, although it had at its disposal the necessary resources to design software with characteristics similar to those of NMPP, NMPP's software had become the industry 'standard'. See Conseil de la Concurrence Decision n. 03-MC-04 of 22 December 2003, *Messageries Lyonnaises de Presse*; and Cour de Cassation, Judgment of 12 February 2004, *NMPP v Conseil de la Concurrence*, BOCCRF n. 5 of 4 May 2004. For a brief analysis of this case see Georges, A. and Matteo F. Bay (2005). *Essential Facilities: A Doctrine Clearly in Need of Limiting Principles?* Intellectual Property & Technology Law Jour 17(12), 1–4.

1318 See ECJ, Case C-393/92 *Municipality of Almelo and others v NV Energiebedrijf Ijsselmij* [1994] ECR I-01477. For a comprehensive overview of the case law on collective dominance see Jones and Sufrin (2008), *supra* n. 104, 918–935

1319 Fraga, I. *Brazilian newspapers leave Google News en masse*. 22 October 2012, Knight Center for Journalism in the Americas. <https://knightcenter.utexas.edu/blog/00-11841-newspapers-say-their-boycott-turned-google-news-"deficient"-brazil-reiterate-request-p> I adopt this approach because saying that

344. Delineating the boundaries of the relevant market is, once again, key to answering the question at hand. Pursuant to the refusal to supply line of case law,[1320] if news outlets and news aggregators operate in the same market, news outlets may not be forced to license their content. In *Volvo*,[1321] for example, which concerned the refusal by the proprietor of a design right covering car body panels to license third parties to sell products incorporating the protected design, the Court ruled that in the *primary* market for which a dominant undertaking has a monopoly owing to its own IP, the exclusive right to produce or sell should be fully respected.[1322] As already discussed above, the issue of whether news aggregators compete with news outlets is still unsettled *and* dependent on the approach to market definition the Commission would adopt in such cases. If news aggregators and news outlets were found to operate in separate markets, the latter could, under certain conditions, be required to license their content. These conditions were dealt with in *Magill*, which concerned the refusal of three Irish broadcasters to license their program listings to a weekly TV guide.[1323] In *Magill*, the Court held that, unless there is an objective justification for the refusal (note that the mere possession of an IPR is not an objective justification for exclusionary behavior[1324]), the dominant company must provide access to its input if the refusal prevents the creation of a new product and results in excluding potential competition in the secondary market.[1325] A broad interpretation of the above criteria could lead to the conclusion that news aggregators requesting access to content produced by news outlets may pass the *Magill* test. A news aggregator such as Google News may qualify as a 'new product'. As opposed to a news outlet's website, Google News does not host the full text of the articles it aggregates[1326] and does not display the content of one source only. Moreover, news aggregators and news outlets may fulfill different needs of the readership. For example, a study found that online news consumers use aggregators 'in apolitical ways'; in other words, they do not want to read opinionated news when they access a news aggregation platform.[1327] This is in sharp contrast to consumption of traditional titles which, as already seen, is often driven by political

a single news outlet should be obliged to license snippets on the grounds that its content is, pursuant to the relevant case law, 'indispensable' for the operation of an aggregation platform would arguably be a stretch

1320 See, for instance, Case T-504/93 *Tiercé Ladbroke SA v Commission* [1997] ECR II-923; Case C-7/97 *Oscar Bronner GmbH & Co. KG v Mediaprint Zeitungs- und Zeitschriftenverlag GmbH & Co. and others* [1998] ECR I-7791; and Joined Cases C-241/91 P and C-242/91 P *Radio Telefis Eireann (RTE) and Independent Television Publications Ltd. v Commission* [1995] ECR I-743

1321 ECJ, Case 238/87 *Volvo v Veng (UK)* [1988] ECR 6211

1322 ibid, paragraph 8

1323 ECJ, Joined Cases C-241/91 P and C-242/91 P *Radio Telefis Eireann (RTE) and Independent Television Publications Ltd. v Commission* [1995] ECR I-743

1324 Examples of acceptable justifications include poor creditworthiness and safety. See Anderman, S. and Hedvig Schmidt (2011). *EU Competition Law and Intellectual Property Rights – The Regulation of Innovation* (Second Edition). Oxford: OUP, 104

1325 *supra* n. 118, paragraphs 54–56

1326 For differences among news aggregators see Huang, Yang, and Hsiang (2013), *supra* n. 50, 4

1327 Lee and Hsiang (2015), *supra* n. 44, 18. Note that this parameter could also inform market definition.

preferences.[1328] And finally, assuming that news aggregators operate in a separate market, a refusal to supply would exclude downstream competition since the alternative (creating an x amount of news outlets to aggregate their content) would not only seem unfeasible but also invalidate the *raison d'être* of the service, that is, the aggregation of content provided by numerous news sources covering a wide variety of topics.

345. From a practical perspective, however, one may question whether establishing the duty to license will produce positive results. There is worrying evidence to suggest that this duty may create more problems than it solves. One way of testing this is to check what happened in cases where a licensing mechanism was established by means of regulation. For example, the Spanish legislator introduced a law requiring news aggregators to pay (through AEDE, the Asociación de Editores de Diarios Españoles) news outlets a fee for the use of their content.[1329] An important aspect of this law is that news outlets may not opt out of the regime, that is, they are not allowed to offer their content for free.[1330] Google exited the market shortly after the law was adopted and traffic to the news outlets' websites was reportedly subsequently reduced by 10–15%.[1331] In Germany, a similar law was introduced in 2013 which apparently also has been far from a success story; publishers reportedly voluntarily relinquished their right to payment from Google *only*.[1332] In this scenario, the obligation to license in effect burdens smaller aggregators, thus impeding the development of a competitive news market.

346. A different path was followed in Belgium and France, where the cases concerning scraping by Google News were settled before regulatory plans materialized. For example, in Belgium, a partnership was established whereby Google committed to contribute to the publishers' efforts to generate revenues via its various advertising services (Google Ads, AdSense, AdExchange), to increase

1328 See, for instance, Chapter 3, Part 4.2.

1329 Ley 21/2014, de 4 de noviembre, por la que se modifica el texto refundido de la Ley de Propiedad Intelectual, aprobado por Real Decreto Legislativo 1/1996, de 12 de abril, y la Ley 1/2000, de 7 de enero, de Enjuiciamiento Civil. [2014] BOE Núm. 268 Sec. I. Pág. 90404. <http://www.boe.es/boe/dias/2014/11/05/pdfs/BOE-A-2014-11404.pdf>

1330 ibid, Article 32(2), which reads as follows: 'La puesta a disposición del público por parte de prestadores de servicios electrónicos de agregación de contenidos de fragmentos no significativos de contenidos, divulgados en publicaciones periódicas o en sitios Web de actualización periódica y que tengan una finalidad informativa, de creación de opinión pública o de entretenimiento, no requerirá autorización, sin perjuicio del derecho del editor o, en su caso, de otros titulares de derechos a percibir una compensación equitativa. *Este derecho será irrenunciable* y se hará efectivo a través de las entidades de gestión de los derechos de propiedad intelectual' [emphasis added]. On this issue see also García, R. R. *Google News solo volverá a España si la tasa por contenidos es voluntaria*. 12 December 2014, La Voz de Galicia. <http://www.lavozdegalicia.es/noticia/vidadigital/2014/12/12/google-news-solo-volvera-espana-tasa-contenidos-voluntaria/0003_201412G12P61991.htm>

1331 D'Elia, D. *Google News Spagna Chiude? Traffico in Calo del 15%*. 17 December 2014, Tom's Hardware. <http://www.tomshw.it/news/google-news-spagna-chiude-traffico-in-calo-del-15-63176>

1332 Malcolm, J. *Google News Shuttered in Spain Thanks to 'Ancillary Copyright' Law*. 10 December 2014, Electronic Frontiers Foundation. <https://www.eff.org/deeplinks/2014/12/google-news-shuts-shop-spain-thanks-ancillary-copyright-law>; and Reda, J. *An EU-wide 'Google Tax' in the Making?* 28 December 2014, juliareda.eu. <https://juliareda.eu/2014/10/an-eu-wide-google-tax-in-the-making/>

the accessibility of the publishers' content through mobile platforms, and to promote reader engagement through Google's social tools such as Google+ and YouTube.[1333] In France, Google made a hefty contribution to a special fund in order to assist the French media with increasing their presence on the Internet.[1334] While it is probably too soon to say whether and, if so, to what extent such initiatives will positively affect the future of news provision, these may be more appropriate than an obligation to license irrespective of whether the latter is imposed as a result of competition law proceedings or by means of regulation.

3.2 The remedies Google proposed to address the Commission's concerns regarding scraping: going too far?

347. We now turn to the assessment of the remedies proposed by Google in the pending antitrust case. In the document outlining the remedies concerned, Google undertook to provide publishers with a technical solution to prevent the display of *snippets* of their articles on Google News, but without preventing the display of *links* to the articles on Google News, and to specify on a webpage-by-webpage basis a particular date by when certain articles should no longer be displayed on Google News.[1335]

348. As regards the first proposal,[1336] one cannot help but wonder whether the remedy is going too far. From a competition perspective, in view of the remarks that were made above regarding the uncertainty surrounding the impact of news aggregation on the original websites, preventing the display of snippets may harm both Google News *and* the publishers. The doubts that were raised by FTC Commissioner Rosch are illustrative in this regard. From a media pluralism perspective, if the small excerpts indeed encourage the user to click through, then 'dry' links to articles may eventually drive consumers to consult the few branded websites they have always consulted. In other words, display of links *only* may ultimately result in discouraging users from discovering alternative sources of information.

349. The second commitment has to do with caching. Caching refers to the 'copying and storing of data from a webpage on a server's hard disk so that the page can be quickly retrieved by the same or a different user the next time that page

---

1333 Google (2012b, December). *Partnering with Belgian news publishers.* <http://googlepolicyeurope.blogspot.it/2012/12/partnering-with-belgian-news-publishers.html>

1334 Kelly, A. *Google to pay 60 million euros into French media fund.* 8 January 2013, Reuters. <http://www.reuters.com/article/2013/02/01/us-france-google-idUSBRE91011Z20130201>

1335 Google (2014, January). *Commitments in Case COMP/C-3/39.740 – Foundem and others*, paragraph 20(b) and (c). <http://services.google.com/fh/files/blogs/google_commitments_full_2014.pdf>

1336 Note that the proposed solution 'borrows' from copyright law. Courts seem to agree with the premise that hyperlinking is not a copyright infringement. See, for instance, BGH, *Paperboy*, Judgment of 17 July 2003, I ZR 259/00; and ECJ, Case C-466/12 *Nils Svensson and others v Retriever Sverige AB* [2014] (not yet reported)

is requested'.[1337] In our case, this means in practice that the user may access a story even after the publisher removed it from its site.[1338] It should be noted that the EU Copyright Directive[1339] and the E-Commerce Directive[1340] provide that caching is not a copyright infringement or an illegitimate restriction on the free movement of information society services respectively provided that it is 'temporary'.[1341] However, courts in France[1342] and Belgium[1343] rejected the argument that Google's caching benefits from the exemptions introduced by (the laws transposing) the above Directives.[1344] This may explain why Google offered the commitment as well as why the Commission was willing to accept it.[1345] This approach may be understandable in that it seeks to introduce a solution with 'harmonizing' effects in order to avoid tension with domestic laws that apply to Google. However, again, this commitment may be going too far. It would be difficult to understand what the anti-competitive effects on the publisher would be if the user were allowed to access an article as it appeared on the original website.

350. The main conclusion to draw from the above is that, under certain conditions, Article 102 TFEU may be invoked by news publishers and news aggregators alike, even if for diametrically opposed purposes. However, the analysis demonstrated that the Commission should intervene with caution. By accepting axiomatically that a news aggregator harms competition in news markets, the Commission runs the risk of penalizing a platform, the conduct of which is not capable of producing exclusionary effects and, by imposing on the aggregator concerned far-reaching obligations, it may deprive the readership of a service that offers convenient access to a variety of news content.[1346] In the more extreme case of news aggregators seeking access to the content produced by news outlets, the Spanish and German experiences show that establishing a licensing duty may produce a less than desirable outcome.

1337 Definition <http://www.alrc.gov.au/publications/issues-paper/caching-indexing-and-other-internet-functions#_ftn55>

1338 Xalabarder (2011), *supra* n. 57, 115

1339 Directive 2001/29/EC of the European Parliament and of the Council of 22 May 2001 on the harmonization of certain aspects of copyright and related rights in the information society [2001] OJ L167/10, Article 5(1)

1340 Directive 2000/31/EC of the European Parliament and of the Council of 8 June 2000 on certain legal aspects of information society services, in particular electronic commerce, in the Internal Market (Directive on Electronic Commerce) [2000] OJ L178/1, Article 13

1341 Article 13 of the e-Commerce Directive poses some additional conditions that need to be fulfilled for cache storing to be legitimate

1342 Cour d'appel du Paris, *Société des Auteurs des Arts Visuels et de L'Image Fixe (SAIF) v Google France*, SARL, and Google Inc. Judgment of 26 January 2011, 08/13423, 8

1343 Court of Appeal of Brussels, *Google Inc v Copiepresse* R. No. 2011/2999, No. 817, 52–55; Court of First Instance of Brussels, *Copiepresse v Google*, No. 06/10.928/C, 18 *et seq.*

1344 On the copyright issues that arose in these cases see Xalabarder (2011), *supra* n. 57, 115 *et seq.*

1345 Commission (2014a, February), *supra* n. 23

1346 Foster (2012), *supra* n. 38, 25

4. Search engines as distribution bottlenecks: retaliation, exclusivity and data exploitation

351. Search engines are undoubtedly evolving into 'the most important gateway used to find content',[1347] including content that seeks to ensure an informed citizenry; search engines seem to be the most popular means of discovering news online.[1348] While not *all* information is nosed out and indexed by search engines, the latter have undeniably broadened our knowledge of the world. Could we imagine an online universe where we would need to find links to websites that could possibly contain interesting content without the help of a search engine? In view of what the alternative would be, it is easy to understand that, in their role as gatekeepers, search engines have made a significant contribution to creating an environment where information, including information on matters of common concern, is instantly and effortlessly available.

352. However, this gatekeeping role does not come without problems. As Foster puts it, 'the fact that [search engines] are now an indispensable part of our lives also means that they have the potential to exert significant influence over public access to different types of content, including news'.[1349] In other words, search engines are not only capable of facilitating the discovery of information we were previously not aware of, but also capable of behaving as bottlenecks, restricting the scope of content that is indeed available. In this latter case, the risk that the user may be prevented from consulting other sources of information is greater if the market is highly concentrated. In the EU, Google is by far the strongest player, holding market shares in general online search 'well above 90%' in most Member States[1350] and the following two practices illustrate how a dominant search engine may act as a bottleneck. First, Google appears to have engaged in 'retaliation' practices; it is claimed that it artificially reduces the information that is available on the web in cases where those providing the information concerned refuse to serve Google's commercial interests in neighboring markets. The second area which illustrates how a search engine may act as an information bottleneck has to do with the gathering and processing of competitors' and customers', including online users', data. More particularly, Google seems to inhibit advertisers from transferring ad campaign data to other advertising platforms, thereby potentially preventing them from reaching audiences that use competing services. Moreover, Google

1347 van Eijk, N. (2009). *Search Engines, the New Bottleneck for Content Access*, 141. In Preissel, B., Justus Haucap and Peter Curwen (eds.), *Telecommunication Markets: Drivers and Impediments*. Berlin: Springer-Verlag

1348 Reuters Institute (2018), *supra* n. 43, 13

1349 Foster (2012), *supra* n. 38, 26

1350 Commission (2013, April), *supra* n. 26; *Google Search* (Case AT.39740) Commission decision of 27 June 2017 relating to proceedings under Article 102 TFEU and Article 54 of the EEA Agreement C (2017) 4444 final, paragraphs 273 *et seq.* (see, for instance, Table 2)

collects and processes a vast amount of user data in order to provide search results that are largely based on the user's individual search history.[1351] While this is supposed to deliver results that best match the user's query, it is unclear whether Google processes data to bring added value to the user or rather to direct her to information that primarily serves its own commercial interests.

353. Prior to discussing the above two practices in more detail, it should be noted that retaliation affects media pluralism in an obvious manner. The other practices, namely those related to the use of data, affect more generally access to information. Hence, the discussion, albeit undoubtedly relevant for our purposes, has a broader focus.

4.1 Retaliation affecting news markets

354. As already mentioned above, one of the main complaints put forward by news publishers is that those publishers that have objected to the display of their content in Google News have been told by Google that the only way for their content not to appear on the News website is to opt out of Google's services, including especially Google's web search results.[1352] Such retaliatory practices could be considered abusive tying. From the statements made throughout the investigation, it may be inferred that the Commission's preliminary assessment was indeed driven by the three requirements which, pursuant to its Guidance Paper on the application of Article 102 TFEU, need to be fulfilled for a conduct to carry the 'tying' tag: a) the firm is in a dominant position in the tying market[1353] ('Google is dominant in the European Economic Area (EEA) both in web search and search advertising'[1354]); b) the tying and tied products are two distinct products[1355] (Google News is a 'specialized service'[1356]); and c) the tying practice is likely to lead to anti-competitive foreclosure[1357] (opting out is 'not a sustainable business option for most websites'[1358]). If broadly interpreted, the case law, as codified in the Guidance Paper, would support the argument that Google may be liable for tying. Usually, tying refers to a situation 'where *customers* that *purchase* one product (the tying product) are required also to *purchase* another product from the dominant undertaking (the tied

1351 Note that this issue is not being investigated by the Commission.

1352 Commission (2013, April), *supra* n. 26

1353 Guidance on the Commission's enforcement priorities in applying Article 82 of the EC Treaty to abusive exclusionary conduct by dominant undertakings [2009] OJ C 45/2, paragraph 50

1354 Commission (2013, April), *supra* n. 26. For the dominance assessment the Commission conducted in the *Google Search* case see *Google Search* (Case AT.39740) Commission decision of 27 June 2017 relating to proceedings under Article 102 TFEU and Article 54 of the EEA Agreement C (2017) 4444 final, paragraphs 271 *et seq*.

1355 *supra* n. 148

1356 Commission (2013, April), *supra* n. 26

1357 *supra* n. 148

1358 Commission (2013, April), *supra* n. 26

product)' [emphasis added].[1359] News publishers are not, strictly speaking, required to 'purchase' Google News in order to 'purchase' access to Google Search. Moreover, while in the case of Google Search publishers could be regarded as 'customers', in the case of Google News they are suppliers of a valuable input. In view of the above, this is not a typical tying case. However, Google does seem to make display in Search entirely conditional upon display in News and, where a news publisher does not allow the use of its content by the aggregating platform, the effects of Google's conduct are 'by definition' exclusionary (news publishers and Google do not compete in the general search market, but a finding of abuse does not depend on whether the anti-competitive effects are manifested in the tied or the tying market[1360]). Ultimately, even if one were reluctant to call this behavior 'tying', there is a plausible theory of harm here, that of leveraging: Google is using its market power in general online search to strengthen its position in an ancillary market, however that latter market is defined (see above on possible market definitions).

355. To address the concerns associated with the retaliation practice, Google undertook to ensure that a news publisher's decision to opt out of Google News will not adversely affect the appearance of the publisher's website in search results delivered by Google Search. As will be seen in greater detail below, Google's suggestions may fall short of providing news publishers with an effective opt-out mechanism.

356. ***Opt out of what?*** In all three submissions, Google explicitly stated that, were a news outlet to opt out of Google News, this would have 'no material adverse impact on ranking in *Generic Search Results*' [emphasis added].[1361] Yet, on no occasion did Google mention how a publisher's decision to opt out would affect the display of 'News Universals'. News Universals are news results that are displayed in a special block following a given query. For example, if a user types inside Google's Search Box 'Google EU antitrust investigation', she will receive, *inter alia*, results directing to DG Competition's website with information on the proceedings, analyses of whether Google should be charged with antitrust violations, and a block of two or three results which originate from the websites of news outlets regarding the investigation. This block of results is

---

1359 Guidance on the Commission's enforcement priorities in applying Article 82 of the EC Treaty to abusive exclusionary conduct by dominant undertakings [2009] OJ C 45/2, paragraph 48. Note that in EU competition law, the term 'customers' encompasses both final consumers as well as undertakings competing with the dominant firm in upstream or downstream markets

1360 ibid, paragraph 52. For a detailed analysis of how Google's behavior fulfills the 'tying' requirements see Edelman, B. (2014). *Leveraging Market Power Through Tying and Bundling: Does Google Behave Anti-Competitively?* Harvard Business School – Working Paper 14-112, 15–17. <http://hbswk.hbs.edu/item/7464.html>

1361 Google (2013, April). *Commitments in Case COMP/C-3/39.740 – Foundem and others*, paragraph 19. Note that the second time around Google expanded the scope of the remedy to cover 'Google Ads results', which remained intact in the third submission. See Google (2013, October). *Commitments in Case COMP/C-3/39.740 – Foundem and others*, paragraph 21 and Google (2014, January). *Commitments in Case COMP/C-3/39.740 – Foundem and others*, paragraph 22

labeled as 'News for [query]'. News Universals are prominently displayed and greatly resemble the Google News service – they contain the headline, sometimes the first few lines of the story, and a link to the story concerned.

357. The way in which the commitment is drafted would arguably give Google considerable room for manoeuvre in disputes that could possibly arise after the closing of the investigation. More particularly, in its submission, Google defines Generic Search Results as Search Results '*not restricted by design* to one or a limited set of pre-defined content categories, *such as news*, product, local businesses, images, travel and video, *and* ... returned in response to a query entered into a Google General Search Input Feature' [emphasis added].[1362] This definition would seem to free Google of the obligation to include in News Universals stories produced by news outlets that opt out of Google News.[1363] Moreover, were news publishers to bring complaints against Google on the grounds that it does not respect the commitment submitted to the Commission, Google could argue that this is how its Universal Search model is designed (note that in May 2007, Google announced that it adopted a 'Universal' model whereby, following a query, the algorithm would search all of its content sources, for instance YouTube, Google News, and Google Maps, rank all the information in its possession and 'deliver an integrated set of results'[1364]). If a news publisher opts out of the News service, so Google's argument could go, then 'by design' it cannot be included in the News Universals block. The way in which News Universals affect news consumption is admittedly far from clear. However, one cannot help but have mixed feelings about this remedy. If the prominent display of News Universals encourages users to click through the websites of (only or predominantly) those publishers that appear on Google News, then the commitment may introduce a different, albeit softer, form of retaliation, thereby falling short of addressing the main concern that arose in the context of the investigation, that is, the 'forced' link of Google News to Google Search. Unsurprisingly, news publishers criticized this proposal, maintaining that News Universals 'attract most user attention [and, since] no publisher can afford to opt out of those results to protect its content from being used elsewhere', the commitment is 'at best useless'.[1365]

358. ***How to opt out?*** Google provided news outlets with two options. First, news outlets may fill in a web-based Notice Form where they state that they wish to opt out of the News service.[1366] This proposal is both superfluous and

1362 Google (2014, January). *Commitments in Case COMP/C-3/39.740 – Foundem and others*, 8

1363 European Press Publishers (2014, September). *Press Publishers 'Response to Google's Third Commitments Proposal. European Commission's Competition Investigation of Google – AT.39740*, 11–12

1364 Google (2007, May). *Google Begins Move to Universal Search*. <http://googlepress.blogspot.com/2007/05/google-begins-move-to-universal-search_16.html>

1365 European Press Publishers (2014, September), *supra* n. 158, 11–12

1366 Google (2014, January). *Commitments in Case COMP/C-3/39.740 – Foundem and others*, paragraph 11

highly likely to be ineffective: superfluous because apparently the Notice Form mechanism was in place long before the Commission opened its investigation.[1367] And likely to be ineffective because Google would cease displaying content on News 'within 30 working days of receipt of a properly completed Notice Form'.[1368] As already explained, news is time sensitive and hence highly perishable. Thus, using the Notice Form is arguably not a viable solution for a news publisher that exercises the right to opt out. Alternatively, Google said it would 'maintain a specific robots exclusion protocol' that would allow publishers to exclude content from display in Google News.[1369] For the sake of clarity, it bears noting that a robots exclusion protocol, as a technical solution, has been available to websites for quite some time. In fact, the mere ability to use a robots exclusion protocol has been one of the oft-repeated arguments put forward by Google in cases concerning copyright infringements, where it has contended that the fact that a website does not implement a robots exclusion protocol should be regarded as an 'implied license' to use the site's content.[1370] In the EU antitrust investigation, the publishers' complaint was that Google would use a system whereby whichever website implemented the robots exclusion protocol to prevent display in News would automatically lose visibility in Google Search.[1371] This may still be a problem since the case has not been resolved yet.

359. ***What to opt out?*** In cases where they indeed use a robots exclusion protocol, publishers are entitled to opt out on a webpage-by-webpage basis. That is to say, in cases where a webpage contains several stories, the news outlet may not choose which stories it wants to see displayed in Google News. Google provided no explanations as to why the opt-out should have such a wide scope.[1372] However, the technical means to support inclusion on an item-by-item basis seems to exist. For example, in the case dealing with the retaliation complaint brought by Italian publishers, AGCom, the Italian media regulator, imposed upon Google the obligation to ensure that publishers are in the position 'to exclude specific articles or images'.[1373]

1367 Edelman (2014), *supra* n. 155, 14

1368 Google (2014, January). *Commitments in Case COMP/C-3/39.740 – Foundem and others*, paragraph 12

1369 ibid, paragraph 20

1370 On this issue and relevant case law see Xalabarder (2011), *supra* n. 57, 155

1371 Sullivan, D. *Debunking The Italian Newspapers' Antitrust Allegations Against Google*. 27 August 2009, Search Engine Land. <http://searchengineland.com/deunking-the-italian-newspapers-antitrust-allegations-against-google-24698>

1372 Note that in the case of the Notice Form, the opt-out would have an even wider scope, allowing website owners to opt out either for their entire domain or for one or some of their sub-domains. See Google (2014, January). *Commitments in Case COMP/C-3/39.740 – Foundem and others*, paragraph 11

1373 AGCom. A420–AS787. *Federazione Italiana Editori Giornali/Google*. Provvedimento n. 21959, paragraph 103. <http://www.agcm.it/dotcmsDOC/allegati-news/p21959.pdf> That this technical measure is possible can also be inferred from how Google proposes to display content of competing (e.g. travel and product) sites. See Google (2014, January). *Commitments in Case COMP/C-3/39.740 – Foundem and others*, paragraph 18

360. Retaliation, as manifested in the Google case, is a worrisome practice, possibly more worrisome than scraping in that, as opposed to the latter, the effects of the former are *per se* exclusionary. It is therefore inexplicable why the Commission appeared willing to accept the commitments proposed by Google which, as the above analysis showed, would be incapable of addressing the concerns they raise.

4.2 Retention and use of data affecting advertisers and online users

361. The other area that illustrates the ways in which digital intermediaries may shape the architecture of information markets in their role as bottlenecks is the gathering and processing of competitors' and customers', including online users', data.[1374] In the case of Google, issues relating to the collection and use of data arise in two contexts that will be examined in this section. First, Google appears to have engaged in practices that prevent advertisers from exporting ad campaign data into competing advertising platforms. This in turn can be seen from two different perspectives. First, content providers, including news outlets, advertise with Google. If the restrictions introduced by Google lead to content providers advertising exclusively with Google, then Google may have prevented them from reaching the user base of other search engines. Second, data portability restrictions may significantly reduce the ability of other search engines to attract advertisers. Data portability restrictions relate to a broader problem that arises in markets where digital intermediaries operate, namely the existence of high switching costs that may amount to customer lock-in. The degree of customer lock-in resulting from data portability restrictions depends, *inter alia*, on the scope of the restrictions and the type of the intermediary. For example, in the case of digital retailers which manufacture the hardware devices to which their digital content stores are tied, and which do not allow the user to transfer the acquired content to a competing device, customer lock-in appears to be high.

362. The second issue that relates to the use of data by powerful digital intermediaries is the (sensitive) information supplied by the online user to the intermediary. Digital intermediaries rely heavily on collecting and processing user data that reveals valuable information about consumer preferences and is used to serve a number of purposes, including targeted advertising. However, online users are in limbo over the vast amount of data they unveil. Moreover, there is considerable uncertainty about whether the intermediary processes data to bring an added value to the user (e.g. 'more relevant' content) or rather to channel her to information that primarily serves its purpose to maximize profit. Consumer

1374 This section was the basis of a piece on whether and, if so, how the collection and processing of consumer data impact may impact EU antitrust and merger control. See Bania, K. (2018). *The Role of Consumer Data in the Enforcement of EU Competition Law*. European Competition Journal 14(1), 38–80

exploitation in this context may give grounds for antitrust intervention that seeks to increase transparency about the ways in which the collection and processing of data may affect the information to which online users are exposed.

4.2.1 Restrictions on data portability

363. Data portability may be defined as the data subject's ability 'to transfer data from one electronic processing system to and into another, without being prevented from doing so by the controller'.[1375] In the case at hand, advertisers licensing Google Ads' API,[1376] an instrument that facilitates the management of an Ads campaign,[1377] seem to be prevented from using tools offered by software developers that allow them to transfer ad campaign data, including keywords, price and targeting information,[1378] to rival advertising platforms such as Microsoft's AdCenter.[1379]

364. Data portability restrictions raise barriers to substituting one service provider for another.[1380] In antitrust parlance, they create switching costs,[1381] that is, 'costs customers actually do or would incur from changing from [one] supplier of a good or service to another'.[1382] Switching costs may become a competition issue if they are high enough to lock-in the customer to a given provider.[1383] In the case at hand, advertiser lock-in may push competing ad-based search engines out of the market or raise (the already high[1384]) barriers

1375 Proposal for a Regulation of the European Parliament and of the Council on the protection of individuals with regard to the processing of personal data and on the free movement of such data (General Data Protection Regulation), COM (2012) 11 final, 9. The proposal refers to natural persons but, for our purposes, we adopt a broader approach to the definition of 'data subjects' to include undertakings.

1376 An API (Application Programming Interface) is '[a] language and message format used by an application program to communicate with the operating system or some other control program such as a database management system (DBMS) or communications protocol.' Definition <http://www.pcmag.com/encyclopedia/term/37856/api>

1377 See https://developers.google.com/adwords/api/>

1378 Federal Trade Commission (2013a, January). *Google Agrees to Change Its Business Practices to Resolve FTC Competition Concerns In the Markets for Devices Like Smart Phones, Games and Tablets, and in Online Search.* Press Release. <https://www.ftc.gov/news-events/press-releases/2013/01/google-agrees-change-its-business-practices-resolve-ftc>

1379 Commission (2014a, February), *supra* n. 23; Commission (2013, April), *supra* n. 26, and Commission (2010, November), *supra* n. 2

1380 Geradin, D. and Monika Kuschewsky (2013). *Competition Law and Personal Data: Preliminary Thoughts on a Complex Issue.* SSRN Working Paper, 10–11 <http://papers.ssrn.com/sol3/papers.cfm?abstract_id=2216088>

1381 On switching costs in new economy markets see, for instance, Edlin, A. S. and Robert G. Harris (2013). *The Role of Switching Costs in Antitrust Analysis: A Comparison of Microsoft and Google.* Yale Journal of Law and Technology 15(2), 171–213

1382 Harris, R. G. *The Role of Switching Costs in the Markets for PC Operating Systems, Online Search, Internet Access and Mobile Service: Implications for Australian Competition and Consumer Protection Policy.* Presented at the Conference on 'Competition in the Online Environment', 28 November 2012, 3. Note that switching costs may take various forms; they can, *inter alia*, be inherent (present in all markets) or strategic (created or raised by a competitor to reduce or eliminate the incentive to switch).

1383 Geradin, D. *Data Portability and EU Competition Law.* Presented at the BITS conference, Brussels, 24 April 2014, 3

1384 See Chapter 2, Part 3.4.2.

to entry,[1385] thereby producing exclusionary effects. Moreover, were the restrictions concerned so stringent as to impede the creation of instruments that allow a more efficient use of ad campaign data, it could also be argued that Google harms innovation. Under this lens, Google's conduct may be caught by Article 102(b) TFEU, which prohibits firms in a dominant position engaging in practices that limit 'production, markets or technical development'.[1386]

365. In view of the above, data portability may be an issue of concern to competition authorities. It bears noting that, while Google's conduct appears to be the first instance in which data portability restrictions were caught on the EU antitrust radar, distortions of competition that may arise from high switching costs are hardly new to competition law. The IBM commitments decision concerning IBM's refusal to supply interface information (impeding interoperability between its central processing unit and operation system and software developed by competing undertakings, thus locking in the customer to IBM products), which dates back to 1984, is illustrative in this regard.[1387] Naturally, markets evolve and new factors come into play. Data has undoubtedly become a valuable input in today's digital economy. This is because, as will be seen in greater detail below, data provides new insights into customers' needs, thereby driving the development of new services. This has not passed unnoticed by the Commission. For example, former Competition Commissioner Almunia stated in a speech that 'a healthy competitive environment in [digital] markets requires that consumers can easily and cheaply transfer the data they uploaded in a service onto another service … [R]etention of these data should not serve as barriers to switching.'[1388] Similarly, in its Impact Assessment Report on the proposed General Data Protection Regulation, the Commission notes that '[p]ortability is a key factor for effective competition'.[1389]

366. Consequently, a remedy imposing the obligation to lift data portability restrictions is nothing more than an adaptation of competition law to the circumstances characterizing today's digital markets. But, while the imposition of the remedy as such is not controversial, a decision finding that a refusal to allow data portability amounts to an abuse can be, because the relevant

1385 Guidance on the Commission's enforcement priorities in applying Article 82 of the EC Treaty to abusive exclusionary conduct by dominant undertakings [2009] OJ C 45/2, paragraph 17

1386 Geradin and Kuschewsky (2013), *supra* n. 175, 11; Graef, I., Jeroen Verschakelen and Peggy Valcke (2014). *Putting the right to data portability into a competition law perspective*. SSRN Working Paper, 7 <http://papers.ssrn.com/sol3/papers.cfm?abstract_id=2416537>

1387 Commission (1984). *Fourteenth Report on Competition Policy*, 77–79. Available at: <https://publications.europa.eu/en/publication-detail/-/publication/3c93e6fa-934b-4fb9-b927-dc9fed71ccfe>

1388 Almunia, J. (2012, November). *Competition and personal data protection*. Speech given at the 'Privacy Platform event: Competition and Privacy in Markets of Data'. <http://europa.eu/rapid/press-release_SPEECH-12-860_en.htm>

1389 Commission (2012). Commission Staff Working Paper. *Impact Assessment accompanying the General Data Protection Regulation and the Directive on the protection of individuals with regard to the processing of personal data by competent authorities for the purposes of prevention, investigation, detection or prosecution of criminal offences or the execution of criminal penalties, and the free movement of such data* SEC (2012) 72 final, 28

assessment will undoubtedly involve examining and weighing complex technical parameters that will ultimately determine whether customers are indeed locked in to the products of the firm under scrutiny. At the time of producing this study, factual information about the restrictions imposed on advertisers is not publicly available. But, the wording of the remedy proposed by Google is very similar to that of the remedy made legally binding on the search giant in the US.[1390] In order to provide the basis of a framework within which the switching costs incurred by advertisers using the Ads platform may be assessed, I shall use the information about the contracts that were scrutinized by the FTC, speculatively inferring that the restrictions set on advertisers in the EU are analogous to those set on advertisers in the US.

367. As already indicated, in order to determine whether the customer is locked in to a service, one would need to measure 'the cost of switching to a different service or adopting a new technology'.[1391] Where the customer has entered into a contract with the provider concerned, one aspect that is key to calculating switching costs is the scope of restrictions introduced by the contract in question.[1392] In the US, apparently, Google Ads advertisers were allowed to use other advertising platforms, including APIs linked to those other platforms.[1393] In other words, they were not bound by exclusive purchasing deals, which, as already seen, may make antitrust bells ring (especially if they involve a dominant firm). Moreover, and perhaps more importantly, advertisers were prevented from using third party tools *only*, that is, they were not prevented from developing their own data portability tools.[1394] Finally, advertisers were allowed to transfer Google Ads campaign data to a competing platform.[1395] Referring to the above, FTC Commissioner Rosch maintained that the restrictions were limited in scope and that, as a result, Google should not be forced to eliminate them.[1396] However, in order to determine the magnitude of switching costs, the analysis should go beyond the assessment of the contract entered into between Google and advertisers, for the lock-in may not necessarily be contractual. That is to say, the same restrictions may lead to *de facto* exclusivity. Therefore, even if not expressly restricted by contract, one would need to check whether it is feasible for an advertiser to develop its own data portability tool[1397] or recreate another campaign (e.g. by inserting

1390 Compare Google (2012a, December). *Commitments Letter From Google Inc to Chairman Leibowitz*, II <https://www.ftc.gov/system/files/documents/closing_letters/google-inc./130103googleletterchairmanleibowitz.pdf> with Google (2014, January). *Commitments in Case COMP/C-3/39.740 – Foundem and others*, paragraphs 33 *et seq*.

1391 Shy, O. (2001). *The Economics of Network Industries*. Cambridge: CUP, 4

1392 ibid.

1393 Federal Trade Commission (2013b, January), *supra* n. 107, 4

1394 ibid, 4–5

1395 ibid, 5

1396 ibid, 4–6

1397 Note that Google acknowledges that 'the [Ads] API is a good option for advertisers who have a developer or programmer who has the technical skills'. However, it does provide small advertisers with the Ads

the data manually or by licensing a competing platform's software[1398]). If associated costs are high, advertisers, including especially small firms, may be discouraged from advertising with another platform. Furthermore, Google has in place 'Required Minimum Functionality Requirements' with which advertisers developing their own portability tools must comply. Depending on how strict they are, these requirements could reduce or eliminate the incentive to multi-home campaigns.[1399] The same effect may be produced by harsh contractual termination provisions combined with ambivalence as to the conditions under which advertisers may exercise their contractual right to export data. For example, Google's competitors contend that the Ads API conditions provide that: 'If you violate any part of this [Ads] API Agreement … your access to the [Ads] API may be suspended or terminated without notice and you have no right to use the [Ads] API.'[1400] According to competitors, in addition to introducing this 'draconian provision', the agreements deliberately do not clarify certain technical aspects (e.g. whether it is allowed to display aggregated campaign data).[1401] If this were indeed the case, 'violation of any part of the AdWords API' would be subject to opportunistic interpretation.

368. However, deciding whether a remedy to lift data portability restrictions should be imposed on Google does not solely depend on the degree of switching costs, but also on what is the relevant market affected by the refusal to eliminate the restriction. In our case, it is not clear whether the relevant market is the broader (online) advertising market[1402] or whether there is a distinct market for (online advertising platform) APIs or even a separate sub-market for the Ads API. This is an important question to answer because the Ads API specifications, that is, 'all information and documentation Google provides specifying or concerning the [Ads] API … and any Google-supplied implementations or methods of use of the [Ads] API' is an IPR-protected asset[1403] and, as already discussed, according to the relevant case law, in the *primary* market for which a dominant undertaking has a monopoly owning to its own IP, the exclusive right to produce or sell should be fully respected.[1404] Hence, pursuant to the relevant case law,[1405] Google should be forced to allow data

Editor tool. Information <https://support.google.com/adwords/answer/15235?hl=en>

1398 Federal Trade Commission (2013b, January), *supra* n. 107, 5

1399 ICOMP (2013, May). *Response to the Remedies Proposed by Google Inc in Case COMP/C-3/39.740*, paragraph 203

1400 ibid, 205

1401 ibid, 204–205

1402 For possible market definitions in the online advertising sector see *Google/Doubleclick* (Case COMP/M.4731) [2008] OJ C 184/6, paragraphs 44 *et seq*. On the broader issue of how competition authorities should define the relevant product markets in the online search sector see Zingales, N. (2013). *Product Market Definition in Online Search and Advertising*. Competition Law Review 9(1), 29–47

1403 See <https://developers.google.com/adwords/api/docs/terms>

1404 ECJ, Case 238/87 *Volvo v Veng (UK)* [1988] ECR 6211, paragraph 8

1405 ibid. See also ECJ, Joined Cases C-241/91 P and C-242/91 P *Radio Telefis Eireann (RTE) and Independent Television Publications Ltd. v Commission* [1995] ECR I-743

portability enabled through third party tools if the market for the Ads APIs or the market for (online advertising platform) APIs (assuming these are two plausible market definitions) is the primary market and the advertising market is the ancillary market. It bears repeating that the Commission's practice and the Courts' case law concerning the refusal to grant licenses for the use of inputs protected by IPRs,[1406] including decisions and judgments dealing with a closely related issue, namely interoperability, such as Microsoft[1407] and IBM,[1408] were based on the same premise, that is, that the dominant firm under scrutiny was leveraging its market power from one market to another market. Were we to interfere with the exercise of IPRs in primary markets, the incentive to innovate would arguably be significantly reduced. A good example that serves our purposes is Google Print Ads, a tool that was introduced to enable advertisers to buy *traditional* newspaper ads through the Ads interface. Advertisers, including local firms, could use Print Ads[1409] to identify newspapers that fit their needs and to organize their campaigns accordingly. If a firm knows in advance that competitors that have not made the investments required (in the Print Ads example these would include e.g. establishing contacts with newspapers interested in participating in the platform, designing and implementing supporting software) to undertake such initiatives may free-ride on its efforts, then why should it bother to innovate in the first place?

369. Furthermore, if the relevant market is the (broader) advertising market, Google may still be found dominant, but establishing the duty to lift the restriction may not be necessary to address any foreclosure concerns that may arise. For example, in the US, search engine marketing firms and advertisers that were surveyed during the investigation stated that the API restriction did not play a role in their decision to choose an advertising platform.[1410] In other words, this was not a factor determining demand-side substitutability.

370. The above remarks on the scope of data portability restrictions and possible market definitions lead to the following conclusion: if the costs of switching to another platform are low or if the market affected by the restrictions is the same market where Google exercises its API-related IPRs, then the duty to lift the restrictions is not proportionate to the allegedly unlawful conduct, namely that Google distorts the market for the Google Ads APIs or the market for (online advertising platform) APIs. If the affected market is the market

1406 See, for instance, ECJ, Case C-418/01 *IMS Health GmbH & Co. OHG v NDC Health GmbH & Co. KG* [2004] ECR I-5039

1407 See CFI, Case T-201/04 *Microsoft Corp. v Commission of the European Communities* [2007] ECR II-03601, and *Microsoft* (Case COMP/C-3/37.792) Commission decision of 24.03.2004 relating to a proceeding under Article 82 of the EC Treaty C (2004) 900 final

1408 Commission (1984), *supra* n. 182, 77–79

1409 While this does not alter the conclusion of the paragraph using the Print Ads example, note that Google discontinued the service two years after its launch.

1410 Federal Trade Commission (2013b, January), *supra* n. 107, fn. 11

for advertising and substitutability does not depend on the API restrictions, then the remedy is not necessary. Pursuant to Article 7 of Regulation 1/2003, 'proportionality' and 'necessity' are the two key conditions under which the Commission must assess and impose remedies[1411] and the above examples regarding data portability restrictions go partway toward explaining why, in complex cases, commitments decisions may fail to find the target.

371. Notwithstanding the possibility that the remedy likely to be imposed upon Google will be disproportionate and/or unnecessary, it should be noted that where customer lock-in concerns indeed arise, establishing the duty to lift data portability restrictions is a powerful tool in the hands of the Commission. This is illustrated by the scope of the remedy envisaged in the Google case, which provided that Google would delete clauses of the API terms that prevented software developers from offering functionalities that allowed advertisers to 'transmit' campaign data to non-Google advertising services.[1412] The wording of the commitment resembles greatly the wording of the General Data Protection Regulation (GDPR), which has recently replaced the EU Data Protection Directive.[1413] More particularly, Article 20(2) GDPR provides that 'the data subject shall have the right to have the personal data *transmitted* directly from one controller to another, where technically feasible' [emphasis added].[1414] The right to data portability applies in cases of copying and transfer of personal data, that is, 'any information to an identified or identifiable natural person'.[1415] As the Google case clearly illustrates, a remedy imposed on a firm that violated the competition provisions is more far-reaching since it may also cover data that is not strictly 'personal'.[1416] Hence, to the extent that the commitment protects the competitive process, EU competition law may address a regulatory gap, to the benefit of the user that will have, as a result, more choice. Moreover, fear

1411 Council Regulation (EC) No. 1/2003 of 16 December 2002 on the implementation of the rules on competition laid down in Articles 81 and 82 of the Treaty [2003] OJ L1/1

1412 Google (2014, January). *Commitments in Case COMP/C-3/39.740 – Foundem and others*, paragraph 33

1413 Directive 95/46/EC of the European Parliament and of the Council of 24 October 1995 on the protection of individuals with regard to the processing of personal data and on the free movement of such data [1995] OJ L281/31.

1414 Regulation (EU) 2016/679 of the European Parliament and of the Council of 27 April of 2016 on the protection of natural persons with regard to the processing of personal data and on the free movement of such data, and repealing Directive 95/46/EC [2016] L119/1 (GDPR). Note that the right to data portability may have far-reaching and – some say – mostly adverse consequences for the consumer. For a comprehensive overview of the potential negative implications arising from establishing a right to data portability as envisaged by the EU legislator see Swire, P. and Yianni Lagos (2013). *Why the Right to Data Portability Likely Reduces Consumer Welfare: Antitrust and Privacy Critique*. Maryland Law Review 72(2), 335–380

1415 GDPR, Article 4(1)

1416 Graef, Verschakelen and Valcke (2014), *supra* n. 181, 8. It goes without saying that remedies intended to lift data portability restrictions may not only concern advertisers and software developers, but also online users. Google seems to have taken some steps to facilitate management of data extracted from email accounts and social networking tool Google+, but Facebook has been severely criticized over the data portability restrictions imposed on users. On the competition concerns that arise from Facebook's practices related to data portability restrictions see Graef, I., Sih Yuliana Wahyuningtyas and Peggy Valcke. *Data Interoperability in Online Social Networks*. Paper presented at the International Workshop on Competition Policy and Regulation in Media and Telecommunications: Bridging Law and Economics, 23 and 24 May 2013, Tilburg Law and Economics Centre, Tilburg

of falling under the EU antitrust microscope for refusing to lift data portability restrictions may produce substantial deterrent effects that (at least for a dominant firm) are larger than those produced by the relevant regulatory framework: under EU competition law, an undertaking which has abused its dominant position may be required to pay a fine up to 10% of its total turnover,[1417] whereas under the GDPR,[1418] an undertaking that falls short of respecting obligations to respect data portability may be required to pay a fine up to 4% of its turnover.[1419]

372. To sum up, data portability restrictions may (artificially) raise the switching costs customers need to incur to change from one intermediary to another. Imposing on a powerful firm the duty to lift these restrictions is not only a manifestation of the flexibility of EU competition law to adapt to the specific circumstances of new economy markets, but also a useful tool in the hands of the Commission to ensure that consumer choice is not reduced. However, the switching costs must be carefully measured, for otherwise they may chill innovation, including the emergence of products that could contribute to the development of content markets.

4.2.2 Exploitative gathering and processing of user data

373. As already mentioned, the second issue that relates to the use of data by powerful digital intermediaries is the collection and processing of information disclosed by the online user. User data is the 'fuel' of digital intermediaries,[1420] including especially advertising-based providers; user data enables a company like Google to strengthen its relationship with its advertising partners because, based on data-disclosing user preferences, advertisers can 'precisely target their audience by combining information regarding geographical location, time of day, areas of interest, previous purchasing record'[1421] and so much more. Moreover, and besides delivering the promise for more effective advertising, intermediaries rely on user data to provide 'more relevant' search results. This relevance does not relate solely to the query, but also (and perhaps primarily) to the interests of a particular user. Customized results that are based on previous searches or information that matches consumer tastes, such as a catalogue on Amazon with 'news apps you may like', undoubtedly bring some value to the user.

1417 Council Regulation (EC) No. 1/2003 of 16 December 2002 on the implementation of the rules on competition laid down in Articles 81 and 82 of the Treaty [2003] OJ L1/1, Article 23(2)(a)

1418 GDPR, Article 83(5)(b)

1419 Graef, Verschakelen and Valcke (2014), *supra* n. 181, 8

1420 The importance of data in today's economy is illustrated in an article from *The Economist* which, after making an overview of the vast amount of information that is currently available to firms, concludes that '[d]ata are becoming the new raw material of business: an economic input almost on a par with capital and labor'. See The Economist. *Data, data everywhere*. 25 February 2010. <http://www.economist.com/node/15557443> Less than three years after this article was published, former Competition Commissioner Joaquin Almunia would acknowledge that, due to the economic benefits they can bring to businesses, 'the ability and the incentive of companies to gather, manipulate and trade personal data have never been stronger'. See *supra* n. 183.

1421 *Google/Doubleclick* (Case COMP/M.4731) [2008] OJ C 184/6, paragraph 45

374. Yet, there exist significant information asymmetries: intermediaries have more often than not covered with a veil of secrecy the practices concerning data collection and processing, confusing consumers over how these practices may affect their content choices. These choices are (to some extent) determined by the inclinations of users, but it is unclear whether they are predominantly driven by the intermediary itself, thereby resulting in serving the commercial interests of the former rather than the information needs of the latter. This latter issue is particularly relevant for our purposes because shady tactics surrounding the mechanisms that lead to the provision of content, including news content, that is based on the user's digital communication history may prevent users from discovering alternative sources of information. In such cases, the user must be adequately informed of the parameters that determine the content that reaches her and be given the necessary instruments that would allow access to the information that is available in a non-personalized universe.[1422] In this section I will demonstrate that Article 102 TFEU equips users with tools to tackle this problem.[1423] While the collection and processing of data was not included in the Commission's investigation, Google is an excellent case study that illustrates how far digital intermediaries can go to gather personal information as well as how far EU competition law can go to address information asymmetries associated with exploitative data-related practices. I will start the analysis by shedding some light on the ways in which Google harvests user data and will then turn to exploring action users may take under Article 102 TFEU.

4.2.2.1 How does Google harvest user data?

375. Google employs a variety of methods to gather and combine user data. First, as far as general online search is concerned, typing queries in the Google search box feeds Google with data on, *inter alia*, our location, language, URLs visited, and date and time of the searches.[1424] Google also checks whether we visited the website of one of Google's advertising partners and how we interacted with it (e.g. whether we purchased goods that Google's advertisers sell). By using the general search engine, Google is also able to identify our hardware model, operating system version, and mobile network information, including our phone

1422 On the issue of how personalized consumption habits may affect democracy see Chapter 2, Part 4.1.2.

1423 On the issue of anticompetitive gathering of data from a different perspective, that of competitors, see Geradin and Kuschewsky (2013), *supra* n. 175, 7–9. Note that, while this section focuses on the negative implications of data gathering for access to information, collection of data may also result in price discrimination. On this issue see Newman, N. (2014). *The Costs of Lost Privacy: Consumer Harm and Rising Economic Inequality in the Age of Google*. William Mitchell Law Review 40(2), 865–73. For a different view see Manne, G. A. and Ben Sperry. *The Problems and Perils of Bootstrapping Privacy and Data into an Antitrust Framework*. CPI Antitrust Chronicle, May 2015(2), 6–8

1424 The user implicitly grants her consent by agreeing to the terms of use of the search engine. Information <http://www.google.com/intl/en/policies/privacy/>; and http://www.google.com/intl/en/policies/> For a comprehensive overview of the user data that Google collects see Dover, D. *The Evil Side of Google? Exploring Google's User Data Collection*. 24 June 2008, Moz Blog. <http://www.seomoz.org/blog/the-evil-side-of-google-exploring-googles-user-data-collection>

number.[1425] Second, Google also assembles a vast amount of information in cases where the consumer uses other services provided by Google for free, such as Google Product Search, YouTube and Google Maps.

376. Accordingly, Google has a clear idea about our favorite brands, music preferences and travel plans. Google can acquire additional information if users decide to use certain services they can access only if they hold a Google Account (e.g. Gmail). Moreover, in 2005, Google introduced a 'personalized search' model whereby only signed-in users, that is users with a Google Account, would get, in response to their queries, results based on their web history.[1426] In 2009, Google announced that it extended the personalized search model to signed-out users worldwide. Google does this through the insertion of a cookie in the browser that allows it to personalize search results based on 180 days of search activity.[1427] Google users may now access information that is not related to their previous queries only if they disable customizations based on search activity.[1428] Finally, in 2012, Google announced that it would modify its Privacy Policy, merging 60+ product-specific privacy policies and generalizing combination of data across services.[1429] This is why the privacy terms of, for instance, Gmail, YouTube and Google Product Search redirect to the privacy terms of Google Search.[1430] This means in practice that Google may use the data it acquires from all additional functionalities to further personalize the search results it delivers through its general search engine and vice versa.

4.2.2.2 Can users rely on Article 102 TFEU to tackle collection and processing of a vast amount of user data?

377. The first issue that needs to be addressed here is that of *locus standi*. Pursuant to Article 7(2) of Regulation 1/2003,[1431] 'natural or legal persons who can show a legitimate interest can bring a complaint' that a firm has acted in violation of Article 102 TFEU. The Commission and the Court[1432] have

1425 See <http://www.google.com/intl/en/policies/privacy/>

1426 Google (2005, June). *Search gets personal.* <http://googleblog.blogspot.com/2005/06/search-gets-personal.html>

1427 Google (2009, December). *Personalized search for Everyone.* <http://googleblog.blogspot.com/2009/12/personalized-search-for-everyone.html>

1428 Via a small tool icon on the Google Search page. One needs to go to web history and disable customizations based on search activity.

1429 Google (2012, January). *Updating our privacy policies and terms of service.* <https://googleblog.blogspot.com/2012/01/updating-our-privacy-policies-and-terms.html>

1430 Information <http://www.google.com/intl/en/policies/privacy/>

1431 Council Regulation (EC) No. 1/2003 of 16 December 2002 on the implementation of the rules on competition laid down in Articles 81 and 82 of the Treaty [2003] OJ L1/1

1432 See, for instance, CFI, Case T-37/92 *Bureau Européen des Unions des Consommateurs (BEUC) v Commission of the European Communities* [1994] ECR II-285, paragraph 36; CFI, Joined cases T-213 and 214/01 *Österreichische Postsparkasse AG and Bank für Arbeit und Wirtschaft AG v Commission of the European* Communities [2001] II-03963. See in particular paragraph 114: 'The Court considers that a final customer who shows that his economic interests have been harmed or are likely to be harmed as a result of the restriction of competition in question has a legitimate interest within the meaning of Article

adopted a broad and flexible interpretation of the term 'persons with a legitimate interest',[1433] holding that 'individual consumers whose economic interests are directly and adversely affected insofar as they are buyers of goods or services that are the object of an infringement can be in a position to show a legitimate interest'.[1434] Consumer associations are also entitled to lodge complaints.[1435]

378. In terms of procedure, an additional remark should be made as regards the burden of proof. Regulation 1/2003 sets out that it should be for the person 'alleging the infringement to prove the existence thereof to the required legal standard'.[1436] To this end, complainants are required to 'submit comprehensive information in relation to their complaint' such as documentation in support of their allegations and further information as to where additional documentation can be obtained by the Commission.[1437] However, in its Notice on the Handling of Complaints under Articles 101 and 102 TFEU, the Commission explicitly states that where it deems appropriate it may waive this obligation.[1438] The Commission explains that 'this possibility can in particular play a role to facilitate complaints by consumer associations where they, in the context of an otherwise substantiated complaint, do not have access to specific pieces of information from the sphere of the undertakings complained of'.[1439] The information submitted by a consumer association may lead to a full-blown investigation by the Commission.[1440] In view of the above, it is not only possible but also less fact-intensive for consumers to bring to the Commission's attention suspected infringements of Article 102 TFEU.

379. Yet, the question remains: could the collection and use of a vast amount of user data by a dominant firm be regarded as an abuse under Article 102 TFEU? Given that the practice concerned impacts consumers directly, that is to say, its effects are not manifested indirectly through foreclosure that may lead to consumer harm in the form of higher prices, lower quality, or less choice, the practice may amount to an exploitative abuse, defined as 'conduct which is directly exploitative of consumers'.[1441] While the focus of the Commission's practice

3 of Regulation No. 17 in making an application or a complaint in order to seek a declaration from the Commission that Articles 81 EC and 82 EC have been infringed'. See also *Greek Ferries* (Case IV/D-2/34.466) [1999] OJ L109/24, paragraph 1

1433 Van Bael, I. (2011). *Due Process in EU Competition Proceedings*. Alphen aan den Rijn: Kluwer Law International, 117

1434 Commission Notice on the handling of complaints by the Commission under Articles 81 and 82 of the EC Treaty [2004] OJ C 101/05, paragraph 37

1435 ibid.

1436 *supra* n, 226, Recital (5)

1437 Commission Notice on the handling of complaints by the Commission under Articles 81 and 82 of the EC Treaty [2004] OJ C 101/05, paragraph 31

1438 ibid.

1439 ibid, paragraph 31

1440 ibid, paragraph 4

1441 Guidance on the Commission's enforcement priorities in applying Article 82 of the EC Treaty to abusive exclusionary conduct by dominant undertakings [2009] OJ C 45/2, paragraph 7

has been on exclusionary abuses, it has long been established that 'Article [102] can properly be applied, where appropriate, to situations in which a dominant undertaking's behavior directly prejudices the interests of consumers, notwithstanding the absence of any effect on the structure of competition'.[1442] As extensively discussed elsewhere, the Commission has been mainly concerned with prices. Hence, unsurprisingly, the example of exploitative behavior given in the Guidance Paper is that of a dominant firm 'charging excessive prices'.[1443] However, it was explained in detail in Chapter 3 that in media markets there are many instances where a transaction does not involve the exchange of a service for money. In the case at hand, the transaction that is relevant for antitrust purposes involves the exchange of user data for access to Google's platform(s). Accordingly, an undertaking that requires the user to disclose 'excessive' user data may, under certain conditions that will be examined below, be liable for exploitative abuse under Article 102 TFEU.[1444]

380. But what could qualify as 'excessive' data? In relevant cases, the Court defined excessive prices as prices that have 'no reasonable relation to the economic value of the product supplied'.[1445] The Court further established a two-step test to determine 'reasonableness' which consists of an assessment of a) whether the profit margin is excessive, which 'may be calculated by making a comparison between the selling price of the product in question and its cost of production',[1446] and b) (if the profit margin is indeed excessive) whether 'a price has been imposed which is either unfair in itself or when compared with competing products'.[1447] This test, albeit seemingly irrelevant, could be applied here: even if no monetary exchange takes place to access user data or the platform, economists are increasingly developing methodologies for calculating the value of personal information. For example, one method consists in conducting surveys and economic experiments with a view to determining the price that individuals would charge the platform in order to reveal the

1442 *1998 Football World Cup* (Case IV/36.888) Commission decision relating to a proceeding under Article 82 of the EC Treaty and Article 54 of the EEA Agreement [2000] OJ L5/55, paragraph 100; ECJ, Case C-6/72 *Continental Can* [1973] ECR 215, paragraph 26

1443 *supra* n. 236

1444 Note that a report produced by the EDPS suggests the same approach without, however, providing a framework within which the assessment of whether the collection and use of data may be regarded as 'excessive' for the purposes of Article 102 TFEU. See European Data Protection Supervisor (2014). *Privacy and competitiveness in the age of big data: The interplay between data protection, competition law and consumer protection in the Digital Economy*, 29. <https://secure.edps.europa.eu/EDPSWEB/webdav/shared/Documents/Consultation/Opinions/2014/14-03-26_competitition_law_big_data_EN.pdf>

1445 ECJ, Case 27/76, *United Brands Company and United Brands Continentaal BV v Commission of the European Communities* [1978] ECR 207, paragraph 250

1446 ibid, paragraph 251

1447 ibid, paragraph 252. For an example of how the Commission carried out this test see *Scandlines Sverige AB v Port of Helsingborg* (Case COMP/A.36.568/D3) [2006] CMLR 1298, paragraphs 145 *et seq.* On other judgments concerning excessive pricing see, for instance, ECJ, Case 26/75, *General Motors Continental NV v Commission of the European Communities* [1975] ECR 01367; Case 226/84, *British Leyland Public Limited Company v Commission* [1986] ECR 3263; Case 78/70, *Deutsche Grammophon Gesellschaft mbH v Metro-SB-Großmärkte GmbH & Co. KG* [1971] ECR 487. For an overview of this case law see Jones and Sufrin (2008), *supra* n. 104, 585–594

information concerned.[1448] Some of the results of empirical studies that have been conducted thus far are particularly relevant here.[1449] A common finding is that the data subjects' willingness to disclose information is highly dependent on context, including especially the nature of information to which access is sought.[1450] For instance, a series of experiments conducted by Frog showed that users are particularly sensitive about their digital history such as their web-browsing history and location-related information.[1451] Frog found that users would charge US$50 *per entry* for disclosing this information.[1452] Other pieces of information such as the online advertising click history are less expensive (users would charge US$3–6 per entry).[1453] An additional parameter that apparently determines the price the user would charge is the data controller. For example, participants in the experiments conducted by Frog replied that social networks are less trustworthy than banks.[1454] Methodologies have also been developed to calculate the data controller's profit. One profit indicator is 'profit per data record', which 'represents the net profit (revenues minus costs) per data record held by the firm'[1455] (note that a record could be a specific piece of information, such as the data subject's gender, or the subject's full profile,[1456] including name, address, age, employment, etc.). For example, the OECD estimates that in 2012 the value of an individual record for Facebook was US$300.[1457] Of course, whether the profit margin is indeed excessive for the first condition of the test set by the Court to be fulfilled is a question of fact. Numerous factors would come into play in relevant assessments. In addition to 'traditional' benchmarks against which the profit margin is measured, such as the costs incurred by the firm in creating and maintaining the platform and the revenues it generates, the above examples illustrate that

1448 OECD (2013b). *Exploring the Economics of Personal Data: A Survey of Methodologies for Measuring Monetary Value*, 29. Note that this would reflect the selling price users, i.e. not the dominant undertaking, would charge. But, the purchase price the dominant firm would be required to pay could inform the analysis of whether the price at which it 'sells' access to its platform is excessive.

1449 See, for instance, Spiekerman, S., Jens Grossklags, and Bettina Berendt (2002). *E-privacy in 2nd generation E-Commerce.* ACM Conference on Electronic Commerce (EC'01), Hrsg. ACM New York, 38–47. Tampa, Florida: ACM Press; Chellapa, R. and Raymond G. Sin (2005). *Personalization Versus Privacy: An Empirical Examination of the Online Consumers' Dilemma.* Information Technology and Management 6(2–3), 181–ekc202; Wathieu, L. and Allan Friedman (2005). *An Empirical Approach to Understanding Privacy Valuation.* Proceedings of the Fourth Workshop on the Economics of Information Security (WEIS '05); Cvrcek, D., Marek Kumpost, Vashek Matyas, and George Danezis (2006). *A Study On The Value Of Location Privacy.* Proceedings of Workshop on Privacy in the Electronic Society (WPES '06), 109–118; Hui, K. L., Hock Hai and Sang-Yong Tom Lee (2007). *The Value of Privacy Assurance: An Exploratory Field Experiment. MIS Quarterly* 31(1), 19–33; and Acquisti, A., Leslie John, and George Loewenstein (2009). *What is Privacy Worth?* Working Paper Carnegie Mellon University. <http://pages.stern.nyu.edu/~bakos/wise/papers/wise2009-6a1_paper.pdf>

1450 OECD (2013b), *supra* n. 243, 31

1451 ibid. referring to Frog Design (2011). *The Value of Personal Data: A Global Perspective.* Presentation at Mobile World Congress, February 2011

1452 ibid.

1453 ibid.

1454 ibid.

1455 ibid, 19

1456 ibid, 18

1457 ibid, 22

parameters such as the nature of information disclosed, the data included in a user's record, and the type of data controller are also relevant. As a result, profit margin valuations should include such variables.

381. With respect to the second condition, that is, that the price charged is 'unfair', thereby not having 'a reasonable relation to the economic value of the product supplied',[1458] the Commission finds that reasonableness should be assessed against the specific circumstances of the case, including non-cost factors that relate to demand.[1459] Since exploitative abuses in the form of collection and use of personal data have not fallen under the EU antitrust microscope thus far, Data Protection Law may provide some guidance here: Article 6(1)(b) of the Data Protection Directive lays down that personal data must be 'collected for specific, explicit and legitimate purposes and not further processed in a way incompatible with those purposes'. In its Opinion on Purpose Limitation, the Article 29 Working Party states that incompatibility should be examined on the basis of, *inter alia*, 'the reasonable expectations of the data subjects at the time of collection'.[1460] Again, surveys can shed light on the users' reasonable expectations as to the use of their data. It should be underlined that this approach has *economic* foundations. The empirical studies referred to above found that the price users would charge is closely related to how they believe the data will be used by the controller.[1461]

382. Clearly, the above analysis does not attempt to suggest a clear-cut standard against which we may assess whether an entity like Google, which gathers and uses a vast amount of personal information, engages in exploitative abuse for the purposes of Article 102 TFEU. It did, however, demonstrate that economic tools that may be used to measure the value of user data and profits earned by firms heavily relying on the extraction of such data are available, thereby making it possible to carry out the two-step test designed by the Court. It further bears noting that by no means does the case law suggest that this test is the only way to determine excessiveness. As the Court put it in *United Brands*, the leading judgment on excessive pricing in which the test was established, 'other ways may be devised – and economic theorists have not failed to think up several – of selecting the rules for determining whether the price of a product is unfair'.[1462]

383. Having established that it is possible to create a framework within which one may examine whether the collection and use of personal information may be

1458 ECJ, Case 27/76, *United Brands Company and United Brands Continentaal BV v Commission of the European Communities* [1978] ECR 207, paragraph 250

1459 *Scandlines Sverige AB v Port of Helsingborg* (Case COMP/A.36.568/D3) [2006] CMLR 1298, paragraph 232

1460 Article 29 Working Party (2013). *Opinion 03/2013 on purpose limitation*, 13. <http://ec.europa.eu/justice/data-protection/article-29/documentation/opinion-recommendation/files/2013/wp203_en.pdf>

1461 OECD (2013b), *supra* n. 243, 32

1462 ECJ, Case 27/76, *United Brands Company and United Brands Continentaal BV v Commission of the European Communities* [1978] ECR 207, paragraph 253

excessive, thereby violating Article 102 TFEU, I will now turn to a specific circumstance under which the Commission may intervene in order to address concerns related to data exploitation. More particularly, the case law appears to have established the condition that antitrust intervention is subject to the condition that the domestic sector-specific regulator has not taken action to remedy such concerns.[1463] This is also implied in the Guidance Paper where the Commission states that, in cases of exploitative abuse, it may act 'where the protection of consumers ... cannot otherwise be adequately ensured'.[1464] There are valid reasons for this approach; a regulator has expert knowledge and, broadly speaking, a clearly defined and specific mandate for dealing with the issues concerned. For our purposes, it bears noting that, over the past three years, data protection authorities across the EU have taken considerable steps towards Google's data collection practices. As already mentioned, in 2012 Google adopted a new privacy policy which '[merged] many product-specific privacy policies and [generalized] combination of data across services'.[1465] This move prompted a pan-European investigation by national Data Protection Authorities, coordinated within the framework of the Article 29 Working Party, which concluded that Google did not provide sufficient information to online users regarding the purposes and types of data it processed and clear tools that would enable users to control the combination of data.[1466] A number of recommendations were addressed to Google, which undertook to take measures to increase the transparency of its data gathering and processing operations.[1467]

384. Had the regulator failed to intervene, there would be room for action under EU competition law. If Google were found to engage in exploitative abuse, certain commitments to remedy the abuse could come near to those made in the context of the data protection proceedings. For example, in the UK, Google undertook, *inter alia*, to explain user rights in clear terms, including their right to object to the combination of data (opt-out), to 'ensure that there is continued evaluation of the privacy impact of future changes to processing', and to 'keep the content of the Privacy Policy and associated web content under review'.[1468] Transparency obligations are far from

1463 Jones and Sufrin (2008), *supra* n. 104, fn. 500; Röller, L. H. (2007). *Exploitative Abuses*. In Ehlermann, C. D. and Mel Marquis (eds.), *European Competition Law Annual 2007: A Reformed Approach to Article 82 EC*. Oxford: Hart Publishing, 525–532 <http://www.eui.eu/Documents/RSCAS/Research/Competition/2007ws/200709-COMPed-Roeller.pdf>

1464 Guidance on the Commission's enforcement priorities in applying Article 82 of the EC Treaty to abusive exclusionary conduct by dominant undertakings [2009] OJ C 45/2, paragraph 7

1465 Article 29 Working Party (2012), *supra* n. 224, 1

1466 ibid, 1–2

1467 See, for instance, Information Commissioner's Office (2014). *Data Protection Act 1998 – Google Inc Undertaking*. ICO Ref: ENF0492064. <https://www.pdpjournals.com/docs/88404.pdf> For action taken by the Italian Data Protection Authority see Garante per la Protezione dei Dati Personali (2013, April). *Google: il Garante per la privacy avvia un'istruttoria sul rispetto della normativa italiana*. <http://www.garanteprivacy.it/web/guest/home/docweb/-/docweb-display/docweb/2348801>

1468 Information Commissioner's Office (2014), *supra* n. 262, 6. On more details about the opt-out mechanism suggested by EU Data Protection Authorities see Article 29 Working Party (not dated). *Appendix – Google Privacy Policy: Main Findings and Recommendations*. <http://www.cnil.fr/fileadmin/documents/

new in the realm of EU competition policy. In antitrust, a good example is *VISA Europe*,[1469] which concerned multilaterally agreed interchange fees, that is, fees which are charged by a cardholder's bank (the issuing bank) to a merchant's bank (the acquiring bank) for each sales transaction made at a merchant's outlet with a payment card. In this case, Visa Europe undertook to introduce certain transparency measures to protect the merchant (i.e. customer), including the establishment of a rule whereby the acquiring banks must 'clearly break down, in their contracts and invoices' the merchant service charges into all their components'.[1470] As regards continuing evaluation, in an abundance of decisions the merged entity or the antitrust offender undertook to appoint independent Monitoring Trustees to check compliance with the obligations imposed in the context of the proceedings.[1471] Naturally, some of the commitments imposed on Google (e.g. Google's duty to ensure that publishers using Google products obtain the required consent) are data protection-specific.[1472] However, the above examples illustrate that competition law may easily adapt to the particularities of a case involving a dominant firm relying excessively on the collection and use of personal data. This is validated by the (still ongoing) investigation the German competition authority (Bundeskartellamt) opened into Facebook's data gathering practices; in 2016, the Bundeskartellamt initiated antitrust proceedings against the social network giant on the grounds that it makes the use of its service conditional upon the user granting the company extensive permission to use his or her personal data.[1473] According to the Bundeskartellamt, although users do not suffer a direct financial loss from Facebook's data-gathering practices, they are not able to control how their personal data is used; Facebook's conduct, the Bundeskartellamt says, may qualify as abusive exploitation.[1474]

en/GOOGLE_PRIVACY_POLICY-_RECOMMENDATIONS-FINAL-EN.pdf>

1469 Commission decision of 26.2.2014 addressed to Visa Europe Limited relating to a proceeding under Article 101 TFEU and Article 53 of the EEA Agreement (Case AT.39398) *VISA MIF*, C (2014) 1199 final, paragraph 33

1470 ibid, paragraph 16. At the time of going to press, the Commission published a proposal for a Regulation promoting fairness and transparency for business users of online intermediation services. It must be noted, however, that the proposal currently applies to platform-to-business relations only. In other words, the transparency obligations it establishes would not govern the relationship between the platform and consumers. Moreover, as the proposal currently stands, the only transparency obligation that binds search engines is Article 5, which imposes on platforms the duty to disclose the main parameters determining ranking. Article 6, which establishes the platforms' obligation to be transparent about whether they grant their own services preferential treatment, and Article 7, which establishes the platforms' obligation to be transparent about whether they grant other providers access to data, do not apply to search engines. See Proposal for a Regulation of the European Parliament and of the Council on promoting fairness and transparency for business users of online intermediation services. COM(2018) 238 final. <https://ec.europa.eu/digital-single-market/en/news/regulation-promoting-fairness-and-transparency-business-users-online-intermediation-services>

1471 ibid, paragraph 34; See also *News Corp/Telepiù* (Case COMP/M.2876) [2004] OJ L110/73, and *Microsoft* (Case COMP/C-3/37.792) Commission decision of 24.03.2004 relating to a proceeding under Article 82 of the EC Treaty C (2004) 900 final

1472 Information Commissioner's Office (2014), *supra* n. 262, 8

1473 Bundeskartellamt (2017). *Background information on the Facebook proceeding*, 4

1474 ibid.

5. Editorial-like judgments: preferential treatment of one's own services

385. As already mentioned, other practices in which digital intermediaries engage and which may impact media pluralism and, more broadly, the fair and free flow of information, concern the editorial-like judgments they perform in selecting, ranking, and in making available the content to which online users are exposed. For example, search engines employ hundreds, if not thousands, of signals,[1475] which are criteria that range from how often a website updates its content to how much traffic the site generates to the number of keywords it contains that match the user's query.[1476] These signals (to which the algorithm assigns different weights) determine the ranking of search results.[1477] Apple subjects the apps that are sold through its iTunes Store to an approval process that is based on guidelines to which software developers must adhere.[1478] Amazon displays a list with the 'Editors' Picks', that is, books that Amazon editors propose to the readership.[1479] Facebook provides 'News Feeds', which is a 'constantly updating list of stories', including news stories, that are shared among users.[1480] While in some cases (e.g. guidelines on app approval) the factors that the intermediaries take into account to perform these editorial-like judgments are published by the intermediaries themselves, usually there is considerable vagueness and haziness over the parameters underpinning their decision whether and, if so, how they will display content.

386. A rather common factor motivating controversial editorial-like judgments is the promotion of the intermediaries' commercial interests.[1481] More particularly,

1475 Foundem (2012). *Remedy Proposals – An Outline of Proposed Remedies to Google's Anti-Competitive Manipulations of its Search Results and Ad Listings*, 10

1476 For examples of ranking signals that may affect Google's ranking see Dean, B. *Google's 200 Ranking Factors: The Complete List (2018)*. 16 May 2018, Backlinko. <http://backlinko.com/google-ranking-factors>

1477 Foundem (2012), *supra* n. 270, 10

1478 See https://developer.apple.com/app-store/review/guidelines/>

1479 See http://www.amazon.com/Editors-Picks-Kindle-eBooks/b?ie=UTF8&node=353898011>

1480 See https://www.facebook.com/help/327131014036297/>

1481 Note that the motivations underpinning editorial-like judgments vary. For example, in 2010, in a controversial move, Apple removed an app which provided instant access to the Wikileaks website. Apple said that it discontinued the service on the grounds that the app failed to comply with its guidelines which provide that '[a]ny app that is defamatory, offensive, mean-spirited, or likely to place the targeted individual or group in harm's way will be rejected'. Apple reportedly declined to make any further comments that could shed some light on this decision. There are other examples of app rejection by Apple and other intermediaries that may be perceived as a form of quasi-censorship. These examples are, however, isolated (for now). For more information on the above see, for instance, Tsotsis, A. *Apple Removes WikiLeaks App From App Store*. 20 December 2010, Techcrunch. <http://techcrunch.com/2010/12/20/apple-removes-wikileaks-app-from-app-store/>; Helft, M. *Why Apple Removed a WikiLeaks App From Its Store*. 21 December 2010, The New York Times. <http://bits.blogs.nytimes.com/2010/12/21/why-apple-removed-wikileaks-app-from-its-store/?_r=0>; BBC. *Apple removes iPhone Wikileaks app from iTunes*. 22 December 2010. <http://www.bbc.com/news/technology-12059577>; Kiss, J. *Apple pulls Wikileaks app, but Android apps remain*. 21 December 2010, The Guardian. <http://www.theguardian.com/media/pda/2010/dec/21/apple-wikileaks-app>; and Gokey, M. *Just say no – Apple and Google reject Flappy Bird Clones*. 17 February 2015, Techtimes. <http://www.techtimes.com/articles/3526/20140217/

integrated digital intermediaries have often been accused of granting their own affiliates preferential treatment to ensure that their services are more visible (or the only one available), thereby increasing the likelihood that consumers will purchase (with money, attention or data) the content they provide. Depending on the type of intermediary, this preferential treatment may be manifested in different ways. For example, Google makes sure that certain services it provides in markets neighboring general online search (e.g. price comparison services) are prominently displayed in the search results page, whilst refusing to apply to its own services penalties that determine ranking.[1482] Apple operates as both retailer selling content through its App Store and manufacturer of the hardware device to which the Store is tied. While apps make it possible for an iPad owner to purchase content using another store, Apple appears to have taken measures to prevent this from happening. For example, it has reportedly rejected the Sony Reader iPhone app, which would have allowed users to purchase and access e-books from the Sony Reader Store.[1483]

387. There is little doubt that preferential treatment in general and prominent display in particular may affect consumer choice. This is as true in the online world as it is in traditional content markets. An example from the offline universe is the so-called 'payola', a common practice in the publishing trade which refers to an arrangement whereby the publisher pays the retailer[1484] to display the book in special areas such as tables near the entrance.[1485] Readers are generally inclined to buy 'payola' books because they link prominent display to success.[1486] As regards online search, the Commission noted in *Google Search* that users 'typically look at the first three to five generic search results on the first general search results page and pay little or no attention to the remaining generic search results'.[1487] Similarly, content that is in a prominent position in Facebook's news feed increases the likelihood of visibility.[1488]

388. The degree to which editorial-like judgments performed by digital intermediaries may impact media pluralism will, of course, depend on various factors, including how successful these practices are in marginalizing competing

---

just-say-no-apple-and-google-reject-flappy-bird-clones.htm>. This lack of transparency regarding preferential treatment may, to some extent, be addressed by the Regulation of the European Parliament and of the Council on promoting fairness and transparency for business users of online intermediation services. COM(2018) 238 final. See *supra* n. 265

1482 These issues will be the focus of the analysis that follows.

1483 Helft, M. *Apple Moves to Tighten Control of App Store*. 1 February 2011, The New York Times. <http://www.nytimes.com/2011/02/01/technology/01apple.html?_r=0>

1484 Canoy, M., Jan C. van Ours and Frederick van der Ploeg (2005). *The Economics of Books*. CESifo Working Paper No. 1414, 16. <https://ideas.repec.org/p/ces/ceswps/_1414.html>

1485 *Lagardère/Natexis/VUP* (Case COMP/M.2978) [2004] OJ L125/54, paragraph 672

1486 Cowen, T. (2000). *What Price Fame?* Cambridge, MA: Harvard University Press, 37

1487 *Google Search* (Case AT.39740) Commission decision of 27 June 2017 relating to proceedings under Article 102 TFEU and Article 54 of the EEA Agreement C (2017) 4444 final, paragraph 455

1488 For examples see Foster (2012), *supra* n. 38, 36

content and the type of content that is downgraded or altogether excluded from the intermediary's platform. For example, in a case similar to the removal of the Sony app from Apple's App Store, iPad owners are locked out of potentially more diverse content made available on the competing platform.[1489] In extreme cases, an intermediary that engages in discriminatory practices to promote a certain political agenda may impact the democratic process. For example, as already mentioned in Chapter 2, an experiment that was conducted by Epstein and Robertson showed that the practice of downgrading may influence voters' preferences.[1490] While arguing that the editorial-like judgments digital intermediaries currently perform are capable of producing such drastic effects on opinion forming is probably a stretch, related issues will gain prominence, especially as intermediaries are increasingly expanding in (news) content markets.

389. This section will deal with – what appears to be – the most common factor that motivates controversial editorial-like judgments, that is, the granting of preferential treatment to one's own services. The analysis that follows focuses on the *Google Search* decision, but the above examples clearly illustrate that the issue of preferential treatment has a much broader relevance for this thesis.

390. In *Google Search*, the Commission found that the conduct under scrutiny decreases traffic from Google's general search results pages to competing comparison shopping services whilst increasing traffic to Google's own comparison shopping service.[1491] It also found that search traffic from Google's general search results pages accounts for a large proportion of traffic to competing services and cannot be effectively replaced by other sources currently available to them.[1492] Along with the effects on internet traffic, the Commission considered that the conduct was capable of leading, or likely to lead, to higher prices (for merchants and consumers alike), less innovation, and lower quality.[1493] It is worth pointing out that, based on user behavior (i.e., users' preference for results ranking higher in the list even if they are less

1489 In a case similar to the removal of the WikiLeaks app (see *supra* n. 276), users would be deprived of an additional tool that would allow access to content on matters of common concern and, perhaps more importantly, they would be prevented from financing a non-profit organization that acts as a watchdog over governments (US$1 from every US$1.99 sale of the app was directed to WikiLeaks).

1490 Epstein, R. and Ronald E. Robertson (2013). *Democracy at Risk: Manipulating Search Rankings Can Shift Voting Preferences Substantially Without Voter Awareness*. American Institute for Behavioral Research and Technology Working Paper Series. Paper presented at the 25th annual meeting of the Association for Psychological Science, Washington, D.C. A summary of the paper is available at: http://aibrt.org/downloads/EPSTEIN_and_Robertson_2013-Democracy_at_Risk-APS-summary-5-13.pdf>

1491 *Google Search* (Case AT.39740) Commission decision of 27 June 2017 relating to proceedings under Article 102 TFEU and Article 54 of the EEA Agreement C (2017) 4444 final, paragraphs 452 *et seq*.

1492 ibid, paragraphs 540 *et seq*.

1493 ibid, paragraphs 593–596. That those other parameters were considered in addition to the effects on internet traffic is arguably explained by the fact that Google argued that the Commission failed to demonstrate that there is a causal link between the conduct and the decrease in traffic to competing providers, on the one hand, and the conduct and the increase in traffic to Google's comparison shopping service, on the other. See paragraphs 605–607

relevant to a query) and Google's failure to effectively inform consumers about the fact that it was granting its own comparison shopping services preferential treatment, the Commission also took account of the effects of the conduct on the consumers' ability to access the most relevant search results.[1494] If one accepts the premise of this study, that is to say, that price is not the only (and perhaps not even the most relevant) dimension of competition in media markets, the non-price factors which drove the Commission's assessment of whether Google abused its dominant position would, in principle, seem to accommodate concerns specific to the markets under investigation.

391. However, while traffic, innovation and relevance undoubtedly play a major role in competing effectively in online search markets, an analysis of the decision reveals that the Commission's reasoning creates considerable confusion about the standards against which self-favoring may amount to exclusionary abuse. This uncertainty is further exacerbated by the Commission's unsuccessful attempt to explain whether and, if so, how the conduct under scrutiny suits the logic followed in decisional practice and case law.

392. This section will unveil the drawbacks of the Commission's analysis and discuss the implications for competition enforcement of the different approaches to assessing whether self-favoring amounts to an abuse that the Commission's inconsistent reasoning implies. In doing so, it will serve the main purpose of this study, which is to showcase that EU competition law is sufficiently flexible to address complex problems arising in digital media markets.

393. Going into the specifics, what led the Commission to conclude that Google's conduct amounts to an abuse of a dominant position? As already mentioned, the Commission found that Google's practices were 'capable of having, or likely to have' anti-competitive effects.[1495] It is not clear from the wording of the decision whether these are two different criteria or whether the Commission uses the terms 'capable of' and 'likely to' interchangeably. For example, the Commission notes that Google's conduct 'is *capable of* leading competing comparison shopping services to cease to provide their services [which] would allow Google to impose and maintain higher fees on merchants for participation in its own comparison shopping service. These higher costs for merchants are *capable of* leading to higher product prices for consumers' [emphasis added].[1496] Subsequently, the Commission mentions that Google's practices are '*likely to* reduce the incentives of competing comparison shopping services to innovate', '*likely to* reduce the incentives of Google to improve the quality of its comparison shopping service', and '*likely*

1494 ibid, see paragraphs 598–599

1495 ibid, paragraph 592

1496 ibid, paragraph 594

to reduce the ability of consumers to access the most relevant comparison shopping services' [emphasis added].[1497] Whether the use of both 'capable of' and 'likely to' makes a difference is *not* an academic question, but a question of major practical importance, for each of these terms may be linked to different evidentiary standards.

394. More particularly, 'likely to' requires an examination of the probable *effects* on competition that the conduct of the dominant firm may create. As already discussed in Chapter 3, in recent years, driven by the idea that competition enforcement seeks to protect competition and not competitors, decisional practice and case law have attempted to establish whether an abuse has taken place by considering the effects on competition in conjunction with other factors (e.g. whether a valuable input which is controlled by the dominant firm and which grants it a significant advantage is *indispensable* to competing in the affected market).[1498]

395. 'Capable of' may imply reliance on the *intent* of the dominant firm to push competitors out of the market, a parameter which in the past influenced several decisions and judgments.[1499] Despite the shift to a more effects-based approach to competition analyses, the Commission may still consider that intent is relevant for antitrust enforcement. For example, in its Guidance on Article 102 TFEU the Commission mentions that it will normally intervene where the exclusionary conduct concerned 'has already been or *is capable of* hampering competition'.[1500] The Guidance refers to *AKZO*, where the Court held that prices below average costs 'must be regarded as abusive if they are determined as part of *a plan for eliminating a competitor*' [emphasis added].[1501] In *Google Search*, the Commission notes that intent is 'one of the criteria which can be used for assessing the abusive nature of behavior under Article 102' and the decision uses indicia of intent. For example, the decision refers to an internal Google email exchange where Google's Engineering Director responsible for Froogle warned that:

1497 ibid, paragraphs 595–597

1498 Chapter 3, Part 4.1.

1499 See, for instance, Commission decision of 29 July 1987 (IV/32.279 – *BBI v Boosey & Hawkes*) [1987] OJ L286/36, paragraph 19; Commission Decision of 18 July 1988 (Case IV/30.178 – *Napier Brown v British Sugar*) [1988] OJ L285/41, paragraph 62. See also Commission decision of 24 July 1991 relating to a proceeding pursuant to Article 86 of the EEC Treaty (IV/31043 – *Tetra Pak II*) [1992] OJ L72/1. In this case, the Commission found that the firm had 'deliberately' sold at a loss 'with the aim' of eliminating competition (paragraphs 150 and 104). For other examples and a comprehensive overview of the role of intent in Article 102 cases see Akman, P. (2014). *The role of intent in the EU case law on abuse of dominance*. European Law Review 39(3), 316–337

1500 Guidance on the Commission's enforcement priorities in applying Article 82 of the EC Treaty to abusive exclusionary conduct by dominant undertakings [2009] OJ C 45/2, paragraph 23 and fn. 1

1501 ECJ, Case C-62/86, *AKZO Chemie BV v Commission of the European Communities* [1991] ECR I-3359, paragraph 72

> (1) [t]he [Froogle] pages may not get crawled without special treatment; without enough pagerank or other quality signals, the content may not get crawled. (2) If it gets crawled, the same reasons are likely to keep it from being indexed; (3) If it gets indexed, the same reasons are likely to keep it from showing up (high) in search results. ... *We'd probably have to provide a lot of special treatment to this content in order to have it be crawled, indexed, and rank well* [emphasis added].[1502]

396. Considering that (at least a part of) the Commission's analysis was indeed effects-based (see the use of 'likely to' referred to above), further confusion is created about whether and, if so, to what extent Google's practices were assessed by reference to the *conditions* set by the case law which was concerned with the effects of the exclusionary conduct under examination on competition.[1503] This confusion stems from the Commission's attempt to reject Google's argument that its practices do not fall under Article 102 TFEU. More particularly, Google contended that 'the conduct could be considered abusive only if the criteria established in the [*Oscar*] *Bronner* case [were] fulfilled'.[1504] By failing to apply those criteria, Google said, the Commission imposed on it a duty to allow competing services to have access to a significant proportion of its general search results pages, despite access to those pages not being *indispensable* in order to compete.[1505] The Commission dismissed this argument on the grounds that '[t]he Bronner criteria are *irrelevant* in a situation, such as that of the present case, where bringing to an end an infringement does not involve a duty on the dominant undertaking to "transfer any asset or to enter into agreements with persons with whom it has not chosen to contract"' [emphasis added].[1506] Contrary to what the Commission says, it will be shown in detail that the condition of 'indispensability' set by *Oscar Bronner* (and other rulings which also dealt with the refusal of the dominant firm to supply) is far from irrelevant in the case at hand. In fact, had the Commission engaged in a careful interpretation of the 'refusal to supply' line of case law, which, in the same way as *Google Search*,[1507] sought to address leveraging of significant market power into a neighbouring

1502 *Google Search* (Case AT.39740) Commission decision of 27 June 2017 relating to proceedings under Article 102 TFEU and Article 54 of the EEA Agreement C (2017) 4444 final, paragraph 491

1503 ECJ, Case C-7/97 *Oscar Bronner GmbH & Co. KG v Mediaprint Zeitungs- und Zeitschriftenverlag GmbH & Co. and others* [1998] ECR I-7791. The conditions set by the Court in *Oscar Bronner* are laid down in paragraph 41, which reads as follows: 'in order to plead the existence of an abuse within the meaning of Article [102] of the Treaty … [it would not only be necessary] that the refusal of the service be likely to eliminate all competition in the daily newspaper market on the part of the person requesting the service and that such refusal be incapable of being objectively justified, but also that the service in itself be indispensable to carrying on that person's business, inasmuch as there is no actual or potential substitute in existence for that home-delivery scheme'

1504 *Google Search* (Case AT.39740) Commission decision of 27 June 2017 relating to proceedings under Article 102 TFEU and Article 54 of the EEA Agreement C (2017) 4444 final, paragraph 645

1505 ibid.

1506 ibid, paragraph 651

1507 ibid, paragraph 649

market, it would have realized that the parameters on which the judgments concerned were based significantly influenced its assessment of Google's practices.

397. The adequacy and implications for competition enforcement of adopting a low or high threshold for finding an abuse are discussed in detail below.

398. Were we to apply a low threshold, we could claim that an integrated firm that enjoys a dominant position is under a *general* obligation to refrain from self-favoring.[1508] This approach could be supported by decisional practice and case law which, as already mentioned, were based on the presumed intent of the firm to push its competitors out of the market.[1509] However, even if it can be backed by precedent, one must still ask whether establishing *ex ante* that dominant firms are bound to refrain from engaging in self-favoring would be desirable. This approach has been criticized on the grounds that intent is not an accurate indicator of the actual or likely impact of the conduct on the market.[1510] In other words, so its opponents say, presumptions of intent run the risk of leading to erroneous outcomes, potentially punishing conduct that is not harmful. While persuasive, this argument is not ultimately conclusive. EU competition law is largely founded on presumptions *and this, in retrospect, is not necessarily a bad thing.*

399. Let us take the example of merger control in the context of which the Commission must assess whether, as a result of the concentration, the merged entity will not only have the ability but also *the incentive* to distort competition.[1511] I have shown in Chapter 4 that a strict approach based on hypotheticals that the merging firms would be incentivized to act anti-competitively post-merger protected rather than harmed competition.[1512] I have also shown that, in recent years, the Commission's permissiveness towards mergers did little to nothing to protect the competitive process. In fact, the adoption of less stringent criteria has not only led to the obvious, that is, higher concentration ratios, but in certain cases it damaged innovation and led to higher prices.[1513] My analysis concerned broadcasting markets only, but if this is any indication of the (positive) role that presumptions of intent may play in avoiding distortions of competition in markets presenting similar characteristics (e.g. a natural tendency to concentration attributed to two-sidedness and the

1508 Ibáñez Colomo, P. (2014). *Exclusionary Discrimination under Article 102 TFEU*. Common Market Law Review 51, 150

1509 ibid, 151–152, referring to Commission decision of 29 July 1987 (IV/32.279 – *BBI v Boosey & Hawkes*) [1987] OJ L286/36, paragraph 19; Commission Decision of 18 July 1988 (Case IV/30.178 – *Napier Brown v British Sugar*) [1988] OJ L285/41, para 62

1510 ibid, 153 and 155

1511 See Guidelines on the assessment of non-horizontal mergers under the Council Regulation on the control of concentrations between undertakings [2008] OJ C 265/7, paragraph 15; and Guidelines on the assessment of horizontal mergers under the Council Regulation on the control of concentrations between undertakings [2004] OJ C 31/3, paragraph 28

1512 See, for instance, Part 3.3.1.

1513 ibid.

resulting network effects and downward spirals), then the scale would seem to tip in favor of a more cautious approach as to how firms *may* behave. The Commission's Merger Study, which analyzed forty decisions adopted in the five-year period 1996–2000[1514] and from which we may clearly infer that behavioral remedies (i.e., remedies that sought to temper the incentive to behave anti-competitively) have been far from a success story, lends further support to the claim that if an integrated firm which enjoys market power was bound by a general obligation not to discriminate, this could be to the benefit of competition. The dominant firm could still defend itself by putting forward objective justifications[1515] or, in a way similar to the restraints 'by object' introduced by an agreement,[1516] efficiencies in support of the discriminatory behavior in question.[1517] Ultimately, whether presumed intent is better than other (higher) thresholds for establishing that a dominant firm has committed an abuse may only be determined if one compares how markets evolved under the former standard with how markets developed under the latter (lower) standard. The above remarks should not be understood to mean that a finding of abuse based on presumptions of intent is devoid of drawbacks. Because finding abuse would (solely) rely on establishing that the conduct concerned contains elements of discrimination and on evidence suggesting that the firm embarked on the conduct in order to eliminate competition, competitors would probably find it easy to free-ride on the dominant firm's efforts. This could ultimately be to the detriment of innovation and consumer choice.

400. We now turn to the other possible method for checking whether preferential treatment of one's own services amounts to an abuse of a dominant position, which consists in measuring the effects that the conduct under scrutiny produces or is likely to produce on competition.[1518] This method would be in line with the more economics-based approach to competition analyses and, compared with the above proposal, complaints and decisions would need to be founded on more robust evidence. However, if we were indeed to go down this path, what would be the threshold above which it may be accepted that the conduct under scrutiny may produce exclusionary effects? Ibáñez Colomo convincingly argues that in such cases it would have to be shown that ceasing

1514 Commission (2005). *Merger Remedies Study*. <http://ec.europa.eu/competition/mergers/legislation/remedies_study.pdf>

1515 Guidance on the Commission's enforcement priorities in applying Article 82 of the EC Treaty to abusive exclusionary conduct by dominant undertakings [2009] OJ C 45/2, paragraphs 28–31. On a comprehensive analysis of how the notion of 'objective justification' has been interpreted by the Court see Albors-Llorens, A. (2007). *The Role of Objective Justification and Efficiencies in the Application of Article 82 EC*. Common Market Law Review 44, 1727–1761 and Loewenthal, P. J. (2005). *The defense of 'objective justification' in the application of Article 82 EC*. World Competition, 28, 455–477

1516 See Commission Guidelines on the Application of Article 101(3) TFEU [2004] OJ C 101/08, paragraph 60; CFI, Case T-168/2001, *GlaxoSmithKline Services Unlimited v Commission* [2006] ECR II-2969, paragraphs 247–252

1517 Guidance on the Commission's enforcement priorities in applying Article 82 of the EC Treaty to abusive exclusionary conduct by dominant undertakings [2009] OJ C 45/2, paragraphs 28–31

1518 Ibáñez Colomo (2014), *supra* n. 303, 155–156

and desisting from engaging in discriminatory practices is 'indispensable' to operating in the affected market.[1519] Adopting the 'indispensability' criterion, he says, would be consistent with the case law concerning other strategies, such as refusal to supply, that essentially seek to achieve the same objective, namely leveraging,[1520] and it would also accord with the principle that only in exceptional circumstances a firm should be forced to deal with its rivals.[1521]

401. Of course, 'indispensability' should be adapted to the specific circumstances of the case, not least because the relevant decisional practice and case law are rather inconsistent. For example, in *Magill*, which concerned a refusal to license IPRs, the decisive factor for establishing abuse was that the conduct prevented the appearance of a new product.[1522] In order to reach this conclusion, the Court took account of the fact that there was no substitute for the product for which there was potential consumer demand and that the raw material to which access was sought was indispensable for its creation.[1523] Put simply, indispensability was integrated in the examination of whether competitors were seeking to offer a new product. This was not the direction the Court followed in *Tiercé Ladbroke*,[1524] which concerned the request by a Belgian owner of betting shops to be granted access to televised transmissions of French horse races. In this latter case, the Court ruled that the refusal to supply would be abusive if 'it concerned a product or service which was *either essential* for the exercise of the activity in question, in that there was no real or potential substitute, *or was a new product* whose introduction might be prevented' [emphasis added].[1525] In *Oscar Bronner*, which concerned access to a newspaper delivery scheme, the Court altogether refrained from referring to the new product requirement.[1526] And in *Microsoft*, the Commission found that the refusal to share the indispensable input, namely interoperability information, was not a refusal that prevented competitors from duplicating Microsoft's (already existing) products, but a 'refusal to allow follow-on innovation', thereby preventing them from improving their own products.[1527] In view of the above, there is considerable uncertainty over how big of a role the provision of a 'new' or a 'better' product would play in determining whether the indispensability criterion is fulfilled.

1519 ibid, 157

1520 ibid, 156

1521 ibid, 158

1522 ECJ, Joined Cases C-241/91 P and C-242/91 P *Radio Telefis Eireann (RTE) and Independent Television Publications Ltd. v Commission* [1995] ECR I-743, paragraphs 54–56

1523 ibid.

1524 CFI, Case T-504/93 *Tiercé Ladbroke SA v Commission* [1997] ECR II-923

1525 ibid, paragraph 131

1526 ECJ, Case C-7/97 *Oscar Bronner GmbH & Co. KG v Mediaprint Zeitungs- und Zeitschriftenverlag GmbH & Co. and others* [1998] ECR I-7791, paragraph 41

1527 *Microsoft* (Case COMP/C-3/37.792) Commission decision of 24.03.2004 relating to a proceeding under Article 82 of the EC Treaty C (2004) 900 final, paragraphs 630 *et seq.*

402. There are differences between the facts of the cases cited above and Google's self-favoring practices. As regards the latter, it is *not access to the facility*, but *equitable access* that is sought. However, some of the parameters that influenced the outcome of the above decisions and judgments, including especially the benchmarks against which indispensability was assessed, appear relevant here. For example, the fact that what competitors seek is not access to the algorithm (which would allow them to design their sites in a way that ensures prominent display), but equal treatment (which would allow their services to somehow communicate with the algorithm in the same way that Google's services do, thereby *potentially* appearing in a more prominent position) establishes a strong resemblance with cases concerning interoperability such as Microsoft. As already mentioned, in this case the Commission did not focus on whether Microsoft's refusal prevented the creation of a new product, but on proving that, absent the refusal, the competitors' work group server operating systems could be better than Microsoft's with respect to, *inter alia*, the reliability of the system and security, two characteristics to which consumers attached particular importance.[1528]

403. Another factor which was decisive in *Microsoft* and which is linked to the Google case is the scope of measures (i.e., levels of intrusiveness) that are capable of striking a balance between the dominant firm's incentive to innovate and competitors' ability to effectively operate in the affected market, thus greasing the wheels of the competitive process. More particularly, Microsoft attempted to rebut its competitor's request to be granted access to the 'indispensable' input by arguing that the request was too invasive; Microsoft said that what the competitor asked was a disclosure of source code written by Microsoft and the right to copy or modify that source code in order to integrate it in its own products (this was referred to in the decision as 'implementation').[1529] Based on expert statements, the Commission drew a distinction between interface information and implementation, noting that 'an interface specification describes *what* an implementation must achieve, not *how* it achieves it'.[1530] The Commission was also keen to clarify that by no means did the decision 'contemplate ordering Microsoft to allow copying ... by third parties'.[1531]

404. Yet another element that appears relevant here is a parameter that influenced the Court in *Tiercé Ladbroke*: the Court held that the televised transmission of French horse races to which the betting shops owner sought access '[was] *not indispensable, since* it [took] place after bets [were] placed, with the

1528 The Commission's findings were upheld by the Court. See CFI, Case T-201/04 *Microsoft Corp. v Commission of the European Communities* [2007] ECR II-03601, paragraph 652

1529 *Microsoft* (Case COMP/C-3/37.792) Commission decision of 24.03.2004 relating to a proceeding under Article 82 of the EC Treaty (2004) 900 final, paragraph 568

1530 ibid, paragraph 570

1531 ibid, paragraph 572

result that *its absence [did] not in itself affect the choices made by bettors and, accordingly, [could not] prevent bookmakers from pursuing their business*' [emphasis added].[1532]

405. Interestingly, while the Commission noted that the criterion of indispensability is 'irrelevant' in the case at hand,[1533] it may be inferred from the decision that its assessment was grounded in the criteria that were discussed above. More particularly, as already mentioned, in *Microsoft* the Commission assessed Microsoft's conduct by reference to whether the refusal to supply interoperability information inhibited 'follow-on innovation' by preventing competitors from offering better products.[1534] Similarly, in *Google Search*, the Commission found that Google's practices are anticompetitive on the grounds that they were likely to reduce the competitors' incentive to innovate, thereby preventing them from 'improving the relevance of their existing services'.[1535] As regards the condition set by *Tiercé Ladbroke*[1536] that there must be a link between the asset to which access is sought and the ability of a competitor to pursue its business, a part of *Google Search* is devoted to the importance of user traffic for comparison shopping services; based on the results of the market investigation, the Commission explained that traffic enhances the ability of comparison shopping services to generate revenue, allows machine-learning effects that improve the relevance of the results they offer, and enables them to generate more original user reviews.[1537] That traffic is a key element of 'pursuing business' in a data-driven (and often ad-based) search market was complemented with evidence about how prominent display affects user behavior and, by extension, traffic.[1538] For example, as already mentioned, the Commission referred to studies that showed that users typically look at the first three to five generic search results on the first page and pay little to no attention to the remaining generic search results.[1539] Finally, as regards the scope of measures (i.e., levels of intrusiveness) that are capable of striking a balance between the dominant firm's incentive to innovate and competitors' ability to effectively operate in the affected market, the remedial order explains in rather broad terms that Google is required to subject its own comparison shopping service to the same underlying processes and methods for the positioning and display in Google's general search results pages as those

1532 CFI, Case T-504/93 *Tiercé Ladbroke SA v Commission* [1997] ECR II-923, paragraph 132

1533 *Google Search* (Case AT.39740) Commission decision of 27 June 2017 relating to proceedings under Article 102 TFEU and Article 54 of the EEA Agreement C (2017) 4444 final, paragraph 651

1534 See CFI, Case T-201/04 *Microsoft Corp. v Commission of the European Communities* [2007] ECR II-03601, paragraph 652

1535 ibid, paragraph 595

1536 CFI, Case T-504/93 *Tiercé Ladbroke SA v Commission* [1997] ECR II-923, paragraph 132

1537 *Google Search* (Case AT.39740) Commission decision of 27 June 2017 relating to proceedings under Article 102 TFEU and Article 54 of the EEA Agreement C (2017) 4444 final, paragraphs 444–451

1538 ibid, paragraphs 454–461

1539 ibid, paragraph 455

used for competing comparison shopping services.[1540] However, Google was not required to disclose its algorithm.

406. In view of the above, the Commission's assessment of whether Google abuses its dominant position appears to have been (at least partly) based on the notion of 'indispensability', as formulated by the relevant jurisprudence. This illustrates that, even under a strict effects-based approach,[1541] EU competition law is sufficiently flexible to address challenges posed by increasingly digitized markets, including algorithm manipulation.

6. Conclusions

407. This Chapter discussed a number of issues that relate to the application of Article 102 TFEU to digital intermediaries. The Chapter used the Google investigation as a case study because it gives rise to a plethora of issues that illustrate the ways in which an intermediary with interests in several markets may impact competition and media pluralism; these issues concern, *inter alia*, 'scraping' and retaliatory behavior that affect news markets, data portability restrictions that affect online advertising and search markets, and prominent display in general search that may affect vertical search markets.

408. As in Chapters 4 and 5, the Chapter examined competition intervention in order to establish whether the Commission has made appropriate use of the tools it has at its disposal to address the competition issues it has identified during the Google investigation, and if not, to explore whether a proper application of Article 102 may remedy concerns over media pluralism in the affected markets. The following conclusions can be drawn from the analysis of the Commission's approach to the complaints against Google. First, as regards the question of how the case has been approached, the assessment of

1540 ibid, paragraph 700

1541 For the avoidance of confusion, while 'indispensability' has been subject to different interpretations, there is a common thread in 'refusal to supply' judgments, namely the (additional) condition that the conduct concerned must further be likely to lead to the exclusion of competition in the affected market. See, for instance, CFI, Case T-504/93 *Tiercé Ladbroke SA v Commission* [1997] ECR II-923, paragraph 133; Case C-7/97 *Oscar Bronner GmbH & Co. KG v Mediaprint Zeitungs- und Zeitschriftenverlag GmbH & Co. and others* [1998] ECR I-7791, paragraph 41; ECJ, Joined Cases C-241/91 P and C-242/91 P *Radio Telefis Eireann (RTE) and Independent Television Publications Ltd. v Commission* [1995] ECR I-743, paragraphs 54–56; *Microsoft* (Case COMP/C-3/37.792) Commission decision of 24.03.2004 relating to a proceeding under Article 82 of the EC Treaty C (2004) 900 final, paragraphs 585–589; ECJ, Joined Cases 6/73 and 7/73 *Istituto Chemioterapico Italiano and Commercial Solvents v Commission* [1974] ECR 223, paragraph 25; and ECJ, Case 311/84 *Centre belge d'études de marché – Télémarketing (CBEM) v SA Compagnie luxembourgeoise de télédiffusion (CLT) and Information publicité Benelux (IPB)* [1985] ECR 3261, paragraphs 26–27. With respect this requirement, it was mentioned that the Commission found, *inter alia*, that Google's practices diverted significant traffic from competing shopping services to Google's services. See *Google Search* (Case AT.39740) Commission decision of 27 June 2017 relating to proceedings under Article 102 TFEU and Article 54 of the EEA Agreement C (2017) 4444 final, in particular paragraphs 452 *et seq*.

the proposed undertakings that are likely to be accepted by the Commission shows that, where a number of complex issues arise, a commitments decision may fail to find the target. As extensively discussed throughout the Chapter, some of the proposed undertakings may be far-reaching and with potentially adverse effects on the markets concerned (scraping), some were poorly designed and hence highly likely to be ineffective (retaliation), and others simply unnecessary (data portability restrictions). This problem arises because in a commitments decision the Commission does not need to define relevant markets or measure the effects of the conduct under scrutiny. The implications of this approach for competition and media pluralism were discussed in detail in Chapter 3, where the *News Corp/BSkyB* decision was used as an example that vividly illustrated how avoiding dealing with complicated matters might jeopardize the accuracy of a competition decision and possibly harm media pluralism. The same conclusions can be drawn with respect to the Google case. For example, the Commission is inclined to prevent Google from displaying snippets of newspaper articles on Google News *without* having appraised the effects of scraping on the traffic of the newspapers' websites. If these effects are positive, there is no harm to competition. From a media pluralism perspective, if the small excerpts indeed encourage the users to click through, then preventing the display of snippets may eventually drive consumers to consult the few branded websites they have always consulted, ultimately disincentivizing them from discovering alternative sources of information.

409. Another issue concerns the management of the case in procedural terms. The Commission justified its decision to pursue the commitments route on the grounds that in fast-moving markets, such as those at issue, the objective is 'to restore quickly the conditions for competition on the merits'.[1542] Yet, eight years after the Commission opened its probe, we are still waiting for a decision addressing many of the practices that were found to raise concerns. Moving at such a slow pace renders the procedure devoid of any benefit.[1543] In view of the above, it would be no exaggeration to say that this case was procedurally mishandled with adverse effects on both competition and media pluralism. As already discussed in Chapter 2, the affected markets have a natural tendency to concentration and, once it acquires a dominant position, the antitrust offender may be difficult to challenge. That is to say, the longer Google is allowed to act anti-competitively, the less likely it is that other firms will be able to exercise effective competitive constraints upon it. With respect to media pluralism, the fact that no measures have been taken yet to address retaliation practices illustrates how the Commission's setbacks may impact the newspapers' ability to reach Google's large user base.

1542 Commission (2014a, February), *supra* n. 23

1543 It would not be an exaggeration to say that this violates the right of the firm that has allegedly breached the EU competition rules to have its affairs handled within a reasonable time, a right enshrined in the CFREU. Charter of Fundamental Rights of the European Union [2000] C 364/1, Article 41(1).

410. That Article 102 has still not managed to address a number of issues which Google's conduct raises should be attributed to the Commission only. The Chapter showed that the provision offers multiple avenues for remedying concerns associated with the practices of a dominant digital intermediary. For example, users can rely on Article 102 to address exploitative practices that largely affect their content choices. Adding to the above, in a Resolution it adopted, the European Parliament notes the significant role that search engines play in ensuring access to information, draws attention to the adverse effects of concentration on the content to which consumers are exposed, and calls upon the Commission 'to consider proposals aimed at unbundling search engines from other commercial services'.[1544] The Resolution was clearly referring to the market power Google enjoys in the EU and the practices that are currently being investigated by the Commission.[1545] Albeit an extreme solution and subject to the condition that no behavioral remedy would be equally effective or less burdensome, breaking up a dominant company is possible under EU competition law.[1546] This is another manifestation of the tools that EU competition law offers to deal with ownership concentration.

1544 European Parliament resolution of 27 November 2014 on supporting consumer rights in the digital single market (2013/2973 (RSP)).

1545 See, for instance, Kanter, J. *E.U. Parliament Passes Measure to Break Up Google in Symbolic Vote*. 27 November 2014, The New York Times. <http://www.nytimes.com/2014/11/28/business/international/google-european-union.html?_r=0>.

1546 Council Regulation (EC) No. 1/2003 of 16 December 2002 on the implementation of the rules on competition laid down in Articles 81 and 82 of the Treaty [2003] OJ L1/1, Article 7(1).

CHAPTER 7
CONCLUSIONS

The Objective

411. This study set out to explore to what extent the enforcement of EU competition rules can contribute to the protection of media pluralism, a value that has long been acknowledged as a condition for and a corollary of democracy.

412. EU law offers multiple avenues for supranational intervention, including the adoption of incentive measures under Article 167(5) TFEU, action against a Member State under Article 7 TEU, and the enactment of instruments containing provisions that seek to ensure that the internal market is not realized at the expense of media pluralism. The strengths and weaknesses of the aforementioned types of action have been extensively discussed in the scholarly literature. However, the potential of EU competition law to protect media pluralism has received limited attention to date. Either due to the shift to a more economics-based approach that has taken place over the past few years, or by virtue of the competence restrictions facing the Commission when dealing with the media, it is generally believed that EU competition law can do little to nothing to safeguard pluralism. But, EU competition law has been ascribed this negligible role without it having been examined whether the Commission has indeed managed to achieve its main goal, namely to protect undistorted competition and, if not, whether an alternative approach that respects the Treaty boundaries would first and foremost benefit competition and possibly, by extension, pluralism. The study aimed to fill this gap in the literature by attempting to answer the following three questions:

a) Has the Commission applied EU competition law to media markets properly, that is, by duly taking account of the parameters that drive competition in the media *and* by using the full toolkit it has at its disposal?

b) If not, what would be an alternative, proper application of EU competition law to media markets?

c) Would this alternative form of competition enforcement deliver an outcome that is more pluralism-friendly?

The Method

413. The study sought to answer the above three questions by examining how EU competition law has been and may be used in cases that concern some of the most widely used platforms through which Europeans access information, such as television, newspapers and search engines. The analysis attempted to cover the main issues the Commission has encountered in older, as well as more recent, cases under the pillars of merger and antitrust control. For that purpose, the decisional practice the Commission has developed in media markets in each pillar was assessed by reference to a specific sector in a way that reflects a business strategy (M&As in broadcasting), pricing model (RPM in books and newspapers), or practice (algorithm manipulation, scraping, data portability restrictions) that has been a major competition and media policy matter in the sector concerned. The common core issue in all the above cases was to determine how EU competition law has been or may be applied to an entity that controls an asset or factor, namely premium content, retail prices, and a popular information gateway, that may somehow affect competition and media pluralism in the affected sector.

Main Findings

414. The main findings regarding the contribution of competition enforcement to the protection of media pluralism are Chapter-specific, that is, related to the provision and sector examined in each Chapter, and were summarized within the respective Chapters. Nonetheless, the following general conclusions arise from the analysis of the Commission's decisional practice as assessed against economic theory and the applicable legal framework.

415. *First, in applying competition law to media markets, the Commission has ignored, to a large extent, sector-specific economics*, including the two-sided nature of advertising-based media markets, demand uncertainty and the resulting tendency to content homogenization, the inelastic price demand for certain media products, and the heterogeneity of consumer preferences. This is mainly attributed to an unjustifiably strong focus on price competition, including especially in cases where price is not the only – and perhaps not the

most relevant – parameter that drives competition in the market concerned. The most notable examples illustrating this focus on price competition are the 'trade relationship' criterion, which guided the Commission in the definition of relevant markets in merger cases involving free-to-air broadcasters, and the assumption that price is the key element in the consumers' decision to purchase a book, which underpinned its reasoning in cases dealing with RPM agreements governing sales of print books. Failure to take account of the sector-specific economics imperils the accuracy of the competition decision, for it falls short of identifying the competitive constraints exercised on the entities concerned. As a result, the decision is condemned from the outset for containing flaws that may range from neglecting an entire market that is relevant for a competition analysis (e.g. the market for audiences) to miscalculating the impact of the transaction or conduct concerned on (price *and* non-price) competition. This is also problematic from a media pluralism perspective. For example, in the case of free-to-air television,[1547] the 'trade relationship criterion' leads to a decision that is limited to discussing the effects of the concentration on advertising prices whilst ignoring altogether the effects on the provision of niche programming, the latter being a key aspect of content diversity. Similarly, in the case of books, the assumption that consumers care more about price than they do about diversity results in a decision that has not properly assessed whether the RPM agreement may generate qualitative efficiencies in the form of a broad range of books or an extensive network of retailers, which would serve content and supply diversity respectively.

416. *Second, it is striking that the Commission has avoided dealing with numerous issues that would determine the outcome of the decision.* In the case of mergers in television, for example, it has identified a market for 'other TV content' that includes news, documentaries and TV series, that is, types of content that are not substitutable for one another. In the case of mergers in newspaper publishing, the Commission has refrained from considering whether online news providers exert competitive constraints on print newspapers. In *Google Search*, it appears inclined to accept remedies without having considered key legal and factual issues that should underpin their design. For example, it is likely that the Commission will prevent Google from displaying snippets of newspaper articles in Google News *without* having considered that the effects of 'scraping' on the traffic to the newspapers' websites may be positive.

417. Irrespective of the reasons that lie behind the Commission's careless or lenient approach to complex and controversial matters, the effects are essentially the same as those resulting from failure to consider media-specific economics: the competition decision is based on inaccurate premises with negative implications for media pluralism. For example, in the case of broad market

1547 Or any other advertising-based market where content is provided for free and where indirect network effects between the advertiser and the consumer need to be taken into consideration.

definitions in merger cases, the decision underestimates the market power of the undertakings under scrutiny. As a result, concentrations have been cleared despite the fact that the merged entity would have the ability and incentive to distort competition in the affected markets post-merger. As regards pluralism, where news provision is included in a broader market for 'other content' or where the market for news provision is not subdivided into smaller markets that would accurately reflect how citizens consume news nowadays, the decision will most likely not address issues that would deliver a pluralism-friendly outcome (e.g. the possible need to divest news assets due to the acquisition by the merged entity of significant power in news markets).

418. The study, as synthesized above, challenged the reasoning underpinning the Commission's decision-making, and, after identifying the loopholes that have been left open, it demonstrated that EU competition law offers plenty of tools which, if used, result in a decision that properly reflects the dynamics of media markets. Moreover, by comparing the drawbacks of the relevant practice against the pro-competitive results that could have been achieved had the Commission applied competition law properly, the study also showcased the potential contribution of competition enforcement to the protection of media pluralism. The study proposed, *inter alia*, a method on the basis of which the Commission may define the relevant free-to-air broadcasting markets in a way that the decision mirrors the viewers' (and not only the advertisers') preferences, including niche programming. It further developed a theoretical framework within which the Commission may measure the effects of a transaction or conduct on non-price competition. In doing so, it shed light on the circumstances under which RPM agreements may deliver qualitative efficiencies in the form of a broad range of book and newspaper titles, the conditions under which a merger between broadcasters may adversely affect the variety or quality of the content broadcast, and the parameters against which to assess a number of business practices potentially harmful to competition and pluralism, such as demotion of competing content of higher quality, restrictions that prevent consumers from seamlessly switching from one content provider to another, and, where news markets are affected, interference with the ability of news outlets to generate (advertising and subscription) revenues.

Policy Implications

419. The study identified two perceptions regarding the role of EU competition law in preserving media pluralism that have underpinned scholarly literature and the Commission's decisional practice. First, media pluralism has been seen as an almost spontaneous result of unhindered market access. Second, media pluralism has been treated as a public policy value that justifies

restrictions of competition under Article 167(4) TFEU. As a result of the shift to a more economics-based approach, which posits that economic efficiency and consumer welfare are the guiding principles of EU competition policy and that concerns over other public policy values should be expelled from competition assessments, the second approach has been abandoned in recent years. While this policy change is arguably ill-founded, it is also true that the extent to which restrictions of competition may be accepted under Article 167(4) is very limited; under no circumstances could pluralism-related considerations supersede competition considerations, for this would be in violation of the Treaty. As regards market access, it is commonly contended that EU competition law contributes to media pluralism either through the prohibition of concentrations that would grant the merging firms significant power or through the imposition of access remedies. However, reality tells a different story. It is noteworthy that, over the past twenty years, the overwhelming majority of concentrations in the media sector were cleared unconditionally. Moreover, drawing on empirical evidence, the study demonstrated that in most cases access remedies are poorly designed and have been incapable of protecting undistorted competition; the analysis of how markets in certain Member States evolved following a series of access remedies that the Commission imposed on entities operating in broadcasting markets, and the appraisal of the remedies likely to be imposed upon Google are indicative of the flaws that are inherent in the Commission's access policy.

420. The theoretical arguments and empirical findings that pinpoint the weaknesses of the above two approaches suggest the need for policy amendments in the enforcement of EU competition law in media markets. The impact of these weaknesses on the competitive process, combined with the possible pro-competitive results that could be achieved by applying competition law as suggested throughout the study, set a sound basis for policy review in this area.

Recommendations for Future Research

421. The scale of the debate over how EU competition law is 'properly' applied to media markets is broad and multifaceted. It involves a number of different product and geographic markets, each of which has its own distinguishing features (size, structure, etc.). Moreover, new business models for the sale of media content have surfaced, the relationship between the consumer and the media content provider has undergone significant changes, and new (potentially anti-competitive) business practices have emerged. In view of the above, competition law is challenged in many respects. To produce sound policy strategies, there is need for more empirical and legal research which would allow further assessment of the various parameters that determine

supply and demand in the modern media landscape. Exploring the following can facilitate the attainment of this goal:

a) Further empirical research on demand-side substitutability: one of the main drawbacks of the Commission's practice that was identified by the present study is that it is not based on empirical data that would enable it to properly measure demand-side substitutability and assess the anti-competitive effects against what consumers value the most. As a result, the outcome of relevant decisions was flawed on a number of occasions. Consumption patterns have changed over the past few years and so has the information economy. The user engages in multisourcing and media multitasking, attaches importance to functionalities that were not available a few years ago (e.g. availability of programming on catch-up TV), and may access content in exchange for personal data. These developments give rise to a number of questions that are relevant for a competition analysis, including whether the user is aware of information asymmetries between the provider and herself, what are the parameters that make a provider more attractive than others, etc. In view of the above, further empirical research on how the media content consumer reacts to changes in quality, variety, and price would undoubtedly benefit decision-making in this area.

b) Research on the role of data, privacy, and artificial intelligence (AI) in competition enforcement: exchange of data for a service is increasingly becoming one of the most common 'transactions' in the modern information economy. But, what role should the accumulation of large reserves of data play in competition enforcement? For example, should competition authorities force firms with access to a vast amount of consumer data to share it with competitors in order to prevent market foreclosure? If protection of consumer data is a parameter of quality in data-driven markets, to what extent should privacy concerns factor into a competition assessment? Related to the above, in recent years, we have seen an exponential growth of AI, which is largely built on algorithms trained on data. Since data is the raw material for AI, how can antitrust agencies ensure that AI technology is competitive? This study illustrated how the collection and processing of user data and the increasing reliance on algorithmic technologies can affect competition and media pluralism. However, given that the use of digital services is only expected to increase, the above and other issues will undoubtedly challenge policymakers in the coming years and are, therefore, worthy of further research.

c) Further empirical research on the impact of RPM on price and non-price competition: in Chapter 5, it was mentioned that while economic theory supports the argument that RPM may generate a number of efficiencies, empirical research dealing with the impact of RPM on price and non-price competition is scarce. This topic is undoubtedly worthy of immediate attention and goes beyond the 'proper' application of Article 101 to media markets. National RPM policies are currently in a state of flux; certain Member States have recently abolished RPM laws governing the sale of print books whereas others have extended their applicability to digital titles. Moreover, NCAs are more and more taking cases involving RPM arrangements for the sale of publications. Hence, it is becoming increasingly important to resolve the uncertainty over the effects of fixed prices on the competitive process and media pluralism.

Limitations of EU competition law in safeguarding media pluralism and how to address them

422. The thesis put forward in the present study is neither that competition enforcement can remedy all the threats currently facing media pluralism nor that competition assessments may substitute pluralism reviews. The study identified the following four limitations, which can be mitigated if relevant assessments are conducted within the framework developed herein. First, competence restrictions prevent the Commission from taking action that would be to the benefit of media pluralism *only*. For example, the Commission may not block a merger that does not raise competition concerns, but is likely to raise pluralism concerns. Nonetheless, if the Commission incorporates in its analysis variety and quality considerations *and* if it acknowledges that in many cases behavioral remedies will not manage to protect undistorted competition in the affected markets, there is a strong likelihood that the outcome of the decision will be friendly to pluralism. Second, there are weaknesses inherent in the design of EU competition law. For example, from a pluralism perspective, centralization of market power, which is the presumed equivalent of opinion-forming power, would be sufficient to trigger the application of media ownership restrictions. Article 102 TFEU, however, does not prevent an undertaking from acquiring and holding, on its own merits, a dominant position but only the abuse thereof. Yet, it bears noting that in most cases this dominant position is not acquired through internal growth but through mergers and acquisitions and agreements with key market players that may contain exclusivity restrictions. By applying stricter criteria in exercising merger control and by keeping an eye on deals between powerful operators, which are no longer subject to notification, the Commission may go a long way towards addressing the acquisition of significant market power by a handful of entities that interferes with the free dissemination of information. Third, the focus of competition assessments and the scope of pluralism reviews are different. This is so for the reason that an authority entrusted with deciding on the impact of a conduct or transaction on pluralism has the power to examine whether the firms or individuals under scrutiny may misrepresent facts and

marginalize opposing viewpoints, in violation of the applicable media laws and principles. The EU competition watchdog is not entitled to carry out these tasks. It may, however, design solutions that would greatly alleviate related concerns. For example, structural remedies, which have been particularly successful in stimulating competition, reduce opinion-forming power, thereby safeguarding supply diversity. The final limitation has to do with the fact that information markets are fast-moving, complex and with a natural tendency to concentration. Hence, by the time competition proceedings are concluded, the harm to competition and media pluralism may already be done. Given the central role that the Commission can play in setting the conditions under which these markets develop, it is crucial to monitor how the practices market players engage in may affect competition and consumer welfare. Addressing anti-competitive conduct at an early stage may significantly influence how these markets will evolve. It is worth noting that one of the main points raised in the Report prepared by the EU Media Futures Forum, an expert group assigned by the Commission to analyze the future of media in the EU, is that one of the major problems in digital content markets is the emergence of new barriers to entry, often fabricated by the market players themselves,. The Report urges competition authorities to 'adjust to the fast-changing world of the Internet' by keeping themselves up-to-date in order to be able to take 'effective' action whenever innovation is threatened.[1548]

Concluding Remark

423. Contrary to general belief, this study demonstrated that the enforcement of EU competition rules may go a long way towards protecting media pluralism without stretching the boundaries of the Treaty. It did so by challenging long-standing assumptions regarding the effectiveness of the Commission's decisional practice, but also by showcasing how EU competition law may be instrumentalized to address problems that have emerged in more recent years. Given the likelihood that action with far-reaching implications under other branches of EU law is low, the normative suggestions put forward in this study may form the only realistic proposal on the contribution that the EU can make to safeguarding diversity in the media.

1548 EU Media Futures Forum (2012). *Fast-forward Europe – 8 solutions to thrive in the digital world*, 4. <http://ec.europa.eu/digital-agenda/sites/digital-agenda/files/forum_final_report_en.pdf>

SELECT BIBLIOGRAPHY

Books, Treatises, Manuals, PhD theses, and Chapters in edited collections

Amato, G. (1997). *Antitrust and The Bounds of Power – The Dilemma of Liberal Democracy in the History of the Market.* Oxford: Hart Publishing.

Anderman, S. (2007). *The Interface between Intellectual Property Rights and Competition Policy.* Cambridge: CUP.

Anderman, S. and Hedvig Schmidt (2011). *EU Competition Law and Intellectual Property Rights – The Regulation of Innovation* (2nd edition). Oxford: OUP.

Antoniadis, A. (2006). *The Financing of Public Service Broadcasting.* In Sanchez Rydelski, M. (ed.). *The EC State Aid Regime: Distortive Effects of State Aid on Competition and Trade.* London: Cameron May.

Appelman, M. *Fixed book price.* In Towse, R. (ed.). *A Handbook of Cultural Economics.* Cheltenham: Edward Edgar.

Areeda, P. E. and Herbert Hovenkamp (2004). *Antitrust Law* (2nd Edition). New York: Aspen Publishers.

Ariño, M. (2005). *Regulation and Competition in European Digital Broadcasting – A study of pluralism through access.* PhD thesis. Florence: European University Institute.

Baker, C.E. (2007). *Media concentration and democracy: why ownership matters.* Cambridge/New York: CUP.

Bardoel, J. and Jan van Cuilenburg (2008). *Strategic Media Management.* In Fourier, P. J. (ed.). *Media Studies – Policy, Management and Media Representation* (2nd edition). Cape Town: Juta & Co.

Besson, S. (2011). *The Human Rights Competence in the EU – The State of the Question after Lisbon.* In Kofler, G., Miguel Poiares Maduro and Pasquale Pistone (eds.). *Taxation and Human Rights in Europe and in the World.* Amsterdam: IBFD.

Biggam, R. (2009). *Public Broadcasting and State Aid in the New Media Environment – Is There A Need to Update the European Commission Broadcasting Communication, and Do 'Public Value Tests' Resolve Long-Running Competition Issues?* In Pauwels, C., Harri Kalimo, Karen Donders and Ben Van Rompuy (eds.). *Rethinking European Media and Communications Policy*. Brussels: VUB Press.

Bishop, S. and Mike Walker (2002). *The Economics of EC Competition Law* (2nd edition). London: Sweet and Maxwell.

Buendia-Sierra, J. L. (1999). *Exclusive Rights and State Monopolies under EC Law*. Oxford: OUP.

Capito, R. and Moira Kettner (2008). *Excursus: EC Merger Regulation*. In Castendyk, O., Egbert J. Dommering and Alexander Scheurer. *European Media Law*. Alphen aan den Rijn: Kluwer Law International.

Carr, N.G. (2010). *The Shallows: What the Internet Is Doing to Our Brains*. New York City: W. W. Norton & Company.

Cavino, M. and Lucilla Conte (2013). *Il diritto pubblico*. Santarcangelo di Romagna: Maggioli.

Chalmers, D. Gareth Davies and Giorgio Monti (2006). *European Union Law: Text and Materials*. Cambridge: CUP.

Compaine, B.M. and Douglas Gomery (2000). *Who owns the media? Competition and concentration in the mass media industry*. Mahwah, NJ: L. Erlbaum Associates.

Cowen, T. (2000). *What Price Fame?* Cambridge, MA: Harvard University Press.

Cruz, J. B. (2002). *Between Competition and Free Movement: The Economic Constitutional Law of the European Community*. Oxford: Hart Publishing.

Davenport, T. H. and John C. Beck (2001). *The Attention Economy: Understanding the New Currency of Business*. Boston: Harvard Business School Press.

de Búrca, G. and Paul Craig (2011). *EU Law: Text, Cases, and Materials* (5th edition). Oxford: OUP.

de Witte, B. (1995). *The European Content Requirement – Five Years After*. In Barendt, E. (ed.). *Yearbook of Media and Entertainment Law*. Oxford: OUP.

de Witte, B. and Gabriel N. Toggenburg (2004). *Human Rights and Membership of the European Union*. In Peers, S. and Angela Ward (eds.). *The EU Charter of Fundamental Rights*. Oxford: Hart Publishing.

Deutsch, A. L. (2010). *Protecting News in the Digital Era: The Case for a Federalized Hot News Misappropriation Tort*. In Advanced Seminar on Copyright Law, (PLI Patents, Copyrights, Trademarks, & Literary Prop., Course Handbook Series No. 1003, 2010).

Docquir, P. F. and Bart Van Besien (2014). *Changing Conditions of Competition for Public Service and Commercial Media in Belgium: Implications for Media Independence*. In Psychogiopoulou, E. *Media Policies Revisited. The Challenge for Media Freedom and Independence*. London: Palgrave Macmillan.

Donders, K. (2011). *Public Service Media and Policy in Europe*. London: Palgrave Macmillan.

Donders, K. (2009). *State Aid and Public Service Broadcasting. How Future Proof is the Remit of Public Broadcasting Organizations?* In Pauwels, C., Harri Kalimo, Karen Donders and Ben Van Rompuy (eds.), *Rethinking European Media and Communications Policy*. Brussels: VUB Press.

Donders K. and Hallvard Moe (2014). *European State-Aid control and PSB: Competition Policy Clashing or Matching with Public Interest Objectives?* In Donders, K., Caroline Pauwels and Jan Loisen (eds.). *The Palgrave Handbook of European Media Policy*. London: Palgrave Macmillan.

Doyle, G. (2002). *Media Ownership: The Economics and Politics of Convergence and Concentration in the UK and European Media*. London: Sage Publications.

Doyle, G. (2002). *Understanding Media Economics*. London: Sage Publications.

Drexl, J., Kerber, W. Podszun, R. (eds.) (2010). *Competition Policy and the Economic Approach – Foundations and Limitations*. Cheltenham: Edward Elgar.

Dyson, K., Peter Humphreys, Ralph Negrine and Jean-Paul Simon (1988). *Broadcasting and New Media Policies in Western Europe*. London: Routledge.

Einstein, M. (2002). *Media Diversity: Economics, Ownership, and the FCC*. New York: Routledge.

Ellis, J. (2002). *Seeing Things: Television in the Era of Uncertainty*. London and New York: I.B. Tauris.

Evans, D.S. (2009). *Two-Sided Market Definition*. American Bar Association, Section of Antitrust Law. *Market Definition in Antitrust: Theory and Case Studies*. Chicago, IL: American Bar Association.

Evans, D. S. and Richard Schmalensee (2008). *The Industrial Organization of Markets with Two-Sided Platforms*. In Collins, W.D. (ed.). *Issues in Competition Law and Policy*. Chicago, IL: American Bar Association.

Everling, U. (1997). *Book Price Fixing in the German Language Area and European Community Law*. Baden-Baden: Nomos.

Feintuck, M. and Mike Varney (2010). *Regulating Media Markets: The Need for Subsidiarity and Clarity of Principle*. In Birkinshaw, P. and Mike Varney (eds.). *The European Union Legal Order after Lisbon*. Alphen aan den Rijn: Kluwer Law International.

Fenton, N. (2010). *Drowning or Waving? New Media, Journalism and Democracy*. In Fenton, N. (ed.), *New Media, Old News. Journalism and Democracy in the Digital Age*. London: Sage.

Geradin, D. and Michel Kerf (2003). *Controlling Market Power in Telecommunications: Antitrust vs Sector-specific Regulation*. Oxford: OUP.

Geradin, D., Anne Layne-Farrar, and Nicolas Petit (2012). *EU Competition Law and Economics*. Oxford: OUP.

Hallin, D. C. and Paolo Mancini (2004). *Comparing Media Systems: Three Models of Media and Politics*. Cambridge: CUP.

Hamelink, C. (1997). *Media, Ethnic Conflict and Culpability*. In Servaes, J. & Lie, R. (eds.). *Media in Transition*. Leuven/Amersfoort: Acco.

Harcourt, A. (2005). *The European Union and the Regulation of Media Markets*. Manchester: Manchester University Press.

Hargittai, E. (2004). *The Changing Online Landscape: From Free-for-All to Commercial Gatekeeping*. In Day, P. and D. Schuler (eds.). *Community Practice in the Network Society: Local Actions/Global Interaction*. New York: Routledge.

Harrison, J. and Lorna Woods (2007). *European Broadcasting Law and Policy*. Cambridge: CUP.

Helberger, N. (2005). *Regulating Conditional Access in Digital Broadcasting*. Alphen aan den Rijn: Kluwer Law International.

Helberger, N. (2015). *Media Pluralism Policies from the User Perspective*. In Valcke, Sükösd and Picard. *Media Pluralism and Diversity. Concepts, Risks and Global Trends*. London: Palgrave Macmillan.

Henning, C. and Karin Renblad (2009). *Perspectives on Empowerment, Social Cohesion and Democracy – An International Anthology*. Jönköping: School of Health Sciences, Jönköping University.

Herold, A. (2009). *The New Audiovisual Media Services Directive*. In Pauwels, C., Harri Kalimo, Karen Donders and Ben Van Rompuy (eds.). *Rethinking European Media and Communications Policy*. Brussels: VUB Press.

Hindman, M. (2008). *The Myth of Digital Democracy*. Princeton, NJ: Princeton University Press.

Humphreys, P. (1996). *Mass media and media policy in Western Europe*. Manchester: Manchester University Press.

Iosifidis, P. (2014). Pluralism, Media Mergers and European Merger Control. In Donders, K., Caroline Pauwels and Jan Loisen (ed.). *The Palgrave Handbook of European Media Policy*. London: Palgrave Macmillan.

Jakubowicz, K. (2015). *New Media Ecology: Reconceptualizing Media Pluralism*. In Valcke, Sükösd and Picard. *Media Pluralism and Diversity. Concepts, Risks and Global Trends*. London: Palgrave Macmillan.

Jones, A. and Brenda Sufrin (2008). *EC Competition Law* (3rd Edition). Oxford: OUP.

Jones, A. and Brenda Sufrin (2014). *EU Competition Law – Texts, Cases and Materials* (5th Edition). Oxford: OUP.

Karpinnen, K. (2007). *Making a difference to media pluralism – A critique of the pluralistic consensus in European media policy*. In Cammaerts, B. and Nico Carpentier (eds.). *Reclaiming the Media*. Bristol: Intellect Books.

Karpinnen, K. (2015). *The Limits of Empirical Indicators: Media Pluralism as an Essentially Contested Concept*. In Valcke, P., Miklós Sükösd and Robert G. Picard. *Media Pluralism and Diversity. Concepts, Risks and Global Trends*. London: Palgrave Macmillan.

Katsirea, I. (2008). *Public Broadcasting and European Law: A Comparative Examination of Public Service Obligations in Six Member* States. Alphen aan den Rijn: Kluwer Law International.

Katsirea, I. (2011). *The Three-Step Test – Three Steps Forwards or Backwards for Public Service Broadcasting in Germany?* In Donders, K. and Hallvard Moe (eds.). *Exporting the Public Value Test. The regulation of public broadcasters' new media services across Europe*. Göteborg: Nordicom.

Keen, A. (2007). *The cult of the amateur*. London: Nicholas Brealey Publishing.

Kjolby, H. (2008). *Denmark*. In Yamey, B. S. (ed.) *Resale Price Maintenance. A Comparative American–European Perspective* (3rd Edition). New Brunswick: Aldine Transaction.

Klimkiewicz, B. (2009). *Is the Clash of Rationalities Leading Nowhere? Media Pluralism in European Regulatory Policies*. In Czepek, A., Melanie Hellwig, and Eva Nowak, *Press Freedom and Pluralism in Europe: Concepts and Conditions*. Bristol: Intellect Books.

Klug, F., Keir Starmer and Stuart Weir (1996). *The Three Pillars of Liberty: political rights and freedoms in the UK*. London: Routledge.

Komorek, E. (2013). *Media Pluralism and European Union*. Alphen aan den Rijn: Kluwer Law International.

Lao, M. (2008). *Free Riding: An Overstated, and Unconvincing, Explanation for Resale Price Maintenance*. In Pitofsky, R. (ed.). *How the Chicago School Overshot the Mark: Effect of Conservative Economic Analysis on U.S. Antitrust*. Oxford: OUP.

Lefever, K. (2012). *New Media and Sport: International Legal Aspects*. The Hague: T.M.C. Asser Press.

Louviere, J.J., D.A. Hensher and J.D. Swait (2000). *Stated choice methods: Analysis and applications.* Cambridge: CUP.

McNair, B. (2006). *Cultural Chaos – Journalism, News and Power in a Globalized World*. London: Routledge.

McQuail, D. (2010). *McQuail's Mass Communication Theory* (6th edition). London: Sage.

Monti, G. (2007). *EC Competition Law*. Cambridge: CUP.

Motta, M. (2004). *Competition Policy: Theory and Practice*. Cambridge: CUP.

Napoli, P. (2015). *Assessing Media Diversity in the U.S.: A Comparative Analysis of the FCC's Diversity Index and the EU's Media Pluralism Monitor*. In Valcke, Sükösd and Picard. *Media Pluralism and Diversity. Concepts, Risks and Global Trends*. London: Palgrave Macmillan.

Negroponte, N. (1995). *Being Digital*. New York: Knopf.

Nicholls, T., Ron Southwell, William Houseley and Peter Block (2001). *Managing in the Media*. Oxford: Focal Press.

Nieminen, H. and Josef Trappel (2011). *Media serving democracy*. In Trappel□, J., Werner A. Meier, Leen D'Haenens□, Jeanette Steemer and Barbara Thomass (eds.). *Media in Europe Today*. Bristol: Intellect.

Nikolinakos, N. (2006). *EU Competition Law and Regulation in the Converging Telecommunications, Media and IT sectors*. Alphen aan den Rijn: Kluwer Law International.

Nitsche, I. (2001). *Broadcasting in the European Union. The Role of Public Interest in Competition Analysis*. Alphen aan den Rijn: Kluwer Law International.

Noam, E.M. (2009). *Media ownership and concentration in America*. Oxford: OUP.

Odudu, O. (2006). *The Boundaries of EC Competition Law: The Scope of Article 81*. Oxford: OUP.

Owen, B. (2006). *The tragedy of broadcast regulation*. In Hassan, R. and Julian Thomas (eds.), *The New Media Theory Reader*. Berkshire UK: Open University Press.

Owen, B. M. and Steven Wildman (1992). *Video Economics*. Cambridge, MA: Harvard University Press.

Pariser, E. (2011). *The Filter Bubble: What the Internet is Hiding from You*. New York: Penguin Press.

Pasquale, F. (2018). *The Automated Public Sphere*. In Seatnan, A. R., Ingrid Schneider, and Nicola Green (eds.). *The Politics of Big Data. Big Data, Big Brother?* Oxon: Routledge.

Prosser, T. (2005). *The Limits of Competition Law: Markets and Public Services*. Oxford: OUP.

Psychogiopoulou, E. (2006b). *The Integration of Cultural Considerations in EU Law and Policies*. PhD Thesis. Florence: European University Institute.

Psychogiopoulou, E. (2008). *The Integration of Cultural Considerations in EU Law and Policies*. Leiden: Martinus Nijhoff Publishers.

Rogers, R. (2004). *Information Politics on the Web*. Cambridge, MA: MIT Press.

Röller, L. H. (2007). *Exploitative Abuses*. In Ehlermann, C. D. and Mel Marquis (eds.), *European Competition Law Annual 2007: A Reformed Approach to Article 82 EC*. Oxford: Hart Publishing.

Shy, O. (2001). *The Economics of Network Industries*. Cambridge: CUP.

Simon, H. A. (1971). *Designing Organizations for an Information-rich World*. In Greenberger, M. (ed.). *Computers, Communications, and the Public Interest*. Baltimore: Johns Hopkins Press. (Cited after reprint in: H.A. Simon (1982). *Models of bounded rationality. Volume 2: Behavioural Economics and Business Organization*. Cambridge, MA: MIT Press).

Spector, D. (2007). *The economic policy of State aids: The assessment criteria*. In Vivier, X. (ed.). *Competition Policy in the EU – Fifty Years on from the Treaty of Rome*. Oxford: OUP.

Stevenson, N. (1995). *Understanding Media Cultures. Social Theory and Mass Communication*. Thousand Oaks, CA: Sage Publications.

Sunstein, C. (2003). *Why Societies Need Dissent*. Cambridge MA: Harvard University Press.

Sunstein, C. (2007). Republic.com 2.0. Princeton: Princeton University Press.

Townley, C. (2009). *Article 81 EC and Public Policy*. Oxford: Hart Publishing.

Ungerer, H. (2014). *The Reasons For Intervention Through Competition Policy.* In Donders, K., Caroline Pauwels and Jan Loisen (ed.). *The Palgrave Handbook of European Media Policy.* London: Palgrave Macmillan

Valcke, P. (2004). *Digitale Diversiteit: Convergentie van Media-, Telecommunicatie- en Mededingingsrecht (Digital Diversity – Convergence of Media, Telecommunications and Competition Law).* Brussels: Larcier.

Van Bael, I. (2011). *Due Process in EU Competition Proceedings.* Alphen aan den Rijn: Kluwer Law International.

Van Bael, I. and Jean-François Bellis (2005). *Competition Law of the European Community* (4th Edition). Aphen aan den Rijn: Kluwer Law International.

van den Bergh, R. and Peter Camesasca (2006). *European Competition Law and Economics – A Comparative Perspective.* Antwerpen, Groningen, Oxford: Intersentia-Hart Publishing.

van Eijk, N. (2009). *Search Engines, the New Bottleneck for Content Access.* In Preissel, B., Justus Haucap and Peter Curwen (eds.), *Telecommunication Markets: Drivers and Impediments.* Berlin: Springer-Verlag.

van Hoboken, J. (2015). *Search Engines, Pluralism and Diversity: What Is at Stake and How to Move Policy Forward?* In Valcke, P., Miklós Sükösd, and Robert G. Picard. *Media Pluralism and Diversity. Concepts, Risks and Global Trends.* London: Palgrave Macmillan.

Van Rompuy, B. (2012). *Economic Efficiency: The Sole Concern of Modern Antitrust Policy?* Alphen aan den Rijn: Kluwer Law International.

Van Rompuy, B. (2014). *The Impact of EU Competition Policy on the Sale of Sports Media Rights: Trends and Developments at the National Level.* In Donders, K., Caroline Pauwels and Jan Loisen (eds.). *The Palgrave Handbook of European Media Policy.* London: Palgrave Macmillan.

Verhulst, S. (2007). *Mediation, Mediators and New Intermediaries. Implications for the Design of New Communications Policies.* In Napoli, P. M. (ed.). *Media Diversity and Localism: Meaning and Metrics.* Mahwah, NJ: Lawrence Erlbaum.

Verouden, V. (2001). *Essays in Antitrust Economics.* PhD thesis. Tilburg: CentER, Center for Economic Research.

Wesseling, R. (2000). *The Modernization of Antitrust Law.* Oxford: Hart Publishing.

Whish, R. and David Bailey (2012). *Competition Law* (7th edition). Oxford: OUP.

Williams, A. (2010). *The Ethos of Europe. Values, Law and Justice in the EU.* Cambridge: CUP.

Xalabarder, R. (2011). *Google News and Copyright*. In Lopez-Tarruella, A. (ed.). *Google and the Law: Empirical Approaches to Legal Aspects of Knowledge-Economy Business Models*. The Hague: T.M.C. Asser Press.

Zimmer, D. (ed.) (2012). *The Goals of Competition Law*, Cheltenham: Edward Elgar.

Journal Articles and Working Papers, including Papers presented at Conferences

Abhishek, V., Kinshuk Jerath and Z. John Zhang (2015). *Agency Selling or Reselling? Channel Structures in Electronic Retailing*. SSRN Working Paper. <http://papers.ssrn.com/sol3/papers.cfm?abstract_id=2013720>.

Acquisti, A., Leslie John, and George Loewenstein (2009). *What is Privacy Worth?* Working Paper Carnegie Mellon University. <http://pages.stern.nyu.edu/~bakos/wise/papers/wise2009-6a1_paper.pdf>.

Akman, P. (2009a). *Consumer Welfare and Article 102 EC: Practice and Rhetoric*. World Competition 32, 71–90.

Akman, P. (2009b). *Searching for the Long-Lost Soul of Article 82 EC*. Oxford Journal of Legal Studies 29 (2), 267–303.

Akman, P. (2014). *The role of intent in the EU case law on abuse of dominance*. European Law Review 39(3), 316–337.

Albors-Llorens, A. (2007). *The Role of Objective Justification and Efficiencies in the Application of Article 82 EC*. Common Market Law Review 44, 1727–1761.

Alegre, S. (2008). *Human Rights and the Future of the European Union*. A Justice Futures Paper. < http://www.antigone.gr/files/en/library/developments-in-human-rights-issues/080606.pdf >.

Alexiadis, P. and Miranda Cole (2004). *Revisiting Competition Law and Regulatory Analyses of Consolidations in the Communications Sector*. Financier Worldwide, Industry Sector Review: Technology, Media & Telecommunications 2004.

Allen, H. and Sara Connolly (2017). *Media pluralism: What matters for governance and regulation?* Journal of Media Economics 30(2), 47–64.

Anderson, C. W. (2010). *What Aggregators Do: Rhetoric, Practice, and Cultures of Digital and Analog Evidence in Web-Era Journalism*. Paper Submitted to the 12th International Symposium for Online Journalism Austin, Texas, 2–3 April.

Andriychuk, O. (2010). *Rediscovering the Spirit of Competition: On the Normative Value of the Competitive Process*. European Competition Journal 6(3), 575–610.

Appelman, M. and Marcel Canoy (2002). *Horses for Courses: Why Europe should not harmonize its book policies*. De Economist 150(5), 583–600.

Argentesi, E. and Lapo Filistrucchi (2007). *Estimating market power in a two-sided market: The case of newspapers*. Journal of Applied Econometrics 22(7), 1247–1266.

Ariño, M. (2004), *Competition Law and Pluralism in European Digital Broadcasting: Addressing the gaps*. Communications and Strategies 54.

Arsenault, A.H. and Manuel Castells (2008). *The Structure and Dynamic of Global Multi-Media Business Networks*. International Journal of Communication 2, 707–748.

Athey, S. and Markus Mobius (2012). *The Impact of News Aggregators on Internet News Consumption: The Case of Localization*. Working Paper. <https://www.law.northwestern.edu/research-faculty/searlecenter/workingpapers/documents/Athey_Impact_News_Aggregators_on_Internet_News_Consumption.pdf>

Baker, C. E. (1992). *Advertising and a Democratic Press*. U. PA. L. REV. 140, 2097–2243.

Baker, J. B. and Judith A. Chevalier (2013). *The Competitive Consequences of Most-Favored-Nation Provisions*. Antitrust Magazine 27(2), 20–26.

Bania, K. (2013). *European merger control in the broadcasting sector: Does media pluralism fit?* In Competition Law Review 9(1), 49–80.

Bania, K. (2014a). *Abuse of dominance in online search: Google's special responsibility as the new bottleneck for content access*. Journal of Competition and Regulation 14, 211–239.

Bania, K. (2014b). *Media concentration and the myth of communicative abundance*. Percorsi Costituzionali 1, 205–218.

Bania, K. (2018). *The Role of Consumer Data in the Enforcement of EU Competition Law*. European Competition Journal 14(1), 38–80.

Bania, K. *The Effects of Broadcasting Digitization on EU Competition Law: A Tale of National and EU Politics*. Paper presented at the 13th Conference of the Academic Society for Competition Law, 21–23 June 2018, New York University.

Bania, K. and Richard Burnley (2014). *Co-operation between broadcasters in the new media age: Rethinking national competition policy*. European Competition Law Review 35(5), 216–222.

Barzanti F. (2012). *Governing the European Audiovisual Space: What modes of governance can facilitate a European approach to media pluralism?* EUI Working Papers RSCAS 2012/49.

Beaton, G. D. (2012). *The Cold Reality of the Ineffective Hot News Remedy, and the Case for Contract.* Columbia Law Review 112, 2068–2109.

Bennett, M. (2013, June). *Online Platforms: Retailers, Genuine Agents or None of the Above?* Competition Policy International. <https://www.competitionpolicyinternational.com/assets/Uploads/EuropeJune.pdf>

Bennett, M., Amelia Fletcher, Emanuele Giovannetti and David Stallibrass (2010). *Resale Price Maintenance: Explaining the controversy, and small steps towards a more nuanced policy.* Fordham International Law Journal 33, 1278–1299.

Berners-Lee, T. *Long Live the Web: A call for continued open standards and neutrality.* 22 November 2010, Scientific American. <http://www.scientificamerican.com/article/long-live-the-web/>.

Berry, S. and Joel Waldfogel (2001). *Do mergers increase product variety? Evidence from radio broadcasting.* Quarterly Journal of Economics 116, 1009–1025.

Boukes, M., Hajo G. Boomgaarden, Marjolein Moorman and Claes H. De Vreese (2014). *News With an Attitude: Assessing the Mechanisms Underlying the Effects of Opinionated News.* Journal of Mass Communication and Society 17(3), 354–378.

Braman S. (2004). *Where Has Media Policy Gone? Defining the Field in the Twenty-First Century.* Communication Law and Policy 9(2), 153–182.

Brogi E., Konstantina Bania, Iva Nenadic, Alina Ostling and Pier Luigi Parcu (2017). *Monitoring Media Pluralism in Europe: Application of the Media Pluralism Monitor 2016 in the European Union, Montenegro and Turkey.* <http://cadmus.eui.eu/bitstream/handle/1814/46786/CMPF-MPM_PolicyReport2017.pdf?sequence=1&isAllowed=y>.

Brynjolfsson, E., Yu J. Hu, and Mohammad S. Rahman (2009). *Battle of the Retail Channels: How Product Selection and Geography Drive Cross-Channel Competition.* Management Science 55(11), 1755–1765.

Burnside, A. *Bob Dylan and Consumer Welfare.* Paper presented at the Centre for Competition Law and Policy Conference, 27 May 2017, Oxford University. *Online Markets and Offline Welfare Effects.* <https://www.law.ox.ac.uk/sites/files/oxlaw/online_markets_and_offline_welfare_effects.pdf>.

Burri-Nenova, M. (2007). *The New Audiovisual Media Services Directive: Television Without Frontiers, Television Without Cultural Diversity.* Common Market Law Review 44(6), 1689–1725.

Butorac Malnar, V (2008). *The Role of Efficiencies in Merger Control: Comparative EU–USA Perspective.* Zb. Prav.fak. Sveuc. Rij 29(2), 851–886.

Caillaud, B. and Bruno Jullien (2003). *Chicken & egg: competition among intermediation service providers.* RAND Journal of Economics 34(2), 309–328.

Camesasca, P.D., Maarten Meulenbelt, Thomas Chellingsworth, Ief Daems and Julie Vandenbuccche (2009). *The Dutch Yellow Pages Merger Case – 2-1 Will Go!* European Competition Law Review 30(1), 4–13.

Canoy, M., Jan C. van Ours and Frederick van der Ploeg (2005). *The Economics of Books*. CESifo Working Paper No. 1414. <https://ideas.repec.org/p/ces/ceswps/_1414.html>

Carpentier, N. and B. Cammaerts (2006). *Hegemony, Democracy, Agonism, and Journalism. An Interview with Chantal Mouffe*. Journalism Studies 7(6), 964–975.

Casey, D. (2009). *Disintegration: Environmental Protection and Article 81 EC*, European Law Journal 15(3), 362–381.

Castells, M. (2007). *Communication, power and counter-power in the network society*. International Journal of Communication 1, 238–266.

Ceron, A. and Sergio Splendore (2016). *From contents to comments: Social TV and perceived pluralism in political talk shows*. New Media and Society 20(2), 659–675.

Chellapa, R. and Raymond G. Sin (2005). *Personalization Versus Privacy: An Empirical Examination of the Online Consumers' Dilemma*. Information Technology and Management 6(2–3), 181–202.

Chickering, A. R. (2008). *Strengthening democracy and personal development through community engagement*. New Directions for Adult and Continuing Education 118, 87–95.

Condorelli, D. Andrea Galeotti and Vasiliki Skreta (2013). *Selling Through Referrals*. NYU Working Paper No. 2451/31774. <http://papers.ssrn.com/sol3/papers.cfm?abstract_id=2260874>.

Cooper, C. and Tang Tang (2009). *Predicting Audience Exposure to Television in Today's Media Environment: An Empirical Integration of Active-Audience and Structural Theories*. Journal of Broadcasting & Electronic Media 53(3), 400–418.

Coyle, D. (2018). *Practical competition policy implications of digital platforms*. Bennett Institute for Public Policy Working Paper 1/2018.

Craufurd-Smith, R. (2001). *State Support for Public Service Broadcasting: The Position Under European Community Law*. Legal Issues of Economic Integration 28(1), 3–22.

Craufurd-Smith, R. (2004). *Rethinking European Union competence in the field of media ownership: The internal market, fundamental rights and European citizenship*. European Law Review 29(5), 652–672.

Craufurd-Smith, R. and Damian Tambini (2012). *Measuring Media Plurality in the United Kingdom: Policy Choices and Regulatory Challenges*. Journal of Media Law 4(1), 54.

de Búrca, G. (2004). *Beyond the Charter: How Enlargement has Enlarged the Human Rights Policy of the European Union*. Fordham International Law Journal 27(2), 679–714.

Deneckere, R., H.P. Marvel, and J. Peck (1997). *Demand Uncertainty and Price Maintenance: Mark-downs as Destructive Competition.* American Economic Review 87(4), 619–641.

De Vany, A. and W. David Walls (1999). *Uncertainty in the Movie Industry: Does Star Power Reduce the Terror of the Box Office?* Paper presented at the annual meeting of the American Economic Association. New York, January 1999. <http://pages.stern.nyu.edu/~wgreene/entertainmentandmedia/Devany&Walls.pdf>.

De Waal, E., Klaus Schönbach and Edmund Lauf (2005). *Online newspapers: A substitute or complement for print newspapers and other information channels?* Communications: The European Journal of Communication Research 30, 55–72.

Donders, K. (2011). *Superficial Harmonization Versus One-Size-Fits-All: The Implementation of European State Aid Principles in Flanders and the Netherlands.* Journal of Media Law 3(2), 237–261.

Doyle, G. (1997, October). *From 'Pluralism' to 'Ownership': Europe's emergent policy on Media Concentrations navigates the doldrums'.* Journal of Information Law and Technology, 3. Available online at: <http://www2.warwick.ac.uk/fac/soc/law/elj/jilt/1997_3>.

Doyle, G. (2010). *From Television to Multi-platform: Less from more or more for less?* Convergence: The International Journal of Research into New Media Technologies 16(4), 431–449.

Drijber, B. J. (1999). *The Revised Television Without Frontiers Directive: Is It Fit For The Next Century?* Common Market Law Review 36(1) 87–122.

Economides, N. (1998). *The incentive for non-price discrimination by an input monopolist.* International Journal of Industrial Organization 16, 271–284.

Edelman, B. (2014). *Leveraging Market Power Through Tying and Bundling: Does Google Behave Anti-Competitively?* Harvard Business School – Working Paper 14-112. <http://hbswk.hbs.edu/item/7464.html>.

Edlin, A. S. and Robert G. Harris (2013). *The Role of Switching Costs in Antitrust Analysis: A Comparison of Microsoft and Google.* Yale Journal of Law and Technology 15(2), 171–213.

Elzinga, K. G. and David E. Mills (2010). *Leegin and Procompetitive Resale Price Maintenance.* The Antitrust Bulletin 55(2), 349–379.

Engesser, S., Nicole Ernst, Frank Esser and Florin Büchel (2016). *Populism and social media: how politicians spread a fragmented ideology.* Journal of Information, Communication and Society 20(8), 1109–1126.

Epstein, R. and Ronald E. Robertson (2013). *Democracy at Risk: Manipulating Search Rankings Can Shift Voting Preferences Substantially Without Voter Awareness*. American Institute for Behavioral Research and Technology Working Paper Series. Paper presented at the 25th annual meeting of the Association for Psychological Science, Washington, D.C. A summary of the paper is available at: <http://aibrt.org/downloads/EPSTEIN_and_Robertson_2013-Democracy_at_Risk-APS-summary-5-13.pdf >.

Esfahani, N. N. and Don-Shin Jeon (2013). *News Aggregators and Competition Among Newspapers in the Internet*. IDEI Working Paper n. 770.

Evans, D. S. (2008). *Competition and Regulatory Policy for Multi-sided Platforms with Applications to the Web Economy*. Concurrences 2, 57–62.

Evans, D. S. and Richard Schmalensee (2007). *Industrial Organization of Markets with Two-Sided Platforms*. Competition Policy International 3(1), 151–179.

Evens, T. and Karen Donders (2016). *Mergers and acquisitions in TV broadcasting and distribution: Challenges for competition, industrial and media policy*. Telematics and Informatics 33(2), 674–682.

Falconieri, S., Frederic Palomino and Joszef Sakovics (2004). *Collective versus Individual Sale of TV Rights in League Sports*. Journal of the European Economic Association 2(5), 833–862.

Falkinger, J. (2005). Attention Economies, CESifo Working Paper, No. 1079. <https://ideas.repec.org/p/ces/ceswps/_1079.html>.

Filistrucchi, L. (2005). *The Impact of Internet on the Market for Daily Newspapers in Italy*. EUI Working Paper ECO No. 2005/12. <http://cadmus.eui.eu/bitstream/handle/1814/3353/ECO2005-12.pdf>.

Filistrucchi, L., Damien Geradin and Eric van Damme (2012). *Identifying two-sided markets*. Discussion Paper, TILEC DP 2012-008.

Filistrucchi, L., Damien Geradin, Eric van Damme, E. and Pauline Affeldt (2012). *Market Definition in Two-Sided Markets: Theory and Practice*. TILEC Discussion Paper No. 2013-009. Available through SSRN at: <http://papers.ssrn.com/sol3/papers.cfm?abstract_id=2240850>.

Fishwick, F. (2008). *Book Prices in the UK Since the End of Resale Price Maintenance*. International Journal of the Economics of Business 15(3), 359–377.

Foa, R. *The Economic Rationale for Social Cohesion: Cross-Country Evidence*. Paper presented at the International Conference on Social Cohesion and Development, Paris, 20 and 21 January 2011. <http://www.oecd.org/dev/pgd/46908575.pdf>.

Foros, Ø., Hans Jarle Kind, and Greg Shaffer (2013). *Turning the Page on Business Formats for Digital Platforms: Does Apple's Agency Model Soften Competition?* CESIFO Working Paper No. 4362. <http://papers.ssrn.com/sol3/papers.cfm?abstract_id=2317715>.

Gabszewicz, J. J., Paolo, G. Garella, and Nathalie Sonnac (2007). *Newspapers' Market Shares and the Theory of the Circulation Spiral.* Information Economics and Policy 19(3–4), 405–413.

Gal, M. and D. L. Rubinfeld (2015). *The Hidden Costs of Free Goods: Implications for Antitrust Enforcement.* NYU Center for Law, Economics and Organization Working Paper Series, Working Paper No. 14-44. Available at SSRN: <http://papers.ssrn.com/sol3/papers.cfm?abstract_id=2529425#%23>.

Garcia Pires, A. (2017). *Media pluralism and competition.* European Journal of Law and Economics 43(2), 255–283.

Gentzkow, M. (2007). *Valuing New Goods in a Model with Complementarity: Online Newspapers.* The American Economic Review 97(3), 713–744.

George, L. (2013). *Local News Online: Aggregators, Geo-Targeting and the Market for Local News.* Time Warner Cable Research Program on Digital Communications. Report Series Winter 2013. <http://www.twcresearchprogram.com/pdf/TWC_George_Report.pdf>.

Georges, A. and Matteo F. Bay (2005). *Essential Facilities: A Doctrine Clearly in Need of Limiting Principles?* Intellectual Property & Technology Law Journal 17(12), 1–4.

Geradin, D. (2005). *Access to content by new media platforms: A review of the competition law problems.* European Law Review 30(1), 68–94.

Geradin, D. *Data Portability and EU Competition Law.* Presented at the BITS conference, Brussels, 24 April 2014.

Gerber, D. J. (2008). *Two Forms of Modernization in European Competition Law.* Fordham International Law Journal 31(5), 1235–1265.

Geradin, D. and Monika Kuschewsky (2013). *Competition Law and Personal Data: Preliminary Thoughts on a Complex Issue.* SSRN Working Paper. <http://papers.ssrn.com/sol3/papers.cfm?abstract_id=2216088>.

Gibbons, T. (2009). *The Future of Public Service Content in the United Kingdom.* Journal of Media Law 1(1), 1–13.

Gippini-Fournier, E. **(2010). Resale Price Maintenance in the EU: in statu quo ante bellum?** SSRN Working Paper. <http://papers.ssrn.com/sol3/papers.cfm?abstract_id=1476443 Also available in Hawk, B. (ed.). *Annual Proceedings of the 36th Annual Conference on International Antitrust Law and Policy – Fordham Corporate Law Institute.* Huntington, NY: Juris Publishing.

Goldhaber, M. H. (1997). *The Attention Economy and the Net.* 7 March 1997, First Monday 2(4). <http://firstmonday.org/article/view/519/440>.

Goodman, E. (2004). *Media Policy Out of the Box: Content Abundance, Attention Scarcity, and the Failures of Digital Markets.* Berkeley Technology Law Journal 19, 1389–1472.

Goolsbee, A. (2001). *Competition in the Computer Industry: Online versus Retail.* The Journal of Industrial Economics 49(4), 487–499.

Graef, I., Jeroen Verschakelen and Peggy Valcke (2014). *Putting the right to data portability into a competition law perspective.* SSRN Working Paper. <http://papers.ssrn.com/sol3/papers.cfm?abstract_id=2416537>.

Graef, I., Sih Yuliana Wahyuningtyas and Peggy Valcke. *Data Interoperability in Online Social Networks.* Paper presented at the International Workshop on Competition Policy and Regulation in Media and Telecommunications: Bridging Law and Economics, 23 and 24 May 2013, Tilburg.

Habermas, J. (2006). *Political Communication in Media Society: Does Democracy Still Enjoy an Epistemic Dimension? The Impact of Normative Theory on Empirical Research.* Communication Theory 16(4), 411–426.

Harcourt, A. (2004). *Institution-driven competition: The regulation of cross-border broadcasting in the EU.* European University Institute Working Papers, RSCAS No. 2004/44. Also published in Journal of Public Policy, 27(3), 293-317. Harris, R. G. (2012). *The Role of Switching Costs in the Markets for PC Operating Systems, Online Search, Internet Access and Mobile Service: Implications for Australian Competition and Consumer Protection Policy.* Presented at the Conference on 'Competition in the Online Environment', 28 November 2012.

Harrison, J. and Lorna Woods (2001). *Television Quotas: Protecting European Culture?* Entertainment Law Review, 12(1), 5–14.

Harvey, S. (2010). *No Jam Tomorrow? State Aid Rules and the Legitimacy of Public Service Media: the Closure of the BBC's Digital Curriculum Project ('Jam').* Draft Paper for RIPE Conference, University of Westminster, London, 8–11 September 2010. Hasebrink, U. (2011), *Giving the audience a voice: The role of research in making media regulation more responsive to the needs of the audience.* Journal of Information Policy 1, 321–336.

Hatton, C. H. and Hector Armengod (2007). *Fair Play: How Competition Authorities Have Regulated the Sale of Football Media Rights in Europe.* European Competition Law Review 28(6), 346–354.

Helberger, N. (2006). *The 'right to information' and digital broadcasting – About monsters, invisible men, and the future of European broadcasting regulation.* Entertainment Law Review 17(2), 70–80.

Helberger, N. (2008). *From Eyeball to Creator – Toying with Audience Empowerment in the Audiovisual Media Service Directive*, Entertainment Law Review 6, 128–137.

Helberger, N. (2011a). *Diversity Label: Exploring the Potential and Limits of a Transparency Approach to Media Diversity*. Journal of Information Policy 1, 337–369.

Helberger, N. (2011b). *Media Diversity from the User's Perspective: An Introduction*. Journal of Information Policy 1, 241–245.

Helberger, N., Guibault, L. and Janssen E. H. (2012). *User-Created-Content: Supporting a Participative Information Society. Understanding the Digital World*. Amsterdam Law School Research Paper No. 2012-32.

Hemphill, S. C. and Tim Wu (2013). *Parallel Exclusion*. Yale Law Journal 122, 1182–1253.

Herold, A. (2002). *Rules Governing the Acquisition by Third Parties of Television Rights for Sporting Events under Eurovision in Breach of the European Competition Law*. International Journal of Communications Law 7, 1–9.

Hill, B. C. (2006). *Measuring media market diversity: concentration, importance, and pluralism*. Federal Communications Law Journal 58, 169–194.

Hilton, J. and David Wiley (2010). *The Short-Term Influence of Free Digital Versions of Books on Print Sales*. BYU Faculty Publications. Paper 1358. <http://scholarsarchive.byu.edu/cgi/viewcontent.cgi?article=2357&context=facpub.

Hitchens, L. P. (1994). *Media Ownership and Control: A European Approach*. The Modern Law Review 57(4), 585–601.

Huang, J. S., M. J. Yang, and Hsiang Iris Chyi (2013). *Friend or foe? Examining the relationship between news portals and newspaper sites in Taiwan*. Chinese Journal of Communication 6(1), 103–119.

Hui, K. L., Hock Hai and Sang-Yong Tom Lee (2007). *The Value of Privacy Assurance: An Exploratory Field Experiment*. MIS Quarterly 31(1), 19–33.

Ibáñez Colomo, P. (2006), *Saving the Monopsony: Exclusivity, Innovation and Market Power in the Media Sector*. Research Papers in Law, 07/2006, Global Competition Law Centre.

Ibáñez Colomo, P. (2014). *Exclusionary Discrimination under Article 102 TFEU*. Common Market Law Review 51, 141–164.

Iosifides, Petros (1997). *Pluralism and media concentration policy in the European Union*. Javnost-The Public 4(1), 85–104.

Isbell, K. (2010). *The Rise of the News Aggregator: Legal Implications and Best Practices*. Berkman Center Research Publication No. 2010-10.

Jeon, Doh-Shin and Nikrooz Nasr (2016). *News Aggregators and Competition among Newspapers on the Internet*. American Economic Journal: Microeconomics 8(4), 91–114.

Jeziorski, P. (2011). *Merger enforcement in two-sided markets*. Economics Working Paper Archive 570, Johns Hopkins University.

Johnson, J. P. (2013). *The Agency and Wholesale Models in Electronic Content Markets*. SSRN Working Paper. <http://papers.ssrn.com/sol3/papers.cfm?abstract_id=2126808>.

Kaiser, U. and Hans Christian Kongsted (2005). *Do Magazines' 'Companion Websites' Cannibalize the Demand for the Print Version?* Centre for Applied Microeconometrics – Institute of Economics University of Copenhagen Working Paper 2005–07. <http://ftp.zew.de/pub/zew-docs/dp/dp0549.pdff>.

Kaiser, U. and Julian Wright (2006). *Price Structure in two-sided markets: Evidence from the magazine industry*. International Journal of Industrial Organization 24, 1–28.

Karppinen, K. (2009). *Rethinking media pluralism and communicative abundance*. Observatorio Journal 3(4), 151–169.

Karppinen, K. and Halvard Moe. (2014). *What we talk about when we talk about 'the market': Conceptual contestation in contemporary media policy research*. Journal of Information Policy 4, 327–341.

Katsirea, I. (2003). *Why The European Broadcasting Quota Should Be Abolished*. European Law Review 28(2), 190–209.

Keane, J. (1999). *Public Life in the Era of Communicative Abundance*. Canadian Journal of Communication 24, 165–78.

Kingston, S. (2010). *Integrating Environmental Protection and EU Competition Law: Why Competition Isn't Special*. European Law Journal 16(6), 780–805.

Komninos, A. P. (2005). *Non-competition concerns: Resolution of Conflicts in the Integrated Article 81 EC*. The University of Oxford Centre for Competition Law and Policy Working Paper No. 08/05.

Ladeur, K. H. (2004), *Guaranteeing the Programming Mandate of Public Broadcasters and Restraints on Private Broadcasters' Programmes in Multimedia Conditions*, German Law Journal 5(8), 907–933.

Lafferty W. M. and Eivind Hovden (2003). *Environmental Policy Integration: Towards an Analytical Framework*. Environmental Politics 12(1), 1–22.

Lao, M. (2009). *Resale price maintenance: A reassessment of its competitive harms and benefits*. SSRN Working Paper. <http://papers.ssrn.com/sol3/papers.cfm?abstract_id=1434984> Also in Drexl, J., Warren S. Grimes, Clifford A. Jones, Rudolph J. R. Peritz and Edward T. Swaine (eds.) (2011). *More common ground for International Competition Law?* Cheltenham, UK: Edward Elgar.

Lascowska, M. (2013). *Dynamic Efficiencies and Technological Progress in EC Merger Control*. The University of Oxford, Centre for Competition Law and Policy Working Paper CCLP (L) 29. The paper is available at: <http://papers.ssrn.com/sol3/papers.cfm?abstract_id=2336956>.

Lee, A. M. and Hsiang Iris Chyi (2015). *The Rise of Online News Aggregators: Consumption and Competition*. International Journal on Media Management 17(1), 3–24.

Lee, E. and Byungtae Lee (2013, June). *Dynamics of Price Elasticity Over Time: Evidence from the E-Book Industry*. PACIS Proceedings. Paper 124.

Lefever, K. and Ben Van Rompuy (2009) *Ensuring Access to Sports Content: 10 Years of Intervention. Time to Celebrate?* Journal of Media Law 1(2), 243–268.

Lianos, I. (2007). *Commercial Agency Agreements, Vertical Restraints, and the Limits of Article 81(1) EC: Between Hierarchies and Networks*. Journal of Competition Law and Economics 3(4), 625–672.

Loewenthal, P. J. (2005). *The defense of 'objective justification' in the application of Article 82 EC*. World Competition 28, 455–477.

Lovdahl-Gormsen, L. (2007). *The Conflict Between Economic Freedom and Consumer Welfare in the Modernization of Article 82 EC*. European Competition Journal 3(2), 329–344.

Lupinacci, T.M. (1991). *The Pursuit of Television Broadcasting Activities in the European Community: Cultural Preservation or Economic Protectionism?* Vanderbilt Journal of Transnational Law 24, 113–154.

Manne, G. A. and Ben Sperry. *The Problems and Perils of Bootstrapping Privacy and Data into an Antitrust Framework*. CPI Antitrust Chronicle, May 2015(2), 6–8.

Massadeh, A. A. (2011). *The Essential Facilities Doctrine Under Scrutiny: EU and US Perspective*. UEA Working Paper Series 2011-AM-1.

Mastrini, G. and Martin Becerra (2011). *Estructura, concentración y transformaciones en los medios del Cono Sur latinoamericano*. Scientific Journal of Media Literacy 36, 51–59.

McDonnell, J. C. (2012). *The Continuing Viability of the Hot News Misappropriation Doctrine in the Age of Internet News Aggregation*. Northwestern Journal of Technology and Intellectual Property, 10(3) 255–276.

Mendes-Perreira, M. *Vertical and horizontal integration in the media sector and EU competition law*. Paper presented at the Workshop 'The ICT and Media Sectors within the EU Policy Framework', Brussels, 7 April 2003.

Michalis, M. (1999). *European Union Broadcasting and Telecoms Towards a Convergent Regulatory Regime?* European Journal of Communication 14(2), 147–171.

Milioni, D., Konstantinos Vadratsikas and Venetia Papa (2012). *Their two cents' worth: Exploring user agency in readers' comments in online news media.* Observatorio (OBS) Journal 6(3), 21–47.

Miller, D. S. (2004). *Limits on Media Ownership: Should the FCC Curb Its Reliance on Deregulation?* U. ILL. J.L. Tech. & Pol'y 2, 345–367.

Montgomery, S. W. (2012). *Extra!! Extra!!: The Viability of the Hot News Misappropriation Claim Is in Jeopardy.* Loyola L.A. Entertainment Law Review 32, 365–398.

Monti, G. (2002). *Article 81 EC and Public Policy.* Common Market Law Review 39(5), 1057–1099.

Mueller, W. F. (1989). *The Sealy Restraints: Restrictions on Free Riding or Output?* Wisconsin Law Review 1293–1296.

Müller, J-W. (2013). *Safeguarding Democracy inside the EU: Brussels and the Future of Liberal Order.* Transatlantic Academy Paper Series 2012–2013, No. 3.

Murray, S. (2005). *Brand loyalties: rethinking content within global corporate media, Media, Culture & Society* 27(3), 415–435.

Napoli, P. (2001, October). *Diversity and Localism: A Policy Analysis Perspective.* Paper presented at an FCC Roundtable on Media Ownership. <http://transition.fcc.gov/ownership/roundtable_docs/napoli-stmt.pdf>.

Napoli, P. M. (1999). *Deconstructing the Diversity Principle*, Journal of Communication 49(4), 7–34.

Napoli, P. M. (2011). *Exposure diversity reconsidered.* Journal of Information Policy 1, 246–259.

Nesvold, P. (1996). *Communication Breakdown: Developing an Antitrust Model for Multimedia Mergers and Acquisitions.* Fordham Intellectual Property, Media and Entertainment Law Journal 6(2), 781–869.

Newman, N. (2009). *The rise of social media and its impact on mainstream journalism: A study of how newspapers and broadcasters in the UK and US are responding to a wave of participatory social media, and a historic shift in control towards individual consumers.* Oxford Reuters Institute for the Study of Journalism Working Paper. <https://reutersinstitute.politics.ox.ac.uk/sites/default/files/2017-11/The%20rise%20of%20social%20media%20and%20its%20impact%20on%20mainstream%20journalism.pdf>.

Newman, N. (2014). *The Costs of Lost Privacy: Consumer Harm and Rising Economic Inequality in the Age of Google.* William Mitchell Law Review 40(2), 865–73.

Norton, S. W. and Will Norton Jr. (1986). *Economies of Scale and the New Technology of Daily Newspapers: A Survivor Analysis.* University of Nebraska – Lincoln College of Journalism & Mass Communications, Working Paper 6.

Odudu, O. (2010). *The Wider Concerns of Competition Law*, Oxford Journal of Legal Studies 30(3), 599–613

Odudu, O. (2011). *Indirect Information Exchange: The Constituent Elements of Hub-And-Spoke Collusion.* European Competition Law Journal 7(2), 205–242.

Odudu, O. and David Bailey (2014). *The Single Economic Entity Doctrine in EU Competition Law.* Common Market Law Review 51, 1721–1758.

Orbach, B. Y. (2008). *Antitrust Vertical Myopia: The Allure of High Prices.* Arizona Law Review 50, 261–287.

Owen, B. M. *Confusing Success with Access: 'Correctly' Measuring Concentration of Ownership and Control in Mass Media and Online Services.* Paper presented at the 'Media Concentration and the Internet – Empirical, Business and Policy Research', a Symposium at the Columbia Institute for Teleinformation (CITI), Columbia Business School, 15 April 2004.

Padilla, J., Matthew Bennett and Wim Koevoets. *Pay-TV prices in Europe – An Econometric Analysis.* London, 18 June 2007.

Palzer, C. and Caroline Hilger (2001). *Media Supervision on the Threshold of the 21st Century – Structure and Powers of Regulatory Authorities in the Era of Convergence.* European Audiovisual Observatory, 8 IRIS plus. <https://rm.coe.int/1680783377>.

Papandropoulos, P. and Alessandro Tajana (2006). *The Merger Remedies Study – In Divestiture We Trust?* European Competition Law Review 27(8), 443–454.

Parlasca, S. and Stefan Szymanski (2002). *The Negative Effects of Central Marketing of Football Television Rights on Fans, Media Concentration and Small Clubs.* Zeitschrift für Betriebswirtschaft 4, 83–104.

Pavlik, J. (2005). *Understanding Convergence and Digital Broadcasting Technologies for the Twenty-First Century.* NHK Broadcasting Studies, 142 <https://www.nhk.or.jp/bunken/english/reports/pdf/05_no4_08.pdf>.

Peepercorn, L. (2008). *Resale price maintenance and its alleged efficiencies.* European Competition Journal 4(1), 201–212.

Petit, N. and David Henry (2010). *Vertical Restraints under EU Competition Law: Conceptual Foundations and Practical Framework.* SSRN Working Paper. <http://papers.ssrn.com/sol3/papers.cfm?abstract_id=1724891>.

Petit, N. and Norman Neyrinck (2011). *Droit de la Concurrence et Instrumentalisation Parasitaire.* Working Paper. Institut d'Etudes Juridiques Européennes, Université de Liège. <http://orbi.ulg.ac.be/handle/2268/98911>.

Picard, R. (2017). *The Sisyphean Pursuit of Media Pluralism: European Efforts to Establish Policy and Measurable Evidence.* Communication Law and Policy 22(3), 255–273.

Picard, R. G. and Bum Soo Chon (2004). *Managing Competition Through Barriers to Entry and Channel Availability in the Changing Regulatory Environment.* The International Journal on Media Management 6(3), 168–175.

Pinelli, C. (2012). Protecting the Fundamentals. Article 7 of the Treaty on the European Union and beyond. Foundation for European Progressive Studies Working Paper.

Polverino, F. (2012). *Hunting the Wild Geese: Competition Analysis in a World of 'Free'.* SSRN Working Paper. <http://papers.ssrn.com/sol3/papers.cfm?abstract_id=2145545> Also in Ghidini, G., Piergaetano Marchetti, Marcello Clarich and Fabiana di Porto (eds.). *Concorrenza e Mercato*. Roma: Giuffrè Editore.

Prior, M. (2005). *News vs. Entertainment: How Increasing Media Choice Widens the Gap in Political Knowledge and Turnout.* American Journal of Political Science 49(3), 577–592.

Psychogiopoulou, E. (2006a). *The Cultural Mainstreaming Clause of Article 151(4) EC: Protection and Promotion of Cultural Diversity or Hidden Cultural Agenda?* European Law Journal 12(5), 575–592.

Raeijmaekers, D. and Pieter Maeseele (2015). *Media pluralism and democracy: what's in a name?* Media, Culture and Society 37(7), 1042–1059.

Rimm, A. M. (2014). *Conditions and Survival: Views on the Concentration of Ownership and Vertical Integration in German and Swedish Publishing.* Publishing Research Quarterly 30(1), 77–92.

Ringstad, V (2004). *On the cultural blessings of fixed book prices.* International Journal of Cultural Policy 10 (3), 351–365.

Rochet, J.C. and J. Tirole (2003). *Platform Competition in Two-sided Markets.* Journal of the of the European Economic Association 1, 990–1029.

Rosenfeld, S. (2014). *How Far Will News Organizations Go to Take the 'Lede?' Hot News Misappropriation in the Digital Age.* Berkeley Journal of Entertainment and Sports Law 3(1), 86–92.

Rysman, M. (2009). *The Economics of Two-sided Markets.* Journal of Economic Perspectives 23(3), 125–143.

Sarikakis, K. (2007). *Mediating Social Cohesion: Media and cultural policy in the European Union and Canada.* European Studies 24, 65–90.

Scherer, F.M. (2005). *Comment on Cooper et al.'s 'Vertical Restrictions and Antitrust Policy'.* Competition Policy International 1(2), 65–74. <http://www2.owen.vanderbilt.edu/lukefroeb/froeb.papers/Vertical/2005.CPI.scherer.pdf>.

Scheuer, A. and Peter Strothmann (2002). *Media Supervision on the Threshold of the 21st Century What are the Requirements of Broadcasting, Telecommunications and Concentration Regulation?* <https://rm.coe.int/1680783385>.

Schmid, C. U. (2000). *Diagonal Competence Conflicts between European Competition Law and National Regulation – A Conflict of Laws, Reconstruction of the Dispute on Book Price Fixing.* European Review of Private Law 8, 155–171.

Schmidt, E. P. (2011). *Hot News Misappropriation in the Internet Age*. Journal on Telecommunications and High Technology Law 9, 313–343.

Schulz, W. (2009). *The Legal Framework for Public Service Broadcasting in Germany: Procrustean Bed or Hammock?* Journal of Media Law 1(2), 219–241.

Schulz, W., Thorsten Held, Stephan Dreyer and Thilo Wind (2008). *Regulation of Broadcasting and Internet Services in Germany. A brief overview*. Working Papers of the Hans Bredow Institute, 2nd edition, No. 13. <http://www.hans-bredow-institut.de/webfm_send/124.

Schweitzer, H. (2007). *Competition Law and Public Policy: Reconsidering an Uneasy Relationship. The Example of Article 81*. EUI Working Paper No. 2007/32.

Sevenster, H.G. and Hans Vedder (2000). *Integreren or concurrenen? De rol van niet-mededingingsbelangen, in het bijzonder milieubescherming, in het kartelbeleid*, Tijdschrift voor Europees en Economisch Rect 2(1), 4–5.

Shen, W. (2012). *Examining Double Marginalization Effect for Innovative Product Supply Chain*. International Journal of Operations Research and Information Systems 3(1), 37–52.

Smith, M. D. and Rahul Telang (2010). *Piracy or Promotion? The Impact of Broadband Internet Penetration on DVD Sales*. Information Economics and Policy 22(4), 289–298. Special Issue: Digital Piracy.

Solberg, H.A. (2007). *Sports Broadcasting: Is it a Job for Public Service Broadcasters? – A Welfare Economic Perspective*. Journal of Media Economics 20(4), 289–309.

Soroka, S., Blake Andrew, Toril Aalberg, Shanto Iyengar, James Curran, Sharon Coen, Kaori Hayashi, Paul Jones, Gianpetro Mazzoleni, June Woong Rhee, David Rowe and Rod Tiffen (2012). *Auntie Knows Best? Public Broadcasters and Current Affairs Knowledge*. British Journal of Political Science 43(4), 1–21.

Spiekerman, S., Jens Grossklags, and Bettina Berendt (2002). *E-privacy in 2nd generation E-Commerce*. ACM Conference on Electronic Commerce (EC'01), Hrsg. ACM New York, 38–47. Tampa, Florida: ACM Press.

Steiner, R. L. (1991). *Sylvania Economics – A Critique*. Antitrust Law Journal 60(1), 41–59.

Streeter, T. (1996). *Selling the Air: A Critique of the Policy of Commercial Broadcasting in the United States*. Chicago, IL: University of Chicago Press.

Stucke, M. and Allen Grunes (2001). *Antitrust and the Marketplace of Ideas*. Antitrust Law Journal 69(1), 249–302.

Sunstein, C. (2000). *Television and the Public Interest.* California Law Review 88(2), 499–564.

Swire, P. and Yianni Lagos (2013). *Why the Right to Data Portability Likely Reduces Consumer Welfare: Antitrust and Privacy Critique*. Maryland Law Review 72(2), 335–380.

Temple Lang, J. (1997). *Media, multimedia, and European Community antitrust law*. Fordham International Law Journal 21(4), 1296–1381. <http://ir.lawnet.fordham.edu/cgi/viewcontent.cgi?article=1569&context=ilj>.

Tonazzi, A. (2002). *Competition Policy and the commercialization of sport broadcasting rights: the decision of the Italian Competition Authority*. International Journal of the Economics of Business 10(1), 17–34.

Toth, B. (2013). *How parallel Most-Favored Nation Clauses in the Television Industry Exclude Competitors and Stifle Innovation.* The Columbia Science and Technology Law Review 15, 194–234.

Valcke, P. (2006). *The Future of Must-Carry to a Concept of Universal Service in the Info-Communications Sector*. Media Law and Policy 15(2), 247–267.

Valcke, P. (2009). *From Ownership Regulation to Legal Indicators of Media Pluralism: Background, Typologies, and Methods*. Journal of Media Business Studies 6(3), 19–42.

Valcke, P. (2011). *Looking For the User in Media Pluralism Regulation: Unraveling the Traditional Diversity Chain and Recent Trends of User Empowerment in European Media Regulation*. Journal of Information Policy 1, 287–320.

van der Ploeg, F. (2004). *Beyond the Dogma of the Fixed Book Price Agreement*. Journal of Cultural Economics 28(1), 1–20.

van der Sloot, B. (2012). *Walking a Thin Line: The Regulation of EPGs*. JIPITEC 3, 138–147.

van Eijk, N. and Bart van der Sloot (2012). *Must-carry Regulation: a Must or a Burden?* foreword. In European Audiovisual Observatory (ed.). *Must-carry: Renaissance or Reformation?* IRIS plus 2012–5.

Van Rompuy, B. and Karen Donders (2012). *Competition Law, Sports, and Public Service Broadcasting: The Legal Complexity and Political Sensitivity of Measuring Market Distortion and Public Value*. Journal of Media Law 4(2), 213–228.

Van Rompuy, B. and Karen Donders (2013). *The EBU's Eurovision System Governing the Joint Buying of Sports Broadcasting Rights: Unfinished Competition Business.* Competition Law Review 9(1), 7–28.

Vanderborre, I. and Michael J. Frese (2014). *Most Favored Nation Clauses Revisited.* European Competition Law Review 12, 588–593.

von Bogdandy, A. (2000). *The European Union as a Human Rights Organization? Human Rights and the Core of European Union.* Common Market Law Review 37(6), 1307–1338.

Vosoughi, S., Deb Roy, and Sinan Aral (2018). *The spread of true and false news online.* Science 359(6380), 1146–1151.

Wand, W. (2011). *Structural Remedies in EU Antitrust and Merger Control.* World Competition 34(4), 571–596.

Wathieu, L. and Allan Friedman (2005). *An Empirical Approach to Understanding Privacy Valuation.* Proceedings of the Fourth Workshop on the Economics of Information Security (WEIS '05).

Webster, J. G. (2005). *Beneath the Veneer of Fragmentation: Television Audience Polarization in a Multi-Channel World.* Journal of Communication 55(2), 366–382.

Wilbur, K. C. (2008). *A Two-Sided, Empirical Model of Television Advertising and Viewing Markets.* Marketing Science 27(3), 356–378.

Williams, A. (2006). *The indifferent gesture: Article 7 TEU, the Fundamental Rights Agency and the UK's invasion of Iraq.* European Law Review 31(1), 3–27.

Williams, B. A. and Michael X. Delli Carpini (2004). *Monica and Bill all the time and everywhere: The collapse of gatekeeping and agenda setting in the new media environment.* American Behavioral Scientist 47(9), 1208–1230.

Wright, J. (2003). *One-Sided Logic in Two-Sided Markets.* Review of Network Economics 3(1), 44–64.

Yang, M. J., and Hsiang Iris Chyi (2011). *Competing with whom? Where? And why (not)? An empirical study of U.S. online newspapers' competition dynamics.* Journal of Media Business Studies 8(4), 59–74.

Zhang, A. H. (2013). *Toward an Economic Approach to Agency Agreements.* Journal of Competition Law and Economics 9(3), 553–591.

Zingales, N. (2013). *Product Market Definition in Online Search and Advertising.* Competition Law Review 9(1), 29–47.

Studies/Reports/Policy Papers

Autorità per le Garanzie nelle Comunicazioni (2012). *Indagine conoscitiva sul settore della raccolta pubblicitaria* (Allegato A alla Delibera 551/12/CONS). <http://www.agcom.it/documents/10179/1/document/bd184d98-cdcd-41e1-b141-9864dcfba8d6>.

BBC (2003). *Facts and Figures*. <http://stakeholders.ofcom.org.uk/binaries/consultations/psb/responses/mceihil_annex.pdf>.

BBC (2012). *Response to Ofcom's Invitation to Comment on Measuring Media Plurality*. <http://stakeholders.ofcom.org.uk/binaries/consultations/measuring-plurality/responses/bbc.pdf>.

BBC Tariff Prices for Independents. <http://www.bbc.co.uk/commissioning/tv/how-we-work/business-requirements/tariff-ranges.shtml>.

BEREC (2018). *Report on the impact of premium content on ECS markets and the effect of devices on* the open use of the Internet. <https://berec.europa.eu/eng/document_register/subject_matter/berec/reports/8013-berec-report-on-the-impact-of-premium-content-on-ecs-markets-and-the-effect-of-devices-on-the-open-use-of-the-internet>.

BNC Research (2013). *The Canadian Book Consumer*.

BNP Paribas (2017, May). *E-Commerce. Online Sales in Europe*.

Broadcasting Authority of Ireland (2010). *Strategy Statement 2011–2013*. <http://www.bai.ie/wordpress/wp-content/uploads/BAI_Strategy_2011-13_v2ENG.pdf>.

Centre for Media Pluralism and Media Freedom (CMPF) (2013). *European Union Competencies in Respect of Media Pluralism and Media Freedom*. <http://cadmus.eui.eu/bitstream/handle/1814/26056/RSCAS_PP_2013_01.pdf?sequence=1&isAllowed=y>.

Comisión Nacional de la Competencia (CNC) (2008). *Informe sobre la competencia en los mercados de adquisición y explotación de derechos audiovisuales de fútbol en España*.

Commissariat voor de Media (2011). *Media Monitor – The Dutch Media in 2010*. <https://www.mediamonitor.nl/wp-content/uploads/2013/08/Mediamonitor-The-Dutch-media-in-20101.pdf>

Commission (not dated). *Common Principles for an Economic Assessment of the Compatibility of State Aid Under Article 87(3)*. <http://ec.europa.eu/competition/state_aid/reform/economic_assessment_en.pdf>

Commission (1984). *Fourteenth Report on Competition Policy*. Available at: <https://publications.europa.eu/en/publication-detail/-/publication/3c93e6fa-934b-4fb9-b927-dc9fed71ccfe>Commission (1986). *Annual Report on Competition Policy 1985*.

Commission. *Report on application of Directive 89/552/EEC and proposal for a European Parliament and Council Directive amending Council Directive 89/552/EEC on the coordination of certain provisions laid down by law, regulation or administrative action in Member States concerning the pursuit of television broadcasting activities* (presented by the Commission). COM (95) 86 final.

Commission (1998). *Report from the High Level Group on Audiovisual Policy: the Digital Age: European Audiovisual Policy.*

Commission (1999). *Report from the Commission to the European Council with a view to safeguarding current sports structures and maintaining the social function of sport within the Community framework* (the Helsinki Report on Sports). <http://eur-lex.europa.eu/LexUriServ/LexUriServ.do?uri=COM:1999:0644:FIN:EN:PDF>.

Commission (2005). *Issues paper for the Liverpool Audiovisual Conference: Media pluralism – What should be the European Union's role?* Brussels: DG Information Society and Media

Commission (2005). *Merger Remedies Study*. <http://ec.europa.eu/competition/mergers/legislation/remedies_study.pdf>.

Commission. *Fifth Report from the Commission to the Council, the European Parliament, the European Economic and Social Committee and the Committee of the Regions on the application of Directive 89/552/EEC 'Television without Frontiers'*, SEC (2006) 160. <http://eur-lex.europa.eu/legal-content/EN/TXT/PDF/?uri=CELEX:52006DC0049&from=EN>.

Commission (2009). *Independent Study on Indicators for Media Pluralism in the Member States – Towards a Risk-based Approach*. <http://ec.europa.eu/information_society/media_taskforce/doc/pluralism/study/final_report_09.pdf>.

Commission (2009). *Independent Study on Indicators for Media Pluralism in the Member States – Towards a Risk-based Approach*. Annex III – Country Reports.

Commission (2009). *Seventh report from the Commission to the European Parliament, the Council, the European Economic and Social Committee and the Committee of the Regions on the application of Directive 89/552/EEC 'Television without Frontiers'* COM 309 final.

Commission (2012). Commission Staff Working Paper. *Impact Assessment accompanying the General Data Protection Regulation and the Directive on the protection of individuals with regard to the processing of personal data by competent authorities for the purposes of prevention, investigation, detection or prosecution of criminal offences or the execution of criminal penalties, and the free movement of such data* SEC (2012) 72 final.

Commission (2012). *Digital Agenda for Europe – Scoreboard 2012*.

Commission. *First Report from the Commission to the European Parliament, the Council, the European Economic and Social Committee and the Committee of the Regions on the application of Directive 2010/13/EU 'Audiovisual Media Service Directive'*. COM (2012) 203 final.

Commission. *First report on the application of Articles 13, 16 and 17 of Directive 2010/13/EU for the period 2009–2010. Promotion of European works in EU scheduled and on-demand audiovisual media services*. COM (2012) 522 final.

Commission (2012). *A vibrant digital single market.* <https://ec.europa.eu/digital-agenda/sites/digital-agenda/files/KKAH12001ENN-chap2-PDFWEB-2.pdf>.

Commission (2016). *Special Eurobarometer 452. Media Pluralism and Democracy.* <http://ec.europa.eu/information_society/newsroom/image/document/2016-47/sp452-summary_en_19666.pdf>.

Commission (2016). *Preliminary Report on the E-Commerce Sector Inquiry.*

Commission (2016). *Media pluralism and democracy: outcomes of the 2016 Annual Colloquium on Fundamental Rights.*

Commission (2017). *Media Use in the European Union.*

Commission pour la nouvelle télévision publique (2008). *Rapport Présenté au Président de la République par Jean-François Copé le 25 juin 2008.* <http://www.culture.gouv.fr/culture/actualites/dossiers/Rapport_Cope/rapport_commission.pdf>.

Competition Commission (2009). *A report on the anticipated joint venture between BBC Worldwide Limited, Channel Four Television Corporation and ITV plc relating to the video on demand sector.* <http://webarchive.nationalarchives.gov.uk/20140402141250/http://competition-commission.org.uk/assets/competitioncommission/docs/pdf/non-inquiry/rep_pub/reports/2009/fulltext/543>.

Council of Europe (2002). *Media Diversity in Europe. Report prepared by the Advisory Panel to the CDMM on media concentrations, pluralism and diversity questions.* <https://rm.coe.int/CoERMPublicCommonSearchServices/DisplayDCTMContent?documentId=0900001680483b2c>.

Council of Europe (2004). *Transnational media concentrations in Europe.* Report prepared by the Advisory Panel to the CDMM on media concentrations, pluralism and diversity questions.

Council of Europe (2008). *Report of high-level task force on social cohesion in the 21st century – Towards an active, fair and socially cohesive Europe*. TFSC (2007) 31E.

Council of Europe (2009). *Methodology for monitoring media concentration and media content diversity.* Report prepared by the Group of Specialists on Media Diversity (MC-S-MD).

Csorgo, L. and Ian Munro (2011). *Market Definition Issues for Audio and Audio-Visual Distribution Products and Services in a Digital Environment, A Report Prepared for the Canadian Radio-television and Telecommunications Commission.* <http://www.crtc.gc.ca/eng/publications/reports/rp110215.htm#_ftn7>.

Cvrcek, D., Marek Kumpost, Vashek Matyas, and George Danezis (2006). *A Study On The Value Of Location Privacy*. Proceedings of Workshop on Privacy in the Electronic Society (WPES '06).

Dahrendorf, R., F. Field and C. Hayman (1995). *Report on Wealth Creation and Social Cohesion in a Free Society* (the Dahrendorf Report). London: Commission on Wealth Creation and Social Cohesion.

Dubai School of Government (2011). *Arab Social Media Report* Vol. 1 No. 2.

EBU (2013). *Reply to the European Commission Green Paper – Preparing for a Fully Converged Audiovisual World: Growth, Creation and Values*. <https://www.ebu.ch/files/live/sites/ebu/files/Publications/Position%20papers/EBU-Position-EN%20reply%20Green%20Paper%20convergence%2010.9.2013.pdf>.

Electronic Frontiers Foundation. *Definition of media*. IRM of 24/11/2009.

ELIAMEP (2010). *MEDIADEM background information report on media policies and regulatory practices in a selected set of European countries, the EU and the Council of Europe.*

ELIAMEP (2010). *MEDIADEM background information report on media policies and regulatory practices in a selected set of European countries, the European Union and the Council of Europe: the case of Belgium.*

ELIAMEP (2010). *MEDIADEM background information report on media policies and regulatory practices in a selected set of European countries, the European Union and the Council of Europe: the case of Denmark.*

ELIAMEP (2010). *MEDIADEM background information report on media policies and regulatory practices in a selected set of European countries, the European Union and the Council of Europe: the case of Germany.*

ELIAMEP (2010). *MEDIADEM background information report on media policies and regulatory practices in a selected set of European countries, the European Union and the Council of Europe: the case of Greece.*

ELIAMEP (2011). *MEDIADEM Case study report: Does media policy promote media freedom and independence? The case of Belgium.*

ELIAMEP (2011). *MEDIADEM Case study report Does media policy promote media freedom and independence? The case of Germany.*

ELIAMEP (2012). *MEDIADEM Comparative Report on Media freedom and Independence in 14 European countries*. <https://www.eliamep.gr/wp-content/uploads/2012/09/media-freedom.pdf>.

eMarketer (2017). *US Simultaneous Media Users*. <https://www.emarketer.com/Report/US-Simultaneous-Media-Users-eMarketers-Estimates-2017/2002163>.

ERG (2009). *Report on price consistency in upstream broadband markets.*

Ernst and Young (2014). *Creating Growth. Measuring cultural and creative markets in the EU.* <http://www.ey.com/Publication/vwLUAssets/Measuring_cultural_and_creative_markets_in_the_EU/$FILE/Creating-Growth.pdf>.

EU Media Futures Forum (2012). *Fast-forward Europe – 8 solutions to thrive in the digital world*, 4. <http://ec.europa.eu/digital-agenda/sites/digital-agenda/files/forum_final_report_en.pdf>.

EU Network of Independent Experts on Human Rights (2003). *Report on the Situation of Fundamental Rights in the European Union and its Member States in 2002.*

EU Network of Independent Experts on Fundamental Rights (2004). *Synthesis Report: Conclusions and Recommendations on the situation of fundamental rights in the European Union and its Member States in 2003.* <https://www.ab.gov.tr/files/ardb/evt/1_avrupa_birligi/1_6_raporlar/1_3_diger/human_rights/report_on_fundamental_rights_2003.pdf>.

EU Network of Independent Experts on Fundamental Rights (2005). *Synthesis Report: Conclusions and Recommendations on the situation of fundamental rights in the European Union and its Member States in 2004.*

EU Network of Independent Experts on Fundamental Rights (2006). *Report on the Situation of Fundamental Rights in the European Union and its Member States in 2005.* <http://www.statewatch.org/news/2006/jun/EU-funrights-report05.pdf>.

Europe Economics (2002). *Market Definition in the Media Sector: Economic Issues. Report for the European Commission, DG Competition.*

European Audiovisual Observatory. Yearbook 2011, T6-01.

European Audiovisual Observatory (2016). *Audiovisual sports rights between exclusivity and right to information.* <https://rm.coe.int/1680788a5d>.

European Data Protection Supervisor (2014). *Privacy and competitiveness in the age of big data: The interplay between data protection, competition law and consumer protection in the Digital Economy.* <https://secure.edps.europa.eu/EDPSWEB/webdav/shared/Documents/Consultation/Opinions/2014/14-03-26_competitition_law_big_data_EN.pdf>.

European Federation of Journalists (2005). *Media power in Europe: The big picture of ownership.*

European Institute for the Media (2004). *The Information of the Citizen in the EU: Obligations for the Media and the Institutions concerning the Citizen's right to be Fully and Objectively Informed.* <http://edz.bib.uni-mannheim.de/daten/edz-ma/ep/04/pe358896-en.pdf>

European Parliamentary Research Service (2017). Access to Culture in the European Union. <http://www.europarl.europa.eu/RegData/etudes/IDAN/2017/608631/EPRS_IDA(2017)608631_EN.pdf>

European Policy Evaluation Consortium (EPEC) (2005). *Preparatory Study for Impact Assessment and Ex Ante Evaluation of Fundamental Rights Agency. Final Report.*

European Press Publishers (2014). *Press Publishers' Response to Google's Third Commitments Proposal. European Commission's Competition Investigation of Google – AT.39740.*

Federal Communications Commission (2003). *Report and Order and Notice of Proposed Rulemaking*, FCC 03-127.

Federal Communications Commission – Waldman, S. and the Working Group on Information Needs of Communities (2011). *The Information Needs of Communities. The changing media landscape in a broadband.* <http://www.fcc.gov/info-needs-communities>.

Foster, R. (2012). *News Plurality in a Digital World – Report prepared for the Reuters Institute for the Study of Journalism.*

Foundem (2012). *Remedy Proposals – An Outline of Proposed Remedies to Google's Anti-Competitive Manipulations of its Search Results and Ad Listings.*

Freedom House (2013). *Report on Spain.* <https://www.freedomhouse.org/report/freedom-press/2013/spain#.VMJr_M016eY>

Frog Design (2011). *The Value of Personal Data: A Global Perspective*. Presentation at Mobile World Congress, February 2011.

Fundamental Rights Agency (2016). *Incitement in media content and political discourse in EU Member States.* <http://fra.europa.eu/en/publication/2016/incitement-media-content-and-political-discourse-member-states-european-union>.

Fundamental Rights Agency (2016). *Violence, threats and pressures against journalists and other media actors in the EU.* <http://fra.europa.eu/en/publication/2016/violence-threats-and-pressures-against-journalists-and-other-media-actors-european>.

Graham, D. and Associates (2009). *Study on the application of measures concerning the promotion of the distribution and production of European works in audiovisual media services (i.e. including television programmes and non-linear services).* <http://ec.europa.eu/archives/information_society/avpolicy/docs/library/studies/art4_5/final_report.pdf>.

Hans Bredow Institute for Media Research *et al.* (2011). *INDIREG Report on Indicators for independence and efficient functioning of audiovisual media services regulatory bodies for the purpose of enforcing the rules in the AVMS Directive.*

High Level Group on Fake News and Online Disinformation (2018). *A multi-dimensional approach to disinformation.* <https://ec.europa.eu/digital-single-market/en/news/final-report-high-level-expert-group-fake-news-and-online-disinformation>.

High Level Group on Media Freedom and Pluralism (2013). *A free and pluralistic media to sustain European democracy.* https://ec.europa.eu/digital-single-market/sites/digital-agenda/files/HLG%20Final%20Report.pdf .

Human Rights Watch (2012, February). *Memorandum to the European Union on Media Freedom in Hungary.* <http://www.hrw.org/news/2012/02/16/memorandum-european-union-media-freedom-hungary>.

IAB (2013). *Mediascope Europe 2012 Pan-European Launch Presentation Summary.* <http://www.iabeurope.eu/files/6713/8720/0955/MEDIASCOPE_2012_PAN-EUROPEAN_SUMMARY_LAUNCH_PRESENTATION_public.pdf>.

International Publishers Association (2014). *Global Fixed Book Price Report.* <http://www.snel.org.br/wp-content/themes/snel/docs/Material/global.pdf>.

Joint Research Centre (2012a). *Statistical, Ecosystems and Competitiveness Analysis of the Media and Content Industries: The Newspaper Publishing Industry.* < http://publications.jrc.ec.europa.eu/repository/bitstream/JRC69881/jrc69881.pdf>.

Joint Research Centre (2012b). *Technical Report on Statistical, Ecosystems and Competitiveness Analysis of the Media and Content Industries: The Book Publishing Industry.* <http://ftp.jrc.es/EURdoc/JRC76642.pdf>.

La Porte Alfaro, M. T. and Teresa Sabada (2001). *Globalization of the Media Industry and Possible Threats to Cultural Diversity – A Study prepared for the European Parliament.* Final Study. Working document for the STOA Panel. <http://www.europarl.europa.eu/RegData/etudes/etudes/join/2001/296704/DG-4-JOIN_ET(2001)296704_EN.pdf>.

Lefever, K., Ellen Wauters and Peggy Valcke (2013, July). *Media Pluralism in the EU – Comparative analysis of measurements systems in Europe and US.* <http://www.steunpunt-media.be/wp-content/uploads/2014/03/Steunpunt-Media_ICRI_Monitoring_D1D2.pdf>.

Microsoft (2009). *Meet Europe's media multi-taskers.*

Milanova, N. (2011). *EU Agency for fundamental rights (FRA): a reality check.* Report prepared for Human Rights Without Frontiers International. <http://www.hrwf.net/index.php/publications/107-policy-and-advocacy-papers>.

Netherlands Competition Authority (1999). *NMa and DTe Annual Report.*

Noll, H.H. (2009). *The Impact of Cultural and Citizenship Education on Social Cohesion.* Input Statement The Impact of Cultural and Citizenship Education on Social Cohesion: Chances – Challenges – Changes, Vilnius, Lithuania.

OECD (1993). *Glossary of Industrial Organization Economics and Competition Law*, compiled by R. S. Khemani and D. M. Shapiro, commissioned by the OECD Directorate for Financial, Fiscal and Enterprise Affairs. <http://stats.oecd.org/glossary/detail.asp?ID=3177>.

OECD (1997). *Policy Roundtable on Resale Price Maintenance.*

OECD (2003a). *Policy Roundtable on Media Mergers.*

OECD (2003b). *Policy Roundtable on Vertical Restraints for Online Sales.*

OECD (2007). *Participative Web: User-Created Content.*

OECD (2009). *Policy Roundtable Report on Two-Sided Markets.*

OECD (2011). *Economic Evidence in Merger Analysis.*

OECD (2012a). *Policy Roundtable on Market Definition.*

OECD (2012b). *E-books: Developments and Policy Considerations.* OECD Digital Economy Papers, No. 208.

OECD (2013a). *Competition Issues in Television and Broadcasting.*

OECD (2013b). *Exploring the Economics of Personal Data: A Survey of Methodologies for Measuring Monetary Value.*

OECD (2013c). *The Role and Measurement of Quality in Competition Analysis.*

Ofcom (2009a). *Wholesale must-offer remedies: International examples.*

Ofcom (2009b). *Pay TV Phase Three Document: Proposed Remedies.*

Ofcom (2009c). *Report on Media Ownership Rules.*

Ofcom (2010a). *Competition issues in premium pay TV movies.*

Ofcom (2010b). *Report on public interest test on the proposed acquisition of British Sky Broadcasting Group plc by News Corporation.*

Ofcom (2012a). *Communications Market Report.*

Ofcom (2012b). *Measuring Media Plurality.*

Ofcom (2012c). *Securing long term benefits from scarce low frequency spectrum.*

Ofcom (2013). *International Communications Market Report.*

Ofcom (2014). *Communications Market Report.*

Ofcom (2018). *News Consumption in the UK: 2018.*

Office of Fair Trading (2008a). *Newspaper and magazine distribution. Opinion of the Office of Fair Trading. Guidance to facilitate self-assessment under the Competition Act 1998.*

Office of Fair Trading (2008b). *An evaluation of the impact upon productivity of ending resale price maintenance on books*. Report prepared for the OFT by the Centre for Competition Policy at University of East Anglia.

Open Society Foundations (2012). *Mapping Digital Media in the European Union – A Report for the High-Level Group on Media Freedom and Pluralism.*

Open Society Institute (2005). *Television across Europe – Monitoring Report.*

OSCE (2003). *The Impact of Media Concentration on Professional Journalism*

OSCE (2010). *Analysis and assessment of a package Hungarian legislation and draft legislation on media and telecommunications.* <http://www.osce.org/fom/71218?download=true>.

Overstreet, T. R. (1983). *Resale Price Maintenance: Economic Theories and Empirical Evidence*. FTC Bureau of Economics Staff Report.

Pavlik, J. (2005). *Understanding Convergence and Digital Broadcasting Technologies for the Twenty-First Century*. NHK Broadcasting Studies. <https://www.nhk.or.jp/bunken/english/reports/pdf/05_no4_08.pdf>.

Radicalization Awareness Network (2012). *Proposed Policy Recommendations for the High Level Conference*. <http://ec.europa.eu/dgs/home-affairs/what-we-do/networks/radicalisation_awareness_network/ran-high-level-conference/docs/proposed_policy_recommendations_ran_at_en.pdf>.

Rainie L. and Jeremy Shermak (2005). *Search Engine Use November 2005*, Technical report. Washington, D.C.: PEW Internet & American Life Project.

Reuters Institute (2018). *Digital News Report 2018.*

The Booksellers Association (2011). *Reports Library RPM-Book Sales in the UK.*

The Bundeskartellamt (2013). *Annual Report*. <http://www.bundeskartellamt.de/SharedDocs/Publikation/EN/Jahresbericht/Jahresbericht_2013.pdf?__blob=publicationFile&v=3>.

Turku School of Economics and Business Administration (2005). *Publishing Market Watch Final Report*. Prepared for DG Enterprise, European Commission.

UK Competition Commission (2007). *Report on the Acquisition by BSkyB plc of 17.9% of the shares in ITV Plc sent to Secretary of State (BERR) of 14 December 2007.*

UK Department for Culture, Media and Sport (2006). *A Public Service for all: the BBC in the digital age.* <https://webarchive.nationalarchives.gov.uk/+/http://www.bbc-charterreview.org.uk/have_your_say/white_paper/bbc_whitepaper_march06.pdf>.

Ward, D. (2006). *Final Report on the Study Commissioned by the MC-S-MD – The Assessment of Content Diversity in Newspapers and Television in the Context of Increasing Trends Towards Concentration of Media Markets*, MC-S-MD (2006) 001, 4. Strasbourg: Council of Europe.

Ward, D., Oliver Carsten Fueg and Alessandro D'Armo (2004). *Mapping Study of Media Concentration and Ownership in Ten European Countries.* <http://citeseerx.ist.psu.edu/viewdoc/download?doi=10.1.1.691.2674&rep=rep1&type=pdf>.

Wardle, C. and Andrew Williams (2008). *ugc@thebbc. Understanding its impact upon contributors, non-contributors, and BBC News.* Cardiff School of Journalism, Media and Cultural Studies. <http://orca.cf.ac.uk/48158/>.

World Radio and Television Council (2000). *Public Broadcasting Why? How?* <http://unesdoc.unesco.org/images/0012/001240/124058eo.pdf>.

Media articles and blog contributions

AOL/Huffington Post. *AOL Agrees To Acquire The Huffington Post.* 7 February 2011, The Huffington Post. <http://www.huffingtonpost.com/2011/02/07/aol-huffington-post_n_819375.html>.

Barraclough, L. *Pay-TV Operator Sky Pays Almost $4 Billion for German Soccer Rights.* 9 June 2016, Variety. <https://variety.com/2016/tv/global/pay-tv-sky-german-soccer-rights-1201792143/>.

Bania, K. *Undermining democracy to save money: The unexpected and illegitimate closure of the Greek public service broadcaster.* 3 July 2013, Media Laws: Law and Policy of the Media in a Comparative Perspective. <http://www.medialaws.eu/undermining-democracy-to-save-money-the-unexpected-and-illegitimate-closure-of-the-greek-public-service-broadcaster/>.

BBC. *Apple removes iPhone Wikileaks app from iTunes.* 22 December 2010. <http://www.bbc.com/news/technology-12059577>.

Berg, M. *The World's Highest-Paid TV Actors: Jim Parsons Leads With $27.5 Million.* 28 September 2017, Forbes. <https://www.forbes.com/sites/maddieberg/2017/09/28/the-worlds-highest-paid-tv-actors-jim-parsons-leads-with-27-5-million/#949d9e851a30>.

Briel, R. *Sky Deutschland wins all live Bundesliga rights.* 18 April 2012, Broadband TV News. <http://www.broadbandtvnews.com/2012/04/18/sky-deutschland-wins-live-bundesliga-rights/>.

Bunz, M. *Rupert Murdoch: 'There's no such thing as a free news story'*. 1 December 2009, The Guardian. <http://www.theguardian.com/media/2009/dec/01/rupert-murdoch-no-free-news>.

Burns, J. F. and Alan Cowell. *Cameron Defends Handling of Murdoch Bid to Take Over Sky Broadcasting*. 25 May 2012, New York Times. <http://www.nytimes.com/2012/05/26/world/europe/e-mail-shows-murdoch-bid-maneuvering.html?_r=0>.

Bury, L. *Young adult readers 'prefer printed to ebooks'*. 25 November 2013, The Guardian. <http://www.theguardian.com/books/2013/nov/25/young-adult-readers-prefer-printed-ebooks>.

Campbell, L. *HC and Hachette UK Refine Agency Model*. 3 April 2013, The Bookseller. <http://www.thebookseller.com/news/hc-and-hachette-uk-refine-agency-model>.

Carlson, N. *Printing The NYT Costs Twice As Much As Sending Every Subscriber A Free Kindle*. 30 January 2009, Business Insider. <http://www.businessinsider.com/2009/1/printing-the-nyt-costs-twice-as-much-as-sending-every-subscriber-a-free-kindle?IR=T#ixzz3PXgJfaiY>.

CellularItalia. *Chiusura definitive offerta 'Infostrada TV' dal 22 giugno 2012*. 30 maggio 2012. <http://www.cellularitalia.com/news/wind1104chiusura-infostrada-tv22-06.php>

Coker, M. *Does Agency Pricing Lead to Higher Book Prices?* 28 March 2012, Smashwords. <http://blog.smashwords.com/2012/03/does-agency-pricing-lead-to-higher-book.html>.

Conn, D. *Sky and BT Sport retain grip on Premier League rights but TV frenzy cools*. 13 February 2018, The Guardian. <https://www.theguardian.com/football/2018/feb/13/sky-bt-sport-premier-league-tv-rights>.

D'Elia, D. *Google News Spagna Chiude? Traffico in Calo del 15%*. 17 December 2014, Tom's Hardware. <http://www.tomshw.it/news/google-news-spagna-chiude-traffico-in-calo-del-15-63176>.

De Moraes, L. *NBC's 'The Blacklist' Tops Annual New-Series Ad Price Survey*. 14 October 2013, Deadline Hollywood. <http://deadline.com/2013/10/nbcs-the-blacklist-tops-annual-new-series-ad-price-survey-610874/>.

Der Spiegel. *Chorus of Criticism: Germany Denounces New Hungarian Media Law*. 22 December 2010, Spiegel. <http://www.spiegel.de/international/europe/chorus-of-criticism-germany-denounces-new-hungarian-media-law-a-736206.html>.

Dover, D. *The Evil Side of Google? Exploring Google's User Data Collection*. 24 June 2008, Moz Blog. <http://www.seomoz.org/blog/the-evil-side-of-google-exploring-googles-user-data-collection>.

El Periódico. *El cierre de Google News no impedirá al ciudadano el acceso a las noticias.* 13 December 2014. <http://www.elperiodico.com/es/noticias/sociedad/cierre-google-news-espana-acceso-noticias-internet-3769029>.

Epstein. R. *Not Proven: The DoJ Suit Against Apple for E-book Pricing.* 10 April 2014, Ricochet. <https://ricochet.com/archives/not-proven-the-doj-suit-against-apple-for-ebook-pricing/>.

Fantz, A. *See yourself as the next Assange? Good luck.* 30 June 2012, CNN. <http://edition.cnn.com/2012/06/29/world/future-leaking-online/index.html>.

Farhi, P. *Washington Post to be sold to Jeff Bezos, the founder of Amazon.* 5 August 2013, The Washington Post. <http://www.washingtonpost.com/national/washington-post-to-be-sold-to-jeff-bezos/2013/08/05/ca537c9e-fe0c-11e2-9711-3708310f6f4d_story.html>.

Fraga, I. *Brazilian newspapers leave Google News en masse.* 22 October 2012, Knight Center for Journalism in the Americas. <https://knightcenter.utexas.edu/blog/00-11841-newspapers-say-their-boycott-turned-google-news-"deficient"-brazil-reiterate-request-p>.

García, R. R. *Google News solo volverá a España si la tasa por contenidos es voluntaria.* 12 December 2014, La Voz de Galicia. <http://www.lavozdegalicia.es/noticia/vidadigital/2014/12/12/google-news-solo-volvera-espana-tasa-contenidos-voluntaria/0003_201412G12P61991.htm>.

Garofalo, A. *'Game Of Thrones' Big Budgets Bring Huge Success; How HBO Series Makes Money With High Cost Per Episode.* 14 August 2014, International Business Times. <http://www.ibtimes.com/game-thrones-big-budgets-bring-huge-success-how-hbo-series-makes-money-high-cost-episode-1658966>.

Gibson, O. *Premier League lands £3bn TV rights bonanza from Sky and BT.* 13 June 2012, The Guardian. <http://www.theguardian.com/media/2012/jun/13/premier-league-tv-rights-3-billion-sky-bt>.

Gil, X. *El Gobierno siete millones de euros al anular la creación del Consejo Estatal de Medios Audiovisuales.* 22 January 2012, Voz Barcelona. <http://www.vozbcn.com/2012/01/22/100013/gobierno-ahorrara-crear-cema/>.

Gokey, M. *Just say no – Apple and Google reject Flappy Bird Clones.* 17 February 2015, Techtimes. <http://www.techtimes.com/articles/3526/20140217/just-say-no-apple-and-google-reject-flappy-bird-clones.htm>.

Goodwin, D. *Top Google Result Gets 36.4% of Clicks.* 21 April 2011, Search Engine Watch. <http://searchenginewatch.com/sew/news/2049695/top-google-result-gets-364-clicks-study>.

Google (2005, June). *Search gets personal.* <http://googleblog.blogspot.com/2005/06/search-gets-personal.html>.

Google (2007, May). *Google Begins Move to Universal Search.* <http://googlepress.blogspot.com/2007/05/google-begins-move-to-universal-search_16.html>.

Google (2009, December). *Personalized search for Everyone.* <http://googleblog.blogspot.com/2009/12/personalized-search-for-everyone.html>.

Google (2012b, December). *Partnering with Belgian news publishers.* <http://googlepolicyeurope.blogspot.it/2012/12/partnering-with-belgian-news-publishers.html>.

Haque, U. *The Attention Economy.* 8 November 2005, Bubblegeneration.com. <http://www.bubblegeneration.com/2005/11/attention-economy-across-consumer.cfm>.

Harris, C. *BSkyB Retains Majority of TV Rights to Premier League On UK TV For 2013–16.* 13 June 2012, World Soccer Talk. <http://worldsoccertalk.com/2012/06/13/bskyb-retains-majority-of-tv-rights-to-premier-league-on-uk-tv-for-2013-16/>.

Heath, E. '*Content is King' – Essay by Bill Gates 1996.* 29 January 2017, Medium <https://medium.com/@HeathEvans/content-is-king-essay-by-bill-gates-1996-df74552f80d9>.

Helft, M. *Apple Moves to Tighten Control of App Store.* 1 February 2011, The New York Times. <http://www.nytimes.com/2011/02/01/technology/01apple.html?_r=0>.

Helft, M. *Why Apple Removed a WikiLeaks App From Its Store.* 21 December 2010, The New York Times. <http://bits.blogs.nytimes.com/2010/12/21/why-apple-removed-wikileaks-app-from-its-store/?_r=0>.

Heritage, S. *Sherlock Holmes's smarter brothers: the best pilots that never made it to air.* 28 May 2010, The Guardian. <http://www.theguardian.com/tv-and-radio/tvandradioblog/2010/may/28/sherlock-holmes-best-pilots-never>.

Holton, K. *UK's Cameron defends role in Murdoch takeover deal.* 25 May 2012, Reuters. <http://www.reuters.com/article/2012/05/25/britain-hacking-cameron-idUSL5E8GP7PN20120525>.

Hom, M. *Why Humans Prefer Print Books.* 4 January 2016, Elsevier SciTech Connect. <http://scitechconnect.elsevier.com/why-humans-prefer-print-books/>.

Hotham, L. and Lucas Nacif. *Article 7 TEU and the Polish case – a recast.* 16 April 2018, KSLR EU Law Blog. <https://blogs.kcl.ac.uk/kslreuropeanlawblog/?p=1274#.W0SGeEiFO71>.

Huang, C. *Facebook and Twitter key to Arab Spring uprisings: report.* 6 June 2011, The National. <http://www.thenational.ae/news/uae-news/facebook-and-twitter-key-to-arab-spring-uprisings-report>.

Hurley, L. *Supreme Court rejects Apple e-books price-fixing appeal.* 7 March 2016, Reuters. <https://www.reuters.com/article/us-usa-court-ebooks-idUSKCN0W91LQ>.

Ibáñez Colomo, P. *The Spanish Google tax, or (twice) the perfect cartel.* 19 March 2014, Chillin' Competition. <http://chillingcompetition.com/2014/03/19/the-spanish-google-tax-or-twice-the-perfect-cartel/>.

Ibáñez Colomo, P. *The Android decision is out: the exciting legal stuff beneath the noise.* 18 July 2018, Chillin' Competition. <https://chillingcompetition.com/2018/07/18/the-android-decision-is-out-the-exciting-legal-stuff-beneath-the-noise-by-pablo/>.

Johnson, T. *The FCC just passed the most significant changes to media ownership regulations in a generation.* 16 November 2017, Business Insider UK. <http://uk.businessinsider.com/fcc-passes-media-ownership-regulations-rules-2017-11?r=US&IR=T>.

Jones, P. *Amazon, Sony agree to agency deals over e-books in US.* 1 April 2010, The Bookseller. <http://www.thebookseller.com/news/amazon-sony-agree-agency-deals-over-e-books-us.html>.

Kahn, J. *Cue on agency model: 'I don't think you understand. We can't treat newspapers or magazines any differently than we treat FarmVille.'* 23 April 2012, 9to5Mac. <http://9to5mac.com/2012/04/23/cue-on-agency-model-i-dont-think-you-understand-we-cant-treat-newspapers-or-magazines-any-differently-than-we-treat-farmville/>.

Kanter, J. *E.U. Parliament Passes Measure to Break Up Google in Symbolic Vote.* 27 November 2014, The New York Times. <http://www.nytimes.com/2014/11/28/business/international/google-european-union.html?_r=0>.

Kassam, A. *Google News says 'adiós' to Spain in row over publishing fees.* 16 December 2014, The Guardian. <http://www.theguardian.com/world/2014/dec/16/google-news-spain-publishing-fees-internet>.

Kelly, A. *Google to pay 60 million euros into French media fund.* 8 January 2013, Reuters. <http://www.reuters.com/article/2013/02/01/us-france-google-idUSBRE91011Z20130201>.

Kelly, L. and Ralph Boulton. *Poland will not yield to EU over court reforms – Kaczynski.* 26 January 2018, Reuters. <https://uk.reuters.com/article/uk-poland-judiciary-kaczynski/poland-will-not-yield-to-eu-over-court-reforms-kaczynski-idUKKBN1FF13X?il=0>Kiss, J. *Apple pulls Wikileaks app, but Android apps remain.* 21 December 2010, The Guardian. <http://www.theguardian.com/media/pda/2010/dec/21/apple-wikileaks-app>.

Krieger, J. *ARD and ZDF establish German VOD portal.* 25 April 2012, RapidTVNews. <http://www.rapidtvnews.com/index.php/2012042521488/ard-and-zdf-establish-german-vod-portal.html>.

Krishna, S. *Facebook's News Feed change may amplify fake news.* 16 January 2018, Engadget. <https://www.engadget.com/2018/01/16/facebook-news-feed-tweak-could-make-fake-news-worse/>.

Koch, T. *La Ley de Propiedad Intelectual será juzgada por el Constitucional.* 5 March 2015, El País. <http://cultura.elpais.com/cultura/2015/03/05/actualidad/1425572373_653722.html>.

MacDonald, M. *Collapse of Net Book Agreement 'within months'*. 26 December 1994, The Independent. <http://www.independent.co.uk/news/uk/collapse-of-net-book-agreement-within-months-collapse-1388530.html>.

Malachiti, A. *Fastweb chiude con Sky e con la Iptv*. 7 September 2012. InfoOggi < https://www.infooggi.it/articolo/fastweb-chiude-con-sky-e-con-la-iptv/31058>.

Malcolm, J. *Google News Shuttered in Spain Thanks to 'Ancillary Copyright' Law*. 10 December 2014, Electronic Frontiers Foundation. <https://www.eff.org/deeplinks/2014/12/google-news-shuts-shop-spain-thanks-ancillary-copyright-law>.

Martin, E. *Here's how much it costs HBO to produce one episode of 'Game of Thrones'*. 6 August 2017, CNBC. <https://www.cnbc.com/2017/08/04/it-costs-millions-to-produce-one-episode-of-hbos-game-of-thrones.html>.

McCabe, M. *YouView will encourage competition, says chief*. 16 September 2010, MediaWeek. <http://www.mediaweek.co.uk/article/1028931/youview-will-encourage-competition-says-chief>.

Microsoft (March, 2011). *Adding our Voice to Concerns about Search in Europe*. <http://blogs.microsoft.com/on-the-issues/2011/03/30/adding-our-voice-to-concerns-about-search-in-europe/>.

Miller, J. *Amazon accused of 'bullying' smaller UK publishers*. 26 June 2014, BBC News. <http://www.bbc.com/news/technology-27994314>.

Nicoli, S. *Vigilanza Rai: tra conflitti di interesse dei commissari e il solito peso di Berlusconi*. 7 June 2013, Il Fatto Quotidiano. <http://www.ilfattoquotidiano.it/2013/06/08/vigilanza-rai-tra-conflitti-di-interesse-dei-commissari-e-solito-peso-di-b/619818/>.

Pearce, J. *Premier League rights sold to BT and BSkyB for £3bn*. 13 June 2012, the BBC. <http://www.bbc.com/news/business-18430036>.

Peeters, T. *Competitive balance in European football leagues*. 14 August 2012, Football Perspectives. <http://footballperspectives.org/competitive-balance-european-football-leagues>.

Perpetuo, J. *El cierre de Google News y la libertad de información en España*. 11 December 2014, El Mundo. <http://www.elmundo.es/blogs/elmundo/jaqueperpetuo/2014/12/11/el-cierre-de-google-news-y-la-libertad.html>.

Peters, J. Y. and Verne G. Kopytoff. *Betting on News, AOL Is Buying The Huffington Post*. 7 February 2011, The New York Times. <http://www.nytimes.com/2011/02/07/business/media/07aol.html?_r=0>.

Pilkington, M. *Simon & Schuster Adopts Refined Agency Pricing with Amazon UK*. 29 April 2013, The Good E-reader. <http://goodereader.com/blog/electronic-readers/simon-schuster-adopts-refined-agency-pricing-with-amazon-uk>.

Powell, M., Jérémie Jourdan, and Strati Sakellariou-Witt. *EU Court annuls a 2014 European Commission merger clearance for insufficient reasoning.* 27 October 2017, White & Case. <https://www.whitecase.com/publications/alert/eu-court-annuls-2014-european-commission-merger-clearance-insufficient-reasoning>.

Prodhan, G. *Financial Times pulls its apps from Apple store.* 31 August 2011, Reuters. <http://www.reuters.com/article/2011/08/31/us-apple-ft-idUSTRE77U1O020110831>.

Pudasaini, P. *Top 10 Sports Leagues With the Highest Attendance Per Game.* 21 March 2014, The Richest.com. <http://www.therichest.com/sports/top-10-sports-leagues-with-the-highest-average-per-game-attendance-in-the-world/5/>.

Reda, J. *An EU-wide 'Google Tax' in the Making?* 28 December 2014, juliareda.eu. <https://juliareda.eu/2014/10/an-eu-wide-google-tax-in-the-making/>.

Robb, A. *92 Percent of College Students Prefer Reading Print Books to E-Readers.* 14 January 2015, New Republic. <http://www.newrepublic.com/article/120765/naomi-barons-words-onscreen-fate-reading-digital-world>.

Roberts, H. *Google made changes to its search algorithm that unintentionally made it vulnerable to the spread of fake news, sources say.* 10 December 2016, Business Insider. <http://uk.businessinsider.com/google-algorithm-change-fake-news-rankbrain-2016-12>.

Rosati, E. *Fordham Focus 9: News Aggregators and Fair Use.* 5 April 2013, The IPKat. <http://ipkitten.blogspot.it/2013/04/fordham-focus-9-news-aggregators-and.html>.

Rowles, D. *Which TV Shows Command The Highest Ad Prices, And How Much Does AMC Make On 'The Walking Dead'?* 21 October 2013, Uproxx. <http://uproxx.com/tv/2013/10/tv-shows-command-highest-ad-prices-much-amc-make-walking-dead/>.

Savage, M. *More buck for your Big Bang Theory: What justifies a $1 million pay packet?* 5 August 2014, BBC News. <http://www.bbc.com/news/entertainment-arts-28658258>.

Schneider, M. *These Are the 100 Most-Watched TV Shows of the 2015-16 Season: Winners and Losers.* 31 May 2016, IndieWire. <https://www.indiewire.com/2016/05/most-watched-tv-show-2015-2016-season-game-of-thrones-the-walking-dead-football-1201682396/>Shaffi, S. *Macmillan US does agency deal with Amazon.* 19 December 2014, The Bookseller. <http://www.thebookseller.com/news/macmillan-us-does-agency-deal-amazon>.

Sharp, E. *The first page of Google, by the Numbers.* 30 April 2014, Protofuse. <http://www.protofuse.com/blog/first-page-of-google-by-the-numbers/>.

Simons, N. *Rupert Murdoch Uses Twitter To Attack David Cameron Over Donor Row.* 26 March 2012, The Huffington Post. <http://www.huffingtonpost.co.uk/2012/03/26/rupert-murdoch-turns-on-david-cameron-over-cash-for-access-allegations_n_1379057.html>.

Smith, P. *Fts Mobile Web App Shows Apples Are Not the Only Fruit.* 8 June 2011, Themediabriefing.com. <http://www.themediabriefing.com/article/fts-mobile-web-app-shows-apples-are-not-the-only-fruit>.

Spangler, T. *Facebook Recruits Eurosport Chief Peter Hutton to Lead Global Sports-Rights Deals.* 21 January 2018, Variety. <http://variety.com/2018/digital/global/facebook-hires-eurosport-peter-hutton-global-sports-deals-1202671505/>.

Spencer, G. *Understanding The Agency Model And The DOJ's Allegations Against Apple And Those Publishers.* 12 April 2012, Mac Stories. <http://www.macstories.net/stories/understanding-the-agency-model-and-the-dojs-allegations-against-apple-and-those-publishers/>Stein, S. *Gibbs On Legal Action Against WikiLeaks: 'I Wouldn't Rule Anything Out'.* 29 November 2010, The Huffington Post. <http://www.huffingtonpost.com/2010/11/29/gibbs-on-legal-action-aga_n_789311.html>.

Stewart, T. *Which 5 Book Genres Make The Most Money?* 31 January 2014, The Richest. <http://www.therichest.com/rich-list/which-5-book-genres-make-the-most-money/?view=all>.

Sullivan, D. *Debunking The Italian Newspapers' Antitrust Allegations Against Google.* 27 August 2009, Search Engine Land. <http://searchengineland.com/deunking-the-italian-newspapers-antitrust-allegations-against-google-24698>.

Surrey, M. *Here's how much it costs to make an episode of 'The Walking Dead'.* 11 December 2016, Mic. <https://mic.com/articles/161740/here-s-how-much-it-costs-to-make-an-episode-of-the-walking-dead#.fjP53F4FP>.

The Economist. *Data, data everywhere.* 25 February 2010. <http://www.economist.com/node/15557443>.

Tsotsis, A. *Apple Removes WikiLeaks App From App Store.* 20 December 2010, Techcrunch. <http://techcrunch.com/2010/12/20/apple-removes-wikileaks-app-from-app-store/>.

Vanderbilt, T. *Why is literary fame so unpredictable?* 21 May 2012, The New Yorker. <http://www.newyorker.com/books/page-turner/why-is-literary-fame-so-unpredictable>.

Venizelos, T. *Greece to liberalize fixed system of book pricing.* 18 March 2014, Press TV News. <https://www.youtube.com/watch?v=cTeRM3Kj-x0>.

WARC.com. *Simultaneous media use rises in Europe.* 1 June 2012, Warc.com. <http://www.warc.com/Content/News/Simultaneous_media_use_rises_in_Europe.content?ID=fed4dca7-bca7-44b6-b42a-dbf941b155c2>.

Wauters, R. *44% Of Google News Visitors Scan Headlines, Don't Click Through.* 19 January 2010, Techcrunch. <http://techcrunch.com/2010/01/19/outsell-google-news/>.

Whithall, Z. *Kobo switches to agency terms with major U.S. publishers.* 1 April 2010, Quill & Quire. <http://www.quillandquire.com/omni/kobo-switches-to-agency-terms-with-major-us-publishers/>.

Williams, C. *Virgin Media urges Ofcom crackdown on Premier League TV prices.* 30 September 2014, The Telegraph. <http://www.telegraph.co.uk/finance/newsbysector/mediatechnologyandtelecoms/media/11131139/Virgin-Media-urges-Ofcom-crackdown-on-Premier-League-TV-prices.html>.

Websites only

http://appsso.eurostat.ec.europa.eu/nui/show.do?dataset=demo_r_d3dens&lang=en

http://appsso.eurostat.ec.europa.eu/nui/submitViewTableAction.do

http://backlinko.com/google-ranking-factors

http://blogs.lse.ac.uk/mediapolicyproject/resources/dossier-media-plurality/

http://chitika.com/insights/2010/the-value-of-google-result-positioning/

http://downloads.bbc.co.uk/bbctrust/assets/files/pdf/about/how_we_govern/charter.pdf

http://downloads.bbc.co.uk/bbctrust/assets/files/pdf/about/how_we_govern/agreement.pdf

http://ec.europa.eu/avpolicy/index_en.htm

http://ec.europa.eu/competition/elojade/isef/index.cfm?fuseaction=dsp_result

http://ec.europa.eu/competition/mergers/statistics.pdf

http://ec.europa.eu/competition/sectors/financial_services/enforcement_en.html

http://ec.europa.eu/competition/sectors/media/decisions_psb.pdf

http://ec.europa.eu/competition/sectors/media/overview_en.html

http://ec.europa.eu/competition/speeches/text/sp2003_009_en.pdf

http://ec.europa.eu/competition/state_aid/overview/state_aid_procedures_en.html

http://ec.europa.eu/culture/calls/index_en.htm

http://epp.eurostat.ec.europa.eu/statistics_explained/index.php/Information_society_statistics_at_regional_level

http://epp.eurostat.ec.europa.eu/tgm/table.do?tab=table&init=1&language=en&pcode=tin00093&plugin=1

http://epp.eurostat.ec.europa.eu/tgm/table.do?tab=table&init=1&language=en&pcode=tin00091&plugin=1

http://europa.eu/legislation_summaries/audiovisual_and_media/l24223a_en.htm

http://europa.eu/legislation_summaries/human_rights/fundamental_rights_within_european_union/l33500_en.htm

http://europa.eu/rapid/pressReleasesAction.do?reference=MEMO/08/671&format=HTML&aged=1&language=EN&guiLanguage=en

http://ketupa.net/espresso2.htm

http://mavise.obs.coe.int/company?id=2093

http://mavise.obs.coe.int/country?id=14

http://mavise.obs.coe.int/country?id=18

http://mavise.obs.coe.int/country?id=2

http://support.google.com/adwords/bin/answer.py?hl=en&answer=1704410

http://support.google.com/adwords/bin/answer.py?hl=en&answer=2454010

http://webarchive.nationalarchives.gov.uk/20140402142426/http://www.oft.gov.uk/OFTwork/competition-act-and-cartels/ca98/closure/e-books

https://widgets.itunes.apple.com/

http://wikileaks.org/About.html

http://www.alrc.gov.au/publications/issues-paper/caching-indexing-and-other-internet-functions#_ftn55

http://www.amazon.com/Editors-Picks-Kindle-eBooks/b?ie=UTF8&node=353898011

http://www.aph.gov.au/About_Parliament/Parliamentary_Departments/Parliamentary_Library/Publications_Archive/archive/mediaregulation

http://www.apple.com/support/mac-apps/ibooksauthor/

http://www.bbc.co.uk/bbctrust/governance/complaints_framework/fair_trading.html

http://www.bbc.co.uk/bbctrust/governance/regulatory_framework/charter_agreement.html

http://www.bbc.co.uk/iplayer/categories/news/highlights

http://www.bbc.co.uk/programmes/b006t1q9

http://www.bbc.co.uk/iplayer/episode/b04v85qt/question-time-11122014

http://www.euralva.wordpress.com

http://www.europarl.europa.eu/workingpapers/tran/105/chap3_en.htm

http://www.fcc.gov/guides/review-broadcast-ownership-rules

http://www.garanteprivacy.it/web/guest/home/docweb/-/docweb-display/docweb/2348801

http://www.google.com/adsense/start/

http://www.google.com/intl/en/policies/

http://www.google.com/intl/en/policies/privacy/

http://www.individual.com/odc/h_idc.html

http://www.investopedia.com/terms/d/del-credere-agency.asp

http://www.legislation.gov.uk/ukpga/1973/41

http://www.pcmag.com/encyclopedia_term/0,1237,t=vertical+search+engine&i=57892,00.asp

http://www.pcmag.com/encyclopedia/term/37856/api

http://www.publications.parliament.uk/pa/cm199394/cmhansrd/1994-03-18/Writtens-5.html

http://www.rte.ie/extra/app/news-now/

http://www.rte.ie/mediasales/digitalsales/advertising-channels/rte-news-now/

http://www.rtlgroup.com/www/htm/AboutUs_History.aspx

http://www.sfgate.com/technology/article/YouTube-will-start-charging-to-see-music-videos-5706889.php

http://www.soccerstats.com/attendance.asp?league=spain

http://www.sporta.de/media/Trustee_Web_EN.pdf

http://www.sporza.be/cm/sporza

http://www.uefa.org/MultimediaFiles/Download/Publications/competitions/Marketing/01/96/76/90/1967690_DOWNLOAD.pdf

http://www.youview.com/

http://www3.ebu.ch/advocacy/initiatives/copyright

https://developer.apple.com/app-store/review/guidelines/

https://developers.google.com/adwords/api/

https://developers.google.com/adwords/api/docs/terms

https://itunes.apple.com/ie/app/irish-independent-news/id335158729?mt=8

https://itunes.apple.com/ie/app/thejournal.ie-news/id409359491?mt=8

https://play.google.com/store/apps/details?id=ie.rte.news&hl=en

https://support.google.com/adwords/answer/15235?hl=en

https://support.google.com/googleplay/android-developer/answer/112622?hl=en

https://www.facebook.com/help/327131014036297/

Concurrences Review

Concurrences is a print and online quarterly peer reviewed journal dedicated to EU and national competitions laws. It has been launched in 2004 as the flagship of the Institute of Competition Law in order to provide a forum for academics, practitioners and enforcers. The Institute's influence and expertise has garnered interviews with such figures as Christine Lagarde, Bill Kovacic, François Hollande and Margarethe Vestager.

CONTENTS

More than 15,000 articles, print and/or online. Quarterly issues provide current coverage with contributions from the EU or national or foreign countries thanks to more than 1,200 authors in Europe and abroad. Approximately 25 % of the contributions are published in English, 75 % in French, as the official language of the General Court of justice of the EU; all contributions have English abstracts.

FORMAT

In order to balance academic contributions with opinions or legal practice notes, Concurrences provides its insight and analysis in a number of formats:

- Forewords: Opinions by leading academics or enforcers
- Interviews: Interviews of antitrust experts
- On-Topics: 4 to 6 short papers on hot issues
- Law & Economics: Short papers written by economists for a legal audience
- Articles: Long academic papers
- Case Summaries: Case commentary on EU and French case law
- Legal Practice: Short papers for in-house counsels
- International: Medium size papers on international policies
- Books Review: Summaries of recent antitrust books
- Articles Review: Summaries of leading articles published in 45 antitrust journals

BOARDS

The Scientific Committee is headed by Laurence Idot, Professor at Panthéon Assas University. The International Committee is headed by Frederic Jenny, OECD Competition Comitteee Chairman. Boards members include Bruno Lasserre, Mario Monti, Howard Shelanski, Richard Whish, Wouter Wils, etc.

ONLINE VERSION

Concurrences website provides all articles published since its inception, in addition to selected articles published online only in the electronic supplement.

WRITE FOR CONCURRENCES

Concurrences welcome spontaneous contributions. Except in rare circumstances, the journal accepts only unpublished articles, whatever the form and nature of the contribution. The Editorial Board checks the form of the proposals, and then submits these to the Scientific Committee. Selection of the papers is conditional to a peer review by at least two members of the Committee. Within a month, the Committee assesses whether the draft article can be published and notifies the author.

INSTITUTE of
Competition Law
Antitrust databases and resources

The Institute of Competition Law

The Institute of Competition Law is a publishing company, founded in 2004 by Dr. Nicolas Charbit, based in Paris and New-York. The Institute cultivates scholarship and discussion about antitrust issues though publications and conferences. Each publication and event is supervised by editorial boards and scientific or steering committees to ensure independence, objectivity, and academic rigor. Thanks to this management, the Institute has become one of the few think tanks in Europe to have significant influence on antitrust policies.

AIM

The Institute focuses government, business and academic attention on a broad range of subjects which concern competition laws, regulations and related economics.

BOARDS

To maintain its unique focus, the Institute relies upon highly distinguished editors, all leading experts in national or international antitrust: Bill Kovacic, Mario Monti, Eleanor Fox, Barry Hawk, Laurence Idot, Fred Jenny, etc.

AUTHORS

3,800 authors, from 55 jurisdictions.

PARTNERS

- Universities: University College London, King's College London, Queen Mary University, Paris Sorbonne Panthéon-Assas, etc.
- Law firms: Allen & Overy, Cleary Gottlieb Steen & Hamilton, DLA Piper, Hogan Lovells, Jones Day, Norton Rose Fulbright, Skadden Arps, White & Case, etc.

EVENTS

More than 350 events since 2004 in Brussels, London, New York, Paris, Singapore and Washington, DC.

ONLINE VERSION

Concurrences website provides all articles published since its inception.

PUBLICATIONS

The Institute publishes Concurrences Journal, a print and online quarterly peer-reviewed journal dedicated to EU and national competitions laws. e-Competitions is a bi-monthly antitrust news bulletin covering 55 countries. The e-Competitions database contains over 12,000 case summaries from 2,600 authors.

www.ingramcontent.com/pod-product-compliance
Lightning Source LLC
LaVergne TN
LVHW052242200926
848481LV00002B/240
* 9 7 8 1 9 3 9 0 0 7 8 5 8 *